ENCYCLOPEDIA OF

THE ANCIENT WORLD

ENCYCLOPEDIA OF

THE ANCIENT WORLD

Volume 2
Coriolanus, Gnaeus Marcius–Pharsalus, Battle of

Editor
Thomas J. Sienkewicz
Monmouth College, Illinois

———————— *Editorial Board* ————————

Lawrence Allan Conrad
North America
Western Illinois University

Katherine Anne Harper
South and Southeast Asia
Loyola Marymount University

Geoffrey W. Conrad
South America
Indiana University

Robert D. Haak
Egypt, Mesopotamia, Near East
Augustana College

Christopher Ehret
Africa
University of California, Los Angeles

Chenyang Li
East Asia
Central Washington University

David A. Crain
Mesoamerica
South Dakota State University

Thomas H. Watkins
Greece, Rome, Europe
Western Illinois University

Managing Editor, **Christina J. Moose**

Salem Press, Inc.
Pasadena, California   Hackensack, New Jersey

Editor in Chief: Dawn P. Dawson

Managing Editor: Christina J. Moose	*Research Supervisor:* Jeffry Jensen
Project Editor: Rowena Wildin	*Research Assistant:* Jeff Stephens
Acquisitions Editor: Mark Rehn	*Production Editor:* Joyce I. Buchea
Assistant Editor: Andrea E. Miller	*Graphics and Design:* James Hutson
Photograph Editor: Philip Bader	*Layout:* William Zimmerman
Administrative Assistant: Dana Garey	*Additional Layout:* Eddie Murillo

Maps by: Electronic Illustrators Group, Morgan Hill, Calif.
Cover Design: Moritz Design, Los Angeles, Calif.

Library of Congress Cataloging-in-Publication Data

Encyclopedia of the ancient world / editor, Thomas J. Sienkewicz.
    p. cm.
Includes bibliographical references and index.
    ISBN 0-89356-038-3 (set) — ISBN 0-89356-039-1 (v. 1) — ISBN 0-89356-040-5 (v. 2) — ISBN 0-89356-041-3 (v. 3)
    1. Civilization, Ancient—Encyclopedias. I. Sienkewicz, Thomas J.

CB311 .E54 2001
930′.03—dc21

2001049896

Second Printing

CONTENTS

KEY TO PRONUNCIATION

Many of the topics covered in the encyclopedia may be unfamiliar to students and general readers. For most of the more unfamiliar topics covered in these volumes, the editors have attempted to provide some guidelines to pronunciation upon first mention of the topic in text. These guidelines do not purport to achieve the subtleties of the languages in question but will offer readers a rough equivalent of how English speakers may approximate the proper pronunciation.

Symbols	Pronounced As In	Spelled Phonetically As
a	answer, laugh, sample, that	AN-sihr, laf, SAM-pul, that
ah	father, hospital	FAH-thur, HAHS-pih-tul
aw	awful, caught	AW-ful, kawt
ay	blaze, fade, waiter, weigh	blayz, fayd, WAYT-ur, way
ch	beach, chimp	beech, chihmp
eh	bed, head, said	behd, hehd, sehd
ee	believe, cedar, leader, liter	bee-LEEV, SEE-dur, LEED-ur, LEE-tur
ew	boot, lose	bewt, lews
g	beg, disguise, get	behg, dihs-GIZ, geht
i	buy, height, lie, surprise	bi, hit, li, sur-PRIZ
ih	bitter, pill	BIH-tur, pihl
j	digit, edge, jet	DIH-jiht, ehj, jeht
k	cat, kitten, hex	kat, KIH-tehn, hehks
o	cotton, hot	CO-tuhn, hot
oh	below, coat, note, wholesome	bee-LOH, coht, noht, HOHL-suhm
oo	good, look	good, look
ow	couch, how	kowch, how
oy	boy, coin	boy, koyn
s	cellar, save, scent	SEL-ur, sayv, sehnt
sh	champagne, issue, shop	sham-PAYN, IH-shew, shop
uh	about, butter, enough, other	uh-BOWT, BUH-tur, ee-NUHF, UH-thur
ur	birth, disturb, earth, letter	burth, dihs-TURB, urth, LEH-tur
y	useful, young	YEWS-ful, yuhng
z	business, zest	BIHZ-ness, zest
zh	vision	VIH-zhuhn

MAPS

COMPLETE LIST OF CONTENTS

Volume 1

OVERVIEWS

ENCYCLOPEDIA

Volume 2

Volume 3

CORIOLANUS, GNAEUS MARCIUS

FLOURISHED: fifth century B.C.E.
RELATED CIVILIZATIONS: Republican Rome,
Corioli, Volsci
MAJOR ROLE/POSITION: Military leader

Life. Little is known of the life of Gnaeus Marcius Coriolanus (NEE-uhs MAHR-shee-uhs kawr-ee-uh-LAY-nuhs). He was immortalized in what is probably a fictitious account by the historian Livy, which was later developed by both the historian Plutarch and English playwright William Shakespeare. According to Livy, Coriolanus was a nobleman and a great soldier who led Rome to many victories. During Coriolanus's lifetime, a drought and poor crops left the commoners of Rome in debt to the nobles. The harsh conditions imposed on them for repayment led to unrest. To quell threats of sedition, the commoners were granted representatives (tribunes) in the government. Coriolanus opposed this development, arguing that the tribunes, backed by the will of the people, would grow in power and overthrow the constitution. Incensed by his words, the commoners tried Coriolanus and banished him from Rome. The Volsicans, enemies of Rome, whom Coriolanus had earlier defeated, welcomed him, hoping for retribution against Rome. Under his command, the Volscian army overtook many towns and eventually made camp at the border of Rome. Although petitioned by many ambassadors from Rome, it was not until entreated by his mother, Venturia, his wife, Volumnia, and their two sons that Coriolanus relented and withdrew his army.

Influence. In all representations, notably William Shakespeare's play *Coriolanus* (pr. c. 1607-1608), Coriolanus symbolizes pride and the dangers inherent in letting pride overrule prudence.

ADDITIONAL RESOURCES

Livy. *The Rise of Rome*. Translated by T. J. Luce. Oxford, England: Oxford University Press, 1999.
Plutarch. *Plutarch's Lives: The Dryden Translation, Edited with Notes by Arthur Hugh Clough*. New York: Modern Library, 2001.

SEE ALSO: Livy; Plutarch; Rome, Republican.

—Sara MacDonald

CORNELIA

ALSO KNOWN AS: Cornelia the Younger; Mother of
the Gracchi
BORN: 195-190 B.C.E.; Italy
DIED: before 100 B.C.E.; Italy
RELATED CIVILIZATION: Imperial Rome
MAJOR ROLE/POSITION: Matriarch

Life. The daughter of Scipio Africanus and Aemilia, Cornelia received an education uncommon for women of the time, reputedly receiving training in poetry, oratory, military tactics, and politics, at the request of her honored father.

In 178 B.C.E., she was married to Tiberius Sempronius Gracchus, a renowned statesman. The goal of their marriage was to produce children who would have the support of patrician resources and connections on their mother's side with the advantage of being eligible for the tribunate, the gift of their father's plebeian blood.

Cornelia survived the birth of her twelve children by Tiberius Sempronius Gracchus, although only three survived to adulthood. The first of these, Sempronia, was married to Scipio Aemilianus. Cornelia is presumed to have said to her sons that she would rather be known as the mother of the Gracchi than the mother-in-law of Scipio Aemilianus.

Through her social connections, Cornelia tried to guide the political lives of her two surviving sons, Tiberius Sempronius Gracchus and Gaius Sempronius Gracchus. She was especially influential with her youngest, Gaius, and outlived both her sons.

Influence. Cornelia illustrated that a Roman woman could affect politics through the Roman social networks. She serves as forerunner to such notable and ambitious Roman mothers as Octavia, Livia Drusilla, and Agrippina the Younger.

ADDITIONAL RESOURCES

Bernstein, Alvin H. *Tiberius Sempronius Gracchus: Tradition and Apostasy.* Ithaca, N.Y.: Cornell University Press, 1978.

Dixon, Suzanne. *The Roman Mother.* London: Routledge, 1990.

SEE ALSO: Agrippina the Younger; Gracchus, Tiberius Sempromius, and Gaius Sempronius Gracchus; Livia Drusilla; Octavia; Rome, Imperial; Scipio Aemilianus; Scipio Africanus.

—*Abigail J. Gertner*

CRASSUS, MARCUS LICINIUS

BORN: c. 115 B.C.E.; place unknown
DIED: 53 B.C.E.; near Carrhae (later Haran, Turkey)
RELATED CIVILIZATIONS: Republican Rome, Parthia
MAJOR ROLE/POSITION: Politician, general

Life. Marcus Licinius Crassus (MAHR-kuhs lih-SIHN-ee-uhs KRAS-uhs) lost his father, a Roman noble, in a civil war in 87 B.C.E. He hid in Spain from 85 to 83 B.C.E., then raised private troops and helped Lucius Cornelius Sulla capture Rome (82 B.C.E.). However, he lost Sulla's support after being accused of profiting improperly from Sulla's proscriptions. He won success through his oratorical ability and financial skill and by doing favors. As praetor in 73 B.C.E., he commanded Rome's war against Spartacus, but Pompey the Great stole the credit for victory (72-71 B.C.E.).

Crassus and Pompey temporarily cooperated to become consuls for 70 B.C.E. and overturn some of Sulla's laws. As censor (65 B.C.E.), Crassus accomplished little. Crassus's supporters, such as Catiline and Julius Caesar, as well as schemes to undercut Pompey, alienated Cicero. Nevertheless, Crassus helped Cicero reveal Catiline's conspiracy (63 B.C.E.).

Crassus joined Pompey and Caesar in the unofficial First Triumvirate (60 B.C.E.) and became consul with Pompey (55 B.C.E.). He made war against Parthia to equal his partners' wealth and military power (54-53 B.C.E.). Defeated by mounted Parthian archers, he lost much of his army and perished near Carrhae (53 B.C.E.).

Influence. Crassus's political ambitions helped destroy the Roman Republic and initiated centuries of Roman hostilities with the Parthians and their successors.

ADDITIONAL RESOURCES

Jiménez, Ramon L. *Caesar Against Rome: The Great Roman Civil War.* Westport, Conn.: Praeger, 2000.

Marshall, B. A. *Crassus, a Political Biography.* Amsterdam: Adolf M. Hakkert, 1976.

Ward, A. M. *Marcus Crassus and the Late Roman Republic.* Columbia: University of Missouri Press, 1977.

SEE ALSO: Caesar, Julius; Catiline; Cicero; Parthia; Pompey the Great; Rome, Republican; Sulla, Lucius Cornelius.

—*Allen M. Ward*

CRATES OF ATHENS

FLOURISHED: c. 449-c.424 B.C.E.
RELATED CIVILIZATIONS: Classical Greece, Athens
MAJOR ROLE/POSITION: Actor, comic playwright

Life. Crates (KRAYT-eez) of Athens acted and wrote comedies in Athens in the middle of the fifth century B.C.E., but nothing is known of his life outside his career. He acted in the plays of Cratinus before producing his own plays. As a playwright, he won in the dramatic competition of the Great Dionysia at least three times. The titles of seven of his plays are known: *Geitones* (*Neighbors*), *Heroes*, *Lamia* (*Goblin*), *Paidiai* (*Games*), *Theria* (*Animals*), *Samioi* (*Samians*), and *Tolmai* (*Courage*). Exact dates for the plays are not known; all were translated into English in 1931. None of his plays survives complete. About sixty fragments are known, none longer than ten lines. *Animals* has the most interesting remains. Fragments refer to a utopia in which furniture and utensils work by themselves and to talking animals who urge humans not to eat meat.

Influence. In *De poetica* (c. 335-323 B.C.E.; *Poetics*, 1705), Aristotle says Crates was the first Athenian to abandon personal abuse in his comedies and instead create plots and stories of universal interest. Crates is also said to have introduced drunken characters to the stage. In *Hippēs* (424 B.C.E.; *The Knights*, 1812), Aristophanes refers to him approvingly as a predecessor.

ADDITIONAL RESOURCES

Kassel, R., and C. Austin. *Poetae Comici Graeci.* Vol. 4. Berlin: Walter de Gruyter, 1983.

Norwood, Gilbert. *Greek Comedy.* London: Methuen, 1931.

SEE ALSO: Aristophanes; Aristotle; Cratinus; Greece, Classical; Performing arts.

—*Wilfred E. Major*

CRATINUS

ALSO KNOWN AS: Kratinos
BORN: date and place unknown
DIED: c. 420 B.C.E.; place unknown
RELATED CIVILIZATIONS: Athens, Classical Greece
MAJOR ROLE/POSITION: Comic playwright

Life. Cratinus (kruh-TI-nuhs) produced comedies successfully for some thirty years, from the 450's to the 420's B.C.E. More than twenty of his plays are known and numerous fragments exist, but there are no complete plays and no fragments more than ten complete consecutive lines. An ancient summary of the *Dionysus Alexander* tells us that the play spoofed the origin of the Trojan War. A clowning Dionysus takes the place of Paris (also known as Alexander) to kidnap Helen and consequently start the Trojan War. Another play, *Nemesis*, told a silly version of the birth of Helen. Besides the mythological travesty, these plays satirized prominent Athenians of the day, most notably Pericles. Cratinus earned a reputation as a vicious satirist, although he was capable of producing apolitical comedy such as the *Odysseuses*, which parodied the Cyclops episode from Homer's *Odyssey* (c. 800 B.C.E.; English translation, 1616). In his later years, Cratinus was mocked by

Aristophanes as a washed-up drunk. Cratinus retaliated in 423 B.C.E. with *Pytine* (*The Bottle*), in which he staged his own rejection of alcoholism in favor of his allegorical wife, Comedy. He resoundingly beat Aristophanes in competition with the play, and this competition is the last known activity of Cratinus.

Influence. Cratinus was the earliest of the great triad of comedians of Old Comedy, along with Aristophanes and Eupolis. He is credited with establishing the vitality and characteristics of the genre.

ADDITIONAL RESOURCES

Heath, Malcom. "Aristophanes and His Rivals." *Greece & Rome* 37 (October, 1990): 143-158.

Kassel, R., and C. Austin. *Poetae Comici Graeci.* Vol. 4. Berlin: Walter de Gruyter, 1983.

Norwood, Gilbert. *Greek Comedy.* London: Methuen, 1931.

Rosen, Ralph Mark. *Old Comedy and the Iambographic Tradition.* Atlanta, Ga.: Scholars Press, 1988.

SEE ALSO: Aristophanes; Crates of Athens; Eupolis; Greece, Classical; Homer; Performing arts.

—*Wilfred E. Major*

CRETE

DATE: 3000 B.C.E.-700 C.E.
LOCALE: Mediterranean Sea
RELATED CIVILIZATIONS: Mycenaean Greece, Egypt, Cyclades
SIGNIFICANCE: The site of one of the earliest civilizations in Greece and of the Minoans during the Bronze Age.

The island of Crete (KREET) is located southeast of mainland Greece, midway between the Greek mainland and Africa or Asia Minor, and bounded on the north by the Aegean Sea and on the south by the Mediterranean Sea. Crete is about 152 miles (250 kilometers) from east to west at its greatest width and 35 miles (57 kilometers) from north to south at its greatest length. Crete is very mountainous but also has grassy plains.

History. The earliest evidence of agriculture in Greece is found at Knossos on Crete and in Thessaly. Neolithic sites on Crete containing evidence of agriculture date back to the seventh millennium B.C.E. Later in the Neolithic period, sites show signs of trade with other peoples across the Aegean. Being an island, Crete was less susceptible to movements and invasions than mainland Greece, and contact with Anatolia, Egypt, and the Near East accelerated the development of a Bronze Age civilization around 2600 B.C.E.. At about this time, it appears that settlers from Egypt or Libya came to Crete. These settlers, however, were not Egyptians or Semites but probably Indo-Europeans.

Crete was the home to the Bronze Age Minoan civilization, first discovered by archaeologist Sir Arthur Evans in 1894. Evans excavated the site of Knossos in the north central area of the island from 1900 to 1941 and partially reconstructed its palace. Evans named the Bronze Age civilization that he discovered "Minoan," after legendary King Minos. One of Evans's major accomplishments was recognizing that the Mycenaean civilization had its roots in the older Minoan civilization. Evans divided the civilization's chronology into Early Minoan (c. 3400-2100 B.C.E.), Middle Minoan (c. 2100-1500 B.C.E.), and Late Minoan (c. 1500-1100 B.C.E.).

Smaller palaces with ground plans similar to the one at Knossos were built at Phaistos, Mallia, Gournia, Khania, and Kato Zakro; all are in an enclosing valley near the sea. The preferred chronology for Minoan civilization during the latter half of the twentieth century is based on the dates of the building of the palaces on Crete, their destruction by an earthquake, their rebuilding, and their eventual final destruction. This chronology is as follows: Pre-Palace period (c. 3100-1925 B.C.E.), Old Palace period (c. 1925-1725 B.C.E.), New Palace period (c. 1725-1380 B.C.E.), and Post-Palace period (c. 1380-1000 B.C.E.).

The fall of the Minoan civilization is attributed to the eruption and implosion of the Aegean island of Thera (modern Thíra) north of Crete. Archaeological remains were first discovered there in 1866. It is theorized that the implosion of Thera (c. 1623 B.C.E.) caused a massive tsunami that destroyed the Minoan fleet, leaving the island vulnerable to Mycenaean occupation. After 1380 B.C.E., the palaces on Crete—with the exception of the palace at Knossos—were damaged by fire and sword. After the fall of the palaces, there is evidence of

Mycenaean occupation on Crete. The written script switched from Linear A to Linear B, which was used on the mainland, and the art became more symmetrical, less colorful, and distinctly Mycenaean. The governance of the island changed to city-states ruled by an assembly consisting of noblemen. Minoan civilization seems to have continued, however, on the western end of the island at Khania. Around 1100 B.C.E., the palace at Knossos was destroyed by the Dorians or by the Sea Peoples, according to legend, corresponding to the fall of Mycenaean civilization on mainland Greece.

Not much is known of Crete between about 1100 and 700 B.C.E. Possibly Mycenaean refugees from the mainland and the Peloponnese settled there during this period, and during the eighth century B.C.E., Greek culture emerged on Crete, which became one of the Greek colonies.

Likewise, not much of significance occurred on Crete during the Greek Classical and Roman eras. In 67 B.C.E., Rome conquered Crete and the island was integrated into the Roman province of Cyrenaica, with Gortyn as the capital. The Romans built majestic structures at Gortyn, including the Praetorium and the Odeion. The law code of Gortyn, carved in blocks, was found next to the Odeion.

In 324 C.E., Crete was annexed into the Eastern Roman Empire, and Christianity was established on the island, which would become an important center for icon painting in the Middle Ages.

Architecture and city planning. The palace at Knossos was built around 1700 B.C.E. on the ruins of an earlier palace, which had been built around 2000 B.C.E. and was destroyed by an earthquake. Both palaces were asymmetrical and labyrinthine in plan, with three or more levels connected by shafts that provided the lower levels with ventilation and light. The second palace was larger than the first. Evans partially reconstructed what he called the "Palace of King Minos" at Knossos, which, including its porches and outbuildings, covers six acres (or roughly two and a half hectares) of land, and he restored many of its fresco paintings.

The unfortified palace was located about three miles (nearly five kilometers) from the sea and was the center of a thriving city of approximately eighty-two thousand people. Although the palace was unfortified, access to it was limited. Its main entrance was on the eastern end through a set of mazelike corridors. Most likely, the legend of the labyrinth originated with this entrance. The northern entrance to the palace went off into the hinterland, and the southern entrance led to a porch.

The palace was composed of distinct areas such as public areas with a throne room, living areas with such amenities as bathtubs and a toilet opening to a drain, and storage areas with giant storage jars (*pithoi*). The drainage system in the palace, with its open stone drains and clay pipes, is remarkably sophisticated. Evans's reconstruction includes red, cast-concrete, downward-sloping columns to replace the original wooden ones, and a grand staircase. The center of the palace was a large, rectangular court measuring 161 by 89 feet (49 by 27 meters). At the northwest corner of the palace is a stepped theatrical area.

Law. In 1884 in Prinia, the site of an important archaic sanctuary dating from the seventh century B.C.E., inscriptions were found of the law code of Gortyn (700-600 B.C.E.) dealing with family law, inheritance, slavery, and punishments for crimes. This is the oldest law code known in Europe.

Language and literature. No literature from ancient Crete survives, but there are numerous references to Minoan cities in Homer's *Iliad* (c. 800 B.C.E.; English translation, 1616), and Crete figures heavily in Greek mythology. In his *Geōgraphica* (c. 7 B.C.E.; *Geography*, 1917-1933), Strabo wrote that Crete was the birthplace of Zeus, who was born in a cave on Mount Ida. (Other legends relate that the cave was on Mount Dicte.) The Cretans viewed Zeus as a seasonal god who died and was reborn again the next season. His legendary tomb is located on Mount Juktas.

Legend relates that Zeus mated with the mortal Europa, who gave birth to three children: Minos, king of Crete, who is mentioned by Homer; Rhadamanthys, another king of Crete; and Sarpedon. Minos's wife, Pasiphae, aided by Daedalus, mated with a bull and gave birth to the monstrous minotaur—a creature half man and half bull, who lived inside the labyrinth. Every year King Minos demanded that the Athenians sacrifice seven youths and seven maidens to the minotaur until it was slain by Theseus, aided by King Minos's daughter, Ariadne. The princess fell in love with Theseus and supplied him with thread, with which he found his way out of the labyrinth.

The creator of the labyrinth was the Athenian Daedalus, who lost favor with the king and was imprisoned in a tower. He fashioned wings from feathers and wax in order to escape Crete but lost his son Icarus in the attempt. Icarus flew too close to the Sun, which melted the wax, and he fell into the sea and was drowned. Minos was also regarded as a wise king and lawgiver and was one of the judges in the Underworld. Heracles fought the Cretan bull as one of his twelve labors. In his *Ethika* (after c. 100 C.E.; *Moralia*, 1603), Plutarch says the word "syncretism" (Greek *synkrētizein*) is derived from *syn* ("together") and *krēte* ("Crete") because the Cretans often quarreled among themselves but united against enemies.

Religion and ritual. Although there is not much firm evidence about religious practices on ancient Crete, artwork yields clues. For example, a Minoan frescoed sarcophagus found in a tomb at Hagia Triada indicates a blood sacrifice associated with funerary rites. One side of the sarcophagus portrays a bull being sacrificed, with its blood draining into a rhyton (a slender, conical ceremonial vessel), as a female (priestess?) worships in front of an altar and a man plays the double flutes. The other side shows men carrying models of two bulls and a boat; men and women carrying vases and pouring a liquid into a bowl flanked by columns topped by double axes; and a shrouded man who has been interpreted as the spirit of the deceased. This indicates belief in an afterlife. In addition, small figu-

The throne room, pictured here, was one of many elaborate rooms in the palace of Minos at Knossos. (Hulton Archive)

PLINY THE ELDER'S FOUR FAMOUS LABYRINTHS OF ANTIQUITY

Cretan

Described as having been built by Daedalus, this labyrinth is associated with the palace at Knossos, although there is no evidence that it ever existed. According to the legend, the Minotaur, a creature with the body of a man and the head of a bull, lived inside the labyrinth. Every year, King Minos demanded that seven Athenian youths and seven Athenian maidens be sacrificed to the bull, until it was killed by Theseus, aided by King Minos's daughter, Ariadne, who helped him find his way out of the labyrinth.

Egyptian

Herodotus and Strabo locate this labyrinth east of the Moeris Lake, near Crocodilopolis. Herodotus described the building as containing three thousand chambers, half above and half below ground, as well as twelve courts. The lower chambers were supposed to contain tombs of the sacred crocodiles as well as tombs of the kings who had built the structure, who included Amenemhet III (r. 1818-1770 B.C.E.).

Lemnian

Reportedly, this labyrinth on Lemnos island off the west coast of Turkey resembled the Egyptian.

Italian

This labyrinth was beneath the tomb of sixth century B.C. king Lars Porsena at Clusium (modern Chiusi in southeast Tuscany).

rines made of faience (earthenware with opaque glazes), have been found in altars in the Minoan palaces. These figurines are women wearing bell-shaped skirts and bolero-style jackets, with their breasts exposed. They are called "snake goddesses" because they are handling snakes and have divine qualities, such as their tall, distinctive hats. Snakes have chthonic associations, so the figures are generally believed to represent fertility goddesses or priestesses involved in fertility rites.

Sports and entertainment. A fresco from the palace at Knossos portrays three young people playing a "bull-leaping" game, which is theorized to have taken place in the theatrical area of the palace. Figurines in the palace also portray participants in a bull-leaping game, and other frescoes portray spectators filling the theatrical area, watching some sort of event, perhaps the bull sport.

Visual arts. Fresco paintings within the palace at Knossos were primarily of curving vegetal and sea life, processions, double axes, and bulls. Evans's recon-

struction attests to the highly decorated character of the interior spaces of the Cretan palaces. The fresco fragments found at the palace at Knossos were all in the lowest level, so the location of the frescoes in his reconstruction has been questioned. A Blue Dolphin fresco that he believed was located in the queen's apartment, for example, may have been actually located on the floor above. The most famous fresco from the palace portrays three young people playing a bull-leaping game. The boys and girls are indistinguishable, except for the darker tone of the boys' skin. Both girls and boys are portrayed in Minoan art with long wavy hair and thin, girdled waists. Men portrayed in art are beardless, in contrast to those in Mycenaean art.

Other artwork associated with the Minoans includes snake goddesses, animal idols, Kamares ware, stoneware, and octopus vases. Kamares ware is found only at the palace at Knossos and in the Kamares cave (after which it is named). Kamares ware is wheel-thrown pottery decorated with a white-on-black design, often with yellow or red accents. The painted decoration is usually organic in nature, with stylized sea life or floral motifs. Other terra-cotta vessels of the New Palace period are decorated in a marine style, with black figures on a white background, and populated with curving, organic octopuses and other sea life. In the Post-Palace period, the designs stiffen and become symmetrical. Finely carved stoneware made in Crete is usually made of serpentine. Surviving pieces include lamps, chalices, rhytons, and small seal stones incised with designs. The most famous Cretan stone pieces include the *Harvester Vase* from Hagia Triada and the *Bull's Head Rhyton* from Knossos. The Minoans also created fine bronze and gold items, including cups and jewelry.

War and weapons. The Minoans do not appear to have been a warring civilization. During the Bronze Age, Crete was probably a thalassocracy (maritime power), as evidenced by representations of fleets of ships in a fresco at the palace at Knossos and by its unfortified palaces. Also, the Minoan civilization's demise has been linked to the destruction of its fleet.

Women's life. Women are depicted more frequently than men in Minoan frescoes, which leads to the theory that women may have had a relatively high status in Minoan society. At one time, it was theorized that Minoan Crete was matriarchal. Snake goddess figurines suggest female participation as priestesses or as divinities in Bronze Age Crete.

Writing systems. The first writing used on Crete was hieroglyphic, as seen on the Phaistos disk (discovered in 1908) in the archaeological museum in Iráklion (Heraklion). Two subsequent scripts dating to the Bronze Age have been discovered on Crete: Linear A, used during the New Palace period, and Linear B, found only at Knossos on Crete and on the Greek mainland. Linear A is found primarily on clay tablets that yield mainly inventories. It is largely a syllabic script consisting of seventy-five signs and a number of ideograms. It has not been deciphered. Linear B, deciphered by Michael Ventris in 1952, appears to be an early form of Greek. It consists of eighty-seven symbols and a number of ideograms and may have been derived from Linear A. The Linear B tablets discovered on Crete are mainly lists and inventories. No written records of Minoan political or social history exist.

Current views. Much of Crete has not been excavated, although the palaces and royal tombs, whose artifacts reflect the wealthiest elite, have been studied. Excavations in the later twentieth century shed light on the palaces at Phaistos and Kato Zakro, a small town of Gournia, the ancient road systems of the Minoans, the cities of Mallia and Palaikastro, necropolises at Arkhanes and Armeni, and Minoan drydocks at Kommos. However, the basic outline of Minoan civilization and chronology laid out by Evans's excavations remains largely unchanged.

Excavation continues at the smaller Minoan palaces at Phaistos, Mallia, and Kato Zakro, which have not been reconstructed like the palace at Knossos. Evans's archaeological methods and reconstructions have been much criticized, but the reconstructed palace at Knossos has also been praised as bringing Bronze Age culture to life for the modern visitor.

ADDITIONAL RESOURCES
Biers, William R. *The Archaeology of Greece: An Introduction.* 2d ed. Ithaca, N.Y.: Cornell University Press, 1996.
Chadwick, John. *Reading the Past: Linear B and Related Scripts.* Berkeley: University of California Press, 1997.
Farnoux, Alexandre. *Knossos: Searching for the Legendary Palace of King Minos.* Translated by David J. Baker. New York: Harry N. Abrams, 1996.
Higgins, Reynold. *Minoan and Mycenaean Art.* Rev. ed. London: Thames and Hudson, 1997.
MacKendrick, Paul. *The Greek Stones Speak: The Story of Archaeology in Greek Lands.* Toronto: W. W. Norton, 1983.
Metropolitan Museum of Art. *Greek Art of the Aegean Islands.* New York: The Metropolitan Museum of Art, 1979.

SEE ALSO: Byzantine Empire; Cyclades; Gortyn, law code of; Greece, Mycenaean; Linear B; Rome, Imperial; Strabo; Thera.

—*Sally A. Struthers*

CRITIAS OF ATHENS

BORN: c. 460 B.C.E.; Athens, Greece
DIED: 403 B.C.E.; Athens, Greece
RELATED CIVILIZATIONS: Athens, Sparta, Classical Greece
MAJOR ROLE/POSITION: Statesman, military leader, writer

Life. Critias (KRIHSH-ee-uhs) of Athens was from an aristocratic family that traced itself to Solon. The uncle of Plato, he associated with Socrates as well as the Sophists and wrote a variety of works in prose and poetry, including a treatise in praise of the Spartan constitution.

In 415 B.C.E., he was implicated in the mutilation of the herms (statues of Hermes) but was released because of information provided by Andocides. His involvement in the Four Hundred remains uncertain. While in exile for proposing a motion to recall Alcibiades of Athens, he lived in Thessaly and allegedly participated in a democratic revolution.

In 404 B.C.E., Critias returned to Athens and became the leader of the Thirty Tyrants, the pro-Spartan oligarchy. He was responsible for their reign of terror, during which fifteen hundred people were killed. According to Xenophon, he had his colleague Theramenes executed for attempting to broaden the oligarchy. In 403 B.C.E., Critias fell in battle against the democratic exiles. After his death, a monument is said to have been erected in his honor, showing a personified Oligarchy setting a torch to Democracy.

Influence. Critias appears in Plato's dialogues, one of which is named after him. He was known throughout antiquity primarily for his brutality and ruthlessness.

ADDITIONAL RESOURCES

Curd, Patricia, and Richard D. McKirahan. *A Presocratic Reader*. Indianapolis, Ind.: Hackett, 1996.

Guthrie, W. K. C. *A History of Greek Philosophy*. 6 vols. New York: Cambridge University Press, 1978-1990.

Krentz, Peter. *The Thirty at Athens*. Ithaca, N.Y.: Cornell University Press, 1982.

SEE ALSO: Alcibiades of Athens; Andocides; Athens; Four Hundred; Greece, Classical; Plato; Socrates; Thirty Tyrants; Xenophon.

—*Andrew Wolpert*

CROESUS

ALSO KNOWN AS: Kroisos
BORN: c. 595 B.C.E.; Lydia (western Anatolia)
DIED: c. 546 B.C.E.; Sardis
RELATED CIVILIZATIONS: Lydia, Archaic Greece, Persia
MAJOR ROLE/POSITION: King

Life. The fifth and final ruler of the Lydian Dynasty, Croesus (KREE-suhs) succeeded his father, Alyattes, after defeating his own half brother. He warred against the Carians, his mother's people, and conquered the Ionian Greeks while seeking peace with those on the mainland. His court at Sardis welcomed Greek intellectuals, especially Solon, the Athenian lawgiver who, however, offended Croesus by refusing to agree that the king was the happiest man on earth.

The richest man in his world, he often gave pure gold to Greek shrines, especially the oracle at Delphi, who announced equivocally that he would bring down a mighty empire if he battled Persia. In battling Cyrus the Great in 546 B.C.E., Croesus did, indeed, bring down an empire—his own.

One legend states that Cyrus ordered, then halted Croesus's execution on a flaming pyre when Croesus called out the name of Solon (the philosopher who had cautioned people about the uncertainty of life). Cyrus then turned him into a vassal. Another legend claims that Croesus was saved by Apollo, who, grateful for rich offerings at Delphi, carried him off to the land of the Hyperboreans to live in perpetual sunshine and plenty.

Croesus stands on the funeral pyre. (North Wind Picture Archives)

Influence. Croesus's interest in Greek religion and philosophy led to a greater Greek influence in western Asia Minor.

ADDITIONAL RESOURCES

Hansmann, George Maxim Anossov. *From Croesus to Constantine: The Cities of Western Asia Minor and Their Arts.* Ann Arbor: University of Michigan Press, 1975.

Pedley, John Griffiths. *Sardis in the Age of Croesus.* Norman: University of Oklahoma Press, 1968.

SEE ALSO: Cyrus the Great; Greece, Archaic; Lydia; Persia; Solon.

—Keith Garebian

CUNAXA, BATTLE OF

DATE: 401 B.C.E.

LOCALE: About 87 miles (140 kilometers) northwest of Babylon, near the Euphrates river

RELATED CIVILIZATIONS: Persia, Classical Greece

SIGNIFICANCE: Cyrus the Younger enrolled 10,400 Greek mercenaries to help him gain the Persian throne from his brother.

Background. Upon the death of Darius II, the elder of his sons, Artaxerxes II, came to the throne. Cyrus the Younger, unhappy with his prospects, revolted and tried to seize the throne. Cyrus's army numbered between 20,000 and 30,000 men, including 2,600 horsemen. Artaxerxes had about 30,000 men, 6,000 of whom were on horses. The disparity in horsemen would cost Cyrus the victory at Cunaxa (kyew-NAK-suh).

Action. Cyrus successfully advanced through Asia Minor and Mesopotamia. He and Artaxerxes met near Babylon. Cyrus posted the Greeks, led by the Spartan Clearchus, on the right with the Paphlagonian horsemen to their right and the Euphrates on the extreme right flank. Cyrus held the center with his 600 horsemen while Ariaeus was placed on the left with the Asiatic troops. The satrap Tissaphernes and Artaxerxes held the center, with the king surrounded by the 6,000 horsemen. In the ensuing battle, Clearchus and the Greeks crushed the Persian left but Cyrus was slain while foolishly attacking his brother head-on. Ariaeus's forces fought well but then fled after the news of Cyrus's death had spread.

Consequences. The victorious Greeks refused to enroll under Artaxerxes and successfully marched home. The expedition demonstrated the vulnerability of the Persian Empire to the Greek hoplite.

ADDITIONAL RESOURCES

Bigwood, J. M. "The Ancient Accounts of the Battle of Cunaxa." *American Journal of Philology* 104 (1983): 340-357.

Cawkwell, G. *Xenophon: The Persian Expedition.* Harmondsworth, England: Penguin Books, 1972.

Hornblower, Simon. *Cambridge Ancient History.* Vol. 6. Cambridge, England: Cambridge University Press, 1994.

SEE ALSO: Greece, Classical; Persia.

—Martin C. J. Miller

CUNOBELINUS

ALSO KNOWN AS: Cymbeline

BORN: first century B.C.E.; Britain

DIED: c. 40 C.E.; Britain

RELATED CIVILIZATIONS: Britain, Imperial Rome

MAJOR ROLE/POSITION: Tribal leader

Life. Cunobelinus (kew-nuh-buh-LI-nuhs) was the greatest and most powerful of the Briton tribal leaders before the Roman invasion (43 C.E.). The historian Suetonius described him as "rex Britannorum," or king of the Britons, probably in reference to his considerable wealth and the extensive lands that he ruled. He was the son of Tasciovanus, king of the Catuvellauni. Cunobelinus became ruler of the Catuvellauni about 10 C.E. and acquired Camulodunum, the capital of the Trinovantes, thus uniting the two tribes. His kingdom was quite large, covering Essex and Hertfordshire.

The great quantity of Roman goods imported into Camulodunum (modern Colchester) and the period of generally peaceful relations between Rome and Britain during Cunobelinus's long reign suggest that he had close links to the Roman world. This relationship may have been threatened, however, in 39 or 40 C.E., when Cunobelinus drove his son Adminius out of Britain, perhaps as part of a dynastic struggle. Adminius fled to the protection of Caligula, then emperor of Rome. After Cunobelinus's death circa 40 C.E., his kingdom was divided between his sons Caratacus and Togodumnus. Both led the Briton resistance against the emperor Claudius's invasion of Britain three years later.

Influence. William Shakespeare's play *Cymbeline* uses Cunobelinus's alternate name and refers to his position as king of the Britons.

ADDITIONAL RESOURCES

Potter, T. W. *Roman Britain*. Cambridge, Mass.: Harvard University Press, 1997.
Salway, Peter. *The Oxford Illustrated History of Roman Britain*. Oxford, England: Oxford University Press, 1993.
Todd, Malcolm. *Roman Britain*. 3d ed. Oxford, England: Blackwell, 1999.

SEE ALSO: Britain; Caratacus; Claudius; Rome, Imperial.

—Alison Taufer

CURTIUS RUFUS, QUINTUS

BORN: first century C.E.; Rome
DIED: late nineties or early second century C.E.; Rome
RELATED CIVILIZATIONS: Imperial Rome, Hellenistic Greece
MAJOR ROLE/POSITION: Historian

Life. Quintus Curtius Rufus (KOORT-see-oos REW-fuhs) is the only Roman historian of the first century C.E. besides Marcus Velleius Paterculus whose work has largely survived. The details of Curtius's life and the exact date of his work are disputed. Most likely a rhetorician or a politician during the reign of Claudius (r. 41-54 C.E.), Curtius wrote *Historia Alexandri Magni* (first and second centuries C.E.; *History of Alexander the Great*, 1553) when he was older, in the early years of Vespasian's reign (r. 69-79 C.E.). Written originally in ten books, but now lacking Books 1 and 2 and sections of Books 5, 6, and 10, Curtius's work blends history and biography and is divided into two parts linked by the themes of "fortune" and "rule." In the first half, Alexander, in contrast with Persian monarch Darius III, appears to be the righteous commander. Yet, once an omnipotent ruler, he becomes progressively more arrogant, and as a result, his good fortune turns against him so that he eventually becomes a tyrant, a duplicate of Darius.

Influence. Curtius's work was an outgrowth of the Roman fascination with Alexander the Great. The first Western conqueror of a vast territory, Alexander became a paradigm for the leaders (Pompey the Great, Julius Caesar, Augustus) of the late Republic, and a figure regarded with a mixture of admiration and hostility in the early empire. Although Curtius is the only Latin author who wrote a literary biography of Alexander and his work was ignored and dismissed as less than serious history by ancient historians and commentators, he gained great popularity among scholars and humanists during the Middle Ages and in the Renaissance.

ADDITIONAL RESOURCES

Atkinson, J. E. "Q. Curtius Rufus' *Historiæ Alexandri Magni.*" *Aufstieg und Niedergang der Römischen Welt* II no. 34. 4 (1997): 3447-3483.
Baynham, E. *Alexander the Great: The Unique History of Quintus Curtius*. Ann Arbor: University of Michigan Press, 1998.

SEE ALSO: Alexander the Great; Claudius; Darius III; Greece, Hellenistic and Roman; Rome, Imperial; Velleius Paterculus, Marcus; Vespasian.

—Sophia Papaioannou

CUSHITES

DATE: eighth millennium B.C.E.-early first millennium C.E.

LOCALE: Northeastern Africa from the far eastern Sahara through Ethiopia and the Horn of Africa to Kenya and Tanzania

RELATED CIVILIZATION: Sudanic civilization

SIGNIFICANCE: The Cushites, who include the modern-day Beja, Somali, Oromo, and Afar, developed a complex agricultural society.

The Cushites (KEW-shits) are a numerous group of peoples who speak the Cushitic languages of the Afrasan (or Afroasiatic) language family. These peoples should not be confused with Kush, an Egyptian term for the Napata kingdom located south of Egypt along the Nile in the last millennium B.C.E.. The most northerly Cushites in ancient times were the Medjay and later the Blemmyes. They were the ancestors of the modern-day Beja, who live in the southern Red Sea region of Africa, extending north from the Ethiopian highlands as far as the southern border of Egypt. A second set of Cushitic peoples, the Agaw, were the majority populations of the northern and north-central parts of the highlands between 4000 B.C.E. and 100 C.E., before the rise of the kingdom of Axum in the first century C.E.. Most widespread of all were the Eastern Cushites, who include today the Somali, the Oromo, and the Afar, as well as many other, smaller societies. These societies together occupy most of the eastern Horn of Africa and the eastern parts of the Ethiopian highlands. A fourth grouping were the Southern Cushites, who occupied large parts of the plains and highlands of Kenya and northern Tanzania from the fourth century B.C.E. to the early first millennium C.E.

The ancestral proto-Cushitic society took shape in areas near the northern edge of the Ethiopian highlands around 8000-6000 B.C.E. The proto-Cushites were already raisers of cattle, sheep, goats, and donkeys by that period. This is known because scholars have been able to show that the proto-Cushitic language contained an extensive vocabulary of words for these animals as well as for the herding and milking of livestock. By around the sixth millennium B.C.E., the early Cushites had begun to move south into the northeastern areas of the Ethiopian highlands. There they began to bring into cultivation two indigenous highland grain crops, t'ef and finger millet, and in this fashion mixed farming entered the economies of many of the Cushitic communities.

As the Cushites spread more widely in the sixth and fifth millennia B.C.E., they gradually diverged into several societies. The ancestors of the Beja remained behind, as livestock raisers in the areas just north of the Ethiopian highlands, and the proto-Agaw society evolved in the northern Ethiopian highlands. Along the Ethiopian Rift Valley, which bisects the highlands from northeast to southwest, two societies took shape, the proto-Eastern Cushites in the middle areas and the proto-Southern Cushites in the far southern region. In the fourth millennium B.C.E., the descendants of both societies expanded still more widely. Eastern Cushitic communities spread across the eastern side of the Ethiopian highlands, evolving over the next two thousand years into a number of distinct societies. The Southern Cushites moved first into the plains of northern Kenya after about 3500 B.C.E. and then south through the middle of Kenya into northern Tanzania from about 1800 B.C.E. onward, bringing the raising of cattle and cultivation of grains for the first time into those regions.

Two major developments in agricultural technology came into being among the Cushites of Ethiopia between the fourth and first millennia B.C.E. One of these took place along the Rift Valley of Ethiopia. There peoples of the Highland branch of the Eastern Cushites began a long and fruitful cultural interchange with Omotic societies living just west of the rift. The Omotic peoples had earlier, probably in about the sixth millennium B.C.E., developed a unique agricultural system based on the raising of the *enset* plant, the inner stalk and bulb of which were edible. In the third and second millennia B.C.E., the Highland Eastern Cushites and the Omotic societies shared in the creation of a new, elaborate irrigation-based agricultural system, building stone-walled terraced fields on the mountainsides, raising both *enset* and grain crops, and using the manure of their cattle to fertilize their farms.

The second major development of the fourth to first millennia was the progressive spread of the Middle Eastern crops of wheat and barley, along with the plow, to most of the northern, central, and southeastern Ethiopian highlands. These additions to agricultural practices enhanced the technological prowess of the ancient Cushitic-speaking populations of that region of Africa. When South Arabian merchants began to visit the lands of the Agaw Cushites of the northern Ethiopian highlands in the last millennium B.C.E., they found already in place complex agriculture, able to produce the kind of surplus that could support states. The most notable of such states was the empire of Axum in the early first millennium C.E.

ADDITIONAL RESOURCES
Ehret, Christopher. "Cushitic Prehistory." In *The Non-Semitic Languages of Ethiopia*, edited by M. L. Bender. East Lansing: Michigan State University, 1976.

_____. "On the Antiquity of Agriculture in Ethiopia." *Journal of African History* 20 (1979).

SEE ALSO: Africa, East and South; Agaw; Axum; Beja; Napata and Meroe; Omotic peoples.

—Christopher Ehret

CYAXARES

ALSO KNOWN AS: Uvakhshtra (Median); Umakishtar (Akkadian)
BORN: seventh century B.C.E.; Media (modern northern Iran)
DIED: 585 B.C.E.; Media
RELATED CIVILIZATIONS: Media, Scythia
MAJOR ROLE/POSITION: King

Life. Cyaxares (si-AK-suh-reez), the son of Phraortes, reigned over the Medes from 625 to 585 B.C.E. According to the historian Herodotus, Cyaxares organized the Median army into three mobile classes of spearmen, bowmen, and cavalry and was able to expel the nomadic Scythians from the area. He made an alliance with Nabopolassar, the king of the Chaldeans. Cyaxares' daughter was given in marriage to the Babylonian prince, Nebuchadnezzar II. It was for her that he built the famous Hanging Gardens of Babylon.

The Medes and the Chaldeans toppled the hitherto invincible Assyrian Empire, capturing Nineveh in 612 B.C.E. An Assyrian remnant, who fled to Haran, were defeated by the Chaldeans and the Medes in 610 B.C.E.

During the last five years of his reign, Cyaxares fought against the Lydians of western Anatolia. Herodotus claimed that the conflict was ended in 585 B.C.E. by the Greek philosopher Thales's prediction of an eclipse. The peace was sealed by the marriage of a Lydian princess to Astyages, the son of Cyaxares.

Influence. The long reign of Cyaxares saw the ascendancy of the Medes.

ADDITIONAL RESOURCES
Cook, J. M. *The Persian Empire*. New York: Schocken, 1983.
Culican, W. *The Medes and Persians*. New York: Praeger, 1965.
Yamauchi, E. *Foes from the Northern Frontier*. Grand Rapids, Mich.: Baker, 1982.
_____. *Persia and the Bible*. Grand Rapids, Mich.: Baker, 1990.

SEE ALSO: Assyria; Astyages; Herodotus; Nebuchadnezzar II; Persia.

—Edwin Yamauchi

CYCLADES

ALSO KNOWN AS: Kikládhes
DATE: 3000 B.C.E.-700 C.E.
LOCALE: Southern Aegean
RELATED CIVILIZATIONS: Neolithic, Mycenaean, Archaic, Classical, Hellenistic, Roman, and Late Antique Greece
SIGNIFICANCE: Although often influenced by outside powers in historical times, these islands were the cradle of many artistic achievements in antiquity.

The Cyclades (si-kluh-DEEZ) are islands and islets whose position on sailing routes across the Aegean Sea has resulted in almost continual occupation from Neolithic times to the present day. Geographers in antiquity were not in complete agreement on which islands should be grouped under this heading (the name refers to their positioning in a circle around the holy island of Delos); all, however, include Andros (Ándros), Ceos (Kéa), Cythnos (Kíthnos), Mykonos (Míkonos), Naxos, Paros

(Páros), Seriphos (Sérifos), Siphnos (Sífnos), Syros, and Tenos (Tínos). Cycladic islands tend to have limited arable land and available water but may have compensated for these scarcities in antiquity by means of sea commerce; the mining of products such as iron, marble (particularly Paros and Naxos), gold and silver (Siphnos especially); and possibly by the terracing of hill slopes to increase their food supply.

The islands were sparsely settled in the Neolithic period, but beginning in the third millennium B.C.E., an influential Bronze Age culture arose in the area. This culture is most noteworthy for having produced strikingly distinctive marble figurines of both stylized and naturalistic types. Art historians have identified several individual artists, such as the Dresden Master, from certain characteristics of these objects. Their function remains speculative, although many have come from graves, and some sort of sacred, ritualized application is likely.

From the middle of the eleventh century B.C.E., nearly all the islands appear to have been abandoned until the Geometric period of the tenth through eighth centuries B.C.E., when they were gradually recolonized by Ionians, who paid homage to the temple of Apollo on Delos. By the Archaic period, oligarchies began to form on the islands, and in some cases, tyrannies, such as that of Lygdamis of Naxos (sixth century B.C.E.), developed. The tradition of sculpture as well as various techniques of monumental architecture continued through Archaic times.

The Greco-Persian Wars saw some islands (such as Paros) contributing to the Persian naval forces. In 478 B.C.E., the Cyclades joined the Delian League. With the collapse of the Athenian Empire in 404 B.C.E., the most important islands appear to have come under the control of Spartan *harmosts*, or garrison commanders. After 394 B.C.E., these Spartan forces were driven out, and most of the Cyclades entered the Second Athenian League soon after its formation in 377 B.C.E. The Hellenistic period saw a succession of various overlords until 133 B.C.E., when Roman control was established. The popular image of the islands as desolate and poverty-stricken, an image that some scholars have recently challenged, arose during this time. A few of the islands were also used as bases by the Byzantine fleet during Late Antiquity. The islands were the site of numerous archaeological surveys and excavations in the 1980's and 1990's.

ADDITIONAL RESOURCES

Barber, R. L. N. *The Cyclades in the Bronze Age.* Iowa City: University of Iowa Press, 1987.

Cherry, J. F., J. L. Davis, and E. Mantzourani. *Landscape Archaeology as Long-Term History.* Los Angeles: University of California Press, 1991.

Reger, Gary. *Regionalism and Change in the Economy of Independent Delos.* Berkeley: University of California Press, 1994.

Renfrew, C., and M. Wagstaff, eds. *An Island Polity: The Archaeology of Exploitation on Melos.* Cambridge, England: Cambridge University Press, 1982.

SEE ALSO: Art and architecture; Greco-Persian Wars; Greece, Archaic; Greece, Hellenistic; Greece, Mycenaean; Thera.

—Brian Rutishauser

CYNOSCEPHALAE, BATTLE OF

DATE: 197 B.C.E.

LOCALE: Southwest Thessaly, Greece

RELATED CIVILIZATIONS: Republican Rome, Macedonia

SIGNIFICANCE: The defeat of King Philip V of Macedonia at Cynoscephalae effectively checked the expansion of Macedonian political influence into southern Greece while contributing markedly to the establishment of Roman power in the region.

Background. In 200 B.C.E., Rome declared war against King Philip V after Rhodes and Pergamum appealed to the senate for aid in stopping Macedonian aggression in the eastern Mediterranean. Roman military activity in Greece through 198 B.C.E. proved largely inconclusive in slowing Philip's territorial ambitions. The following year, Roman and Macedonian armies clashed in a climactic battle at Cynoscephalae (sih-nuh-SEH-fuh-lee).

Action. Philip V and an army of 20,000 men engaged a Roman force of equal size under the proconsul Titus Quinctius Flamininus. The battle spontaneously developed after the armies unexpectedly encountered each other in fog on Cynoscephalae ridge. Philip, advancing on the Roman formation with only the right wing of his phalanx fully assembled, drove back the Roman left, but broken ground disrupted the cohesion of the Macedonian left wing, permitting the forces of Flamininus's right to gain a complete victory in that quarter. With the defeat of Philip's left assured, a Roman tribune detached twenty maniples from the legions' right and attacked the successful portion of the phalanx in the rear. This action completely shattered the Macedonian formation. Philip's losses included 8,000 killed and 5,000 captured. Roman casualties amounted to 700 dead.

Consequences. Following his defeat at Cynoscephalae, Philip was forced by Rome to surrender his fleet, relinquish all claims to territorial possessions in Greece and the Aegean Sea, and pay a sizable war indemnity. Rome became the primary political arbiter in the region.

ADDITIONAL RESOURCES

Adcock, F. E. *The Roman Art of War Under the Republic*. New York: Barnes & Nobles, 1995.

Walbank, F. W. *Philip V of Macedon*. Hamden, Conn.: Archon Books, 1967.

SEE ALSO: Flamininus, Titus Quinctius; Greece, Hellenistic and Roman; Macedonia; Philip V; Rome, Republican.

—Donathan Taylor

CYPRIAN OF CARTHAGE, SAINT

ALSO KNOWN AS: Thascius Caecilius Cyprianus
BORN: c. 200 C.E.; Carthage, North Africa
DIED: September 14, 258 C.E.; Carthage, North Africa
RELATED CIVILIZATION: Imperial Rome
MAJOR ROLE/POSITION: Christian bishop

Life. Born into a pagan family of wealth and social standing, Cyprian (SIHP-ree-uhn) of Carthage received a first-rate education and later became a distinguished rhetorician. Converted to Christianity about 246 C.E., he soon was elected bishop of Carthage, a leading city in North Africa. When the emperor Decius commenced his persecution of Christians in about 249 C.E., Cyprian was forced to flee but maintained the governance of his church through correspondence. Returning in 251 C.E., he was confronted with the issue of Christians who had lapsed from their faith during the persecution. Arguing for a middle course of penance and delay before reconciliation to the Church, Cyprian was opposed by both rigorists and a more moderate faction. This debate, in turn, led to quarrels with the bishop of Rome, Stephen, on the matter of the rebaptism of

schismatics. In the meantime, a new emperor, Valerian, renewed the persecution of Christians in 257 C.E. Again Cyprian fled but soon returned to Carthage and was martyred there.

Influence. Although Cyprian was not an original theologian, his writings reveal a remarkably talented and focused church administrator and pastor. As a martyr, his memory was revered for centuries by the North African church.

ADDITIONAL RESOURCES

Hinchcliff, P. *Cyprian of Carthage and the Unity of the Christian Church*. London: Chapman, 1974.

Robeck, Cecil M. *Prophecy in Carthage: Perpetua, Tertullian, and Cyprian*. Cleveland, Ohio: Pilgrim Press, 1992.

Sage, M. M. *Cyprian*. Cambridge, Mass.: Philadelphia Patristic Foundation, 1975.

SEE ALSO: Africa, North; Carthage; Christianity; Rome, Imperial; Valerian.

—Craig L. Hanson

CYPRUS

DATE: 6000 B.C.E.-700 C.E.
LOCALE: Northeastern Mediterranean Sea, fifty miles south of modern Turkey
SIGNIFICANCE: An important stop between the East and West with safe harbors and abundant agricultural products and mineral resources, particularly copper.

Cyprus is an island located in the northeastern corner of the Mediterranean Sea, fifty miles south of the coast of Cilicia, near the Levant. It is approximately 140 miles (225 kilometers) long by 60 miles (97 kilometers) wide. The island, because of its strategic location, was seen throughout history as an important possession and found itself involved in many conflicts through the ages. The island was also seen as a valuable economic resource because of its plentiful production of wheat, olives, and wine and its extensive copper deposits. The ancient writer Ammianus Marcellinus noted that Cyprus was so fertile that it could completely build and stock cargo ships solely from its own resources. According to myth, Aphrodite (Greek goddess of love, beauty, and fertility) emerged from the sea at Cyprus, and numerous temples to her can be found throughout the island, especially near Paphos.

Early history. Archaeological excavations on the island have uncovered evidence for a preceramic early Neolithic culture at sites such as Khirokitia and Kalavasos (Tenta), dating back to the sixth millennium B.C.E. Small, circular buildings constructed from little stones, sun-dried mud bricks, and wood characterize these small farming sites. This early phase was followed by a Late Neolithic period (c. 4500-3500 B.C.E.) characterized by square buildings, often partially underground, and the use of pottery as seen at the sites of Sotira (Teppes) and Ayios Epiktitos (Vrysi). The daily life in those Neolithic villages was devoted to farming, hunting, and animal husbandry. The Chalcolithic period (c. 4500-2500/2300 B.C.E.) saw the first evidence of metalworking on the island with the appearance of copper implements. The copper industry on the island began to flourish, and commercial contacts were established with other regions around the eastern Mediterranean.

In the Early Bronze Age (2500/2300-1900 B.C.E.), settlers from western Anatolia began to arrive in large numbers and soon replaced the indigenous culture with their Near Eastern culture. Economic prosperity continued, and urbanization began in the coastal regions. In the Late Bronze Age (c. 1600-1050 B.C.E.), Cyprus became more commercial as trade with Egypt and the Levant increased. The increased commercial traffic resulted in the growth of large cities on the eastern and southern coasts, such as Enkomi and Maroni (Vournes). These cities were constructed from large ashlar blocks, similar to Near Eastern cities. During this period, as Cyprus became known as a rich source for copper, Mycenaean merchants first visited the island. Soon Mycenaean colonists started arriving in large numbers, and the local culture developed a significant Aegean influence.

Around the year 1250 B.C.E., the island began to suffer from the same problems that resulted in the general collapse of Bronze Age civilizations around the eastern Mediterranean. Piracy increased, resulting in decreased commercial traffic, and in 1190 B.C.E., the coastal cities were attacked and destroyed by raiders referred to in Egyptian sources as the Sea Peoples. The local culture was further changed with the arrival of new Greek colonists fleeing the collapse of the Mycenaean civilization on mainland Greece. From this point on, Greek culture, religion, and language were to be dominant on the island as the Greek colonists controlled the major Cypriot kingdoms of Kourion, Lapithos, Marion, Pahos, Salamis, Soli, and Tamassos.

Prosperity and outside rule. As Cyprus entered the Iron Age (c. 1050-323 B.C.E.), it lost contact with Greece and strengthened its ties to the Near East. Phoenicians from Tyre settled on the island and founded a colony at Kition during the ninth century B.C.E. In the eighth century B.C.E., contact with Greece was reestablished. Cyprus became extremely prosperous, as can be seen by the wealth and splendor of items discovered during the archaeological investigation of the royal tombs at Salamis. From 709 to 663 B.C.E., the Cypriot kingdoms were part of the Assyrian Empire but were allowed to keep their local autonomy. Following the end of Assyrian rule, the Cypriot kingdoms enjoyed a brief period of independence until the Egyptian pharaoh Amasis annexed them around 560 B.C.E.

After a short period of Egyptian control (c. 560-540 B.C.E.), Cyprus became part of the Persian Empire during the reign of Cambyses II (r. 529-522 B.C.E.). Other than a few brief attempts at rebellion, such as the Ionian Revolt in 500 B.C.E. and the revolt of Evagoras I of Salamis in the late fifth/early fourth century B.C.E., Cyprus remained part of the Persian Empire until the latter's destruction by Alexander the Great. In gratitude for the assistance rendered to him by Cypriot naval forces at the siege of Tyre, Alexander granted the Cypriot kingdoms their freedom.

After Alexander the Great's untimely death in 323 B.C.E., the leading city-states of Cyprus formed an alliance with Ptolemy I Soter against the advances of the Antigonids. Demetrius Poliorcetes captured the island in 306 B.C.E., only to see it recaptured by the Ptolemies in 294 B.C.E. When the Ptolemies regained control of the island, they made the city of Nea Paphos, founded by Nikokles I, their new administrative center. Continuing the economic trend begun in the classical period, Cyprus continued to experience increased economic prosperity—a trend seen throughout the eastern Mediterranean during this period.

Roman rule. In the year 100 B.C.E., the Roman senate, concerned about the problem of piracy in the eastern Mediterranean and its effect on trade, passed a *senatus consultum* that encouraged all friends and allies of Rome, including Cyprus, to give no assistance or aid to pirates. This was followed by the sudden annexation of Cyprus in 58 B.C.E. A Roman tribune for that year, Publius Clodius Pulcher, was able to secure the passage of a law that reduced Cyprus to a province and confiscated the wealth of Cyprus's king. For the next ten years, Cyprus was considered part of or an addition to the province of Cilicia. In 48/47 B.C.E., Julius Caesar gave Cyprus to Egypt to be ruled by the two children of Auletes, but in actuality Cleopatra VII governed the island. Marc Antony confirmed Egypt's control over Cyprus and Cilicia in 36 B.C.E. Augustus reclaimed the island for Rome when he assumed control of Egypt after his victory at Actium over Cleopatra and Antony in 31 B.C.E. In 22 B.C.E., Augustus ceded the island to the Roman senate to become a senatorial province but a minor one governed only by a praetor. To aid in its government, the island was divided into twelve or thirteen regions, each controlled by the major city in its area.

Throughout the Roman period, the island was fairly quiet, with little political or military disruption. Tradition claims that the Christian apostles Paul and Barnabas visited the island during their first missionary journey in 45 C.E. and converted the Roman governor Sergius Paulus to Christianity. In 116 C.E., the Jewish insurrection of Artemion devastated part of the island, including the cities of Paphos and Salamis. Roman troops were sent to the island and harshly put down the revolt. In 164 C.E., a plaguelike illness ravished the island, killing many inhabitants. This was followed by an invasion of the Goths in 269 C.E. A series of plagues struck the island during the last half of the sixth century C.E.

Arabs and Byzantines. After the plagues, the island remained relatively peaceful until the Arab empire began to mobilize for an attack upon the Byzantine Empire. In 647 C.E., the island became the first step for the Arabs in their attempt to use sea power to defeat the Byzantines because Cyprus would make an ideal staging area for a naval force that intended to attack Constantinople. The Arab raids on the island resulted in the destruction and abandonment of many coastal cities, and the economy suffered tremendously. Two years later, in 649 C.E., the Arabs attacked Cyprus with a large naval fleet under the leadership of Mu'āwiyah I. He captured and looted the capital city of Salamis and pillaged the rest of the island. In 654 C.E., another large Arab invasion further devastated the island and depressed the economy. Following this attack, the Arabs left a garrison of 12,000 men stationed on Cyprus. In 683 C.E., the garrison was withdrawn, and five years later a treaty between the Byzantine emperor Justinian II and the Arab caliph ʿAbd al-Malik resulted in the island of Cyprus becoming a neutral area, with no troops stationed there and the taxes being equally divided between the Arab caliph and the Byzantine emperor.

ADDITIONAL RESOURCES

Hill, George Francis. *A History of Cyprus.* 4 vols. Cambridge, England: Cambridge University Press, 1940-1952.

Karageorghis, Vassos. *Ancient Cyprus: Seven Thousand Years of Art and Archaeology.* Baton Rouge: Louisiana State University Press, 1981.

———. *Cyprus: From The Stone Age to the Romans.* New York: Thames and Hudson, 1982.

Panteli, Stavros. *A New History of Cyprus, from the Earliest Times to the Present Day.* London: East-West Publications, 1984.

Tatton-Brown, Veronica. *Ancient Cyprus.* London: British Museum Press, 1997.

SEE ALSO: ʿAbd al-Malik; Alexander the Great; Ammianus Marcellinus; Antigonid Dynasty; Antony, Marc; Arabia; Assyria; Augustus; Byzantine Empire; Caesar, Julius; Christianity; Cleopatra VII; Egypt, Ptolemaic and Roman; Goths; Greece, Mycenaean; Judaism; Persia; Phoenicia; Rome, Republican.

—*R. Scott Moore*

CYPSELUS OF CORINTH

ALSO KNOWN AS: Kypselos of Korinthos
BORN: early seventh century B.C.E.; Corinth
DIED: 627 B.C.E.; place unknown
RELATED CIVILIZATIONS: Corinth, Archaic Greece
MAJOR ROLE/POSITION: Tyrant

Life. Archaic Corinth was ruled by the Bacchiadae, a tight-knit aristocratic clan, of which Cypselus's (SIHP-suh-luhs) mother was a member. Cypselus of Corinth seems to have held both military and civil office under their rule. Sensing growing hostility toward the Bacchiadae, he led an insurrection and established himself as tyrant. Although this was done primarily with the assistance of wealthy Corinthians dissatisfied with Bacchiad rule, Cypselus seems also to have enjoyed popular support. During the thirty years of his rule, circa 657-627 B.C.E., he reorganized Corinthian political institutions, founded colonies in northwestern Greece, and built the Corinthian treasury at Delphi. Growing trade and external contacts brought prosperity and artistic innovation. Cypselus was succeeded by his son Periander of Corinth and then his grand-nephew

Psammetichus, who was soon deposed and killed (c. 585), ending the Cypselid dynasty.

Influence. Cypselus founded one of the earliest and longest-lasting tyrant dynasties. He would serve as a model for other Greek tyrants and as an archetype of the cruel, ruthless dictator for those who opposed tyranny—despite the fact that he almost certainly enjoyed a good reputation in his native Corinth.

ADDITIONAL RESOURCES

Herodotus. *The Histories*. Translated by Robin Waterfield. New York: Oxford University Press, 1998.

McGlew, J. *Tyranny and Political Culture in Ancient Greece*. Ithaca, N.Y.: Cornell University Press, 1993.

Salmon, J. B. *Wealthy Corinth*. New York: Oxford University Press, 1984.

SEE ALSO: Greece, Archaic; Periander of Corinth; Thirty Tyrants.

—Shawn A. Ross

CYRIL OF ALEXANDRIA, SAINT

BORN: c. 375 C.E.; place unknown
DIED: June 27, 444 C.E.; place unknown
RELATED CIVILIZATIONS: Roman Egypt, Imperial Rome
MAJOR ROLE/POSITION: Patriarch of Alexandria

Life. Cyril (SIH-ruhl) of Alexandria was born into an influential Christian family that included his uncle Theophilus, patriarch of Alexandria (385-412 C.E.). Raised near the capital, Cyril appears to have been groomed as the successor to his uncle's important ecclesiastical position. Indeed, when after a vicious struggle Cyril became patriarch (412 C.E.), he continued both his uncle's aggressive antipagan policies in Egypt and his attempts to make Alexandria the most influential of the urban centers in the Roman Empire. His position and policies were furthered through his extensive writings and his participation in doctrinal controversies, such as the Nestorian controversy, which included the Council of Ephesus (431 C.E.). Cyril formed strong bonds with the imperial household, making his political

and religious influence in Alexandria even greater. Though he was not entirely responsible for violence against those who followed non-Christian religious beliefs and philosophies, he has been consistently associated with the violent atmosphere that prevailed in Alexandria and that produced greater anti-Jewish sentiment in that city as well as the murder of Hypatia (415 C.E.), a Neoplatonic philosopher.

Influence. The work of the highly educated Cyril was crucial in the establishment of orthodox Christian theology and the advancement of orthodoxy in the halls of political power in Constantinople. In later years, his work found greater appreciation and therefore had greater influence on Western Christianity.

ADDITIONAL RESOURCES

Burghardt, Walter J. *The Image of God in Man According to Cyril of Alexandria*. Washington, D.C.: Catholic University of America Press, 1957.

Cyril, Saint. *Cyril of Alexandria*. Translated by Norman Russell. New York: Routledge, 2000.

Kerrigan, Alexander. *St. Cyril of Alexandria: Interpreter of the Old Testament.* Rome: Pontificio Instituto Biblico, 1952.

Prestige, George Leonard. *Fathers and Heretics.* Reprint. London: SPCK, 1985.

Wilken, Robert Louis. *Judaism and the Early Christian Mind: A Study of Cyril of Alexandria's Exegesis and Theology.* New Haven, Conn.: Yale University Press, 1971.

See also: Alexandrian patriarchs; Christianity; Egypt, Ptolemaic and Roman; Hypatia; Jewish diaspora; Judaism; Nestorius; Rome, Imperial.

—*Kenneth R. Calvert*

Cyrus the Great

Born: c. 601-590 B.C.E.; Media (modern northern Iran)
Died: c. 530 B.C.E.; Scythia (southern Russia)
Related civilizations: Persia, Mesopotamia
Major role/position: Monarch

Life. Legend shrouds the origins of Shah Cyrus (SIH-ruhs) the Great, founder of the Persian Empire. The most reliable sources connect him to Achaemenes, founder of a Persian tribal confederation and vassal to the king of the Medes. Cyrus became king of Anshan, the western Persian lands, circa 559 B.C.E. at a time when the Median ruler, Astyages, was facing popular opposition. Cyrus declared himself independent, and in either 553 or 550 B.C.E., Astyages marched against him. Before they clashed, however, the Median army mutinied, arrested Astyages, and transferred their loyalty to Cyrus.

Cyrus immediately displayed one of the many appealing personal traits that made him a charismatic leader—magnanimity. He spared Astyages and retained most of his officials while discreetly "Persianizing" the ruling elite. Nonetheless, Croesus, king of Lydia and ally of Astyages, was determined to cross swords with Persia. Allied with Egypt, Sparta, and Babylon, the Lydians invaded Persian Cappadocia in 547 B.C.E. Cyrus marched his army twelve hundred miles (nineteen hundred kilometers) and repelled the invaders. Then, to Croesus's shock, the shah pursued him into Lydia and captured Sardis, capital of Lydia. Cyrus thereby gained all Anatolia, including the Greek towns on Anatolia's coast. Again, along with his military prowess, generosity to the defeated allowed Cyrus to win over his enemies.

After occupying what became modern Afghanistan and Turkmenistan, Cyrus turned to Babylon, where King Nabonidus and his son, Belshazzar, had alienated their subjects through incompetence, financial irresponsibility, and religious persecution. About 540 B.C.E., Cyrus declared that Babylon's chief

Cyrus the Great. (North Wind Picture Archives)

god, Marduk, had commissioned him to rescue the Babylonian people. Trusting in the Persian reputation for moderate rule, Babylonian priests, generals, and officials openly aided the shah. As Cyrus entered Babylon in 539 B.C.E., Phoenicia, Palestine, and much of Syria voluntarily submitted to him. Shortly afterward, the shah authorized Babylon's hostage Jewish community to return to Israel, restored Jewish property looted during the 589 B.C.E. Babylonian conquests, and encouraged reconstruction of the temple in Jerusalem. That Cyrus credited his actions to the direct command of Israel's God is directly and frequently noted in several Old Testament sources.

After conquering the Levant, the shah appeared to be planning an expedition to subjugate the Nile Valley. However, in about 530 B.C.E., Cyrus was fighting nomads in Turkmenistan at the other end of his empire. In a monumental battle near the Jaxartes River, the tribesmen overcame the Persians. Shah Cyrus died alongside thousands of his soldiers. His son, Cambyses II, inherited the throne that same year and went on to conquer the Egyptians and move eastward into the Indus Valley.

Influence. Cyrus and his Achaemenian Dynasty ruled the largest empire in the western Afro-Eurasian world before Alexander the Great. In addition, they pioneered techniques of rule that other empires later imitated, seeking to integrate subject peoples into the state and economy instead of exploiting them. Persia also became a conduit between India, China, and the west. Zoroastrianism, the tolerant monotheism of the Persian people, profoundly influenced the religions of the empire, including Judaism.

ADDITIONAL RESOURCES

Cook, J. M. *The Persian Empire*. New York: Schocken, 1983.
Herodotus. *The Histories*. Translated by Robin Waterfield. New York: Oxford University Press, 1998.
Wiesehöfer, J. *Ancient Persia*. New York: Tauris, 1996.

SEE ALSO: Achaemenian Dynasty; Astyages; Babylonia; Croesus; Jerusalem, temple of; Persia; Zoroastrianism.

—Weston F. Cook, Jr.

— D —

DALLÁN FORGAILL

ALSO KNOWN AS: Saint Dallán; Dallán of Cluain
   Dallain
BORN: sixth century C.E.; Connaught, Ireland
DIED: 598 C.E.; Inniskeel, Ireland
RELATED CIVILIZATION: Ireland
MAJOR ROLE/POSITION: Bard, monk

Life. A kinsman of Saint Aidan, Dallán Forgaill
(dah-LAHN FAWR-gil) was renowned for his scholarship. He is said to have become blind from intensive
study while rising to power as chief bard of Ireland, a
position he attained in 575 C.E.

Shortly after Dallán gained power, the high king of
Ireland sought to pressure the assembly of Dunceat into
disbanding the bardic guild. However, Saint Columba
successfully argued to the assembly that bards were
necessary to the preservation of Irish history. In gratitude, Dallán wrote the panegyric *Ambra Choluim Kille*
(sixth century C.E.; English translation, 1871). Dallán
thereafter reformed the order of bards, instituting practices that turned the focus of bardship toward preservation of the culture. In later life, Dallán retired to a monastery at Inniskeel and was killed there during a break-in by pirates.

Influence. Along with other scholars associated
with Saint Columba, Dallán was instrumental in the
preservation of knowledge in Ireland and Scotland
through the Dark Ages. His reformation of the bardic
order enabled that pagan institution to survive the
Christian conversion of Ireland. The bardic guild actively contributed to the preservation of Irish culture
until the last bard died in 1738.

ADDITIONAL RESOURCES
Adamnan. *Life of St. Columba.* Translated by Richard
   Sharpe. New York: Penguin Books, 1995.
Clancy, Thomas, and Gilbert Markus. *Iona: The Earliest Poetry of a Celtic Monastery.* Edinburgh, Scotland: Edinburgh University Press, 1995.
Sellner, Edward. *Wisdom of the Celtic Saints.* Notre
   Dame, Ind.: Ave Maria Press, 1993.

SEE ALSO: Christianity; Columba, Saint; Ireland.
   —*Michael W. Simpson*

DALTON TRADITION

DATE: 8000-7400 B.C.E.
LOCALE: Much of the southeastern United States,
   from North Carolina and Alabama to Illinois and
   as far north as New England
SIGNIFICANCE: The Dalton tradition, identified by a
   distinctive style of projectile point, was a dominant
   hunting tradition in the southeastern United States
   during the Early Archaic period.

Chert or flint Dalton points (called Hardaway in North
Carolina) mark a hunting tradition prevalent throughout the American southeast from about 8000 to 7400
B.C.E. They are distinguished by a slender triangular
shape, a concave base, and sometimes by "ears" projecting from either side of the base. The North Carolina variant, the Hardaway point, has a truer triangular form,
as well as side notches and flaring ears. These projectile
points were often repeatedly resharpened and, when
too reduced by sharpening to tip a spear, recycled
as knives, scrapers, or chisels. Dalton and Hardaway
points remained in use until about 7400 B.C.E., when
they were replaced by new styles.

Although it is impossible to paint an in-depth portrait of the peoples associated with the Dalton tradition,
it is known that their world was marked by deciduous
forests, which had gradually replaced jack pines and
spruces as glacial sheets receded northward throughout
the early Holocene epoch. It is likely that the people of
the Dalton tradition supplemented their diet of wild
meat with nuts and other vegetable matter present in

these oak-dominated woodlands.

Excavations of Dalton sites in the Little Tennessee Valley and northeastern Arkansas have produced stone tools—points, hammerstones, knives, and choppers—primarily associated with hunting and butchering. The Sloan site in Arkansas, believed to have been a burial site, has produced bone fragments and artifacts that were probably interred as grave goods, including groups of Dalton points (probably originally hafted and placed in bundles).

ADDITIONAL RESOURCES

Chapman, Jefferson. *Tellico Archaeology.* Knoxville: University of Tennessee Press, 1985.

Smith, Bruce. "The Archaeology of the Southeastern United States: From Dalton to De Soto, 10,500 to 500 B.P." *Advances in World Archaeology* 5 (1986): 1-92.

SEE ALSO: Archaic North American culture; Deptford culture.

—*Jeremiah R. Taylor*

DAMASCUS DOCUMENT

AUTHORSHIP: unknown
DATE: oldest fragments, c. 100 B.C.E.
LOCALE: Khirbat Qumran, Israel, and Cairo, Egypt
RELATED CIVILIZATION: Jewish sectarians
SIGNIFICANCE: The document gives details of the organization and beliefs of a peripheral Judaean group, which originated in the second century B.C.E. and survived in Egypt until the twelfth century C.E.

Originally discovered as two fragments in a Jewish synagogue in Cairo in 1896-1897, the Damascus document was compiled for a community, probably of Essenes, who identified themselves with the old Zadokite priesthood in Jerusalem. Five additional fragments were discovered later among the Dead Sea Scrolls. They dated from about 100 B.C.E. Differences among the fragments suggest that their two major types of materials, admonitions and laws, originally circulated independently.

The document begins with a reference to Judaeans' going into exile in Damascus (a symbol for Babylon) under Nebuchadnezzar II in 587 or 586 B.C.E. and describes God's rescue of a group of them 390 years later

under their founder, called the Teacher of Righteousness. The rest of the book is cast as the sayings of the Teacher. Roughly one half consists of the citation of and commentary on a selection of passages from the Hebrew Bible designed to warn the Teacher's community to remain faithful to God and to its traditions. The other half is a collection of laws designed to instruct the community in how to live in the towns of Israel.

ADDITIONAL RESOURCES

Davies, Philip R. *The Damascus Covenant: An Interpretation of the Damascus Document.* Sheffield, England: Sheffield Academic Press, 1983.

Hempel, Charlotte. *The Damascus Texts.* Sheffield, England: Sheffield Academic Press, 2000.

Schechter, Solomon. *Fragments of a Zadokite Work.* Cambridge, England: Cambridge University Press, 1910.

SEE ALSO: Bible: Jewish; Dead Sea Scrolls; Israel; Judaism; Nebuchadnezzar II.

—*Paul L. Redditt*

DAṆḌIN

FLOURISHED: late sixth and early seventh centuries C.E.
RELATED CIVILIZATION: India
MAJOR ROLE/POSITION: Sanskrit writer

Life. Daṇḍin (DAHN-deen) was a Sanskrit writer, probably of south Indian origin. He authored *Kāv-*

yādarśa (sixth or seventh century C.E.; *Kavyadarsa of Dandin*, 1924), considered a valuable contribution to Sanskrit poetry, and a *gadya* (prose) romance titled *Daśakumāracarita* (sixth or seventh century C.E.; *The Adventures of the Ten Princes*, 1927), which is written in elegant, polished, and involved Sanskrit. Daṇḍin uses verbal tricks and grammatical devices to show his mastery of the language. To illustrate, he relates an episode in which a lover is bitten on the lip and must speak without the use of labials, which he is unable to pronounce.

Influence. Daṇḍin's novel, *The Adventures of the Ten Princes*, is long and rambling and full of wonder and magic, like adventures of medieval princes in Western fairy tales. It provides a glimpse of the luxury and depravity of the age. Love is portrayed at its most sordid level, wholly of the senses, of violent and unrestrained lusts that arise and demand immediate fulfillment, regardless of the obstacles. Indian and European critics have censured Daṇḍin for his vulgar puns, suggestive innuendos, graphic details of seduction, and general departure from good taste.

ADDITIONAL RESOURCES

Chandrasekharan, K., and B. H. S. Sastri. *Sanskrit Literature*. Bombay, India: International Book House, 1951.

Majumdar, Ramesh Chandra, Achut Dattatraya Pusalkar, and Asoke Majumdar. *The Vedic Age*. Bombay, India: Bharatiya Vidya Bhaban, 1951.

Tripathi, Jayasankara. *Dandin*. New Delhi, India: Sahitya Akademi, 1996.

Walker, Benjamin. *Hindu World: An Encyclopedic Survey of Hinduism*. London: George Allen and Unwin, 1968.

SEE ALSO: Hinduism; India.

—Arthur W. Helweg

DAOISM

ALSO KNOWN AS: *Wade-Giles* Taoism
DATE: beginning in 300 B.C.E.
LOCALE: China
RELATED CIVILIZATIONS: China, Korea
SIGNIFICANCE: One of the major world religious traditions, Daoism inspires, shapes, and infuses much of Chinese culture, philosophy, medicine, art, calligraphy, and spiritual disciplines.

Daoism (DOW-ih-zuhm) is a complex and multifaceted part of the traditional landscape of Chinese culture. Typically exclusively associated with the philosophically oriented teachings of the classic text *Dao De Jing* (possibly sixth century B.C.E., probably compiled late third century B.C.E.; *The Speculations on Metaphysics, Polity, and Morality of "the Old Philosopher, Lau-Tsze,"* 1868; better known as the *Dao De Jing*), Daoism in fact draws upon and incorporates an extensive range of religious and cultural elements. As one of China's three principal religions (Confucianism and Buddhism being the others), Daoism has exercised tremendous influence on the political, cultural, and social life of the Chinese.

Daoism as an institutionalized religion began in 142 C.E., when the incarnated god of the Dao, Taishang Laojun, appeared to Zhang Daoling, a Daoist philosopher. Taishang, considered to be the deified Laozi, revealed that Zhang was to receive the mandate to rule the chosen people of Daoism and become the first Celestial Master and founder of the first organized Daoist school.

Initially known as the Five Bushels of Rice movement for the contributions required of all members, the Celestial Masters school placed heavy emphasis on ritual, exorcisms, and moral purity.

Zhang Daoling drew heavily on the philosophical teachings contained in the *Dao De Jing* and *Zhuangzi* (traditionally c. 300 B.C.E., probably compiled c. 285-160 B.C.E.; *The Divine Classic of Nan-hua*, 1881; also known as *The Complete Works of Chuang Tzu*, 1968; commonly known as *Zhuangzi*, 1991). Both texts are traditionally dated to the fourth and third centuries B.C.E., although their authorship is a matter of some dispute. Although scholars discount the association, tradition holds that Laozi (the Old Master) composed the approximately five-thousand-character *Dao De Jing* as he was departing China riding on an ox. The common theme in both works revolves around the concept of the Dao, from which the tradition derives its name. By its very definition, the Dao is indescribable, ineffable, and unnamable. Simultaneously immanent and transcendent, the Dao is the original source of and natural order present in all things. De represents the efficacious power of the Dao, the means by which generation takes place and is manifested.

Daoism advocates the pursuit of the simplicity and naturalness inherent in Dao through spiritual cultivation. By returning to the freedom and spontaneity of the Dao, the Daoist adept strives to become a sage or perfected person (*zhenren*), thereby achieving immortality through transcendence of the human condition. Although some sought transcendence by means of alchemical elixirs and pills, the majority of Daoist practitioners relied on meditation, ritual, and medical techniques such as acupuncture and dietetics.

Following the establishment of the Celestial Masters school, Daoism continued to grow and flourish. By the sixth century C.E., it had become a highly diversified religion with numerous doctrinal and sectarian traditions, initiated and ordained priesthoods, countless rituals, and a growing body of canonical literature. Eventually, Daoist scriptures would be compiled into a canon of more than one thousand volumes. The heyday of Daoist political influence came during the Tang Dynasty (618-907 C.E.), when the deified Laozi was proclaimed head of the dynasty's ancestral line and every emperor heavily patronized Daoism.

ADDITIONAL RESOURCES
Kohn, Livia, ed. *Daoism Handbook*. Boston: E. J. Brill, 2000.
_____. *The Taoist Experience: An Anthology*. Albany, N.Y.: State University of New York Press, 1993.
Pregadio, Fabrizio, ed. *The Encyclopedia of Taoism*. Richmond, Surrey, England: Curzon Press, 2000.
Robinet, Isabelle. *Taoism: Growth of a Religion*. Stanford, Calif.: Stanford University Press, 1997.
Schipper, Kristofer. *The Taoist Body*. Berkeley: University of California Press, 1994.

SEE ALSO: China; Laozi; Tang Dynasty; Zhou Dynasty; *Zhuangzi*.

—*Jeffrey Dippmann*

DARIUS THE GREAT

ALSO KNOWN AS: Darius I
BORN: 550 B.C.E.; place unknown
DIED: 486 B.C.E.; Persepolis, Persia
RELATED CIVILIZATIONS: Persia, Classical Greece, Mesopotamia, Pharaonic Egypt
MAJOR ROLE/POSITION: Emperor

Life. Darius (DAH-ree-uhs) the Great seized power and became ruler of the Achaemenian Empire in 522 B.C.E. It is uncertain whether he killed Bardiya, brother of Cambyses II, or a usurper called Gaumata, although he proclaims the latter to be the case in a trilingual inscription at Behistun in Iran, and the historian Herodotus supports his assertion. In the inscription, he mentions suppressing many revolts against his rule.

The six companions of Darius who aided him in his accession were given privileged positions in the reorganization of the empire, and their descendants continued in high regard until the end of the empire. Darius divided the empire into satrapies and extended the boundaries of Achaemenian domains into Thrace and India. Herodotus described his unsuccessful expedition into south Russia against the Scythians. He ordered subject nations, such as the Egyptians, to codify their laws, and he allowed the Jews to rebuild their temple in Jerusalem. Above the local laws was a king's law, more secular than the local religious laws, that was applied throughout

Darius the Great. (Library of Congress)

the empire. These actions caused him to be known as a great lawgiver.

He built a canal from the Nile River to the Red Sea, and he erected a symbolic or religious center at Persepolis in his homeland (modern Fārs province of Iran), although the administrative capital was at Susa. In addition to constructing many buildings, Darius issued a gold coin, called the *daric* after his "throne name" Darius, meaning "possessing good." His personal name is unknown. He also reorganized the postal and information services as well as the army and the central bureaucracy. It is thought that he also ordered the creation of a cuneiform writing system for the Old Persian language, in which many inscriptions exist.

The last expedition ordered by Darius was the attack on Greece, which ended with the Battle of Marathon (490 B.C.E.), in which the Persians were decisively de-feated. Soon afterward, he died and was succeeded by his son Xerxes I.

Influence. Darius established the features of the Achaemenian Empire, many of which continued after the empire was conquered by Alexander the Great.

ADDITIONAL RESOURCES

Briant, Pierre. *From Cyrus to Alexander: A History of the Persian Empire*. Winona Lake, Ind.: Eisen-brauns, 1998.

Dandamaev, Muhammad. *A Political History of the Achaemenid Empire*. Leiden: E. J. Brill, 1989.

SEE ALSO: Achaemenian Dynasty; Alexander the Great; Darius III; Greece, Classical; Egypt, Pharaonic; Jerusalem, temple of; Marathon, Battle of; Persia; Xerxes I.

—*Richard N. Frye*

DARIUS III

ALSO KNOWN AS: Codommanus
BORN: c. 380 B.C.E.; Persia
DIED: 330 B.C.E.; Bactria
RELATED CIVILIZATION: Persia
MAJOR ROLE/POSITION: King

Life. Darius (DAH-ree-uhs) III won fame as a young man by killing an enemy champion in battle. For this feat, his uncle, Artaxerxes III, king of Persia, awarded him the satrapy of Armenia. Darius was crowned king in 336 B.C.E. after Artaxerxes III and the royal family were poisoned by one of the king's generals, Bagoas. When Darius became king, he wisely forced Bagoas to drink one of his own lethal drafts.

In 334 B.C.E., Alexander the Great invaded the Middle East. Darius faced Alexander at the Battle of Issus in 333 B.C.E. but fled before the battle had been decided. His army was defeated, and Alexander captured the royal family and the king's treasury. Attempts by Darius to ransom his family were rebuffed by Alexander. During the next two years, Alexander was occupied with conquering Syria, the Levant, and Egypt. Darius faced him in battle once more, in 331 B.C.E., this time on the eastern side of the Tigris River. Once again Darius fled. Darius was killed by his own men the following summer, shortly before Alexander's men overtook him.

Influence. The short reign of Darius III brought the Persian Empire to a close. The conquests of Alexander the Great, which Darius proved unable to withstand, ushered in the new age of Hellenism.

ADDITIONAL RESOURCES

Cook, J. M. *The Persian Empire*. New York: Schocken Books, 1983.

Nylander, Carl. "Darius III." In *Alexander the Great: Reality and Myth*, edited by Jasper Carlsen. Rome: L'Erma di Bretschneider, 1993.

SEE ALSO: Alexander the Great; Bactria; Darius I; Egypt, Pharaonic; Issus, Battle of; Persia.

—*Kriston J. Udd*

DAVID

BORN: c. 1032 B.C.E.; Bethlehem, Judah
DIED: c. 962 B.C.E.; Jerusalem, Israel
RELATED CIVILIZATION: Israel
MAJOR ROLE/POSITION: King, military leader, musician, prophet

Life. The biblical David was born the eighth son of Jesse and a descendant of Ruth. During his early life as a shepherd, the prophet Samuel anointed him to be king to replace Israel's first king, Saul. David's musical skills brought him into Saul's service, and he quickly distinguished himself by killing the Philistine giant Goliath and becoming a notable warrior. Despite being the king's son-in-law and his son Jonathan's close friend, David was forced by Saul's raging jealousy to flee for his life with a small band of outlaws. After the death of Saul and Jonathan at the Battle of Mount Gilboa, David was anointed king over the tribe of Judah and seven years later ruler over all Israel.

David's first move as king of Israel was to establish Jerusalem as the political and religious capital. His forty-year reign was marked by triumph—he greatly expanded Israel's borders and was undefeated in battle—and tragedy—adultery with Bathsheba, the murder of her husband, and the death of his son Absalom in a failed coup attempt.

Influence. David left an inspirational legacy: He was underdog against the giant, prototypical friend, military genius, and wise ruler, and dozens of his psalms are still sung. Religiously, he is considered a messianic prophet and the ancestor of Jesus Christ.

King David. (North Wind Picture Archives)

ADDITIONAL RESOURCES
Fox, E. *Give Us a King: Samuel, Saul, and David.* New York: Schocken Books, 1999.
McKenzie, Steven L. *King David: An Unauthorized Biography.* New York: Oxford University Press, 2000.

SEE ALSO: Bathsheba; Christianity; Israel; Jesus Christ; Philistines; Samuel; Saul.

—Paul John Chara, Jr.

DEAD SEA SCROLLS

AUTHORSHIP: probably Essene monks
DATE: fourth century B.C.E.-first century C.E.
LOCALE: Northwestern shore of the Dead Sea
RELATED CIVILIZATION: Essenes
SIGNIFICANCE: The scrolls reveal the teaching of a long-lost Jewish group that combined a central concern for law, as in later Judaism, with messianic and apocalyptic beliefs similar to those of early Christianity.

The Dead Sea Scrolls are a collection of some eight manuscripts, mostly fragmentary, recovered from eleven caves in the 1940's and 1950's. They were probably composed or collected by Essene monks living at the nearby site of Khirbat Qumran. The scrolls are written in three languages: Hebrew (about 80 percent), Aramaic (about 20 percent), and Greek (a few).

Almost two hundred biblical manuscripts were found, representing every book of the Old Testament except Esther. These scrolls are five hundred to eight hundred years older than the oldest copies previously known. They show that the text had been copied with great care through the centuries. Here and there, however, there are some interesting variations.

Two of the most important texts found at Khirbat Qumran are the Rule of the Community and the Damascus document. These functioned as the constitution of the group and indicate that the Qumranites believed they were living in the end of days and that they alone remained true to the law of God. These works also outline membership procedures, rules for daily conduct, and penalties for various transgressions. Other compositions include previously known works such as the Book of Tobit from the Apocrypha, as well as many previously unknown works.

ADDITIONAL RESOURCES
Schiffman, Lawrence. *Reclaiming the Dead Sea Scrolls*. New York: Doubleday, 1994.
VanderKam, James. *The Dead Sea Scrolls Today*. Grand Rapids, Mich.: Eerdmans, 1994.

SEE ALSO: Christianity; Damascus document; Essenes; Judaism.

—*Erik W. Larson*

A portion of the Dead Sea Scrolls, which were discovered in jars in caves in Israel between 1947 and 1956. (Hulton Archive)

DELPHI

DATE: c. fourteenth century B.C.E.-390 C.E.
LOCALE: On the slopes of Mount Parnassus in Central Greece
RELATED CIVILIZATIONS: Mycenaean, Archaic, Classical, Hellenistic, and Roman Greece
SIGNIFICANCE: Site of the temple and oracle of Apollo, the quadrennial Pythian Games, and a theater of Dionysus, Delphi was a major Panhellenic shrine.

Greek tradition suggests that Delphi was an ancient oracular site where a holy stone called the *omphalos*, or "navel," located in the temple of Apollo, marked the center of the earth. The Homeric *Hymn to Apollo* describes how Apollo captured the oracle from the goddess Earth by defeating the monster Python. The shrine

was also considered a place of purification where those inflicted with blood guilt, such as the mythical Orestes, who committed matricide, could seek physical and spiritual cleansing.

From about 1100 B.C.E., the shrine was administered by a Panhellenic association called the Amphictyonic League. Delphi's greatest oracular influence occurred as the city-states of Archaic Greece devised law codes and established colonies. Such issues were both easy to affirm and conducive to the oracle's good reputation. Two famous law codes, those of Lycurgus in Sparta and of Solon in Athens, were both closely associated with Delphi. Even Croesus of Lydia is said to have consulted the oracle.

Representatives of cities (or, less frequently, private

individuals) made inquiry of the Pythia while she sat on a tripod in Apollo's temple, but only on the seventh day of each nonwinter month. Women were not permitted to consult the oracle directly. The typical response was probably not a riddle but a simple yes or no to a policy question previously deliberated by a city; moreover, replies were almost always affirmative. Those who accept as genuine some of the longer responses traditionally associated with the oracle speculate that the Pythia induced self-hypnosis or inhaled narcotic fumes emitted from a chasm in the earth, but that is unlikely.

The temple of Apollo, destroyed by fire in 548 B.C.E., was rebuilt under the direction of the great Athenian family of Alcmaeonids. The *temenos*, or sanctuary, was filled with about twenty treasuries erected by individual city-states as well as numerous commemorations of military victories and individual accomplishments. One noteworthy monument was the Portico of the Athenians, built to display plunder captured from the Persians in the Battle of Marathon (490 B.C.E.).

Pythian Games were held at Delphi in honor of Apollo from antiquity. After 582 B.C.E., the games occurred in the third year after the Olympic Games and were considered one of the four sets of Crown Games. Events included musical as well as athletic events. A stadium was located above the *temenos* on the slope of Parnassus. Apollo possessed the shrine only during the summer months. In winter, Delphi belonged to Dionysus, the Greek god of wine, and a theater dedicated to the god was located just to the north of Apollo's temple.

Despite plundering by the Persians, the Gauls, and the Romans, the shrine continued to serve as an oracular site until it was closed in 390 C.E. by the Christian emperor Theodosius the Great.

ADDITIONAL RESOURCES

Burkert, Walter. *Greek Religion*. Translated by John Raffan. Cambridge, Mass.: Harvard University Press, 1985.
Golding, William. *The Double Tongue*. New York: Farrar, Straus and Giroux, 1995.
Morgan, Catherine. *Athletes and Oracles: The Transformation of Olympia and Delphi in the Eighth Century* B.C. New York: Cambridge University Press, 1990.

SEE ALSO: Croesus; Lycurgus of Sparta; Marathon, Battle of; Olympic Games; Solon; Sports and entertainment; Theodosius the Great.

—*Thomas J. Sienkewicz*

DEMETRIUS PHALEREUS

ALSO KNOWN AS: Demetrius of Phalerum; Demetrius of Phaleron
BORN: c. 350 B.C.E.; Phaleron, near Athens, Greece
DIED: 283 B.C.E.; Egypt
RELATED CIVILIZATION: Hellenistic Greece
MAJOR ROLE/POSITION: Ruler, philosopher

Life. Demetrius Phalereus (duh-MEE-tree-us fuh-LEE-rews) was born to the Athenian deme Phaleron and reportedly educated under Aristotle and Theophrastus. In 317 B.C.E., a few years after Athens fell to Macedonia, Cassander took over Athens and put Demetrius in charge of the city. Demetrius governed Athens and largely stayed out of the wars that raged among the successors to Alexander the Great. He became best known for his legislative and social reforms, which seem broadly guided by his philosophical education. These reforms included curbing extravagances, canceling subsidies for the poor for public functions, and instituting a census. All these reforms responded to the desires of the wealthy Athenian aristocracy. In 307 B.C.E., Demetrius Poliorcetes ("the Besieger") took Athens, and Demetrius Phalereus fled. He subsequently served Cassander and Ptolemy I Soter. Under Ptolemy II Philadelphus, he fell into disfavor and died in 283 B.C.E.

Influence. Demetrius remains an example of a successful combination of ruler and philosopher. He governed Athens during a crucial period after the loss of the democracy and as it became a cultural center for Greece. He is also credited with persuading Ptolemy I Soter to build the Alexandrian library. Although almost all of his writing is now lost, he was a widely read and respected Peripatetic philosopher in antiquity.

ADDITIONAL RESOURCES
Green, Peter. *Alexander to Actium: The Historical Evolution of the Hellenistic Age*. Reprint. Berkeley:

University of California Press, 1993.

Habicht, Christian. *Athens from Alexander to Antony.* Translated by Deborah Lucas Schneider. Cambridge, Mass.: Harvard University Press, 1999.

SEE ALSO: Alexander the Great; Alexandrian library; Aristotle; Athens; Cassander; Demetrius Poliorcetes; Diadochi; Greece, Hellenistic and Roman; Philosophy; Ptolemaic Dynasty; Theophrastus.

—*Wilfred E. Major*

DEMETRIUS POLIORCETES

BORN: 336 B.C.E.; Macedonia
DIED: 283 B.C.E.; Cilicia (later in Turkey)
RELATED CIVILIZATION: Hellenistic Greece
MAJOR ROLE/POSITION: King

Life. The son of Antigonus I Monophthalmos, Demetrius Poliorcetes (duh-MEE-tree-us pahl-ee-ohr-SEET-eez) served as his general against Ptolemy I Soter (312 B.C.E.) and Seleucus I (311 B.C.E.) and later against Cassander (307 B.C.E.) when Demetrius took over several cities, including Athens and Corinth. His victory over the Ptolemaic fleet allowed Antigonus to claim kingship for himself and Demetrius (306 B.C.E.). His year-long unsuccessful siege of Rhodes (305-304 B.C.E.) gave Demetrius his nickname "Besieger of Cities." He reconstituted the Corinthian League (302 B.C.E.), and the isthmus remained his power base after the collapse of the Antigonid kingdom following the defeat of Antigonus and Demetrius at Ipsus (301 B.C.E.).

After marrying his daughter to Seleucus, Demetrius received Cilicia in return (299-298 B.C.E.). His star rose again when he reestablished control over Athens, defeated Sparta, and occupied the Macedonian throne (294-293 B.C.E.). However, his preparations to recover the Antigonid kingdom caused Seleucus, Ptolemy,

Lysimachus, and Pyrrhus to ally against him and attack Macedonia from the east and west (288 B.C.E.). Despoiled of almost everything in Europe in accordance with the treaty of 287 B.C.E., Demetrius tried to contest Anatolia but had to surrender to Seleucus (286 B.C.E.). He died in captivity, indulging in drinking and other vices.

Influence. Demetrius's life reflects the tumultuous period following the death of Alexander the Great, which consisted of almost incessant wars of the Diadochi before relative stabilization in the late 280's B.C.E.

ADDITIONAL RESOURCES

Billows, Richard A. *Antigonos the One-Eyed and the Creation of the Hellenistic State.* Berkeley: University of California Press, 1990.

Duggan, Alfred Leo. *Besieger of Cities.* New York: Pantheon, 1963.

Wehrli, C. *Antigone et Démétrios.* Geneva: Droz, 1968.

SEE ALSO: Alexander the Great; Antigonid Dynasty; Athens; Cassander; Demetrius Phalereus; Diadochi; Greece, Hellenistic and Roman; Lysimachus; Macedonia; Seleucid Dynasty; Seleucus I.

—*Sviatoslav Dmitriev*

DEMOCRITUS

ALSO KNOWN AS: Democritus of Abdera
BORN: c. 460 B.C.E.; Abdera (Avdira), Thrace
DIED: c. 370 B.C.E.; Abdera, Thrace
RELATED CIVILIZATION: Classical Greece
MAJOR ROLE/POSITION: Philosopher

Life. Democritus (dih-MAHK-riht-uhs) was born to a wealthy family in the city of Abdera on the Greek mainland. He is believed to have traveled widely in Egypt and Asia Minor. He was a disciple of Leucippus,

who is believed to have proposed the atomic hypothesis between 440 and 430 B.C.E., but about whom little is known. Democritus was a prolific author, writing more than seventy works on a wide range of subjects, including ethics, music, astronomy, and mathematics. He is thought by some to have reached the age of one hundred.

Influence. Democritus elaborated the atomic theory as formulated by Leucippus. His atoms were of several different kinds and were both indestructible and indivisible. The atoms had definite shapes and properties.

Democritus. (Library of Congress)

Because the world consisted of only atoms and empty space, there was no room for the gods or survival of the individual after death. Democritus's atomic theory was adopted by Epicurus and his disciples. Much later, its materialism made it unacceptable to the authorities of the Catholic Church, who found Aristotle's metaphysics of form and (infinitely divisible) substance more compatible with Catholic theology. Scientific acceptance of the atomic hypothesis would not come until the eighteenth century.

ADDITIONAL RESOURCES

Bailey, Cyril. *The Greek Atomists and Epicuris.* New York: Russell and Russell, 1964.

McKirahan, Richard D., Jr. *Philosophy Before Socrates.* New York: Hackett, 1994.

SEE ALSO: Greece, Classical; Leucippus.

—*Donald R. Franceschetti*

DEMOSTHENES

BORN: c. 384 B.C.E.; Athens, Greece
DIED: 322 B.C.E.; Calauria, Greece
RELATED CIVILIZATION: Classical Greece
MAJOR ROLE/POSITION: Politician, orator

Life. Demosthenes (dih-MAHS-thuh-neez) is the most famous of ten authors whom Alexandrian critics included in the canon of Attic orators. Orphaned in childhood, he supposedly developed his skills as a writer and speaker to sue trustees who mismanaged his estate. Despite a weak voice and physique, he trained himself and studied until he won his lawsuit. He then became a leading politician at Athens from about 351 B.C.E. until his death.

The issue of the day was whether Athens and other city-states should resist the expansion of Macedonia under Philip II and Alexander the Great. Demosthenes' speeches tried to rally unity; the best known are the three speeches against Philip II's policies—*Kata Philippou A*, *B*, and *G* (351 B.C.E., 344 B.C.E., and 341 B.C.E.; *First Philippic, Second Philippic, Third Philippic*, all 1570)—and the three *Olynthiacs—Olunthiakos A*, *B*, and *G* (349 B.C.E., 349 B.C.E., and 348 B.C.E.; *First and Second Olynthiacs, Third Olynthiac*, all 1570).

Demosthenes fought at the Battle of Chaeronea (338 B.C.E.), which Macedonia won; nonetheless, he was later awarded a crown in recognition of his services to Athens. In 324 B.C.E., he was charged with appropriating money deposited at Athens by a Macedonian turncoat. Although the charge may have been politically inspired, he was found guilty and went into exile. He re-

Demosthenes. (North Wind Picture Archives)

turned to Athens after the death of Alexander the Great in 323 B.C.E., was arrested again in 322 B.C.E., and committed suicide by taking poison.

Influence. Demosthenes was considered the supreme exponent of Classical Greek rhetoric. About sixty of his political and legal speeches survive. His work was repeatedly quoted and taken as a model by rhetorical theorists such as Hermogenes.

ADDITIONAL RESOURCES

Demosthenes. *Orations*. 6 vols. Translated by J. H. Vince, C. A. Vince, and A. T. Murray. Cambridge, Mass.: Harvard University Press, 1939.
Murphy, James Jerome, ed. *Demosthenes' On the Crown: A Critical Case Study of a Masterpiece of Ancient Oratory*. Reprint. Translated by John J. Keaney. Davis, Calif.: Hermagoras Press, 1983.
Sealey, Raphael. *Demosthenes and His Time*. New York: Oxford University Press, 1993.

SEE ALSO: Alexander the Great; Athens; Chaeronea, Battle of; Greece, Classical; Macedonia; Philip II.

—Janet B. Davis

DENIS, SAINT

ALSO KNOWN AS: Saint Dionysius
BORN: date unknown; Italy
DIED: c. 250 C.E.; near Paris
RELATED CIVILIZATIONS: Gaul, Imperial Rome
MAJOR ROLE/POSITION: Bishop, missionary

Life. Saint Denis became a bishop and was sent to convert the Franks in Gaul. He established his mission around Paris. He built a church, converted many people, and performed miracles. He became recognized as the first bishop of Paris. He was imprisoned with a priest, Rusticus, and a deacon, Eleutherius, all of whom were beheaded. Their bodies were later recovered and buried outside Paris. A church built at their burial site became the abbey of Saint Denis.

In the ninth century C.E., a life of Saint Denis conflated this third century bishop and martyr with Dionysius the Areopagite, who was converted by Saint Paul in Athens in the first century C.E. By this conflation, Dionysius (Denis) traveled to Rome, where Pope Clement consecrated him as bishop. He then came to Paris, where he was beheaded. Afterward, he picked up his head and carried it to the site outside Paris where he was buried. The life of Saint Denis thus assumed a legendary quality.

Influence. Medieval French kings regarded Saint Denis as their patron and the protector of France. The abbey church of Saint Denis became the French royal abbey and mausoleum.

ADDITIONAL RESOURCES

Lacaze, Charlotte. *The Vie de St. Denis Manuscript*. New York: Garland, 1979.
Spiegel, Gabrielle M. "The Cult of Saint Denis and Capetian Kingship." *Journal of Medieval History* 1 (1975): 43-69.

SEE ALSO: Christianity; Gauls; Rome, Imperial.

—Karen K. Gould

DEPTFORD CULTURE

DATE: 500 B.C.E.-500 C.E.
LOCALE: The coastal plain in the southeastern United States, including southeastern Alabama, northern and west-central Florida, southeastern South Carolina, and eastern Georgia
SIGNIFICANCE: The first Indians to adapt to the modern coastal environment of the eastern United States, the Deptford people were dominant in the southeast during the Early Woodland period.

The Deptford (DET-fuhrd) people had two different ways of life: coastal and riverine. Those who lived near the coast enjoyed a diet of fish, shellfish, and other marine foods as well as the nuts, turkey, deer, and other woodland edibles that sustained inland peoples. By 100 B.C.E., the Deptford culture had penetrated the interior, where the riverine tradition flourished in the Chattahoochee and Alabama Valleys.

Deptford villages were characterized by two dwelling types: a walled oval hut inhabited during cool weather and a warm-season shelter with open walls. Major riverine sites also display large, earthen platform mounds, which may have been designed for feasts or communal eating. Deptford ceramics were made of coiled sandy clay and decorated with impressions made by cords, fabric, or wooden stamps. Numerous types of stone were used for projectile points, axes, blades, and other tools. In coastal settlements, shell was widely used for decorative and utilitarian purposes.

Among the Deptford people, certain dead (the majority of whom were women) were buried beneath earthen mounds, which were often enlarged by later interments. Excavations have revealed an even distribution of grave goods (most commonly, projectile points) in these mound burials, suggesting that the Deptford culture was egalitarian—that is, persons were born relatively equal, distinction being based on personal achievement, not heredity.

ADDITIONAL RESOURCES

Bense, J. A. *Hawkshaw: Prehistory and History in an Urban Neighborhood in Pensacola, Florida.* Pensacola: Archaeology Institute, University of West Florida, 1985.

Milanich, J. T. *Archaeology of Precolumbian Florida.* Gainesville: University of Florida Presses, 1994.

Thomas, D. H. "The Anthropology of St. Catherine's Island: 2. The Refuge—Deptford Mortuary Complex." *Anthropological Papers* 56, no. 1. New York: American Museum of Natural History, 1979.

SEE ALSO: Dalton tradition; Eastern peoples; Middle Woodland traditions.

—Jeremiah R. Taylor

DHAMMAPADA

ALSO KNOWN AS: *Dharmapada* (Sanskrit)
AUTHORSHIP:: Attributed to Siddhārtha Gautama (the Buddha)
DATE: second century B.C.E.-third century C.E.
LOCALE: Indian subcontinent
RELATED CIVILIZATIONS: India, Southeast and Far East Asia
SIGNIFICANCE: One of the canonical Pāli texts of Theravāda (Hīnāyāna) Buddhist literature that contains important teachings of the founder.

The *Dhammapada* (English translation in *Buddhist Legends*, 1921; the name means "path of truth/virtue/morality" in the Pāli languages; the Sanskrit is *Dharmapada*) is a collection of 423 verses in 26 chapters that treats the way or teaching of the dharma. The word "dharma" is central to Buddhist teachings and has many meanings depending on context. It can mean variously the teachings of the Buddha, the truth, ultimate reality, the moral law or the right way, duty, and the true religion. The *Dhammapada* (DAH-mah-PAH-dah) is the best known and most widely esteemed text in the Pāli *Tipiṭaka* (collected c. 250 B.C.E.; English translation in *Buddhist Scriptures*, 1913), the sacred scriptures or canon of Theravāda (Hīnāyāna) Buddhism, which is the conservative southern Asian school of Pāli Buddhism found in Sri Lanka, Burma, Thailand, Laos, Vietnam, and Cambodia, in contrast to the Mahāyāna Buddhism of the East Asian countries of China, Korea, and Japan. It is included in the *Khuddaka Nikāya* ("minor collection") of the *Sūtra Piṭaka*.

Its popularity has raised it far above the place it occupies in the Pāli scriptures to the status of a world religious classic. This short anthology of verses constitutes a perfect compendium of the Buddha's teaching, containing between its covers all the essential principles elaborated at length in the forty volumes of the Pāli canon. According to the Theravāda Buddhist tradition, each verse in the *Dhammapada* was originally spoken by the Buddha in response to a particular episode (reputedly on 305 separate occasions).

The *Dhammapada* contains certain of the Buddha's central teachings such as that of *anātman* or the idea that no real self (personality or soul) exists. There is only the ultimate reality or "true suchness" of being. The Buddha taught in a time of Vedantic mysticism that maintained that absolute reality (*brahman*) exists, as does the individual soul or self (*ātman*), and that they are identical. The Buddha resolutely denied the concept of the individual personality because suffering—another pivotal notion in his teachings—is produced by the mistaken attachment to this "idea" of a self that is in truth only the product of illusory sense perceptions. The self must be discarded in order to perceive absolute reality (*tathata*) and to overcome suffering.

ADDITIONAL RESOURCES

Brough, John, ed. *The Gandhari Dhartnapada*. London: Oxford University Press, 1962.

Norman, K. R., trans. *The Word of the Doctrine*. Oxford, England: The Pali Text Society, 1997.

Radhakrishnan, Sarvepalli, ed. *The Dhammapada: With Introductory Essays, Pali Text, and English Translation and Notes*. London: Oxford University Press, 1997.

Robinson, Richard H., and Willard L. Johnson. *The Buddhist Religion: A Historical Introduction*. Belmont, Calif.: Wadsworth, 1982.

Von Hinuber, O., and K. R. Norman, eds. *Dhammapada*. Oxford, England: The Pali Text Society, 1995.

SEE ALSO: Buddha; Buddhism; China; India; Japan.
—*Thomas F. Barry*

DIADOCHI

DATE: coined c. 323 B.C.E.
LOCALE: Greece and the Eastern Mediterranean
RELATED CIVILIZATIONS: Hellenistic and Roman Greece

The Greek word *diadochi* (di-uh-DOH-chee; or *diadochoi*) means "successors" and refers to the lieutenants of Alexander the Great who partitioned his empire after his death in 323 B.C.E. Antipater was declared regent of Macedonia. Lysimachus, Antigonus I Monophthalmos, Seleucus I, and Ptolemy I Soter were made satraps or governors of Thrace, Phrygia, Babylon, and Egypt, respectively. Macedonian by birth, all eventually ruled as independent monarchs and fought one another in a futile effort to reunify the empire. Several founded dynasties that lasted for several centuries.

A few years after Antipater's death in 319 B.C.E., his son Cassander gained control of Macedonia and most of Greece, which he ruled until his death in 297 B.C.E. Cassander's descendants, however, lost the kingdom to Demetrius Poliorcetes, the son of Antigonus I Monophthalmos. Their dynasty, the Antigonids, ruled Macedonia and Greece until 168 B.C.E. At his death in 281 B.C.E., Lysimachus had extended his rule of Thrace to include large portions of Asia Minor (Anatolia) and even Macedonia but had not managed to establish a lasting dynasty. Seleucus I founded the Seleucid Empire in Syria and Mesopotamia, which his descendants ruled until the Roman conquest of Syria in 64 B.C.E. Ptolemy I Soter founded the Ptolemaic Dynasty, which ruled Egypt until the death of Cleopatra VII in 30 B.C.E.

THE DEATHS OF THE DIADOCHI
(ALL DATES B.C.E.)

Perdiccas	321, slain by mutineers who were bribed by Ptolemy
Craterus	321; killed by Eumenes while invading Cappadocia
Antipater	319, died
Eumenes	316, slain by own men who were bribed by Antigonus
Polysperchon	310?, died
Antigonus	301, killed in battle with Seleucus and Lysimachus, allies of Cassander
Cassander	297, died after being recognized as king of Macedonia
Demetrius	283, died in prison
Ptolemy	283/282, died
Lysimachus	281, killed in hand-to-hand combat by Seleucus at Battle of Corus
Seleucus	281, murdered by Ptolemy Keraunos, disinherited son of Ptolemy

ADDITIONAL RESOURCES

Billows, Richard A. *Antigonos the One-Eyed and the Creation of the Hellenistic State*. Berkeley: University of California Press, 1990.

Lund, Helen S. *Lysimachus: A Study in Early Hellenistic Kingship*. New York: Routledge, 1992.

SEE ALSO: Alexander the Great; Antigonid Dynasty; Antipater; Cassander; Demetrius Poliorcetes; Egypt: Ptolemaic and Roman; Greece, Hellenistic and Roman; Lysimachus; Ptolemaic Dynasty; Seleucid Dynasty; Seleucus I.

—*Thomas J. Sienkewicz*

DIDO

ALSO KNOWN AS: Elissa
FLOURISHED: Legendary figure; between c. 1200 B.C.E. and the tenth century B.C.E.
RELATED CIVILIZATIONS: Carthage, Prerepublican Rome
MAJOR ROLE/POSITION: Queen of Carthage

Life. Dido (DI-doh) was the legendary Phoenician queen of ancient Carthage, located on the coast of North Africa across from Italy. Various traditions about her life circulated in the Greco-Roman world. According to the Greek historian Timaeus, her Phoenician name was Elissa. Following her husband's political murder, she fled to North Africa and founded the city of Carthage. The Libyans called her Dido ("wanderer"). By the third century B.C.E., the Roman historian Gnaeus Naevius had linked her to Aeneas, the Trojan hero who escaped the fall of Troy.

However, it was the epic poet Vergil, who, in Books 1 and 4 of the *Aeneid* (c. 29-19 B.C.E.; English transla-

In this sketch of an opera scene, Dido, founder of Carthage, receives a visit from Aeneas. Their romance is a fiction created by the poet Vergil. (North Wind Picture Archives)

tion, 1553), gave full expression to the most famous (and probably fictional) story of Dido and Aeneas. Vergil relates the voyage of Aeneas after the fall of Troy and his subsequent landing at Carthage to escape a storm. He and his men are offered hospitality by Dido. As Aeneas tells the famous story of Troy's end, Dido falls desperately in love with him. Aeneas is eager to stay in Carthage and marry Dido until he is reminded of his destiny in Italy. As he sails to Italy, Dido curses Aeneas and then commits suicide on her bed, which she has had placed atop a funeral pyre. Vergil underscores Dido's tragic situation in Book 6 when Aeneas speaks to her during his visit to the underworld.

Influence. For many Romans, Vergil's story fore- shadowed the wars between Rome and Carthage in the third century B.C.E.

ADDITIONAL RESOURCES

Desmond, Marilyn. *Reading Dido: Gender, Textuality, and the Medieval Aeneid*. Minneapolis: University of Minnesota Press, 1994.

Virgil. *The Aeneid*. Translated by Robert Fitzgerald. New York: Random House, 1983.

SEE ALSO: Aeneas; Carthage; Naevius, Gnaeus; Phoe- nicia; Rome, Prerepublican; Troy; Vergil.

—*Steve O'Bryan*

DIO CASSIUS

ALSO KNOWN AS: Cassius Dio Cocceianus; Cassius Dio
BORN: c. 150 C.E.; Nicaea, Bithynia (later İznik, Turkey)
DIED: c. 235 C.E.; place unknown
RELATED CIVILIZATION: Imperial Rome
MAJOR ROLE/POSITION: Administrator, historian

Life. Dio Cassius was born into a family distin- guished for imperial service and literary composition. He received a standard rhetorical education and by the mid-180's C.E. had entered public service at Rome, where he became a member of the senate about 189 C.E. Dio observed many political developments at first hand and was remarkably adept at shifting with changing po- litical winds. He described the assassination of the em- peror Lucius Aurelius Commodus in 192 C.E. as the be- ginning of the "most violent wars and civil strife." He found favor under Lucius Septimius Severus (r. 193- 211), for whom he composed his first known work, "On Dreams and Portents" (now lost). Its success encour- aged Dio to embark on the composition of a Roman his- tory. Dio was named replacement consul around 205 C.E. and was a member of Severus's imperial council. In the late 220's C.E., he was given military commands in Dalmatia and Upper Pannonia, and in 229 C.E., he was rewarded with a second consulate. He then retired from public service, pleading age and poor health, and re- turned home to Nicaea, where he spent the rest of his life.

Influence. Dio is known primarily for his eighty- book *Romaika* (probably c. 202 C.E.; *Roman History*, 1914-1927), which begins with the arrival of Aeneas in Italy circa the eleventh century B.C.E. and continues to 229 C.E. Surviving sections include Books 36-54, 55- 60, and 78-79; the rest must be reconstructed from Byz- antine fragments. Dio's history provides eyewitness coverage of a critical period of Roman history and is as much a record of political events as an account of his own personal experiences.

ADDITIONAL RESOURCES

Cary, E. *Dio's Roman History*. 9 vols. New York: Macmillan, 1927.

Gowing, Alain M. *The Triumviral Narratives of Appian and Cassius Dio*. Ann Arbor: University of Michi- gan Press, 1992.

Millar, Fergus. *A Study of Cassius Dio*. Oxford, En- gland: Clarendon Press, 1964.

SEE ALSO: Languages and literature; Rome, Imperial; Septimius Severus, Lucius.

—*Ralph W. Mathisen*

Dio Chrysostom

ALSO KNOWN AS: Dio Cocceianus of Prusa
BORN: c. 40 C.E.; Prusa, Bithynia
DIED: after 112 C.E.; probably Bithynia
RELATED CIVILIZATION: Imperial Rome
MAJOR ROLE/POSITION: Rhetorician, philosopher

Life. Dio Cocceianus, trained in rhetoric, was given the name "Chrysostom" (DI-oh krihs-OHS-tuhm; golden-mouthed) and won fame throughout the Roman Empire because of his eloquence in speech and writings. As his fame grew, he began to travel, and he reached Rome during the reign of the emperor Vespasian (r. 69-70 C.E.). Dio arrived in Rome a Sophist opposed to many of the philosophers. However, he soon accepted the philosophies of the Stoics and Cynics. His writings began to reflect a Stoic and Cynic moralizing tone, most clearly seen in *Euboicus* (n.d.; *Euboean Discourse*, 1932) and *Discourse on Kingship* (translation 1932), in which he discusses the evils of self-indulgence. In style, he took the philosophers Antisthenes, Demosthenes, Plato, and Xenophon as his models.

Open criticisms of the emperor Domitian (r. 81-96) led to his banishment in 82 C.E. from Rome, Italy, and Bithynia. He eventually settled in Viminacium, a Roman camp on the Danube, and lived among the native Getae, whose history he later wrote.

Dio's exile ended in 96 C.E. with the death of Domitian. He returned to his native Prusa in 103 C.E. and died there about 112 C.E.

Influence. Dio's writings, along with those of the philosopher Plutarch, are part of a brief revival of Greek writings in the second century C.E.

ADDITIONAL RESOURCES
Cohoon, J. W. *"Dio Chrysostom" with an English Translation.* Cambridge, Mass.: Harvard University Press, 1961-1964.
Mussies, G. *Dio Chrysostom and the New Testament.* Leiden, Netherlands: E. J. Brill, 1972.
Swain, Simon, ed. *Dio Chrysostom: Politics, Letters, and Philosophy.* New York: Oxford University Press, 2000.

SEE ALSO: Demosthenes; Domitian; Plato; Plutarch; Rome, Imperial; Vespasian; Xenophon.

—*Roger S. Evans*

Diocles of Carystus

BORN: c. 375 B.C.E.; Carystus, Greece
DIED: c. 295 B.C.E.; Athens?, Greece
RELATED CIVILIZATION: Classical Greece
MAJOR ROLE/POSITION: Physician

Life. Diocles of Carystus (DI-uh-kleez of kuh-RIHS-tuhs) on the island of Euboea became a famous and respected physician, sometimes ranked second only to Hippocrates. The exact dates of his life remain uncertain, but he lived after the Hippocratic school was well established and may have been a contemporary of Aristotle. No full writings of his survive, but later writers credit him with the first handbook on anatomy, along with works on physiology, aetiology, diagnoses, dietetics, and botany. He was best known for promoting the importance of practical experience in making sensible diagnoses. Diocles' insistence on practical experience may explain one fragment that calls for more complex assessments of pathological effects, rather than simply assuming a certain smell or substance always reflects the same condition in every patient. Another fragment provides detailed daily and seasonal regimens for healthy living.

Influence. Careful observation allowed Diocles to distinguish for the first time among different types of diseases of the lungs and intestines. He also established that a fever was a symptom of disease, not a disease itself. Two ancient inventions also bore his name: a type of head bandage and a spoon for removing arrowheads. Later physicians such as Galen praised Diocles both for his practical knowledge and for his theoretical positions.

ADDITIONAL RESOURCES
Eijk, Philip J. van der. *Diocles of Carystus: A Collection of the Fragments with Translation and Com-*

mentary. Boston: Brill, 2000.

Lyons, A. S., and R. J. Petrucelli. *Medicine: An Illustrated History.* New York: Abrams, 1978.

SEE ALSO: Greece, Classical; Hippocrates; Medicine and health.

—*Wilfred E. Major*

DIOCLETIAN

ALSO KNOWN AS: Gaius Aurelius Valerius Diocletianus; Diocles (before accession)
BORN: c. 245 C.E.; possibly Salona
DIED: December 3, 316 C.E.; Salona
RELATED CIVILIZATION: Imperial Rome
MAJOR ROLE/POSITION: Roman emperor

Life. Diocletian (di-oh-KLEE-shuhn), of humble birth, grew up during the anarchy of the soldier emperors. An accomplished soldier mentored by Lucius Domitius Aurelianus (Aurelian), he became consul suffect in 283 C.E. and bodyguard commander for the emperor Numerian. Diocletian was named emperor in Nicomedia in 284 C.E. after executing Numerian's assassin, praetorian prefect Lucius Aper.

Diocletian stabilized the fractured empire by restructuring it. In 286 C.E., Diocletian, stationed in the East, appointed Maximian as fellow Augustus to oversee the West. In 293 C.E., Diocletian imposed tighter control by adopting two Caesars (Gaius Galerius Valerius Maximianus and Constantius I), thus creating the tetrarchy. From provincial capitals, each tetrarch governed a quadrant of the empire. Diocletian fortified the provinces, which he grouped into twelve dioceses, with additional soldiers and defensive architecture.

His religious and legal reforms restored traditional Roman religion and classical jurisprudence. Diocletian revived the cult of Jupiter, proclaiming himself "Jovius," thus sanctifying the tetrarchy. He revived the rescript system and codified law. To bolster the economy, he instituted a tax system based on land units and in 301 C.E. issued the Edict on Maximum Prices. In 303 C.E., Diocletian renewed persecution of the Christians in an attempt to eliminate the religion. In May, 305 C.E., a weary Diocletian resigned his throne to his caesar, Gaius Galerius Valerius Maximianus. He returned to the Adriatic coast to reside in his retirement palace at Split.

Influence. Having created a new world order, Diocletian was the first emperor to abdicate. His tetrarchic system survived thirty years. Justinian's law code derived from Diocletian's. Diocletian's retirement palace spawned the concept of the castle.

ADDITIONAL RESOURCES

Barnes, T. D. *The New Empire of Diocletian and Constantine.* Cambridge, Mass.: Harvard University Press, 1982.

Williams, Stephen. *Diocletian and the Roman Recovery.* New York: Routledge, 1997.

SEE ALSO: Aurelianus, Lucius Domitius; Christianity; Galerius Valerius Maximianus, Gaius; Justinian I; Maximian; Rome, Imperial.

—*Joanne Mannell Noel*

DIOGENES OF SINOPE

ALSO KNOWN AS: Diogenes the Cynic
BORN: c. 412/403 B.C.E.; Sinope, Paphlygonia (in present-day Turkey)
DIED: c. 324/321 B.C.E.; probably Corinth, Greece
RELATED CIVILIZATIONS: Classical Greece, Republican Rome
MAJOR ROLE/POSITION: Cynic philosopher

Life. Diogenes of Sinope (di-AHJ-uh-neez of si-NOH-pee) was a major early Cynic philosopher. Cynicism ("doggishness") predated Diogenes and may be discerned in Plato's portrait of Socrates and in the precepts espoused by Antisthenes, a notable figure in Socrates' circle, who may or may not have been Diogenes' mentor. However, Diogenes' penchant for playing like a dog, flaunting the insult of "doggishness" embodied in the name of Cynicism as though it were a compliment, linked him permanently with the philosophy. The ancient biographical tradition relates that Diogenes fled to Athens after being exiled from Sinope, a prosperous Greek Black Sea trading metropolis, where he was involved in defrauding the currency, along with his father, an alleged financier. More data regarding Diogenes' background and the details of this particular incident have not been preserved; the extant information largely consists of an assortment of aphoristic traditions contained in a treatise entitled *Peri biōn dogmatōn kai apophthegmatōn tōn en philosophia eudokimēsantōn* (third century C.E.; *The Lives and Opinions of the Philosophers*, 1853) and attributed to Diogenes Laertius, about whom exceedingly little is known.

Although all genuine early Cynic documents have been lost, it is still possible to create a profile of the ancient Cynic movement. Unlike other contemporary philosophical systems, Cynicism was more a method of social critique grounded in antiestablishment principles than a school with a doctrine that cultivated adherents. Caustic commentary on normative modes of thinking, exhibitionist acts that mocked all social trappings, and a choice of lifestyle based on simple essentials made the Cynic sage the essence of Cynicism. Metaphysical theory was regarded as useless and scientific speculation as an elitist sport. Practice and principle were fundamentally equivalent. Cynicism itself was a vocation or calling, the object of which was to challenge assumptions by accosting the public with words and deeds contrived to instigate rude awakenings.

Evidently, Diogenes viewed himself as a man who had experienced deliverance from delusion. In his view, this delusion was a state of malaise that generally characterized the plight of humanity in its endless pursuit of material gain, status, prestige, and pretensions to power. In this context, the phrase "defacing the currency," the accusation faced by Diogenes and his father, became a motto of Cynic intent. This phrase both described Diogenes' past transgression, which served as antecedent to his engagement with wisdom, and served as a summary statement of the civic role the Cynics perceived as their debt to society. Diogenes made a lasting impression in Athens by living in a great tub on charitable donations and publicly performing bodily acts otherwise deemed indecent by custom. Numerous anecdotes yield a consistent profile. When Alexander the Great approached Diogenes and asked what he wished for, Diogenes asked the king to step out of the path of the sunlight that had been reaching him; when coming from the baths and asked if they were crowded, Diogenes said he saw many bathers but very few people. Ostentatiously hostile toward all common judgments, Di-

Diogenes of Sinope. (Hulton Archive)

ogenes proclaimed himself a "citizen of the cosmos." In the Cynic view, heritage constructs and identity claims were pompous illusions that spawned discord and conflict. They rated among the many and varied futile pursuits that sapped human agency from moral virtue. The classic Cynic outlook, in this regard, assessed human practice most negatively but looked at human potential in a positive light. Cynic eccentrics existed on earth to endorse a reordering of human priorities.

Influence. Cynicism had an effect on Greek and Roman philosophy (especially Stoic and Epicurean ethics), literature (especially parody and polemics via the Cynic diatribe and anecdotal tradition), religion, ruler ideology, Christian asceticism, and Continental European philosophy.

ADDITIONAL RESOURCES

Branham, R. Bracht, and Marie-Odile Goulet-Caze, eds. *The Cynics: The Cynic Movement in Antiquity and Its Legacy.* Berkeley: University of California Press, 1996.

Dudley, D. R. *A History of Cynicism: From Diogenes to Sixth Century* A.D. London: Methuen, 1937. Reprint. London: Bristol Classical Press, 1998.

Green, Peter. *Alexander to Actium: The Historical Evolution of the Hellenistic Age*. Reprint. Berkeley: University of California Press, 1993.

Navia, Louis E. *Classical Cynicism: A Critical Study*. Westport, Conn.: Greenwood Press, 1996.

SEE ALSO: Alexander the Great; Greece, Classical; Philosophy; Plato; Rome, Imperial; Socrates.

—*Zoe A. Pappas*

DIONYSIUS I THE ELDER OF SYRACUSE

BORN: c. 430 B.C.E.; Sicily
DIED: 367 B.C.E.; Sicily
RELATED CIVILIZATIONS: Sicily, Classical Greece
MAJOR ROLE/POSITION: Tyrant of Syracuse

Life. Born into the aristocracy of the Sicilian Greek polis of Syracuse, Dionysius I the Elder (di-uh-NISH-ee-uhs) brushed aside the opposition of his peers to become tyrant of the city in 406 B.C.E. Throughout his life, he fought a series of campaigns aimed at driving the Carthaginians from Sicily and constructing a Syracusan empire on the island. He also took an active interest in the affairs of the Greek mainland and eastern Aegean, forming ties with Sparta and Corinth, although he was often viewed with suspicion. In 388 or 384 B.C.E., he sent chariot teams and orators to the Olympic Games, but the teams lost, and Dionysius's poetry was ridiculed. In 368 B.C.E., in gratitude for his hostility to the Boeotians, the Athenians granted him citizenship and a crown. His play *The Ransom of Hector* (367 B.C.E.; now lost) defeated its competitors at the Lenaea festival in Athens the following year, shortly before his death.

Influence. Dionysius I can be seen as the fourth century B.C.E. version of Archaic Greek tyrants such as Pisistratus and Polycrates of Samos, skilled not only in military tactics but also in diplomacy and the arts. Many ancient philosophers (that is, at Plato's Academy) and other authors (Ephorus, Polyaenus) devoted space in their works to him. Although not responsible for large-scale conquests, he occupies a position among the great military leaders of world history.

ADDITIONAL RESOURCES
Caven, Brian. *Dionysius I: War-Lord of Sicily*. New Haven, Conn.: Yale University Press, 1990.
Sanders, L. J. *Dionysius I of Syracuse and Greek Tyranny*. New York: Croom Helm, 1987.

SEE ALSO: Carthage; Dionysius the Younger; Greece, Classical; Olympic Games; Philosophy; Pisistratus; Plato; Polycrates of Samos.

—*Brian Rutishauser*

DIONYSIUS THE YOUNGER

BORN: c. 396 B.C.E.; Sicily
DIED: late fourth century B.C.E.; probably Corinth
RELATED CIVILIZATIONS: Classical Greece, Sicily
MAJOR ROLE/POSITION: Tyrant

Life. Son of Dionysius I the Elder, the militarily successful tyrant of Syracuse, Dionysius the Younger (di-uh-NISH-ee-uhs) succeeded his father in 367 B.C.E. Not as gifted as his father, he was greatly influenced by his uncle Dion, a devoted follower of Plato, and by the historian Philistius. Dion persuaded his nephew to invite Plato to the Syracusan court, no doubt in the hope that Plato would carry out some of his politi-

cal dreams there. Plato imposed a course of mathematical and philosophical studies on Dionysius, studies perhaps not suited to the young man's nature, and when Plato was rumored to be plotting to turn Syracuse over to Athens, Dionysius banished both Plato and Dion. In 357 B.C.E., Dion defeated his nephew in battle, but the Syracusan assembly, perhaps frightened at the prospect of a strong leader, removed Dion from command. After more turmoil, Dion was murdered, and Dionysius resumed his despotism, now hardened or jaded into cruelty. The Corinthian hero Timoleon organized an army of volunteers and liberated Syracuse from Dionysius, sending the deposed tyrant to Corinth, where he lived the remainder of his life teaching and begging for a living.

Influence. Dionysius made his mark on history as a cautionary example of the folly of philosophers who think that they can change the world by influencing a prince and as an example of the power of a capricious fortune that could change a man from a tyrant to a beggar to a tyrant and again to a poor man.

ADDITIONAL RESOURCE

Caven, Brian. *Dionysius I: War-Lord of Sicily.* New Haven, Conn.: Yale University Press, 1990.

SEE ALSO: Athens; Dionysius I the Elder of Syracuse; Greece, Classical; Plato; Timoleon of Corinth.

—*James A. Arieti*

DIVINITY

DATE: beginning about the ninth millennium B.C.E.
LOCALE: Eastern and central parts of the Sudan belt of Africa and the Horn of Africa
RELATED CIVILIZATIONS: Sudanic civilization, Cushitic civilization

"Divinity" is the word scholars use to translate the indigenous terms for the one god of the ancient monotheistic religion of the eastern and central Sudan regions of Africa. This Sudanic belief system can be traced far back in the history of the peoples of the Sudanic civilization, most of whom spoke languages of the Nilo-Saharan family. They identified Divinity with the heavens, and they commonly viewed lightning and rain as metaphors for the power of Divinity in life. They had no other category of spirits or deities. In some recent versions of the Sudanic religion, Divinity might choose to manifest itself to human beings in the form of seemingly particular, lesser spirits. However, the followers of Sudanic religion understood these spirits to be just other guises of Divinity. Sudanic beliefs viewed evil as a divine judgment or retribution for the wrong that a person, or a person's forebears, had done in this life.

The ancestors passed after death into an afterlife, but they had no functional role in religious observance or ritual and were not venerated.

The idea of Divinity was adopted into the religion of the Cushites of the Horn of Africa at a very early period. Among the Cushites, this monotheistic idea apparently displaced a more ancient henotheism, centered on belief in the deity of one's own particular community. Despite changing over to the monotheistic idea of Divinity, the Cushitic peoples continued to recognize the existence of a category of lesser, dangerous spirits, treating them as an additional explanation of the problem of evil.

ADDITIONAL RESOURCE

Ehret, Christopher. "Sudanic Civilization." In *Agricultural and Pastoral Societies in Ancient and Classical History*, edited by Michael Adas. Philadelphia: Temple University Press, 2001.

SEE ALSO: Cushites; Henotheism; Napata and Meroe; Nilo-Saharans.

—*Christopher Ehret*

DJANGGAWUL CYCLE

DATE: possibly as old as 50,000 B.C.E.
LOCALE: Oceania document of the Bawinanga region, Arhhem Land, northern coastal Australia
RELATED CIVILIZATIONS: Australian Aborigine, Yolngu
SIGNIFICANCE: The Djanggawul cycle, one of the world's oldest continuously told myths of origin, concerns two sisters and a brother who arrived on earth via the island of the dead and created the landscape.

The Djanggawul song cycle tells the story of three ancestral beings and their travels through the Millingimbi region. Made up of 188 songs, it chronicles how three children of the Sun, the two sisters Bildjiwuaroju and Miralaldu (who taught human beings to hunt and gather in Dreamtime), and the brother Djanggawul fertilized the ancient landscape with their dreamings and brought the world into being by naming the plants, animals, and places they crossed over.

Aboriginal narratives are primarily about land, the

journeys of the Ancestors to creation sites where they created the different clans and animals and plants, battles for power and knowledge among them, and the ritual journeys of the totems that represent each clan. Individual songs, usually acted out, dealing with one or two totems associated with a specific area, may constitute a song cycle. Each clan knows only a song cycle segment, and these are exchanged at meeting points to maintain the continuity of dreaming, creation, time, space, and human life.

Besides covering the mythic fertilizing and creation of the world, the cycle clarifies and defines the nature and meaning of relationships between men and women and their respective powers and knowledge, making it clear that the original source of all power in the Dreaming comes from, and through, the women.

ADDITIONAL RESOURCES

Isaacs, Jennifer. *Australian Dreaming: Forty Thousand Years of Aboriginal History.* Sydney: Lansdowne Press, 1980.

Narogin, Mudrooroo. *The Indigenous Literature of Australia: Milli Milli Wangka.* South Melbourne, Australia: Hyland House, 1997.

SEE ALSO: Dreaming; Australia, Tasmania, New Zealand.

—*Michael W. Simpson*

DOMITIAN

ALSO KNOWN AS: Titus Flavius Domitianus; later Caesar Domitianus Augustus
BORN: October 24, 51 C.E.; place unknown
DIED: September 18, 96 C.E.; Rome
RELATED CIVILIZATION: Imperial Rome
MAJOR ROLE/POSITION: Emperor

Life. Domitian's youth, although not aristocratic, was far from the literary tradition associating him with poverty. Well regarded as a poet and writer, he authored a book on baldness and gave public recitals of his works. After the fall of Vitellius in 69 C.E., Domitian (duh-MIHSH-uhn) greeted the invading Flavian forces and represented Vespasian until he was recalled to Rome. He led forces against the insurgent Batavian auxiliaries in the Rhine, but the revolt was suppressed before his arrival. He married Domitia Longina in 70 C.E.

Domitian held minor posts during the reign of Vespasian and Titus (his brother). Upon the death of Titus in 81 C.E., Domitian was proclaimed emperor and received the titles Augustus and *pontifex maximus* (chief priest). Although he celebrated triumphs in the Dacian Wars, his successes were mostly in repelling invaders and suppressing internal uprisings.

Influence. Domitian raised the silver content of coinage back to Augustan levels and, even after its debasing in 85 C.E., maintained Vespasianic levels. He made copious civic improvements, constructed roads in Asia Minor, and improved defensive fortifications in North Africa. These projects, funded by heavy taxation in the provinces, his elevation of freedmen and expansion of the role of the equestrian class at the expense of the aristocracy, and his harsh despotism offset his efficient and practical rule, leaving an unsympathetic impression of his reign.

ADDITIONAL RESOURCES

Southern, Pat. *Domitian: Tragic Tyrant.* Bloomington: Indiana University Press, 1997.

Suetonius. *The Twelve Caesars.* Translated by Robert Graves. London: Viking Press, 2000.

SEE ALSO: Rome, Imperial; Titus; Vespasian.

—*David B. Pettinari*

DONATISM

DATE: c. 309-c. 750 C.E.
LOCALE: Roman Africa (northwest Africa)
RELATED CIVILIZATIONS: Imperial Rome, Vandals, Byzantine Empire
SIGNIFICANCE: Long-lived movement stemming from tendencies in African Christianity.

"Donatism" (DOH-nuh-tin-zuhm), named by "Catholic" opponents, refers to an African schism in the Christian Church that stemmed from Donatus (d. c. 355 C.E.), who claimed the Carthaginian see from 313/314 to 355 C.E. Donatus succeeded Majorinus, whom a group of Numidian bishops had elected (c. 309 C.E.) after rejecting Caecilian's earlier election by Carthagian Christians. Because transmarine churches still recognized Caecilian, two lines of succession lasted into the Arab conquest. Each communion viewed itself as the catholic church and therefore contested the other's catholicism, churches, and martyrs.

Primatial rivalry between Caecilian's predecessor, Mensurius of Carthage, and Secundus of Tigisis contributed to the schism, but Diocletian's persecution (303-305 C.E.) coined its terms. This persecution had demanded the surrender (*traditio*) of Scripture, and those surrendering seemed to be *traditores*, or traitors, to Christianity. The followers of Donatus rejected these traitors' sacraments and argued that Caecilian's consecrator was impure for having surrendered his copy of the Holy Scriptures to Romans during the prosecution. Though "Christian" by transmarine standards, Constantine the Great and later emperors who enforced transmarine canon seemed to be persecutors and Antichrists to the Donatists.

Saint Augustine regarded Donatist rebaptism as schismatic rejection of the one baptism, which existed even outside the catholic church. In 411 C.E., the Council of Carthage ruled against the Donatists, officially condemning the heresy. After a Vandal invasion in 429 C.E., Donatists and Catholics began a peaceful coexistence.

ADDITIONAL RESOURCES

Brown, Peter. *Augustine of Hippo: A Biography.* Berkeley: University of California Press, 1967.

Field, Lester L., Jr. *Liberty, Dominion, and the Two Swords: On the Origins of Western Political Theology (180-398).* Notre Dame, Ind.: University of Notre Dame Press, 1998.

Frend, W. H. C. *The Donatist Church: A Movement of Protest in Roman North Africa.* New York: Clarendon Press, 1985.

SEE ALSO: Africa, North; Augustine, Saint; Byzantine Empire; Christianity; Diocletian; Rome, Imperial; Vandals.

—Lester L. Field, Jr.

DONATUS, AELIUS

BORN: perhaps c. 310 C.E.; perhaps Africa
DIED: probably second half of fourth century C.E.; probably Rome
RELATED CIVILIZATION: Imperial Rome
MAJOR ROLE/POSITION: Grammarian

Life. Aelius Donatus (EE-lee-uhs duh-NAYT-uhs), who taught in Rome, composed a Latin grammar consisting of two sections. The first, *Ars minor* (n.d.; English translation, 1926), introduces beginners to the eight parts of speech in a handy, innovative question-and-answer form, and the more substantial second section, *Ars major* (n.d.; English translation, 1926), contains matter pertaining to literary style. Donatus also wrote commentaries on the Roman comic dramatist Terence and on the greatest of all Latin poets, Vergil. The Terence commentary, which survives only in a condensed version, presents an intriguing mixture of valuable information, good sense, and silliness. Donatus's commentary on Vergil, the most important work of literary exegesis to be produced in late antiquity, has perished except for the introduction; however, its content is to some degree preserved in the extant commentary of Donatus's imitator Servius.

Influence. In the Middle Ages, Donatus's grammar exercised a vast influence. It was printed by Johannes Gutenberg even before the Bible. Its author's name became a synonym for the subject itself: Any Latin "grammar" was simply a "Donatus."

ADDITIONAL RESOURCES

Daintree, D. "The Virgil Commentary of Aelius Donatus: Black Hole or 'Éminence Grise'?" *Greece and Rome* 37 (1990): 65-79.

Kaster, R. A. *Guardians of Language: The Grammarian and Society in Late Antiquity.* Reprint. Berkeley: University of California Press, 1997.

SEE ALSO: Languages and literature; Rome, Imperial; Vergil.

—Neil Adkin

DONG ZHONGSHU

ALSO KNOWN AS: *Wade-Giles* Tung Chung-shu
BORN: c. 179 B.C.E.; Hebei, China
DIED: c. 104 B.C.E.; Hebei, China
RELATED CIVILIZATIONS: China, Western Han
Dynasty
MAJOR ROLE/POSITION: Philosopher, politician

Life. Dong Zhongshu (doong joong-SHEW) was born into a rich family of landowners but reportedly was never concerned about his family property, preferring scholarship. Before he was thirty-nine years old, he became known as the "Confucius of the Han Dynasty." Later, his erudition was noticed by the emperor Wudi, who appointed him chancellor. He resigned when he was fifty-eight years old and returned to his hometown to focus on study and writing.

Dong Zhongshu proposed a theory of the interaction between humans and heaven that demonstrated that the emperor was appointed by heaven. His philosophy involved three essential principles—that the emperor was the host of chancellors, the father of sons, and the husband of a wife—and five ethical regulations—benevolence, righteousness, courtesy, wisdom, and sincerity. Politically, he advocated limiting the gap between the rich and poor and making moral education the main measure and penalty a secondary measure in ruling. He viewed only Confucianism to be the right ideology.

Influence. Dong Zhongshu developed the thought of Confucius, creating a systematically feudal ideology. Therefore, his theories were used by almost all feudal dynasties in Chinese history and deeply affected the culture and society of China for hundreds of years.

ADDITIONAL RESOURCES
Fung, Yu-lan. *A Short History of Chinese Philosophy.* New York: Free Press, 1997.
Queen, Sarah Ann. *From Chronicle to Canon: The Hermeneutics of the Spring and Autumn, According to Tung Chung-shu.* New York: Cambridge University Press, 1996.

SEE ALSO: China; Confucianism; Confucius; Han Dynasty.

—*Lihua Liu*

DORSET PHASE

DATE: c. 700 B.C.E.-900 C.E.
LOCALE: Arctic and subarctic Canada
SIGNIFICANCE: A general term referring to the Eskimo/Inuit peoples who inhabited most of northern Canada for about fifteen hundred years.

The Dorsets were descendants of the last wave of immigrants from Siberia, the Inuits, or Eskimos. They were bounded on the west by the Norton Eskimos, a similar culture, and on the south by Athapaskans; they probably reached as far as the Atlantic coast in Labrador and Newfoundland.

The Dorset appear to have emerged about three thousand years ago from the Sarqaq stage of Eskimo development, which in turn had emerged from the Arctic Small Tool tradition. The Dorset themselves were hardly a "culture" in the usual sense of the term, having no centralized government, but rather were a loose group of tribes spread out over a huge territory.

The dwellings of the Dorset were usually small and round, made of a wide variety of found materials, including skins supported by whale bones, driftwood, packed snow, and occasionally sod. They traveled by sea in small boats called kayaks and larger ones known as *umiaks* that could support an entire family.

The Dorset culture was submerged by the later Thule Eskimo culture between 700 and 900 C.E. during the Medieval Maximum, a period of warmer weather that also brought the Norse to the shores of North America. There are no surviving traces of the Dorset, in either language or customs.

ADDITIONAL RESOURCES
Clark, Donald Woodforde. *Western Subarctic Prehistory.* Hull, Quebec: Canadian Museum of Civilization, 1991.
Friedel, Stuart J. *Prehistory of the Americas.* Cambridge, England: Cambridge University Press, 1987.
Snow, Dean. *The Archaeology of North America.* New York: Viking Press, 1976.

SEE ALSO: Arctic Small Tool tradition; Subarctic peoples.

—*Marc Goldstein*

DRACO

ALSO KNOWN AS: Dracon
BORN: seventh century B.C.E.; possibly Athens
    Greece
DIED: c. 600 B.C.E.; possibly Athens, Greece
RELATED CIVILIZATION: Archaic Greece
MAJOR ROLE/POSITION: Lawgiver

Life. Little is known of Draco's (DRAY-koh) personal life. According to Aristotle, Draco gave Athens its first legal code at the request of the archons. The fragment that remains deals with homicide. Before Draco's code, the tribes and phraties (aristocratic brotherhoods) meted out punishment for murder. In cases in which the murderer and victim belonged to different families, retaliation by the victim's clan against a member of the murderer's, not necessarily the perpetrator, led to extended blood feuds. Draco established a court system in which the murderer was judged depending on whether the homicide was accidental or intentional. If the killing was accidental, the victim's family could pardon the culprit or order him out of the country. Intentional murderers were executed. Modern scholars are uncertain whether Draco actually wrote other laws, but writings created several centuries later attribute a complete code to him. His punishments were said to be so harsh, including execution for minor crimes, that his name has given English speakers the word "draconic."

Influence. Draco's code was an advance over a lawless system. However, it left the administration of the law in the hands of the archons, a closed aristocratic group of magistrates.

ADDITIONAL RESOURCES

Carawan, Edwin. *Rhetoric and the Law of Draco.* Oxford, England: Oxford University Press, 1998.
Gagarin, Michael. *Drakon and Early Athenian Homicide Law.* New Haven, Conn.: Yale University Press, 1981.
Stroud, Ronald S. *Drakon's Law on Homicide.* Berkeley: University of California Press, 1968.

SEE ALSO: Aristotle; Government and law; Greece, Archaic.

—Frederick B. Chary

DREAMING

ALSO KNOWN AS: Dreamtime
DATE: possibly as old as 50,000 B.C.E.
LOCALE: Oceania
RELATED CIVILIZATION: Australian Aborigine
SIGNIFICANCE: Part creation myth and part affiliation-identifier, talk of Dreaming defines Aborigine cultural identity and property rights.

In discussions of Aborigine cultures, Dreaming has two chief senses. In the first sense, the Dreaming (or the Dreamtime) is an eternal "time-out-of-time" in the creation myth central to the religious beliefs of Australia's indigenous (aboriginal) population. According to this myth, supernatural quasi-ancestors walked the land, creating the world in its present form, and in the process marking out tracks and signs ("songlines"), which later generations must commemorate (in song) and follow (for example, on "walkabout"), in order for creation to be ritually renewed and sustained.

In the second sense, a particular kind of Dreaming (such as Kangaroo Dreaming or Wallaby Dreaming) signifies an individual's chief totem figure, and so indicates the person's clan, religious duties, and relation to the Dreamtime; in a similar sense the term applies to an individual's "song." The songs and stories describing the Dreaming are central to the sense of identity of a clan and its members and are carefully guarded against misappropriation by outsiders. In recent times, such stories have also served as evidence supporting a clan's legal claim to a traditional territory.

ADDITIONAL RESOURCES

Charlesworth, Max, ed. *Religious Business: Essays on Australian Aboriginal Spirituality.* Cambridge, England: Cambridge University Press, 1998.
Chatwin, Bruce. *The Songlines.* New York: Viking Penguin, 1987.
Flood, Josephine. *Archaeology of the Dreamtime.* Rev. ed. New Haven, Conn.: Yale University Press, 1991.
Keen, Ian. *Knowledge and Secrecy in an Aboriginal Religion.* Oxford, England: Oxford University Press, 1994.

McIntosh, Ian S. *Aboriginal Reconciliation and the Dreaming*. Boston: Allyn and Bacon, 2000.

SEE ALSO: Australia, Tasmania, New Zealand; Djanggawul cycle.

—Edward Johnson

DZIBILCHALTÚN

DATE: 800 B.C.E.-700 C.E.
LOCALE: Yucatán Peninsula, Mexico
RELATED CIVILIZATION: Maya
SIGNIFICANCE: One of the largest, oldest, and longest occupied Maya population centers.

Dzibilchaltún, a very large and important archaeological site in the northern part of Mexico's Yucatán Peninsula, has been occupied almost continuously from around 800 B.C.E. By 500 B.C.E., small farming villages with thatched-roof huts were giving way to formally arranged public buildings. Eventually a well-planned urban center arose. The site's later growth may have been connected with the production of salt used in long-distance coastal trade with other Maya sites. The most dramatic growth spurt occurred between 600 and 900 C.E., when Dzibilchaltún developed into one of the region's largest cities, containing about 8,400 structures within a 7.3-square-mile (18.9-square-kilometer) area, a population approaching 25,000, and an agricultural area extending around 38 square miles (99 square kilometers).

Dzibilchaltún's most thoroughly restored building is the Temple of the Seven Dolls located in the main plaza. This structure sits astride a major east-west roadway at whose western end is a large stela aligned perfectly with the temple.

After 700 C.E. Dzibilchaltún began to decline after 1000 C.E., and although some modest building resumed before the Spanish Conquest (1521), the site was reduced to the status of ceremonial center, with less than 10 percent of its former population.

ADDITIONAL RESOURCES

Andrews, E. Wyllys IV. "Dzibilchaltún." In *Archaeology*. Vol. 1 of *Supplement to the Handbook of Middle American Indians*. Austin: University of Texas Press, 1981.
Kelly, Joyce. *An Archaeological Guide to Mexico's Yucatan Peninsula*. Norman: Oklahoma University Press, 1993.

SEE ALSO: Chichén Itzá; Cobá; Maya.

—David A. Crain

— E —

EASTERN AFRICAN MICROLITHIC/KHOISAN PEOPLES

DATE: beginning c. 17,000 B.C.E.
LOCALE: Eastern Africa
RELATED CIVILIZATION: Khoisan
SIGNIFICANCE: This ancient African archaeological complex lasted for many thousands of years.

The Eastern African Microlithic was an exceedingly ancient African archaeological complex, lasting from around 17,000 B.C.E. down to the first few centuries C.E. The makers of this tradition, wherever adequate evidence is available, turn out to have spoken languages of the Khoisan (KOY-sahn) family. At 8000 B.C.E., Khoisan peoples and their Microlithic tool kits could be found across 965,000 square miles (2.5 million square kilometers) of territory, from Kenya and Somalia in the north to the Limpopo River in the south. Between 8000 and 7000 B.C.E., the Southern Khoisan peoples spread south and west across most of southern Africa, expanding their way of life across another 772,000 square miles (2 million square kilometers).

The Khoisan peoples built up a variety of highly successful and adaptive strategies for exploiting the wild resources of the widely differing environments in which they lived. Among the earliest users of bows and arrows in the world, they also invented many different arrow poisons to increase the effectiveness of these weapons.

The Khoisan for thousands of years have been remarkable rock artists. In southern Africa, the earliest rock art goes back at least 26,000 years, long before the Khoisan arrived with their Eastern African Microlithic culture. However, it was Khoisan painters, skilled in conveying both movement and perspective, who were responsible for the great florescence of the rock art tradition in southern Africa after 3000 B.C.E. Scholarship has revealed that the artists were shamans, religious healers whose paintings depicted the visions they saw while in a state of trance.

Between 3500 B.C.E. and 700 C.E., the expansion of agricultural societies gradually brought an end to the long era of the Khoisan and their Microlithic tradition. In East Africa, Cushites and Nilotes expanded into former Khoisan lands. After 300 B.C.E., the Mashariki Bantu spread across Khoisan areas in both eastern and southern Africa. By 700 C.E., Khoisan societies remained a major historical force only far south in Africa.

ADDITIONAL RESOURCES
Diagram Group. *Peoples of Southern Africa*. New York: Facts On File, 1997.
Heine, Bernd, and Derete Nurse. *African Languages: An Introduction*. New York: Cambridge University Press, 2000.
Vossen, Rainer, and Klaus Keuthmann, eds. *Contemporary Studies on Khoisan*. Hamburg, Germany: H. Buske, 1986.

SEE ALSO: Afrasans; African rock art, southern and eastern; Bantu, Mashariki; Cushites; Khoisan; Nilotes.

—*Christopher Ehret*

EASTERN PEOPLES

DATE: 8000 B.C.E.-700 C.E.
LOCALE: Eastern North America
RELATED CIVILIZATIONS: Adena culture, Hopewell, Mississippian
SIGNIFICANCE: During the Holocene epoch, most aboriginal populations in eastern North America were transformed from mobile hunter-gatherers to fully sedentary and, occasionally, quite complex societies wholly or partially dependent on cultigens.

The initial occupation of eastern North America is now known to extend back to at least the fifteenth millennium B.C.E., as evidenced by sites such as Meadowcroft Rockshelter, Pennsylvania, and probably Cactus Hill, Virginia. Much more widespread though still ephemeral evidence of human presence occurs about 11,000-10,000 B.C.E. with the Clovis, or fluted point, horizon. The signature of humanity remains relatively light, however, until the end of the Pleistocene period, which is conventionally fixed at about 8500-8000 B.C.E.

Throughout the last six millennia of the Late Pleistocene, aboriginals in eastern North America were apparently highly mobile and targeted a wide array of now extinct as well as modern animal species while exploiting a range of plant resources. Environments were often ecologically anomalous by modern standards and have no precise analogues today.

Archaic period. By 8000 B.C.E., the Pleistocene megafauna were extinct throughout the east, and ecological conditions were similar to those of the present. In archaeological terms, the Paleo-Indian period was succeeded by the Archaic, which would last in a few areas well into historical times but in most regions would grade into the Woodland period.

The Early Archaic period (c. 8000–5500 B.C.E.) is signaled by the appearance of a variety of side- and corner-notched projectile point styles that succeed the fluted and unfluted lanceolate forms of the preceding Paleo-Indian period. Ground and pecked stone implements, rare in earlier times, become common, and in the few places where preservation permits, basketry, cordage, sandals, and related plant fiber and wood-derived products are represented. The number of sites across the eastern woodlands increases markedly, presumably reflecting population increase. However, groups are still quite small in most areas and remain highly mobile as they pursue a wide range of forest products. By the end of the Early Archaic period, seasonal aggregation sites can be found in major river valleys and other favored habitats.

The Middle Archaic period (c. 5500–3050 B.C.E.) witnesses a continuation of the trends of the earlier period. Large middens composed of shell and other occupational detritus mark the locations of large seasonal aggregation sites, and many contain numerous burials suggestive of substantial population sizes. Although the inferred settlement/subsistence regimes still involve considerable mobility, occupational stability is clearly reflected in many areas where riverine, maritime, or plant resources are abundant. Important developments in the Middle Archaic period include conclusive evidence for long-distance trade and exchange as well as the first appearance of ceremonial earthmound constructions in widely separated parts of the east. Elaborate ritual behavior is also suggested by complex funerary rites as evidenced at Windover, Florida, where Middle Archaic foragers buried more than 170 individuals, many of whom were wrapped in elaborate textiles.

The tendencies toward a more sedentary lifestyle, elaborate ceremonial architecture, intensive long-distance exchange, and higher population densities continued into the Late Archaic period (3050–1050 B.C.E.) with unprecedented site densities in virtually all habitat zones. Although scattered hunter-foragers with high mobility still existed (and would continue to exist) on the margins of the eastern woodlands, notably in Canada, the Late Archaic is typified in many areas by genuinely complex sociocultural manifestations such as Poverty Point in Louisiana and the Old Copper sites in the upper Midwest.

By the Late Archaic period, seasonal use of increased amounts of wild plants had turned into local cultivation of indigenous species such as sumpweed, sunflowers, gourds, and various chenopods such as goosefoot. Additionally, extensive exploitation of both riverine and coastal maritime resources heavily augmented the acquisition of forest products and facilitated higher population aggregates.

The Late Archaic grades almost imperceptibly into the Early Woodland period (1050-100 B.C.E.), which is marked by the widespread use of ceramics, year-round sedentism in many areas, and the appearance, in minor quantities, of nonlocal domesticates such as corn and squash. Village sites are rather small (about six to ten structures; fifty to seventy-five people), but clear evidence of nascent stratification is apparent in groups such as the Adena of the Midwest.

Middle Woodland period. During the Middle Woodland period (100 B.C.E.-1000 C.E.), many populations across eastern North America were loosely connected in a techno-economic and, possibly, religious and political exchange network known as the Hopewell Interaction Sphere. Named for a spectacular complex in southern Ohio, the Hopewellian efflorescence involved the incorporation into regionally distinct and essentially local cultures with a veneer of shared behaviors that includes complex burial and effigy mound construction; long-distance acquisition, use, and ritual disposal of high-status trade goods; and an almost standardized iconography.

The Hopewell phenomenon began to decline in many parts of its range by 300-400 C.E., although in restricted areas, notably the lower Mississippi Valley and parts of the southeast, it was succeeded by an even more dramatic development known as Mississippian (1000 B.C.E.-450 C.E.). This entity—actually a series of separate ethnic and linguistic units like Hopewell—represents the most complex cultural expression to appear in

ANCIENT NORTH AMERICAN SITES AND AREAS

North America, north of central Mexico. Mississippian society was centered on large, town-size communities that dominated extensive territories. Organized hierarchically into stratified chiefdoms, these Mississippian centers are typified by sites such as Cahokia near St. Louis, Moundville in Alabama, and Etowah in Georgia.

Though the Mississippian began to unravel well before European contact, some of its lineal descendants, such as the Natchez, remained organizationally complex well into the early historic period. Elsewhere, Eastern Woodland groups were in the process of evolving into the more or less egalitarian, maize-based societies that would soon be overwhelmed by Europeans with their introduced diseases.

ADDITIONAL RESOURCES

Anderson, David G., and Kenneth E. Sassaman. *The Paleoindian and Early Archaic Southeast*. Tuscaloosa: University of Alabama Press, 1996.

Fagan, Brian M. *Ancient North America: The Archaeology of a Continent*. 2d ed. New York: Thames and Hudson, 1995.

Smith, Bruce D. *Rivers of Change: Essays on Early Agriculture in Eastern North America*. Washington, D.C.: Smithsonian Institution Press, 1992.

SEE ALSO: Adena culture; Archaic North American culture; Clovis technological complex; Middle Woodland tradition; Old Copper complex; Paleo-Indians in North America; Poverty Point.

—*J. M. Adovasio*

EDWIN

ALSO KNOWN AS: Eadwine
BORN: sixth century C.E.; northern England
DIED: October 12, 632 C.E.; Hatfield Chase, England
RELATED CIVILIZATIONS: England, Anglo-Saxon
MAJOR ROLE/POSITION: Military leader and statesman

Life. Son of King Ælle of Deira, Edwin found himself in exile as a youth after his kingdom was conquered and annexed by Æthelfrith of Northumbria. Edwin, after some time of moving about, was ultimately taken in by King Rædwald of East Anglia; with his aid, Edwin fought and defeated Æthelfrith in 616 C.E. and assumed the throne of Northumbria.

As king, Edwin expanded both north and far to the south and even somewhat into Wales. By forging alliances, he extended his influence throughout most of England, becoming overlord of the most extensive political organization to date. For his political achievements, he was included by the eighth century C.E. historian Bede among the seven most powerful kings (or *bretwaldas*) to have held power in England. Importantly, Edwin converted to Christianity in 627 C.E. and

encouraged the spread of the faith within Northumbria and elsewhere. Edwin died in battle against a Welsh force in 632 C.E.

Influence. With Edwin's death, both the kingdom of Northumbria and Christianity struggled—but only briefly, as the political structures Edwin put into place managed to provide cohesion. Soon Northumbria would rise as a center for learning and the arts in the late seventh through early eighth centuries (the age of Bede).

ADDITIONAL RESOURCES

Blair, Peter Hunter. *An Introduction to Anglo-Saxon England*. 2d ed. Cambridge, England: Cambridge University Press, 1995.

Campbell, James, ed. *The Anglo-Saxons*. New York: Penguin Books, 1982.

Stenton, Frank. *Anglo-Saxon England*. 3d ed. Oxford, England: Clarendon Press, 1971.

SEE ALSO: Angles, Saxons, Jutes; Britain; Christianity.

—*Alexander M. Bruce*

EGYPT, PHARAONIC

DATE: c. 3050-305 B.C.E.
LOCALE: Nile River Valley in northeastern Africa
SIGNIFICANCE: Creators of one of the earliest civilizations, the ancient Egyptians emphasized practical knowledge and produced the world's first national government, large cities, irrigation projects, gigantic pyramids, beautiful temples, a written language, a paperlike writing material made from papyrus plants, and a 365-day calendar.

The ancient Greek historian Herodotus called Egypt "the gift of the Nile," which recognized the country's total dependence on the river. Flowing through an arid desert, the Nile each year overflowed and deposited fertile mud that made agriculture possible. Because of the dark soil, the ancient Egyptians called the country Kemet, which meant "black land." In addition to providing food, the Nile was a means of transportation and commerce, and it also had a tendency to encourage the unification of the region into a single political entity. With desert sand to its east and west, the Nile cataracts to its south, and the Mediterranean to its north, Egypt had the advantage of natural defenses from outside invasion.

History. The Egyptian priest Manetho, writing about 280 B.C.E., arranged the long history of Egyptian pharaohs into thirty-one dynasties (or hereditary rulers), extending from legendary times until Alexander the Great. Manetho's arrangement, despite its problems, is still used. The thirty dynasties are usually divided into seven periods as shown in the table: Archaic Period (First to Second Dynasties), Old Kingdom (Third to Sixth Dynasties), First Intermediate Period (Seventh to Tenth Dynasties), Middle Kingdom (Eleventh to Twelfth Dynasties), Second Intermediate Period (Thirteenth to Seventeenth Dynasties), New Kingdom (Eighteenth to Twentieth Dynasties), and Post-empire (Twenty-first to Thirty-first Dynasties). Earlier dates in Egyptian history are only approximations, but fairly precise dates are possible after the Persian conquest of 525 B.C.E.

Even in the predynastic era, the Egyptians had taken fundamental steps toward the creation of an advanced civilization. Settled in farming villages, they had learned to dig irrigation canals, to make tools made of copper and stone, to use written symbols to preserve records, and to exchange goods and services based on a specialization of labor. In time, Egyptian villages were organized into two political systems: the delta area was known as Lower Egypt, and the southern region was called Upper Egypt.

The First Dynasty was established about 3050 B.C.E., when a legendary southern king, Menes (also known as Narmer or Aha), conquered the northern region and united all Egypt into a single national monarchy. Unification was important because it meant that a single government was able to maintain order and regulate trade from the Mediterranean to the first cataract of the Nile. Menes established a new city, later called Memphis (near present-day Cairo), as the capital of his kingdom. Probably Menes was also known as Narmer, the name written on a famous slate palette in the Cairo museum.

Beginning about 2700 B.C.E., the kings of the Old Kingdom greatly strengthened the central government, and they constructed the famous pyramids of Egypt. King Djoser (also known as Zosher), the founder of the Third Dynasty, constructed the first pyramid, which was the Step Pyramid at Saqqara. Khufu and other kings of the Fourth Dynasty were responsible for the largest pyramids. The king was considered a divine being, having powers that were almost unlimited. After five hundred years, the united kingdom was broken up for a combination of reasons: climatic changes resulting in crop failures, discontent with high taxes, conflict between priests and secular rulers, and the usurpation of power from provincial strongmen.

The First Intermediate Period was a time of weak central government, with numerous invasions by desert tribes and regional leaders often at war with one another. About 2050 B.C.E., the rulers of Thebes gradually reestablished centralized rule, so that Thebes became the capital for most of the next millennium. The kings of the Middle Kingdom achieved only a limited authority over regional warlords and nobles, but they were able to promote trade and prosperity. These kings were recognized as dispensers of justice and had a reputation for being concerned about the welfare of the people.

About 1790 B.C.E., Egypt again became disunited and entered its Second Intermediate Period. Soon thereafter, the country was conquered by the Hyksos (called Shepherd Kings), who were apparently a Semitic people from Syria. The Hyksos introduced the horse-drawn chariot, knowledge of casting bronze

THE SEVEN PERIODS OF THE THIRTY-ONE EGYPTIAN DYNASTIES

Name of Period	Dynasty	Years
Archaic Period	First to Second	c. 3050-c. 2700 B.C.E.
Old Kingdom	Third to Sixth	c. 2700-c. 2200 B.C.E.
First Intermediate Period	Seventh to Tenth	c. 2200-c. 2050 B.C.E.
Middle Kingdom	Eleventh to Twelfth	c. 2050-c. 1790 B.C.E.
Second Intermediate Period	Thirteenth to Seventeenth	c. 1790-c. 1570 B.C.E.
New Kingdom	Eighteenth to Twentieth	c. 1570-c. 1085 B.C.E.
Post-empire	Twenty-first to Thirty-first	c. 1085-305 B.C.E.

EIGHTEENTH DYNASTY EGYPT, CIRCA 1550-1352 B.C.E.

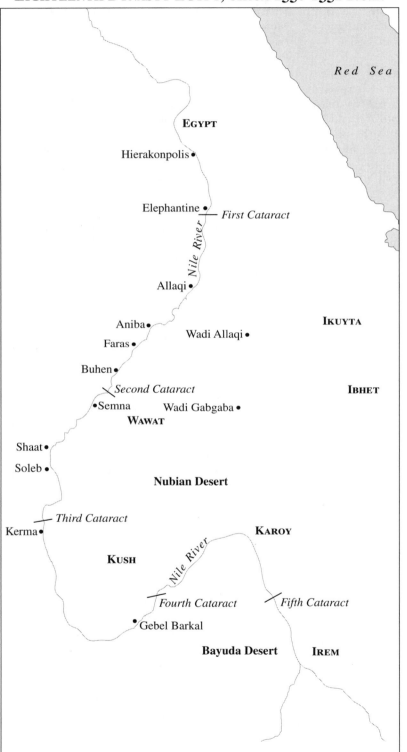

tools and weapons, the composite bow made of laminated wood and horn, and Asian ideas of religion and government. Under Hyksos hegemony, which lasted about a century, the Nile Delta became the capital. Although the Hyksos accepted most aspects of Egyptian culture, they were nevertheless resented as foreign intruders.

Ahmose I, founder of the Eighteenth Dynasty, expelled the Hyksos about 1570 B.C.E., which marked the beginning of the New Kingdom. During the next five hundred years, Egypt ruled over a large empire extending from the Euphrates River in the east to the fourth cataract of the Nile River. The many gold artifacts in Tutankhamen's preserved tomb give testimony to the ostentatious wealth of the time. The temples and other buildings of the Eighteenth Dynasty are recognized as the zenith of Egyptian architecture. Rameses II, probably the pharaoh mentioned in the Hebrew Bible, was especially notable for his many monuments, such as the impressive temples at Karnak, Luxor, and Abu Simbel.

Following the end of the Twentieth Dynasty (about 1085 B.C.E.), Egypt's power and level of cultural achievement declined rapidly. During the next seven hundred years, foreign invaders often ruled over Egypt. From 931 to c. 711 B.C.E., Libyan kings controlled most of the northern half of the country. They were followed by Nubians from the southern deserts, but the Nubians were soon driven out by Assyrian invaders. Following another period of independence, Persians took command of Egypt in 525 B.C.E. The Persians exercised hegemony over Egypt on and off until

Alexander the Great added Egypt to his empire in 332 B.C.E., the same year that he began building the city of Alexandria. After Alexander's death, his general Ptolemy I Soter established a Greek-speaking dynasty in 305 B.C.E., which is usually considered the end of the pharaonic age.

Agriculture and animal husbandry. Sometime before 5000 B.C.E., people in the Nile River Valley were planting seeds and domesticating animals. It is not known whether this practice evolved independently in Egypt or was brought to Egypt from elsewhere in the Mediterranean world. Because of almost a total lack of rainfall, large-scale agriculture was possible only with the use of irrigation. The building of canals required a great deal of difficult labor and social cooperation, which promoted centralized government and authoritarian rule.

The work of farm laborers did not change much during the history of ancient Egypt. To prepare their fields for planting, the Egyptians usually used wooden plows pulled by oxen. The vast majority of farm laborers did not own their own land, but they were forced to work on the large estates of the nobility. Usually such laborers were sharecroppers who received a small amount of the crops as pay, with most of the wealth going to land owners and to the government in the form of taxes.

Because of the importance of bread to the diet, wheat and barley were the major crops. The cultivation of dates and grapes was also important for the making of wine. Flax was grown to make linen and cotton for clothing. Other crops included beans, lentils, onions, melons, figs, lettuce, and cucumbers. In addition, the ancient Egyptians raised beef and dairy cattle, goats, donkeys, geese, and ducks.

Government and law. During periods of centralized rule, the kings of ancient Egypt had few restrictions on their authority to make and enforce laws, although priests and nobles exercised considerable political influence. During the New Kingdom, the king became known as the pharaoh, a term that originally meant "great house" or "palace." The position of kingship was inherited by the eldest son of the king's chief wife. Sometimes the eldest daughter of a chief wife would claim the right to the throne, and at least four women became monarchs. The Egyptian religion taught that the royal family descended from the falcon-headed god Horus, a belief that strengthened royal authority.

The king's highest officials were called viziers. They acted as the highest judges of the land and also supervised the collection of taxes, a difficult task that was crucial to the preservation of centralized power. For local government, the country was usually divided into forty-two provinces called nomes. The king appointed an official called a nomarch to administer each of the provinces.

As in other early civilizations, the Egyptian political system was usually harsh and dictatorial. There is no evidence that the Egyptians ever developed the concepts of representation and democracy. Often, however, they did maintain a rule of law, with written rules and impersonal enforcement in national courts. It is not known whether the common people ever believed in the official ideology that was supported by the ruling elite.

Class and gender. An enormous gulf separated the upper from the lower classes. Wealthy people lived in elegant palaces, while the poor lived in mud-brick shanties. The class system, however, was not rigid when compared with those of other ancient societies, and there were limited opportunities for individuals to advance to more prestigious positions. The upper class included the royal family, government officials, rich landowners, and priests. The middle class consisted of merchants, skilled craftspeople, and soldiers. The lower class, which included the majority of the population, was made up of unskilled workers. Most of the slaves were foreigners who had been captured in warfare.

Class distinctions were more important than gender distinctions. Compared with other ancient societies, women were not especially subordinate to men. Although polygamy was permitted, most families were monogamous. Women were not secluded and could own property and operate businesses. Women of the upper classes enjoyed significant privileges. During the New Kingdom, Egyptians queens often acted as royal regents and were sometimes depicted on an identical scale as their husbands. In Egyptian art, women of the lower classes are commonly seen engaging in agricultural work and the manufacture of clothing.

Education. A small percentage of children from the upper classes were able to attend schools and learn to read and write. Schools concentrated on the skills necessary for practical occupations, which included scribes, physicians, priests, and builders. Among the common people, most Egyptian boys were taught to follow the occupations of their fathers. Sometimes boys were placed with master craftspeople in order to learn professions, although the majority of the people became simple farmers. Girls were almost always taught by their mothers to become wives and mothers.

Writing systems. The dominant type of writing used in ancient Egypt is called hieroglyphics, which means "sacred inscriptions." Scholars are not certain whether Egypt's development of a writing system was influenced by Mesopotamia. Once begun, hieroglyphics developed rapidly, and it was largely perfected by the beginning of the Old Kingdom. The developed system utilized more than six hundred conventionalized pictures, or pictograms, each representing an idea, a syllable, or the sound of a single consonant. The Phoenicians probably acquired the basic idea of an alphabetic system from the Egyptians.

During the Middle Kingdom, a cursive form of writing called hieratic (from the Greek word for "priestly") began replacing hieroglyphics. Later, during the New Kingdom, a more developed style of handwriting, the demotic (from the Greek word for "popular"), was widely used except on monuments and in funeral texts. By the time of Roman rule, knowledge of how to read Egyptian hieroglyphics was entirely lost, and it was regained only after 1799, when French investigators discovered a stone slab containing both Greek and Egyptian writings outside Rosetta, a city near Alexandria.

Religion. The religion of ancient Egypt had a profound impact on all aspects of life. In general, the Egyptians believed in some version of polytheism, with a variety of deities that resembled humans, animals, or objects of nature. It appears likely that each city or region originally had its own local deity but that the unification of the country resulted in a fusion into several main deities. Therefore, many of the guardian deities were merged into the Sun deity Re (also called Amun or Amun-Re). The gods personifying the vegetative forces of nature were gradually combined into the god of the Nile, called Osiris.

The Egyptians sometimes appeared almost obsessed with issues relating to an afterlife, although particular beliefs and rituals did change over time. During the Old Kingdom, the cult devoted to the Sun god Re seemed to show little concern for the fate of most individuals, but the immortality of the king was considered important for the survival and prosperity of the society. During the Middle Kingdom, there was a widespread belief that each individual soul (*ka*) could survive in an afterlife. Osiris was recognized as the judge of the dead. Presumably Osiris had been murdered, but his sister and wife, Isis, had miraculously resurrected his body to life. During the New Kingdom, images of Osiris judging the dead were commonly found in funerary texts, many of which were collected and are now known as

the *Book of the Dead* (compiled and edited in the sixteenth century B.C.E.; English translation, 1842). While emphasizing ritual and magical formulas, the texts indicated that future happiness in the afterlife was also dependent on the deceased having lived a virtuous life on earth.

Because of its polytheistic nature, Egyptian religion was generally tolerant toward different beliefs. The priests of the dominant cults were among the small elite who had the advantage of formal education, and they enjoyed a great deal of prestige. About 1375 B.C.E., the devotion of Pharaoh Akhenaton (also known as Amenhotep IV) to the Sun deity Aton is now considered an early form of monotheism. Akhenaton's new capital of Amarna prohibited worship of any other deities. Most Egyptians, however, were not prepared for such a radical change. Following Akhenaton's death, his successors returned the capital to Thebes and brought back traditional polytheism.

Science and technology. Ancient Egyptians were interested in the practical applications of science, with only limited concern for theoretical explanations. They made important observations in the field of astronomy, making it possible to produce a calendar of 365 days a year. They noted that the annual flooding began shortly after the star Sirius reappeared about June 20 each year. In mathematics, they devised a system of counting by tens, and they could calculate area and volume. Although having no zero, they were able to use complex fractions. They formulated principles of geometry to design buildings and to determine boundaries. Egyptian physicians used empirical observations and measurements in studying the human body. They could set broken bones, sew up wounds, and treat many illnesses.

Ancient Egyptians also made important advances in industrial technology. In predynastic times, they learned to mine and smelt copper. Probably copper was the only metal available during the Old Kingdom, but there are indications that Egyptians were making some bronze tools before the Hyksos invasion. Apparently Egypt had to import its iron and silver from Asia. It is possible that Egyptians were the first to invent glass, which became an Egyptian specialty about 1500 B.C.E. For constructing buildings, they developed a large assortment of tools, including drills, pulleys, rollers, and lathes. One of Egypt's most important innovations was a writing material made from strips of the stems of papyrus plants.

Architecture. The ancient Egyptians used two principal materials for constructing buildings, unbaked mud bricks and stone. Tombs and religious temples were generally constructed in stone, while private houses, towns, and fortresses were usually made of mud brick. Most of the ancient towns have been lost because they were located in the flooded regions of the Nile River Valley. Numerous tombs and temples, in contrast, have survived because they were located in the desert regions. The modern study of Egyptian architecture, therefore, places an inordinate emphasis on religious funerary constructions.

The pyramids of the Old Kingdom are the largest and oldest stone structures of the world. An individual king built his own pyramid in order to preserve his body throughout eternity. A small passage in the northern wall usually led to the body of the dead king, located deep below the surface. The three pyramids of Giza are ranked as one of the Seven Wonders of the World. The largest of the three, built for Khufu, covers thirteen acres and originally rose 482 feet (147 meters). It is composed of 2.3 million limestone blocks, weighing an average of more than two tons each.

During and after the Middle Kingdom, the temple became the dominant architectural form. The largest temples were built for the worship of major deities, but funeral temples were also built to honor dead kings. The temples of Karnak and Luxor are especially notable for their massive size and richly carved columns. The Karnak temple has 130 columns that rise 80 feet (24 meters), and it is 1,300 feet (396 meters) long, encompassing the largest area of any religious edifice ever constructed. The famous temple at Abu Simbel was carved out of a sandstone cliff, with three consecutive halls extending 185 feet (56 meters) into the cliff. The entrance contains four seated statues of Rameses II, each rising 66 feet (20 meters).

Visual arts. Egyptians liked to decorate their tombs and temples with paintings and other works of art. The colorful pictures were typically related to religious themes and conceptions about the afterlife. Apparently the Egyptians believed that the future life would be similar to known experiences, so the walls of tombs were often covered with scenes of daily life and work. In addition to paintings, tombs and temples also included statues, which demonstrated the patience and skill of Egyptian craftspeople. The most impressive statues were large representations of kings, proclaiming their power and divine grandeur. The Great Sphinx, for example, represented the king with a human head and the body of a powerful lion.

Current views. The ancient Egyptians maintained an orderly way of life and an essential continuity for an amazingly long period of time. Like the majority of their contemporaries, they showed almost no interest in speculative philosophy or theoretical science, and their culture did not encourage the production of great works of literature or theater. Whatever the limitations of the culture, however, Egyptian achievements in art, architecture, and technology were among the most impressive of the ancient world. Clearly Egyptian civilization had a significant influence on later developments in the Mediterranean world, although the direct and indirect influences are difficult to determine in specific instances.

During the 1990's, there was considerable controversy about the racial makeup of ancient Egyptian society. The best evidence suggests that most Egyptians had relatively dark hair and dark skin, but paintings also seem to indicate that they were somewhat lighter in complexion than the Nubians to the south. Because of frequent contact with diverse peoples from southwest Asia, southern Europe, and Nubia, the Egyptian population included a diversity of physical traits. There is no evidence that the Egyptians had a concept of race or that their social positions were based on physical attributes such as skin color or hair texture.

ADDITIONAL RESOURCES

Aldred, Cyril. *The Egyptians*. London: Thames and Hudson, 1998.

Clayton, Peter. *Chronicle of the Pharaohs*. London: Thames and Hudson, 1994.

Johnson, Paul. *The Civilization of Ancient Egypt*. New York: HarperCollins, 1999.

Quirke, Stephen. *Ancient Egyptian Religion*. London: British University Press, 1992.

Reeves, Nicholas, and Richard Wilkinson. *The Complete Valley of the Kings*. London: Thames and Hudson, 1996.

Siliotti, Alberto. *Egypt: Splendor of an Ancient Civilization*. London: Thames and Hudson, 1994.

Silverman, David, ed. *Ancient Egypt*. New York: Oxford University Press, 1997.

SEE ALSO: Akhenaton; Alexander the Great; Assyria; Egypt, Prepharaonic; Egypt, Ptolemaic and Roman; Herodotus; Hyksos; Nubia; Persia; Pyramids and the Sphinx; Rameses II; Rosetta stone; Tutankhamen.

—Thomas T. Lewis

EGYPT, PREPHARAONIC

DATE: 8000-c. 3050 B.C.E.

LOCALE: Nile River Valley and Delta

SIGNIFICANCE: The foundation and essential elements of one of the earliest and most important civilizations in the history of the world developed in Egypt many centuries before the more famous pharaohs began to reign.

The ancient Greek historian Herodotus observed that Egypt was "the gift of the Nile," meaning that the development of civilization in Egypt, as well as the special flavor or character of that civilization, was the result of the life-giving waters of the great river that flowed through the midst of a desert wasteland. The essential characteristics of Egyptian culture developed sometime between 8000 and 3050 B.C.E. Because the people living in the Nile River Valley were surrounded by desert and therefore isolated from other cultures, they developed feelings of security and insulation. Because of the regular, yearly, predictable cycle of flooding along the Nile, they became a conservative, happy, optimistic people who enjoyed the present life enough to believe it should and would continue forever. During the period before 3050 B.C.E., the Egyptian people became obsessed with the quest for eternal life and came to believe in the goodness of their gods and the benevolence of the universe. These beliefs and concepts then continued to be represented in their art, architecture, and literature on and off for the next thirteen hundred years during the periods of the three Egyptian kingdoms (Old, Middle, and New).

Predynastic history. Historians and archaeologists recognize two main periods of Egypt's prehistoric past—the Neolithic and Chalcolithic Ages—meaning, respectively, New Stone and Copper Stone Ages, and so called primarily on the basis of the kind of tools used by the inhabitants. Usually these two periods are lumped together and referred to simply as the predynastic period of ancient Egypt. Over several thousands of years, people began leaving their settlements in regions now part of the Sahara, and migrating to the Nile Valley as more and more areas turned into inhabitable desert following the end of the wet phases of the Paleolithic (Old Stone) Age and as the Nile Valley began to dry out, making it more hospitable. People lived primarily as nomadic hunters and gatherers until sometime around 5000 B.C.E., when settled agriculture took hold.

The earliest known Neolithic cultures have been found on the southwest edge of the Nile Delta region, and farther to the southwest in the region called the Fayum. The different phases of cultural development have been given names by anthropologists, usually based on the places where remains of material culture (pottery, tools, jewelry, rock drawings, burial remains) have been found. Important cultures found in Upper Egypt date from the late fifth millennium B.C.E. and are called Tasian and Badarian. The most important predynastic culture-type of ancient Egypt is called Naqadah II, also named Gerzean. It spread gradually throughout the land and is identified by a special type of pottery made of desert clay decorated in red with images of boats and certain animals. Ceremonial knives made of flint by craftspeople possessing tremendous skill were characteristic of this cultural phase, and they continued to be manufactured during later periods of Egyptian history.

During the late Naqadah II culture, contacts with other civilizations of the Near East, especially Mesopotamia, became more frequent and important. Although many details are not known about the political developments of Egypt during this time, it is likely that small districts, called nomes (after the Greek word for law), were evolving into administrative regions. At the same time (at least as Egyptians of later periods believed), the whole of Egypt coalesced into two larger areas eventually called the Two Kingdoms, each consisting of a confederation of nomes, and each ruled from a principal center of power. Upper Egypt in the south was controlled by a king from Naqadah, who wore the white crown and whose patron or tutelary deity was the god Seth. Lower Egypt in the north was ruled by a king from Behdet in the Delta, who wore the red crown, and whose tutelary deity was the now-famous falcon god Horus. As time went on, new capitals were established at Hierakonpolis in Upper Egypt and Buto in the Delta. The names of the predynastic kings of the Two Lands were recorded on the Palermo stone, a fragmentary presentation of royal annals manufactured during the Fifth Dynasty (latter half of the Old Kingdom).

Early dynastic period. About 3050 B.C.E. (as historians reckon), the king of Upper Egypt conquered Lower Egypt and united the two kingdoms, becoming the King of the Two Lands. According to tradition, this ruler became the first king of the First Dynasty (the term pharaoh did not come into use as a designation for the king until the later reigns of the New Kingdom,

c. 1570-c. 1085 B.C.E.) and was named Menes or Narmer (both are recorded). His conquest was graphically portrayed on the so-called Narmer palette. He is also credited with establishing united Egypt's first capital, Memphis, on what was the border between the Two Lands.

Historians regard this conquest as the beginning of Egypt's historical period, the time from which writing first seems to be in use, and the time from which the succession of Egypt's thirty-one dynasties began to be measured. The king during this early historical period was regarded as the embodiment of a living god on earth—the Horus falcon. The last king of the First Dynasty apparently introduced the wearing of the double crowns of Upper and Lower Egypt as the symbol of the unified country. How the Second Dynasty began is not known, but it seems to have occurred around 2850 B.C.E. and lasted until the inauguration of the Old Kingdom under the leadership of the Third Dynasty in about 2700 B.C.E.

Current views. At one time, the scarcity of evidence and lack of historical records for this period, plus the fact that two and a half millennia of pharaonic culture followed it, tended to cause some students to regard it as only an unimportant preface to the "real" achievements of ancient Egypt. Such is not the case. As more archaeological fieldwork is being completed, advances in scholars' understanding of the importance of this developmental period have been forthcoming. Also, archaeological evidence seems to indicate that the unification of ancient Egypt may have been more gradual than the traditional portrayals handed down from the Old Kingdom and later.

ADDITIONAL RESOURCES

Hoffman, Michael A. *Egypt Before the Pharaohs: The Prehistoric Foundations of Egyptian Civilization.* New York: Alfred A. Knopf, 1991.

Kemp, B. J. *Ancient Egypt: Anatomy of a Civilization.* New York: Alfred A. Knopf, 1989.

Wilson, John A. *The Culture of Ancient Egypt.* Chicago: University of Chicago Press, 1956.

SEE ALSO: Egypt, Pharaonic; Egypt, Ptolemaic and Roman.

—*Andrew C. Skinner*

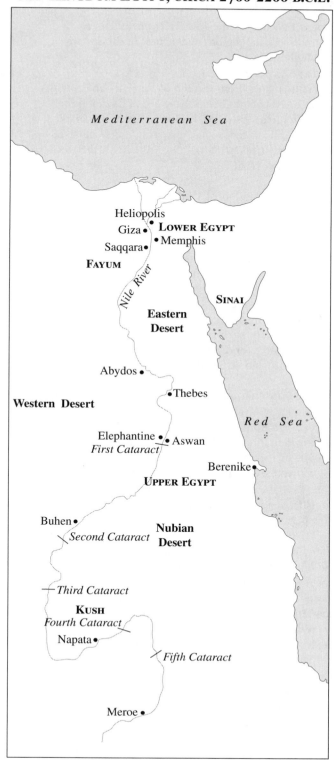

OLD KINGDOM EGYPT, CIRCA 2700-2200 B.C.E.

EGYPT, PTOLEMAIC AND ROMAN

LOCALE: Valley of the Nile River, including, at times, coastal regions and islands of the eastern Mediterranean

DATE: 323 B.C.E.-639 C.E.

SIGNIFICANCE: From the end of Persian control with the arrival of the Greeks to the end of Byzantine control with the arrival of the Arabs, Egypt was marked by political and social upheaval, intellectual advancement, and wide-ranging influence in the Mediterranean world.

"Ptolemaic" (tah-leh-MAY-ihk) refers to the dynasty ruling Egypt from the death of Alexander the Great in 323 B.C.E. until the death of Cleopatra VII in 30 B.C.E. The succession of kings and queens, spanning almost three hundred years, were all descendants of Ptolemy I, a Macedonian general of high rank. The kings went by the name Ptolemy and most of the queens by the name Cleopatra. Although Roman numerals are used to distinguish among them, members of the dynasty used Greek epithets such as Soter ("savior"), Euergetes ("benefactor"), or Epiphanes ("made manifest") for this purpose and also to denote how they wanted to be perceived.

The transition to Roman authority resulted in little immediate interruption in ordinary affairs in Egypt, although the Romans introduced fundamental changes during their three hundred years of rule. As an imperial province, the exports of agricultural products from Egypt were especially vital to the economy of the empire. Both the Ptolemaic and Roman periods were Hellenistic, and the dominant force in Egypt in the Byzantine period was the Church and its patriarchs.

History. When Alexander the Great led his army from Macedonia and Greece into Egypt in 332 B.C.E., no one could have anticipated the lasting impact such an unopposed "invasion" would have. It was not until a decade later, when Alexander died in Babylon, that it started to become clear how complete the change would be. Because no one was ready to succeed Alexander either as commander of the army or king on the throne, a struggle began to resolve the complex issue, lasting more than four decades. Ptolemy I Soter partly preempted the struggle by gaining possession of the great leader's corpse and securing control over Egypt. He immediately began building a tomb in the new city of Alexandria for Alexander's body. Acting at first like a successor to the Persian satrap, he did not use the title

king. Nevertheless, he was clearly ready to defend his position of supreme ruler, as in 321 B.C.E. when one of Alexander's generals unsuccessfully attacked. By 305 B.C.E., Ptolemy I Soter was officially king of Egypt, and subsequent events in his reign were dated from that year.

Building on the foundation of his father, Ptolemy II Philadelphus along with his son Ptolemy III Euergetes achieved remarkable success in transforming Egypt into a world power. Their combined rule of sixty years (285-221 B.C.E.) is the best documented and the most important period of the Ptolemaic Dynasty. They maximized Egypt's natural resources and manpower and carefully managed agricultural enterprises, yet they left in place as much native control as possible. As a result, the Ptolemaic kingdom was prospering and the Ptolemies were gaining dominion over other regions around the Mediterranean, including Palestine and Cyrenaica, coastal areas of Asia Minor, as well as Cyprus and most of the Aegean islands.

Although this all happened within one hundred years of when Ptolemy I first entered Egypt, the next one hundred years would see the undoing of much of what had been accomplished. Natives revolted against the government. An army that had been largely staffed by Greek and Macedonian soldiers became increasingly and dangerously dependent on native draftees. Territories outside Egypt were lost to more powerful kingdoms.

In 168 B.C.E., a Seleucid army invaded Egypt, and the Seleucids were poised to take absolute control when the Romans appeared on the scene. The Romans had come to protect the balance of power, as well as their own interests, and demanded that the Seleucids withdraw. It was a sign of things to come, when Rome would become increasingly involved in the affairs of the Ptolemaic kingdom.

During the first century B.C.E., Egypt was a client-kingdom of Rome. That meant that the Ptolemaic kings and queens were free to rule, as long as nothing was done to threaten the interests of the growing Roman Republic. The dynasty ended with Queen Cleopatra VII, a remarkable woman and ruler. She aligned herself and her kingdom first with Julius Caesar and after his death with Marc Antony. When she and Antony were defeated in a naval battle by Octavian (later Augustus), it was time for the future emperor to annex Egypt as a Roman province.

Roman Egypt was very important to the empire for the huge shipments of grain arriving in the port of Rome. Egypt also provided other agricultural products, papyrus, and quarried stone. In addition, the merchants of Egypt offered many rarities to the wealthy Romans.

It was common for Roman emperors to make imperial visits to Egypt. Vespasian, Caracalla, and Hadrian, for example, toured the land and sought the allegiance of the masses but with only partial success. Early in the second century, a revolt of Jews who were living in Egypt led to fierce fighting throughout the land and the near annihilation of the prominent Jewish community.

In the mid-third century, the control of Egypt was temporarily lost to foreign kings descended from the Persians. However, the emperor Aurelian (Lucius Domitius Aurelianus) defeated them and reclaimed Egypt as a Roman province. Late in the third century, internal revolts forced the emperor Diocletian to besiege the city of Alexandria for eight months before he could regain control. Diocletian was responsible for the infamous Great Persecution of Christians, later known among Christians as the era of martyrs.

Soon after Diocletian's rule, the emperor Gaius Galerius Valerius Maximianus issued the Edict of Toleration, which marked the end of persecution of Christians. Based in part on other policies of liberalization toward Egypt, the antipathy toward Rome quickly changed to friendship. Under the emperor Constantine the Great, Christianity became an increasingly powerful force, and within fifty years, Egypt was largely Christian.

The point at which Egypt entered the Byzantine era is not clear, but it definitely occurred by early in the fourth century. Egypt was increasingly aligned with Constantinople, both economically and religiously. The Christian patriarchs of Alexandria, who in this period were the most powerful individuals in Egypt, played important roles in the history of eastern Christianity, especially in interaction with the patriarchs of Constantinople. Unfortunately, two problems resulted. The struggle of the patriarchs to maintain their influence within Egypt and in the Mediterranean world led to political intrigue more than religious influence. An increasing lack of trust between Alexandria and the rest of Egypt undermined the stability of the region. Bitter struggles between patriarchs and rioting masses became common. In addition, tribes to the south of Egypt were threatening southern cities. These conditions persisted into the sixth century.

By the seventh century, Egypt was vulnerable to attack from foreign armies and to unrest from native discontents. In 632 C.E., Muḥammad proclaimed a holy Islamic war against Byzantium. In 639, an Arab army marched into Alexandria without resistance, largely because the Byzantine forces had fled. Though some areas of Egypt remained under Christian influence, the Islamic presence was there to stay.

Settlements and social structures. Were it not for the Nile River, Egypt would be little more than uninhabitable desert. Even with the Nile, the inhabitable part is limited to three relatively small areas: the narrow strip of land on either side of the Nile, the delta of the Nile, and the Fayum, a depression watered by the Nile. Therefore, the only settlements in Egypt were near these sources of water.

The most important city in Egypt in the Hellenistic period was also one of the newest. When Alexander entered Egypt late in the fourth century B.C.E., he founded a city that was "outside" Egypt. It would soon become the leading city of Egypt and, at times, of the whole Mediterranean area. That was especially true intellectually. The Ptolemies spared no effort to encourage the development of the highest levels of learning, providing almost unlimited funds to attract scholars to move from Athens and elsewhere to Alexandria. The result was a library with an unrivaled collection of scrolls and a museum where numerous advances were made in mathematics, science, technology, and Homeric scholarship. Later, Alexandria was home to some of the leading fathers of the early Church.

Egypt, Alexandria in particular, drew thousands of immigrants: merchants, fortune seekers, soldiers for the army, craftsmen, educators, and scholars. Those who emigrated to Egypt from more than two hundred cities around the Mediterranean were favored over the natives in the social hierarchy. One of the largest ethnic groups that took up residence in Egypt was the Jews. Reportedly, two of the five quarters in Alexandria in the first century C.E. were populated by Jews.

Languages and writing materials. The presence of foreign rulers and the numerous immigrants in Egypt created a language barrier. Since the lingua franca of the Mediterranean world was Greek, the problem was primarily that of Egyptians who did not know Greek. Unless they were content to stay out of touch with their changing world, they needed to learn Greek. How many actually did is hard to judge, but it did not displace the use of Egyptian. Hieroglyphic, hieratic, and demotic (different scripts of essentially the same language) are all attested in this period. A trilingual inscription from

196 B.C.E. known as the Rosetta stone—with the same text in hieroglyphic, demotic, and Greek—was key to deciphering the Egyptian hieroglyphs.

The daily writing materials during this millennium of history in Egypt are an unusual source of information about the people and their culture. Preserved in the dry sands on the fringes of the Nile valley, papyri were used for every form of writing imaginable, from official documents to personal notes. They provide a wealth of information about the day-to-day lives of the people.

Government and law. Ptolemaic and Roman officials sought to micromanage all aspects of Egypt that could affect the economy, including agriculture, industry, banking, trade, currency, and shipping. This required close cooperation between native workers and foreign officials. Though not always successful, when it was, the economy prospered and money flowed freely. However, because of high taxes, the government was the primary beneficiary. In order to generate as much revenue as possible, the government auctioned off to independent tax farmers the right to collect taxes in different areas. Using thorough censuses and land surveys as well as numerous agents, taxes were assessed on almost everything, including people, livestock, and crops.

Local affairs during the Roman period were not handled by salaried officials as in the Ptolemaic period but by landowners, supposedly as volunteers. These public servants increasingly had responsibility for such things as supervising agriculture, maintaining dikes, and collecting taxes. These liturgies bordered on being obligatory.

For legal problems, the natives were permitted to keep a separate system of courts and judges. This allowed them a measure of their own identity, but because the foreigners were tried in a different court, it often meant favored status for nonnatives.

Religion and ritual. Traditional Egyptian cults were largely left alone by the Ptolemies and Romans. A number of new religions also arose. One of these religions, the cult of Sarapis, was a syncretism of Greek and Egyptian religious elements and provided a patron

Traditional and new cults flourished during Ptolemaic Egypt. This early drawing depicts the Sun setting out on its daily journey through Egypt. (North Wind Picture Archives)

deity for the Ptolemaic Dynasty. In addition to its religious side, the cult had political overtones, leading to the Ptolemies being recognized as descendants of the gods and supporting the imperial cult.

Current views. The Hellenistic period is so named because of the spread of Greek culture and ideas throughout the Mediterranean world. That phenomenon has been subject to exaggeration, but current scholarship is seeking a balance on the extent of hellenization, as well as the how and the why. Whatever the answers, the multicultural environment in Egypt raises questions of ethnicity. The tendency was for those from the Greek world to be given special privileges, and the natives to be treated as second-class. That led to efforts by Egyptians toward upward mobility, through intermarriage and mastery of the Greek language. Some Egyptians succeeded in acquiring dual identities. However, the real question facing scholars is how the different ethnicities coexisted in the same towns and villages.

ADDITIONAL RESOURCES

Bagnall, R. S. *Egypt in Late Antiquity.* Princeton, N.J.: Princeton University Press, 1993.

Bowman, A. K. *Egypt After the Pharaohs, 332 B.C.-A.D. 642: From Alexander to the Arab Conquest.* Berkeley: University of California Press, 1986.

Hölbl, Günther. *History of the Ptolemaic Empire.* New York: Routledge, 2000.

Lewis, N. *Greeks in Ptolemaic Egypt: Case Studies in*

the Social History of the Hellenistic World. Oxford, England: Clarendon Press, 1986.

———. *Life in Egypt Under Roman Rule.* Oxford, England: Clarendon Press, 1983.

Rostovzeff, M. *The Social and Economic History of the Hellenistic World.* 3 vols. Oxford, England: Clarendon Press, 1941.

Thompson, D. J. *Memphis Under the Ptolemies.* Princeton, N.J.: Princeton University Press, 1988.

SEE ALSO: Actium, Battle of; Alexander the Great; Alexandrian library; Antony, Marc; Aurelianus, Lucius Domitius; Caesar, Julius; Caracalla; Christianity; Cleopatra VII; Constantine the Great; Diocletian; Galerius Valerius Maximianus, Gaius; Greece, Hellenistic and Roman; Hadrian; Jewish Diaspora; Macedonia; Muḥammad; Ptolemaic Dynasty; Rome, Republican; Seleucid Dynasty; Vespasian.

—*D. Brent Sandy*

EL TAJÍN

DATE: 200-700 C.E.
LOCALE: Veracruz, Mexico
RELATED CIVILIZATIONS: Huastec, Totonac
SIGNIFICANCE: El Tajín was the primary center of Classic Veracruz civilization and the heart of a thriving commerce in Gulf coast obsidian.

El Tajín (ehl tah-HEEN) was the principal civic-ceremonial center of the Classic Veracruz civilization of the north-central Gulf coast of Mesoamerica. Culturally, the site represents an amalgamation of Mesoamerican cultures that occupied that area later identified with the Huastec, Totonac, and Otomi. The site's development, which spans the whole of the Middle (300-600 C.E.) and Late Classic (600-900 C.E.) periods and culminates in the Postclassic (c. 1200 C.E.), was dependent on the obsidian trade between Teotihuacán, Puebla, and the Gulf coast and Maya regions. As such, El Tajín's architecture and culture reflect Teotihuacán, Nuiñe, Maya, Zapotec, and coastal Guatemalan influences.

Though initial developments at this site were heavily influenced by central highland civilization, El Tajín rose to distinguish itself as the paramount center of a Veracruz-based obsidian procurement network. The site's distinctive architecture, particularly the Pyramid of the Niches, incorporates a number of Classic Veracruz traits, including masonry entablatures, niches, and everted cornice elements. Other features include elaborately carved stucco and rock panels and a diverse array of ball courts and ball court paraphernalia pointing to cultural and economic interactions with the sites of Copán, Teotihuacán, Xochicalco, Cotzumalhuapa, Monte Albán, and Palenque.

ADDITIONAL RESOURCES
Brüggemann, Juergen, Sara Ladrón de Guevara, and Juan Sánchez Bonilla. *Tajín.* Mexico City: El Equilibrista, 1992.

Kelly, Joyce. *The Complete Visitor's Guide to Mesoamerican Ruins.* Norman: University of Oklahoma Press, 1982.

SEE ALSO: Ball game, Mesoamerican; Copán; Maya; Monte Albán; Palenque; Teotihuacán; Zapotecs.

—*Ruben G. Mendoza*

ELEUSINIAN MYSTERIES

DATE: seventh century B.C.E.-395 C.E.
LOCALE: Eleusis, in the region of Attica, Greece
RELATED CIVILIZATIONS: Archaic, Classical, Hellenistic, and Roman Greece
SIGNIFICANCE: These religious ceremonies in honor of the agricultural goddesses Demeter and her daughter, Kore (also known as Persephone), revealed secret rites to initiates.

Archaeological evidence indicates that the worship of Demeter began at Eleusis as early as the Mycenaean period and lasted until 395 C.E. This mystery cult was created to celebrate the two gifts of Demeter: grain and the promise of a better life after death. The Homeric *Hymn to Demeter* (n.d.; *The Homeric Hymn to Demeter*, 1902) is the major literary source for the myth behind the ritual at the sanctuary, which consisted of nine days of purification, processions, ritual abuse, fasting, sacrifices, special meals and drinks, dancing, and the final revelatory experience.

These Greater (Eleusian) Mysteries (ehl-yoo-SIH-nee-uhn), held at Eleusis in late September or early October, were under the control of specially chosen priests (*hierophantai*). On the ninth day, the ultimate experience of the event, occurring in the Telesterion, was the disclosure of the unspeakable rite (*arretos tells*) to the initiates (*mystai*). The nature of this revelation remains unknown as the initiates were sworn to secrecy. The revealed item may have been as simple as a sheaf of wheat. Roman scholar Marcus Terentius Varro is quoted in Saint Augustine's *De civitate Dei* (413-427; *The City of God*, 1610) as saying "Much is transmitted in the mysteries of Demeter, which has only to do with the invention of grain."

ADDITIONAL RESOURCES

Foley, Helene P. *The Homeric Hymn to Demeter: Translation, Commentary, and Interpretive Essays*. Princeton, N.J.: Princeton University Press, 1999.

Meyer, Marvin W. *The Ancient Mysteries: A Sourcebook of Sacred Texts*. Philadelphia: University of Pennsylvania Press, 1987.

Mylonas, George E. *Eleusis and the Eleusinian Mysteries*. Princeton, N.J.: Princeton University Press, 1961.

Richardson, N. J. *The Homeric Hymn to Demeter*. Oxford, England: Oxford University Press, 1974.

SEE ALSO: Greece, Archaic; Greece, Classical; Greece, Hellenistic and Roman; Religion and ritual; Varro, Marcus Terentius.

—Christina A. Salowey

ELIJAH

ALSO KNOWN AS: Elias; Elia; Eliyyahu
FLOURISHED: ninth century B.C.E.
RELATED CIVILIZATION: Ancient Israel
MAJOR ROLE/POSITION: Hebrew prophet

Life. The ninth century B.C.E. prophet Elijah (ih-LI-juh) appears in the Old Testament (1 Kings 17-19 and 2 Kings 1-2) during a religious crisis. After the death of King Solomon (930 B.C.E.), the kingdom of Israel had been split in two: Judah in the south, Israel in the north. The northern capital, Tirzah, deemed inadequate by 850 B.C.E., was replaced by Samaria, constructed by Phoenician artisans hired by King Omri (r. c. 882-871 B.C.E.). To defray costs, Omri's son and successor Ahab arranged to marry a Phoenician princess, Jezebel, who agreed only on condition that her religion, Baal-Melkart, be established. The result was confusion in a people already disaffected with Jerusalem.

Elijah ranks with Moses in saving the religion of the Old Testament god Yahweh from corruption, functioning as Ahab's nemesis and the Lord's champion. Four stories in Kings present Elijah. First, he prophesies a great drought, which God sends to punish Israel for idolatry. The drought is broken after a contest arranged atop Mount Carmel challenging Baal to send fire to ignite a sacrifice; frenzied pagan behavior avails nothing, and Elijah's

Elijah's prayers ignite a sacrifice on Mount Carmel. (North Wind Picture Archives)

calm prayer produces results: victory for Yahweh and death for Baal's prophets. Second, Jezebel covets a vineyard belonging to her neighbor Naboth, who refuses Ahab's purchase offer. She arranges Naboth's murder and then sends a willing Ahab to take possession of the land. Elijah confronts Ahab with a prophecy of doom. Third, Ahab's successor, Ahaziah, falls ill and sends for help from Baal. Elijah intervenes and sends messengers home with another doom prophecy. Finally, Elijah's flight from Jezebel into the wilderness and his despair under the juniper tree are answered by food and drink from God; after forty days in the wilderness (compare the Israelites' wanderings with Moses and Jesus's similar sojourn), Elijah climbs Mount Horeb and is taken by a great wind, or tornado, to heaven. To his companion Elisha is passed the mantle,

both literal and figurative, of Elijah's prophecy.

Influence. Elijah emerged as a fierce champion of Yahweh and of social justice. Later biblical tradition sees Elijah as herald of the end of history. He is recognized not only as a Hebrew and Christian prophet but also as a prophet of Islam.

ADDITIONAL RESOURCES

Uffenheimer, Benjamin. *Early Prophecy in Israel*. Jerusalem: Magnes, 1999.

Wilson, Robert R. *Prophecy and Society in Ancient Israel*. Philadelphia: Fortress, 1980.

SEE ALSO: Ahab; Bible: Jewish; Israel; Jesus Christ; Moses.

—John M. Bullard

ENNIUS, QUINTUS

BORN: 239 B.C.E.; Rudiae, southern Italy
DIED: c. 169 B.C.E.; possibly Rome
RELATED CIVILIZATION: Republican Rome
MAJOR ROLE/POSITION: Poet

Life. Quintus Ennius (KWIHN-tuhs EHN-ee-uhs) was born in Rudiae of Calabria, an Italian town permeated with Greek culture. His birthplace was near the Latin colony of Brundisium and the Greek city of Tarentum, and he himself attests his multilingual proficiency. Brought to Rome in 204 B.C.E. by Cato the Censor, he spent at least his early years in the city in teaching and elucidating Greek literature as well as in writing. There is testimony that he was on friendly terms with a number of prominent Roman citizens, and he was granted citizenship in 184 B.C.E. through Marcus Fulvius Nobilior. Ennius wrote an epic on the history of Rome, *Annales* (first century B.C.E.; *Annals*, 1935), as well as tragedy and comedy and works in various other genres, including satire and philosophy. In tragedy, the titles and fragments indicate that he modeled his adaptations

more on Euripides than on the other Greek dramatists.

Influence. Ennius represents the final victory of Greek literature in Rome. He abandoned the attempts to keep alive the native Saturnian meter and instead employed the Greek hexameter for his epic, upon which his fame principally rested and which was the national epic of Rome until Vergil wrote his *Aeneid* (c. 29-19 B.C.E.; English translation, 1553). His works survive only in fragments.

ADDITIONAL RESOURCES

Jocelyn, H. D. *The Tragedies of Ennius*. Cambridge, England: Cambridge University Press, 1993.

Vahlen, Iohannes. *Ennianae Poesis Reliquiae*. Amsterdam: Hakkert, 1967.

Warmington, E. H. *Remains of Old Latin*. Cambridge, Mass.: Harvard University Press, 1987.

SEE ALSO: Cato the Censor; Rome, Republican; Vergil.

—C. Wayne Tucker

EPAMINONDAS

BORN: c. 410 B.C.E.; Thebes
DIED: 362 B.C.E.; Mantinea, Greece
RELATED CIVILIZATIONS: Macedonia, Persia
MAJOR ROLE/POSITION: Political and military
  leader

Life. Of a venerable family, Epaminondas (ih-pam-uh-NAHN-duhs) received an excellent education and became prominent in Boeotian politics. In 371 B.C.E., he was ambassador to the peace conference at Sparta, at which he opposed the Spartan king Agesilaus II. War ensued, and at the Battle of Leuctra (371 B.C.E.), he decisively defeated the Spartans. He thus initiated a period in which Thebes became the leading power in Greece. In 370 B.C.E., he encouraged a Theban alliance with Elis, Arcadia, and Argos to combat Sparta; and in the following year, he led a devastating allied invasion of Laconia, after which he liberated the Messenians, whom Sparta had enslaved for 230 years.

Upon his return home, he won easy acquittal of charges of misconduct leveled by jealous rivals, but despite his fame, he never dominated local politics. Nonetheless, in 369 B.C.E., he again invaded the Peloponnese, attacked Corinth, and won over several major cities. Another invasion in 366 B.C.E. brought him little success. Equally disappointing were his efforts to sponsor with Persia a common peace in Greece. Nonetheless, again with Persian support, he led a naval campaign to win Greek allies in the Aegean. At last in 362 B.C.E., he conducted his final campaign to Mantinea to regain allied support for Thebes. At the ensuing Battle of Mantinea, he again defeated Sparta but was killed in battle.

Influence. His military genius influenced subsequent warfare. The conqueror of Sparta, he created the Theban hegemony. Despite his many military campaigns, he genuinely but unsuccessfully sought a solution to the political problems of Greece.

ADDITIONAL RESOURCES

Buckler, J. *The Theban Hegemony, 371-362* B.C.E. Cambridge, Mass.: Harvard University Press, 1980.
Hanson, Victor Davis. *The Soul of Battle*. New York: Free Press, 1999.

SEE ALSO: Greece, Classical; Leuctra, Battle of; Mantinea, Battle of; Persia.

—John Buckler

EPHIALTES OF ATHENS

BORN: date and place unknown
DIED: 461 B.C.E.; place unknown
RELATED CIVILIZATION: Classical Greece
MAJOR ROLE/POSITION: Politician

Life. Ephialtes of Athens (ehf-ee-AL-teez) remains obscure and controversial. Surviving ancient sources are fragmentary, providing only a bare outline. Ephialtes exercised a naval command in 465/464 B.C.E. In 462/461 B.C.E., as a partisan of Pericles, Ephialtes took advantage of the absence of the conservative politician Cimon (then attempting to lend military support to Sparta against an insurrection of helots, or state-owned serfs) in order to "break the aristocracy" by transferring jurisdiction over public magistrates from the Areopagus to the popular courts. No longer would popular politicians have to appear before the aristocrats who dominated the Areopagus. Aristocrats themselves, moreover, would (when accused of bribery or malfeasance) now appear before juries dominated by common citizens. Ephialtes, exceptional in his immunity to bribery, was himself remorseless in his attacks on corrupt officials. The resulting atmosphere of political terror led to nocturnal assassination. Ephialtes was entombed among Athens' other heroes at the city's expense.

Influence. Modern scholars question every aspect of this historical tradition. Did Ephialtes act independently or on behalf of Pericles? Was the reform of the Areopagus in 462/461 B.C.E. as constitutionally significant as the ancient sources claim? Was Ephialtes assassinated or did he die naturally? Was Pericles implicated in the murder? The case remains open.

ADDITIONAL RESOURCES

Mueller, H. F. "Ephialtes Accusator: A Case Study in Anecdotal History and Ideology." *Athenaeum* 87 (1999): 425-445.
Wallace, R. W. *The Areopagus Council to 307* B.C. Baltimore: Johns Hopkins University Press, 1989.

SEE ALSO: Cimon; Government and law; Greece, Classical; Pericles.

—Hans-Friedrich Mueller

EPICTETUS

ALSO KNOWN AS: Epiktetos
BORN: c. 55 C.E.; Hieropolis, Phrygia, Asia Minor
DIED: c. 135 C.E.; Nicopolis, Epirus (later Greece)
RELATED CIVILIZATIONS: Hellenistic and Roman Greece, Imperial Rome
MAJOR ROLE/POSITION: Slave, philosopher

Life. Born a slave, Epictetus (ehp-ihk-TEET-uhs) was brought to Rome at an early age and became the slave of Nero's freedman and secretary, Epaphroditus, a cruel master. According to theologian Origen's anecdote, Epictetus did not flinch when Epaphroditus broke his leg. Epictetus learned Stoicism from Gaius Musonius Rufus and at some point became a freedman. When Domitian expelled all philosophers from Rome (c. 89 C.E.), Epictetus went to Nicopolis, Epirus, Greece, where he established a school. He may have returned to Rome during the reign of Hadrian.

Epictetus wrote nothing himself. His *Enchiridion* (n.d.; known as the *Manual*, 1916) and four books of *Discourses* (translation 1916) were transcribed by his student, Arrian (also known as Flavius Arrianus).

Influence. Epictetus and the emperor Marcus Aurelius were the two greatest Stoic ethicists. Much of the emperor's thought derived from that of the slave. Both Stoics, especially Epictetus, had exceptional influence on Western culture. Epictetus was most popular in times when military virtues, secular values, self-reliance, individualism, forbearance, equanimity, and persistence were most honored. Thinkers and leaders in the Italian and French Renaissances, Enlightenment Prussia, and Victorian England all held him in high esteem.

ADDITIONAL RESOURCES

Barnes, Jonathan. *Logic and the Imperial Stoa.* New York: E. J. Brill, 1997.
Bonhöffer, Adolf Friedrich. *The Ethics of the Stoic Epictetus.* New York: Peter Lang, 1996.
Xenakis, Iason. *Epictetus: Philosopher-Therapist.* The Hague, Netherlands: Nijhoff, 1969.

SEE ALSO: Arrian; Domitian; Greece, Hellenistic and Roman; Hadrian; Marcus Aurelius; Origen; Rome, Imperial.

—Eric v.d. Luft

EPICURUS

ALSO KNOWN AS: Epikouros
BORN: 341 B.C.E.; Island of Samos, Greece
DIED: 270 B.C.E.; Athens, Greece
RELATED CIVILIZATION: Hellenistic Greece
MAJOR ROLE/POSITION: Philosopher

Life. Born an Athenian citizen on the isle of Samos, Epicurus (ehp-ihk-KYOOR-uhs) began his philosophical education at fourteen and continued in Asia Minor after the conquests of Alexander the Great. He was tutored by the Platonist Pamphilus and the Democritean-Skeptic Nausiphanes but developed his own philosophy based on the thought of Democritus, incorporating the popularizing tendencies of Hellenistic philosophy. In his early thirties, he founded a school, which he eventually moved to Athens in 307 B.C.E., when it became known as The Garden. Epicurus wrote numerous books and letters, some of which survive. Remarkably for the time, he accepted both women and slaves as students. He also became highly revered by his pupils and was treated as an earthly savior by later adherents. He died at the age of seventy-one from a painful illness, encouraging his students to the very end. Loyal Epicureans continued to celebrate his birthday.

Epicurus taught that the only reliable guide to truth was the evidence of the senses, that everything in the universe was made of various kinds of atoms or resulted from their accidental collision or combination, and that the good life consisted of freedom from pain and fear. In his view, the soul did not survive the death of the body, but because death meant the end of all sensation, it was not to be feared. Likewise, his atomism and empiricism led him and his followers to deny the reality of supernatural phenomena and to oppose superstition as an enemy of human happiness. Epicurus defined happiness as tranquillity of mind, a kind of simple contentment with life, achieved by reducing or simplifying one's desires and living a life of quiet retirement and contemplation, while cultivating true friendships. Because most ancient philosophy had the practical aim of securing human happiness, Epicurus's methods of getting at the truth, his doctrines regarding the nature of the universe, and his ethical teachings were all carefully designed to that end, but also as a response to Platonism and Pyrrhonism.

Epicurus. (Library of Congress)

Influence. In creating a system of philosophy both admired and hated, Epicurean thought remained an important intellectual current throughout the Western world until the fall of the Roman Empire. It had a profound effect on such men as the poets Lucretius and Vergil, and philosopher Lucian, and it forced opponents, especially the Stoics, to address its arguments. Even Saint Augustine noted in his *Confessiones* (397-400; *Confessions*, 1620) that he would have been an Epicurean if Epicureans did not deny the immortality of the soul. When Epicureanism was recovered during the Renaissance and taken up by French scientist and philosopher Pierre Gassendi, it had a significant impact on the scientific revolution and Enlightenment humanism.

ADDITIONAL RESOURCES

Asmis, E. *Epicurus' Scientific Method*. Ithaca, N.Y.: Cornell University Press, 1983.

Bailey, Cyril. *Epicurus: The Extant Remains*. Oxford, England: Clarendon Press, 1926.

Mitsis, P. *Epicurus' Ethical Theory*. Ithaca, N.Y.: Cornell University Press, 1988.

Rist, J. M. *Epicurus: An Introduction*. Cambridge, England: Cambridge University Press, 1972.

Sharples, R. W. *Stoics, Epicureans, and Sceptics*. New York: Routledge, 1996.

SEE ALSO: Athens; Augustine, Saint; Democritus; Greece, Hellenistic and Roman; Lucian; Lucretius; Philosophy; Plato; Pyrrhon of Elis; Vergil.

—*Richard C. Carrier*

ERASISTRATUS

BORN: c. 304 B.C.E.; Iulis, Island of Ceos (later Kéa, Greece)
DIED: c. 250 B.C.E.; place unknown
RELATED CIVILIZATION: Hellenistic Greece
MAJOR ROLE/POSITION: Physician

Life. Erasistratus (ur-uh-SIHS-treht-uhs) studied medicine in Athens and Cnidus and practiced in Alexandria until his death. His writings, including works on fevers, hygiene, hemoptysis, abdominal pathology, and comparative anatomy, have not survived.

Best known for his anatomical and physiological research, he dissected both animals and people, drawing parallels from his finds. For example, from the cavities in the brains of men, stags, and hares, he inferred a connection with intelligence. His dissections of recently deceased humans led him to conclude that blood is carried by the veins while the arteries carry air or *pneuma*, tiny particles of air that account for muscular movements. He was attempting to explain physiology naturalistically.

He recognized the difference between motor and sensory nerves and that the heart is a pump. He also theorized that the veins and arteries were joined by capillary tubes too small to be observed (to explain how blood could appear in a severed artery). He discovered the function of the epiglottis in swallowing. Erasistratus considered plethora (hyperemia) as the primary cause of disease, which led him to prescribe dietary and exercise regimens to his patients.

Influence. Erasistratus laid the foundations for the study of anatomy and physiology as well as anatomical investigations undertaken by later physicians such as Galen.

ADDITIONAL RESOURCES

Bourgey, L. "Greek Medicine from the Beginnings to the End of the Classical Period." In *History of Science*, edited by Renee Taton. Vol. 1. New York: Basic Books, 1963.

Galen. *On the Natural Faculties*. 1916. Reprint. Cambridge, Mass.: Harvard University Press, 1991.

Longrigg, James. *Greek Rational Medicine: Philosophy from Alcmaeon to the Alexandrians*. New York: Routledge, 1993.

Wright, John P., and Paul Potter. *Psyche and Soma: Physicians and Metaphysicians on the Mind-Body Problem from Antiquity to Enlightenment*. New York: Oxford University Press, 2000.

SEE ALSO: Galen; Greece, Hellenistic and Roman; Science.

—*Terry R. Morris*

ERATOSTHENES OF CYRENE

BORN: c. 285 B.C.E.; Cyrene (later in Libya)
DIED: c. 205 B.C.E.; Alexandria, Egypt
RELATED CIVILIZATION: Hellenistic Greece
MAJOR ROLE/POSITION: Geographer, mathematician

Life. Following his education in Athens, Eratosthenes of Cyrene (ur-uh-TAHS-thuh-neez of si-REE-nee) spent most of his life in Alexandria as head of the great library there. His areas of accomplishment included geography, math, astronomy, and literary criticism. Contemporaries regarded him highly. Archimedes dedicated a work to him. Later writers (including Strabo) were more critical. It is difficult to judge his works independently because only fragments of Eratosthenes' many titles survive.

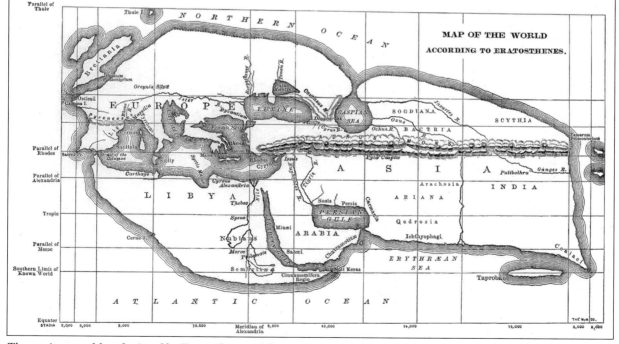

The ancient world as depicted by Eratosthenes of Cyrene, a geographer and mathematician. (North Wind Picture Archives)

Most recognized for his work in geography, Eratosthenes established this study on a mathematical basis, dividing Earth into five climate zones. He also developed an accurate method for calculating the circumference of Earth, noting the difference between the shadow cast by the Sun on March 21 at Syene (none) and some 5,000 stadia away in Alexandria (roughly one-fiftieth the circumference of a circle, or 7 degrees and 12 minutes). He realized (by Euclidian geometry) that the angle the Sun's rays made in Alexandria was the same as the angle made by lines extended to the center of the earth from Syene and Alexandria (opposite interior angles are equal). In other words, the distance from Syene to Alexandria was one-fiftieth of the distance around Earth, and so Earth's circumference was 250,000 stadia, about 29,000 miles, close to modern estimates.

In mathematics, Eratosthenes solved the problem of doubling the cube and developed an algorithm for finding prime numbers, his "sieve."

Influence. Not only did he lay the foundations for a mathematical geography, but also, by using geometry, Eratosthenes calculated the size of Earth to a degree of accuracy that would not be improved on until the modern era.

ADDITIONAL RESOURCES
Calinger, Ronald. *A Contextual History of Mathematics.* Englewood Cliffs, N.J.: Prentice Hall, 1999.
Dyer, J. E. *History of the Planetary Systems from Thales to Kepler.* New York: Dover, 1953.
Hogben, Lancelot. *Mathematics for the Millions.* New York: W. W. Norton, 1983.

SEE ALSO: Alexandrian library; Archimedes; Greece, Hellenistic and Roman; Science; Strabo.

—*Terry R. Morris*

ERINNA

FLOURISHED: mid-fourth century B.C.E.; Greece
RELATED CIVILIZATION: Classical Greece
MAJOR ROLE/POSITION: Lyric poet

Life. Though Erinna (ih-RIHN-uh) wrote for only a short period of time, she and her work were praised by the ancients; Antipater lists her as one of the "nine earthly Muses." Of her works, only six fragments survive, the best of which is fifty-four lines of *Elakate*, or *The Distaff*, a lament for her childhood friend Baucis. Erinna's poetry celebrated the domestic life using "heroic language," and she even moved beyond her native Doric dialect perhaps to mimic the works of Sappho. Her style ranged from puns to laments to metaphors, covering both lyric and epigrammatic forms.

Influence. Today she is cited as one of only a few women writers in the ancient world whose works survive. Her work is a source for study about everyday life in Greece in the Classical period.

ADDITIONAL RESOURCES
Balmer, Josephine. *Classical Woman Poets.* Newcastle-upon-Tyne, England: Bloodaxe Books, 1996.
Rayor, Diane. *Sappho's Lyre: Archaic Lyric Women Poets of Ancient Greece.* Berkeley: University of California Press, 1991.
Snyder, Jane McIntosh. *The Woman and the Lyre: Women Writers in Classical Greece and Rome.* Carbondale: Southern Illinois University Press, 1989.

SEE ALSO: Greece, Classical; Languages and literature; Sappho.

—*Tammy Jo Eckhart*

ESARHADDON

ALSO KNOWN AS: Assurakhidina; Sacherdonos
BORN: c. 704 B.C.E.; Assyria
DIED: 669 B.C.E.; Assyria
RELATED CIVILIZATIONS: Assyria, Babylonia
MAJOR ROLE/POSITION: Monarch

Life. Esarhaddon (ee-sahr-HAD-uhn) was the youngest son of the Assyrian monarch Sennacherib, and his selection as heir-apparent in 689 B.C.E. evoked the homicidal ire of at least two older brothers, identified as Adrammelech and Sharezer in the biblical books of I Kings and Isaiah. Upon learning of the assassination of his father by his brothers, Esarhaddon entered Ashur and assumed the throne in 680 B.C.E. His vengeance on the fugitive parricides was delayed for seven years by affairs of state, including the restoration of the city of Babylon (destroyed by Sennacherib in 698 B.C.E.) and the expansion of the Assyrian Empire as far abroad as Egypt.

In 672 B.C.E., Esarhaddon attempted to secure a peaceful succession by designating his sons Ashurbanipal and Shamashshumukin as kings of Ashur and Babylonia, respectively. Esarhaddon's adult years were marred by an illness to which he finally succumbed during a military campaign against Egypt.

Influence. Under Esarhaddon, Assyria achieved its greatest territorial expansion. Biblical authors remember him as a king who settled foreigners in northern Israel. In spite of Esarhaddon's provision for a peaceful succession, an internecine civil war between his sons Ashurbanipal and Shamashshumukin severely weakened the Assyrian Empire.

ADDITIONAL RESOURCES

Gwaltney, William C., Jr. "Assyrians." In *Peoples of the Old Testament World*, edited by Alfred J. Hoerth et al. Grand Rapids, Mich.: Baker, 1994.

Leichty, Erle. *Esarhaddon, King of Assyria.* In *Civilizations of the Ancient Near East*, edited by Jack M. Sasson. New York: Charles Scribner's Sons, 1995.

SEE ALSO: Ashurbanipal; Assyria; Babylonia; Sennacherib.

—Walter C. Bouzard, Jr.

ESSENES

DATE: c. 100 B.C.E.–c. 100 C.E.
LOCALE: Palestine
RELATED CIVILIZATION: Israel
SIGNIFICANCE: Ascetic Jewish society prevalent during the Hasmonean era and widely considered the writers of the Dead Sea Scrolls found at Khirbat Qumran.

The Essenes (i-SEENS) were a messianic sect of Jews that broke from traditional society most likely during the religious upheaval caused by the Maccabean revolts. Their history has been recovered from classical sources such as Pliny the Elder, Philo of Alexander, and Flavius Josephus. The Essenes settled in remote locations in Palestine where they could escape Jewish and Roman persecution, practice communal living, and adhere to a simple life of work and prayer. Full society membership was reserved for males who went through several years of probation and generally vowed celibacy. A body of strict elected officials governed each community and doled out agricultural resources. At their height, the Essene movement numbered around four thousand.

Essenian theology was based on predestination and focused on obedience, piety, justice, honesty, and secrecy. They claimed to be direct descendants of the high priest Aaron and often served as apocalyptic prophets with, according to Josephus, a remarkable ability to predict the future. It is widely accepted that the Essenes were the writers of the Dead Sea Scrolls, considered one of the most important archaeological discoveries in the twentieth century. The Essenes ceased to exist independently after the Jewish revolt in the mid-first century, when their theology was absorbed into the beginnings of rabbinic Judaism.

ADDITIONAL RESOURCES

Cohen, Shaye. *From the Maccabees to the Mishnah.* Philadelphia: Westminster John Knox Press, 1995.

Stemberger, Gunter. *Jewish Contemporaries of Jesus: Pharisees, Sadducees, Essenes.* Translated by Allan Mahnke. Minneapolis, Minn.: Fortress Press, 1995.

SEE ALSO: Dead Sea Scrolls; Josephus, Flavius; Judaism; Maccabees; Philo of Alexander; Rome, Imperial.

—John Grady Powell

ETHIOPIA

ALSO KNOWN AS: Abyssinia
DATE: 8000 B.C.E.-700 C.E.
LOCALE: Horn of Africa
RELATED CIVILIZATIONS: Egypt, Nubia, Cush, Mesopotamia
SIGNIFICANCE: Ethiopia is the site of the earliest human beings and, next to Cush, of the earliest human civilization as well as, perhaps next to Armenia, the earliest country to adopt Christianity.

The anglicized name "Ethiopia" is derived from the Greek *Aethiopes*, or "burnt faces," probably referring to black Africans, in the New Testament. First millennium C.E. sources related the Ethiopians to the Habashat people of ancient South Arabia, from whose name was later derived the name "Abyssinia." Ethiopia lies in the eastern part of Africa adjacent to the Red Sea (the Erythraean Sea), which separates the African continent from the Arabian Peninsula. The country is divided into three major relief regions: western highlands, eastern highlands, and the comparatively low-lying Rift Valley as well as western lowlands. The Rift Valley region is marked by a series of lakes at an elevation of about five thousand feet (fifteen hundred meters).

Prehistory. Archaeological finds in the Omo Valley in the southwest and the Afar lowlands in eastern Eritrea provide evidence of hominids called *Australopithecus afarensis* about 2.5 million to 4 million years old. Another skeleton from Hadar in the Welo province of Ethiopia is estimated to be 3.6 million years old. *Australopithecus africanus*, the successor of *afarensis*, developed about 3 million years ago in the Omo Valley. *Africanus* was followed by *Homo habilis* in the next million years, and his remains have been unearthed at Melka Kontoure, a few miles south of Addis Ababa. *Homo habilis* evolved into the brainier *Homo erectus* of the Paleolithic Age about 1.5 million years ago, and their remains have been discovered in Harer and the Awash Valley in the east as well as in the Omo Valley. The more highly evolved *Homo sapiens* lived about 60,000 years ago in Dire Dawa in the east, the Awash Valley, and Melka Kontoure.

Languages traditionally spoken by the people of Ethiopia and Eritrea developed as the two principal branches of the Afroasiatic (Hamitic and Semitic) family: Cushitic and Omotic. The Cushitic languages are Agaw languages in the northern highlands and Oromo language. Kafa, spoken in the southwestern highlands, is the best known Omotic language. The African Semitic languages (introduced from southern Arabia during the first half of the last millennium B.C.E.) of the northern highlands are Amharic and Tigrinya. Two other members of this group are ancient Ge'ez, the liturgical language of the Ethiopian Orthodox Church, and Tigre, spoken by a predominantly Muslim population of northern Eritrea.

Most scholars believe that the prosperous Land of the Punt mentioned in Egyptian sources dating from the third millennium B.C.E. lay on the African side of the Red Sea coast, especially parts of the Sudan and Eritrea. At some time during the third quarter of the last millennium B.C.E., strong connections were established between south Arabia and the regions of Eritrea, as is attested by writing, stone architecture, and sculpture. Those civilizational traits had developed earlier in south Arabia and were unearthed by archaeologists at Yeha, some twenty miles northeast of Adowa (Adwa). Most probably, iron also came to be used at about the same time.

History. According to the *Kebre Nagast* (fourteenth century C.E.; *The Glory of Kings*, 1995), based on a twelfth century mythopoeic legend, King Menelik I, the son of the Queen of Sheba in Yemen and King Solomon of Jerusalem, was the founder of the royal dynasty of Ethiopia (Axum). In actuality, the earliest Ethiopian civilization developed in the highlands of the province of Tigray in the northeast part of Ethiopia between 500 B.C.E. and 100 C.E., and no evidence supports the idea that the actual site of the city of Axum was occupied before this time. Axum flourished under rulers of South Arabian descent and religious beliefs into the fourth century C.E. At the height of their power, the kings of Axum ruled an empire that extended from the Upper Nile Valley in the west to Yemen in the east. They styled themselves as "kings of kings" and ruled their somewhat federally structured empire by exercising central control over regions ruled by local princes and chiefs. The anonymous sea captain from Roman Egypt who wrote the *Periplus Maris Erythraei* (also known as *Periplus*, first century C.E.; *Periplus of the Erythraean Sea*, 1980) mentions the prosperous port of Adulis, some fifty miles (eighty kilometers) northeast of the metropolis of Axum and two miles (slightly more than three kilometers) inland from the harbor of Massawa.

By the third century C.E., the elites of Axum had learned of Christianity from some of the traders. By the early fourth century C.E., the new faith had been estab-

An Ethiopian princess travels in a cart drawn by oxen. (North Wind Picture Archives)

lished as the religion of the Eastern Roman Empire. Naturally, the faith of the Roman traders who dominated the Red Sea would influence Axum. The Axumite coins of the first third of the fourth century C.E. were embossed with a cross and by monuments carrying inscriptions prefaced by Christian incantations. According to the account of the fourth century Byzantine theologian Rufinius, the Axumite emperor Ella Amida (fl. fourth century C.E.) employed two Christian Syrian boys—Aedisius and Frumentius, victims of a shipwreck—as his court slaves. The monarch was so taken by the piety, honesty, and sagacity of the youths, particularly of Frumentius, that his will called for their manumission. The two Syrians were retained by the Empress Dowager—Aedisius as cupbearer and the wittier Frumentius as councilor—until the infant incumbent to the throne, Ezana, came of age. The latter ascended the throne circa 330 C.E., whereupon Frumentius traveled to Alexandria to request the patriarch to send a bishop to Ethiopia to aid its conversion. Saint Frumentius returned to Axum circa 335 as the bishop and converted Ezana.

The Axumite empire thrived from the Red Sea and Indian Ocean trade. However, beginning in the sixth century C.E., problems arose in the Middle East that affected Axum's political-economic status. Followers of Judaism there harassed the Christians, who applied to the Ethiopian emperor for help. In 525 C.E., Emperor Kaleb defeated the Jewish leader Dhu Nuwas. However, this victory was to be the last flicker of the dying lamp of Axumite glory. With the rise of Islam in Arabia in the mid-seventh century C.E. and the subsequent Arab conquest of Egypt and the Near East, Axum's maritime economy declined. The decline of Ethiopian shipping in the Red Sea and Indian Ocean waters isolated the Axumite empire from the eastern Mediterranean, resulting in loss of trade. Adulis and other commercial centers were slowly marginalized. Axum lost its contact with the outside world, and Ethiopian civilization began to turn inward and southward.

Agriculture and animal husbandry. In the absence of archaeological research in prehistoric Ethiopian plant cultivation, most of the information in this area comes from botanical studies. These studies confirm an extensive cultivation of teff (*ragrostis teff*), wheat, finger millet (*dagussa*), enset (*ensete edulis*), coffee, and the narcotic chat (*catha edulis*). Archaeological data on domestic animals yield evidence of such animals as cattle, donkeys, sheep, goats, dogs, camels, and chickens.

Rock art. Ethiopia and Eritrea abound in rock art sites. The extant rock art specimens include representations of people, animals, and inanimate objects or weapons. In the Harer region, fat-tailed sheep are depicted. An interesting painting at Ba'ati Facada near Adigrat shows a man guiding a plow drawn by a pair of yoked oxen.

Architecture. Monumental temples dating back to 500 B.C.E. at Yeha, Haoulti, and Mantara contain altars dedicated to Sabaean gods. At an early stage of its development, Axum adopted the practice of burying its kings in tombs and marking their graves with monumental stelae. Of more than 140 stelae in Axum, the largest—a single block of granite 69 feet (21 meters) long—stands in a park of the city.

Writing. The earliest inscriptions, dating back to the seventh century B.C.E. and discovered on the northern plateau, are boustrophedon (script that reads from left to right and right to left on alternate lines), and the text uses Sabaean terms. Ethiopian inscriptions evolved their own style, abandoning boustrophedonic style and eventually developing Ge'ez.

Current views. Archaeology is the primary source for the history of Ethiopia of this period, and David W. Phillipson's book, *Ancient Ethiopia: Aksum, Its Antecedents and Successors* (1998), rejects the stereotyped picture of Ethiopia and Eritrea as countries noteworthy for civil war and famine and suggests that Ethiopian civilization, though geographically part of sub-Saharan Africa and culturally linked with ancient Egypt and South Arabia, was essentially autonomous and unique.

ADDITIONAL RESOURCES

Beckwith, Carol, and Angela Fisher. *African Ark: People and Ancient Cultures of Ethiopia and the Horn of Africa*. New York: Harry N. Abrams, 1990.

Burstein, Stanley M., ed. *Ancient African Civilizations: Kush and Axum*. Princeton, N.J.: Markus Wiener, 1998.

Marcus, Harold G. *A History of Ethiopia*. Berkeley: University of California Press, 1994.

Phillipson, David W. *Ancient Ethiopia: Aksum, Its Antecedents and Successors*. London: British Museum Press, 1998.

SEE ALSO: Africa, East and South; Axum; Christianity; Ezana; Frumentius, Saint; Islam; Judaism; Kaleb; Nubia; Sheba, Queen of; Solomon.

—*Narasingha P. Sil*

ETRUSCANS

DATE: 800 B.C.E.-400 B.C.E.
LOCALE: Central Italy
SIGNIFICANCE: The Etruscans were a unique people who founded the first advanced and most powerful civilization in Italy. They had a strong influence on the Romans, who rose to dominate the Italian peninsula.

There is continuing scholarly debate about the origins of the Etruscans (ih-TRUHS-kuhns). Some scholars view the Etruscans as indigenous to central Italy and direct descendants of Villanovan culture. Others trace the origins of the Etruscans to Asia Minor. However, scholars agree that the Etruscan language and culture were very different from those of other peoples living in Italy and that their level of technology was very advanced.

History. Between 800 and 600 B.C.E. the Etruscans expanded into west central Italy, establishing Etruria (later called Tuscany) as a home base. The Etruscans became neighbors of the Latins in Rome, who had established villages there as early as 1000 B.C.E. They also became neighbors of the Greeks, who were expanding their commercial empire into Corsica, Sicily, and northwest coastal Italy. The Etruscans were considered as barbarians by the Greeks and were banned from participating in the Olympic Games.

The Etruscans grew wealthy on the copper, tin, zinc, lead, and iron deposits in Etruria. Fertile soil and favorable climate led to abundant crops of wheat, olives, and grapes. The Etruscans traded widely within the ancient world. They were trading partners and periodic hostile adversaries of two other maritime powers, the Greek city-states and the Phoenicians. The Etruscans built a loose confederation of twelve independent city-states such as Veii, Caere, Tarquinia, Vuki, and a number of large towns. Etruscan cities were linked by an elaborate system of roads. Meetings on matters of common interest were held at Velsna (in modern Orvieto). Clearly the city was the main center of population and life in Etruscan Italy.

Militarily, the Etruscans developed an excellent navy and a formidable army based on heavy body armor and the use of bronze chariots. Cities were built on defensible hilltops, protected by heavy walls and gates as well as ravines to provide security. Their military power was projected south into the Bay of Naples and toward the Latin villages of Rome, which the Etruscans easily dominated as an aristocratic military ruling elite from 616 to 509 B.C.E. Rome's geographical location—with seven hills situated in the middle of a coastal plain—and its potential as the hub of major trade routes, was not lost on the Etruscans.

Politically, the Romans were ruled by Etruscan kings. The king's power was called *imperium* and was conferred by a popular assembly. *Imperium* was symbolized by an eagle-headed scepter and an ax bound in a bundle of rods (*fasces*). After the Etruscans, both these symbols continued as Roman symbols, as did the concept of *imperium*.

According to tradition, the first Etruscan king, Lucius Tarquinius Priscus (r. 616-579 B.C.E.), consolidated Roman villages and began the building of the city. His successor, Servius Tullius (r. 578-535 B.C.E.), extended the city boundaries and continued building structures, including fortified city walls. He also implemented social reform, dividing the population into six classes according to wealth. He introduced the system of centuries into the Roman citizen army, grouped in phalanx formation into legions. According to historian Livy, he also cemented bonds with the Latin nobles (patricians), who formed an advisory council to the king. The patricians were grouped into clans and were known by both personal name and clan name. The common people (plebeians) were divided into thirty wards, which as a committee could discuss only matters placed by the king on the agenda. In embryonic form, Rome's second king set up the senate and assembly of tribes.

The third and last Etruscan king, Lucius Tarquinius Superbus (r. 534-509 B.C.E.), reversed the Servian reforms, established absolute rule, and succeeded in an-

tagonizing both plebeians and patricians. Arrogant, tyrannical, and a lavish spender, Tarquinius built a temple to Jupiter larger than the Parthenon. He is also credited with building Rome's great sewer, the Cloaca Maxima.

According to legend, Tarquinius's son Sextus raped Lucretia, the wife of a friend. To regain her honor, Lucretia fatally stabbed herself, inspiring a friend, Lucius Junius Brutus, to lead a revolt against Tarquinius's tyranny. In 509 B.C.E., the revolt was successful. In reaction to monarchical tyranny, the Romans turned legislative power over to the senate. Preventing overbearing executive power, Rome established a system of two consuls, elected only for a single one-year term, each with the power to veto the other. Junius Brutus was the first consul of the newly established Republic of Rome.

Following its defeat in Rome, Etruscan power received a serious setback. In 474 B.C.E., the Etruscan navy was defeated by the Greeks off Cumae. Rome and its Latin allies gradually expanded toward the Etruscan cities. In 396 B.C.E., Veii fell after a long siege. By 250 B.C.E., what was left of Etruscan autonomy was integrated into the Roman system. However, what had been integrated long before was the Etruscan concept of civilization and technological know-how to make advanced civilization possible.

Language and literature. Etruscan (like Finnish, Hungarian, and Basque) is not part of the family of Indo-European languages. It is unrelated to any other language spoken in Italy. By 700 B.C.E., the Etruscans had adapted the Greek alphabet to produce their first writing. To date, archaeologists have uncovered about thirteen thousand Etruscan inscriptions, most of which state simple facts about individual lives or instructions about ritual. The Etruscans have left behind no known literature and a language that is still incompletely known in relation to the meaning of words or grammatical forms. Hence what is known about the Etruscans comes from their monuments and artifacts or descriptions produced by other ancient civilizations, most of which were written at a later date.

Architecture and city planning. The Etruscans brought urban life to Italy and were a powerful influence for the development of civilization. In the course of the seventh century C.E., Etruscan Rome rapidly developed from a collection of villages into a major city. For Rome, the Etruscan cultural and technological legacy was immense. In building the city, the arch and vault, which could support considerable weight, were first used by the Etruscans. Later the arch would be used with great proficiency by the Romans. The practice of placing temples on a high platform (podium) at the far end of a sacred enclosure so as to elevate both the structure and the gods, making the individual feel relatively insignificant, would later become a standard Roman practice. The Romans also adopted the science of boundaries (*limitatio*), which divided land into rectangular grids. Also the marking of formal city boundaries in a circle (*pomerium*), to define a holy and protected space, became a basic Roman preoccupation. To expand land for cultivation and to eliminate unhealthy marshlands, the Etruscans employed the tunnel method of draining river bottoms (*cuniculus*), a method that the Romans would continue. The general use of drainage and irrigation systems, the construction of excellent hydraulic works, and the building of roads, bridges, and sewers were all aspects of Etruscan technology that the Romans would borrow and continue.

Art. Etruscan artistic achievement was expressed in wall frescoes and graphic terra-cotta portraits found in their tombs. They greatly admired Greek pottery and attempted to imitate it. However, the Etruscans also developed their own native style of pottery (*buchero*), with decorations on a shiny black background.

Daily life and death. Judging from paintings depicting scenes from everyday life, the realistic figures of the dead placed on top of sarcophagi or funerary urns, and artifacts uncovered from tombs, the Etruscans were a luxury- and pleasure-loving people with much leisure time and were voracious consumers. The banquet was a way of showing family status. Elaborate banquets are portrayed in tomb reliefs, along with sporting events, hunting, and dancing. Splendor was enjoyed even in death, for the Etruscans built large cities of the dead (necropolises), laid out in grid fashion. Such a necropolis, with streets, squares, and rectangular tombs cut into rock, can be toured at Cerveterei. Pleased with urban life on earth, the Etruscans appear to have envisioned the afterlife as a continuation. Etruscan houses were built of wood and clay, but tombs were built to last forever. Tombs were filled with favorite possessions of the deceased, a fact known to grave robbers through the ages. The Tomb of the Baron at Tarquinia is one of the best-preserved painted tombs and provides an insight into Etruscan life and anticipations of the afterlife.

Women's life. Etruscan women enjoyed the luxury of fine jewelry, elegant clothing, elaborate hairstyles, decorated bronze mirrors, and diverse cosmetics and appear to have been granted a high degree of equality in Etruscan life. They were given individual first names and participated freely in all aspects of public life. That women's bronze mirrors had inscriptions carved into them is an indication that Etruscan women were literate.

Religion and ritual. In relation to religious beliefs, the Etruscans had a major impact. Their preoccupation with foretelling the future (divination) also became a Roman preoccupation, though one that was usually relegated only to times of emergency. Examination of animal entrails, most commonly the liver, became a pseudoscience designed to uncover the will of the gods. The liver was considered as the seat of life. An inscribed bronze model of a sheep's liver, found near Piacenza, appears to have been used as a teaching device for diviners.

Similarly, the interpretation of lightning and thunder was used by the Etruscans to decipher the will of the gods, a practice the Romans would continue. In fact, the Romans would insist on discovering signs (*auspices*) before making any major decision.

Like the Greeks, the Etruscans pictured their gods as having human form. The three major Etruscan gods, Tinia, Uni, and Menrva, were adapted by the Romans. Having much leisure time, the Etruscans celebrated many official holidays in honor of their gods. The Romans also would mark the year with many religious festivals. Undoubtedly, the major event in Etruscan Rome was the elaborate, semi-religious procession following victorious campaigns, containing victors, captive prisoners, displays of seized treasures, musicians, and dancers. This ritual of the triumphant victory processional would continue throughout the Roman Republican and Imperial eras.

Medicine. The Etruscans were known for their medical skills. Numerous surgical and dental instruments can be found among funerary objects in tombs. The Etruscans also had a reputation in the ancient world for the medicinal use of plants and the use of thermal springs for therapeutic purposes.

Sports and entertainment. For recreation on religious festivals, the Etruscans staged gladiator duels. Although they may seem to have been basic martial contests in comparison with the later Roman gladiatorial extravaganzas, still the Romans appear to have first developed their love of gladiator shows from the Etruscan experience. Tomb paintings also indicate that chariot racing was a favorite Etruscan recreation. This also became popular in Rome, with the Circus Maximus later outdoing anything the Etruscans could have fantasized.

The Etruscan propinquity toward rampant consumerism, fine foods, exciting sports, and elaborate banquets provided a hedonistic model that the Romans would later perfect to an extent that would have made the Etruscans envious. However, these are not the aspects of Etruscan life that would make Roman civilization probable. The Romans, adopting Etruscan technology—and even the togas that they wore—added their own original contribution, the citizen-based legion, which was used to defeat the Etruscans, conquer Italy, and then most of the Western world. This would be a world of cities, roads, and conspicuous consumption, one that the Etruscans helped shape.

ADDITIONAL RESOURCES

Banti, Luisa. *Etruscan Cities and Their Culture*. Berkeley: University of California Press, 1973.
Barker, Graeme, and Tom Rasmussen. *The Etruscans*. Malden, Mass.: Blackwell Publishers, 1998.
Grant, Michael. *The Etruscans*. New York: Scribners, 1980.
Hus, Alain. *The Etruscans*. New York: Grove Press, 1963.
Keller, Werner. *The Etruscans*. New York: Knopf, 1974.
Pallottino, Massimo. *A History of Earliest Italy*. Translated by M. Ryle and K. Soper. Ann Arbor: University of Michigan Press, 1991.
Scullard, H. H. *A History of the Roman World 753 to 146 B.C.* New York: Routledge, 1991.
Spivey, Nigel J., and S. Stoddart. *Etruscan Italy*. London: Batsford, 1990.

SEE ALSO: Junius Brutus, Lucius; Livy; Lucretia; Rome, Republican; Tarquins.

—Irwin Halfond

EUCLID

ALSO KNOWN AS: Euclid of Alexandria
BORN: c. 330 B.C.E.; probably Greece
DIED: c. 270 B.C.E.; Alexandria, Egypt
RELATED CIVILIZATION: Hellenistic Greece
MAJOR ROLE/POSITION: Mathematician

Life. Euclid taught at the museum in Alexandria. He compiled results from earlier geometry textbooks and the works of contemporary Greek mathematicians into thirteen books of *Stoicheia* (compiled c. 300 B.C.E.; *Elements*, 1570). *Elements* covered plane geometry, the theory of proportion, solid geometry, and number theory. The text culminated with constructions of the five Platonic solids. It immediately superseded all previous geometry manuals.

The most notable feature of *Elements* was the special attention Euclid paid to the deductive structure of the work. In general, he accepted no facts about geometrical concepts without proof. The proof of each theorem or problem depended on earlier propositions and on the few axioms and postulates Euclid claimed to be self-evident.

Euclid wrote several other works that survived in fragments, if at all. In addition to the philosophy of how to solve mathematical problems, Euclid was interested in astronomy, optics, music, and conic sections.

Influence. No book besides the Bible has appeared in as many translations, editions, and commentaries as

Euclid. (Library of Congress)

Elements. Since antiquity, mathematicians, students, and historians have equated Euclid's name with the rational order and deductive structure associated with Greek mathematics. Euclidean geometry was believed to be the only possible geometry until the nineteenth century.

ADDITIONAL RESOURCES
Artmann, Benno. *Euclid: The Creation of Mathematics*. New York: Springer Verlag, 1999.
Heilbron, John L. *Geometry Civilized: History, Culture, and Technique*. Oxford, England: Clarendon Press, 1998.
Knorr, Wilbur. *The Evolution of the Euclidean Elements*. Dordrecht, Netherlands: Reidel, 1975.

SEE ALSO: Alexandrian library; Greece, Hellenistic and Roman.

—*Amy Ackerberg-Hastings*

EUDOCIA

ALSO KNOWN AS: Athenais; Eudokia
BORN: c. 401 C.E.; Athens
DIED: October 20, 460 C.E.; Jerusalem
RELATED CIVILIZATIONS: Imperial Rome, Byzantine Empire
MAJOR ROLE/POSITION: Empress, poet, religious figure

Life. Originally named Athenais, Eudocia (yoo-DOH-shee-uh) was the daughter of the pagan scholar Leontius. The name Athenais may be derived from her birthplace, Athens, or it may honor Athena as the patron divinity of Athens. When she was about twenty years old, Athenais came to Constantinople in connection with a dispute over inheritance. There, her beauty attracted the young emperor Theodosius II. After she was baptized, taking the name Eudocia, she married the emperor in 421 C.E. Prominent at court for many years, Eudocia fell into disfavor in 441 C.E. because of her supposed adultery; actually, the charge may have been fabricated by her enemies. She thereupon retired to Jerusalem, where she was instrumental in building various churches.

Early in her life, Eudocia wrote a poem on a Roman victory over the Persians. Later, she wrote religious poetry, including a life of Christ in a cento, built up from lines from Homer.

Influence. Eudocia's poetry reflects the transitional period when Christianity, in the process of being established as the religion of the Roman Empire, actively appropriated material of Classical writers such as Homer.

ADDITIONAL RESOURCES
Cambridge Medieval History: The Christian Roman Empire and the Foundation of the Teutonic Kingdoms. Cambridge, England: Cambridge University Press, 1967.
Usher, Mark David. *Homeric Stitchings: The Homeric Centos of the Empress Eudocia*. Lanham, Md.: Rowman and Littlefield, 1998.

SEE ALSO: Byzantine Empire; Christianity; Constantinople; Homer; Rome, Imperial.

—*Edwin D. Floyd*

EUDOXIA, AELIA

ALSO KNOWN AS: Eudoxia the Elder
BORN: 370's C.E.; France or Italy
DIED: October 6, 404 C.E.; Constantinople (Istanbul)
RELATED CIVILIZATIONS: Imperial Rome, Byzantine Empire
MAJOR ROLE/POSITION: Empress

Life. Daughter of the pagan Frankish general Bauto who served the West Roman emperor Gratian, Aelia Eudoxia (yoo-DAHK-see-uh) may have fled in 387 C.E. with Gratian's widow Justina and her son Valentinian II from the usurper Maximus to the East Roman emperor Theodosius the Great at Salonika. On April 27, 395 C.E., she married Arcadius, the sixteen-year-old son of Theodosius. She gained a controlling influence when he became emperor in 395 C.E.

In July, 399 C.E., Eutropius, the all-powerful adviser of Arcadius, was exiled at Eudoxia's insistence. On

January 9, 400 C.E., she was proclaimed Augusta. She supported the pro-Roman party of Lucius Domitisu Aurelianus (Aurelian), prefect of the praetorium of the Orient, against those who supported the barbarians. She favored the proscription of pagan cults. At the birth of her son Theodosius in 401 C.E., she obtained through a clever stratagem the destruction of the Marneum at Gaza, a pagan temple tolerated by Arcadius. Conflicts between her and the archbishop of Constantinople, Saint John Chrysostom, resulted in his exile. She died in childbirth.

Influence. Eudoxia's upholding of the Roman and Christian traditions and her imposition on a strong religious hierarchy set the pace for East Rome. She raised the position of empress to equality. The consorts of Theodosius II and Valentinian III would carry her name.

ADDITIONAL RESOURCES
Diehl, Charles. *Byzantine Empresses*. New York: Studion, 1999.
Jones, A. H. M. *The Later Roman Empire, 284-602*. Norman: University of Oklahoma Press, 1986.
Oost, Stewart Irvin. *Galla Placidia Augusta*. Chicago: University of Chicago Press, 1968.

SEE ALSO: Byzantine Empire; Christianity; Gratian; John Chrysostom, Saint; Theodosius the Great; Theodosius II; Valentinian III.

—Reinhold Schumann

EUDOXUS

BORN: 390 B.C.E.; Cnidus
DIED: c. 350 B.C.E.; Cnidus
RELATED CIVILIZATION: Classical Greece
MAJOR ROLE/POSITION: Mathematician, astronomer, doctor, lawyer

Life. Eudoxus (yew-DAHK-suhs) studied mathematics with Archytas in Tartenum and in Athens under Plato. Later, he founded a school in Cyzicus. Eudoxus made two main mathematical contributions: expanding the application for an area-finding method and creating a new theory of incommensurables. First, he took Antiphon's "method of exhaustion," used to find the area of a circle, and proved that it could be applied to finding the areas and volumes of other figures. This method "exhausts" the area inside an unknown figure by inscribing multiple figures with known areas inside it. Second, he solved a problem created by Greek mathematics' conception of numbers as lengths of lines. This idea works well for rational numbers but encounters difficulty with irrational numbers. As a solution, Eudoxus created the theory of incommensurables. This is the subject of Book 5 of Euclid's *Stoicheia* (compiled c. 300 B.C.E.; *Elements*, 1570), probably written by Eudoxus.

In astronomy, Eudoxus calculated the circumference of the earth, reported by Aristotle to be 40,000 miles (64,400 kilometers). Eudoxus also originated a theory that the complex movement through the sky of the Sun, Moon, planets, and stars is dependent on their positions on rotating concentric celestial spheres.

Influence. Eudoxus's method of exhaustion presaged integral calculus by almost two thousand years. His theory of incommensurables foreshadowed the nineteenth century formulation of the real numbers by German mathematicians Julius Wilhelm Richard Dedekind and Karl Theodor Wilhelm Weierstrass. His celestial sphere theory was held as the true description of the universe until the rise of the heliocentric theory during the Renaissance.

ADDITIONAL RESOURCES
Euclid. *The Elements, Book V*. Translated by Sir Thomas Heath. New York: Dover, 1956.
Lindberg, David. *The Beginnings of Western Science*. Chicago: University of Chicago Press, 1992.
Smith, D. E. *History of Mathematics*. New York: Dover, 1951.

SEE ALSO: Euclid; Greece, Classical; Plato.

—Andrius Tamulis

EUMENES II

BORN: date unknown; Pergamum
DIED: 160-159 B.C.E.; Pergamum
RELATED CIVILIZATION: Hellenistic Greece
MAJOR ROLE/POSITION: Ruler

Life. Eumenes II (YEW-muh-neez) inherited the kingship of Pergamum from his father, Attalus I, in 197 B.C.E. On his accession, Eumenes was faced by threats from Philip V of Macedonia to his west and Antiochus the Great of Syria to his south. By this time, Rome had become the dominating power in the Greek world, and Eumenes' policy of friendship with Rome paid off handsomely. For his support of the Romans against Antiochus in 192 B.C.E. and then at the Battle of Magnesia ad Sipylum in 189 B.C.E., he was rewarded with parts of Seleucid Asia Minor and the Thracian Chersonese, a substantial elephant corps, and a large monetary sum. Pergamum suddenly became a strong and rich kingdom in Asia Minor. Eumenes continued his friendship with Rome, although his power excited suspicion, and helped Rome defeat the last Macedonian king, Perseus, in 168 B.C.E.

Eumenes introduced economic reforms, increased the size of the city, and inaugurated a building program. The Great Altar of Zeus at Pergamum (180-175 B.C.E.), with its frieze depicting battle between the gods and giants to symbolize the Attalids' victories over the Gauls, was a product of his reign.

Influence. Under Eumenes II, Pergamum became a powerful and rich kingdom. The Great Altar of Zeus, which he commissioned, is one of the marvels of ancient art.

ADDITIONAL RESOURCES

Allen, R. E. *The Attalid Kingdom: A Constitutional History.* Oxford, England: Oxford University Press, 1983.

Green, Peter. *Alexander to Actium: The Historical Evolution of the Hellenistic Age.* Reprint. Berkeley: University of California Press, 1993.

SEE ALSO: Antiochus the Great; Attalid Dynasty; Greece, Hellenistic and Roman; Macedonia; Magnesia ad Sipylum, Battle of; Philip V; Zeus at Pergamum, Great Altar of.

—*Ian Worthington*

EUPALINUS OF MEGARA

BORN: c. 575 B.C.E.; Megara, Greece
DIED: c. 500 B.C.E.; place unknown
RELATED CIVILIZATION: Archaic Greece
MAJOR ROLE/POSITION: Civil engineer

Life. In the middle of the seventh century B.C.E., Theagenes, the tyrant of Megara, built a famous waterworks, evidently a conduit and water fountain, or spring house, that brought water to the middle of the city. Eupalinus of Megara (YEW-pah-lihn-uhs of ME-gahruh), the son of Naustrophus, was probably hired by the tyrant Polycrates of Samos (d. c. 522 B.C.E.) to build, or at least design, one of the three greatest Hellenic public works known to historian Herodotus, a 3,300-foot (1,005-meter) tunnel over 6 feet (1.9 meters) high through the watershed of Samos to pipe water from springs beyond the mountain into the capital city. His work gangs started from both sides of the ridge and met in the middle with an error of only about 6 feet (2 meters).

Influence. Eupalinus's achievement at Samos proved the accuracy of Greek geometry and the practicality of the civil engineering that built on it.

ADDITIONAL RESOURCES

Burn, A. R. *The Lyric Age of Greece.* London: Edward Arnold, 1960.

DeCamp, L. Sprague. *The Ancient Engineers.* New York: Dorset, 1990.

Jeffery, L. H. *Archaic Greece: The City-States c. 700-500 B.C.* New York: St. Martin's Press, 1976.

SEE ALSO: Greece, Archaic; Herodotus; Polycrates of Samos.

—*O. Kimball Armayor*

EUPOLIS

BORN: c. 445 B.C.E.; place unknown
DIED: c. 411 B.C.E.; place unknown
RELATED CIVILIZATIONS: Athens, Classical Greece
MAJOR ROLE/POSITION: Comic playwright

Life. Eupolis (YEW-puh-luhs) first competed as a comic playwright at the young age of sixteen, in 429 B.C.E. He won in dramatic competition several times with the nearly twenty plays he wrote. No complete play survives, but a number of fragments do, including some lengthy ones. In the *Demes* (after 418 B.C.E.; precincts), famous Athenian leaders from the past, including Solon and Pericles, are recalled from the dead to restore Athens to its glory. In *Cities* (c. 420 B.C.E.; cities), Athens' imperial subjects are personified, apparently in an appeal for more lenient treatment for them. Controversy surrounds his *Maricas* (421 B.C.E.; maricas), which attacked the Athenian politician Hyperbolus extensively. Aristophanes charged Eupolis with stealing the idea from his own *Hippēs* (424 B.C.E.; *The Knights*, 1812), but Eupolis claimed he had, in fact, helped Aristophanes first. Fanciful stories abound about Eupolis's death, some involving his play *Baptae* (after 424 B.C.E.; dippers), which mocked Alcibiades of Athens. Evidence does suggest he died relatively young, probably in his thirties.

Influence. Eupolis was the last of the great triad of comedians of Old Comedy, along with Cratinus and Aristophanes. Much of what survives shows the creativity but not the charm for which he had a reputation in antiquity.

ADDITIONAL RESOURCES
Kassel, R., and C. Austin. *Poetae Comici Graeci.* Vol. 5. Berlin: Walter de Gruyter, 1986.
Norwood, Gilbert. *Greek Comedy.* London: Methuen, 1931.
Sidwell, Keith. "Authorial Collaboration? Aristophanes' 'Knights' and Eupolis." *Greek, Roman, and Byzantine Studies* 34, no. 4 (Winter, 1993): 365.

SEE ALSO: Alcibiades of Athens; Aristophanes; Athens; Cratinus; Greece, Classical; Performing arts; Pericles; Solon.

—*Wilfred E. Major*

EURIPIDES

BORN: c. 485 B.C.E.; Phlya, Greece
DIED: 406 B.C.E.; Macedonia, Greece
RELATED CIVILIZATION: Classical Greece
MAJOR ROLE/POSITION: Playwright

Life. The disproportion between what little can be ascertained about Euripides' (yoo-RIHP-uh-deez) life and the richness and completeness of his texts is immense. Plutarch gives his date of birth, dramatically but probably incorrectly, as the day of the Battle of Salamis in 480 B.C.E. Born to the farmer Mnesarchus (or Mnesarchides) and his wife Clito, he rose from rather humble beginnings to gain an education in Athens, perhaps in the schools of Anaxagoras and Protagoras. His sympathy with Sophistic philosophy lends credibility to a friendship with Socrates, which is suggested by ancient biographers. He was married to Melito, with whom he had three sons. The youngest, also named Euripides, followed his father into the theater. Although he may once have been sent on an embassy to Syracuse, he generally disdained public life and held no political or religious office, as other playwrights did. He is said to have been studious and withdrawn by nature and probably spent much time in his large private library.

Euripides turned to playwriting young and was awarded his first chorus at the dramatic competitions of the Athenian City Dionysia in 455 B.C.E. He did not win, and indeed his later career was marked by a paucity of victories. He achieved his first victory in 441 B.C.E. Although he entered the *agōn*, or contest, twenty-two times, he took first prize on only four occasions, far fewer than either Aeschylus or Sophocles. However, the fact that he continued to receive choruses, which were apportioned by the state and privately sponsored, suggests that audiences were thrilled by his plays, even if they found them unworthy of formal recognition. It is perhaps on account of such rejection that in 408 B.C.E. Euripides followed the invitation of King Archelaus of Macedonia to leave war-torn Athens and spend his last years at the Macedonian court as a confidant of the

Euripides. (North Wind Picture Archives)

king. He died there in 406 B.C.E. and is buried in Pella. Ironically, he won his fifth victory at the City Dionysia posthumously, with a trilogy of plays written in exile and brought back to Athens by his son.

Euripides wrote as many as ninety-two plays, of which eighteen of certain authorship remain—the largest body of extant work by any ancient playwright. Most were written and staged in the shadow of the Peloponnesian War (431-404 B.C.E.); his *Mēdeia* (431 B.C.E., *Medea*, 1781) was first performed the year the war broke out. His plays are suffused with irony and pessimism and characterized by an often radical rejection of classical decorum and rules. Among the most famous

are *Hippolytos* (428 B.C.E., revised version of an earlier play; *Hippolytus*, 1781), *Trōiades* (415 B.C.E.; *The Trojan Women*, 1782), and *Bakchai* (405 B.C.E.; *The Bacchae*, 1781).

Influence. Together with the Archaic Aeschylus and the Classical Sophocles, Euripides provided the canon of Greek tragedy and so no less than the foundation of Western theater. Following his death, Euripides' reputation soon began to eclipse that of the older playwrights. He is perceived today to be the most "modern" of the Greek tragedians; his plays revel in moral ambiguity and complexity of motivations and have been a direct stimulus both to Neoclassical writers such as French dramatist Jean Racine and to the twentieth century avant-garde.

ADDITIONAL RESOURCES

Collard, C. *Euripides*. Oxford, England: Clarendon Press, 1981.

Euripides. *Euripides: Plays One*. Translated by David Thompson and Michael J. Walton. London: Methuen, 2000.

Michelini, Ann Norris. *Euripides and the Tragic Tradition*. Madison: University of Wisconsin Press, 1987.

Zimmermann, Bernhard. *Greek Tragedy: An Introduction*. Baltimore: Johns Hopkins University Press, 1991.

SEE ALSO: Aeschylus; Greece, Classical; Peloponnesian War; Performing arts; Plutarch; Protagoras; Salamis, Battle of; Socrates; Sophocles.

—*Ralf Erik Remshardt*

EUSEBIUS OF CAESAREA

BORN: c. 260 C.E.; probably Caesarea, Palestine
DIED: May 30, 339 C.E.; Caesarea, Palestine
RELATED CIVILIZATION: Imperial Rome
MAJOR ROLE/POSITION: Christian scholar, bishop of Caesarea

Life. Eusebius (yew-SEE-bee-uhs of sehs-uh-REE-uh) was born in Caesarea Maritima, the provincial capital of Roman Palestine. Besides being a political and economic center, Caesarea was a seat of Christian learning. The speculative theologian Origen had worked there in the middle decades of the third century C.E., and the renowned teacher Pamphilus built a great

library there in the later decades of that century. As a priest and disciple of Pamphilus, Eusebius was given control of the library and drew on its resources to compose the first editions of his *Chronicon* (c. 300, 325 C.E.; *Chronicle*, 1583) and *Historia ecclesiastica* (c. 300, 324 C.E.; *Ancient Ecclesiastical Histories*, 1576-1577; better known as Eusebius's *Church History*). The former compiled the records of pagan (Egyptian, Greek, and Roman) and sacred (Hebrew and Christian) history and provided a comparative chronology of human history from its beginnings to late antiquity. The latter contained the traditions of the early Church and gave a history of Christianity from the first through the third centuries C.E. It was filled with information about the episcopal successors of the Apostles, the heretical attackers and orthodox defenders of the faith, the fate of the Jews, the evolution of the New Testament, and the imperial persecutions and heroic martyrs of the Church.

Eusebius survived the Great Persecution (303-313 C.E.) and was elected bishop of Caesarea when the Edict of Milan gave peace to the Church (313 C.E.). Over the next decade, he expanded his *Church History* to include the tetrarchic persecutions and Constantine's conversion (c. 315 C.E.) and wrote defenses of the Christian faith. By the time Constantine the Great conquered the east and made Christianity the favored religion in the empire (324 C.E.), Eusebius was one of the most famous leaders of the Church. He published a final edition of his *Church History* and expanded his *Chronicle* to bring events up to 324 C.E. He attended the Council of Nicaea and helped devise an official creed for the Christian faith and a common day for the Easter festival (325 C.E.). In his later years, Eusebius guided the empress mother Helena on her Holy Land pilgrimage (326-327 C.E.), supervised the making of luxury Bibles for the new Christian capital of Constantinople (330 C.E.), and gave the *Oratorio de laudibus Constantini* (335-336 C.E.; *In Praise of Constantine*, 1976) for the thirtieth anniversary of Constantine's reign (336 C.E.). After the death of Constantine, Eusebius composed a four-book *Vita Constantini* (339 C.E.; *Life of Constantine*, 1845), which recounted the pious actions of the emperor Constantine in favor of the Christian Church.

Influence. Eusebius laid the groundwork for the B.C.(before Christ)-A.D.(anno Domini) dating system with his chronological studies and provided the fundamental data for the historical study of early Christianity.

ADDITIONAL RESOURCES

Barnes, Timothy D. *Constantine and Eusebius*. Cambridge, Mass.: Harvard University Press, 1981.

Chesnut, Glenn F. *The First Christian Histories*. 2d ed. Macon, Ga.: Mercer University Press, 1986.

Kofsky, Arieh. *Eusebius of Caesarea Against Paganism*. Boston: Brill, 2000.

SEE ALSO: Christianity; Constantine the Great; Constantinople; Milan, Edict of; Nicaea, Council of; Origen; Rome, Imperial.

—*Charles M. Odahl*

EUTROPIUS

BORN: date and place unknown
DIED: c. 399 C.E.; place unknown
RELATED CIVILIZATION: Imperial Rome
MAJOR ROLE/POSITION: Grand chamberlain, consul

Life. Eutropius (yoo-TROH-pee-uhs) was a former slave, possibly of Armenian origin, and a eunuch. He had been a chamberlain and a court eunuch for Theodosius the Great and was once sent to consult an ascetic holy man in Egypt about that emperor's forthcoming battle with the usurper Eugenius. After Theodosius's death in early 395 C.E., Eutropius outmaneuvered Rufinus, praetorian prefect of the East, who was murdered later that year, and then, as grand chamberlain (*praepositus sacri cubiculi*) for the young emperor Arcadius, Eutropius became the most influential man in the Eastern Empire for the next several years. He defeated the Huns and allied with Alaric I the Goth as a move against Flavius Stilicho, the most influential man in the West (under the emperor Honorius, Arcadius's even younger brother). In 399 C.E., he became consul.

Eudoxia, Arcadius's wife, was trying to lessen Eutropius's influence with her husband. Some reactions to Eutropius's consulship were negative, a fact exploited by Stilicho, resulting in the strong opposition of the general Gainas and the senator Aurelian. Soon Eutropius was overthrown, exiled, recalled, and killed.

Influence. Although former slaves and even eunuchs had long been influential in the imperial court, none before Eutropius had ever reached the consulship. One measure of his influence and power is the violent invective written against him by the poet Claudian.

ADDITIONAL RESOURCE

Long, Jacqueline. *Claudian's "In Eutropium": Or, How, When, and Why to Slander a Eunuch*. Chapel Hill: University of North Carolina Press, 1996.

SEE ALSO: Alaric I; Claudian; Goths, Ostrogoths, Visigoths; Huns; Rome, Imperial; Stilicho, Flavius; Theodosius the Great.

—*Mark Gustafson*

EXODUS

DATE: traditionally c. 1450-c. 1430 B.C.E.
LOCALE: Egypt
RELATED CIVILIZATIONS: Pharaonic Egypt, Israel
SIGNIFICANCE: Marked the beginning of Israel as a people dedicated to ethical monotheism.

The dates of the Jewish Exodus from Israel are a matter of debate; traditionally the Exodus is dated at circa 1450 B.C.E., but scholars also agree that two key figures in the Exodus, the Jewish leader Moses and the Egyptian pharaoh Rameses II, were contemporaries of the thirteenth century B.C.E. Today, scholars agree to disagree, some believing that the Exodus may be a matter of myth. In about the seventeenth century B.C.E., the Israelites had migrated into Egypt and settled in the eastern Nile Delta as guests of the pharaoh. Eventually, however, the Israelites fell out of royal favor, and they had even become state slaves by the end of the fifteenth century B.C.E.

Moses was divinely commissioned to lead the Israelites out of Egyptian bondage. His mission became a contest with the pharaoh, perhaps Rameses II. A series of ten plagues that visited Egypt and culminated in the deaths of the firstborn sons of Egyptian families, persuaded the pharaoh to release the Israelites. Nevertheless, he later changed his mind and tried to stop them at the Reed (traditionally the Red) Sea. Then, according to the Bible, a miracle occurred: God parted the waters, allowing the Israelites to cross in safety; the pursuing Egyptians were drowned when the waters returned.

After the Israelites' escape, Moses shaped the refugees into a distinctive, cohesive community. At Mount Sinai, the Israelites made a covenant with God, whom they credited with liberating and choosing them as his special people. Later, the successors of Moses established a monotheistic Israelite state in Palestine.

ADDITIONAL RESOURCES

Bright, John. *A History of Israel.* 3d ed. Philadelphia: Westminster, 1993.
Finegan, Jack. *Let My People Go.* New York: Harper and Row, 1963.

SEE ALSO: Egypt, Pharaonic; Israel; Judaism; Moses.

—Ronald W. Long

Moses and the Israelites walk through the wilderness as he leads them out of Egyptian bondage. (North Wind Picture Archives)

EZANA

ALSO KNOWN AS: Ēzānā; Ezanas; Aezana
BORN: fourth century C.E.; Axum, Abyssinia (now in Ethiopia)
DIED: fourth century C.E.; Sudan
RELATED CIVILIZATIONS: Axum, Napata, Egypt, Greece
MAJOR ROLE/POSITION: Emperor

Life. Ezana (AY-zah-nah) ascended the throne of Axum circa 330 C.E., after being tutored by Saint Frumentius. He supported the spread of Christianity and converted later in his reign. Ezana's expansion policy moved Axum from one of several Red Sea kingdoms to a position as the dominant empire in the region. Axum, the basis of later Ethiopia, extended to both sides of the Red Sea, west into the Sudan, and south into Somalia. In the process, Ezana conquered the kingdoms of Meroe and Kush (Napata). By ending the custom of enslaving conquered peoples and by guaranteeing their land rights, Ezana won loyalty and support across his new empire. The economy prospered under his policies, and international trade in ivory, gold, hides, and spices flourished. He awarded himself the ti-

tle "king of kings," used by Ethiopian emperors until the 1980's. Although Ezana ushered in an era of peace for the Red Sea coastal area, he died in battle. His body is enshrined in a rock-hewn church in Axum.

Ezana made Ge'ez the national language to help forge an Ethiopian identity. He also fostered the creation of a uniquely Ethiopian Christianity and extended it into his empire. Ezana is regarded as a saint in the Ethiopian and Catholic Churches.

Influence. Ezana created the outlines for Abyssinia (Ethiopia) and left it with a common language and religion.

ADDITIONAL RESOURCES

Burstein, Stanley, ed. *Ancient African Civilizations: Kush and Axum*. Princeton, N.J.: Markus Wiener, 1998.
Munro-Hay, Stuart. *Aksum, An African Civilization of Late Antiquity*. Edinburgh, Scotland: University of Edinburgh, 1992.

SEE ALSO: Africa, East and South; Axum; Ethiopia; Frumentius, Saint; Napata and Meroe.

—Norbert Brockman

EZEKIEL

BORN: c. 627 B.C.E.; Jerusalem
DIED: c. 570 B.C.E.; Babylonia
RELATED CIVILIZATIONS: Israel, Judah, Babylon
MAJOR ROLE/POSITION: Religious leader

Life. Ezekiel, the son of Buzi, most likely came from a prominent, influential family. A priest in Jerusalem, he was taken captive to Babylon in 597 B.C.E. along with Jehoiachin, king of Judaea, and ten thousand other captives. From 597 to 587 or 586 B.C.E., he served as a prophet among the exiles at Tel-Abib in Babylon. His prophecies, which are preserved in the biblical book of Ezekiel, emphasize the sinfulness and associated punishment of the Israelites, as well as the impending destruction of Jerusalem, which took place in 587 or 586 B.C.E. Ezekiel also prophesied of a glorious future for Israel, which was partially fulfilled by the return from captivity in 536 B.C.E. and 458 B.C.E.

With the restoration of Israel, Ezekiel served as a lawmaker, codifier, and designer of the form and structure of Hebrew worship. He exhibited an ardent love for

Ezekiel. (Library of Congress)

his countrymen, dwelling among the people, watching over them, encouraging them to live better lives, and warning them of the consequences of sinful living. His writings include vivid descriptions of the resurrection of the dead and details of the restored temple to be built in Jerusalem.

Influence. Ezekiel served God, comforted and inspired the Israelite people, and described the future history of Israel and the world.

ADDITIONAL RESOURCES

Block, Daniel I. *The Book of Ezekiel*. Grand Rapids, Mich.: Wm. B. Eerdmans, 1998.

Clements, Ronald E. *Ezekiel*. Louisville, Ky.: Westminster John Knox Press, 1996.

SEE ALSO: Israel; Judaism.

—Alvin K. Benson

EZRA

BORN: late sixth or early fifth century B.C.E.;
  southern Mesopotamia
DIED: date unknown; probably Jerusalem
RELATED CIVILIZATIONS: Babylon, Judaea
MAJOR ROLE/POSITION: Scribe

Life. Ezra is mentioned in the Bible in Ezra 7-10 and Nehemiah 8. According to Ezra 7-8, he led a group of Jews from Babylon to Jerusalem under the authority of the Persian emperor Artaxerxes, probably Artaxerxes I (r. 464-424 B.C.E.), in the seventh year of his reign or 458 B.C.E. Ezra's two recorded activities were to read the "law" to an assembly of Jewish people in Jerusalem and to require Jewish men, particularly priests and Levites, who had married "foreign wives" to divorce them. The law read by Ezra appears to have been the law of Moses, that is, Genesis through Deuteronomy, or the legal texts included within those books, though Nehemiah 8:15 refers to a law not actually found in those books. It may have been an inference from Leviticus 23:40-42, which reflected later practice. The issue of divorce in Ezra 9-10 (and Nehemiah 10 and 13) perhaps arose from the perceived need of Jews who came from Babylon to keep themselves separate from others in Palestine to ensure purity in worship and theology.

Influence. Rabbinic Judaism viewed Ezra as a second Moses, who passed on the law to later scribes. By the first century C.E., he was seen as the one entrusted by God with preserving seventy secret books.

ADDITIONAL RESOURCES

Grabbe, Lester L. *Ezra-Nehemiah*. New York: Routledge, 1998.

Smith, Morton. *Palestinian Parties and Politics That Shaped the Old Testament*. 2d ed. London: Student Christian Movement Press, 1987.

SEE ALSO: Bible: Jewish; Judaism.

—Paul L. Redditt

Ezra receives a letter from Artaxerxes. (North Wind Picture Archives)

— F —

FABIUS

ALSO KNOWN AS: Quintus Fabius Maximus
   Verrucosus; Cunctator ("the Delayer")
BORN: c. 275 B.C.E.; place unknown
DIED: c. 203 B.C.E.; possibly Rome
RELATED CIVILIZATIONS: Republican Rome,
   Carthage
MAJOR ROLE/POSITION: Military leader, statesman

Life. Fabius (FAY-bee-uhs) enjoyed a fabulously successful career, holding the highest political offices at Rome and earning military victories over a number of Rome's enemies. He is most famous for his activities during the Second Punic War (218-201 B.C.E.). After the Roman defeat at Lake Trasimene (217 B.C.E.), the Romans elected Fabius dictator and placed him in command of all the Roman armies in Italy. During his period as dictator, Fabius practiced his legendary "Fabian strategy" against Hannibal. He avoided full-scale battles on disadvantageous terms and sought to train his raw recruits through a series of small skirmishes. In the middle years of the war, Fabius served as a general in central and southern Italy, recapturing several towns that had rebelled against Rome. He never lived to see the final defeat of Hannibal, however, dying in 203 B.C.E. after a long and distinguished career.

Influence. Later Romans believed that Fabius's strategy saved Rome by successfully checking Hannibal's army and thwarting Hannibal's attempts to supply his army. It is more likely, however, that Fabius did not harm the Carthaginian army but simply provided the Romans with a temporary respite after two major defeats. In any event, Fabius became a legend of traditional Roman strength and patriotism.

ADDITIONAL RESOURCES
Erdkamp, Paul. "Polybius, Livy, and the 'Fabian Strategy.'" *Ancient Society* 23 (1992): 127-147.
Plutarch. *Fabius Maximus.* In *Makers of Rome*, translated with an introduction by Ian Scott-Kilvert. London: Penguin Books, 1965.

SEE ALSO: Carthage; Hannibal; Punic Wars; Rome, Republican.

—Jeremiah B. McCall

FABIUS MAXIMUS, QUINTUS

ALSO KNOWN AS: Quintas Fabius Maximus
   Rullianus
BORN: c. 360 B.C.E.; place unknown
DIED: c. 290 B.C.E.; Rome
RELATED CIVILIZATION: Republican Rome
MAJOR ROLE/POSITION: Politician and general

Life. The life of Quintus Fabius Maximus (KWIHN-tuhs FAY-bee-uhs MAK-suh-muhs) illustrates three trends: Rome's emergence from legend to history, the establishment of the patrician-plebeian aristocracy based on personal achievements as well as birth, and the extension of Roman power throughout peninsular Italy by 275 B.C.E. subsequent to the dissolution of the Latin League in 340 B.C.E. Fabius (Rullianus) is more historical than his ancestors but less so than his grandson or great-grandson Fabius (the Cunctator). A fresco from his tomb survives, and the outline of his career is clear, but uncertainties remain, according to the historian Livy. A patrician, Fabius was consul five times between 322 and 295 B.C.E., dictator at least once, Master of the Horse twice, censor, and *princeps senatus*. In 304 B.C.E. as censor, he earned the *cognomen* Maximus by thwarting Appius Claudius Caecus, builder of Rome's first paved highway and aqueduct. Although Appius had registered the freedmen in all tribes, Fabius Maximus confined them to the four urban tribes. Holding repeated commands and a rare prorogation,

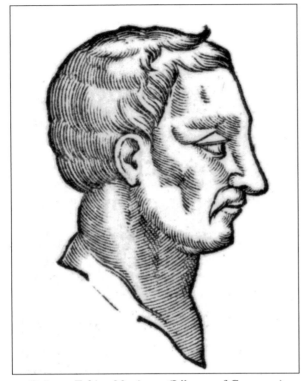

Quintus Fabius Maximus. (Library of Congress)

Fabius Maximus was a hero of the Second and Third Samnite Wars.

Influence. Fabius Maximus, a political conservative and stalwart campaigner, embodies traditional Roman values.

ADDITIONAL RESOURCES

Cornell, T. J. *The Beginnings of Rome*. London: Routledge, 1995.

Hornblower, S., and A. Spawforth, eds. *The Oxford Classical Dictionary*. 3d ed. Oxford, England: Oxford University Press, 1996.

Salmon, E. T. *Samnium and the Samnites*. Cambridge, England: Cambridge University Press, 1967.

Torelli, M. *Tota Italia*. New York: Oxford University Press, 1999.

Walbank, F. W., and A. E. Astin et al., eds. *The Cambridge Ancient History*. 2d ed. Cambridge, England: Cambridge University Press, 1989-1996.

SEE ALSO: Claudius Caecus, Appius; Fabius; Rome, Republican.

—*Thomas H. Watkins*

FABIUS PICTOR, QUINTUS

ALSO KNOWN AS: Pictorinus
FLOURISHED: c. 200 B.C.E.
RELATED CIVILIZATION: Republican Rome
MAJOR ROLE/POSITION: Historian

Life. Quintus Fabius Pictor (KWIHN-tuhs FAY-bee-uhs PIHK-tur) is called the first Roman historian. The name Pictor ("painter") refers to a grandfather who painted the walls of a temple around 302 B.C.E. Fabius Pictor was a member of the senate who fought in the Second Punic War (218-201 B.C.E.) and went on an embassy to Delphi in 216 B.C.E. after Hannibal's defeat of the Romans at Cannae. He wrote in Greek because that was the language of the world, but he also intended to present the Romans to the Greek world and convey Roman ideals. His history of Rome (now lost) started with stories from the founding of the city and continued up until his own time.

Influence. Fabius Pictor made Rome known to the Greek world. His work was used by Polybius in his writings of the First and Second Punic Wars, although he was criticized by Polybius for his pro-Roman bias that Hannibal and his family were responsible for the Second Punic War. Fabius was also quoted by Livy.

ADDITIONAL RESOURCES

Hadas, M. *A History of Latin Literature*. New York: Columbia University Press, 1952.

Hornblower, S., and A. Spawforth, eds. *The Oxford Classical Dictionary*. 3d ed. Oxford, England: Oxford University Press, 1996.

Mellor, Ronald. *The Roman Historians*. New York: Routledge, 1999.

SEE ALSO: Cannae, Battle of; Greece, Hellenistic and Roman; Livy; Polybius; Punic Wars; Rome, Republican.

—*Sherwin D. Little*

FAUSTINA I

ALSO KNOWN AS: Annia Galeria Faustina; Faustina
the Elder
BORN: c. 104 C.E.; place unknown
DIED: October or November, 140 C.E.; Rome
RELATED CIVILIZATION: Imperial Rome
MAJOR ROLE/POSITION: Wife of emperor

Life. Faustina I (faw-STI-nuh), the daughter of the
senator Marcus Annius Verus and Rupilia Faustina (the
aunt of Marcus Aurelius), was born during the reign of
Trajan. She married Antoninus Pius, and when he became emperor in 138 B.C.E., she was immediately designated Augusta. The marriage was happy, and he was
devoted to her in life and in death. The couple had four
children, but by 138 C.E., three of them, Marcus Galerius, Marcus Aurelius Fulvius, and Aurelia Fadilla,
had died. The remaining child, Annia Galeria Faustina,
became the wife of Marcus Aurelius. An account of
questionable veracity in the *Historia Augusta* (c. 325
C.E.; English translation, 1921-1932) describes her behavior as reckless and immoral, but there is no evidence
that Antoninus Pius found any fault in her.

Influence. Upon Faustina's death, she was deified,
games were held in her honor, and by senatorial decree,
a temple was constructed in the Roman Forum for her.
When Antoninus Pius died (March 7, 161 C.E.), it was
rededicated to both of them. The structure survives today as the Church of San Lorenzo in Miranda (1602).

In her honor, Antoninus Pius had millions of coins
bearing her image struck, whose range of types and variety of their reverse legends offer valuable evidence for
the period. He also established an alimentary fund in
her name, the Puellae Faustinianae, for poor girls.

ADDITIONAL RESOURCES
Balsdon, J. P. V. D. *Roman Women: Their History and
Habits*. London: Bodley Head, 1962.
Bauman, Richard A. *Women and Politics in Ancient
Rome*. New York: Routledge, 1992.

SEE ALSO: Antoninus Pius; Faustina II; Marcus
Aurelius; Rome, Imperial; Trajan.
—*Michele Valerie Ronnick*

FAUSTINA II

ALSO KNOWN AS: Annia Galeria Faustina; Faustina
the Younger
BORN: c. 129 C.E.; place unknown
DIED: 175 C.E.; Halala in Cappadocia
RELATED CIVILIZATION: Imperial Rome
MAJOR ROLE/POSITION: Wife of emperor

Life. Faustina II (faw-STI-nuh; Annia Galeria
Faustina) was the younger of two daughters born to
Antoninus Pius and Annia Galeria Faustina, her name-
sake. After Hadrian's death, Antoninus Pius broke off
her betrothal to Lucius Verus and matched her with his
wife's nephew and his adopted son, Marcus Aurelius.
The couple were married in 145 C.E.; the bride was
about fifteen years old and the groom was twenty-four.
A daughter born in November of 147 C.E. was followed by thirteen other children. Seven of these died
in infancy. Only four daughters and one son survived

their father. Historian Dio Cassius and the *Historia
Augusta* (c. 325 C.E.; English translation, 1921-1932)
provide unflattering reports concerning Faustina II's
lusty interest in sailors and gladiators. These include
the rumor that her son, Lucius Aurelius Commodus
was a gladiator's bastard and that she actually had
committed suicide in 175 C.E. in shame and fear over
her involvement in Gaius Avidius Cassius's attempted
coup d'état. However, her husband remained unper-
turbed.

Influence. In 174 C.E., Faustina's husband gave her
the title *mater castorum* and followed Antoninus Pius
in establishing an alimentary fund, the Novae Puellae
Faustinianae, for poor girls. When she died in Halala,
the Cappadocian town was renamed Faustinopolis. Her
husband had her deified, and the posthumous coinage
that was struck for her forms one of the most extensive
memorial series in Imperial times.

ADDITIONAL RESOURCES
Balsdon, J. P. V. D. *Roman Women: Their History and Habits*. London: Bodley Head, 1962.
Bauman, Richard A. *Women and Politics in Ancient Rome*. New York: Routledge, 1992.

SEE ALSO: Antoninus Pius; Faustina I; Marcus Aurelius; Rome, Imperial.

—*Michele Valerie Ronnick*

FAXIAN

ALSO KNOWN AS: *Wade-Giles* Fa-hsien
BORN: 337 C.E.?; place unknown
DIED: 422 C.E.?; place unknown
RELATED CIVILIZATION: China
MAJOR ROLE/POSITION: Buddhist monk, translator

Life. Little is known about Faxian's (fah-SHEE-en) early life. Faxian felt that China lacked Buddhist scriptures and decided to go India to study Buddhism. In 399 C.E., he and his Buddhist fellows, Hui Jing and Dao Zheng, went west. They started from Chang'an (modern Xi'an), crossed Liusha River and Congling Mountain, and traveled in northern, western, central, and eastern India. They also visited Sri Lanka and Java. They returned to China by sea in 414 C.E., bringing with them a large volume of Buddhist scriptures in Sanskrit. The whole trip took fourteen years. After he returned to China, Faxian settled in Jiankang (modern Nanjing) and devoted the rest of his life to translating Buddhist scriptures.

Influence. Faxian was one of the pioneers who went on a pilgrimage for Buddhist scriptures and one of the earliest Buddhist translators. His *Fo Guo Ji*, also known as *Faxian Zhuan* (fourth century C.E.; *Fo Koue Ki*, 1836; also known as *The Travels of Fa-hsien*), is an important document for studying Buddhism in the fourth century C.E. and for studying the history, geography, and cultures of South Asia. It was translated into English and French in the nineteenth century.

ADDITIONAL RESOURCES
Fa-hsien. *A Record of Buddhistic Kingdoms*. Translated and annotated by James Legge. New York: Dover, 1991.
_____. *The Travels of Fa-hsien*. Re-translated by H. A. Giles. Westport, Conn.: Greenwood Press, 1981.

SEE ALSO: Buddhism; China.

—*Zhaolu Lu*

FERTILE CRESCENT

DATE: 8000-3900 B.C.E.
LOCALE: Near East
RELATED CIVILIZATIONS: Natufian culture, Pre-Pottery Neolithic A and B cultures, Halafian culture, Chalcolithic period cultures
SIGNIFICANCE: This region witnessed the emergence of sedentary village life and the evolution of plant and animal domestication, creating the subsistence foundations for complex Bronze Age agrarian civilizations.

The Fertile Crescent extends northward in a great arc from the Persian Gulf, through the foothills of the Zagros Mountains in modern Iran, through Iraq, westward through the Taurus Mountains, and then southward along the Mediterranean coast to southern Israel and Jordan. It is a rain-fed region exhibiting a wet and dry, two-season climate. The topography is variable, occasionally rugged, and complex: desert, woodland steppe, and alluvial plains. Both rainfall and soil fertility have decreased over the past five millennia. Much of the region does not exhibit the conditions that prevailed when domestication and village communities were evolving.

The ancestors of humankind's first cultivated cereals and legumes are native to the region, including emmer and einkorn wheat, barley, rye, and lentils. Similarly, the region was home to a range of fauna, including the first domesticates: sheep, goats, cattle, and pigs.

Subsistence and settlement patterns deviating from traditional hunters and foragers are evident in the pre-Neolithic Natufian culture (11,000-8300 B.C.E.). The Natufians, while probably not initiating cereal cultivation, developed a sedentary lifestyle in the Levant. Archaeological evidence suggests an economy based on intensive gathering of wild vegetal foods, particularly cereals, and hunting. The Natufians, situated in the southwestern corner of the Fertile Crescent, elaborated a stone-tool technology of mortars, pestles, and sickles that had been gradually developing among earlier Mesolithic hunters and gatherers. In addition, the Natufians used lined storage pits to preserve vegetal surplus.

Early farming cultures that succeed the Natufians are known as Pre-Pottery Neolithic A (PPNA). At Jericho in the Jordan Valley, PPNA levels reveal a Natufian foundation of intensive collecting (to about 8300 B.C.E.) followed by the emergence of cereal cultivation. All early farming cultures continued to practice hunting or fishing.

Spectacular features at PPNA Jericho were the massive 12-foot-high (3.7-meter-high) walls and a 28-foot-tall (8.5-meter) stone tower. These works may have functioned for either defense or water control. Pre-Pottery Neolithic B (PPNB) at Jericho documents an agrarian economy, which included domesticated sheep and goats by circa 7300-6000 B.C.E. The massive walls were not maintained during this period. Complex social organization and social stratification are inferred from burials and monumental building projects that required labor coordination and a leadership hierarchy. Hence, by PPNA times, the productivity of the Fertile Crescent fostered occupational specialization and centralized authority, prerequisites for monumental building, town planning, and surplus food management.

In the Zagros region, the site of AliKosh (c. 7500 B.C.E.) documents a progression from hunting and foraging to cereal cultivation. Simple village life was tied to these economic pursuits, and circa 7000-6500 B.C.E., the population at AliKosh was cultivating emmer wheat and barley.

Neolithic archaeological sites within the Fertile Crescent demonstrate considerable economic, organizational, and architectural variability. For example, Jarmo (c. 6750-5000 B.C.E.), a farming village located in the eastern Fertile Crescent (modern Iraqi Kurdistan), contrasts sharply with Jericho. Monumental building projects, such as fortifications, are absent at Jarmo, as are burials, suggesting no status differentiation. The members of this village of perhaps two hundred to three hundred individuals grew lentils, peas, wheat, and barley; raised goats; and perhaps domesticated the pig. Hunting, as in other Neolithic farming communities, supplemented the diet. Although production appears to have been primarily for consumption, Jarmo's population possessed ceramic technology and a substantial tool kit, with many types being made from obsidian.

Early Neolithic (PPNA) archaeological sites lack evidence for domesticated animals. However, by late PPNB times (c. 7500-6500 B.C.E.), sheep and goats had been domesticated and were followed by cattle and pigs. The later Neolithic (PPNB) evidence indicates interest in cult activity. Plastered skulls and mother-goddess figurines suggest perhaps ancestor worship and social concerns over fertility.

Archaeological sites from the PPNB can be found over much of the Fertile Crescent. Archaeological evidence suggests trade in both shells and lithic materials had increased. The need for various agricultural tools may have fostered exchange in lithic material. Within the Fertile Crescent, fairly large settlements emerged during PPNB times. The site of Ain Ghazal (c. 6900 B.C.E.) in modern Jordan, for example, is larger than thirty acres. Controversy surrounds the cause of the demise of the large Neolithic (PPNB) sites in the Levant: deliberate deforestation or draught? Late Neolithic village sites are characterized by small settlements of less than three acres (c. 6500 B.C.E.).

By 6500 B.C.E., the manufacture of pottery had become common in agricultural communities within the Fertile Crescent. The use of ceramic wares such as vessels for storage, cooking, brewing, and ceremonial use is of great importance in sedentary agrarian settlements. Ceramics and agriculture diffused together into the alluvial regions of the Tigris-Euphrates drainage.

By the sixth millennium B.C.E., the "secondary products revolution" was in effect: Animal traction was employed for plowing and transport in northern Mesopotamia. In the northern Fertile Crescent, the Halafian culture (c. 5700-5600 B.C.E.) produced impressive ceramics that enjoyed a widespread distribution throughout the Near East. This culture, of which there is limited knowledge, was based on cereal cultivation and stock breeding.

The archaeology of the Chalcolithic period suggests a centralized chiefdom level of political organization. Settlements had enlarged to PPNA dimensions (twenty-five acres). The introduction of metallurgy is an attribute of this period. Tools manufactured from copper (axes, adzes, chisels) are found, as are items that imply ritual and elite usage. Chalcolithic sites in modern Israel have produced crowns and maceheads dating to about 4500-3500 B.C.E.

ADDITIONAL RESOURCES
Harris, D. R., and G. Hillman, eds. *Foraging and Farming: The Evolution of Plant Domestication.* London: Unwin Hyman, 1989.

Levy, Thomas E., ed. *The Archaeology of Society in the Holy Land.* New York: Facts On File, 1995.
Mellaart, James. *The Neolithic of the Near East.* London: Thames and Hudson, 1975.

SEE ALSO: Halafian culture; Natufian culture.
—*Rene M. Descartes*

FIGULUS, PUBLIUS NIGIDIUS

BORN: before 97 B.C.E.; place unknown
DIED: 45 B.C.E.; place unknown
RELATED CIVILIZATION: Republican Rome
MAJOR ROLE/POSITION: Scholar, statesman

Life. Very little about the life of Publius Nigidius Figulus (puhb-LEE-uhs nu-GIHD-ee-uhs FING-yuh-lus) is directly attested. His career path suggests aristocratic birth and a fine education. He entered the senate by 63 B.C.E. and was a praetor (Rome's second highest office) in 58 B.C.E. He also served as a legate in Asia Minor in 51 B.C.E. Shortly thereafter, he took up Pompey the Great's side in the civil war, apparently never reconciled with Julius Caesar, and died in exile.

Figulus is known primarily through reports of his extensive scholarly production. He wrote many works, some of them quite lengthy and allegedly marked by an obscure style. These are all now lost; a modest number of small fragments and references are preserved by later grammarians, writers of miscellanies, and writers of natural history. Attribution of particular material to Figulus is often a matter of scholarly dispute. His topics included grammatical notes, the gods, dreams, the "sphere" (astronomy and astrology), winds, animals, augury, and perhaps rhetoric. His astrological expertise and position as the leading Pythagorean thinker of his day have given him a reputation as a mystic.

Influence. In most respects, Figulus is overshadowed by his contemporary Marcus Terentius Varro, but he is still noted for esoteric knowledge. The two were among the first Romans to engage in serious scholarship.

ADDITIONAL RESOURCE
Rawson, Elizabeth. *Intellectual Life in the Late Roman Republic.* London: Duckworth, 1985.

SEE ALSO: Caesar, Julius; Pompey the Great; Pythagoras; Rome, Republican; Varro, Marcus Terentius.
—*Andrew M. Riggsby*

FINNIC PEOPLES

DATE: 1-700 C.E.
LOCALE: Coast of Baltic Sea, Finland
SIGNIFICANCE: The Finns immigrated from other areas around the Baltic Sea at about the beginning of the common era, largely displacing the Lapps, a related culture that still exists in northern Scandinavia to some extent.

The early history of Finland is somewhat mysterious because of a lack of written materials, but the area seems to have been inhabited for several thousand years. At the beginning of the common era, the ancestors of the people known as Finns migrated into the area, probably from the area that is now Estonia.

The Finnish language is part of the Finno-Ugric family, which also includes Lappish, Estonian, Lithuanian, Latvian, and a few obscure languages spoken in northwestern Russia. These languages are not known to be related to the Indo-European family, which gave rise to most of the languages spoken today in Europe. It appears to be distantly related to the Magyar languages, the only modern example of which is Hungarian.

The words "Finn" and "Finnish" arise from the term used by the Roman historian Tacitus in his *De origine et situ Germanorum* (c. 98 C.E., also known as *Germania*; *The Description of Germanie*, 1598). His reference to the "Fenni" consists of only about one hundred words, and his description of a primitive, forest-dwelling tribe suggests that he may very well have been referring to the Lapps rather than the Finns. The term "Fenni" probably comes from the Latin "finis," suggesting that the area was considered an edge of civilization, or a borderland.

This description is, in a way, accurate. The Finnish people are situated between the much more powerful and numerous Slavs to the east, Germans to the south, and Scandinavians to the west. From about 1 to 400 C.E., Finland was occupied by the Roman Empire. After the Romans left, the area was dominated by invading Vikings, and by the twelfth century C.E. was actually a part of Sweden. Swedes still make up a significant part of the population, and both Finnish and Swedish are official languages of modern Finland.

Therefore, it is somewhat difficult to isolate a Finnic culture, as such. The earliest archaeological evidence of the period, primarily grave sites, already shows a mixture of Finnish, Roman, and Germanic cultures. Most of the tools, weapons, and ornaments found in the early graves are of bronze or iron and may well have been imported as completed objects from other areas around the Baltic Sea.

The original Finns were primarily hunters and fishermen, and their settlements were concentrated in the southwestern part of the country. The north was, and remains, sparsely populated and represents the greatest concentration of Lapps.

Finland was never a political unit and did not exist as an independent nation until the twentieth century. The Finns have always referred to their land as "Suomi," a name that translates roughly as "marshland" and is probably a distant cognate of the English "swamp."

ADDITIONAL RESOURCES

Aini, Ranjanen. *Of Finnish Ways*. Minneapolis, Minn.: Dillon Press, 1981.

Derry, T. K. *A History of Scandinavia*. Minneapolis: University of Minnesota Press, 1979.

Kivikoski, Ella. *Ancient Peoples and Places: Finland*. New York: Praeger, 1967.

Singleton, Frederich Bernard. *A Short History of Finland*. New York: Cambridge University Press, 1998.

SEE ALSO: Rome, Imperial; Tacitus.

—Marc Goldstein

FLAMININUS, TITUS QUINCTIUS

BORN: c. 229 B.C.E.; place unknown
DIED: 174 B.C.E.; place unknown
RELATED CIVILIZATIONS: Republican Rome, Hellenistic Greece
MAJOR ROLE/POSITION: General, politician

Life. On being elected consul (198 B.C.E.), Titus Quinctius Flamininus (TIT-uhs KWIHNK-shee-uhs flam-uh-NEE-nuhs) was entrusted with military command in the war against Philip V of Macedonia. His good knowledge of Greek culture and negotiation skills allied to him many Greek states that were resentful of Philip's power. After negotiations with Philip failed, he defeated Philip in the Battle of Cynoscephalae (197 B.C.E.) and proclaimed the liberty of the Greeks (196 B.C.E.). Together with a special senatorial commission, he reorganized the administration of Greek cities. The latter offered him numerous honors, including those associated with divinity, put up his statue at Rome, and issued a coin with his portrait (the earliest known image of a living Roman on a coin).

His slogan of Greek liberty was used by the Romans in the wars against the Spartan tyrant Nabis (195-193 B.C.E.) and Antiochus the Great (192-188 B.C.E.). He took part in the negotiations with, and the war against, Antiochus and in the subsequent organization of affairs in Greece. His demand to the Bithynian king Prusias to extradite Hannibal led to the latter's suicide (182 B.C.E.), causing a public outcry in Rome.

Influence. Flamininus embodied a Roman philhellene who remained conscious of Rome's political interests. He is credited with establishing the system of *clientela* (clientage) of the Greeks to Rome and laying the foundations for the later cooperation between Roman politicians and Greek intellectuals.

ADDITIONAL RESOURCES
Gruen, Erich S. *The Hellenistic World and the Coming of Rome*. Berkeley: University of California Press, 1984.
Montagu, John Drogo. *Battles of the Greek and Roman Worlds*. Mechanicsburg, Pa.: Stackpole, 2000.

SEE ALSO: Antiochus the Great; Cynoscephalae, Battle of; Greece, Hellenistic and Roman; Hannibal; Macedonia; Rome, Republican; Philip V.

—*Sviatoslav Dmitriev*

FLAVIAN AMPHITHEATER

ALSO KNOWN AS: Colosseum
DATE: constructed c. 72-96 C.E.
LOCALE: Rome
RELATED CIVILIZATION: Imperial Rome
SIGNIFICANCE: The Flavian Amphitheater, which combines ancient Greek orders with Roman architectural developments, has stood nearly two thousand years as a memorial to the prowess and power of the Roman Empire.

This 206-by-171-yard (188-by-156-meter) elliptical structure, built from poured concrete, Travertine marble, and iron, was named for the three members of the Flavian Dynasty: Vespasian, Titus, and Domitian. It was commissioned in 72 C.E., dedicated in 80 C.E., and completed in 96 C.E. It seated approximately fifty thousand people and was the site of frequent gladiatorial competitions. It has been damaged by frequent earthquakes and lightning strikes. The name "Colosseum" is derived from a colossal statue of Nero that formerly stood on the location. The last gladiatorial contests were held in 404 C.E.

The 94-by-59-yard (86-by-54-meter) arena floor, below which was a complex system of corridors, gladiator and animal cells, and a medical facility, could be filled with water, and, until 248 C.E., was the site of nu-

The Flavian Amphitheater, dedicated in 80 C.E., was the site of gladiatorial competitions and Christian executions. (PhotoDisc)

merous naval contests. Superimposed on its four levels are the three Greek orders (Doric, Ionic and Corinthian). The upper attic pilasters feature composite Corinthian capitals with alternating windows. Twenty rows of seats, in two main sections, radiate outward, and barrel arches form level seating areas and crowd exits. Valeria focused light, through an oculus, onto the arena floor, while keeping the sun, wind, and elements off of the crowd.

ADDITIONAL RESOURCES

Luciani, Roberto. *The Colosseum.* Novara, Italy: Instituto Geografico De Agostini, 1990.

Nardo, Don. *The Roman Colosseum.* San Diego: Lucent Books, 1998.

SEE ALSO: Art and architecture; Domitian; Rome, Imperial; Sports and entertainment; Vespasian.

—*David B. Pettinari*

FOLSOM TECHNOLOGICAL COMPLEX

DATE: 10,900-10,000 B.C.E.

LOCALE: Folsom, New Mexico; North American Plains; Rocky Mountains; and Southwest

RELATED CIVILIZATION: Paleo-Indian tradition

SIGNIFICANCE: The people of the Folsom technological complex, a group of bison hunters, may have been derived from those of the earlier Clovis technological complex.

The Folsom technological complex was named after a town in New Mexico near Wild Horse Arroyo where George McJunkin, an African American cowboy, discovered the remains of an extinct form of bison, *Bison bison antiquus*, and a distinctive style of flaked stone weapon in 1908. The association was later confirmed on July 14, 1926, by an excavation conducted under the direction of Jesse Figgins and the Colorado Museum of Natural History. Although the evidence was incontrovertible, it was not widely accepted until Barnum Brown, a paleontologist at the American Museum of Natural History, Frank H. H. Roberts, an archaeologist at the Smithsonian Institution, and A. V. Kidder, an archaeologist at the Robert S. Peabody Foundation for Archaeology, examined artifacts in place among fossil bison bones in September, 1927, and subsequently presented their findings at the annual meeting of the American Anthropological Society.

In the summer of 1928, excavations resumed as a joint venture between the Colorado and American Museums of Natural History. As during the previous summers, more artifacts were found among skeletons of the extinct bison. Experts in archaeology, paleontology, and geology were once again invited to examine the artifacts in place, and thus, Folsom became the single most important American archaeological discovery of the twentieth century.

Folsom sites consist of bison-kill sites, overlooks, campsites, and stone procurement and workshop sites. Distinctive artifacts include thin, delicate, pressure-flaked spear points with channel flakes removed from one or both sides, spurred end-scrapers, gravers, incised bone, needles, beads, and red ochre. Because these artifacts are shared with pan-North American Clovis sites, Folsom may be derived from the earlier and preceding Clovis technological complex. Radiocarbon dates from Folsom sites overlap with both Clovis and Goshen sites on the plains, and their exact relationship remains poorly understood. Folsom bifaces are stylistically and technologically similar to the Cumberland and Barnes points of eastern North America. Stone used in the production of Folsom weapons and tools was frequently transported over distances upward of 250 miles (400 kilometers). Although bison was the base of the Folsom economy, antelope, deer, rabbits, prairie dogs, ground squirrels, and marmots were also exploited. Bison-kill sites range from a few animals to almost sixty bison, and important strategic locations to dispatch game were frequently reused. Most Folsom habitation sites include small hearth features, and a small circular structure was discovered at the Agate Basin site in Wyoming. Ritual items include a painted bison skull with a zigzag line, a stacked bison bone feature, and red ochre. Additional cultural aspects of the Folsom complex are yet to be discovered.

Important Folsom sites include Lindenmeier and Cattle Guard, Colorado; Agate Basin and Hansen, Wyoming; Adair-Steadman, Lipscomb, Lake Theo, and Lubbock, Texas; Cooper, Oklahoma; and Lake Ilo, North Dakota.

ADDITIONAL RESOURCES

Agogino, G. "The McJunkin Controversy." *New Mexico Magazine* 49, no. 3 (1971): 41-44.

Frison, G. C. "Paleoindian Large Mammal Hunters on the Plains of North America." *Proceedings of the National Academy of Science* 95 (1998): 14576-14583.

Frison, G. C., and B. Bradley. *Folsom Tools and Technology at the Hanson Site, Wyoming.* Albuquerque: University of New Mexico Press, 1980.

Haynes, C. V. "Clovis-Folsom Geochronology and Climatic Change." In *From Kostenki to Clovis: Upper Paleolithic-Paleo-Indian Adaptations*, edited by O. Soffer and N. D. Praslov. New York: Plenum Press, 1993.

Taylor, R. E., C. V. Haynes, and M. Stuiver. "Clovis and Folsom Age Estimates: Stratigraphic Context and Radiocarbon Calibration." *Antiquity* 70 (1996): 515-525.

SEE ALSO: Archaic North American culture; Clovis technological complex; Paleo-Indians in North America.
—*Kenneth B. Tankersley*

FORTUNATUS, VENANTIUS

ALSO KNOWN AS: Venantius Honorius Clementianus Fortunatus
BORN: c. 530-540 C.E.; near Treviso, Italy
DIED: c. 600 C.E.; Poitiers, France
RELATED CIVILIZATIONS: Merovingian Gaul, Rome
MAJOR ROLE/POSITION: Poet, bishop

Life. After completing his studies at Ravenna, Venantius Fortunatus (veh-NAHN-shee-uhs fuhr-chew-NAY-tuhs) left Italy for Merovingian Gaul (c. 565 C.E.). There Fortunatus frequented the royal courts in northern Gaul and wrote poetry for kings and politically prominent bishops. In 567 C.E., Fortunatus arrived in Poitiers, where he was to spend the rest of his life. He soon acquired the patronage of such local luminaries as Saint Radegunda, for whom he wrote the famous hymns *Vexilla regis* and *Pange lingua* among many other works, and Gregory of Tours, who encouraged him to publish his poetry. Although Fortunatus continued to write poetry for royal patrons on occasion, religious figures such as Radegunda and Gregory were his primary patrons. Fortunatus's ordination as a priest by 576 C.E. emphasizes the ecclesiastical focus of his career, which culminated in his consecration as bishop of Poitiers in the 590's C.E.

Influence. Fortunatus is best known as a prolific author of verse and saints' lives. In his own day, both Gallo-Romans and Franks regarded Fortunatus as the most accomplished writer in Gaul. Fortunatus's ornate poetic style is no longer widely admired, but his works remain important not only for their historical value but also because they represent a transitional stage in Latin literature from the classical to the medieval.

ADDITIONAL RESOURCES

George, Judith. *Venantius Fortunatus: A Latin Poet in Merovingian Gaul.* Oxford, England: Clarendon Press, 1992.

_____. *Venantius Fortunatus: Personal and Political Poems.* Liverpool, England: Liverpool University Press, 1995.

SEE ALSO: Christianity; Gauls; Languages and literature; Merovingian Dynasty; Radegunda, Saint.
—*Martha G. Jenks*

FOUR EMPERORS, YEAR OF THE

DATE: June, 68-July, 69 C.E.
LOCALE: Rome
RELATED CIVILIZATION: Imperial Rome
SIGNIFICANCE: The lack of a legal or constitutional means of succession proved to be one of the great weaknesses of the Roman Empire.

Background. The incompetence of the Roman emperor Nero helped produce rebellions in Gaul, Africa, and Judaea. In Rome, the Praetorian Guard abandoned Nero as the senate proclaimed him an enemy of the state. On June 9, 68 C.E., Nero committed suicide, setting into motion a bloody contest to succeed the last emperor of the Julio-Claudian line.

Action. The first of the contenders was Servius Sulpicus Galba, a respected patrician and governor of the province Hispania Tarraconensis. His troops proclaimed him "legate of the senate and Roman people" when he allied himself with the rebellion in Gaul as well as with Marcus Salvius Otho, the governor of Lusitania. Though this revolt failed, Galba was proclaimed Nero's successor by the praetorians as well as by the senate, which saw an opportunity to regain its traditional power. Unfortunately, Galba offended many by imitating the abuses of Nero. He had opponents executed and angered the Praetorian Guard by refusing to pay for their protection.

In the end, already weakened by a new rebellion in Upper Germany, Galba alienated Otho when he announced another man as his successor. Otho conspired with the praetorians against Galba and had the emperor murdered on January 15, 69 C.E. All was for naught, however, because by this time another would-be emperor had emerged among the legions of the Rhine. Though heavily outnumbered, the general Aulus Vitellius moved against Otho, whose efforts to defend Italy and the capital were hampered by his own profligate lifestyle and the tyranny of the Praetorian Guard. After being defeated at the Battle of Bedriacum on April 16, Otho killed himself.

Because of the disorganized nature of his campaign, Vitellius did not reach the capital until July. Once there, he arranged for the senate to proclaim him consul for life, and he replaced the Praetorian Guard with sixteen cohorts drawn from his own German legions. In that same month, however, Titus Flavius Vespasianus (Vespasian) was proclaimed emperor by his allies in the East. The son of a tax collector, Vespasian had worked his way up in politics as well as in the military, including participation in the invasion of Britain in 43 C.E. By 66 C.E., Nero had assigned him to suppress the revolt in Judaea, which he had successfully accomplished by 68 C.E. It was then that he turned his attention to the drama unfolding in the West. At first he supported Galba, Otho, and then Vitellius. However, in the spring of 69 C.E. while Vitellius attempted to organize his reign, Vespasian and his Eastern allies began to plot an overthrow. On July 1, Vespasian was proclaimed emperor, and on December 20, his supporters gained control of the capital. Vitellius was dragged through the streets, brutally tortured, and killed. With the support of an overwhelming number of troops and with Egypt's grain under his control, Vespasian became the undisputed successor to the imperial throne.

Consequences. The Flavian Dynasty begun by Vespasian further strengthened the Roman Empire. However, the events of this tumultuous year illustrate Rome's inability to establish a consistent means of succession as well as the obvious domination of military power in the process of choosing new emperors. Such important weaknesses would be crucial factors in the eventual collapse of the empire.

ADDITIONAL RESOURCES

Levick, B. M. *Vespasian.* New York: Routledge, 1999.
Wellesley, K. *The Long Year:* A.D. *69.* 2d ed. Bristol, England: Bristol Classical Press, 1989.

SEE ALSO: Africa, North; Gauls; Judaism; Nero; Rome, Imperial; Vespasian.

—Kenneth R. Calvert

FOUR HUNDRED

DATE: spring-summer, 411 B.C.E.
LOCALE: Athens, Greece
RELATED CIVILIZATION: Classical Greece
SIGNIFICANCE: The Four Hundred briefly replaced Athenian democracy with an oligarchy and weakened Athens' ability to fight the Peloponnesian War (431-404 B.C.E.).

Background. A failed Sicilian expedition (415-413 B.C.E.) left Athens militarily weak and financially desperate.

Action. The revolution began in the Athenian fleet at Samos when Alcibiades of Athens promised to win Persian support for Athens if he was recalled from exile and limits were imposed on the democracy. After fruitless negotiations with the Persian satrap Tissaphernes, the oligarchical leaders broke with Alcibiades and carried through a *coup d'état* at Athens, putting power in the hands of a handpicked Council of Four Hundred. Their promise to share power with an assembly of Five Thousand (citizens with full rights) was not kept.

Diplomatic missions to Sparta produced no peace

agreement but inspired rumors of a plot to betray the harbor of Piraeus. Civil war seemed possible. Under pressure, the Four Hundred agreed to enroll the Five Thousand. After a naval defeat off Euboea, the Four Hundred fell; some leaders fled or were executed. The Five Thousand, led by moderates, soon gave way to full democracy.

Consequences. Bitter memories of 411 B.C.E. continued to divide Athens. After Athens' defeat, former members of the Four Hundred participated in the Thirty Tyrants.

ADDITIONAL RESOURCES
Kagan, Donald. *The Fall of the Athenian Empire.* Ithaca, N.Y.: Cornell University Press, 1987.
Sealey, Raphael. *A History of the Greek City States.* Berkeley: University of California Press, 1976.
Stockton, David. *The Classical Athenian Democracy.* New York: Oxford University Press, 1990.

SEE ALSO: Alcibiades of Athens; Greece, Classical; Peloponnesian War; Thirty Tyrants.

—*George E. Pesely*

FRANCE

DATE: 8000 B.C.E.-700 C.E.
LOCALE: Present-day France
RELATED CIVILIZATIONS: Celts (Gaul), Franks
SIGNIFICANCE: France, which possesses some of the world's earliest archaeological sites, had experienced considerable economic and cultural development by the early Middle Ages.

France, derived from the Late Latin *Francia,* is named for the Franks who were members of a Germanic tribe, especially the Salian Franks who conquered Gaul about 500 C.E. In antiquity, the region consisted of the territory south and west of the Rhine, west of the Alps, and north of the Pyrenees, and included present-day Belgium.

History. Traces of prehistoric humans go back as far as one million years or more in the territory of modern France. The Mesolithic, or Middle Stone Age, period began about 10,000 B.C.E. and extended to about 7500 B.C.E. During this period, a warming of temperatures encouraged the development of forested regions. Animals such as the reindeer and the seal tended to migrate or disappear. The people lived from hunting wild boar and oxen and from gathering fruit. Tanning made its appearance as well as pottery and basket weaving.

The Neolithic, or Recent Stone Age, extends from about 6500 B.C.E. to about 2000 B.C.E. and is characterized by a movement away from hunting and gathering to a more sedentary life. The growing of grains and the raising of animals began and villages were established. The art of polishing stones developed. The oldest known inhabitants of the territory of France were the Iberians, who came north from the peninsula of Spain

about the year 2000 B.C.E. The later Stone Age was influenced by two different cultural groups. The first came from the area of the Danube and was primarily felt in the eastern part of the Paris Basin. The second was Mediterranean and established itself more in the southeast. Paradoxically, although people in this period exhibited a tendency to be attached to the land, there was also considerable migration. Coastland areas began to experience significant growth in population. About 2000 B.C.E., the area of the Massif Armorican became one of the main areas for the erection of megaliths in what is now France. The end of the Neolithic period is marked by the introduction of the use of metals.

The Bronze Age in Western Europe began about 2000 B.C.E. and lasted until about 850 B.C.E. Some scholars argue that bronze was introduced into France slowly, and by the time that bronze objects appeared in some quantity, it was already the age of iron. What seems certain is that these periods overlap to some extent. The periods also differ from region to region. In any event, this was the period of the birth of metallurgy in the territory of France. It is also the era of the empire of the Ligurians, who had come from northern Italy (around Genoa) and established themselves in much of Western Europe.

The Iron Age extends from about 900 or 800 B.C.E. until about 50 B.C.E. and the era of Augustus. The Celts drove out the Ligurians in about 800 B.C.E. The first part of this period, until about 500 B.C.E, is sometimes referred to as the Hallstatt period from the name of an archaeological site in the Austrian Alps. The second Iron Age is referred to as La Tène period, named for a site on the extreme north end of Neuchâtel Lake in Switzerland. The use of iron expanded quickly because deposits of ore are numerous in Europe and were often easy to extract. A large selection of tools and weapons made of iron (and bronze) has been found in more than two thousand graves at the Hallstatt site. One particularly characteristic iron weapon was a sword with a tapered blade.

The Celts, who were the inhabitants of the territory when it was first referred to as Gaul, were invaders who had come from central Europe about 1000 B.C.E. They did not constitute one nation but were made up of some sixty different groups, dominated by the wealthier among them who owned land and flocks. One of these

Clovis, the young Frankish king, is baptized as a Christian. (North Wind Picture Archives)

tribes was named the Parisii, who gave their name to the capital, Paris (later called *Lutèce* under Roman domination). In the sixth century B.C.E., Greek merchants founded the city of Marseille, and the region was opened to influences of the Greek civilization.

After some two or three centuries of friction between the Gauls and the Romans, the latter settled in the southern part of Gaul in the second century B.C.E. and created a province that had Narbonne as its capital. The province extended from the Alps to the Pyrenees. Most of the rest of Gaul remained independent until the military campaign lead by Julius Caesar from 58 to 51 B.C.E. The defeat of the Gauls' chief, Vercingetorix, in the year 52 B.C.E. at Alesia marked the end of the resistance of the Gauls and the integration of Gaul into the Roman Empire. The Romans, who were adept builders of roads, monuments, and public and private buildings, spread their civilization throughout all of Gaul but most visibly in the southeast quadrant of the "hexagon." For about five centuries, this region developed significantly along the model of the influence of Rome. Excellent examples of Roman influence are found in cities such as Orange, Aries, and Nimes. Temples, theaters, public baths, triumphal arches, arenas, and aqueducts are characteristic of this region, as they were in typical Roman cities and villages.

In 406 C.E., the Vandals, who themselves were being pushed by the Huns from Eastern Europe, invaded Gaul from across the Rhine. Among them were the Visigoths who settled in southwestern Gaul and the Burgundians who settled in the area of Savoy and latter marched north into the area of Besançon. Meanwhile, two branches of Frankish tribes—the Ripuarians and the Salians—were settling in the northeast and in the area of Flanders, respectively. Although the Visigoths in the southwest seemed to be the most powerful of the groups, the bishops of Gaul withheld their support from them because of their acceptance of Arian beliefs, heretical according to the Christian Church, and the episcopal support was given to the Salian Franks in the north after their leader, Clovis, accepted Christianity.

Attila, king of the Huns, continued his expansion westward from the area of the Caspian Sea and led his armies of Huns, Alani, and Germans into Gaul in 451 C.E. They advanced through Metz as far as Orléans, but the Visigoths joined the Gallo-Romans to oppose Attila. Genevieve, the patroness of Paris, supposedly played a prayerful role in preventing Attila from capturing the city before he led his retreating armies back to the area of the Rhine.

The middle of the fifth century C.E. saw the rule of the first of the Frankish kings, and in 481 C.E., Clovis, a member of the Merovingian Dynasty, came to power. He was only fifteen years old when he succeeded his father, Childeric I, and only five years later (486 C.E.) he won a victory over Syagrius at Soissons, the last bastion of Roman authority in Gaul. In 493 C.E., Clovis married Clotilda, a Burgundian princess who had converted to Christianity. After his victory over the Allemanni at Tolbiac, Clovis had himself baptized a Christian. The king of the Visigoths, Alaric II, was defeated and killed by the soldiers of Clovis in a battle in 507 C.E. at Vouillé near Poitiers.

Clovis was probably the most influential of the Merovingian kings. He was clever and scheming and able to extend his authority, by force of arms or by assassination, over areas neighboring his own. Clovis was also able to get the support of the bishops who, in the disarray of the collapse of the Roman Empire, were able to exert considerable influence. Although Clovis had embraced Christianity, his cruelty was legendary, as illustrated by the famous incident of revenge for the "vase of Soissons." At the death of Clovis in 511 C.E., the realm was divided between his four sons, Thierry, Clodomir, Childebert, and Chlotar I. Sons, grandsons, and nephews of Clovis struggled, plotted, and murdered one another until Dagobert I became king in 629 C.E.

Dagobert was successful in uniting most of the Frankish kingdoms. It is said that he reconstituted the unity of the Regnum Francorum (Frankish kingdom) for the second time since the death of Clovis. The assistance that Dagobert gave to the monastery of Saint Denis near Paris helped make it one of the most influential religious centers of the Middle Ages in France. Dagobert's death in 639 C.E. led to a succession of weak

Frankish kings, until Charles Martel defeated the Saracens at Poitiers in 732 C.E. The grandson of Charles Martel became Charlemagne.

Agriculture. As early as 4000 B.C.E., farming appeared along the coast of the Mediterranean and spread northward through the Rhone Valley to the forested areas of central France and westward to Brittany. The invention of improved tools contributed to deforestation for the sake of agriculture. Fire was also used to remove forests. Traces of grains have been found in the Dordogne, and wheat and barley were cultivated in Roussilon. The cave of Murée de Montpezat (Basses-Alpes) has yielded certain legumes and even a variety of peas.

Settlements. Prehistoric humans had taken shelter in caves and under the protection of large rocks. In regions where there were no natural shelters, tentlike structures were built in the open air with bones of mammoths serving as framing, and skins and twigs as coverings. As the population became more sedentary, shelters became more permanent. In the Danubian cultures, huts became rectangular and showed a more regular framework. Each house had a hearth where fire could be used but controlled.

Navigation and transportation. Some of the slow-flowing rivers of northern France, such as the Seine, the Saône, and the Somme, were probably used for transportation. In the south, the Garonne and certainly the Rhone were much less navigable. On land, horses were used to pull two-wheeled carts and chariots. During the era of the Romans, the high-quality and long-lasting roads, especially in the southeast, aided land transportation.

Economics. Manufacturing and transportation became more important as certain techniques were developed. As people became more familiar with alloys used in tools for deforestation and as raw materials were needed to make these alloys, small industries began to develop.

Government and law. When Gaul came under Roman rule, the area was divided into provinces, each ruled by a Roman governor. The barbarians, especially the Visigoths, opposed the leadership of Rome. Clovis, however, was able to establish the first widespread unity in the country, referred to as the Regnum Francorum.

Religion and ritual. Gallic society was greatly dominated by the Druids, who were the priests of the Gauls. The Druids met in the forests, especially that of the Carnutes (Chartres), and believed in several gods.

They attached mysterious powers to certain plants. The judicial powers of the Druids gave them a political and social as well as a religious influence. In some areas, for example in the southeast at Mount Bego (north of Nice), engravings of horned bulls suggest that this animal was the object of religious cults.

Death and burial. As early as 4500 B.C.E., Stone Age people were erecting funeral monuments under gigantic mounds with huge vertical markers (menhirs and stelae) and horizontal stones (dolmens). The best known of these monuments are those of Carnac, which possesses the most dense concentration of megaliths in all the world. Some of these stones are the size of large trucks, and the techniques used to elevate these megaliths remain speculative.

More common in other areas of France were burials in mounds (tumuli) and in caves. The burial mounds of Haguenau (Bas-Rhin) show a strong aristocratic influence. In the oldest graves of the Bronze Age, one person was buried alone. In later periods, collective graves of women and children are found; usually three or four, but sometimes up to eight people were placed together. Some burial sites in the urnfields (les Champs d'Urnes) show the dead person's place in society because of the quality and quantity of objects placed with the body.

War and weapons. The need for additional lands and the desire to control deposits of minerals necessary for the making of tools and weapons led to attacks on communities by neighboring peoples. Increasing demographics meant that more land was disputed, and archaeologists have found skeletons with arrows. The warrior became an important individual in society, and many different kinds of swords, daggers, and various metal weapons have been found in burial sites.

Women's life. In prehistoric France during the hunter-gatherer era, it is quite probable that the woman guarded the dwelling place and looked after the children while the male was absent. The woman's role as caregiver is also suggested by the bodies of women and children that have been buried together. During the Bronze Age, women wore the jewelry that has been found in tombs, usually necklaces, bracelets, leg bands, and hairpins.

Writing systems. Images and picture writing are found in much prehistoric art. Stick animals and people are engraved in polished stones of the southeast of France. Some figures, such as crosses and swastikas, are also found. In the Roman era, inscriptions on coins and pottery are good examples of the writing of the times.

ADDITIONAL RESOURCES

Haine, W. Scott. *The History of France*. Westport, Conn.: Greenwood Press, 2000.

Kuhn, Herbert. *The Rock Pictures of Europe*. Translated from the German by Alan H. Brodrick. Fair Law, N.J.: Essential Books, 1956.

Milisauskas, Sarunas. *European Prehistory*. New York: Academic Press, 1979.

Wertime, Theodore A., and James D. Muhly, eds. *The Coming of the Age of Iron*. New Haven, Conn.: Yale University Press, 1980.

SEE ALSO: Alani; Alaric II; Alesia, Battle of; Arianism; Attila; Caesar, Julius; Celts; Chlotar I; Christianity; Clovis; Franks; Gauls; Goths; Halstatt culture; Huns; La Tène; Rome, Imperial; Rome, Republican; Vandals; Vercingetorix.

—*John P. Doohen*

FRANKS

DATE: c. 400-700 C.E.

LOCALE: Northern Europe, modern France, Belgium, and the Rhineland

SIGNIFICANCE: The Franks conquered Gaul and established the earliest version of what would become France.

Originally a collection of small, Germanic tribes living just north and east of the lower Rhine in what later became the Netherlands and the northwestern part of Germany, the Franks were composed of several subgroups, traditionally the Chamavi, Bructeri, Chattuari, Salyii, Amsivarii, and Tubantes, although the fluid nature of early Germanic tribal affiliations makes such subdivision problematical. The term "Frank," which apparently meant "fierce" and later "free," first begins to appear in Roman sources in the mid-third century C.E., in reference to the peoples menacing the Roman Empire's

The Franks invade Gaul. (North Wind Picture Archives)

borders. By 306 C.E., Constantine the Great had sub-dued them, and Frankish personages show up routinely in Roman military service throughout the fourth century C.E., often in quite high positions. In the late 350's C.E., the emperor Julian settled the Salian Franks just south and west of the mouths of the Rhine in Toxandria, modern Belgium, as allies of the empire.

With the slow dissolution of Roman power in Gaul during the fifth century C.E., the Franks moved to fill the vacuum with their first powerful king, Childeric I (r. 456-481 C.E.), who may have cooperated with the remnants of Roman rule in the north as represented by Count Aegidius of Soissons (d. 463 C.E.). It was Childeric's son, Clovis (r. 481-511 C.E.), who projected Frankish presence throughout Gaul.

Beginning a career of conquest and consolidation, Clovis took Soissons in 486 C.E. and eliminated the last vestige of Roman rule by executing Aegidius's son, Syagrius. He then defeated the Thuringians circa 491 C.E., thereby securing his northern border, and inter-vened in Burgundian affairs by forcing King Gundobad (r. 474-516 C.E.) to pay tribute. The highwater mark of

Frankish power under Clovis came in 507 C.E., when he defeated the Visigoths at Vouillé outside Poitiers, killed their king himself, and took over southern Gaul. In the subsequent two years, he disposed of rival Frankish kings, particularly at the important northern centers of Cambrai and Cologne.

The Franks became the preeminent people in the West, a fact attested by the Byzantine emperor's grant-ing of the title of consul to Clovis in the aftermath of Vouillé, and the pope's bestowing of the pallium, the sa-cred vestment exclusive to the pontiff until this time, on Caesarius of Arles (470-543 C.E.), a new Frankish ally in southern Gaul.

Although the Frankish kingdom was partitioned upon Clovis's death, his sons finalized the conquest of Burgundy in 534 C.E., and the kingdom was reunited under the surviving son, Chlotar I (r. 511-561 C.E.), in 558 C.E. Although this realm of "Francia" would co-alesce and fragment repeatedly during succeeding years and would eventually devolve into four compo-nent parts—Austrasia (east of the Rhine), Neustria (north and central Gaul), Burgundy (southeastern

Gaul), and Aquitaine (southwestern Gaul)—by 700 C.E., the Franks were recognized as an enduring force in the barbarian West.

ADDITIONAL RESOURCES
Bachrach, Bernard S., trans. *Liber Historiae Francorum.* Lawrence, Kans.: Coronado, 1973.
James, Edward. *The Franks.* Oxford, England: Basil Blackwell, 1991.

Thorpe, Lewis, trans. *Gregory of Tours: The History of the Franks.* Harmondsworth, England: Penguin, 1982.

SEE ALSO: Byzantine Empire; Chlotar I; Clovis; Constantine the Great; France; Gauls; Goths; Merovingian Dynasty; Rome, Imperial.

—Burnam W. Reynolds

FREMONT CULTURE

DATE: c. 400-700 C.E.
LOCALE: Eastern Great Basin and western Colorado plateau
RELATED CIVILIZATIONS: Great Basin peoples, Southwest peoples
SIGNIFICANCE: A village-farming pattern only peripherally related to Southwestern pueblo culture, which appeared in the midst of the foraging traditions of the Great Basin and then disappeared for unknown reasons.

Around 400 C.E., the foraging tradition (Desert Archaic) of the Great Basin was temporarily replaced by a relatively sedentary population that lived in scattered villages and farms. Labeled Fremont culture, these people built stone dwellings and granaries, practiced horticulture, and developed a unique artistic style that was manifested in their rock art and anthropomorphic figurines. Authorities debate whether the culture was a diffusion and adaptation of Southwestern culture or the intrusion of a new population.

Characteristic cultural elements included hide moccasins, one-rod-and-bundle basketry, anthropomorphic figurines, incised stone tablets, and a unique trough-and-shelf metate. Five geographic variants existed. The Parowan, Sevier, and San Rafael were all located near arable land and reliable water sources (rivers or marshes) in south and central Utah. They relied on horticulture, particularly maize, supplemented with hunting and gathering. The northern Great Salt Lake and Uinta variants both appear to have been only seasonal hunting-gathering camps because of poor (salty) soil or short growing seasons. Sites within the Escalante River drainage shared the area with the culturally distinct Kayenta Anasazi.

After 700 C.E. During the mid-1300's, the Fremont culture disappeared, possibly displaced by incoming Numic-speaking people or forced out of the area—or the horticultural tradition—by climatic changes.

ADDITIONAL RESOURCES
Marwitt, John P. "Fremont Cultures." In *Handbook of North American Indians.* Vol 11. Washington, D.C.: Smithsonian Institution Press, 1986.
Noble, David Grant. *Ancient Ruins of the Southwest.* Flagstaff, Ariz.: Northland, 2000.

SEE ALSO: Anasazi; Cochise culture; Southwest peoples.

—Sondra Jones

FRONTINUS, SEXTUS JULIUS

BORN: c. 35 C.E.; place unknown
DIED: c. 103 C.E.; place unknown
RELATED CIVILIZATION: Imperial Rome
MAJOR ROLE/POSITION: Senator, soldier, supervisor of aqueducts

Life. Sextus Julius Frontinus's (frahn-TI-nuhs) birthplace is unknown, though southern Gaul is often mentioned. After serving as urban praetor in 70 C.E., he helped crush the revolt of Gaius Julius Civilis. After a consulship in 72 or 73 C.E., he succeeded Gnaeus Julius

Agricola, Tacitus's father-in-law, as governor of Britain. Frontinus was proconsul of Asia in 86 C.E. and held second and third consulships in 98 and 100 C.E. with Trajan. In 97 C.E., Marcus Cocceius Nerva appointed him *curator aquarum* (superintendent of aqueducts), and it is his account of that service that has brought him the most acclaim. The words of his *De aquis urbis Romae* (n.d.; *Aqueducts*, 1925) reveal a high-level civil servant and military expert operating at his technical and rhetorical best. They show him to be a clear and direct thinker. His work on the art of war is lost, but a handbook of military procedure, *Strategemata* (n.d.; *Strategems*, 1925), survives. He is thought to have written several books on land surveying, parts of which remain in the *Corpus Agrimensorum* (n.d.). Frontinus was esteemed by his contemporaries. Pliny the Younger described him as one of the two most distinguished men of his time. The poet Martial called him a friend, and historian Tacitus referred to him as a great man.

Influence. The waterworks of modern Rome are Frontinus's legacy, for the rediscovery of his treatise by Poggio Bracciolini in 1429 instructed the Renaissance popes about refurbishing the aqueducts.

ADDITIONAL RESOURCE

Evans, Harry B. *Water Distribution in Ancient Rome: The Evidence of Frontinus.* Ann Arbor: University of Michigan Press, 1994.

SEE ALSO: Agricola, Gnaeus Julius; Martial; Pliny the Younger; Rome, Imperial; Science and technology; Tacitus; Trajan.

—*Michele Valerie Ronnick*

FRONTO, MARCUS CORNELIUS

BORN: c. 100 C.E.; Cirta, Numidia (later Constantine, Algeria)
DIED: c. 166 C.E.; possibly Rome
RELATED CIVILIZATION: Imperial Rome
MAJOR ROLE/POSITION: Orator, rhetorician, tutor

Life. After completing his education in Rome, Marcus Cornelius Fronto (FRAHN-toh) became a leading orator and civil servant under Hadrian. Although he is famous for his speeches, only fragments of them have survived, and for centuries he was praised on the basis of sparse evidence. In 138 C.E., he was chosen by Antoninus Pius to tutor princes Lucius Verus and Marcus Aurelius in Latin and oratory. In 1815, his letters to and from his pupils, their parents, and certain friends were found in Rome, and they form the basis of the modern study of Fronto. Filled with details of contemporary life, they demonstrate Fronto's own distinctive tastes and antipathies in literature. Ancient locutions attracted him, and he preferred older authors such as Plautus, Quintus Ennius, Gnaeus Naevius, and Cato the Censor. Although the letters are often overly affectionate, they point to Fronto's interest in making his charges men of action and his distaste for Marcus's preoccupation with Stoicism.

Influence. In Fronto is preserved a window into the Antonine period. His philological interests have also preserved valuable evidence from earlier authors.

ADDITIONAL RESOURCES

Champlin, Edward. *Fronto and Antonine Rome.* Cambridge, Mass.: Harvard University Press, 1980.
Ronnick, Michele Valerie. "Substructural Elements of Architectonic Rhetoric and Philosophical Thought in Fronto's Letters." In *Roman Eloquence*, edited by William J. Dominik. New York: Routledge, 1997.
Van den Hout, Michel P. J. *A Commentary on the Letters of M. Cornelius Fronto.* Boston: E. J. Brill, 1999.

SEE ALSO: Antoninus Pius; Cato the Censor; Ennius, Quintus; Marcus Aurelius; Naevius, Gnaeus; Plautus; Rome, Imperial.

—*Michele Valerie Ronnick*

FRUMENTIUS, SAINT

ALSO KNOWN AS: Abba Salama ("Father of Peace");
   Abuna ("Our Father")
BORN: fourth century C.E.; Tyre, Phoenicia
DIED: fourth century C.E.; Axum
RELATED CIVILIZATIONS: Axum/Abyssinia, Arabia
MAJOR ROLE/POSITION: Religious figure

Life. Saint Frumentius (frew-MEHN-shee-uhs) was
a Syrian student en route to India with his master when
pirates hijacked their ship. He and his brother were
brought as slaves to the court of the queen regent of
Axum, the founding state of Ethiopia. The two brothers
became court administrators and tutors for Prince
Ezana, to whom they introduced Christianity. As administrators, they supported Christian merchants and
increased trade with Greece and Rome, thus identifying
economic prosperity with the new faith.

When Ezana came to the throne, tradition says that
Frumentius went to Alexandria to plea for a bishop for
Axum, but the patriarch Saint Athanasius of Alexandria
instead ordained Frumentius himself around 333 C.E.
By dint of forceful preaching and pastoral care, Fru-
mentius succeeded in converting the country to ortho-
dox Christianity. His credentials were challenged in
356 C.E. by Emperor Constantius II, who was pro-
Arian, an indication of the importance of the young
Ethiopian Church. The Ethiopians remained faithful to
Athanasius and orthodoxy, however.

Influence. Frumentius introduced Christianity to
Ethiopia, Africa's only historically Christian nation,
and cemented its ties with Egypt and the West. He is
recognized as a saint by both the Ethiopian and Catholic Churches. His feast day is October 27.

ADDITIONAL RESOURCES
Baur, John. *Two Thousand Years of Christianity in Af-
rica.* Nairobi, Kenya: Paulines, 1998.
Brown, C. F. *The Conversion Experience in Axum Dur-
ing the Fourth and Fifth Centuries.* Washington,
D.C.: Howard University Press, 1973.

SEE ALSO: Africa, East and South; Athanasius of Alexander, Saint; Axum; Christianity; Constantius I-III;
Ethiopia; Ezana.

—Norbert Brockman

FU HAO'S TOMB

DATE: c. 1200 B.C.E.
LOCALE: Anyang, the last capital city of the Shang
   Dynasty
RELATED CIVILIZATIONS: Shang Dynasty, China
SIGNIFICANCE: The tomb provides a clearer insight as
   to royal burials during the Shang Dynasty.

Fu Hao (FEW HAH-oh) was one of the sixty-four consorts of King Wu Ding, the twelfth ruler of the Shang
Dynasty (1600-1066 B.C.E.). Her tomb, excavated in
1976, is the only royal tomb that has been discovered
intact and the only Anyang burial whose occupant can
be confidently identified. More than a hundred bronzes
bear the name of Fu Hao.

The relatively modest tomb consists of a shaft 13
feet (4 meters) by 18.4 feet (5.6 meters) at the mouth
and 24.6 feet (7.5 meters) deep. Other Shang tombs excavated in the same area also had four access ramps,
usually two short and two long, in the shape of a cross,
but these tombs were looted and therefore hold few
clues for archaeologists. Fu Hao's tomb contained
more than sixteen hundred objects, including the largest assemblage of jade ever unearthed. Other items include carved marble, carved bone, ivory cups inlaid
with turquoise, seven thousand cowry shells, and
eleven pieces of pottery. Among them are some of the
best art objects of the Shang Dynasty.

The Shang Dynasty practiced human sacrifice. In Fu
Hao's tomb, sixteen human skeletons and the skeleton
of a dog were found arranged in various locations.

ADDITIONAL RESOURCES
Chang, K. C., ed. *Studies of Shang Archaeology.* New
Haven, Conn.: Yale University Press, 1986.

Loewe, Michael, and Edward L. Shaughnessy, eds. *The Cambridge History of Ancient China from the Origins of Civilization to 221* B.C.E. Cambridge, England: Cambridge University Press, 1999.

SEE ALSO: China; Shang Dynasty.

—*Juliana Y. Yuan*

FULGENTIUS, FABIUS PLANCIADES

ALSO KNOWN AS: Fabius Furius Planciades Fulgentius; Fulgentius the Mythographer
FLOURISHED: late fifth and early sixth century C.E.; probably North Africa
RELATED CIVILIZATIONS: Imperial Rome, North Africa
MAJOR ROLE/POSITION: Grammarian

Life. Nothing is known of the life of Fabius Planciades Fulgentius (FAY-bee-uhs plahn-KEE-ah-deez fuhl-JEHN-shee-uhs). His era and native country are inferred from his writings. His mediocre Latin diction and his broad knowledge of Greek language and culture were typical of educated North Africans under the Vandals. At least three and perhaps four or five of his works survive. Medieval manuscripts attribute *Mythologiae* (n.d.; *Mythologies*, 1971), *Expositio continentiae Virgilianae secundum philosophos moralis* (n.d.; *Explanation of the Content of Vergil According to Moral Philosophy*, 1971), and *Espositio sermonum antiquorum* (n.d.; *Explanation of Obsolete Words*, 1971) specifically to Fabius Planciades Fulgentius; however, they attribute *De aetatibus mundi et hominis* (n.d.; *On the Ages of the World and of Humankind*, 1971) to Fabius Claudius Gordianus Fulgentius and *Super Thebaiden* (n.d.; *On the Thebaid*, 1971) to Sanctus Fulgentius Episcopus. Scholars debate whether these works were written by one Fulgentius, or two, or three. The author of *Mythologies* was certainly a North African Christian, but whether he was also Saint Fulgentius, bishop of Ruspe, Tunisia, in the sixth century, remains in dispute.

Influence. Fulgentius was continually popular from his own time through the Renaissance but neglected thereafter. His appeal stemmed from his subject matter, his sense of humor, and his erudition.

ADDITIONAL RESOURCE
Whitbread, Leslie George. *Fulgentius the Mythographer*. Columbus: Ohio State University Press, 1971.

SEE ALSO: Africa, North; Languages and literature; Rome, Imperial; Vandals.

—*Eric v.d. Luft*

FULVIA

BORN: c. 85/80 B.C.E.; place unknown
DIED: 40 B.C.E.; Sicyon, Greece
RELATED CIVILIZATION: Republican Rome
MAJOR ROLE/POSITION: Political leader

Life. Fulvia (FUHL-vee-ah) hailed from a conservative Optimate family, but became a leader of the Populares upon marriage to the radical politician Publius Clodius Pulcher in 62 B.C.E. Upon his murder ten years later, Fulvia assumed full leadership when she dragged her husband's bloody body into the street, thus inciting a riot that ended in the destruction of the senate house. She married Gaius Scribonius Curio the next year, and he, while tribune in 50 B.C.E., followed her tactics to such a degree that civil war between Julius Caesar and Pompey the Great became inevitable. Upon Curio's death in 48 B.C.E., Fulvia then married Marc Antony. Through her, Antony also became a political force with whom Caesar was forced to reckon. After Caesar's death in 44 B.C.E. and Antony's defeat at Mutina in 43 B.C.E., Fulvia managed to save her husband from outlawry by the senate, and by 41 B.C.E., she effectively ruled Rome alongside Antony and Octavian.

By the end of 41 B.C.E., she was engaged in a war (the Perusine War) with Octavian. As the first Roman woman to command an army in battle, she nearly succeeded in toppling Octavian, and would have done so if Antony had only attacked Italy as she had planned. Even after the fall of Perusia, she nearly succeeded by allying with Sextus Pompeius Magnus and Gnaeus Domitius Ahenobarbus, but, yet again, the effort collapsed when Antony abandoned her for Cleopatra VII. Heartbroken, she took ill in Athens, and by the end of the year, she was dead.

Influence. Fulvia was the driving force behind the events that led to the collapse of the Roman Republic and, hence, was responsible for the institution of Octavian Augustus as the first Roman emperor.

ADDITIONAL RESOURCES

Arkenberg, Jerome S. "Licinii Murenae, Terentii Varrones, and Varrones Murenae: A Prosopographical Study of Three Roman Families." *Historia* 42, no. 3 (1993): 326-351.

Bauman, R. A. *Women and Politics in Ancient Rome.* London: Routledge, 1992.

Welch, Kathryn E. "Antony, Fulvia, and the Ghost of Clodius in 47 B.C." *Greece and Rome* 42, no. 2 (1995): 182-201.

SEE ALSO: Antony, Marc; Augustus; Caesar, Julius; Cleopatra VII; Clodius Pulcher; Pompey the Great; Publius; Rome, Republican.

—Jerome S. Arkenberg

FUNAN

ALSO KNOWN AS: Kurung-bnam, "Kingdom of the Mountain"

DATE: first-sixth centuries C.E.

LOCALE: Present-day Cambodia

SIGNIFICANCE: Funan, the first great power of mainland Southeast Asia, was absorbed by Chenla, which in turn was annexed by the kingdom of Angkor into what later became the modern state of Cambodia.

The reputed founder of the state of Funan (few-NAHN; the Chinese rendering of Bnam) was Kaundinya, who sailed up the Mekong River in the first century C.E., based on a dream. When he arrived at a place near modern Phnom Penh, Liu-yeh, the queen of the country, unsuccessfully tried to seize his ship. He then married her and founded a dynasty that ruled for nearly two centuries. The Funanese were Malay peoples.

One of Kaundinya's grandsons decided to turn over the conduct of state affairs to Fan Shih-man, who built a fleet, attacked ten kingdoms, and established vassal states along the Mekong from Tonle Sap Lake to the Mekong Delta. Funan had walled cities containing palaces with engraved ornaments. By 270 C.E., Funan allied with Champa, the coastal state to the east, to attack the Chinese-controlled Tonkin state in the north, but the two attacking states later became rivals.

Funan went on to become the first great power in mainland Southeast Asia, having established many artistic traditions that persist to the present and vast irrigation works that enabled cultivation of wet rice as the kingdom expanded. Among the Funanese traditions that are typically Cambodian are the *sampot*, the piece of cloth wrapped around the waist, and the legends of the Naga princess and the sacred mountain. The canals, which extended for more than 124 miles (200 kilometers), permitted seagoing ships to pass along the Mekong to the Gulf of Siam. During its apogee, Funan occupied the territory from what is now southern Cambodia and Vietnam to most of the Malay peninsula. One of the Funan's vassal states to the north was Chenla, which occupied what is now northern Cambodia and southern Laos.

In the middle of the sixth century C.E., Bhavavarman, the king of Chenla, rebelled against its vassal status, conquered the capital of Funan, and assumed dominance in the region through constant warfare. Funan then moved the capital south, while Bhavavarman's successors continued conquests, seeking to subdue the rest of what is now known as Laos.

The two kingdoms of Chenla and Funan coexisted until 627 C.E., when King Isanavarman of Chenla annexed Funan. The kingdom of Angkor, in turn, absorbed Chenla in 802 C.E., but in 877 C.E., the ruler of Angkor chose as his queen a member of the royal line of both the Funan and Chenla kingdoms. Accordingly, Angkor, the precursor to the present state of Cambodia, may be said to have superseded both Chenla and Funan.

CENTERS OF POWER IN ANCIENT SOUTHEAST ASIA

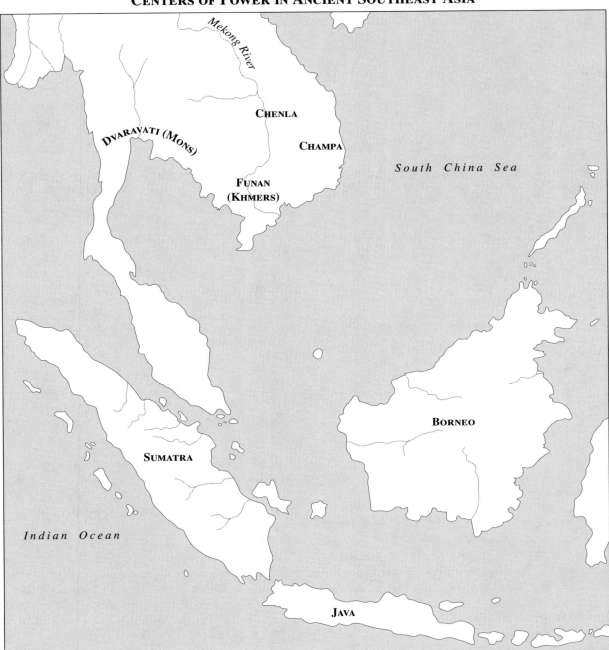

ADDITIONAL RESOURCES
Beri, K. K. *History and Culture of South-East Asia: Ancient and Medieval*. New Delhi, India: Sterling, 1994.
Briggs, Lawrence Palmer. *The Ancient Khmer Empire*. Philadelphia: American Philosophical Society, 1951.

Hall, D. G. E. *A History of South-East Asia*. 3d ed. London: Macmillan, 1968.

SEE ALSO: Laos; Malay; Vietnam.

—*Michael Haas*

— G —

GALEN

ALSO KNOWN AS: Galen of Pergamum
BORN: 129 C.E.; Pergamum, Mysia, Anatolia
DIED: c. 199 C.E.; possibly Rome or Pergamum
RELATED CIVILIZATION: Hellenistic and Roman Greece
MAJOR ROLE/POSITION: Physician

Life. The son of Nicon, a prosperous architect, Galen spent his youth at Pergamum, which featured both a great library and a temple of Asclepius (god of healing). According to tradition, when he was sixteen, his father had a dream in which Asclepius appeared and announced that Galen would become a physician. Galen traveled to Egypt and Asia Minor to study and returned to Pergamum as physician to the gladiators. In 162 C.E., he left for Rome. He returned home in 166 C.E. but was recalled by the emperor two years later. He was a self-promoter, often alluding to his high-ranking patients. With public opposition to the dissection of cadavers, Galen developed many anatomical ideas based on his dissection of animals.

Influence. With the exception of Hippocrates, Galen was the most influential physician of ancient times. His works, translated into Arabic in the ninth century, were then translated into Latin in the eleventh. Because he recognized a benevolent creator god, his works were acceptable to Church authorities. In matters of anatomy, his word was accepted without question until the Renaissance. Some plant-derived remedies are known, even today, as "galenicals" because they first appear in his medical writings.

ADDITIONAL RESOURCES
Porter, Roy. *The Greatest Benefit to Mankind: A Medical History of Humanity, from Antiquity to the Present*. New York: W. W. Norton, 1997.
Smith, Wesley D. *The Hippocratic Tradition*. Ithaca, N.Y.: Cornell University Press, 1979.

SEE ALSO: Greece, Hellenistic and Roman; Hippocrates; Science.

—*Donald R. Franceschetti*

Galen. (Library of Congress)

GALERIUS VALERIUS MAXIMIANUS, GAIUS

BORN: c. 250 C.E.; Serdica, Thrace (later Sofia, Bulgaria)

DIED: May 311 C.E.; Romulianum (later Gamzigrad, Serbia)

RELATED CIVILIZATION: Imperial Rome

MAJOR ROLE/POSITION: Military commander, Caesar, Augustus

Life. Gaius Galerius Valerius Maximianus (GAY-uhs guh-LIHR-ee-uhs vuh-LIHR-ee-uhs mak-sihm-ee-AY-nuhs) became a Caesar in the tetrarchy on March 1, 293 C.E. His father-in-law Diocletian (r. 284-305 C.E.), one of two Augusti, awarded him an appointment for demonstrated loyalty as a military commander. Galerius was Caesar to Diocletian in the East, and Constantius I was Caesar to Maximian in the West. From his residence in Sirmium (near modern Sremska Mitrovica, Yugoslavia), Caesar Galerius successfully campaigned against the Germans (293-295 C.E.) in Pannonia (modern Hungary) and the Persians (296-298 C.E.) in Syria. Around 300 C.E., numerous structures were built at Thessalonica (modern Thessaloníki, Greece), including a triumphal arch to honor his victory over the Persians, a rotunda, a palace, an octagon, and hippodrome.

Galerius encouraged Diocletian to begin persecuting Christians in 303 C.E. In 305 C.E., Diocletian and Maximian resigned, leaving the Caesars, particularly Galerius, in power. Constantius died in 306 C.E. The new Augustus was constantly challenged by rebels inside the provinces and criticized for his cruelty toward the Christians. Maximian's son Maxentius seized Rome, Italy, and part of Africa, so Galerius sent Augustus Severus (Flavius Valerius Severus) against him. Severus was defeated, then Galerius invaded Italy but was forced to retreat (307 C.E.). Galerius declared Maxentius a public enemy. Maxentius was defeated in 312 C.E. by his father, Maximian. On April 30, 311 C.E., in Nicomedia (later İzmit, Turkey), a gravely ill Galerius revoked his anti-Christian policy and issued an Edict of Toleration permitting Christians to practice their religion. A few days later, he died and was buried in Romulianum, named after his mother Romula.

Influence. Some Christians, including Lucius Caelius Firmianus Lactantius, regarded the painful illness that caused Galerius's death to be a form of divine intervention. Galerius's edict, issued shortly before his death, enabled Christianity to flourish in the Roman Empire.

ADDITIONAL RESOURCES

Lactantius. *The Minor Works.* In *The Fathers of the Church: A New Translation*, translated by Mary Francis McDonald. Washington, D.C.: Catholic University of America Press, 1965.

Pollitt, J. J. *The Art of Rome c. 753 B.C.-A.D. 337: Sources and Documents*. Cambridge, England: Cambridge University Press, 1995.

SEE ALSO: Christianity; Constantius I-III; Diocletian; Lactantius, Lucius Caelius Firmianus; Maximian; Rome, Imperial.

—*Rozmeri Basic*

GALLIC WARS

DATE: 58-50 B.C.E.

LOCALE: Gaul (modern France and the Low Countries)

RELATED CIVILIZATIONS: Republican Rome, Gaul

SIGNIFICANCE: A major imperial conquest, this war was also central to the career of Julius Caesar and thus to the fall of the Roman Republic. The resulting partition of Gaul from Germania helped form the modern nations of France and Germany.

Background. Romans had fought Celtic tribes from Gaul and northern Italy since the fourth century B.C.E.

They established provinces in Italy and in southern Gaul (modern Provence). Tensions continued, however, and Julius Caesar arranged a five-year governorship of the Roman provinces for himself and soon found an opportunity for war.

Action. In 58 B.C.E., a large group of Helvetii (from modern Switzerland) attempted a migration westward near Roman territory and fought tribes allied with the Romans. Caesar engaged and defeated them. Then, at the request of certain Gallic tribes, he engaged and defeated Ariovistus, a German chieftain who had also invaded Gaul.

Caesar spent most of 57 B.C.E. fighting Belgian tribes in northeast Gaul, while a sub-commander brought the tribes of the northeast coast to formal submission. In the following year, several of the maritime tribes revolted and were subdued only after considerable difficulty. The tribes of Aquitania (southwestern Gaul) were also beaten by Roman forces.

In 55 B.C.E., Caesar repulsed another incursion by Germans. Then he crossed the Rhine in force to terrorize the tribes on the other side. This adventure was followed by a small invasion of Britain, from which Caesar retired after declaring victory. Back in Rome, Caesar's command was extended for five years.

The next year's campaigns began with a much larger invasion of Britain. After initial difficulties, the Romans were able to obtain the surrender of several tribes. However, Caesar was forced to return to Gaul when a major uprising broke out behind him in northwest Gaul. Roman forces, in scattered encampments, were attacked and in one case annihilated. Caesar, along with his lieutenant Titus Labienus, was able to restore the situation and engage in reprisals.

In 53 B.C.E., the reprisals continued. In response to German-supported resistance, Caesar again crossed the Rhine on a terror campaign. The Germanic Sugambri nonetheless invaded and were repulsed only after threatening another Roman encampment.

The following year was marked by an uprising of most of Gaul led by Vercingetorix. After a serious repulse at the stronghold of Gergovia, Caesar cornered Vercingetorix at Alesia. There he defeated the besieged troops and a large relieving force. Some resistance continued for the next two years, most notably in central Gaul in 51 B.C.E., but Caesar and his lieutenants put them down decisively.

Virtually the only source of information is Caesar's own account. Although there is no reason to question the general outline, his veracity in detail has been a matter of considerable dispute.

Consequences. Gaul was quickly integrated into the Roman Empire, ending centuries of conflict. The wealth, glory, and military loyalty Caesar gained in Gaul enabled him to seize his dictatorship.

ADDITIONAL RESOURCES

Caesar, Julius. *The Gallic War*. Translated by Carolyn Hammond. Oxford, England: Oxford University Press, 1996.

Gelzer, Matthias. *Caesar: Politician and Statesman*. Translated by Peter Needham. Cambridge, Mass.: Harvard University Press, 1968.

Jiménez, Ramon L. *Caesar Against Rome: The Great Roman Civil War*. Westport, Conn.: Praeger, 2000.

SEE ALSO: Alesia, Battle of; Britain; Caesar, Julius; Celts; Gauls; Germany; Rome, Republican; Vercingetorix.

—*Andrew M. Riggsby*

GALLIENUS

ALSO KNOWN AS: Publius Licinius Egnatius Gallienus
BORN: c. 218 C.E.; place unknown
DIED: 268 C.E.; place unknown
RELATED CIVILIZATION: Imperial Rome
MAJOR ROLE/POSITION: Roman emperor

Life. Gallienus (gal-ee-EE-nuhs) ruled jointly with his father Valerian from 253 to 260 C.E. and then alone until 268 C.E. During his early career, Gallienus ruled the Western Roman Empire, fighting Germanic tribes along the Danube and the Rhine. After his father was taken captive by the Persians in 260 C.E., the emperor solidified his control over the central portion of the empire, consisting of Italy, North Africa, Egypt, Greece, and Eastern Europe, at the expense of leaving the Roman East to an allied client ruler, Septimius Odenaethus. The West was ostensibly held by the usurper Marcus Cassianus Latinius Postumus, who suffered no reprisals from Rome. Gallienus's inaction might have been an intentional policy that allowed stable rule for the areas under the emperor's control. The last years of Gallienus's reign were spent fighting the Goths in the Balkans until 268 C.E. when he was assassinated by his officers while besieging a renegade general in Milan.

Influence. Gallienus enacted some important administrative reforms such as the exclusion of senators from military command, while replacing them with professional equestrian officers. He also increased the use of a strategic reserve of cavalry, which heralded the large field armies of the fourth century. Reversing Valerian's anti-Christian edicts, Gallienus allowed Christians access to their cemeteries and restored the bishops to their parishes. Increased patronage of the arts, literature, and Neoplatonic philosophy during the emperor's reign indicates some evidence of a "Gallienic Renaissance."

ADDITIONAL RESOURCE
Den Blois, L. *The Policy of the Emperor Gallienus.* Leiden, Netherlands: E. J. Brill, 1976.

SEE ALSO: Christianity; Goths, Ostrogoths, Visigoths; Persia; Rome, Imperial; Valerian.

—*Byron J. Nakamura*

GANDHĀRA ART

DATE: 100 B.C.E.-700 C.E.
LOCALE: North India, northwest Pakistan, and the eastern part of Afghanistan
RELATED CIVILIZATIONS: India, Central Asia
SIGNIFICANCE: Gandhāra art may be the possible origin of the anthropomorphic image of the Buddha.

The term Gandhāra (gahn-DAH-rah) art is derived from a geographic region in Central Asia, once the crossroads of different religious and cultural influences. It was a territory ruled by Indian emperors and non-Indian dynasties with a predominantly Buddhist population and with artists who created work in the Roman style of the late first or early second century C.E.

There is strong evidence to support a controversial theory that the earliest anthropomorphic image of Buddha was executed at the same time: the late first or early second century C.E. in Gandhāra (compare the theory of Mathurā origin). This development was instigated by the contemporary Western tradition of depicting divinities in human forms, significantly foreign to the local aniconic representations. In addition to the monumental stone sculptures, the Gandhāra masters produced stone and stucco bas reliefs narrating events from the life of Buddha modeled on the Roman examples. The backgrounds of these works encompass typical non-Indian motifs such as atlases, garlands, laurel wreaths, and vine scrolls. The major figures are dressed according to locally altered Roman fashion, including garments, hairstyles, and adornments. The psychological state of mind of these characters is conveyed by insisting on their physical dynamism and vivid facial expressions. The scenes of starvation, temptation, or death were especially popular. The earliest iconic images of Buddha in Gandhāra art include later standard elements of his hand gestures (*mudras*) and physical marks of *urna* (a small protuberance between his eyebrows), and *ushnisha* (cranial bump on the top of his head).

ADDITIONAL RESOURCES
Marshall, John. *The Buddhist Art of Gandhara: The Story of the Early School, Its Birth, Growth, and Decline.* Cambridge, England: The Syndics of the Cambridge University Press, 1960.
Nehru, Lolita. *Origins of the Gandhara Style: A Study of Contributory Influences.* New York: Oxford University Press, 1989.

SEE ALSO: Buddha; Buddhism; India; Rome, Imperial.

—*Rozmeri Basic*

GARAMANTES

ALSO KNOWN AS: Garamantis
DATE: 600 B.C.E.-300 C.E.
LOCALE: Fezzan and Sahara Desert
SIGNIFICANCE: The Garamantes, a seminomadic people in the region of Libya, are the ancestors of the Berbers of North Africa.

The Garamantes (gah-rah-MAN-teez) were a seminomadic tribe that the Greek historian Herodotus located along the eastern coastal area of Libya, along with eleven other groups. Historians Pliny the Elder and Strabo and geographer Ptolemy all refer to the Garamantes as a nomadic tribe known to reside in North Africa. The Garamantes also occupied an area along the Saharan caravan route that Herodotus describes as spanning "from Thebes of Egypt to the Pillars of Heracles." The presence of the Garamantes both on the interior, desert route and along the coast suggests that they were one of the more powerful Libyan tribes in North Africa. Their capital, Garama (modern Germa), has been located and excavated in the Wadi el Agial.

Periodic agriculturalists and nomadic traders, the Garamantes were known in Roman times as desert pirates who were difficult to subdue. Historian Tacitus records that the Garamantes were accomplices to Tacfarinas, a Numidian warrior who sponsored an insurrection against Rome in Africa. By 80 C.E., however, the Romans relied on the assistance of the Garamantes in exploring southern routes into the Libyan Desert.

ADDITIONAL RESOURCES

Ayoub, M. S. *The Rise of Germa*. Tripoli, Libya: Kingdom of Libya, Ministry of Tourism and Antiquities, 1968.

Daniels, Charles. *The Garamantes of Southern Libya*. Stoughton, Wis.: Oleander Press, 1970.

Reynolds, Dana. "The African Heritage and Ethnohistory of the Moors." *Journal of African Civilizations*, no. 11 (Fall, 1991): 93-150.

SEE ALSO: Africa, North; Berbers; Herodotus; Pliny the Elder; Rome, Imperial; Strabo.

—Darlene L. Brooks Hedstrom

GASH CIVILIZATION

DATE: 2700-1400 B.C.E.
LOCALE: Gash Delta, southeast of the fifth cataract near the border of modern Sudan and Ethiopia
SIGNIFICANCE: One of the Nubian chiefdoms that emerged along the important land routes to the Red Sea during the time of the Egyptian kingdoms.

The Gash civilization can be divided into three major periods: early Gash civilization, 2700-2300 B.C.E.; the middle Gash civilization, 2300-1900 B.C.E., which corresponds to the First Intermediate period in Egyptian historiography; and finally late Gash civilization, 1700-1400 B.C.E.

The Gash civilization arose from the settlement of Butuan descendants in the Gash Delta lowlands in the third millennium B.C.E. Gash Delta trade was early tied to activity in the kingdoms of Egypt and later Kerma in upper Nubia. Despite its early dependence on Egypt and Kerma, trade in the Gash Delta survived even after the decline of those larger states. After 2300 B.C.E., traders of the delta region were able to tap into the vibrant trade networks in the southeast, which had previously been dominated first by Egypt and then by Kerma. By shifting away from the north and focusing on trade taking place on the edge of the northern Ethiopian plateau (modern Eritrea and Tigray), the Gash Delta continued to participate in and benefit from Red Sea trade.

Remarkably, two separate pottery styles were traded to the western shores of Arabia via the Gash Delta: Kerma and Tigray pottery. The earliest pottery of Kerma, a coastal region, has decorative motifs that appear to be variants of one complex. Tigray pottery displays signs of Egyptian influence that were most likely brought in through Gash knowledge of Egyptian fashions. The coastal pottery complex has been dated to between the late fourth and mid-second millennia B.C.E. The Gash Delta was the corridor that linked the Horn of Africa, the Sudan, Arabia, and Egypt. The link provided by the Gash civilization was both physical and cultural.

The Gash Delta valley was settled by the Butana, who had been gatherers and hunters of wild plants and animals. After relocating in the area, the Butana embarked on a new economy of cattle breeding and cereal cultivation as early as the fourth millennium B.C.E. Archaeologists have uncovered lidded pots at these sites as well as maces, staffs, and items common to hierarchical bureaucracies. In the Classical Gash period, increases occur in the presence of stones marking burial sites and the number of large residential settlements. This archaeological evidence demonstrates a shift in types of material wealth and settlement patterns. The more sedentary lifestyle of the Gash civilization was the result of less food collection and more food production. This brought about stratification and a more hierarchical social system. Some archaeological evidence exists that camels may have been domesticated in this region as early as the fourth millennium B.C.E. and were kept as domesticated pack animals as early as the second millennium B.C.E.

ADDITIONAL RESOURCES

Burstein, Stanley M., ed. *Ancient African Civilizations: Kush and Axum*. Princeton, N.J.: Markus Wiener, 1998.

Connah, Graham. *African Civilizations: Precolonial Cities and States in Tropical Africa, an Archaeological Perspective.* Reprint. Cambridge, England: Cambridge University Press, 1994.

Iliffe, John. *Africans: The History of a Continent.* Cambridge, England: Cambridge University Press, 1995.

SEE ALSO: Africa, East and South; Axum; Egypt, Pharaonic; Kerma; Nubia.

—*Catherine Cymone Fourshey*

GAUDAPĀDA

BORN: c. 725 C.E.; place unknown
DIED: date and place unknown
RELATED CIVILIZATION: India
MAJOR ROLE/POSITION: *Advaita* (monism) philosopher

Life. Gaudapāda (goh-dah-PAH-dah) wrote a commentary on Sāṁkhya (an orthodox system of Hindu philosophy that influenced the Buddha, who later influenced Sāṁkhya philosophy) in which he set forth the principles of *advaita*, a doctrine of monism (nondualism) that teaches that only the ultimate principle is integral, whole, and unsplit and that it alone has real existence; all other phenomena are either ephemeral or illusive. Gaudapāda was deeply influenced by Buddhism, especially Yogācara philosophy.

Influence. Gaudapāda was a very strict monist, denying the possibility of change, causation, creation, destruction, bondage, or liberation. He argued the doctrine of *ajātivāda*, which held that the Absolute, a being self-existent, is neither a creator nor a destroyer and is changeless. Therefore, neither was the world created nor will it be destroyed. If the Absolute did not exist at the beginning or the end, it did not exist in the middle.

Life, he argued, was like a torch, which when it is rapidly moved around, creates the illusion of a ring of fire. The purpose of philosophy, he maintained, was to quench the flame. The Vedantic philosopher Śaṅkara was strongly influenced by Gaudapāda.

ADDITIONAL RESOURCES

Mahadevan, T., ed. *Gaudapada: A Study of Early Advaita.* 2d ed. Madras, India: University of Madras, 1954.
Sarma, Candradhara. *The Advaita Tradition in Indian Philosophy: The Study of Advaita in Buddhism, Vandanta, and Kashmri Shaivism.* Delhi, India: Motilal Banarsidass, 1996.
Walker, Benjamin. *Hindu World: An Encyclopedic Survey of Hinduism.* London: George Allen and Unwin, 1968.

SEE ALSO: *Advaita*; Buddha; Buddhism; Hinduism.

—*Arthur W. Helweg*

GAUGAMELA, BATTLE OF

DATE: October 1, 331 B.C.E.
LOCALE: Plain of Gaugamela, north of modern Baghdad
RELATED CIVILIZATIONS: Macedonia, Classical Greece, Persia
SIGNIFICANCE: Alexander the Great's victory effectively destroyed the Persian Empire.

Background. Alexander the Great invaded the Persian Empire in 334 B.C.E. After defeating a Persian satrap at the Granicus, then defeating Darius III of Persia at Issus, Alexander took control of the eastern Mediterranean coast and Egypt. With his rear secured, he marched east looking for Darius, who had just raised a new army.

Action. Darius gathered his 200,000-man army on raised ground on the plain of Gaugamela (gaw-guh-MEE-luh), with level ground before him so he could deploy his elephants and scythed chariots. Alexander arrayed his 47,000 men in two parallel lines of infantry with cavalry on the flanks.

Alexander led his right wing cavalry at the Persian left flank, creating a gap in his lines that Persian chariots immediately attacked. Greek light infantry negated their effort but created an even bigger gap in the Greek line. Persian cavalry in the center broke through the gap but rode past the battle to loot the Greek camp. Alexander charged the space left by the Persian cavalry and drove directly at Darius. The Persian emperor stood briefly, then fled. Leaderless, the Persian army began to disintegrate.

Consequences. Alexander seized the Persian treasury at Persepolis, then pursued Darius to Ecbatana (Agbatana, later Hamadān). Darius's death, coupled with the acquisition of the empire's wealth, gave Alexander both an eastern empire and the means to invade India.

ADDITIONAL RESOURCES

Arrian. *The Campaigns of Alexander.* Translated by Aubrey de Selincourt. Baltimore: Penguin, 1958.

Keegan, John. *The Mask of Command.* New York: Little, Brown, 1982.

Livesey, Anthony, and Randal Gray. *Great Commanders and Their Battles*. London: Greenwich Editions, 1997.

SEE ALSO: Alexander the Great; Darius III; Granicus, Battle of; Greece, Classical; Issus, Battle of; Macedonia; Persia.
—Paul K. Davis

This Greek relief depicts the victory of Alexander the Great over the Persians at the Battle of Gaugamela. (Library of Congress)

GAULS

ALSO KNOWN AS: Celts, Ligurians, Salyii
DATE: c. 500-50 B.C.E.
LOCALE: Liguria, southern part of modern France
SIGNIFICANCE: The Gauls were the precursors of European, especially French, civilization.

The Gauls descended from the Celts of the late Iron Age or, to identify it with the site of its excavation, La Tène culture. The name "Gaul" is derived from the Latin *Galli*, as the Romans called the Celts. The Gauls inhabited the regions known, since the sixth century C.E., as Liguria, covering approximately the southern part of modern France: the Côte d'Azur and Provence.

The Greeks called them *Galatai* (whence the Biblical reference to them as Galatians).

They lived in fortified stone encampments (*oppidum* or towns) on the hills. Those excavated in Ambrussum, Nages, and Entremont contain some very sophisticated military architecture characterized by curtain walls, projecting towers, posterns, sally ports, and ditches. The houses were of various sizes, from single-room shacks to multi-room residences surrounded by stone or mud-brick walls. The streets were usually of beaten earth and occasionally laid out on a grid plan. There are no monuments or public buildings; the city walls and ramparts were apparently used for public functions.

The language of the Celts belongs to the Indo-European language family, and the principal dialects include Gaulish and Goidelic (Irish, Scottish Gaelic, and Manx). However, the Gauls were illiterate although they cultivated eloquence. Roman Cato the Censor praised the Cisalpine Gaul for their eloquence.

It is noteworthy that Gaul was not Celticized with any degree of uniformity. Even at the time of the Roman conquest in the first century B.C.E., Gaul appears to have been settled by three distinct peoples, as noted by Julius Caesar: Galli (in the region from the Garonne to the Seine and the Marne), Aquitani (between the Pyrenees and the Garonne), and Belgae (from the Marne to the Rhine via the Seine). The most recent arrivals in Gaul were the Belgae, who probably crossed the Rhine into northeastern Gaul in the fourth and third centuries B.C.E.

Before the Roman conquest, Gaul was divided into sixteen separate large groups. These political units, known to classical writers as *civitates*, *populi*, *nationes*, or *gentes*, consisted of smaller subdivisions known as *pagi*. According to Julius Caesar's *Comentarii de bello Gallico* (52-51 B.C.E.; translated with *Comentarii de bello civili*, 45 B.C.E., as *Commentaries*, 1609), the Gauls had become disunited and weakened in the second and first centuries B.C.E. This explains their conquest by the Romans.

The Gauls, especially the Ligurians, were traditionally regarded as cruel barbarians—a view that had become popular since the days of colonization of the southern region (Massilia) by the Greeks. The Romans echoed this Greek bias in their estimate of the Gauls. Admittedly, the life of the Gauls was hard and rough, yet they impressed the Greeks and the Romans with their volatile exuberance, dancing and singing at one moment and slaughtering one another at the next. They were famous for their drinking. Their religion of nature worship was controlled by the Druids, bards, and soothsayers. Human sacrifice, sometimes allied to divination, was part of their religion.

ADDITIONAL RESOURCES

Chadwick, Nora. *The Celts*. New York: Penguin, 1997.

Hubert, Henri. *The Greatness and Decline of the Celts*. Translated by M. R. Dobie. 1934. Reprint. New York: Benjamin Blom, 1972.

Woolf, Greg. *Becoming Roman: The Origins of Provincial Civilization in Gaul*. Cambridge, England: Cambridge University Press, 1998.

SEE ALSO: Caesar, Julius; Cato the Censor; Celts; Gallic Wars; Greece, Hellenistic and Roman; La Tène culture; Rome, Republican.

—Narasingha P. Sil

Two Gallic warriors on horseback consult each other. (North Wind Picture Archives)

GE HONG

ALSO KNOWN AS: *Wade-Giles* Ko Hung; Baopuzi
(*Wade-Giles* Pao-p'u-tzu)
BORN: c. 283 C.E.; Danyang, China
DIED: c. 343 C.E.; Danyang, China
RELATED CIVILIZATION: China
MAJOR ROLE/POSITION: Military officer, Daoist
scholar, alchemist, medical theorist

Life. Ge Hong (go HOONG) was born in an aristocratic family (the Shi class). He began to study various Confucian classics when he was sixteen years old. Later, he shifted his interest to Daoism, especially to alchemy and other longevity techniques, and went to study alchemy from Zheng Yin, a disciple of a famous alchemist, Ge Xuan. In 303 C.E., he was appointed to the post of junior military officer to help subdue a peasant uprising and was promoted to senior officer for his military achievement. In his later years, except for briefly being a military adviser, Ge Hong concentrated on Daoist studies and alchemical practice.

Influence. Ge Hong was a key link in the history of Daoism. His works *Baopuzi* and *Shenxianzhuan* (both fourth century C.E.; both partial English translation in *Alchemy, Medicine, and Religion in China of* A.D. *320*, 1967) were important scriptures of Daoism. They summarized Daoist myths of gods and alchemy as they existed before the Western Jin Dynasty (265-316 C.E.) and exerted a great influence on later development of Daoist religion. Ge Hong was also an important figure in the history of traditional Chinese medicine.

ADDITIONAL RESOURCES

Ko, Hung. "Laozi: Ancient Philosopher, Master of Immortality and God." Translated and edited by Livia Kohn. In *Religions of China in Practice*, edited by Donald S. Lopez, Jr. Princeton, N.J.: Princeton University Press, 1996.
Sailey, Jay. *The Master Who Embraces Simplicity: A Study of the Philosopher Ko Hung.* San Francisco: Chinese Materials Center, 1978.

SEE ALSO: China; Daoism; Laozi.

—Zhaolu Lu

GELLIUS, AULUS

BORN: c. 125-128 C.E.; possibly Rome
DIED: date and place unknown
RELATED CIVILIZATION: Imperial Rome
MAJOR ROLE/POSITION: Scholar, writer

Life. What little is known of Aulus Gellius's (AW-luhs JEHL-ee-uhs) life derives from his surviving work, the *Noctes Atticae* (c. 180 C.E.; *Attic Nights*, 1927). Gellius spent most of his life in Rome and studied under some of the best instructors of the age. He also spent time touring Greece. In fact, Gellius states that he originally compiled the materials for his work in order to while away long winter nights in Athens and later worked up his notes in twenty books (or chapters) in order to provide instruction for his children. The work treats an incredible variety of topics, including, for example, morality, philosophy, natural science, medicine, law, religion, history, biographical anecdotes, literary history, textual criticism, and etymology. Gellius's style is lively, and he includes dramatic dialogues and demonstrates a fondness for both archaism and neologism. Of the twenty books, the beginning of the preface, book eight, and the end of book twenty are no longer extant.

Influence. Gellius was popular in later antiquity. In the Middle Ages, excerpts from his work were often included in anthologies. During the Renaissance, his work was very highly valued. No longer as popular as he once was, Gellius continues to attract readers mainly for his work's vast store of curious information.

ADDITIONAL RESOURCES

Holford-Strevens, L. A. *Aulus Gellius.* London: Duckworth, 1988.
Rolfe, J. C. *The Attic Nights of Aulus Gellius.* Cambridge, Mass.: Harvard University Press, 1927.

SEE ALSO: Aesop; Greece, Hellenistic and Roman; Languages and literature; Phaedrus; Rome, Imperial.

—Hans-Friedrich Mueller

GELON OF SYRACUSE

BORN: c. 540 B.C.E.; place unknown
DIED: c. 478 B.C.E.; place unknown
RELATED CIVILIZATION: Classical Greece
MAJOR ROLE/POSITION: Tyrant of Syracuse

Life. Gelon (JEE-lahn) of Syracuse, son of Deinomenes, rose to prominence as bodyguard and then master of the cavalry for Hippocrates, ruler of the city of Gela on the island of Sicily roughly 498 to 491 B.C.E. Hippocrates steadily built a small empire, and when he died, Gelon snatched the monarchy from Hippocrates' heirs. Gelon continued to build power through alliance and conquest, culminating in control of Sicily's grand prize, the city of Syracuse in 485 B.C.E. Gelon governed Syracuse himself and handed over Gela to his brother Hieron. He maintained an alliance with another tyrant, Theron of Acragas, which included marrying Theron's daughter Damarete. Gelon commanded the largest military force in Greece and therefore caught the attention of the Carthaginians. When Xerxes I led Persian troops against mainland Greece, Gelon could provide only limited assistance because the Carthaginian general Hamilcar attacked Sicily itself. In conjunction with Theron, Gelon repelled the Carthaginians at the Battle of Himera, reportedly at the same time as the Greeks overwhelmed the Persian attack at Salamis in 480 B.C.E. Upon Gelon's death in about 478, his brother ruled Syracuse as Hieron I.

Influence. Gelon increased the power and prestige of Sicily, and his reign was later considered a golden age. He especially enhanced the city of Syracuse with an increased population, public works, and prosperity.

ADDITIONAL RESOURCE
Finley, M. I. *A History of Sicily.* Vol. 1. London: Chatto & Windus, 1968.

SEE ALSO: Carthage; Greco-Persian Wars; Hieron I of Syracuse; Xerxes.

—*Wilfred E. Major*

GERMANY

DATE: 3000 B.C.E.-700 C.E.
LOCALE: Southern Scandinavia, France, Germany, Austria, Switzerland
SIGNIFICANCE: Germanic tribes from northern Europe replaced the dominant Celtic culture in central Europe, eventually establishing kingdoms in all Western Roman provinces.

A jawbone discovered near Heidelberg reveals that humanlike creatures called *Australophicines* lived in the region of modern Germany. Remains of Neanderthals, early *Homo sapiens* who lived between 100,000 and 30,000 B.C.E., were first discovered in the Neander Valley in Germany. Archaeological findings reveal that human beings lived in Hamburg by 10,000 B.C.E. and in other parts of modern Germany by 8000 B.C.E.

By the third millennium B.C.E., Corded Ware culture dominated northern Germany. One millennium later, the Beaker people appeared in the Rhineland and in the upper Elbe River Valley, where they mixed with the Corded Ware people. By the second millennium B.C.E., both social inequality and social centralization appear in Germany. In Achsolshausen, Bavaria, one grave site dated 1250 B.C.E. included a four-wheeled vehicle. For protection, hill forts appeared. Skeletal types from sites in southern and central Germany reveal a short, stocky, round-headed individual, who differed from the meagerly muscled Neolithic people found in earlier graves.

Between 1200 and 800 B.C.E., the population increased, and people remained in settlements for a much longer time. However, most settlements, including Hascherkeller, Bavaria, had fewer than fifty people. Between the eighth and fifth centuries B.C.E., much of southern and central Germany shared Celtic Hallstatt and La Tène cultures. The Celts who spread from central Europe to other parts of Europe dominated southern and central German culture between 600 and 200 B.C.E. However, between 200 B.C.E. and 500 C.E., Romans and Germanic invaders pushed the Celtic people to the peripheries of Europe.

Both Celts and Romans faced Germanic tribes who would occupy and transform all of Western Europe. The ancient Greeks named the people of western and central Europe Keloi (Celts), but they did not mention Germanic people. It was not until the second century C.E. that Roman writers described Germans as being different from Celts. In 98 C.E., Tacitus wrote a particularly detailed commentary on the lifestyle and behavior of the German tribes.

The Germans did not call themselves Germani but used tribal names such as Goths or Franks. They can be traced to the first millennium B.C.E. and located in the north German plain between the Rhine and Oder and in southern Scandinavia. Germanic Jastorf culture was contemporary with the Hallstatt and La Tène cultures in southern and western Germany. Beginning in 500 B.C.E., German tribes migrated south and east. Eastern Germans such as the Goths migrated to the northern regions of the Black Sea. Western German tribes moved to the borders of the Roman Empire, which ran along the Danube and Rhine rivers. By the second century B.C.E., Germans encroached on the Roman Empire, and in 9 C.E. at Teutoburg Forest, they stopped Roman expansion toward the Elbe River. The Allemanni moved into southwestern Germany in 213 C.E., but the Visigoths were the first to establish a Germanic kingdom on Roman soil. By the beginning of the sixth century C.E., all old Western Roman provinces had Germanic kingdoms.

For modern Germany, the most important Germanic people were the Franks, who originated along the North Sea and on the banks of the lower Rhine River before moving into Gaul (modern France). Like many Germans, the Franks fought as allies (*foederati*) of the Roman army. However, unlike other Germanic kingdoms, the Frankish kingdom established in Gaul in the late fifth century C.E. survived. Clovis and his sons defeated two important southern and central German tribes, the Allemanni and the Thuringians, and extended Frankish power to the east of the Rhine River.

The Franks also expanded their power in northern Germany over the Frisians in the sixth century C.E. The Saxons, the strongest force in northern Germany between the Weser and the Elbe Rivers, were not defeated until the eighth century by the Frankish ruler Charlemagne. The Bavarians in southern Germany also submitted to Charlemagne in the late eighth century. Not until 870 C.E. did the German medieval empire, composed of various Germanic regions from Saxony to Bavaria, emerge as separate entity from the Frankish realm.

War and weapons. Most Germanic soldiers in the second century B.C.E. were foot soldiers who carried lances and javelins. They had no body armor, although the chiefs wore helmets. Eastern Germans such as the Goths, however, had an impressive cavalry, and the aristocrats wore armor. The Comitatus, a sworn warrior band of young warriors who followed a leader, was organized for constant fighting.

Religion and ritual. Before the Germanic people migrated south, they usually cremated their dead, although inhumation was common among the Goths. With the exception of the Anglo-Saxons, the Germans in the Roman regions adopted inhumation by the fourth century C.E. Tacitus wrote that the Germans had sacred trees rather than temples. The Germanic people also sacrificed people in peat bogs. Originally the Germans had old Indo-European gods, but they adopted specific gods such as Tiu, Wodan, and Thor, who represented a variety of natural forces.

Only the Goths converted to Christianity in the early fourth century C.E. before they entered the Roman Empire. However, within one or two generations after coming into the Roman provinces, other German tribes also converted. The Franks were the only German tribe to convert to Roman Catholicism, and most other Eastern Germans accepted Arian Christianity, which was rejected by Rome. The conversion of Germans east of the Rhine took much longer. In the eighth century, Charlemagne forcibly converted the Saxons to Christianity, and Saint Boniface, an English monk, attempted to convert Saxons, Bavarians, and Frisians.

Daily life, customs, and traditions. Aside from warfare, much of daily life centered on the village. The Romans described the Germans' addiction to heavy beer drinking and gambling. The Germans kept time by using solar years and lunar months until they adopted the week from the Mediterranean people. A six-foot-long (nearly two-meter-long) bronze S-shaped horn was used to create music.

Settlement and social structure. In northern Germany, German tribes built timber houses that were inhabited by both people and livestock. Unlike Germans in southern, Celtic regions, northern Germans generally did not built hill forts or fortified settlements.

Aside from the tribe, the key social organization was the clan of perhaps fifty households. The function of the tribe was to keep peace between clans. The English word "friend" is related to the German word for peace (*Frieden*). There was a social hierarchy in the tribes and clans, and Germans kept slaves.

Language and literature. Germanic languages belonged to the Indo-European language family. First century B.C.E. inscriptions on helmets with Runic letters adopted from a northern Italian alphabet reveal little about the German language. The first written German language was Gothic, because a fourth century C.E. Gothic bishop translated the Bible into Gothic. Most

Germanic tribes that entered the Roman provinces in the West eventually adopted the local vulgar Latin language. Only the Germans between the Rhine Valley and the Oder retained their German dialects.

Government and law. Tribal councils were not legislative assemblies but rather pep rallies because decisions had already been made by the aristocrats. After entering the Roman Empire, Germanic kings governed by using personal power and the loyalty of dukes rather than Roman institutions. They also used German customary law to reduce violence by imposing fines (*Wergild*) or ordering trial by ordeal or combat to decide innocence or guilt.

Agriculture and animal husbandry. Agriculture and animal husbandry played a crucial role in German society. Cattle were the most important domesticated animals. Horses were not prominent among western Germans, although they were important to the eastern Germans. Barley, which was essential for brewing beer, was the most important crop, followed by wheat and flax.

Women's life. Patriarchal Germanic society was dominated by male warriors. A woman's infidelity was punished by banishment or death, while a man's adultery resulted only in a fine. Kingship was traced through both male and female lines. However, there are more words for male than female relatives in Anglo-Saxon. Germans did have a female god concerned with love and marriage.

Current views. Historians have discarded the interpretation that the Germanic people lived in a democratic, classless society. Furthermore, no serious historian still adheres to theories about German racial and tribal homogeneity, which were popular long before the Third Reich. Instead of discussing a "Nordic race," scholars stress how tribes intermingled with a variety of people. Long before the Germanic people penetrated the Western Roman Empire, they were influenced by both Celtic and Roman culture.

ADDITIONAL RESOURCES
Collins, John. *The European Iron Age*. New York: Routledge, 1997.
Geary, Patrick J. *Before France and Germany: The Creation and Transformation of the Merovingian World*. New York: Oxford University Press, 1988.
MacKendrick. *Romans on the Rhine: Archaeology in Germany*. New York: Funk and Wagnalls, 1970.
Musset, Lucien. *The Germanic Invasions: The Making of Europe* A.D. *400-600*. University Park: Pennsylvania State University, 1975.
Sherratt, Andrew. *Economy and Society in Prehistoric Europe: Changing Perspectives*. Princeton, N.J.: Princeton University Press, 1997.
Todd, Malcolm. *The Early Germans*. Oxford, England: Blackwell, 1992.
Wells, Peter S. *Rural Economy in the Early Iron Age: Excavations at Hascherkeller, 1978-1981*. Cambridge, Mass.: Harvard University Press, 1983.

SEE ALSO: Allemanni; Angles, Saxons, Jutes; Arianism; Beaker people; Celts; Christianity; Clovis; Franks; Goths; Hallstatt culture; La Tène culture; Rome, Imperial; Rome, Republican; Tacitus; Teutoburg Forest, Battle of.

—Johnpeter Horst Grill

GHANA

ALSO KNOWN AS: Wagadu Empire; Ouagadou; Aoukar
DATE: c. 300-1200 C.E.
LOCALE: The Western Sudan
SIGNIFICANCE: Ghana, the first West African empire, became a conduit between sub-Saharan Africa and the Mediterranean and Islamic worlds.

Ghana (GAH-nah) was the ancient kingdom of the Soninke, who were among the earliest Sudanic groups to develop farming, ironworking, and permanent communities. With the desiccation of the Sahara, pressure from nomadic groups and the development of desert trade stimulated organization into a larger political entity.

The kingdom's early history has been sketched from oral traditions, archaeological evidence, and Islamic authors. The Soninke referred to their kingdom as "Wagadu," or "place of herds." Their ruler was known as "Ghana," or "warrior king." Many referred to the empire by this royal title. Earliest written references describe it as the land of gold.

Ghana was located between the upper Niger and Senegal Rivers, just below the Sahara. Its capital was Koumbi. Not to be confused with present-day Ghana, the empire encompassed parts of modern Senegal, Mali, and Mauritania. Growth paralleled trans-Saharan trade route expansion, which accelerated with the fifth century C.E. introduction of the camel. The empire provided a stable commercial environment between North African salt mines and caravan routes and gold- and ivory-producing regions to the south.

After suffering Muslim incursions and shifts in gold sources, Ghana declined. The twelfth century C.E. marked a southward movement in the region's political center of gravity, with Mali emerging as a successor state.

ADDITIONAL RESOURCES
Davidson, Basil. *West Africa Before the Colonial Era.* New York: Longman, 1998.
Levtzion, Nehemiah. *Ancient Ghana and Mali.* New York: Africana, 1980.

SEE ALSO: Africa, West; Islam.

—Cassandra Lee Tellier

GIGAKU

ALSO KNOWN AS: *Kuregaku*
DATE: 612-800's C.E.
LOCALE: Japan
RELATED CIVILIZATION: Japan
SIGNIFICANCE: This early form of masked dance and entertainment was one of the many cultural arts introduced into Japan from Korea and China.

Gigaku (GEE-gah-kew) is a form of dance drama, performed wearing masks, which was most popular during the late Kofun and Nara periods. According to the *Nihon shoki* (compiled 720 C.E.; *Nihongi: Chronicles of Japan from the Earliest Times to* A.D. *697,* 1896), Mimaji (Mimashi) from Paekche, Korea, introduced *gigaku* to Japan in 612 C.E. Mimaji, who became a naturalized citizen of Japan, learned this art in the Chinese kingdom of Wu. Its Chinese origins give it its alternative name, *kuregaku,* or "Wu music." Shōtoku Taishi, the regent of Japan, gave Mimaji a place in Sakurai in Yamato, to encourage the propagation of *gigaku* as part of Buddhist ceremonies and rituals. It is difficult to trace the history of *gigaku,* as it lost its popularity by the Heian period, when it was replaced by *bugaku,* a more solemn form of dance and drama introduced from China. By the 1200's, *gigaten* was gone. During the middle of the Heian period, *gigaku* reached commoners through performances at Buddhist temples and influenced their art.

Gigaku is believed to have derived from Indian or Tibetan masked dances and dramas. Its plots emphasized humor, and the accompanying music was created with flutes, drums, and gongs. The performers used masks that covered the entire head and were much larger than those used for *bugaku* or Nō. The masks' features were exaggerated and often grotesque. The human mask was adorned with a tall Aryan-like nose and the animal mask with that of a monstrous beast. Tōdaiji, a temple in Nara, owns more than two hundred *gigaku* masks, including the ones used for the "opening eye ceremony" of Roshana Buddha in Tōdaiji in 752 C.E. Hōryūji, a temple in Nara Prefecture, houses thirty-two masks from the late Kofun and Nara periods.

ADDITIONAL RESOURCE
Nogami, Toyoichiro. *Masks of Japan: The Gigaku, Bugaku, and Noh Masks.* Tokyo: Kokusai Bunka Shinkokai, 1935.

SEE ALSO: Buddhism; Japan; Mimaji; *Nihon shoki*; Performing arts; Shōtoku Taishi; Yamato court.

—Hiroko Johnson

GILGAMESH EPIC

AUTHORSHIP: Unknown
DATE: 2000 B.C.E.
LOCALE: Ancient Babylon
RELATED CIVILIZATION: Babylonia
SIGNIFICANCE: The first written myth in the Western tradition, the Gilgamesh epic attempted to answer the great questions about life and death.

About ten thousand years ago, humankind began what is now known as the Neolithic revolution, which took place in the fertile river valleys of the ancient world. This newfound wealth brought about many important changes. Governmental control was required to direct the distribution of this bounty and to protect citizens both from each other and from foreign invasion. The necessity for accounting for this wealth led to the invention of writing. Over time, a sophisticated language system evolved that enabled the Babylonians to express abstract thoughts. In turn, a new class of intellectuals arose whose members spent time thinking about the great questions of life. This was the beginning of the disciplines of theology, philosophy, and literature.

The Gilgamesh epic (GIHL-guh-mehsh; translated into English as *Gilgamesh Epic*, 1917) is the first recorded attempt to create a written myth that possesses answers to life's most troubling questions. The hero Gilgamesh characterizes this revolutionary time. His skill, strength, and beauty reflect the dominant position of this new civilization, and his total dominance of the city represents the power of the new class of absolute monarchs.

In the epic, Enkidu, the swift, strong human from the wilderness, represents the last remnants of a noble but dying way of life. He loses his natural innocence after sleeping with a woman from the city. After the encounter, Enkidu is no longer as fast and strong as he once was. This represents the great change that took place in human society as the result of the Neolithic revolution. Natural strength, power, and speed were no longer needed to supply the necessities of life, and over time, the sedentary culture reduced humans' proficiency in these traditional areas. Initially, Enkidu is the enemy of Gilgamesh, but Gilgamesh defeats him and they become great friends. This episode is a metaphor for the process of the absorption of the peripheral nomadic bands into the dominant civilization.

The final part of the epic concerns the ultimate questions of the origin and purpose of life and the finality of death. When his best friend Enkidu dies, Gilgamesh begins a journey to find the answers to these important questions. His quest brings him into the company of Utnapishtin, a man who has achieved immortality. He tells Gilgamesh a story about a great flood that destroyed all life on earth. He describes how the gods directed him to build a great boat and to place in it one pair, male and female, of every living creature on earth. When the flood subsided, he released them to repopulate the earth; this explains the origin of life. Utnapishtin also informed Gilgamesh that a certain plant could bestow immortality. After a considerable struggle, Gilgamesh managed to acquire one plant, but a serpent stole it, and he lost his chance at defeating death.

Gilgamesh finally realizes that the secret to happiness is the realization that life consists of sorrow as well as joy, and in the end, no matter how much people struggle and achieve, they must all die. This great epic is the first attempt to pass this knowledge from generation to generation.

ADDITIONAL RESOURCES

George, Andrew, trans. *The Epic of Gilgamesh*. London: Penguin, 2000.

Nissen, Hans. *The Early History of the Ancient Near East 9000-2000* B.C. Chicago: University of Chicago Press, 1988.

Oppenheim, A. L. *Ancient Mesopotamia*. Chicago: University of Chicago Press, 1977.

SEE ALSO: Babylonia.

—*Richard D. Fitzgerald*

GNOSTICISM

DATE: c. 100-200 C.E.
LOCALE: Roman Greece, Eastern Mediterranean
RELATED CIVILIZATIONS: Roman Greece, Imperial Rome

Gnosis (knowledge) was the pursuit of a constellation of religious societies in the early common era Mediterranean. Though their mythology and practices were diverse, Gnostics united in the belief that they had secret knowledge about the universe that freed them from constrictions of human existence.

According to one Gnostic myth, the original, spiritual world was disrupted when one spiritual being (Wisdom) turned from spiritual reality, resulting in the physical world. Materiality was the source of evil, most vivid in the passions of the flesh. Bodies imprisoned sparks of divinity capable of recalling the lost spiritual world. Gnostic myths featured a heavenly messenger who delivered secret knowledge to initiates, allowing them to rise to their original fullness.

Scholars debate Gnosticism's (NAHS-tuh-sih-zuhm) origins. Many posit its beginnings in forms of

Judaism in which biblical narratives of creation were retold in mythic form. The Nag Hammadi library, a collection of documents unearthed in 1946, supports this view. Combined with elements from Greek and Persian philosophies, Gnosticism made inroads within the early church. Jesus Christ was interpreted by Gnostic Christians as a liberator imparting secret knowledge. Views on embodiment led some Gnostics to fleshly license but most to a rigorous asceticism. As the popularity of Christianity surged in the fourth century, Gnosticism waned, though it survived in some forms of esotericism in late antiquity.

ADDITIONAL RESOURCES
Robinson, J. M., ed. *The Nag Hammadi Library in English.* San Francisco: Harper and Row, 1988.
Roukema, Riemer. *Gnosis and Faith in Early Christianity.* Harrisburg, Pa.: Trinity Press International, 1999.
Rudolph, Kurt. *Gnosis: The Nature and History of Gnosticism.* San Francisco: Harper and Row, 1983.

SEE ALSO: Christianity; Irenaeus, Saint; Judaism.

—*William P. McDonald*

GORGIAS

BORN: c. 480 B.C.E.; Leontini, Sicily
DIED: c. 370 B.C.E.; Greece (perhaps Thessaly)
RELATED CIVILIZATION: Classical Greece
MAJOR ROLE/POSITION: Teacher, practitioner of rhetoric

Life. Gorgias (GAWR-jee-uhs), who may have been a pupil of the philosopher Empedocles, taught and practiced rhetoric in his native Sicily until he was about fifty. After traveling to Athens with a diplomatic delegation in 427 B.C.E., he became one of the most successful of the mainland Sophists (itinerant teachers of rhetoric). He taught the Athenian orator Isocrates, amassed considerable wealth, and lived to be over a hundred years old. Reliable documentation exists of several of his speeches, including defenses of Helen of Troy (against a charge of adultery) and of Palamedes (for treachery), and a philosophical speech *On Nature* (alternatively, *On Not-Being*; only summaries of this speech exist). In the dialogue by Plato named *Gorgias* (399-390 B.C.E.; English translation, 1804), he appears as a competent and successful rhetor who is nonetheless unable to withstand cross-examination by Socra-

tes. Surviving texts display an exceptionally florid style (called "Gorgianic") that makes use of unusual vocabulary, many figures of speech, and incantatory formulations. His *Encomium of Helen* attributes almost magical powers to speech, describing it as "a powerful lord" and comparing its effect to that of a drug.

Influence. Gorgias, the most celebrated fifth century exponent of a highly stylized type of rhetoric, was long admired for his worldly success and criticized for his philosophical shortcomings.

ADDITIONAL RESOURCES
Jarratt, Susan. *Rereading the Sophists: Classical Rhetoric Refigured.* Carbondale: Southern Illinois University Press, 1991.
Kennedy, George, trans. "Gorgias." In *The Older Sophists*, edited by Rosamond Kent Sprague. Columbia: University of South Carolina Press, 1972.

SEE ALSO: Greece, Classical; Isocrates; Philosophy; Plato; Socrates; Troy.

—*Janet B. Davis*

GORTYN, LAW CODE OF

DATE: 700-600 B.C.E.
LOCALE: Island of Crete, Greece
RELATED CIVILIZATION: Archaic Greece
SIGNIFICANCE: The oldest preserved law code in Europe.

Gortyn (GOHR-tihn) is considered the most important Roman town on Crete, located on the fertile Mesara plain. It was founded about 1100 B.C.E. at the end of the Bronze Age. According to some sources, the city owes its name to the hero Gortys, the son of Rhadamanthys, who was the brother of King Minos, and to others, he was the son of Tegeates. In 68 B.C.E., the island was conquered by the Romans, and in 27 B.C.E., the city was made the capital of the province and the seat of the Roman governor. During the Byzantine period, Gortyn continued to be the capitol of Crete until it was heavily damaged by the earthquake of 670 C.E. The invasion of Arabs in 824 C.E. destroyed the city completely.

The Gortyn law code, which dates between 700 and 600 B.C.E., is the oldest preserved law code in Europe. It is inscribed in twelve columns carved on porous stone blocks. These slabs were later incorporated into the exterior walls of the Odeion, a theater. Each column is five feet (one and a half meters) high and, except for the last one, consists of fifty-three to fifty-six lines, in total more than six hundred lines. The text is in Cretan Doric dialect, and the writing technique used is boustrophedon, in which alternate lines are written in opposite directions. The code addresses a variety of important issues of family law, civil rights, and trade relations, with no references to cruel disciplinary measures or capital punishment.

Cretans are assumed to have established a tradition in just government because of the rule of King Minos. Minoan laws were still valid at this later date during Dorian rule. Therefore, it is highly probable that the code incorporates older principles of justice.

ADDITIONAL RESOURCES
Camp, John McK., II. "Gortyn: The First Seven Hundred Years." In *Polis and Politics: Studies in Ancient Greek History*, edited by Pernille Flensted-Jensen, Thomas Heine Nielsen, and Lene Rubinstein. Copenhagen: Museum Tusculanum Press, 2000.
Willetts, R. F. *The Law Code of Gortyn*. Berlin: Walter de Gruyter, 1967.

SEE ALSO: Crete; Government and law; Greece, Archaic.

—Rozmeri Basic

GOSĀLA MASKARĪPUTRA

ALSO KNOWN AS: Gosāla Makkhali; Gosāla Mankhaliputto
BORN: sixth century B.C.E.; place unknown
DIED: c. 467 B.C.E.; place unknown
RELATED CIVILIZATION: Upaniṣadic India
MAJOR ROLE/POSITION: Founder of Ājīvika sect

Life. A contemporary of the Buddha and Vardhamāna (Mahāvīra), Gosāla Maskarīputra (goh-SHAH-lah MAS-kah-ree-PEW-trah) was a materialist, atheist, and fatalist who roamed the eastern Gangetic Valley preaching a non-Vedic doctrine of materialism and fatalism. As a fatalist, he stressed that all human effort was ineffective in determining the goals and ends of life, and humans are powerless to change their lives in any way. He denied free will and moral responsibility. Rebirth was limited, and there was nothing humans could do to shorten or lengthen their allotted births until the various states were used up.

Little is known about his early life. Jain scripture places his birth circa 540 B.C.E. He led an ascetical life for twenty-four years, during which time he joined Vardhamāna for six years until a breach occurred over his doctrine of predestination. He resumed his wanderings and assumed leadership of the Ājīvika sect, whose members abided by rigid moral observances, severe asceticism and austerities, strict dietary regimens, self-denial, and solitude. Western scholars estimate that Gosāla passed away circa 467 B.C.E.

Influence. The Ājīvika doctrine, although severely criticized and condemned by Buddhists and Jains alike, flourished in south India after Gosāla's death until the fourteenth century C.E.

ADDITIONAL RESOURCES
Basham, A. L. *History and Doctrines of the Ājīvikas.* Delhi, India: Motilal Banarsidass, 1981.
_____. *The Wonder That Was India.* New York: Grove Press, 1959.

SEE ALSO: Ājīvikas; Buddha; Buddhism; India; Jainism; Vardhamāna.

—George J. Hoynacki

GOTHS

ALSO KNOWN AS: Ostrogoths; Visigoths
DATE: c. 50-c. 730 C.E.
LOCALE: Poland, Ukraine, Balkans, Italy, Southern Gaul, Iberia
SIGNIFICANCE: Rome's failure to deal successfully with the Goths led to their invasion and establishment of kingdoms in Iberia, southern Gaul, and Italy.

Contemporary scholarship dismisses ancient stories of Gothic origins in Scandinavia and places the Goths firmly among other Germanic tribes in Poland. Together, these peoples constituted the Wielbark culture. Literary evidence for the Goths dates only to the first century C.E. The second century C.E. Marcomannic War caused Goths to move southward toward the Danube River and Black Sea, affecting, and perhaps spawning, the Cernjachov (Cherniakhov) culture.

In the mid-third century C.E., Goths expanded contacts with Rome and broke into the Balkans and Aegean Sea, raiding Attica, Ephesus, and Cyprus. Driven back, they remained in the region from the Danube to the Don River and developed ties of trade and military assistance with Rome. They were loosely organized around petty kings in small agricultural settlements dominated by an upper freeman class and worked by lower class freemen and slaves. Pagan until converted by Ulfilas in the later fourth century C.E., they practiced inhumation, but generally without weapons. Ulfilas provided a written language centered on the Gothic Bible, but his semi-Arian Christianity, to which Goths came to adhere, created friction with Roman (Catholic) communities.

Pressure from the expanding Hun empire to the east in the later fourth century C.E. forced the movement of large numbers of western tribespeople (largely Tervingi), or Visigoths, into Roman territory. Clashes with Rome led to Emperor Valens's great defeat at Adrianople in 378 C.E. Visigoths settled in the Balkans, and the Huns dominated the eastern Goths (largely Greuthungi), or Ostrogoths. These became the two ma-

The Visigoths enter Spain, where they would develop a landed nobility. (North Wind Picture Archives)

jor divisions of the Gothic peoples. Each developed stronger senses of ethnic identity and stronger monarchies.

Rebellious King Alaric I led the Visigoths to sack Rome in 410 C.E. His successor Ataulphus then moved his people into southern Gaul, establishing a kingdom in Toulouse (Septimania) and, after 416 C.E., in Spain. By the mid-470's C.E., a Visigothic kingdom emerged in Spain that replaced a Roman administration with which it had generally cooperated. The Frank leader Clovis absorbed much of southern Gaul after his victory at Vouillé in 507 C.E. The Hispanic Visigoths de-

WESTERN EUROPE, CIRCA 500 C.E.

veloped an entrenched landed nobility based on the Roman *latifundia*. Under King Reccared, the Arian Visigoths converted to Catholicism (Third Council of Toledo, 589 C.E.). Muslim conquests from 711 C.E. ended Visigothic control of Iberia.

As Hunnish power waned, the Ostrogoths organized around a central ruling family (Amal). Under King Theoderic the Great, they moved into Italy with the blessing of Eastern Roman emperor Zeno (489 C.E.) and destroyed the power of the Germanic Herulians. Theoderic tried to mimic Roman ways in establishing this third Gothic kingdom and exercised authority over the Iberian Visigoths. The Gothic Wars of Emperor Justinian I (535-555 C.E.) destroyed the Ostrogothic state and people, but their twenty-year resistance suggests their strength and resolution.

ADDITIONAL RESOURCES

Burns, Thomas. *A History of the Ostrogoths*. Bloomington: Indiana University Press, 1991.
Heather, Peter. *The Goths*. New York: Blackwell, 1996.
Wolfram, Herwig. *History of the Goths*. Berkeley: University of California Press, 1988.

SEE ALSO: Adrianople, Battle of; Alaric I; Christianity; Clovis; Cyprus; Germany; Huns; Islam; Justinian I; Rome, Imperial; Valens.

—Joseph P. Byrne

GRACCHUS, TIBERIUS SEMPRONIUS, AND GRACCHUS, GAIUS SEMPRONIUS

GRACCHUS, TIBERIUS SEMPRONIUS
BORN: 163 B.C.E.; probably Rome
DIED: June, 133 B.C.E.; Rome

GRACCHUS, GAIUS SEMPRONIUS
ALSO KNOWN AS: Gracchi
BORN: 153 B.C.E.; probably Rome
DIED: 121 B.C.E.; Grove of Furrina, near Rome
RELATED CIVILIZATION: Republican Rome
MAJOR ROLE/POSITION: Statesmen

Life. Tiberius Sempronius Gracchus (ti-BIHR-ee-uhs sehm-PROH-nee-uhs GRAK-uhs) and Gaius Sempronius Gracchus (GAY-uhs sehm-PROH-nee-uhs GRAK-uhs), offspring of Tiberius Sempronius Gracchus, twice consul, and Cornelia, daughter of Scipio Africanus, conqueror of Hannibal, had notable careers as Roman tribunes of the *plebs* (common people).

As tribune in 133 B.C.E., Tiberius proposed an agrarian reform law in order to alleviate a number of related social ills, particularly the decline of small farmers and Rome's consequent difficulty in recruiting sufficient numbers of men for its armies. Tiberius's law sought to enforce a long-ignored statute limiting individuals to hold no more than 500 iugera (about 300 acres, or 120 hectares) of Roman public land. Although he faced considerable opposition from elements of the elite who stood to have their excess holdings of public land confiscated, Tiberius had the support of the *plebs* and enough of the aristocracy to pass his law. Afterward, a commission consisting of Tiberius, his father-in-law Appius Claudius Pulcher, and his brother Gaius began to reclaim surplus public land for redistribution to the Roman poor.

When Tiberius sought successive reelection to the tribunate, he was assassinated by a mob led by Publius Cornelius Scipio Nasica Serapio, who allegedly feared that Tiberius intended to establish a tyranny. Yet in spite of the murder of Tiberius, the work of the agrarian commission continued, largely unhampered by his opponents.

Besides serving on the agrarian commission, Gaius was elected as a tribune for 123 and again for 122 B.C.E., meeting with greater success than his brother did. In his tribunates, Gaius embarked on an even more extensive program of reform. After some initial measures designed to exact revenge on the enemies of Tiberius, the laws that Gaius passed included measures establishing new colonies, government-subsidized grain purchases, a public works program, and minimum-age requirements for army service. In order to gain the support of the equestrian class, he legislated their control of tax collection in Asia and the empaneling of Roman juries. Gaius also unsuccessfully proposed legislation to extend full Roman citizenship to Rome's Latin allies and more limited political rights to Rome's Italian allies. After failing to win election to a third tribunate in 121 B.C.E., Gaius and his supporters sought to defend his colonial legislative program by force of arms. It was at this juncture, that Gaius unfortunately met the fate of his brother and was killed through the machinations of his political opponents.

Influence. Overall, through their legislation, Tiberius and Gaius had the positive effect of helping to relieve many of the social and economic ills that plagued Rome, and it is for this that they have largely been heralded by posterity. However, both tribunes' legislative programs unwittingly contributed to other problems at Rome that would be confronted by another generation. These problems included the growing tendency of the *plebs* to question senatorial leadership, the elevation of the equestrian class as a political force in competition with the senate, and the demands of Rome's allies in Italy for greater political rights.

ADDITIONAL RESOURCES

Badian, E. "Tiberius Gracchus and the Beginning of the Roman Revolution." *Aufstieg und Niedergang der Römischen Welt* 2 (1972): 668-731.

Bernstein, A. H. *Tiberius Sempronius Gracchus*. Ithaca, N.Y.: Cornell University Press, 1978.

Stockton, D. *The Gracchi*. Oxford, England: Clarendon Press, 1979.

SEE ALSO: Rome, Republican; Scipio Aemilianus.

—*Leah Johnson*

GRANICUS, BATTLE OF

DATE: spring, 334 B.C.E.
LOCALE: Granicus (Kocabaş) River, in Hellespontine Phrygia
RELATED CIVILIZATIONS: Macedonia, Persia, Classical Greece
SIGNIFICANCE: Alexander's first victory over the Persians illustrated the power of the superbly drilled Macedonian phalanx and his strategic genius.

Background. In 334 B.C.E., Alexander the Great invaded Persia, fulfilling the plans laid by his father Philip II. Close to the Hellespont (Dardanelles), the invader was met by a Persian army.

Action. The Persian force—led by satraps, not the Persian king Darius III—was hastily levied and outnumbered by the Macedonians. The Persians faced Alexander on the steep east bank of the river, evidently expecting that the Macedonian army, on the opposite bank would become disarrayed when marching down that bank, crossing the river, and then pushing uphill against them.

Although the sources are somewhat confused on the details, it seems that Alexander attacked quickly. Parmenion commanded the Macedonian left and Alexander the right. The steepness of the river banks prevented the army attacking in extended line, so it crossed the river with two cavalry charges, the first to disrupt the Persian line and the second to protect the infantry, and then in fierce fighting routed the Persians. The Persian's Greek mercenaries, which had not been deployed, were defeated by Alexander, and many slaughtered.

Alexander the Great (mounted and brandishing a sword, center), defeats the Persians at the Granicus. (Library of Congress)

Consequences. The battle at Granicus (grah-NI-kuhs) allowed Alexander to establish his own satrap in Hellespontine Phrygia and move further inland in his conquest of Persia. It also served to alert Darius III to the need of leading the Persian army himself.

ADDITIONAL RESOURCES
Bosworth, A. B. *Conquest and Empire: The Reign of Alexander the Great.* Cambridge, England: Cambridge University Press, 1988.
Dodge, Theodore Ayrault. *Alexander.* London: Greenhill Books, 1993.

SEE ALSO: Alexander the Great; Darius III; Gaugamela, Battle of; Greece, Classical; Issus, Battle of; Macedonia; Persia; Philip II.

—Ian Worthington

GRATIAN

ALSO KNOWN AS: Flavius Gratianus
BORN: 359 C.E.; Sirmium, Pannonia (near modern Sremska Mitrovica, Serbia)
DIED: August 25, 383 C.E.; Lugdunum, Lugdunensis (later Lyon, France)
RELATED CIVILIZATION: Imperial Rome
MAJOR ROLE/POSITION: Emperor

Life. Born in the late Roman Empire to the emperor Valentinian I, Gratian (GRAY-shuhn) became co-emperor at the age of nine, to the dismay of the army, as he showed more interest in books than in war. In 375 C.E., when Valentinian I died and Gratian succeeded him as senior Western emperor, the army named his half brother, Valentinian, a child of four, to be his co-emperor. Gratian agreed, but it was a sign of the army's continuing distrust.

In 376 C.E., Gratian ordered the legions from the West sent to assist his uncle, the Eastern emperor Valens, against a Gothic uprising. One of his generals, Merobaudes, countermanded his instructions, insisting that some of the troops remain in the West in case another Germanic tribe, the Allemanni, rebelled. Again, Gratian yielded.

By 377 C.E., the Gothic rebellion had become so severe that Gratian felt he must go to his uncle's aid. When word of his intentions spread, the Allemanni did revolt, but the troops left behind defeated them, and Gratian departed. However, for reasons that are unclear, rather than wait for help, Valens attacked the Goths and was killed at the Battle of Adrianople in 378 C.E.

Gratian, needing an able military assistant in the eastern half of the empire, perhaps under pressure from the military, appointed a popular general, Theodosius the Great, and returned to the West. However, shortly afterward, a British general, Magnus Maximus, rebelled. Gratian's armies deserted him, and he was killed.

Influence. Gratian continued several trends of the late Roman Empire. He came to rely on barbarians for soldiers and, like Valens, settled barbarians in Moesia and Pannonia. His inability, like that of most late Roman emperors, to control the army encouraged its anarchic tendencies. Gratian also advanced Christianity while suppressing paganism. He was the first emperor to refuse to wear the insignia of *pontifex maximus*, or chief priest, and over much protest, he ordered the statue of Victory removed from the Roman senate. He abolished the support for the state cults, which cost paganism financial support and influence. Finally, he sided with orthodox Trinitarians against the Arians.

By temperament and inclination, Gratian was ill-suited to be emperor in the time in which he lived. In another, more settled time, his reign might have been more successful.

ADDITIONAL RESOURCES
Burns, Thomas S. *Barbarians Within the Gates of Rome: A Study of Roman Military Policy and the Barbarians, c. 375-425* A.D. Bloomington: Indiana University Press, 1994.
Marcellinus, Ammianus. *The Later Roman Empire.* Translated by Walter Hamilton. New York: Penguin Classics, 1986.
Vogt, John. *The Decline of Rome.* New York: The New American Library, 1965.

SEE ALSO: Adrianople, Battle of; Allemanni; Arianism; Britain; Christianity; Goths, Ostrogoths, Visigoths; Rome, Imperial; Theodosius the Great; Valens; Valentinian I.

—Terry R. Morris

GREAT BASIN PEOPLES

DATE: 9500 B.C.E.-700 C.E.
LOCALE: Interior western North America
RELATED CIVILIZATIONS: Fremont culture,
Southwest peoples
SIGNIFICANCE: For more than eleven thousand years,
the Great Basin was peopled by mobile foragers
who exploited wild plants and animals, exhibiting
astonishing persistence and flexibility in a changing, harsh desert environment.

The Great Basin is ecologically diverse, marked by
shrubby deserts, sweeping grasslands, broad intermon-
taine valleys, resource-rich wetlands, piñon- or juniper-
dotted hill slopes, high steppes, alpine tundra, and dramatic mountain ranges. The region is framed by the
Sierra Nevada, the Southern Cascades, and the Wasatch
Range and the Columbia and Colorado Rivers. The
Great Basin ranges over nearly 165,000 square miles
(428,000 square kilometers) and includes all Nevada
and portions of California, Oregon, Idaho, Utah, and
Wyoming. Lying in the rain shadow of the Sierras, this
arid to semiarid terrain receives an average of only 10
inches (25 centimeters) of rainfall per year.

The first peoples moved into the Great Basin about
9500 B.C.E. They left behind tools, quarry workshops,
and the large fluted (broadly grooved) stone tips of
their hunting spears on the area's ancient lake terraces.
They soon occupied caves and rock shelters. Ancient
stemmed spear points in cave deposits in Oregon, Nevada, and Utah have been dated to about 9200 B.C.E.
Over the next several thousand years, people lived on
the shores of the shallow lakes and marshes that formed
in the early Holocene period (8000-5500 B.C.E.). These
early Holocene foragers most likely enjoyed a life of
relative plenty, pursuing large game, waterfowl, fish,
shellfish, roots, and abundant marsh plants.

By the Middle Holocene period (5500-2500 B.C.E.),
dramatic changes in the region's climate were underway.
As the region became warmer and drier, the lowland
valleys and productive marshes that once provided an
Eden-like existence dried up and became markedly less
inviting to prudent foragers. Plant and animal distributions shifted, and people began to exploit a greater
range of environments to sustain life in an increasingly
uncertain world. Population densities declined locally
as people moved upland to intensify their use of critical
water sources and dryland plants (especially grass
seeds) and large and small mammals. Grinding stones

for processing seeds in bulk became essential components of the toolkit.

Small game and grass seeds required considerably
more effort to procure and process than the large game
and marsh resources of earlier times. Therefore, Middle
Holocene foragers of the Great Basin worked harder
than their ancestors, moved regularly in pursuit of food,
lived lives of considerable stress, and no doubt often
faced starvation.

By the Late Holocene (beginning in 2500 B.C.E.), the
harsh conditions of life appear to have eased considerably. The climate became cooler and moister, and population growth surged. People were broadly distributed,
and archaeological sites from this time are numerous.

The distribution of water and food across the landscape determined where, when, and how often bands of
closely related kin traveled and camped. Several hundred plant species (roots, berries, grass and shrub seeds,
sedges, tule and cattail seeds, and, where available,
piñon nuts and agave) made up the largest share of the
diet. Large and small game (deer, antelope, mountain
sheep, bison in some locales, rabbits, marmots, go-
phers, waterfowl) and fish provided less than one-third
of the subsistence base. Men and women probably cooperated in the food quest during communal rabbit
drives, fishing activities, piñon nut gathering, insect
collecting, and waterfowl hunting. Storage of food was
critical for winter survival.

In some locations, where productive marshes and
riverine habitats provided dense food resources, social
groups based on large, extended families (perhaps up to
fifteen people) were able to settle almost year-round.
They exploited the nearby wetland resources, building
houses covered in bark, tule, or grass mats. Where food
resources were sparse and widely scattered, small nuclear family groups established only brief encampments, occupying small, domed brush wickiups. Such
camps, occupied for a few days at a time, were set down
in far-flung habitats as food became available season-
ally.

Great Basin foragers developed an ingenious material culture for the day-to-day requirements of a mobile
life in the desert. Plant processing tools were made
from coarse stone. Seed-collecting baskets, paddle-
shaped seed beaters, winnowing/parching trays, soft
bags, and cradles were woven from plant fibers. Fiber
cordage was used to fashion snares and nets for catch-
ing birds, rabbits, and fish. Cutting and scraping tools

and the points on spears, darts, and arrows were flaked from stone (obsidian, chert, chalcedony, and basalt). Sinew was used for hafting tools and making bowstrings. Wood was carved into dart shafts, digging sticks, atlatls (spear-throwers). Bone was shaped into awls, flakers, tubes, and pipes. Clothing was manufactured from leather (moccasins and garments), rabbit skins (robes), grass, and shredded sagebrush bark (sandals).

Works of art, symbol, and ritual were also important. The Great Basin peoples produced figurines, ornaments, and flutelike musical instruments. They distributed shell beads, turquoise, and obsidian through extensive trade networks. Elaborate rock art was pecked, incised, or painted on boulders and cave walls near hunting zones, seed and root harvesting fields, and ceremonial areas.

After 700 C.E. A few hundred years after the beginning of the common era, Great Basin culture began to experience significant change. The bow and arrow was introduced around 300 C.E., and a few centuries later, pottery made its appearance in parts of the basin but remained a scarce commodity overall. Around this time, villagelike settlements were pushed by lowland population pressures to the extraordinary alpine tundra zones of high mountain ranges. Some archaeologists have suggested that about 1000 C.E., significant migrations of peoples from southeastern California fanned out and up through the Great Basin, bringing new technologies, foraging patterns, and languages with them (accounting for the distribution of modern Numic languages). Between 500 and 1350 C.E., the Fremont peoples of the eastern Great Basin, probably influenced by the Anasazi horticulturalists of the Southwest, settled into small, year-round villages and supplemented hunting and gathering with cultivation of maize, beans, and squash.

ADDITIONAL RESOURCES

Beck, Charlotte, ed. *Models for the Millennium: Great Basin Anthropology Today.* Salt Lake City: University of Utah Press, 1999.

D'Azevedo, Warren L., ed. *Great Basin.* Vol. 11 in *Handbook of North American Indians.* Washington, D.C.: Smithsonian Institution Press, 1986.

Grayson, Donald K. *The Desert's Past: A Natural Prehistory of the Great Basin.* Washington, D.C.: Smithsonian Institution Press, 1993.

SEE ALSO: Fremont culture; Southwest peoples.

—*Melinda Leach*

GREAT WALL OF CHINA

DATE: c. 221 B.C.E.

LOCALE: China

RELATED CIVILIZATIONS: Warring States, Qin Dynasty

SIGNIFICANCE: For China, which faced the threat of attacks from nomadic tribes to its north, successful fortification in the form of a wall meant preservation of a way of life.

The danger of raids by mobile pastoral tribes of the steppes of Northern Asia led some of the northern states in central China to build defensive walls. These walls were partially dismantled and linked to form the first Great Wall after the state of Qin was unified by King Zheng in 221 B.C.E.

According to historian Sima Qian's *Shiji* (first century B.C.E.; *Records of the Grand Historian of China*, 1960, rev. ed. 1993), at the conclusion of his campaigns against six rival states (Chu, Chao, Han, Wei, Yan, and Qi), King Zheng, who renamed himself Shi Huangdi (first emperor), decided to send some of the discharged troops to work on various public works projects rather than send them home without any hope of employment. General Meng Tian was put in command of the Great Wall project. The labor force consisted of 300,000 soldiers and hordes of forced laborers, mostly peasants. When the work was terminated with the death of the emperor in 210 B.C.E., the laborers had completed an astonishing 2,600 miles of construction. Superior organization and discipline no doubt played a part; however, in Shi Huangdi's world, efficiency often meant getting a job done no matter what the cost in human life.

Research by scholar Arthur Waldron, however, indicates that what is known as the Great Wall of China was largely built during the Ming Dynasty in the sixteenth century, not in the Qin Dynasty. Walls during the earlier period were formed from earthen ramparts, not stone, and most likely were destroyed. Records on wall building in the Qin Dynasty are scarce, and the exact location of the wall constructed by Shi Huangdi is not known for certain.

ADDITIONAL RESOURCES

Needham, Joseph. *Science and Civilization in China.* Vols. 1-7. London: Cambridge University Press, 1954-1999.

Ssu-ma Ch'ien. *Historical Records.* Translated by Raymond Dawson. New York: Oxford University Press, 1994.

Twitchett, Denis, and Michael Loewe, eds. *The Ch'in and Han Empires.* Vol.1 in *The Cambridge History of China.* Cambridge, England: Cambridge University Press, 1986.

Waldron, Arthur. *The Great Wall: From History to Myth.* New York: Cambridge University Press, 1990.

Yu Jin. *The Great Wall.* Beijing: Cultural Relics Publishing House, 1980.

SEE ALSO: China; Qin Dynasty; Shi Huangdi; Zhou Dynasty.

—*Sugwon Kang*

Great Wall of China, as it appears in modern times. (Corbis)

GRECO-PERSIAN WARS

DATE: 499-449 B.C.E.
LOCALE: Greece
RELATED CIVILIZATIONS: Persia, Classical Greece
SIGNIFICANCE: Greece preserved its independence from Asia, allowing Athenian civilization to flower.

Background. War between the independent Greek states and the growing Persian Empire was perhaps inevitable because Persia wished to expand its empire into Europe.

Action. The Ionian Greeks of the eastern Aegean, conquered in the first half century of the sixth century B.C.E. by Cyrus the Great, rebelled in 499 B.C.E. and enlisted Athens and Eretria as allies. In a swift raid inland, the Athenians burned Sardis (498 B.C.E.), a Persian provincial capital. Darius the Great demanded from Greece "earth and water" as symbols of submission.

In 495 B.C.E., Persia sacked Miletus, the most important Greek city in Asia. The psychological effect of the loss of Miletus was immense and perhaps inspired the independent Greeks to cooperate against Persia.

The Persian expeditionary force took Eretria and expelled its population to Persia. When, with help from only Plataea, Athens defeated the Persian army at Marathon (490 B.C.E.), Darius determined to return with a much larger force.

Rebellions in Egypt and Babylonia distracted Persia from executing an immediate assault on Greece, as did Darius's death in 486 B.C.E. In 481 B.C.E., his successor, Xerxes I, organized a large attack on Greece. After building a pontoon bridge over the Hellespont, he led an immense land force into Europe and also sent a huge fleet.

Athens was led by Themistocles, who had persuaded Athens to use new wealth from its silver mines at Laurium to construct a fleet of warships. An indecisive naval battle at Artemesium (480 B.C.E.) showed that although Persia might have a vast number of ships, it lacked the skill to use them effectively. At the Battle of Thermopylae, a small band of Spartans under King Leonidas retarded the advance of the Persian infantry. However, in a decisive naval battle at Salamis, the

Greeks destroyed most of the Persian fleet and forced the remnant to withdraw to Asia. A final land battle in Greece, the Battle of Plataea (479 B.C.E.), ended the hopes of Persia for victory in Europe, and a final Persian naval defeat at Mycale foreshadowed the dominance of the Athenian navy.

Consequences. Fear of another attack from Persia dominated Greek politics for the next half century. Athens organized the Delian League to protect the island states. In 466 B.C.E., Athens won the Battle of Eurymedon, liberating the remaining Asiatic Greeks from Persia. The relative amity among the Greek cities, a result of their fear of the common enemy Persia, lasted until a general peace with Persia was negotiated by Callias in 449 B.C.E.

In the fifty years following the war, a period celebrated as the Pentecontaetia, democracy, tragedy, comedy, rhetoric, history, philosophy, and medical science all came into their own. Had Greece succumbed to Persia, it is doubtful that any of these accomplishments would have occurred.

ADDITIONAL RESOURCES

Belcer, Jack Martin. *The Persian Conquest of the Greeks.* Konstanz, Germany: Universitatsverlag Konstanz, 1995.

Lazenby, John Francis. *The Defence of Greece, 490- 479 B.C.* Warminster, England: Aris & Phillips, 1993.

SEE ALSO: Athens; Cyrus the Great; Darius the Great; Greece, Classical; Marathon, Battle of; Persia; Plataea, Battle of; Salamis, Battle of; Themistocles; Thermopylae, Battle of; Xerxes I.

—James A. Arieti

GREECE, ARCHAIC

DATE: 800-500 B.C.E.

LOCALE: Greek peninsula, Crete, Cyprus, Cyclades

SIGNIFICANCE: Between 800 and 500 B.C.E., Greece, which already had achieved a remarkably advanced civilization, saw the city-state organization of its society grow and adopted a more advanced economy that promoted trade.

During Greece's Archaic period, the economy was transformed by the invention of coinage, which inevitably led to an expansion of trade and commerce. As its population grew and prospered, Greece, hungry for land, colonized Mediterranean areas and moved into the territories surrounding the Black Sea. The relatively unsophisticated economy of the ancient Greek villages was much disturbed by this expansion. Land wars were common.

History. The ancient Greeks called themselves Hellenes, but the Roman name for the area in southern Italy to which thousands of Hellenes migrated in the period of great colonization between 750 and 500 B.C.E. was Magna Graecia, from which the words "Greek," "Greece," and "Grecian" are derived. During the Archaic period, which began around 800 B.C.E. and continued until the Golden Age of Athens shortly after 500 B.C.E., there was considerable emigration from the Greek islands and the Peloponnese.

Population growth, combined with a growing shortage of land, led many of the country's citizens to colonize areas ranging from southern Spain to the Black Sea, North Africa, and the Near East. In the first half of the eighth century alone, the population of Attica quadrupled. In the next half century, it doubled.

The only city-states that did not engage in colonization were Athens and Sparta. During the early Archaic period, Athens had sufficient fertile land to support its population, so it did not establish external colonies. When Sparta needed land to accommodate its swelling population, it used military might to overcome Messenia to its west (725 and 668 B.C.E.) and Arcadia to its north (560 and 550 B.C.E.), making colonization unnecessary.

The historian Herodotus recounts how famine struck the island of Thera, causing the Therans to exile some of their number. When these exiles failed to find a suitable place in which to begin a new colony, they returned to Thera, only to be rebuffed by arrows that prevented their landing, forcing them to depart hastily.

Archaic Greece had scores of city-states. The topography of the area lent itself to the establishment of isolated enclaves that originally were tribal but, by the beginning of the archaic period, were centered around the polis, or city. The population in the outlying areas were also considered part of the political unit that was called the city-state. High mountain ranges separated many of the city-states from each other. Others grew on the islands of the Aegean and Mediterranean Seas.

Most of the cities around which the city-states formed were small. Sparta, geographically the largest of the city-states with an area of 3,360 square miles (8,712 square kilometers), had fewer than five thousand residents. Athens, during its Golden Age, with an area of 1,060 square miles (2,749 square kilometers), claimed an adult male population of forty-three thousand. Small villages existed outside the major cities. Their inhabitants were citizens of the city-state. Boeotia, whose major city was Thebes, had twelve villages in its outlying areas, each with an average size of 52 square miles (135 square kilometers).

Even though conflicts arose and border wars were fought among the city-states, an underlying unity existed, particularly as colonization in far-off venues became more common. A major unifying thread was Greek mythology, the basis for the religion of most Greeks regardless of their citizenship in individual city-states. The temple of Apollo at Delphi became a center to whose oracle most Greeks turned for advice.

Four major Panhellenic religious festivals united the citizens of disparate areas. Festivals and games held at Olympia and Nemea honored Zeus, the father of the gods. Corinth regularly honored Poseidon, god of the sea. Apollo was similarly honored at Delphi. The Olympic, Nemean, Isthmian, and Pythian Games were Panhellenic events during which any warring factions observed an inviolable truce. The Greeks measured time by Olympiads, using 776 B.C.E., the date of the first Olympic Games, as a starting point.

Archaic Greece provided the blueprint for Western civilization. In approximately three hundred years, the country moved from a collection of tribes to federations of city-states. During this period, governments were formed, laws were codified, a simplified alphabet was adopted, enabling large numbers of Greeks to gain literacy, money was coined for the first time, and education became available to increasing numbers of citizens.

The art of the period moved from the stiff, geometrical art of the preceding period to a more fluid art that reflected Asian influences. Intellectual Greeks studied rhetoric and oratory, developing skills that enabled them to pose searching questions concerned with the position of humans in the universe and to articulate complex ideas according to the rules of formal logic.

Government became stratified according to class during this period. Initially ruled monarchically by kings, in time, the government became oligarchic, ruled by a wealthy, landed aristocracy that ruled autocratically, much as the kings had. They denied political power to those who did not own land. Following 680 B.C.E., when the first coinage of money took place, commerce developed, and the economy changed, creating new groups of landless but affluent people, a rising middle class, who, beginning around 650 B.C.E., grasped political power.

From among these citizens, mostly engaged in trades, crafts, and agriculture, emerged tyrants who wrested control from the aristocrats. These tyrants usually had the support of the slaves and the serfs. Among the city-states, only Sparta continued to be controlled by aristocrats. Many of the early tyrants were shrewd rulers. They spearheaded significant social improvement and offered hope to the serfs and the slaves who supported them. In time, however, many of them became autocratic and isolated from their constituencies, only to be overthrown by the lower classes on whom their power depended. After 500 B.C.E., no tyrants remained in the Greek city-states.

Government and law. In the early Archaic period, the Greek city-states, originally ruled by monarchs who inherited their kingships, often became oligarchies, ruled by a landed gentry that excluded from the power structure those who did not own land and were not, therefore, aristocratic. As commerce grew during the mid-seventh century, a middle class of merchants, tradesmen, and farmers began to gain power. Supported by serfs and slaves seeking to improve their bleak lives, tyrants emerged as the rulers.

Although the tyrants initially were usually well-qualified men who engineered desirable change, many of them eventually became as autocratic as their aristocratic and monarchical predecessors had been. As they lost touch with the people, they were usually overthrown.

As early as the ninth century B.C.E., Lycurgus of Sparta, a lawgiver, had created a representative form of government that became a model for many city-states. This government consisted of a bicameral body. Its upper house, the *gerousia*, had twenty-eight elders, each over sixty years old. The lower house, the *apella*, was composed of citizens who were qualified to serve if they were more than thirty years old. Two kings ruled, but five powerful magistrates, called ephors, supervised and controlled these kings, whose tenure was in their hands.

The lawgivers in the city-states had almost unlimited power. The citizens chose them and trusted them, abiding by their judgment. The most renowned law-giver, Solon, served Athens at the beginning of the sixth century B.C.E., a critical time in its existence. The Athenians had suffered a severe drought and an ensuing famine. Many Athenians who had borrowed money were unable to pay their debts and were enslaved by fellow citizens.

Solon resolved this dilemma through the controversial expedient of canceling all debts, thereby restoring some order to a society in crisis. He also mandated that no Athenian could incur further indebtedness but that any who did so and failed to repay his debts could be enslaved. Any son whose father failed to teach him a trade or profession was absolved from having to support that father in his old age. Solon also prohibited the export of all agricultural products except olive oil, of which Athens had an abundance. Under Solon, an assembly of citizens met regularly and a court of appeals was established to limit the power of magistrates. Solon's laws represent the most significant steps Athens took toward establishing a democracy.

Religion and ritual. Throughout the Greek city-states of the Archaic period, religion was a major unifying force. The mythology that had been imparted in oral form from a time when Greek society was largely tribal is recorded in the Homeric epics, the *Iliad* (c. 800 B.C.E.; English translation, 1616) and *Odyssey* (c. 800 B.C.E.; English translation, 1616). In these epics, the hierarchy of the ancient gods of the sea, of fertility, of war, and of various other elements of human existence was established, with Zeus, the king or father of the gods, holding the preeminent position.

Even into the fifth century B.C.E., when Euripides' dramas were mocking the gods as they were presented in the Homeric epics, polytheism flourished. One could mock the gods much as modern comedians mock prominent political figures, but it was unthinkable to deny them.

Settlements and social structure. As Greece's city-states grew during the eighth century B.C.E., land became scarce and people had limited means of earning their livelihoods. As a result, hundreds of citizens from every city-state except Athens and Sparta were forced to leave their homes to colonize other places that offered them greater opportunities and less crowded conditions. Considerable numbers sailed west to Sicily and southern Italy, where numerous Greek colonies were established. Others traveled east to the shores of the Black Sea and the Sea of Mamara.

Each new colony maintained a sentimental and usually a commercial connection with the original city-state, often carrying a sacred flame from the mother city to the new colony. Nevertheless, these colonies were independent and, unlike Roman colonies, were not connected politically to the city-state from which they came.

Usually about two hundred men from an overcrowded city-state would set out to establish a colony elsewhere. Once they had set down some roots, they would bring their women—mothers, wives, daughters, sweethearts—to the new colony.

Economics. Unlike the economies of many ancient societies, the Archaic Greek economy was not wholly agricultural, although agriculture played an important role in it. Manufacturing, which flourished during the Bronze Age and the Iron Age, was a major economic factor in many Greek city-states. A turning point in commerce came with the first coinage of silver in the mid-seventh century.

During this century, small villages grew into cities as manufactured goods such as pottery, textiles, metal utensils, and weapons found ready markets throughout the areas that bordered the Mediterranean and Black Seas. The rise in manufacturing created jobs for many who had previously been unemployed and in a number of city-states reduced considerably the pressure to colonize. Some exiles from the colonies were also able to return to their native homes to work in manufacturing.

Philosophy. Until the sixth century B.C.E., Greeks explained natural and social phenomena in terms of the myths that had been handed down through the ages. During the sixth century, however, thinking Greeks began to seek deeper explanations for phenomena they could not easily understand. The pre-Socratic philosophers, notable among them Heraclitus, Thales of Miletus, Pythagoras, Anaximenes, and Anaximander, pondered such questions as the source and meaning of life. They sought the "worldstuff," or basis of all the material world. Heraclitus, considered the founder of metaphysics, postulated the philosophy that everything changes, that nothing ever remains the same.

Essentially, the early Greek philosophers had a pessimistic view of life. During the sixth century B.C.E., despite the notable strides they had made, most of the philosophers were still steeped in the myths with which they had been brought up and found it difficult to assess the world in other than the mythical terms that were so familiar to them.

Women's lives. Although many city-states bestowed citizenship on their female residents, Greece was largely a male-dominated society. Women generally did not serve in public office. Colonizing was done by males, who usually established their colonies and then sent for their women. Women's activities were usually domestic in nature, although some notable women, such as Sappho in the sixth century B.C.E., gained recognition as poets. Women were unable in most city-states to vote. Most married early because they required men in their lives as protectors.

Writing systems. In the ancient Greek script, now designated Linear B, each sign represented a single syllable. This script, recorded on clay tablets by using sharp instruments, died out around 1200 B.C.E. Greece was essentially illiterate for the next four hundred years. At the beginning of the Archaic period, however, the Greeks began to trade with the Phoenicians, from whom they adapted a sixteen-letter alphabet to which they added seven vowel sounds. The earliest extant examples of the Greek alphabet date to about 740 B.C.E.

War and weapons. With its vast coastline, Greece was vulnerable to naval attack. As a result, various city-states that bordered the sea had substantial navies manned partly by citizens who were given land and money in return for their services and partly by mercenaries. Such was also true of the armies formed for the protection of individual city-states, the strongest of which was Sparta.

Sparta, being inland, had more need for foot soldiers and cavalry than for a strong navy. Its soldiers were armed mostly with spears, clubs, and bows and arrows. Many mercenaries came to Greece to fight for various city-states. They accounted for the first coinage of money in Greece, but the currency minted for them was in denominations too large to be of much use to ordinary citizens. Within a short time, however, silver coins had become trading vehicles.

Although Athens is not renowned for its army or navy, it will be forever remembered for its victory at the Battle of Marathon in 490 B.C.E. Vastly outnumbered by a fierce contingent of Persian troops, the Athenians, aided only by a small contingent from Plataea, a nearby polis, scored an incredible victory. The Persians lost more than 6,400 men; the Athenians suffered 192 casualties.

ADDITIONAL RESOURCES

Boardman, John. *Early Greek Vase Painting, Eleventh-Sixth Centuries B.C.: A Handbook*. New York: Thames and Hudson, 1998.

Cartledge, Paul. *The Greeks: Crucible of Civilization*. New York: TV Books, 2000.

Durando, Furio. *Ancient Greece: The Dawn of the Western World*. New York: Stewart, Tabori, and Chang, 1997.

Garland, Robert. *Daily Life of the Ancient Greeks*. Westport, Conn.: Greenwood Press, 1998.

Osborne, Robin. *Archaic and Classical Greek Art*. New York: Oxford University Press, 1998.

Pomeroy, Sarah B., Stanley M. Burstein, Walter Donlan, and Jennifer Tolbert Roberts. *Ancient Greece: A Political, Social, and Cultural History*. New York: Oxford University Press, 1999.

Shanks, Michael. *Art and the Greek City State: An Interpretive Archaeology*. New York: Cambridge University Press, 1999.

SEE ALSO: Athens; Delphi; Euripides; Government and law; Herodotus; Homer; Linear B; Lycurgus of Sparta; Magna Graecia; Marathon, Battle of; Messenian Wars; Olympic Games; Philosophy; Pre-Socratic philosophers; Pythagoras; Religion and ritual; Solon; Thera.

—*R. Baird Shuman*

GREECE, CLASSICAL

DATE: 500 B.C.E.-323 B.C.E.

LOCALE: Greek peninsula, southern Italy, Sicily, eastern Mediterranean

SIGNIFICANCE: Greek culture reached its apex, producing philosophers, tragedians, orators, and buildings such as the Parthenon. Its city-states rose and fell as military powers, and Greek dominion reached the eastern and western basins of the Mediterranean.

History. The Panhellenic religious and cultural developments of the seventh and sixth centuries B.C.E. provided impetus, but two events played a signal role in the making of Classical Greece, giving it a definition and figure that differentiates it from its Archaic antecedent. The first was the deposition of the tyrants. Tyrants (from *tyrannos*, a word possibly of Lydian extraction) had dominated the poleis, or city-states, during the late seventh and sixth centuries. Tyrants usually came to power at the instigation of the lower economic classes and were in many cases a forerunner to democratic government. Although tyrants were usually no worse than their aristocratic predecessors (and in some cases they were considerably better), tyranny seldom lasted more than two generations. The tyrants were for the most part gone by the end of the sixth century B.C.E., although tyranny did last longer in Sicily, where it was even revivified in the fourth century B.C.E.

By the end of the sixth century B.C.E., the best-known Greek states had developed the system of government they would maintain throughout the Classical period: Athens had democracy, put in place by Cleisthenes; Sparta was ruled by a dual kingship and military aristocracy; Corinth had an elected council and a board of magistrates; and Thebes and the other cities of Boeotia were governed by the somewhat enigmatic Boeotarchs. Sparta in this period took the lead in Greek affairs, helping to depose many of the tyrants, developing the Spartan Alliance, and entering into international relations with Lydia.

The second major event was the conflict with Persia. When Persia defeated the Lydian kingdom of Croesus and gained control of the lucrative Greek cities of Ionia and western Asia Minor, a collision with the mainland Greeks became inevitable. The conflict was accelerated by the expansionist policies of the Persian king Darius the Great, who crossed over into Europe and annexed portions of Thrace and eventually extended Persian rule to the Danube. When the Ionian states rebelled against Persia in 499 B.C.E., the Athenians and Eretrians exacerbated a volatile situation by assisting their fellow Ionians and sending troops to aid the rebels. One detachment sacked the Persian regional capital, Sardis, in 494 B.C.E.

Darius suppressed the revolt and determined to punish the Athenians and Eretrians for their role in aiding the rebels. He also intended an eventual annexation of mainland Greece. In 490 B.C.E., a Persian expedition sacked Eretria and deported the population to Asia but was subsequently defeated at Marathon by the combined forces of Athens and Plataea.

Under Darius's successor, Xerxes I, Persia mounted a true invasion. The Persians won a victory at Thermopylae and killed the Spartan king Leonidas in 480 B.C.E., but the Greeks won a subsequent naval victory at Salamis later that same year and then scored a decisive victory on land at Plataea in 479 B.C.E. A subsequent engagement at Mycale crippled the Persian fleet. At the same time, Gelon, the tyrant of Syracuse, crushed a synchronously timed invasion of Sicily by Carthage, defeating the Carthaginians at Himera and breaking Carthaginian power in the west for two generations.

The defeat of the Persians left Athens and Sparta as the dominant powers in mainland Greece. Sparta did little to exploit its advantage, content to preserve the status quo. By contrast, the Athenians, whose city had been sacked twice by the Persians during the invasion, resolved to continue the war in order to liberate the Greek cities of Asia Minor. Athens and the Greek maritime powers created an alliance known as the Delian League because the treasury of the league was kept at Delos, the island sacred to Apollo. Under the leadership of the Athenian Cimon, the league vigorously prosecuted the war, winning a great double victory at the Eurymedon River circa 466 B.C.E.

At home, Athens radicalized its democracy under Ephialtes and Pericles. It continued to pursue an aggressive foreign policy against Sparta and Persia, consolidated its leadership of the Delian League, and transformed it into an Athenian empire. Athens removed the treasury of the league from Delos to Athens and used the revenues to finance its own building projects, imposed terms and garrisons on the other cities in the league, required all members to use Athenian coinage and standards, and ordered the other cities to bring offerings to the Great Panathenaic festival every four years. These policies caused rebellions throughout the league and eventually caused Sparta to bring an army into Attica. Pericles, the architect of Athenian policy, was able to negotiate a withdrawal of the Spartan army and a Thirty Years' Peace (445 B.C.E.). The peace left Athens free to consolidate its empire but laid the groundwork for the Peloponnesian War by essentially dividing Greece into two armed camps.

Hostilities with Sparta and its allies exploded in 431 B.C.E. for a variety of reasons. The first ten years of the war, known as the Archidamian War (431-421 B.C.E.), were inconclusive, although Athens suffered greatly from the plague in 429-428 B.C.E. The Peace of Nicias guaranteed a fifty-year truce, but Athens opted to break the peace by invading Syracuse, the wealthiest Greek city in the west. The invasion ended disastrously for Athens and renewed the general war with Sparta. Athens suffered a final humiliating defeat at Aegospotami in 405 B.C.E. and surrendered the next year, enduring the loss of its democracy and the imposition of a Spartan garrison on the Acropolis.

Sparta was unable to hold Athens for long, and the

CLASSICAL GREECE, FIFTH CENTURY B.C.E.

democracy was restored in 401 B.C.E. Sparta embarked on an interventionist foreign policy under Agesilaus II, who was forced ultimately to sell out the Greek cities in Ionia in order to gain Persian aid in controlling affairs in mainland Greece. Athens, Thebes, Argos, and Corinth, in a rolling system of alliances, opposed Sparta. Spartan power was finally broken at Leuctra in 371 B.C.E., and Thebes and the Boeotian League enjoyed a brief hegemony under Epaminondas, but he was killed at the indecisive Battle of Mantinea (362 B.C.E.), and Thebes never recovered its position.

The last few decades of the Classical era witnessed the growth of Macedonia under Philip II. He first consolidated his own power in Macedonia, then exploited the chaotic conditions in Greece after Mantinea to gain a foothold in Greece. He intervened in the Third Sacred War (357 B.C.E.-346 B.C.E.), was invited by Isocrates to

lead a Greek invasion of Persia, and eventually overwhelmed Greek opposition to Macedonian domination at Chaeronea in 338 B.C.E. His son and successor Alexander the Great took two years to consolidate his own position, defeating Celtic tribes in the north and west of Macedonia and then quelling any possible Greek opposition by annihilating Thebes. Alexander then led his army into Persia, where he overwhelmed Persian opposition at Granicus, Issus, and Gaugamela. He took over Darius III's throne and reached as far as southern Russia, Afghanistan, and India before returning to Babylon and dying in 323 B.C.E.

In western Greece, Syracuse remained the dominant state. After the invasion by Athens, internal difficulties led to a restoration of the system of tyranny that had been jettisoned sixty years earlier when Syracuse overthrew the unfortunate Thasyboulos. The new tyrant,

Dionysius I the Elder, warred almost incessantly against Carthage and gained control of much of Sicily and Magna Graecia before a serious defeat at Cronium (375 B.C.E.). His son Dionysius the Younger, briefly a student of Plato, attempted to consolidate Syracusan power in Sicily but saw his position usurped by his uncle, Dion, who held Syracuse until his murder in 354. Dionysius the Younger eventually recovered Syracuse but was defeated by the Corinthian Timoleon, who sent Dionysius the Younger into exile at Corinth. Timoleon made peace with Carthage and was able to consolidate his power at Syracuse until his retirement from public life, caused by encroaching blindness. He died about 334 B.C.E.

Performing arts. In Athens, the fifth century was the era of the theater. At the festival of the City Dionysia, Athenian citizens watched the tragedies of Aeschylus, Sophocles, and Euripides. The tragedians competed with one another, both for the right to have plays funded and to perform them. The *Oresteia* (458 B.C.E.; English translation, 1777) of Aeschylus is the only surviving trilogy from ancient Greece, and Sophocles' *Oidipous Tyrannos* (c. 429 B.C.E.; *Oedipus Tyrannus*, 1715) remains the most famous of all Greek plays. Aristophanes was the leading comic poet of Athens. His comedies mocked the leading citizens of Athens and denounced the excesses of the prowar parties. His most famous work, the *Lysistratē* (411 B.C.E.; English translation, 1837), has remained a staple of pacifism to the present day.

Language and literature. The fifth century was the age of Pindar, whose *Epinikia* (498-446 B.C.E.; *Odes*, 1656) celebrated the glories of athletic victory. Bacchylides of Ceos, a proximate contemporary, wrote epinician (victory) odes and dithyrambs, while Simonides, also of Ceos, wrote hymns and epitaphs to celebrate and to mourn the fallen of the Greco-Persian Wars. The same century also saw the development of historical writing. Herodotus wrote *Historiai Herodotou* (c. 424 B.C.E.; *The History*, 1709), focusing on the war against Persia and recording a great deal of ethnographic, religious, and sociological information on Greece as well as Egypt, Persia, and other states of the Near East. Thucydides wrote the definitive history of the Peloponnesian War, and where his account breaks off in about 410 B.C.E., it is picked up by Xenophon, whose *Ellēnika* (411-362 B.C.E.; *History of the Affairs of Greece*, also known as *Helenica*, 1685) extends the account to the second Battle of Mantinea in 362 B.C.E. Xenophon also gave the world one of the

great "true" adventure stories, the *Kurou anabasis* (between 394 and 371 B.C.E.; *Anabasis*, also known as *Expedition of Cyrus* and *March Up Country*, 1623), an account of the expedition of 10,000 Greek mercenaries against the Persian king Artaxerxes II, and their subsequent escape.

The late fifth and fourth centuries B.C.E. also saw the development of oratory as an art form. The canonical Attic orators practiced at this time. Lysias, a metic (resident noncitizen) of Athens was the master of the simple, smooth style of Attic Greek. Demosthenes, who spoke out repeatedly against Philip II of Macedonia, earned a place in history for himself with his Philippic orations, which were later copied by Cicero in his writings against Marc Antony.

Philosophy. The three most famous figures of Greek philosophy belong to this period. Socrates was an Athenian stonecutter who abandoned his trade to inquire into the nature of humankind, thus moving philosophy from natural science to ethics. He wrote nothing, and his greatest contribution was as a teacher to Plato. He was executed by the state for impiety and corruption of the youth. His great disciple, Plato, authored a number of works in dialogic form in which Socrates challenges the conventional wisdom of his interlocutor and works through logical analysis to educate. Plato's greatest works are the *Politeia* (388-368 B.C.E.; *Republic*, 1701), *Symposion* (388-368 B.C.E.; *Symposium*, 1701), *Phaedros* (388-368 B.C.E.; *Phaedrus*, 1792), and *Phaedōn* (388-368 B.C.E.; *Phaedo*, 1675).

Aristotle, born in Stagirus in Chalcidice, came to Athens at the age of seventeen to study with Plato and remained at the Academy until Plato's death in 347 B.C.E. He later tutored Alexander the Great (then a boy) and finally returned to Athens in 335 B.C.E., establishing his own school at a grove sacred to Apollo Lyceius and the Muses. His extensive works include the *Physica* (335-323 B.C.E.; *Physics*, 1812), *Metaphysica* (335-323 B.C.E.; *Metaphysics*, 1801), *Technē rhetorikēs* (335-323 B.C.E.; *Rhetoric*, 1686), and *Ethica Nicomachea* (335-323 B.C.E.; *Nicomachean Ethics*, 1797).

Religion and ritual. The Panhellenic aspects of Greek religion focused on the major festivals and shrines. From the eighth century B.C.E., Delphi had been predominant for the worship of Apollo, and its influence grew in the Classical period as it became the place to which the Greek cities resorted for information, approbation, and direction from the god. It played a particularly important part in the Greco-Persian Wars, although it did lose some of its authority. It was pro-

Spartan during the Peloponnesian War and later was pro-Macedonian, suggesting either a great conservatism or a keen if sometimes errant estimate of comparative military force by Apollo and his minions.

The city of Athens opened its Panathenaic and Dionysia festivals to foreigners, but perhaps its most famous ritual was the Eleusinian mysteries, held at the village of Eleusis and sacred to Demeter. Other significant sites included Delos, sacred to Apollo, the Heraion at Argos, the temple of Artemis Orthia at Sparta, and the shrine of Zeus at Dodona.

The great spiritual longing that would characterize the Hellenistic age seems not yet apparent in the Classical period, although, in addition to the rites of Demeter at Eleusis, there is substantial evidence for Orphic and Dionysiac practice at this time.

Women's life. The condition of women varied considerably from one Greek state to another, and it is a mistake to view any one instance as paradigmatic. In Athens, women were generally isolated from men, to the extent that the better houses included separate women's quarters. Nonetheless, women did play a central role in family ritual and held important roles in burial practices. The principal female festival at Athens was the Thesmophoria. Spartan women were, by contrast, able to own property and were noted for the extensive freedom of behavior and movement they enjoyed. Educated women from Ionia and the Greek cities of Asia Minor were actively sought as courtesans, and it is from this group that Aspasia of Miletus, the mistress of Pericles, was drawn. Women were also noted for acts of great heroism. The poet Telesilla of Argos (whose work survives in nine fragments only) led a group of women who repelled Spartan invaders under Cleomenes after the Argive army was defeated at Sepeia.

Economics. By the Classical period, most of the Greek world had adopted coined money. The availability of coinage made easier the acquisition and preservation of capital and encouraged both commerce and private wealth. Trade was conducted on an international basis, with Greek cities acquiring goods from across the Mediterranean basin, the Black Sea, inland Europe, and Asia. Greek wares reached the Atlantic coast and India. Athens, Corinth, Rhodes, and the cities of the Asiatic coasts (depending on political conditions) were all leading market cities.

Government and law. The major cities of Greece had, for the most part, established forms of government before the Classical period. Each city was essentially self-governing, although owing to victory or defeat in war or the dominance of one power or another in the shifting alliances that characterized the period, the larger powers sometimes gained control of the internal government and foreign policy of their allies. Nor were the governments entirely static. Athens revised its democratic practices on more than one occasion, even going so far as to vote the democracy out of existence in 411 B.C.E. under the stress of the Greco-Persian Wars. The Thebans and the other states of the Boeotian confederacy were under the rule of the Boeotarchs. Sparta was governed by two kings who operated at the direction of the board of ephors (magistrates), a *gerousia* (council of elders), and an assembly of citizen-soldiers. Corinth enjoyed for the most part a rule of stable oligarchy, although it did flirt briefly with democracy. Argos established a type of democracy sometime after 480 B.C.E.

The famous law code of Gortyn, in Crete, which dates from the fifth century, gives an idea of both the substantive and procedural laws that might have been common throughout the Greek states. Most knowledge about the laws in Athens, however, comes from the large number of speeches preserved from the law courts of the late fifth and fourth centuries B.C.E.

War and weapons. Greece defeated Persia in no small part because of its naval supremacy. Athens built a substantial fleet of triremes (warships) to keep its maritime empire in charge. On land, hoplite warfare reigned supreme during the Classical period. The later fifth and the fourth centuries B.C.E. saw the first widespread use of mercenary soldiers in Greece. The preferred weapon of the hoplite was the spear, backed by the use of a short, straight sword. Hoplite armies were effective against cavalry on even terrain, but when scattered or on broken ground, they were much more vulnerable. The Thebans under Epaminondas proved the ultimate effectiveness of cavalry backed by heavy infantry, particularly at Leuctra in 371 B.C.E. Philip II and Alexander the Great perfected such tactics.

Education and training. Sparta demanded that every boy enter the army at age seven and remain there until his retirement from active service. In addition to military skills, young men learned to read and write and received some instruction in music. Women were educated in gymnastics, dancing, and music. Elementary education at Athens might consist of a boy hearing a *grammatistes*, who taught reading, writing, literature, and the elements of arithmetic; a *kitharistes* who taught music; and a *paidotribes*, who taught physical education. Evidence from vase painting suggests that upper-class young women might receive education in all three areas as well. Higher education in professional fields was available, as was advanced study at the philosophical schools. Plato's Academy, Aristotle's Lyceum, and Isocrates' school of rhetoric were the most famous. Professional itinerant educators known as Sophists taught rhetoric, logic, and other skills. Schools are mentioned in other cities as well (for example, Troezen and Mycalessus), but little is known of how they functioned.

Architecture and city planning. The fifth century B.C.E. witnessed the great period of Athenian building. A wall was built around the city in 479 B.C.E., replacing an Archaic wall, and long walls were built to connect the city to the Piraeus in the 450's. The Piraeus, a harbor complex built to accommodate the new Athenian navy as well as to foster trade, was laid out on a rectangular plan by the architect Hippodamus of Miletus, who was also responsible for planning the Panhellenic colony at Thurii (443 B.C.E.).

On the Acropolis, most of the original buildings had been destroyed by Persian invaders. In the 450's B.C.E., the major building projects were begun, and Phidias's colossal statue of Athena Promachus was erected. Phidias superintended the overall work on the Acropolis. The Parthenon was completed by 432 B.C.E.: Ictinus and Callicrates were the architects. Mnesicles was responsible for the Propylaea, finished in the same year, and the latter part of the fifth century B.C.E. saw the completion of the Erechtheum. An earlier building program under Cimon had seen a substantial rebuilding of the Agora, including the famous Stoa Poecile. The shape of the fifth century B.C.E. Theater of Dionysus is a matter of considerable dispute. In imitation of Athens, however, substantial theaters were built at Epidaurus and Megalopolis. Megalopolis, founded by Epaminondas as the center of the Arcadian League, was perhaps the most ambitious foundation of the fourth century B.C.E. until Alexander founded Alexandria in Egypt to provide him communication by sea with Europe.

Calendars and chronology. The Greek world had no universal calendar. The Athenian calendar, the best known, was a twelve-month lunar calendar of approximately 354 days with an occasional thirteenth month added to restore pace with the solar year. The names of some individual months are known from other cities. Years were generally reckoned on the four-year cycle of the Olympic Games, while an individual year might be known from a particular officeholder (in Athens, for example, the Archon Eponymous).

Medicine and science. Medicine developed greatly during the Classical period. Hippocrates of Cos was said by Plato to be the first who attempted to treat the body as a whole, although the body of works that have come down in the Hippocratic corpus show no overt signs of such concern. It is likely that the peripatetic Hippocrates left disciples throughout the Greek world who followed in outline, at least, his theories. However, the popularity of the cult of Asclepius at Epidaurus, the use of incubation in Asclepian rites, and the persistent use of charms and amulets suggest that nonrational elements continued to exercise a strong influence on Greek medical practice. The great scientific and astronomical discoveries of the Hellenistic age lay in the future, but some progress was made in mathematics and natural science by Plato and by Aristotle. The expedition of Alexander the Great into Persia and Central Asia greatly increased knowledge in geography, botany, and biology.

Transportation and navigation. The Greeks of the Classical period continued to improve on their shipbuilding. The trireme was the principal warship in Classical times, replacing the *pentekontor* in the late sixth century B.C.E. It was fairly narrow, with a removable mast that was taken down and sometimes put ashore before battle. The regular merchant vessels were much squarer, relying primarily on sail power, although they could use long sweeping oars for maneuverability. The original merchant ships had one mast, although later a forward mast was added. The sailing season generally fell between March and October. Ships did not tack well, and there were no instruments such as the sextant or compass to assist in finding position at sea.

Sports and entertainment. The Olympic Games, celebrated every fourth year, remained the most important of the athletic festivals of this period. In addition, Panhellenic games were celebrated at Corinth (Isthmian Games), Nemea (Nemean Games), and Delphi (Pythian Games). Two of the most famous athletes of the Classical period were Theagenes of Thasos, who won nine Nemean and ten Isthmian Games, and Dorieus of Rhodes, whose victories in boxing and the *pankration* (a type of "no-holds-barred" wrestling) extended over a career of at least twenty-six years.

Visual arts. Athenian red-figured pottery came into use around 530 B.C.E. and dominated throughout the classical period. Vase painting became less stiff although still idealized. A freer style of painting characterized fourth century B.C.E. vases. In sculpture, Phidias completed the monumental Athena Promachos for the

Acropolis in the 450's. The sculptures of the pediment are either his work or were done under his direction. There was some larger painting done on walls at this period, particularly by Micon and Polygnotus, who decorated the Stoa Poecile and the Theseum. Zeuxis of Heraclea was perhaps the best known of all the painters of the Classical period, known for his use of shading and highlighting. A famous story alleges that his painting fooled birds.

Current views. Much scholarship has focused on integrating the cultural and religious elements of the Classical period with the more familiar politics and literature. There has been a rejection of the Apollonian/Dionysian split favored by philosopher Friedrich Nietzsche in favor of an attempt to find the unity that underlies the rationalism of Plato and Aristotle, the mysticism of Eleusis, the superstition of Delphi, and the ordinary savagery of Greek warfare and politics. In addition, comparative evidence is being mined for insights into the lives of women and the political underclasses in Greek society, and much more work is being done on those elements that connect Classical Greece to its own Archaic past. There has also developed a greater appreciation of the role that cultural exchange with Asia, other parts of Europe, and Egypt played in the development of Classical Greece.

ADDITIONAL RESOURCES

Bryant, Joseph M. *Moral Codes and Social Structure in Ancient Greece: A Sociology of Greek Ethics from Homer to the Epicureans and Stoics*. Albany: State University of New York Press, 1996.

Gagarin, Michael. *Early Greek Law*. Berkeley: University of California Press, 1986.

Hammond, Nicholas G. L. *A History of Greece to 322 B.C.* 3d ed. Oxford, England: Oxford University Press, 1986.

Roberts, J. W. *The City of Sokrates: An Introduction to Classical Athens*. London: Routledge and Kegan Paul, 1998.

Stockton, D. *The Classical Athenian Democracy*. New York: Oxford University Press, 1990.

Wiles, David. *Tragedy in Athens: Performance Space and Theatrical Meaning*. Cambridge, England: Cambridge University Press, 1997.

SEE ALSO: Aegospotami, Battle of; Aeschylus; Agesilaus II of Sparta; Alexander the Great; Archidamian War; Aristophanes; Aristotle; Aspasia of Miletus; Athens; Bacchylides; Callicrates; Chaeronea, Battle of; Cimon; Darius the Great; Delphi; Demosthenes; Dionysius I the Elder of Syracuse; Dionysius the Younger; Eleusinian mysteries; Epaminondas; Euripides; Gaugamela, Battle of; Gelon of Syracuse; Gortyn, law code of; Granicus, Battle of; Greco-Persian Wars; Herodotus; Hippocrates; Ictinus; Isocrates; Issus, Battle of; Leonidas; Leuctra, Battle of; Lysander of Sparta; Lysias; Macedonia; Mantinea, Battles of; Marathon, Battle of; Olympic Games; Parthenon; Pericles; Phidias; Philip II; Pindar; Plataea, Battle of; Plato; Polygnotus; Sacred Wars; Simonides; Socrates; Sophocles; Thermopylae, Battle of; Thucydides; Timoleon of Corinth; Xenophon; Xerxes I.

—*Joseph P. Wilson*

GREECE, HELLENISTIC AND ROMAN

DATE: 323 B.C.E.-330 C.E.

LOCALE: Greek peninsula, Italy, Sicily, eastern Mediterranean

SIGNIFICANCE: The Hellenistic period is marked in Greece by a futile struggle to maintain independence from outside powers, the spread of Greek language and culture throughout the eastern half of the Mediterranean, and the assimilation into Greek culture of foreign or non-Greek features.

"Hellenistic," derived from *Hellenistes* (the Greek word for "one who speaks Greek"), is more a temporal than a geographical term and refers to the period from the death of Alexander the Great in 323 B.C.E. until the beginning of the reign of the Roman emperor Augustus in 31 B.C.E. Hellenistic Greece included not only the Greek peninsula but also Greek communities in Italy and Sicily known as Magna Graecia, as well as vast areas of western Asia, North Africa, and Egypt. Roman Greece began with Augustus and ended with the founding of Constantinople as the new capital of the Roman empire in 330 C.E.

History. The traditional independent Greek city-state disintegrated in the Hellenistic period as Alexander's Diadochi, or successors, struggled to create dynastic kingdoms and waged nearly continuous warfare with one another and with various leagues of Greek cities. It is impossible to consider the history of Greece in this period separately from the affairs of powerful ruling families such as the Seleucids in Syria, the Ptolemies in Egypt, the Antigonids in Macedonia, and, eventually, Rome.

At the time of Alexander the Great's death, Greece was controlled by Antipater, a general who had served under Alexander's father Philip II. Antipater's death in 319 B.C.E. was followed by factional warfare among Antigonus I Monophthalmos, Ptolemy I Soter of Egypt, and Antipater's son Cassander. In 311 B.C.E., all three signed a treaty giving Macedonia and Greece to Cassander and acknowledging their separate spheres of influence as independent monarchs.

Greece in general and Athens in particular were mere pawns in this struggle. An aristocratic faction under the peripatetic philosopher Demetrius Phalereus ruled Athens for Cassander. In 307 B.C.E., Antigonus' son Demetrius Poliorcetes seized Athens and restored the democracy. In 301 B.C.E., Cassander, Ptolemy, and Seleucus defeated Antigonus and Demetrius Poliorcetes at Ipsus, and Athens returned to Cassander, who allowed the city self-rule until it was recaptured by Demetrius in 295 B.C.E.

Cassander died in 298 B.C.E. Rivalries among his sons enabled Demetrius Poliorcetes to control Macedonia from 294 B.C.E. until his death in 288 B.C.E. Lysimachus then ruled Macedonia and northern Greece until he fell in battle in 281 B.C.E. Two years later, Macedonia was invaded by the Galati, a Gallic tribe from the Danube. Greece proper avoided a similar fate only by the brave defense of the Aetolians. After thwarting Galatian conquest of Asia Minor, Antigonus II Gonatas, son of Demetrius Poliorcetes, returned in 276 B.C.E. to Macedonia, where he established himself as king. At first Antigonus's control of Greece was limited to Corinth and Piraeus. A revolt by Athens, Sparta, and other cities, called the Chremonidean War (268/267-262/261 B.C.E.), led to Athens' capture by Antigonus in 262 B.C.E.

The second half of the third century B.C.E. is marked by a futile struggle to attain Greek independence, first from Macedonia and then from Rome, complicated by inter-Greek conflicts among the Achaean League, the Aetolian League, and Sparta. An Aetolian alliance with Rome against Philip V of Macedonia in 212 B.C.E. led to a series of Macedonian wars between Rome and Macedonia. In 197 B.C.E., Macedonia was defeated by Titus Quinctius Flamininus at Cynoscephalae. In the follow-

ing year, at the Isthmian Games, Flamininus declared free all Greeks formerly ruled by Philip. This brilliant stroke of propaganda led to widespread support for Rome throughout Greece, except in the cities of the Aetolian League, which encouraged the Seleucids to support an unsuccessful war of liberation against Roman rule of Greece. Following the defeat of the Macedonian king Perseus at Pydna in 168 B.C.E. by the Roman Quintus Marcius Philippus, the Aetolian League was dissolved and many Greeks, including the historian Polybius, were exiled to Rome. In 146 B.C.E., the Achaean League declared war on Rome. The consul Lucius Mummius, sent by Rome to deal with the uprising, defeated the league and destroyed Corinth as its political center. Greece became Roman territory.

In the first century B.C.E., Greece was caught in the middle of Roman conflicts, first with the ambitious Mithradates VI Eupator of Pontus and then in the series of Roman civil wars between Julius Caesar and Pompey the Great, between Caesar's heir and his assassins, and finally between Octavian and Marc Antony. Cities and shrines such as Delos, Delphi, and Olympia were sacked by all sides, and there was great loss of Greek life. Peace finally came to ravaged Greece in 27 B.C.E. when the emperor Augustus declared Greece to be the Roman province of Achaea. In this new Roman order, Athens retained its status as a university town, and the cities of Corinth and Patrae became major commercial centers. The Greek economy recovered slowly. During the long period of Roman rule, however, no Greek cities ever regained their former political or economic prominence. Greek culture and language continued to flourish only to be transformed after the fourth century C.E. into a Byzantine world focused on Constantinople (later Istanbul).

War and weapons. The warfare of the period was marked by the use of cavalry, elephants, and mercenaries, especially Greeks or soldiers trained in the Greek fashion. It was also an age of large warships and sophisticated naval warfare based on ramming or the use of the grappling hook.

Government and law. In the Hellenistic period, the Greek polis, or city, continued to maintain its own law code, but cities sometimes shared judges in order to ensure impartiality. Citizenship was usually localized in the city, but in some areas of Greece, especially Aetolia, citizenship was regional and based on league membership. During the Roman period, Greece was administered by a governor from Rome, but many cities were declared free states and were exempt from Roman taxation. Local citizenship remained important until 212 C.E., when the Edict of Caracalla granted Roman citizenship to all free-born inhabitants of the Roman Empire.

Settlements and city planning. Greek cities such as Alexandria in Egypt and Antioch in Syria were founded by Hellenistic rulers throughout the eastern Mediterranean. Two such foundations in Greece proper were Cassandreia (formerly Potidaea) and Demetrias (near modern Volos). Civic architecture and town planning became more scientific, and temples such as Olympian Zeus in Athens and Apollo at Didyma, became more monumental. The street-grid system and the Corinthian order became standardized. Arches, cupolas, pillared colonnades, and round buildings such as the Tholos in Delphi were popular. During the Roman period, older Greek cities such as Athens benefited from public works projects subsidized by rich or powerful patrons. The Roman agora (gathering place) in Athens, for example, blended traditional Greek and Roman architectural features under the sponsorship of the emperor Hadrian.

Education and training. Most Hellenistic cities made elementary education available to both males and females in the public gymnasium, which served as a center of learning as well as physical training. More advanced education, especially the study of philosophy and rhetoric, was an option for the wealthy. From the first century B.C.E. onward, many famous Romans, including Cicero and Horace, completed their education in Athens.

Women's life. The visible role of women in Greek society increased markedly during the Hellenistic period. Olympias, Berenice, and Cleopatra VII, as members of important dynasties, wielded great political power both indirectly and directly. The Thracian Hipparchia, for example, was a prominent student and companion of the late fourth century Cynic philosopher Crates of Thebes. Many contemporary documents testify to the prominence of women in commerce and everyday life, their occasional great wealth, and their ability to manage their own affairs.

Economics. Hellenistic Greece was essentially an urban culture. Few could support themselves in rural communities, and Greece relied heavily on grain imports, especially from Egypt. Greece was part of an elaborate trade network including not only the Mediterranean world but also east Africa and the Red Sea, where there were significant exploration and expansion.

Trade with the western Mediterranean, especially Rome, increased dramatically in the last few centuries B.C.E. Other major trade routes ran through Mesopotamia to India and from the Mediterranean coast into Africa. Sea traffic and commerce were widespread despite threats from pirates. Some coinage was issued by individual Greek cities and more by dynastic rulers. Eventually all coinage was issued from Rome. In addition to grain, important commodities included precious gems and metals, timber, textiles, and slaves. Greece was an important exporter of marble and artwork.

Slavery was a fact of life and an economic mainstay. Anyone, rich or poor, could suddenly become a slave because of the prevalence of piracy on the high seas and capture in war. Slave revolts were not common, as were bankruptcy and calls for cancellation of debts.

Religion and ritual. A general sense of the precariousness of life encouraged a religious revival, especially focused on mystery cults such as that of Dionysus or the goddess Demeter at Eleusis. Such cults promised initiates temporary release from present troubles or at least special treatment in the afterlife. The goddess Tyche (Chance) was also popular in the Hellenistic and Roman periods, as were foreign cults such as those of the Phrygian mother goddess Cybele, the Egyptian goddess Isis, and eventually Christianity. In the midst of such religious syncretism, traditional shrines like those at Delphi and Olympia were maintained but were frequently plundered in war or invasion.

Outside these mystery religions, Greek beliefs in the afterlife offered little solace or promise of a better existence after death. Burial practices show a tendency to demonstrate affection for the deceased and to celebrate their individuality. This is evident both in the modest grave steles of the middle class and in extravagant tombs such as the famous mausoleum of Halicarnassus.

Philosophy. Philosophy was another recourse in a troubled age. Athens served as the intellectual center for Greek philosophical schools throughout the Hellenistic and Roman periods. In the fourth century B.C.E., Aristotle's Peripatetic school produced a scholarly giant in Theophrastus and a political power in Demetrius Phalereus. The same century saw the foundation of several major philosophical movements—Skepticism, Epicureanism, and Stoicism —as well as the career of the great Cynic philosopher Diogenes of Sinope.

Sports and entertainment. The quadrennial Olympic Games and the other traditional Crown Games at Delphi, Nemea, and Corinth, open only to Greek athletes, served as another important symbol of Hellenic

The Greeks were fond of games and competitions. Here, the winner of a competition is crowned with laurel. (North Wind Picture Archives)

the political authority to make it universal. Only with the advent of Roman rule did Greece attain some semblance of calendar uniformity, based on the Roman system and the Julian calendar.

Language and literature. The political chaos of Hellenistic Greece contrasts with its linguistic and cultural unity. During this period, the many dialects of ancient Greece merged into a single, common language known as Koine Greek, which became the lingua franca of a polyglot eastern Mediterranean. Literacy was not unusual, and Hellenistic cities were filled with public documents inscribed in stone. Papyrus (imported from Egypt), slates, and clay tablets served as material for more temporary records.

The cultural center of the Hellenistic world was not Greece but Alexandria in Egypt, where the Ptolemies sponsored a literary and scientific revival. Greek texts were collected from Athens and elsewhere for the library and museum. Several early Alexandrian librarians, representing diverse parts of the Hellenistic world, dominated scholarship and literature in the third and second centuries B.C.E. Zenodotus of Ephesus and Aristarchus of Samothrace were great philologists. Eratosthenes of Cyrene was a great mathematician and geographer. Apollonius Rhodius and Callimachus of Cyrene were scholarly poets of sophisticated verse. Other major authors of the period included the pastoral poet Theocritus of Syracuse and the historian Polybius. The novelists Chariton of Aphrodisias and Xenophon of Ephesus developed a popular prose genre of romance and adventure.

In the second century C.E., Greek learning and literature were revitalized in a movement called the Second Sophistic, which strove to re-create the glory of Classical Athens by the use of archaism in style and Atticism, a form of Greek similar to the Attic dialect of the fifth

culture. Special dispensation was granted for the Roman emperor Nero to compete during his progress through Greece in 66 C.E. The Olympic Games continued to be held until 393 C.E., when they were abolished by the emperor Theodosius the Great.

Calendars and chronology. The Hellenistic world had no universal calendar. A method of recording time based on the four-year cycle of the Olympic Games had been invented, but most cities still preferred their own idiosyncratic systems. The Seleucids developed a calendar based on the history of their dynasty but lacked

century B.C.E. Noteworthy in this movement were the orators Aristides and Dio Chrysostom. Their contemporaries included the biographers Plutarch and Flavius Philostratus, Pausanias the Traveler, the historians Appian, Arrian, Dio Cassius, and the novelists Longus and Lucian.

In the third century C.E., Heliodorus of Emesa produced a major novel of romance and adventure called *Aethiopica* (third century C.E.; *An Aethiopian Historie*, 1569?). Epigrammatic poetry, on subjects such as love and religious hymns, was revitalized after the fourth century C.E., especially by Gregory of Nazianzus and other Christian authors. Quintus Smyrnaeus wrote an epic poem *Posthomerica* (c. 375 C.E.; English translation, 1821), which followed the mythological narrative between Homer's *Iliad* (c. 800 B.C.E.; English translation, 1616) and the *Odyssey* (c. 800 B.C.E.; English translation, 1616). The *Dionysiaca* (fifth century C.E.; English translation, 1940) of Nonnus of Panopolis celebrated the myths of the god Dionysus.

Performing arts. Although some tragedies were written in this period and the plays of the great fifth century B.C.E. masters were still performed, the major performing art of the Hellenistic period was comedy. One of the few Athenian voices in the Hellenistic period was the comic playwright Menander. Mime was popular long into the Roman period but, like music for voice and instruments, is essentially lost. Displays of rhetoric were also popular forms of public entertainment throughout the Hellenistic and Roman periods.

Visual arts. Major schools of Hellenistic art were located at Alexandria, Rhodes, and Pergamum. The art of the period is marked by a transition from the idealism of the Archaic and Classical periods to the striking realism of works such as the Great Altar of Zeus at Pergamum or the sculpture *Nike of Samothrace*. Classical restraint and anonymity gave way to individualism, especially in portrait sculpture, numismatics, and mosaics, in which the artist strove to emphasize personal characteristics and to celebrate the patron. One major area of Hellenistic art, wall paintings, is virtually lost and can be appreciated only through its Roman imitations.

Science and technology. The Hellenistic world saw advances in medicine, science, and technology. Prominent physicians included Herophilus of Chalcedon and Erasistratus of Iulis on Ceos. The emphasis was on anatomy and physiology with a strong interest in poisons and antidotes. Philinus of Cos was more empirical. The close alliance of medicine and religion is illustrated by the popularity of sanctuaries of the god Asclepius at healing centers.

Scientific advances in astronomy and geographic measurements by Aristarchus of Samos, Eratosthenes of Cyrene, Hipparchus of Nicaea, and Posidonius of Apamea showed the influence of Babylonia, as well as outstanding Hellenistic research, scholarship, and ingenuity. The mathematical works of Euclid remained basic points of reference for centuries.

Archimedes of Syracuse made advances in practical mechanics with his invention of a water clock and the dioptra, a portable water level. Aristotle's student Theophrastus produced works of careful observation and analysis in botany and zoology.

Current views. Although the Greek-speaking world expanded dramatically in the Hellenistic period, it is questionable that this resulted from a deliberate policy of cultural propaganda on the part of Alexander the Great and the Diadochi. Greek military skill and rulers of Greek ancestry certainly dominated the eastern Mediterranean between the death of Alexander and the Roman conquest, and Greek language and Greek culture spread widely as Greek cities were founded throughout the region. Although nineteenth century historians often sought to explain Greek expansionism during the Hellenistic period in terms of Christian missionary zeal and European colonial imperialism, more modern scholars have understood the spread of Greek culture in a less programmatic way and have described a much more multicultural environment in which the Greeks borrowed as much as they loaned to their neighbors.

ADDITIONAL RESOURCES

Green, Peter. *Alexander to Actium: The Historical Evolution of the Hellenistic Age.* Reprint. Berkeley: University of California Press, 1993.

_____, ed. *Hellenistic History and Culture.* Berkeley: University of California Press, 1993.

Habicht, Christian. *Athens from Alexander to Antony.* Translated by Deborah Lucas Schneider. Cambridge, Mass.: Harvard University Press, 1999.

Martin, Thomas R. *Ancient Greece: From Prehistoric to Hellenistic Times.* New Haven, Conn.: Yale University Press, 1998.

Tarn, W. W., and G. T. Griffith. *Hellenistic Civilisation.* 3d ed. New York: World, 1952.

SEE ALSO: Achaean League; Achaean War; Aetolian League; Alexander the Great; Alexandrian library;

Antigonid Dynasty; Antipater; Antony, Marc; Appian; Appollonius of Rhodes; Archimedes; Aristarchus of Samothrace; Aristides; Arrian; Athens; Augustus; Caesar, Julius; Callimachus of Cyrene; Cassander; Cicero; Cleopatra VII; Cynoscephalae, Battle of; Demetrius Phalereus; Demetrius Poliorcetes; Diadochi; Dio Cassius; Dio Chrysostom; Diogenes of Sinope; Epicurus; Eratosthenes of Cyrene; Flamininus, Titus Quinctius; Gauls; Hadrian; Herophilus; Hipparchus; Horace; Lucian; Lysimachus; Macedonia; Magna Graecia; Menander (playwright); Mithradates VI Eupator; Mummius, Lucius; Nonnus of Panopolis; Olympias; Olympic Games; Pausanias the Traveler; Philip V; Philostratus, Flavius; Polybius; Pompey the Great; Posidonius; Ptolemaic Dynasty; Quintus Smyrnaeus; Rome, Republican; Seleucid Dynasty; Seleucus; Theocritus of Syracuse; Theophrastus; Zeus at Pergamum, Great Altar of.

—Thomas J. Sienkewicz

GREECE, MYCENAEAN

DATE: 2100-1000 B.C.E.

LOCALE: Ancient city of Mycenae, other places on the Greek mainland

SIGNIFICANCE: During the Mycenaean age, Greek-speaking city-states created the first great civilization of the Greek mainland, producing large fortified cities, beautiful works of art, and a written language.

According to legend, the city of Mycenae was the capital of Agamemnon, the Achaean king who supposedly led the campaign against Troy. Ancient writers said that Perseus, the mythological hero of Argos and Tiryns, was the founder of the city, which derived its name from the eponymous heroine Mycene, the wife of Arestor. Contemporary historians now apply the adjective "Mycenaean" to all the settlements on the Greek mainland during the late Bronze Age, although the settlements were not united into a single state. This label has been commonly used since the late nineteenth century, when Heinrich Schliemann's archaeological discoveries brought to light the high level of civilization that once existed at the site of Mycenae.

History. About 2100 B.C.E., the first Greek-speaking tribes probably arrived in the area. Apparently these fierce invaders already had a relatively advanced culture and knew how to use bronze, and they learned many additional skills from the non-Greek people they conquered, including shipbuilding, stone masonry, and the cultivation of olives. The invaders had no knowledge of writing, and archaeologists have discovered few objects that can be traced to their first five hundred years on the mainland.

By about 1600 B.C.E., archaeological evidence reveals that the Mycenaeans were building large stone cities located on high hills for protection. At this time, they also had powerful rulers, probably kings, who were buried in elaborate graves and tombs rather than the simple graves of earlier centuries. The objects left in the burial sites demonstrate that the Mycenaeans had advanced skills in metallurgy and that they made numerous weapons, tools, and decorations out of bronze, gold, silver, and other metals (but not iron).

The Mycenaean Greeks were divided into regional kingdoms: Mycenae in the plain of Argos, Pylos in the plain of Messenia, Thebes in the plain of Boeotia, Iolcus in the great plain of Thessaly, and Athens (a minor kingdom) in Attica. The wealthiest and most powerful of the kingdoms were Mycenae and Pylos. In Homer's *Iliad* (c. 800 B.C.E.; English translation, 1616), the Mycenaean king Agamemnon ruled as the supreme commander over a united Greek campaign, but most historians think it is unlikely that Mycenae ever exercised any real influence over the other kingdoms.

The Mycenaeans borrowed heavily from the Minoan civilization of Crete. Using architectural techniques from Knossos, they constructed high-walled castles at Mycenae and Tiryns. They also obtained the idea of a written language from Crete. For many years, the relations between the two societies were peaceful, but about 1450 B.C.E., the Mycenaeans invaded Crete and occupied the palace at Knossos. After remaining in Crete for some fifty years, they took over the Minoans' foreign trade and established trading colonies in the Aegean Sea and on the Asian coast, including Miletus.

The period from 1400 to 1250 B.C.E. was the heyday of Mycenaean civilization. These years were immortalized in Homer's epic poems, written more than four hundred years later. Scholars disagree about whether Homer, who had to depend on oral traditions, possessed much accurate information about particular events and customs. Although Homer's purpose was not to record the factual events of history, he apparently preserved memories of Mycenaean mythology and cultural values, including the notion of a warrior code of honor and bravery.

The decline of the Mycenaean civilization began during the thirteenth century B.C.E., probably the result of multiple causes. Perhaps the most basic factor was internal rivalry and civil conflict. In addition, upheavals in Asia Minor, especially the decline of the Hittite kingdom, made it more difficult to obtain raw materials from the eastern trade routes. As the Mycenaeans became less prosperous, they presented an invitation to invaders from the so-called Sea Peoples. Archaeological research reveals that the cities of Mycenae, Thebes, and Pylos suffered a succession of devastating military defeats in the years after about 1250 B.C.E.

The Mycenaeans, therefore, were in a condition of exhaustion and depopulation when the Dorians invaded the Greek mainland about 1100 B.C.E. These invasions marked the demise of Mycenaean civilization, the end of its undertaking of large building projects, its use of written records, and its thriving commerce. The various peoples of the region entered a period that historians call the Dark Age of Greece, during which the Aegean world returned to a more primitive level of culture.

Written language. The written script used by the Mycenaeans is known as Linear B, a modified version of the Minoan Linear A system adapted for writing in the Greek language. Most of the signs of Linear B stand for vowels and syllables, but there are also pictorial symbols representing animals and many objects. Scholars generally agree that the language is an archaic dialect of Greek, but with many ambiguities. The script was finally deciphered in 1952 by Michael Ventris with the assistance of John Chadwick.

The largest collection of tablets written in Linear B comes from Pylos, where numerous tablets of unbaked clay survived because the building that housed them was burned. The Pylos tablets consist of administrative and business records. Because the documents were written just before a destruction of the palace, they provide a glimpse into how the Mycenaeans prepared for an emer-

gency. It is fairly certain that Linear B was never used for recording poetry or other forms of creative literature.

Religion. Evidence suggests that the origins of classical Greek religion may lie in the Mycenaean period. The Linear B texts, for example, present Zeus as the dominant deity, and they also appear to mention a number of other familiar Olympian deities. Sacred buildings for religious rituals have been discovered on the acropolis of Mycenae. Most scholars now agree that the deities and the cultic practices of the Mycenaeans were quite different from those of the Minoans.

Mycenaean priests and priestesses made offerings of agricultural products to the recognized deities, and less frequently, they conducted sacrifices of sheep, cattle, and pigs. Both legends and Linear B texts indicate that the Mycenaeans practiced human sacrifices, but they probably performed these sacrifices only in emergency situations. One Pylos tablet mentioned that thirteen gold objects and eight humans had been offered to the deities.

Shaft graves and tombs. In 1874-1876, Schliemann discovered six large pits in Mycenae that served as royal graves, dated at about the sixteenth century B.C.E. Several of the skeletons were adorned with beautiful and realistic face masks hammered out of gold.

Realistic gold masks like this were found covering the faces of the bodies in the graves at Mycenae. (North Wind Picture Archives)

The graves also contained a variety of jewelry, weapons, and tools made of gold, silver, and bronze. One famous dagger contained a vivid scene of a lion hunt inlaid on the blade. The large number of weapons in the graves testifies to the important role of warfare in Mycenaean culture.

Members of the nobility were buried in underground beehive-shaped tombs, called *tholoi*, throughout the Mycenaean region. Some of these vaulted tombs were quite large. The most impressive structure, the Treasury of Atreus, measures forty-eight feet (fifteen meters) in diameter and forty-four feet (thirteen meters) high. Many of the tombs give indications that dead leaders and warriors were venerated, probably anticipating the hero cults that later became important. Unfortunately, most of the contents of the tombs were robbed in antiquity.

Art and architecture. The Mycenaeans often decorated their buildings and tombs with relief sculpture. A large lion gate at the entrance to the citadel at Mycenae is especially impressive. Craftspeople also carved small realistic statues out of stone and ivory. The beautifully decorated pottery of the Mycenaeans was highly prized throughout the Mediterranean world. The fresco decorations on Mycenaean palaces were greatly influenced by Minoan styles.

The palaces were usually built around a large hall with a vestibule and central hearth. In contrast to Minoan palaces, there were no open central courts, perhaps because the Mycenaeans had a cooler climate. They constructed fortified walls, bridges, and tombs out of megalithic blocks, with individual blocks sometimes weighing as much as a hundred tons (ninety metric tons). The blocks were not joined by mortar. The Mycenaeans never constructed arches but used huge lintels, often rounded at the top, to support the weight above entrances and windows. Mycenae obtained its water supply from an impressive cistern with steps leading forty feet (twelve meters) underground.

Social classes. Although the evidence concerning classes is limited, it appears that the Mycenaeans had authoritarian rulers and that their society was stratified into relatively rigid social classes. A small number of elite warriors constituted a military aristocracy, and all male citizens were expected to render military service. The middle class was made up of farmers and skilled craftspeople. The land system was both communal and privately owned, with a wealthy elite owning large estates. The bulk of the population consisted of unskilled laborers. The Pylos tablets suggest that slavery

was a familiar institution, mostly consisting of female slaves.

Agriculture and animal husbandry. Like other peoples of the Mediterranean, the Mycenaeans produced a diversity of agricultural products. The primary grain crops were barley and wheat. In addition, farmers grew olives, figs, grapes, and spices such as cumin and coriander. They also grew flax for making linen and cords. They had domesticated oxen for plowing, sheep for wool, and a small breed of horses for pulling light wagons and chariots. Other domesticated animals included pigs and goats. With the relatively dense population that existed during the height of Mycenaean civilization, their need for additional supplies of food, especially during periods of drought, was an important motivation for trade and specialization of labor.

Industry and commerce. The Mycenaeans made many objects out of bronze and also worked with gold and silver. With their large number of smiths, they produced a surplus of such products for export. They had few natural resources and had to import metallic ores from either Asia Minor, Egypt, or Europe. Their pottery has been found all over the eastern half of the Mediterranean and as far west as Italy. In addition, the Mycenaeans were known for their luxurious furniture, with tables and chairs inlaid with gold, ivory, and blue glass. Other exports included jewelry, ornamented textiles, perfumes, and blue glass.

Surviving records suggest that the palace strictly regulated commerce. It is thought that the merchants did not constitute an important social class. A lack of coinage or another standard medium of exchange hindered the growth of trade.

Warfare. The Mycenaeans had to maintain constant vigilance against the threat of external invaders. Homer's description of felt helmets covered by rows of small plates of boar's tusks has been confirmed in art and archaeological discoveries. In the later Mycenaean period, these helmets were replaced by stronger ones made of bronze. One full suit of bronze armor has been discovered at Dendra, but such heavy armor was probably rare. Soldiers were usually equipped with long throwing spears, short two-edged swords, daggers, shields, and sometimes bows. When roads were available, elite soldiers traveled in light, two-wheeled chariots pulled by two horses.

From the 1300's, many important locations such as Mycenae and Gla had imposing stone fortifications, and most cities had at least small walled citadels, usually in a place with a secure supply of water. Mycenaean art depicts the use of warships propelled by oars and of merchant ships that relied on sails.

Current views. Given the limited number of written records, specialists in Mycenaean history are cautious about making generalizations. Although historians of the nineteenth century tended to assume the uniqueness of the early Greek-speaking peoples, contemporary historians tend to focus on the cultural influences coming from Crete, Egypt, and even western Asia. Contemporary historians also tend to minimize the degree of continuity between the Mycenaean age and later Greek accomplishments. Although cultural practices in art, architecture, and religion apparently survived until Homer's day, no firm evidence exists that the Mycenaeans made any direct contribution to the later growth of Greek philosophy, literature, or science. Contemporary historians disagree about the reasons for the fall of Mycenaean civilization, but there is a consensus that the Dorian invasions were only one of many factors.

ADDITIONAL RESOURCES

Chadwick, John. *The Mycenaean World*. Cambridge, England: Cambridge University Press, 1976.

Higgins, Reynolds, and Lyvia Morgan. *Minoan and Mycenaean Art*. London: Thames and Hudson, 1997.

Mylonas, George E. *Mycenae and the Mycenaean Age*. Princeton, N.J.: Princeton University Press, 1966.

Palmer, L. R. *The Interpretation of Mycenaean Greek Texts*. New York: Oxford University Press, 1998.

Taylor, Lord William. *The Mycenaeans*. Rev. ed. London: Thames and Hudson, 1999.

Wardle, K. A., and Diane Wardle. *The Mycenaean World: Cities of Legends*. Bristol, England: Bristol Classic Press, 1998.

SEE ALSO: Art and architecture; Athens; Crete; Greece, Archaic; Homer; Linear B; Mycenae, palace of; Religion and ritual; Troy; Writing systems.

—*Thomas T. Lewis*

GREGORY OF NAZIANZUS

ALSO KNOWN AS: Gregory Nazianzen
BORN: 329/330 C.E.; Arianzus, Cappadocia
DIED: 389/390 C.E.; Arianzus, Cappadocia
RELATED CIVILIZATION: Imperial Rome
MAJOR ROLE/POSITION: Religious leader

Life. Often called "the Theologian," Gregory of Nazianzus (GREHG-uh-ree of nay-zee-AN-zuhs) is among the leading figures of the patristic period. A child of wealth, Gregory was educated in rhetoric and theology and studied in several schools in the Eastern Empire. Gregory's life is a study in tension. Though his rhetorical skills yielded oratorical excellence, he desired monastic seclusion and often retreated from worldly duties. He became bishop of Constantinople (380-381 C.E.), where he delivered his famous *Orationae* (362-381 C.E.; *Theological Orations*, 1894).

Gregory demonstrated theological sophistication by couching ideas in classical verse. He also rose to the occasion of theological controversy with the Eunomians, who contended that humans could comprehend the divine essence. Gregory countered that divinity was a mystery, though God was revealed in mediate terms through Scripture.

Controversy at the Council of Constantinople in 381 C.E. moved him to resign his post and move to Nazianzus, where he served as bishop until illness forced his retirement to writing, which he did until his death.

Influence. Along with Gregory of Nyssa and Saint Basil of Cappadocia, Gregory stressed the coeternity and equality of the Trinity, against heretics who taught a Trinity of unequally divine persons. This defense of orthodoxy, along with his poetic abilities, earned Gregory an honored place in church history.

ADDITIONAL RESOURCES

McGuckin, I. *Gregory Nazianzen: Selected Poems*. Oxford, England: SLG, 1986.

Norris, F. W. *Faith Gives Fullness to Reasoning: The Five Theological Orations of Gregory Nazianzen*. New York: Brill, 1997.

SEE ALSO: Basil of Cappadocia, Saint; Christianity.

—*William P. McDonald*

GREGORY THE GREAT

ALSO KNOWN AS: Saint Gregory I
BORN: c. 540 C.E.; Rome
DIED: 604 C.E.; Rome
RELATED CIVILIZATION: Rome
MAJOR ROLE/POSITION: Theologian, pope

Life. Gregory the Great was the son of a Roman senator. His mother, Sylvia, was a devout Christian, and like her son, she would later be canonized. He became a priest and founded seven monasteries. In 578 C.E., he began writing his commentaries on the Old Testament Book of Job, *Moralia in Job* (after 578 C.E.; *Morals on the Book of Job*, 1844-1850; commonly called *Moralia*). In this work, he explained that readers needed to take into account both the literal and symbolic meanings of biblical texts. Gregory the Great gave numerous practical applications of the Book of Job to people's daily lives. In his lengthy discussion of the suffering of the just Job, Gregory the Great illustrated the relevance of biblical stories for believers. This book, his *Dialogues* (c. 593 C.E.; *Dialogues of Gregory*, 1942), and his writings on monasticism, *Regulae pastoralis liber* (sixth century C.E.; *Pastoral Care*, 1950), established his reputation as the leading Christian theologian of his era.

After the death of Pope Pelagius II in 590 C.E., Gregory the Great was elected pope and chose the name of Gregory I. During the fourteen years of his papacy, he implemented reforms so that the training of priests became more rigorous, and he also made sure that the church met both the religious and material needs of Christians.

Influence. He reformed Christian monasticism and had a profound influence on later Christian theologians such as Saint Thomas Aquinas.

ADDITIONAL RESOURCES
Evans, G. R. *The Thought of Gregory the Great.* Cambridge, England: Cambridge University Press, 1986.

Gregory the Great. (Library of Congress)

Gregory the Great, Saint. *Dialogues.* Translated by Odo John Zimmerman. New York: Fathers of the Church, 1959.
Straw, Carole, and Roger Collins. *Gregory the Great.* Brookfield, Vt.: Ashgate, 1996.

SEE ALSO: Christianity; Rome, Imperial.

—Edmund J. Campion

GU KAIZHI

ALSO KNOWN AS: *Wade-Giles* Ku K'ai-chih
BORN: c. 345 C.E.; Wuxi, Jiangsu Province, China
DIED: c. 406 C.E.; place unknown
RELATED CIVILIZATION: China
MAJOR ROLE/POSITION: Painter

Life. Gu Kaizhi (GEW KAHI-jee) was the most distinguished early post-Han painter. He was first a military adviser and, in his last two years, an attendant of Emperor Andi of the Eastern Jin Dynasty (317-420 C.E.). Highly versatile in verse, calligraphy, and painting, he won the title of Sanjue ("three uniques" for his talent, painting, and artistic infatuation). He painted figures, celestial beings, birds and beasts, and landscapes but has been primarily regarded as a figure painter. Most distinctive was his rendering of eyes, which sharply contrasted to the dull portrayals popular since the Han Dynasty and produced expressions so lifelike that they led to a saying, "An eye touch makes a figure speak." His fresco *Weimojie Xiang* ("the portrait of Vimalakirti") in Waguan Temple in Nanjing was unimaginably vivid and dazzlingly brilliant. His authentic masterpiece was *Nushi Zhen* ("the admonitions of the instructress to the court ladies"), now in the British museum. The originals of his paintings are lost but copies survive. Also extant are three of his articles, all from the fourth century C.E.: *Lun Hua* (on painting), *Weijin Shengliuhua Zan* (ode to the best paintings since Wei and Jin), and *Hua Yuntaishan Ji* (notes of paintings of Mount Yuntai), in which he holds that the spirit of a figure lies in the eyes and that forms are used to depict the spirit.

Influence. His paintings and artistic theory have had lasting effects on the later development of Chinese painting.

ADDITIONAL RESOURCES

Fang, Hsüan-ling. *Biography of Ku K'ai-chih.* Translated by Shih-hsiang Ch'en. Berkeley: University of California Press, 1961.

Perkins, Dorothy. *Encyclopedia of China: The Essential Reference to China, Its History and Culture.* New York: Roundtable, 1999.

SEE ALSO: China; Han Dynasty; Xie He; Yan Liben.

—*Charles Xingzhong Li*

GUANG WUDI

ALSO KNOWN AS: *Wade-Giles* Kuang-wu-ti; Liu Xiu (*Wade-Giles* Liu Hsin)
BORN: c. 5 B.C.E.; Nanyang, China
DIED: March 29, 57 C.E.; Luoyang, China
RELATED CIVILIZATION: China
MAJOR ROLE/POSITION: Military and political ruler

Life. Probably descended paternally from Gaozu (Liu Bang), founder of the former Han Dynasty, Guang Wudi (gwang woo-DEE; "shining martial emperor") was the third son of a local magistrate and his wife, the daughter of a wealthy landowner in Nanyang. His personal name was Liu Xiu.

Guang Wudi served under his older brother Liu Bosheng in his revolt against Wang Mang and personally led the successful assault against the city of Kunyang in 23 C.E. The rebel forces proclaimed Liuxuan emperor, and Liu Bosheng was executed shortly after the battle at Kunyang. Liuxuan was overthrown by the peasant movement known as the Red Eyebrows. Guang Wudi proclaimed himself emperor, entered Luoyang in eastern China, and made it his capital in 25 C.E. For the next decade, Guang Wudi suppressed uprisings and consolidated power throughout the country. His last rival, Gongsun Shu, was defeated in 36 C.E.

Guang Wudi used both diplomacy and force to pacify the Xiongnu along China's northern borders. He encouraged expansion into South Asia and by 51 C.E. had accepted the submission of the Ailao people near Yunnan. The last years of his reign were marked by military peace but intense political rivalry among powerful clans and court intrigues that led him to replace his empress Guo Shentong with Yin Lihua in 41 C.E. Two years later, Mingdi, Yin Lihua's son, became heir-apparent.

Influence. Guang Wudi's restoration of the Han Dynasty, gained through his vast military and political skills, lasted until 220 C.E.

ADDITIONAL RESOURCES

Dubs, Homer H. *The History of the Former Han Dynasty by Panku.* Baltimore: Waverly Press, 1938-1955.

Perkins, Dorothy. *Encyclopedia of China: The Essential Reference to China, Its History and Culture.* New York: Roundtable, 1999.

SEE ALSO: China; Han Dynasty; Wudi; Xiongnu.

—*Thomas J. Sienkewicz*

GUṆĀḌHYA

FLOURISHED: third or fourth century C.E.
RELATED CIVILIZATION: India
MAJOR ROLE/POSITION: Writer

Life. Guṇāḍhya (gew-NAHD-yah) wrote a major classic of Indian literature, a collection of tales in the Paiśācī dialect of Prākrit called the *Bṛhatkathā* (n.d., original in Prākrit lost; "great story"). The *Bṛhatkathā* consisted of 700,000 couplets describing the world from its beginnings. Supposedly, the legends were whispered into Guṇāḍhya's ear while he was dreaming by primordial beings who wanted the ancient wisdom preserved, and he wrote the latter part of the work to make it current.

According to tradition, Guṇāḍhya presented his work to King Sātavāhana, who disdained it because it was written in the plebian Paiśācī language. Guṇāḍhya climbed a hill and, by the light of a fire, read the text aloud. As he read, the sky became overcast, the earth shook, deities hovered around him, trees bent toward him, and birds wept silently. He burned the manuscript as he read.

When King Sātavāhana heard of the extraordinary happenings, he sent messengers to obtain the book, but only a few thousand verses, called the *Bṛhatkathā*, remained. These focused on the modern period.

Influence. Even though the *Bṛhatkathā* was lost, Sanskrit translations of fragments dating back to the fourth century C.E. still exist, including *Bṛhatkathā manjari* (c. 1037 C.E.) and *Bṛhatkathā saṃgraha* (c. 1064-1081 C.E.; *The Brhatkatha*, 1974). In addition, stories from the masterpiece are included in Sanskrit works.

ADDITIONAL RESOURCES

Chandrasekharan, K., and B. H. S. Sastri. *Sanskrit Literature*. Bombay, India: International Book House, 1951.
Prasad, S. N. *Studies in Gunadhya*. Varanasi, India: Chaukhamhha Orientalia, 1977.
Walker, Benjamin. *Hindu World: An Encyclopedic Survey of Hinduism*. London: George Allen and Unwin, 1968.

SEE ALSO: Budhasvāmin; India; Sātavāhana Dynasty.
—*Arthur W. Helweg*

GUPTA EMPERORS

DATE: c. 300-500 C.E.
LOCALE: India
RELATED CIVILIZATION: India
SIGNIFICANCE: The Guptas reigned over what is traditionally considered to be ancient India's golden or classical age.

The Gupta Dynasty is considered to be the greatest of Indian history, although some archaeological evidence suggests that the post-Mauryan period may have enjoyed greater material wealth. At its peak, the Gupta Empire encompassed virtually all of subcontinent north of the Deccan Plateau. Gupta greatness was not limited to territorial acquisition but also included prosperity and the flourishing of science, astronomy, arts, philosophy, and religion.

The collapse of the Kushān Dynasty in the third century left the Ganges River Valley under the control of several small kingdoms. Chandragupta I (r. 320-c. 330 C.E.), the son of a Magadha ruler, united the valley from Magadha (southern Bihār) to Pryaga (Allah-abad, Uttar Pradesh). He gained prominence at the court of Pāṭaliputra and secured support of the powerful Licchavi clan by marrying the Licchavian princess Kumāradevī.

Chandragupta I's son Samudragupta (r. c. 330-c. 380) was a brilliant military strategist who extended the empire to the Kushān Empire in the northwest, to the Bay of Bengal in the east, and down the eastern side of the subcontinent as far south as modern Tamil Nādu. He then shifted the capital from Pāṭaliputra to Ayodhya, whose central location made it easier to control the remote provinces.

Samudragupta's second son, Chandragupta II (r. c. 380-c. 415), had one of the most glorious reigns of Indian history. He loosened the foreign influence on western India and established direct rule to the mouth of the Indus River in the west as a result of his most important campaign, against the Śaka rulers of Ujjain. Hill states like Nepal and Kamarupa in the northeast as well as the Punjab in the northwest became feudatories, and other realms, such as that of the Vākāṭakas in the southwest, were brought into a state of respectful recognition. His reign is noted mainly for a flourishing of the arts, as attested by a Chinese Buddhist monk named Faxian (337?-422? C.E.) who traveled in India and left an account of his impressions.

Kumāragupta (r. c. 415-455), Chandragupta II's son by Dhruvadevī, patronized Buddhism and endowed Buddhist monasteries. However, during his reign and that of his son Skandagupta (r. c. 455-467), the Huns commenced their depredations from the northwest. Although Skandagupta held them back, his successors could not, and the Gupta Empire went into decline.

The Guptas marked the climax of the Hindu imperial tradition. They inherited and perfected the Mauryan administrative system—one wonders whether the identical names of the founding ruler of the Mauryan Dynasty (c. 320 B.C.E.), Chandragupta, and the founding ruler of the Gupta line (c. 320 C.E.), also Chandragupta, are merely coincindental. The Guptas compiled law books and ruled over highly organized, well-governed, and prosperous dominions. The Guptas were first to stamp their images on coins, and in fact numismatics provides much information about the era. It was also the classical period of Sanskrit, including early redactions of the *Mahābhārata* (400 B.C.E.-400 C.E., present form by c. 400 C.E.; *The Mahabharata of Krishna-Dwaipayana Vyasa*, 1887-1896), *Rāmāyaṇa* (c. 500 B.C.E., some material added later; English translation, 1870-1889), and ancient *Purāṇas* (fourth to sixth centuries C.E.) and the writing of India's greatest poet and dramatist, Kālidāsa. Astronomy, mathematics, and surgery developed and flourished, while Hindu architecture and sculpture reached their zenith.

Although orthodox adherents to the Vedas and emergent Hinduism, the early Guptas favored Buddhists and endowed their monasteries and places of learning. Gupta kings had Buddhist advisers, and later rulers converted to Buddhism. Also, many eminent Buddhists of the period were foreigners. In fact, the extraordinary intellectual and artistic output was in some

EMPERORS OF THE GUPTA DYNASTY, C. 320-550 C.E.

Emperor	Reign
Chandragupta I	c. 320-330 C.E.
Samudragupta	c. 330-c. 380
Chandragupta II	c. 380-c. 415
Kumāragupta I	c. 415-455
Skandagupta	c. 455-467
Kumāragupta II	467-477
Budhagupta	477-496
Chandragupta III?	496-500
Vainyagupta	500-515
Narasimhagupta	510-530
Kumāragupta III	530-540
Vishnugupta	540-550

measure caused by culture and trade contacts with outlying civilizations including China, Rome, and Persia.

ADDITIONAL RESOURCES

Ganguly, Dilip Kumar. *The Imperial Guptas and Their Times*. New Delhi, India: Abhinav Publications, 1987.

Hinds, Kathryn. *India's Gupta Dynasty*. New York: Benchmark Books, 1996.

Keay, John. *India: A History*. New York: Atlantic Monthly Press, 2000.

Saran, Santosh. *History of Science and Technology During the Gupta Period*. New Delhi, India: Prachi Prakashan, 1994.

Schwartzberg, Joseph E., ed. *A Historical Atlas of South Asia*. Chicago: University of Chicago Press, 1975.

SEE ALSO: Buddhism; Faxian; Hinduism; Huns; India; Kushān Dynasty; *Mahābhārata*; Mauryan Dynasty; *Purāṇas*; *Rāmāyaṇa*; Vedas.

—Arthur W. Helweg

GYGES

BORN: c. 705 B.C.E.; place unknown
DIED: c. 645 B.C.E.; Lydia
RELATED CIVILIZATIONS: Lydia, Assyria, Archaic Greece
MAJOR ROLE/POSITION: King, military leader, Mermnad Dynasty founder

Life. Gyges' (JI-jeez) early life is sketchy, although it is known that he was the son of Dascylus. Historian Herodotus and philosopher Plato relate his unusual coming to the throne of Lydia. King Candaules of Sardis was proud of his wife and thought her the most beautiful woman in the world. Gyges was a trusted royal bodyguard, but the king felt Gyges did not share his opinion of his queen's surpassing beauty. The king forced reluctant Gyges to observe the queen's nakedness while hidden in her chamber. The disgraced queen took vengeance on her husband—nudity was a Lydian taboo—by summoning Gyges and compelling him to choose: Slay Candaules and become king or die immediately himself. Astonished but ultimately persuaded, Gyges took the queen's challenge, slew his predecessor, and married the queen, ruling Lydia from roughly 680 to 645 B.C.E.

Plato's *Politeia* (388-368 B.C.E.; *Republic*, 1701) claims that Gyges was a shepherd who found a magic ring, making him invisible and thus able to pursue seduction and accomplish murder. Herodotus also tells how Gyges was among the first barbarians known to send offerings to Delphi after the oracle confirmed him as king. Gyges also collaborated with the Assyrian king Ashurbanipal in Anatolia and invaded the Ionian Greek city of Miletus.

Influence. The story of Gyges' succession to the Lydian throne is famous to the Greeks.

ADDITIONAL RESOURCES

Herodotus. *The Histories*. Translated by Robin Waterfield. New York: Oxford University Press, 1998.

Plato. *The Republic*. Edited by G. R. F. Ferrari, translated by Tom Griffith. Cambridge, England: Cambridge University Press, 2000.

SEE ALSO: Ashurbanipal; Assyria; Greece, Archaic; Herodotus; Lydia; Plato.

—Patrick Norman Hunt

— H —

HADRIAN

ALSO KNOWN AS: Publius Aelius Hadrianus
BORN: January 24, 76 C.E.; Italica, Spain
DIED: July 10, 138 C.E.; Baiae, Bay of Naples, Italy
RELATED CIVILIZATION: Imperial Rome
MAJOR ROLE/POSITION: Roman emperor

Life. Hadrian (HAY-dree-uhn) was born to a prominent family originally from Italy but which settled in Italica. His father, Publius Aelius Hadrianus Afer, was the son of one of Trajan's cousins. When his father died in 85 C.E., Hadrian resided with Trajan and his wife Pompeia Plotina, who had been childless. Hadrian married Sabina Augusta, Trajan's grandniece, in 100 C.E. They had no children. He was educated in Rome during Domitian's reign, a time of cosmopolitanism and Hellenic tastes. Hadrian became an accomplished soldier and early in his career (95-102 C.E.) served as tribune of legions in Italy, Germany, and the

Hadrian. (Library of Congress)

Balkans; imperial quaestor; and staff officer in Trajan's first Dacian War. He served as plebeian tribune in 105 and as a legion commander in the second Dacian War (105-106 C.E.) while concurrently serving as praetor. Hadrian was governor of Lower Pannonia in 107 C.E. and in 112 C.E. was elected archon of Athens. In 114 C.E., during Trajan's Parthian war, Hadrian was appointed governor of Syria, the base for military operations in the East. Upon Trajan's death in isolated Cilicia in August 117 C.E., Hadrian, who was in Antioch, assumed the title of emperor. Allegedly, Trajan officially adopted Hadrian as his heir only from his deathbed.

Modeling himself after Augustus, Hadrian was reserved in his military policy. He was a pacifist who sought to consolidate the empire after Trajan's conquests. Hadrian's administration brought tranquillity, financial recovery, and urban well-being. The Romans enjoyed gladiatorial shows, extra public largesse, and cancellation of all debts to the state. He did not raise taxes or impose any new taxes. Conditions of slavery improved. Hadrian, with Sabina's endorsement, ardently supported education and charity for the children of Rome and oversaw adoption proceedings.

Hadrian, renowned for his intellectual curiosity and his philhellenism, was accomplished in literature, music, art, and architecture. In his villa at Tivoli, he entertained his courtly circle of rhetoricians, scholars, and philosophers with musical banquets and poetry readings along with riding and hunting. Fascinated by natural history and committed to diplomacy, Hadrian traveled extensively, especially in the East. With Sabina and an entourage of secretaries, advisers, and orators, Hadrian toured the provinces from 120 to 125 and 128 to 132 C.E. Hadrian gave visibility to his reign by restoring and commissioning public works, buildings, and monuments in Rome and throughout the provinces. Pan Mediterranean industries of brick making, quarrying, shipping, and marble import brought prosperity to the empire. The Pantheon, the Temple of Venus and Rome, his mausoleum in Rome, and his villa at Tivoli reveal architectural innovations typical of the era. Hadrian was influenced by Epicurean and Stoic philosophy as well as astrology. Like Augustus, Hadrian was tolerant of foreign religious cults and was initiated in the Eleusinian mysteries.

Hadrian died at a mineral spa while under treatment for consumption. His successor Antoninus Pius inherited a peaceful empire and deified Hadrian.

Influence. Hadrian ushered in an era of urban well-being. He elevated the provinces to the status of the capital. Hadrianic architecture left a prolific legacy.

ADDITIONAL RESOURCES
Birley, A. *Hadrian: The Restless Emperor.* London: Routledge, 1997.
Henderson, B. W. *Life and Principate of the Emperor Hadrian.* New York: Brentano, 1923.

SEE ALSO: Antoninus Pius; Eleusinian mysteries; Hadrian's villa; Parthia; Rome, Imperial; Trajan.

—Joanne Mannell Noel

HADRIAN'S VILLA

DATE: c. 125-138 C.E.
LOCALE: Tivoli, Italy
RELATED CIVILIZATION: Imperial Rome
SIGNIFICANCE: The villa sheds light on Hadrian's personality and lifestyle, about which little is recorded, and expresses the era's cosmopolitan spirit. It has influenced architects from antiquity to the twenty-first century.

The 300-acre (121-hectare), 900-room, landscape villa just east of Rome was the primary residence of the emperor Hadrian. Hadrian probably participated in aspects of its design. The hilly terrain dictated a decentralized plan of structures clustered along disparate axes. Hadrian's private quarters, disposed along terraces and enhanced with gardens and fountain courts, consisted of apartments, a triclinium, library, ceremonial precinct, a belvedere, and a nymphaeum. Hadrian's circular intimate island retreat with drawbridge served as a hinge between the residential complex and the public areas of the villa, where Hadrian and guests conducted business while enjoying leisure activities. These areas included a porticoed terrace with reflecting pool, a ceremonial reception room, an imposing triclinium

prefaced by a fountain court, a stadium-shaped garden with elevated pool building, a porticoed canal (Canopus) with triclinium, several baths, two theaters, underground galleries (perhaps for Eleusinian rites), and a park.

The villa's protean nature features the staid Doric order alongside exuberant curvilinear walls and porticoes crowned by vaults and domes of revolutionary designs. The wealth of sculpture, mosaics, and imported colored marble veneer that embellished the villa attests to Hadrian's devotion to the arts. Overt references to Hadrian's travels pervade the villa. Hadrian's villa provided a microcosm of the vast but peaceful empire and mirrored the universality espoused by the emperor.

ADDITIONAL RESOURCE
MacDonald, William Lloyd, and John A. Pinto. *Hadrian's Villa and Its Legacy.* New Haven, Conn.: Yale University Press, 1995.

SEE ALSO: Art and architecture; Hadrian; Rome, Imperial.

—Joanne Mannell Noel

HAGHIA SOPHIA

DATE: consecrated in 537 C.E.
LOCALE: Istanbul, Turkey
RELATED CIVILIZATION: Byzantine Empire
SIGNIFICANCE: Haghia Sophia was the jewel of the capital of the Byzantine Empire, a church without peer in the Christian world. Its magnificence persuaded many pagans to convert to Christianity.

Haghia Sophia (ah-YEE-ah soh-FEE-ah) was the cathedral of Constantinople (Istanbul) built in 537 C.E. at a site along the Bosporus by Justinian I (r. 527-565 C.E.). Earlier, at the same site, Constantius II (r. 337-361 C.E.) built his Great Church in 360 C.E. near the Great Palace and the Hippodrome race track. During the civil strife of 404 C.E., rioters destroyed it, but the emperor Theo-

Haghia Sophia. (Hulton Archive)

dosius II (r. 408-450 C.E.) rebuilt it in 415 C.E. Around 430 C.E., it became known as Holy Wisdom or Haghia Sophia.

In 532 C.E., during the infamous Nika Riots against Justinian and Theodora, the church was destroyed a second time. In his plans for rebuilding the city after the riots, Justinian had his architects make the new church the masterpiece of his empire. The architects, Anthemius of Tralles and Isidoros of Miletus, had a variety of skilled workers at their disposal, including masons, marble carvers, and carpenters. Justinian also decreed that they should have any type of material they wished to employ. The finest marble was brought from all over the empire. Patriarch Menas (r. 536-552 C.E.) consecrated the building on December 27, 537 C.E. However, according to some accounts, work on it continued another twenty years, employing thousands of craftsmen, and Patriarch Eutychius (r. 552-565 and 577-582 C.E.) consecrated it a second time in 552 C.E.

Haghia Sophia is a domed basilica of almost square construction (256 feet by 236 feet, or 78 meters by 72 meters). Its central nave was covered by a dome of more than 100 feet (30 meters) and two semidomes. Four immense bases supported the dome with four arches and four pendatives between them. The supports were arranged in such a way as to be hidden from observers entering the church, and the dome seemed to float on air. The church also had two galleries and two narthexes that divided it into three aisles. In 558 C.E., the dome collapsed, and a new, even bigger dome was constructed several years later. The cathedral has forty single arched windows on the dome and twenty-four large windows in two rows along the galleries to bathe it in light. The structure is buttressed from the outside.

On the west of the church, the architects built an atrium and fountain. There were also two baptisteries and a sacristy. The church was near the palace of the patriarch and connected to it by an overground passageway. The administration of the church included more than five hundred clergy and three nearby churches.

The church served as the main center for elaborate imperial ceremonies and contained the Metatoria, or imperial rooms, for this purpose.

During the latter centuries of the Byzantine Empire, a few repairs were necessary because of earthquake or structural damage, but the church has remained mostly intact. In the Ottoman period, it was turned into a mosque, but during the time of the Turkish republic after 1922, it was converted to a museum.

ADDITIONAL RESOURCES

Altay, A. S. *St. Sophia*. Istanbul: Basimevi, 1978.
Ousterhout, Robert. *Master Builders of Byzantium*. Princeton, N.J.: Princeton University Press, 2000.

SEE ALSO: Anthemius of Tralles; Byzantine Empire; Christianity; Constantinople; Justinian I; Theodora; Theodosius II.

—*Frederick B. Chary*

HALAFIAN CULTURE

DATE: 5700-5600 B.C.E.
LOCALE: Northern Mesopotamia, present-day northern Syria and Iraq
SIGNIFICANCE: Halafian culture flourished in northern Mesopotamia in the sixth millennium B.C.E.

In 1899, German diplomat Max Frieherr von Oppenheim first investigated Tell Halaf, an ancient mound located on the headwaters of the Khabur River at the present-day Syrian/Turkish border. Von Oppenheim returned again to the site to conduct excavations between 1911 and 1913 and also in 1927 and 1929. He discovered two major periods of occupation at Halaf. The first dated to the prehistoric sixth millennium B.C.E. and the second to the Aramean and Assyrian Iron Age.

The ceramic assemblages first associated with the earlier occupation at Halaf have been subsequently recovered from a significant number of sites across northern Mesopotamia. Because the first examples of this particular Neolithic culture were found at Tell Halaf,

the name "Halafian" has been employed to designate this distinctive civilization.

The Halafian culture is characterized by beautifully decorated polychrome ceramic vessels. A large number of decorative motifs are painted mainly on jars and bowls in distinctive forms. Copper items, flint tools, stone vessels, figurines, and other objects are also found in this distinctive type of prehistoric culture.

ADDITIONAL RESOURCES

Dornemann, Rudolph H. "Halaf, Tell." In *The Oxford Encyclopedia of Archaeology in the Near East*, edited by Eric M. Meyers. Oxford, England: Oxford University Press, 1997.
Lloyd, Seton. *The Archaeology of Mesopotamia: From the Old Stone Age to the Persian Conquest*. Rev. ed. New York: Thames and Hudson, 1984.

SEE ALSO: Fertile Crescent; Natufian culture; Samarran culture.

—*Stephen J. Andrews*

HALICARNASSUS MAUSOLEUM

DATE: c. 367-351 B.C.E.
LOCALE: Halicarnassus in the region of Caria, Asia Minor
RELATED CIVILIZATION: Classical Greece
SIGNIFICANCE: One of the Seven Wonders of the World and the first mausoleum.

The mausoleum at Halicarnassus was a monumental tomb commissioned by and for Mausolus, satrap of Caria, from whom it derives its name. When Mausolus

began building the new Carian capital, his monumental tomb was to be the central attraction. The tomb was completed about two years after his death in 353 B.C.E. The Greek sculptors Scopas, Bryaxis, Leochares, Timotheus, and perhaps Praxiteles worked with Pythius, the state architect, and Satyrus, a local sculptor-architect, in the design and creation of the tomb. Pythius and Satyrus wrote a book about the mausoleum but it does not survive.

The structure lasted until the fifteenth century C.E.

SEVEN WONDERS OF THE ANCIENT WORLD

Colossus of Rhodes (292-280 B.C.E.)	Large bronze statue, probably a standing nude man wearing a crown of Sun rays, built in the harbor of Rhodes to commemorate the raising of the siege of that city
Halicarnassus Mausoleum (c. 367-351 B.C.E.)	Monumental tomb commissioned by Mausolus, satrap of Caria, and completed by his widow, Artemisia II
Hanging Gardens of Babylon (500's B.C.E.)	Series of landscaped terraces, reportedly built by Nebuchadnezzar II in honor of his wife
Temple of Artemis at Ephesus (c. 700 B.C.E.-262 C.E.)	Temple dedicated to Artemis, goddess of the hunt, sponsored by King Croesus of Lydia and designed by the architect Chersiphron
Pharos of Alexandria (c. 300-285 B.C.E.)	Three-tiered lighthouse on the island of Pharos in the harbor of Alexandria designed by Sostratus of Cnidus, commissioned by Ptolemy I
Pyramids of Giza (c. 2575-2465 B.C.E.)	Three pyramids on the West Bank of the Nile River near Giza built during the Fourth Dynasty; the largest was built for Khufu and the others for Khafre and Mankaure
Statue of Zeus at Olympia (c. 400 B.C.E.)	Colossal seated statue of Zeus, fashioned of gold and ivory over a wooden core, designed by the Athenian sculptor Phidias

when the Knights of Rhodes quarried the building for stone used in the castle-fort at modern Bodrum. Modern excavations at the site have supplemented ancient accounts that describe the tomb so that its general form can be reconstructed. The tomb, which stood at least 140 feet (43 meters) high, was composed of a high podium on which a colonnade of thirty-six Ionic columns stood. Above the colonnade, the structure bore a pyramid of at least twenty-four steps, crowned with a chariot group.

Both freestanding sculpture and carved reliefs decorated the building. Carved relief blocks from the building that depict an Amazonomachy are displayed in the British Museum.

ADDITIONAL RESOURCES

Clayton, Peter A., and Martin Price, eds. *The Seven Wonders of the Ancient World*. New York: Routledge, 1998.

Jeppesen, K. *The Maussolleion at Halikarnassos*. Aarhus, Denmark: Aarhus University Press, 1986.

Waywell, G. B. *The Freestanding Sculpture of the Mausoleum at Halicarnassus*. New York: Farrar, Straus, and Giroux, 1979.

SEE ALSO: Art and architecture; Greece, Classical; Mausolus; Scopas.

—Christina A. Salowey

HALLSTATT CULTURE

DATE: c. 1100-450 B.C.E.
LOCALE: Northern Europe, present-day Austria
RELATED CIVILIZATION: Celts
SIGNIFICANCE: Hallstatt ushered in Europe's Iron Age, setting the pattern of urban civilization for the next two thousand years.

In 1824, K. P. Pollhammer uncovered an ancient tomb outside the Austrian town of Hallstatt, by a lake in an Alpine valley some thirty miles (forty-eight kilometers) southeast of Salzburg. In 1846, a salt-mine manager, George Ramsauer, excavated nearly one thousand graves there, along with pottery, bronze vessels of

Greek and local origins, gold and Baltic amber jewelry, and weapons of an unexpected material—iron. More graves were later discovered.

They fell into two periods: Hallstatt A and B covered the late Bronze Age Urnfield culture (1300-800 B.C.E.). The Urnfield peoples, who cremated the bodies of their dead and placed the ashes in urns for burial, had helped spread bronze-working throughout Europe. Hallstatt C and D covered the early Iron Age (800-500 B.C.E.) and can be identified with early Celts, since the advent of iron-working was accompanied by the custom of inhumation (burial of the entire body) instead of cremation. In these graves, often found in hill forts, chiefs were buried with costly goods, including four-wheeled carts, indicating the emergence of social differentiation based on trade.

Hallstatt culture developed where passes and rivers made it possible to trade with the Mediterranean. Mediterranean wine, oil, bronzes, jewelry, and iron-working skills moved north, paid for with tin, copper, hides, textiles, amber, salt, and salt-cured fish and pork. Salt was so important that Rome later paid its legionnaires with it, a *salarium argentum* (money for salt), the origin of the word "salary." From Spain to Hungary, hill forts and settlements arose along these trade routes, evolving into industrial centers.

In eastern France, a Hallstatt D hill fort on Mont Lassois dominated the headwaters of the Seine River. In an associated barrow at the nearby village of Vix in 1953, René Joffroy discovered the remains of a Celtic princess on a dismantled wagon wearing a golden crown, its ends terminating in winged horses. Her grave goods included bronze and amber jewelry, a Greek Black Figure pot, silver and bronze vessels, and a huge two-handled bronze jar, or krater, weighing 460 pounds (209 kilograms) on which a frieze showed a Greek charioteer, four horses, and hoplite infantrymen. Celtic art of this period shows a concern with nature, with humans portrayed almost abstractly using triangles and circles. The "Hallstatt duck" and solar disc motifs are found on pottery and other artifacts.

Iron continued to be relatively rare during the Hallstatt period, but its impact was evident in materials excavated from the 40-foot-tall (12-meter-tall) Hohmichelle barrow, located near the Heuenburg hill fortress overlooking the Danube River in southern Germany. The planks used to construct the main chamber had been sawn from logs with a two-man iron saw. Another burial excavation, in 1978 at Hochdorf, Germany, revealed an iron-plated wagon along with an iron drinking horn more than three feet (one meter) in length.

ADDITIONAL RESOURCES

Freidin, Nicholas. *The Early Iron Age in the Paris Basin: Hallstatt C and D*. Oxford, England: B.A.R., 1982.

Hodson, Frank Roy. *Hallstatt: Dry Bones and Flesh*. Oxford, England: Oxford University Press, 1986.

Mason, Philip. *The Early Iron Age of Slovenia*. Oxford, England: Tempus Reparatum, 1996.

Raymond, Robert. *Out of the Fiery Furnace: The Impact of Metals on the History of Mankind*. University Park: Pennsylvania State University Press, 1986.

SEE ALSO: Celts; La Tène culture; Neolithic Age Europe.

—*Thomas J. Sienkewicz*

HAMMURABI'S CODE

AUTHORSHIP: Compiled by Hammurabi (also known as Hammurapi; c. 1810-1750 B.C.E.)
DATE: compiled c. 1770 B.C.E.
LOCALE: Babylon
RELATED CIVILIZATIONS: Sumer, Akkad, Babylonia
SIGNIFICANCE: The code demonstrates the existence of stable, urban civilization in the second millennium B.C.E. and probably influenced the law of ancient Israel.

Hammurabi, ruler of Babylon, established a kingdom that extended up from the Persian Gulf, through the valleys of the Tigres and Euphrates Rivers, and to the Mediterranean Sea in the northwest. This region, known as Mesopotamia, was inhabited by a series of civilizations. The Sumerian civilization was succeeded by an Akkadian civilization when the Akkadians, a Semitic people, conquered the city-states of Mesopotamia. Hammurabi was the first king of his line who did not have an Akkadian name. His city-state of Babylon was not dominant when he assumed its rule. By military conquest over other city-states, he established an extensive Babylonian empire. Hammurabi was, however, much more than a conqueror. He gave his personal attention to the construction of buildings, to agriculture and irrigation, and to oversight of the bureaucracy. There was much commercial activity in his empire.

Hammurabi is best known for his law code. The large black stele, or obelisk, on which it was written shows Hammurabi receiving the law from Shamash, the Sun god. Hammurabi referred to himself as an exalted prince who was called to bring righteousness to the land and prevent the strong from harming the weak. The code contains nearly three hundred sections and recognizes three classes of people: chieftans or aristocrats, ordinary free people, and slaves. They were not equal under the law, but all had rights. Section 196 of the code states that if a man puts out the eye of another man (presumably his equal), then his eye shall be put out. Section 200 states that if a man knocks out the teeth of his equal, then his teeth shall be knocked out. This principle of an eye for an eye and a tooth for a tooth found its way into the law of Israel some five centuries later. Israelites could have become familiar with Hammurabi's code during their Babylonian captivity.

When the code of Hammurabi was discovered during an archaeological excavation in 1901-1902, it was the earliest known law code. Since then, earlier law codes have been discovered. Some scholars have interpreted Hammurabi's code as a true law code that was actually applied to the various situations it described. Others, however, have considered it more like a work of social criticism in which Hammurabi set forth his responsibility as king to dispense justice to all classes of people.

On the stele with Hammurabi's law code, Hammurabi is shown standing before the Sun god. (North Wind Picture Archives)

ADDITIONAL RESOURCES

Kramer, Samuel Noah, and the editors of Time-Life Books. *Cradle of Civilization*. New York: Time, 1967.

Oates, Joan. *Babylon*. Rev. ed. New York: Thames and Hudson, 1986.

Oppenheim, A. Leo. *Ancient Mesopotamia: Portrait of a Dead Civilization*. Compiled by Erica Reiner. Rev. ed. Chicago: University of Chicago Press, 1977.

Spodek, Howard. *The World's History: To 1500*. Upper Saddle River, N.J.: Prentice Hall, 1998.

SEE ALSO: Babylonia; Fertile Crescent; Israel; Sumerians.

—*Patricia A. Behlar*

HAN DYNASTY

DATE: c. 206 B.C.E.-220 C.E.
LOCALE: Southern to northern China, extending to Indochina and Central Asia
RELATED CIVILIZATION: China
SIGNIFICANCE: Fostered an age of prosperity, power, and cultural development in China.

Amid the downfall of the strictly Legalist Qin Dynasty (221-206 B.C.E.), the Han family earned the mandate of heaven (the authority from heaven to rule) in approximately 206 B.C.E. The Han promoted Confucianism as a sociopolitical philosophy and restored political unity during this period through the establishment of a well-organized government. An examination system was developed to determine the most desirable candidates for government jobs. Young men studied required subjects such as Chinese law, history, and traditions, as officials had to be knowledgeable not only in the area of policies but also in Confucian ideals. Furthermore, fundamental to Confucianism is the relationship of superiors and inferiors. Kowtowing—bowing deeply until the head touches the floor to show respect for authority—dates from this period. The Han felt that a skilled and obedient bureaucracy fostered an efficient one.

The Han rulers established overland trade routes known as the Silk Road, over which Chinese silks and spices reached the Roman-dominated Mediterranean. The Han rulers expanded their empire to Indochina—resulting in the introduction of Buddhism to the Chinese people—as well as Central Asia, southern Manchuria, and northern Korea. The Han Dynasty marked a time of great prosperity and growth. Literature, art, science, and industry flourished like never before. For example, paper was created during the Han reign around 105 C.E.

ADDITIONAL RESOURCES
Eberhard, Wolfram. *A History of China.* Berkeley: University of California Press, 1977.
Sima Qian. *Records of the Grand Historian: Han Dynasty.* Translated by Burton Watson. New York: Columbia University Press, 1993.

CHINA DURING THE HAN DYNASTY

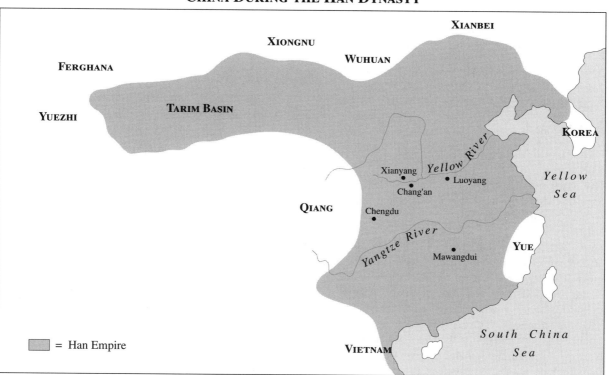

FERGHANA

XIONGNU

XIANBEI

WUHUAN

TARIM BASIN

YUEZHI

KOREA

Xianyang *Yellow River*

Luoyang

Yellow Sea

QIANG

Chang'an

Chengdu

Yangtze River

Mawangdui

YUE

VIETNAM

South China Sea

= Han Empire

Taton, Rene, ed. *Ancient and Medieval Science*. New York: Basic Books, 1963.

SEE ALSO: Buddhism; Cai Lun; China; Confucianism; Confucius; Qin Dynasty; Silk Road.

—Noelle Heenan

HAN FEIZI

ALSO KNOWN AS: Wade-Giles *Han Fei-tzu*
AUTHORSHIP: Han Fei (c. 280-233 B.C.E.) and anonymous Imperial-period Legalists
DATE: traditionally later half of third century B.C.E., probably compiled c. 235-c. 160 B.C.E.
LOCALE: Capitals of the Qin and Han Dynasties
RELATED CIVILIZATIONS: Qin Dynasty, Han Dynasty, China
SIGNIFICANCE: The *Han Feizi* is the most mature expression of early Legalist thought.

Han Fei, a native of the state of Han (not related to the Han Dynasty), met death in Qin during a failed intrigue against Yao Jia. Later legend portrays him as betrayed by the evil Qin minister Li Si. Of the fifty-five chapters of *Han Feizi* (han fay-DZEW; *The Complete Works of Han Fei Tzu: A Classic of Chinese Legalism*, 1939-1959, 2 vols.; commonly known as *Han Feizi*), only the pedestrian third is probably his. The rest is by Han Dynasty Legalists "sheltering under" his name, and from that position—a Legalism not tainted by identification with Qin policies—opposing a resurgent Confucianism.

The usual view is that the work blends earlier theories of law (chapters 6, 43), bureaucratic control (8, 11, 52), and intrinsic authority (40); scholars Hsiao-po Wang and Leo S. Chang see its mystical strain (21-22) as basic. Its literary merits, though spotty, are widely acknowledged. Chapter 12, on the "Art of the Courtier," is especially admired.

ADDITIONAL RESOURCES

Fu, Zhengyuan. *China's Legalists*. Armonk, N.Y.: M. E. Sharpe, 1996.

Han Feizi. *The Complete Works of Hai Fei Tzu*. Translated by W. K. Liao. 2 vols. London: Probsthain, 1939-1959.

Wang, Hsiao-po, and Leo S. Chang. *The Philosophical Foundations of Han Fei's Political Theory*. Honolulu: University of Hawaii Press, 1986.

SEE ALSO: China; Confucianism; Legalists; Qin Dynasty; Shang Yang.

—E. Bruce Brooks

HANIWA

DATE: fourth-seventh centuries C.E.
LOCALE: Japan
RELATED CIVILIZATION: Kofun period, Japan
SIGNIFICANCE: This clay art is associated with Japanese burial mound culture.

Haniwa (HAH-nee-wah) are the unglazed hollow clay artifacts placed around the burial mounds for the elite, most of which were constructed during the Kofun period (c. 300-710 C.E.). *Haniwa* fall into two categories: cylindrical *haniwa*, which have simple tubular shapes, and figure *haniwa*, which take the shape of humans, animals, buildings, and goods. The human figures include warriors, farmers, and females in formal attire. The animals include horses, boars, deer, monkeys, chickens,

waterfowl, eagles, and fish. The buildings include residences with windows and entrances and windowless warehouses. The types of roofs included hip, gable, and hip and gable. Goods included hats, swords, halberds, armors, ships, and talismanic shields. The general belief is that cylindrical *haniwa* developed from offering stands used in the Yayoi period; however, their purpose or use remains unknown.

The shapes of *haniwa* and the techniques used to make them changed as the burial mounds developed during the Kofun period. Halberds and chicken-shaped *haniwa* began to appear along cylinders and houses during the fourth century. Horses, deer, and humans were added in the fifth century and became popular during the sixth century. During the early fifth century, the Sue ware technique from Korea was introduced, changing the techniques used to make traditional reddish Haji ware. Until the sixth century, *haniwa* were arranged systematically at the top of the burial mound in a rectangular or circular arrangement and in a line along the shoulder and middle or bottom slopes. When the horizontal-style tombs developed during the sixth century, figure *haniwa* were placed at the entrances.

ADDITIONAL RESOURCES
Imamura, Keiji. *Prehistoric Japan*. Honolulu: University of Hawaii Press, 1996.
Miki, Fumio. *Haniwa*. Translated by Gina Lee Barnes. Arts of Japan 8. New York: Weatherhill, 1974.

SEE ALSO: Japan; Kofun period; Yamato court.

—Hiroko Johnson

HANNIBAL

ALSO KNOWN AS: Hannibal Barca
BORN: 247 B.C.E.; probably Carthage, North Africa
DIED: 182 B.C.E.; Libyssa, Bithynia, Asia Minor
RELATED CIVILIZATIONS: Carthage, Republican Rome
MAJOR ROLE/POSITION: Military leader

Life. Hannibal left Carthage for Spain with his father Hamilcar in 238 B.C.E. He became commander of the Carthaginian forces in Spain in 221 B.C.E. After consolidating Carthaginian control in Spain, he

Hannibal. (Library of Congress)

marched through southern France over the Alps into northern Italy with troops and elephants in 218 B.C.E. There he recruited soldiers from among the Celts. He defeated Roman armies at the Trebia River, Lake Trasimene, and Cannae. Capua, Syracuse, and Macedonia allied with him. Though the Romans never defeated him in battle, they pushed Hannibal into southern Italy and defeated invasions by Hannibal's brothers Hasdrubal in 207 B.C.E. and Mago in 205 B.C.E. In 203 B.C.E., Scipio Africanus invaded Africa. After Scipio Africanus defeated the Carthaginian defensive army, Hannibal was called home. Carthage lost the Battle of Zama in 202 B.C.E., ending the Second Punic War (218-201 B.C.E.). Hannibal fled east to the Seleucids and finally to Bithynia, where he drank poison in 182 B.C.E. rather than be turned over to the Romans.

Influence. Hannibal tested Rome more than any other enemy general. Rome's military innovations to defeat Hannibal helped it spread throughout the Mediterranean. Fighting Hannibal increased Rome's hatred of Carthage, leading them to destroy the city after the Third Punic War.

ADDITIONAL RESOURCES
De Beer, G. *Hannibal: Challenging Rome's Supremacy*. New York: Viking Press, 1969.
Lancel, Serge. *Hannibal*. Oxford, England: Blackwell, 1998.
Lazenby, J. F. *Hannibal's War: A Military History of the Second Punic War*. Warminster, England: Aris & Phillips, 1978.

SEE ALSO: Cannae, Battle of; Carthage; Celts; Punic Wars; Rome, Republican; Scipio Africanus; Zama, Battle of.

—James O. Smith

HARIVAṂŚA

AUTHORSHIP: Composite; attributed to legendary
author Vyāsa
DATE: third or fourth century C.E.
LOCALE: India
RELATED CIVILIZATION: India
SIGNIFICANCE: A epic poem that relates an early version of the Krishna (Kṛṣṇa) legend, differing in
many details from later and more widely known stories.

The *Harivaṃśa*—(hah-ree-VAHM-shah) "the dynasty
(or lineage) of Hari," the latter an epithet of either
the god Vishnu (Viṣṇu) or Krishna—is most widely
known as an appendix to the longer epic *Mahābhārata*
(400 B.C.E.-400 C.E., present form by c. 400 C.E.; *The
Mahabharata of Krishna-Dwaipayana Vyasa*, 1887-
1896). The earlier epic had dealt with a dynastic struggle in the clan of the Kurus, but the *Harivaṃśa* (translated in English as *A Prose English Translation of
Harivamsha*, 1897) deals with the Vrsni-Andhaka clan
to which Krishna belongs. Sometimes, however, the
Harivaṃśa is said to belong to a later class of epic texts
known collectively as the *Purāṇas*, whose contents pro-

mote the worship of Vishnu and Śiva, still prominent in
modern Hinduism.

Besides the lengthy legend of the hero and deity
Krishna, the *Harivaṃśa* contains other legends and
myths, such as accounts of the incarnations of the god
Vishnu. The text is composed in Sanskrit of roughly the
same epic or poetic dialect as found in the *Mahābhārata*
and the *Rāmāyaṇa* (c. 500 B.C.E, some material added
later; English translation, 1870-1889). In its longest
version, the *Harivaṃśa* consists of about 18,000 stanzas, although its most recent editors have separated out
a text one-third that length that they argue is significantly older than the remainder.

ADDITIONAL RESOURCES
Brockington, John. *The Sanskrit Epics*. Leiden: E. J.
Brill, 1998.
Hiltebeitel, Alf. *Rethinking India's Oral and Classical
Epics*. Chicago: University of Chicago Press, 1999.

SEE ALSO: Hinduism; India; *Mahābhārata*; Purāṇas;
Rāmāyaṇa.
—*Burt Thorp*

HARKHUF

ALSO KNOWN AS: Harkuf; Horkhuf
FLOURISHED: c. 2300-2200 B.C.E.
RELATED CIVILIZATIONS: Pharaonic Egypt, Nubia
MAJOR ROLE/POSITION: Provincial governor, leader
of trade expedition

Life. Governor of Upper Egypt in the late Old Kingdom (in the reigns of Merenre and Pepy II of the Sixth
Dynasty), Harkhuf (HAHR-kewf) led four trading expeditions to Nubia. His autobiography, including the
account of this activity, is recorded on the facade of his
tomb at Aswan. The most complete report is that of his
fourth expedition, completed early in the reign of Pepy
II, when he returned from Nubia with incense, ivory,
ebony, panther skins, and "all good things." The boy
king, delighted with these new acquisitions, wrote a letter asking Harkhuf to hurry north to the capital. This letter is reproduced in Harkhuf's tomb inscription.

Influence. The accounts of Harkhuf provide some
of the most complete inscriptional information on
Egyptian/Nubian relations in the Old Kingdom. In addition to the Nubian information, the letter Harkhuf re-
produces in his tomb provides one of the few glimpses
available of the personality of a king, as his childhood
excitement is not hidden behind the formulaic narrative
that is more typical of Egyptian letters.

ADDITIONAL RESOURCES
Lichtheim, Miriam. *The Old and Middle Kingdoms*.
Vol. 1 in *Literature of Ancient Egypt*. Berkeley: Uni-
versity of California Press, 1973.
O'Connor, David. *Ancient Nubia: Egypt's Rival in Af-
rica*. Philadelphia: The University Museum, 1993.

SEE ALSO: Egypt, Pharaonic; Nubia.
—*Sara E. Orel*

HARMODIUS AND ARISTOGITON

BORN: dates and places unknown
DIED: both 514 B.C.E.; Athens, Greece
RELATED CIVILIZATION: Archaic Greece
MAJOR ROLE/POSITION: Tyranicides

Life. Harmodius (hahr-MOH-dee-uhs) and Aristogiton (uh-rihs-TOH-ji-tahn) assassinated Hipparchus, the brother of the ruling tyrant Hippias of Athens, at the Panathenea in 514 B.C.E. The pair belonged to the same Athenian aristocratic clan and were committed homosexual lovers. After attempting to seduce Harmodius and failing twice, Hipparchus took revenge by defaming Harmodius's sister. She was summoned as a potential basket-bearer in a religious procession (possibly connected to the same Panathenea), but she was sent home as unworthy, probably because she was—allegedly—no longer a virgin. This public insult motivated Harmodius, but according to the historian Thucydides, Aristogiton, the elder of the pair, also intended "to pull down the tyranny." They enlisted a few friends and planned to kill Hippias and Hipparchus at the Panathenea on the only day they could appear armed in the streets without provoking suspicion. However, at the set hour an accomplice was seen talking with Hippias. Fearing betrayal, they assassinated Hipparchus in the Agora, where he probably was acting as marshal for the grand parade for the festival. Harmodius was killed on the spot. Aristogiton was arrested later and tortured; he died without betraying a single coconspirator. Four years later, Hippias was expelled, and the tyranny overthrown.

Influence. Almost immediately, Harmodius and Aristogiton were deemed patriots; bronze statues of them were soon erected in the Agora; and in the Ceramicus, a tomb was built for the Tyrannicides, as they were known when, in the fifth century B.C.E., the murdered Hipparchus was misremembered as the actual tyrant. Drinking songs hailed their liberation of Athens, and their descendants were honored and exempted from certain public obligations.

ADDITIONAL RESOURCES
Moudson, S. Sara. "The Allure of Harmodius and Aristogeiton." In *Greek Love Reconsidered*, edited by Thomas K. Hubbard. New York: W. Hamilton Press, 2000.
Taylor, Michael W. *The Tyrant Slayers*. Salem, N.H.: Ayer, 1991.

SEE ALSO: Greece, Archaic; Hippias of Athens; Thucydides.

—*F. E. Romer*

HARṢA

ALSO KNOWN AS: Harṣavardhana; Shilāditya; Harsha
BORN: c. 590 C.E.; probably Thāneswar, India
DIED: c. 647 C.E.; possibly Kanauj, India
RELATED CIVILIZATIONS: Cālukya, Pallava Dynasties
MAJOR ROLE/POSITION: Monarch

Life. The Thāneswar kingdom of Prabhākaravardhana emerged victorious after the Gupta period in its struggle against Huns and rival states. Rājyavardhana II succeeded to his father's throne in 604 C.E., was slain by Śaśāṅka, king of Bengal, but revenged in 606 C.E. by his sixteen-year-old brother Harṣa (HUHR-suh), who added to the empire until checked by the Cālukya king Pulakeśin II in the Deccan.

Harṣa ruled an empire across north India as Sakalottarāpatheshvara, or "Sovereign of the Entire Earth," supervised all matters personally, and replaced anarchy with peace. Intensely energetic, self-disciplined and punctilious in his duties, the last emperor of India established an organized reign with justice, prosperity, and security. He was tolerant of all religions, worshiped Śiva, Vishnu (Viṣṇu), and Buddha, convened the Malāmoksha Parishad to support all religious charities, honored Buddhist scholars, discussed doctrinal matters with them, prohibited animal slaughter, erected stupas and monasteries, and supported the Buddhist University of Nālānda. A great advocate of learning, he patronized his court poet Bāṇa, who immortalized him in the poetic romance *Harṣacarita* (seventh century C.E.; *The Harsa-carita*, 1897), and wrote the three dramas *Nāgānanda* (seventh century C.E.; *Nāgānanda: Or, the Joy of the Snake-World*, 1872), *Priyadarśika* (seventh century C.E.; *Priyadarsika: A Sanskrit Drama,*

1923), and *Ratnāvāli* (seventh century C.E.; *Retnavali: Or, The Necklace*, 1872). He honored the Chinese pilgrim Xuanzang, who recorded his reign. Because Harṣa died without heirs, the throne was usurped by his minister Arjuna, but anarchy quickly disintegrated the empire.

Influence. Harṣa's energetic and prosperous empire restored Gupta glory for a time, but it was the last empire of India.

ADDITIONAL RESOURCES
Basham, A. L. *The Wonder That Was India*. New York: Grove Press, 1959.
Majumdar, R. C. *Ancient India*. Delhi, India: Motilal Banarsidass, 1971.

SEE ALSO: Bāṇa; Gupta emperors; India.

—*George J. Hoynacki*

HATSHEPSUT

ALSO KNOWN AS: Hatshipsitu; Hatchepsut; Maatkare
BORN: c. 1525 B.C.E.; probably near Thebes, Egypt
DIED: c. 1482 B.C.E.; place unknown
RELATED CIVILIZATION: Pharaonic Egypt
MAJOR ROLE/POSITION: Pharaoh

Life. Hatshepsut (hat-SHEHP-sewt) endures as one of the most enigmatic women in ancient history because she became one of only a handful of female rulers in pharaonic Egypt. She was the daughter of Thutmose I and Queen Ahmose of the Eighteenth Dynasty. When her two brothers, Wadjmose and Amenmose, died as children, Hatshepsut became coregent with her father Thutmose I. In her early teens, she married Thutmose II, her half brother and her father's oldest son by Moutnofrit. During the marriage, Hatshepsut bore one daughter, Neferure, who may have been the offspring of her lover, Senenmut. After her father's death, Hatshepsut ruled with her half brother/husband as queen. Judging from his mummy, Thutmose II died of a skin disease only a few years after the marriage. His heir and oldest son was Thutmose III, the son of a minor wife, Isis. Because the boy was very young, Hatshepsut remained in the position of regent for a few years, before taking the reins as pharaoh around 1502 B.C.E.

Hatshepsut ruled for nearly two decades, bringing a cessation in military activities as she turned to domestic building projects, one of the largest being her temple at Deir el-Bahri in the Valley of the Kings. To preserve her sovereignty, Hatshepsut adopted the attributes of her male predecessors, including wearing male clothing and a fake beard. She convinced the priests of Amun-Re of her divinity, claiming the god himself had

Hatshepsut. (Library of Congress)

visited her mother while she was pregnant with Hatshepsut. With this ploy, she invented the notion of divine kingship. She actively pursued broadening the trade network of the Egyptians throughout Africa and Asia. One particularly vaunted expedition embarked for Punt, most likely located near modern Somalia. The trade junket yielded ebony, cinnamon, ivory, furs, gold, perfumes, and myrrh trees.

Despite her successes, her rule was never secure. She arranged the marriage of her daughter to her stepson, who began to scheme in earnest to acquire the throne. Senenmut, her consort and chief architect, died, some postulate at the hand of Thutmose III. By 1483 B.C.E., her daughter was also dead, and Hatshepsut and her mummy vanished, aided by the concerted attempts of her son-in-law/stepson Thutmose III who broke her stelae and chiseled out her name as pharaoh wherever he could find it.

Influence. Women in Egypt enjoyed comparatively high status for females in the ancient Near East.

Hatshepsut stands with Nitokerty, Sobeknofru, and Twosret as female rulers of pharaonic Egypt. She brought peace to her land and increased the power of Egypt through trade. The female pharaoh left numerous works of art, many of which have been rediscovered despite the efforts of Thutmose III. These works of art demonstrate innovations in engineering and decoration. When Hatshepsut died, she left a powerful and united empire as well as the notions of divine kingship and public investiture of royal heirs.

ADDITIONAL RESOURCES
Tyldesley, Joyce. *Hatchepsut: The Female Pharaoh.* New York: Penguin Books, 1996.
Wells, Evelyn. *Hatshepsut.* Garden City, N.Y.: Doubleday, 1969.

SEE ALSO: Egypt, Pharaonic; Thutmose III.
—*Michaela Crawford Reaves*

HATTUSILIS I

ALSO KNOWN AS: Labarnas II
FLOURISHED: seventeenth century B.C.E.
RELATED CIVILIZATION: Hittite
MAJOR ROLE/POSITION: King

Life. Hattusilis I (hat-uh-SIHL-uhs; r. c. 1650-c.1620 B.C.E.) is known as the second king of the Hittites. The edict of the later king Telipinus mentions him immediately after Labarnas I, the founder of the Old Hittite Kingdom. His name was Labarnas II, but after he moved the administrative capital from the city Kussara to Hattusas (modern Bogazköy, Turkey), he adopted the throne name of Hattusilis, meaning "(man) from Hattusas."

The earliest inscriptions in the Old Kingdom were created under Hattusilis I. An annalistic bilingual inscription in the Hittite and Akkadian languages deals with his acts over six years. He reportedly conducted campaigns against more than twenty cities. Hattusilis I undertook a military expedition to Arzawa in southwestern Anatolia, then fought against the Hurrians on the southeastern borders. He destroyed the important city Alalah (later Tell-Açana) in the plain of Antioch. Thereafter, Hattusilis I collided with the famous Hurro-

Amorite kingdom of Yamhad, with its capital Aleppo, which at that time dominated northern Syria. However, against this powerful enemy, he could not achieve a full success and was forced to retreat, probably because of a serious battle injury. He spent his final years in his old capital Kussara as an ill man and there wrote a political will. This document reveals conflicts between Hattusilis I and the members of the royal family, which would indicate a weakened authority of the king. According to the offering lists from Hattusa, the queen of Hattusilis I was Kaddusis. He was succeeded by his adoptive son Mursilis I.

Influence. Hattusilis's conquests created the Hittite state, which would again experience expansion in the fourteenth century B.C.E.

ADDITIONAL RESOURCES
Bryce, Trevor. *The Kingdom of the Hittites.* Oxford, England: Clarendon Press, 1998.
Gurney, Oliver R. *The Hittites.* 2d ed. London: Penguin Books, 1990.

SEE ALSO: Anatolia; Hittites; Labarnas I; Telipinus.
—*Oguz Soysal*

HAWAII

DATE: probably colonized fifth century C.E.
LOCALE: North central Pacific Ocean Islands
SIGNIFICANCE: Polynesians who migrated to Hawaii developed a unique culture on the islands.

Because of conflicts with the Malay peoples, Polynesians living on the Indonesian archipelago migrated in small groups eastward into the Pacific Ocean, using their knowledge of seacraft derived from single-outrigger voyages in the Indonesian archipelago. They followed a northern and southern route, but on both routes, they encountered resistance from the indigenous peoples and were forced to migrate farther east until they located unoccupied lands. The northern route took the Polynesians through the Philippines and Micronesia. Two accounts claim that the first Polynesians reached the Hawaiian Islands from the Marshall Islands in Micronesia, perhaps by the year 450 C.E. The southern route took the Polynesians past New Guinea through Melanesia to Fiji and on to Samoa, Tonga, and Tahiti. The second wave of Polynesians sailed to Hawaii from the Marquesas, which are part of Tahiti, from the eleventh to the thirteenth centuries. The Hawaiian Islands were among the last places on earth to receive humans for settlement, and they were isolated from contact outside Polynesia for about a thousand years.

The original peoples of Hawaii, known as Menehune, engaged in subsistence agriculture. The stronger men established political dominance, exacting food as tribute from the commoners. Warriors were able to carry spears that were thirty feet (about nine meters) in length. The ruling classes reportedly were lazy and often cruel, insisting that the commoners pay homage to them. Below the commoners were slaves, who had been captured in warfare; they performed the most menial tasks. Land was the property of the king of each island and was divided among the chiefs, who were in charge of districts of each island.

The ruling classes established a rigid system of laws (taboos) to protect the lives, property, and dignity of the chiefs and the priests. The chiefs and priests exclusively used certain places to live, fish, bathe, and drink water, and they wore distinctive decorative clothing. The Hawaiians believed in a supreme being, but four gods were in charge of various aspects of the earth, and each in turn was in charge of four lesser gods. Temples of lava rock were erected on hilltops and on seacoasts. Idols of gods were carved from trees to watch over the places where commoners engaged in agriculture, fishing, weaving, and other economic activities.

When the king of each island died, often a war of succession occurred among the chiefs. The winner would then redivide the land among newly appointed followers, who were appointed as the new chiefs. The king's main adviser was an older man with experience in governance and warfare. Tax collectors collected levies once each year in the form of feathers, food, and cloth during festivals.

ADDITIONAL RESOURCES

Handy, E. S. Craighill, et al. *Ancient Hawaiian Civilization.* Rev. ed. Rutland, Vt.: Tuttle, 1970.
Kirch, Patrick Vinton. *Feathered Gods and Fishhooks: An Introduction to Hawaiian Archaeology and Prehistory.* Honolulu: University of Hawaii Press, 1997.
Wyndette, Olive. *Islands of Destiny: A History of Hawaii.* Rutland, Vt.: Tuttle, 1968.

SEE ALSO: Melanesia; Micronesia; Polynesia; Sea Peoples.

—*Michael Haas*

HE YAN

ALSO KNOWN AS: *Wade-Giles* Ho Yen
BORN: date and place unknown
DIED: 249 C.E.; Luoyang, China
RELATED CIVILIZATION: China
MAJOR ROLE/POSITION: Government official, Daoist scholar

Life. Little is known about He Yan's (hoh YUHN) life. He was a grandson of He Jin, a famous general of the Han Dynasty. He was later adopted by Cao Cao (155-220 C.E.), the founder of the Wei Dynasty. In Cao's imperial family, He Yan was treated as a prince. After he was married to a princess, He Yan was given the title of Lie Hou, which was the highest rank of nobility at the time. He Yan was appointed the minister of official personnel affairs, but not long afterward, he was killed in a power struggle. For most of his life, He Yan studied Daoism, particularly the works of Laozi and Zhuangzi. He wrote several dozen essays, but most of them were lost.

Influence. He Yan was one of the main figures in the Xuan Study movement, a Daoist intellectual movement in the Wei and Jin Dynasties. He was as well known as Wang Bi (226-249 C.E.) and was responsible for the development and elaboration of the Daoist theory of nothingness or nonexistence as the foundation, the root, the source, and the essence of existence.

ADDITIONAL RESOURCES

Chan, Wing-tsit, ed. and trans. *A Sourcebook in Chinese Philosophy.* Princeton, N.J.: Princeton University Press, 1963.

Fung, Yu-lan. *A Short History of Chinese Philosophy.* New York: Free Press, 1997.

SEE ALSO: Cao Cao; China; Daoism; Laozi; Wang Bi; *Zhuangzi.*

—Zhaolu Lu

HECATAEUS OF MILETUS

FLOURISHED: sixth to fifth centuries B.C.E.; Ionia
RELATED CIVILIZATION: Persia
MAJOR ROLE/POSITION: Genealogist, mythographer, geographer, cartographer, protohistorian

Life. Born of an old family in Ionia, Hecataeus of Miletus (hehk-uh-TEE-uhs), the son of Hegesander, built an atlas based on Anaximander's map of the world (Europe and Asia, including Africa) using poetry, mythology, and his own investigations of Greek and Persian trade routes. This work, *Periēgēsis* (sixth or fifth century B.C.E., also known as *Periodos gēs*; known as "journey round the world") contained information on geographical features such as mountains, seas, and cities, roads, and rivers as well as descriptions of peoples and gods, kings and customs, etymologies, and economies. As a prominent member of Miletus's insurgent political faction and a foremost proponent of sea power, he advised Histiaeus of Miletus's rebel kinsman Aristagoras during the disastrous Ionian Revolt of 499-494 B.C.E. After the war, Hecataeus served as emissary to the victorious Persians. Later, he wrote of the revolt and the Persian Empire, including the military, in his *Genealogia* (sixth or fifth century B.C.E., also known as *Historiai*; known in English as *Genealogies* or *Histories*). Only fragments of both Hecataeus's atlas and histories survive, and only parts have been translated into English.

Influence. Hecataeus was the most significant of the early Ionian narrators, preeminent in the Western transition from poetry to prose, from mythology to rationalism, from genealogy to chronology, from ethnocentrism to cosmopolitanism, and from Olympian creationism to secular enquiry. His is the first Western, personal sense of humor extant. He may have been the real father of history and anthropology a generation before the Greek historian Herodotus.

ADDITIONAL RESOURCES

Bury, J. B. *The Ancient Greek Historians.* London: Macmillan, 1909.

Drews, Robert. *The Greek Accounts of Eastern History.* Cambridge, Mass.: Harvard University Press, 1973.

Luce, T. James. *The Greek Historians.* New York: Routledge, 1997.

Pearson, L. *Early Ionian Historians.* Oxford, England: Clarendon Press, 1939.

SEE ALSO: Histiaeus of Miletus; Ionian Revolt; Persia.

—O. Kimball Armayor

HELENA, SAINT

ALSO KNOWN AS: Mother of Constantine the Great
BORN: c. 248 C.E.; Drepanum (modern Herkes),
    Bithynia, Asia Minor
DIED: c. 328 C.E.; Nicomedia
RELATED CIVILIZATIONS: Imperial Rome,
    Byzantine Empire
MAJOR ROLE/POSITION: Empress, Christian saint

Life. Born an innkeeper's daughter, Helena became one of the world's most powerful women when her husband, the general Constantius I, became coregent of the Western Roman Empire. In spite of the birth of their son Constantine in about 272-285 C.E., Constantius divorced Helena to marry Emperor Maximian's stepdaughter in 292 C.E. Constantine the Great restored honor to his mother when he became emperor in 306 C.E. He immediately bestowed upon Helena the title of Augusta and had coins struck in her honor. Constantine also converted his mother to Christianity. In her eighties, Helena made a pilgrimage to the Holy Land, where she discovered many important relics, including the True Cross, nails of the Crucifixion, and Christ's seamless gown.

Influence. Helena fed the poor, housed pilgrims, and founded many churches throughout the Holy Land. She is associated with the medieval legend of the True Cross and is depicted in art by artists such as the Italian painters Paolo Veronese and Piero della Francesca with her symbol, the cross. Helena is venerated on August 18 by the Catholic Church and is invoked as a healer of depression.

ADDITIONAL RESOURCES

Drijvers, Jan Willem. *Helena Augusta: The Mother of Constantine the Great and the Legend of Her Finding of the True Cross*. New York: E. J. Brill, 1992.
Eusebius of Caesarea. *Life of Constantine*. Translated by Averil Cameron and Stuart G. Hall. Oxford, England: Oxford University Press, 1999.

SEE ALSO: Byzantine Empire; Christianity; Constantine the Great; Constantius I-III; Maximian; Rome, Imperial.

—*Laura Rinaldi Dufresne*

HELIODORUS OF EMESA

ALSO KNOWN AS: Heliodoros
FLOURISHED: third century C.E.
RELATED CIVILIZATIONS: Hellenistic and Roman
    Greece
MAJOR ROLE/POSITION: Greek novelist

Life. At the end of the novel *Aethiopica* (c. 320 C.E.; *Heliodorus His Æthiopian History*, 1622), the author is identified as Heliodorus (hee-lee-oh-DOHR-uhs of i-MAY-suh), from the Phoenician city of Emesa, Theodosius's son, whose family was linked with the Sun. The question of the dating of the novel is still open. The novel, in ten books, traces how Charicleia, born a white baby to the black king and queen of Ethiopia, exposed at birth by her mother, and raised by Apollo's priest at Delphi, returns home to her birth parents. Notable characteristics include the start midstory, the lengthy retrospective first-person narratives, and the movement away from the Greek world to end in Ethiopia. The novel focuses on themes of piety and chastity and differences of ethnicity, race, and language. The fifth century Byzantine church historian Socrates Scholasticus claims that Helidorus eventually became a bishop.

Influence. Heliodorus's novel was influential in the twelfth century Byzantine Greek revival of the novel. In the sixteenth century, translations of this novel began to appear in Latin and in modern languages, beginning with French. The novel had influence on such varied works as Sir Philip Sidney's *Arcadia* (1590, 1593, 1598, originally entitled *The Countess of Pembroke's Arcadia*), Miguel de Cervantes' *Los trabajos de Persiles y Sigismunda* (1617; *The Travels of Persiles and Sigismunda: A Northern History*, 1619), and French dramatist Jean Racine's tragedies.

ADDITIONAL RESOURCES

Bartsch, Shadi. *Decoding the Ancient Novel: The Reader and the Role of Description in Heliodorus and Achilles Tatius*. Princeton, N.J.: Princeton University Press, 1989.

Hunter, Richard, ed. *Studies in Heliodorus*. Cambridge, England: The Cambridge Philological Society, 1998.

SEE ALSO: Greece, Hellenistic and Roman; Languages and literature.

—*Joan B. Burton*

HELTON PHASE

DATE: 3500-2900 B.C.E.
LOCALE: North America, lower Illinois valley
RELATED CIVILIZATIONS: Adena, Hopewell
SIGNIFICANCE: The Helton phase marks the transition from Late Archaic to Early Woodland civilization on the American plains.

The latter part of the Middle Archaic period saw the rise of the Helton phase in the lower Illinois Valley. The artifacts discovered at the Koster site in west-central Illinois were remarkable because of the evidence of ground and pecked chert implements such as woodworking adzes, stemmed points, grooved axes, and improved weights for atlatls. Technological innovations possibly resulted from shrinking territory, climatic changes, or other unknown factors.

Evidence gathered from burial sites indicates a gradual movement from roving hunting bands to more settled peoples who engaged in some primitive agricultural practices and left behind camp debris, middens, and mounds full of lithic and bone remains. Some of those remains include antler hooks, handles, projectile points, stone atlatl weights, axes of at least three types, bone awls, and engraved pins. Most remains are those of women and children, with an occasional dog, leaving modern investigators with little more than intriguing bits and pieces of the picture of Helton phase life.

ADDITIONAL RESOURCES

Brown, James A., and Robert K. Vierra. "What Happened in the Middle Archaic? Introduction to an Ecological Approach to Koster Site Archaeology." In *Archaic Hunters and Gatherers in the American Midwest*, edited by James L. Phillips and James A. Brown. New York: Academic Press, 1983.
Cook, Thomas Genn. *Koster: An Artifact Analysis of Two Archaic Phases in West Central Illinois*. Evanston, Ill.: Northwestern University Archaeological Program, 1976.

SEE ALSO: Adena culture; Archaic North American culture; Middle Woodland traditions.

—*Michael W. Simpson*

HENOTHEISM

DATE: coined c. 1880 to describe some religious systems dating back to 8000 B.C.E. or earlier
LOCALE: Africa, Middle East, India
RELATED CIVILIZATIONS: Afrasan, Egypt, early Hebrew, India

Henotheism (heh-noh-THEE-i-zuhm) is a religious system that accepts the existence of many gods but worships only one. Often worshipers concentrate their attention on a chief god who is regarded as representing all the others. In a henotheistic system, the believer devotes all attention to one god, who becomes the only god for that person. It is sometimes described as a monotheism of mind and belief. However, it differs from true monotheism, which denies the existence of other gods rather than merely refraining from worshiping them.

The term was originated by Max Müller (1823-1900) to describe the Vedic religion of India, which recognized a multitude of deities but lacked a fixed hierarchy of deities such as that of the Greeks and Romans. It was also found in Egypt, among the Afrasans, and in early stages of Hebrew religion, in which Yahweh was the patron deity of the Children of Israel and was jealous of their attention to other nations' gods, rather than being regarded as the only deity in existence. However, henotheism is not considered to be a stage in evolution of religion or a particular religion but rather a particular pattern of belief within a number of religions.

ADDITIONAL RESOURCES

Ephirim-Donkor, Anthony. *African Spirituality: On Becoming Ancestors.* Trenton, N.J.: Africa World Press, 1997.

Lawson, E. Thomas. *Religions of Africa: Traditions in Transformation.* San Diego: Harper & Row, 1984.

SEE ALSO: Afrasans; Africa, North; Egypt, Pharaonic; India; Judaism; Vedism.

—*Leigh Husband Kimmel*

HERODAS

ALSO KNOWN AS: Herondas
FLOURISHED: third century B.C.E.; place unknown
RELATED CIVILIZATION: Hellenistic Greece
MAJOR ROLE/POSITION: Poet

Life. Herodas (huh-ROH-duhs) wrote literary mimes (short dramatic scenes) in iambic verse for reading or possibly performance by small groups. Extant works are seven full poems, one partial poem, and additional fragments. Internal evidence in the poems strongly suggests that Herodas was writing in the middle of the third century B.C.E. His poetry shows familiarity with Alexandria, Egypt, and the island of Cos. Herodas's poems focus on everyday events and feature ordinary characters: housewives, slaves, cobblers, a matchmaker, a pander, a schoolmaster. Themes include gender roles and power relationships: A jealous mistress threatens an unfaithful slave, a mother asks a schoolmaster to punish her son, housewives discuss dildos, and women visit a temple sanctuary. In "Poem 8," Herodas connects his poetry with Hipponax, a sixth century writer of satirical iambic poetry.

Influence. In the first century C.E., Pliny the Younger, in a private letter, pairs Herodas with Callimachus of Cyrene, a third century B.C.E. poet of considerable influence on Roman literature. However, Herodas's poetry was mostly lost until a papyrus was discovered in Egypt in 1891. His poetry has been admired for its ancient realism as well as its learned qualities. The modern Greek poet Constantine P. Cavafy wrote a graceful homage to Herodas.

ADDITIONAL RESOURCES

Herodas. "Mimiambi." In *Characters.* 2d ed. Cambridge, Mass.: Harvard University Press, 1993.

Hutchinson, G. O. *Hellenistic Poetry.* Oxford, England: Clarendon Press, 1988.

Mastromarco, Giuseppe. *The Public of Herondas.* Amsterdam, Netherlands: J. C. Gieben, 1984.

SEE ALSO: Callimachus of Cyrene; Greece, Hellenistic and Roman; Languages and literature; Pliny the Younger.

—*Joan B. Burton*

HERODIAN

BORN: c. 178 C.E.; possibly Antioch, Asian Minor
DIED: c. 250 C.E.; place unknown
RELATED CIVILIZATION: Imperial Rome
MAJOR ROLE/POSITION: Historian

Life. What little is known about Herodian's (huh-ROH-dee-uhn) life is inferred from his writings, including the approximate year of his birth and length of his life. Born in the eastern, Greek half of the Roman Empire, Herodian spent considerable time in Rome and the provinces as a minor official in the imperial civil service. This gave him access to imperial correspon-

dence, senatorial archives, and eyewitness accounts and an opportunity to travel on official business to various parts of the empire. After his retirement, Herodian wrote in Greek a history in eight books of the events of his lifetime, from the death of Marcus Aurelius to the accession of Gordian III, translated into English in 1969 as *History of the Empire After Marcus.*

Although his history dealt with recent events, it contains errors of chronology and geography and reveals a poor grasp of military strategy. A rhetorical and moralizing strain runs through the history, in which style becomes more important than historical accuracy. Marcus

Aurelius is described as the ideal emperor, against whom his many successors are compared and found wanting. Despite these drawbacks, Herodian often used documentary sources, eyewitness accounts, and personal observations that are contained in no other source.

Influence. Herodian provides a detailed history of his time. Though perhaps an inferior historian to Dio Cassius, Dio's history of the period survives only in fragments and ends nine years earlier. Despite its errors, Herodian's history is more accurate than most of the other historical narratives of that period.

ADDITIONAL RESOURCE
Whittaker, C. H., trans. *Herodian.* 2 vols. Cambridge, Mass.: Harvard University Press, 1969-1970.

SEE ALSO: Dio Cassius; Marcus Aurelius; Rome, Imperial.

—*Robert Rousselle*

HERODIAN DYNASTY

DATE: 37 B.C.E.-c. 70 C.E.
RELATED CIVILIZATIONS: Judaea, Imperial Rome
SIGNIFICANCE: Appointed Jewish rulers by Rome, the Herodians (huh-ROH-dee-uhns) brought Roman culture to Jewish lands.

Herod, son of Antipater of Idumaea, was appointed king of Judaea (r. 37- 4 B.C.E.) by Rome because of his father's assistance to Pompey the Great in conquering Jerusalem in 63 B.C.E. His Idumean roots offended Jewish nobility as did various offenses against Jewish law. He was known as "the Great" because of his building projects, including a remodeling of the Jerusalem temple and seaport city Caesarea that involved the creation of Roman temples, a stadium, and a harbor linking Judaea commercially with the entire empire. Six of Herod's sons were educated in Rome. The paranoid Herod executed numerous male relatives, including his sons and his brother-in-law, a high priest.

At Herod's death, his kingdom was divided among three surviving sons: Herod Archelaus ruled Judaea until deposed after a decade; Herod Antipas ruled Galilee; and Herod Philip ruled the Golan for four decades spanning the years of Jesus of Nazareth. Herod Antipas beheaded the popular prophet John the Baptist.

Under Herod Agrippa I, grandson of Herod the Great and the noble Mariamme, the kingdom was reunited and the title of king restored. Schooled in Rome with the future emperor Claudius, Agrippa assisted in his accession to the throne and was favored in return. Illness took him after a short reign (r. 41-44 C.E.). Herod Agrippa II's loyalty to Rome led him to send his army against Jerusalem to end the Jewish nation (70 C.E.). With sister Bernice as mistress of the emperor Titus, Agrippa II retired in luxury.

ADDITIONAL RESOURCES
Jones, A. H. M. *The Herods of Judaea.* Oxford, England: Clarendon Press, 1967.
Richardson, Peter. *Herod: King of the Jews and Friend of the Romans.* Columbia: University of South Carolina Press, 1996.

SEE ALSO: Antipater of Idumaea; Claudius; Jerusalem, temple of; John the Baptist, Saint; Pompey the Great; Rome, Imperial; Titus.

—*Fred Strickert*

HERODOTUS

ALSO KNOWN AS: Herodotus of Halicarnassus
BORN: c. 484 B.C.E.; Halicarnassus (later Bodrum, Turkey)
DIED: c. 425 B.C.E.; Thurii, Lucania (later southern Italy)
RELATED CIVILIZATIONS: Classical Greece, Persia
MAJOR ROLE/POSITION: Historian

Life. Little is known about the early life of Herodotus (heh-RAHD-uh-tuhs), the son of Lyxes and Dryo. His family fled Halicarnassus in the chaotic years after the Greco-Persian Wars (499-448 B.C.E.) and ultimately settled on the island of Samos. He traveled widely as a young man and ascertained a great deal of information

Herodotus. (Library of Congress)

regarding various lands, customs, and people. This learning enabled him to make a living as a traveling orator, reciting stories of foreign cultures to the masses.

A visit to Athens inspired him to use his learning to write a history of the Greco-Persian Wars, and in the 440's B.C.E., he settled in Thurii to research and write this epic. He died before its completion, however, and a concluding chapter was completed by his contemporaries.

The result of this effort is a book in nine sections, written in literary Ionic, and entitled *Historiai Herodotou* (c. 424 B.C.E.; *The History*, 1709). Herodotus stated that the purpose of the study was to preserve a memory of the war, to record the achievements of the Greeks and the Persians, and to explain why the conflict

began. To do this, he presented all the information available, whether he believed it or not.

The first section is a history of the Persian leader Cyrus the Great. It tells of his accession to power and his conquests and also contains geographic and ethnologic information on Persia, Mesopotamia, and Egypt. The second section is a history of Cyrus's son Cambyses II and his conquests. Sections three through six describe Cyrus's son Darius the Great and the opening battles of the war. Darius's advance into Greek territory is described in depth but so too are the efforts of the Greeks to unite and repel the Persian invaders. These sections include descriptions of the famous Athenian victory at Marathon (490 B.C.E.) and of Darius's defeat. Sections seven through nine tell the story of Darius's son Xerxes I. His efforts to raise an army and invade Greece, the battles at Thermopylae and Salamis, and the Greek victory are described in these sections and complete the study.

Influence. Herodotus is usually dubbed "the father of history" and is considered the first person to use ethnology, geography, and intensive research to describe the actual course of past events. Although he did include numerous references to oracles, divine intervention, and fate, the factual basis of his work separated him from popular storytellers whose epics were mythological. His studies were very popular and sparked an active interest in history among other ancients, including Thucydides. His descriptions of numerous cultures also provide modern scholars with some of the best information on the ancient Near East.

ADDITIONAL RESOURCES

Evans, James A. S. *Herodotus*. Boston: Twayne, 1982.

Gould, John. *Herodotus*. New York: St. Martin's Press, 1989.

Myers, Sir John L. *Herodotus, Father of History*. Chicago: H. Regency, 1971.

Romm, James. *Herodotus*. New Haven, Conn.: Yale University Press, 1998.

SEE ALSO: Cyrus the Great; Darius the Great; Greco-Persian Wars; Greece, Classical; Marathon, Battle of; Salamis, Battle of; Thermopylae, Battle of; Thucydides; Xerxes I.

—Gregory S. Taylor

HERON

ALSO KNOWN AS: Hero of Alexandria
FLOURISHED: c. 62 C.E.
RELATED CIVILIZATIONS: Roman Greece, Imperial Rome
MAJOR ROLE/POSITION: Mathematician, surveyor

Life. The ancient world brought forth two kinds of mathematicians. The first was the kind typified by Euclid and Pythagoras, the pure mathematicians. The other kind of mathematician was an applied mathematician. Applied mathematics had its roots in Babylon and Egypt, where mathematics was used yearly to redraw property boundaries after the Nile's flood, and was a necessity in the ancient world.

Heron (HIHR-ahn) was a prime example of an ancient applied mathematician. His writings were in an Egyptian style. He wrote of the calculation of areas of pieces of land and of volumes of frustums of pyramids. He is best known for the formula for the area of a triangle, where a, b, and c are the lengths of the side of the triangle, and s is half the perimeter.

$$\sqrt{s(s-a)(s-b)(s-c)}$$

Heron also applied his calculating prowess to tabulating the areas of regular figures from three through twelve sides. Heron wrote on *caloptrics*, or reflection, and also about his various inventions. These include approximately a hundred small machines and toys, among them a steam engine. He also discussed increasing the power of catapults and how to move a given weight with a given power.

Influence. The formula for the area of a triangle is still known as Heron's formula. In tabulating areas of regular figures, Heron is considered to have created one of the first trigonometric tables, anticipating modern trigonometry by a millennium.

ADDITIONAL RESOURCES

Boyer, Carl. *A History of Mathematics*. New York: John Wiley and Sons, 1969.
Lewinter, Marty, and William Widulski. *The Saga of Mathematics*. Upper Saddle River, N.J.: Prentice-Hall, 2001.
Smith, D. E. *History of Mathematics*. New York: Dover, 1951.

SEE ALSO: Euclid; Greece, Hellenistic and Roman; Pythagoras; Rome, Imperial.

—*Andrius Tamulis*

HEROPHILUS

ALSO KNOWN AS: Herophilus of Chalcedon
BORN: c. 335 B.C.E.; Chalcedon, Bithynia (later Kadiköy, Turkey)
DIED: c. 280 B.C.E.; probably Alexandria, Egypt
RELATED CIVILIZATIONS: Pharaonic and Ptolemaic Egypt
MAJOR ROLE/POSITION: Scientist, physician

Life. Herophilus (heh-RAHF-uh-luhs) began his medical apprenticeship on Hippocrates' native island of Cos, studying under the famous physician Praxagoras. Cos had a close relationship with Alexandria, which was rapidly becoming the business, intellectual, and medical center of the ancient world.

At Alexandria, Herophilus was able to conduct research by practicing human dissection and even vivisection on live prisoners awaiting execution. His research resulted in eight major books dealing with ophthalmology, respiration, reproduction, blood circulation, digestion, the nervous system, general physiology, therapeutics, and causal theory. Conclusions drawn underscore Herophilus's original genius. He distinguished between motor and sensory nerves and defined the structure of the brain and its central role in human intelligence. Also, he described the structure and function of the heart and the vascular system.

Influence. The Herophileans, or Methodists, as his followers came to be known, continued the work of the great medical researcher for many centuries. Herophileans were still identifiable at the height of the Roman Empire. However, what rapidly disappeared after Herophilus's death was human dissection, the practice that led to his original discoveries. Also all of Herophilus's writings were lost in the great fires that destroyed the great library of Alexandria. His conclusions, particularly on blood circulation, had to be rediscovered in the seventeenth century. Herophilus's work is known through references in several ancient sources that did survive, particularly the works of Galen.

ADDITIONAL RESOURCES

Longrigg, James. *Greek Rational Medicine: Philosophy from Alcmaeon to the Alexandrians*. New York: Routledge, 1993.

Von Staden, Heinrich. *Herophilus: The Art of Medicine in Early Alexandria*. New York: Cambridge University Press, 1989.

SEE ALSO: Egypt, Pharaonic; Egypt, Ptolemaic and Roman; Galen; Hippocrates; Medicine and health.

—Irwin Halfond

HESIOD

FLOURISHED: c. 700 B.C.E.
RELATED CIVILIZATION: Archaic Greece
MAJOR ROLE/POSITION: Singer/poet, farmer

Life. According to Hesiod's (HEE-see-uhd) own testimony, his father moved from Cyme in Asia Minor to Boeotia. There, the Muses visited Hesiod while he tended sheep on Mount Helicon and "gave" him a song about the gods. In a poetic contest at the Funeral Games of Amphidamas, Hesiod won first prize, some say beating Homer himself. In *Erga kai Emerai* (c. 700 B.C.E.; *Works and Days*, 1618), the poet lambasts his brother, Perses, concerning land inheritance. Of the many works attributed to Hesiod, only the *Theogonia* (c. 700 B.C.E.; *Theogony*, 1728) and the *Works and Days* are considered authentic. The *Theogony* traces the movement from female Earth to Olympian Zeus, telling a story of familial violence, including Cronos's castration of Uranus and Zeus's overthrow of Cronos before Zeus creates civic order. In the *Works and Days*, Hesiod's tone is more plaintive and chastising, warning of divine retribution for greedy kings and lazy people. This work includes stories about Prometheus, the birth of Pandora, and the Five Ages of Man. Both the *Theogony* and the *Works and Days* are concerned with jus-

tice, each showing extensive influence from Near Eastern literature. *The Shield* (c. 580-570 B.C.E.; English translation, 1815), about Heracles' shield and his fight with Cycnus, is no longer considered Hesiodic. Lengthy fragments from *Ehoiai* (c. 580-520 B.C.E.; *The Catalogue of Women*, 1983), describing heroic genealogies, also survive. This work was believed to be Hesiod's in antiquity, but apparently this continuation of the *Theogony* was written later.

Influence. Hesiod, with Homer, established for the Greeks their understanding of the gods. The influence of the *Theogony* is seen throughout Greek literature; influence of the *Works and Days* is especially evident in poet Vergil's *Georgics* (c. 37-29 B.C.E.; English translation, 1589).

ADDITIONAL RESOURCES

Caldwell, Richard, ed. *Hesiod's Theogony.* Cambridge, Mass.: Focus, 1987.

West, M. L. *The East Face of Helicon.* Oxford, England: Clarendon, 1997.

SEE ALSO: Greece, Archaic; Homer; Languages and literature.

—Stephen Scully

HESYCHIUS OF ALEXANDRIA

FLOURISHED: fifth century C.E.
RELATED CIVILIZATION: Imperial Rome
MAJOR ROLE/POSITION: Grammarian, lexographer

Life. No information exists concerning the particulars of the life of Hesychius (huh-SIHK-ee-uhs) of Alexandria. Therefore, all attempts at placing him in a particular time and identifying him with a particular religion are purely conjecture. Most scholars agree that his work comes from the fifth century C.E., and while most scholars hold that Hesychius was pagan, internal evidence mitigates against a strong conclusion as to his religious affiliation.

The only information historians have about Hesychius is the place of the authorship of his lexicon entitled *Synagōgē pasōn lexeōn kata stoicheion* (fifth century C.E.; alphabetical collection of all works). The preface reads that this lexicon was written by "Hesychius of Alexandria, grammarian, to his friend Eulogius." The author states that he based his work on that of the lexographer Diogenianus of Heraclea who lived during the reign of the emperor Hadrian (r. 117-138 C.E.). However, although Diogenianus's lexicon covers the vocabularies of poetry, medicine, and history along with Homeric, comic, tragic, and lyric literature, Hesychius's lexicon provides Greek scholars with a vocabulary of otherwise unknown words and rare usages of words along with information about lost authors.

The only surviving manuscript (from the fifteenth century) shows a disturbance in the alphabetical order, and it contain numerous biblical and ecclesiastical glosses.

Influence. Hesychius's lexicon contains about 51,000 entries, making it the richest surviving Greek lexicon until the invention of printing. Numerous words from the Greek dialects are important, not only for Greek but also for Indo-European philology.

ADDITIONAL RESOURCES

Hornblower, S., and A. Spawforth, eds. *The Oxford Classical Dictionary.* 3d ed. Oxford, England: Oxford University Press, 1996.

Phillimore, J. S. "Hesychius of Alexandria." *The Catholic Encyclopedia.* New York: Robert Appleton Press, 1910.

SEE ALSO: Rome, Imperial.

—*Roger S. Evans*

HEZEKIAH

ALSO KNOWN AS: Ḥizqiyya
BORN: c. 740 B.C.E.; Judah
DIED: c. 687 B.C.E.; Judah
RELATED CIVILIZATIONS: Judah, Israel
MAJOR ROLE/POSITION: King of Judah

Life. When Hezekiah (hehz-uh-KI-uh) succeeded his father Ahaz to Judah's throne in 715 B.C.E., he persevered to free his people from the Assyrian yoke that had sorely stifled their political and religious independence. The biblical editor in 2 Kings 18 extols Hezekiah for his nationalistic bent in foreign policy and far-reaching religious reform mandating centralized worship in Jerusalem. Circumspect in its origins, this reform escalated once it became obvious that Assyria's newly challenged status in the Near East rendered it incapable of further intrusion into Judaean affairs. Intent on purging Judah's worship of any foreign dross, Hezekiah initiated a reform that entailed a repudiation of various Assyrian gods that his father in his vassalage had tolerated.

Hezekiah's dream of reuniting northern Israel and southern Judah into a single state went unre-

Hezekiah. (North Wind Picture Archives)

alized. In 701 B.C.E., King Sennacherib led his Assyrian army westward and conquered many of Hezekiah's fortified cities. Jerusalem, Judah's capital, was severely besieged but not taken. Jerusalem was aided by Hezekiah's earlier resolve to repair its walls and construct a new water tunnel and by the fact that Sennacherib had business elsewhere.

Influence. Whereas Hezekiah's bid for Judah's independence saw no lasting results, his fidelity to his religious heritage was intense, and his talent as an administrator and strategist was extraordinary.

ADDITIONAL RESOURCES
Coogan, Michael D., ed. *The Oxford History of the Biblical World*. New York: Oxford University Press, 1998.
Miller, J. Maxwell, and John H. Hayes. *A History of Ancient Israel and Judah*. Philadelphia: Westminster Press, 1986.
Provan, Iain. *Hezekiah and the Book of Kings*. New York: Walter de Gruyter, 1988.

SEE ALSO: Assyria; Bible: Jewish; Israel; Judaism; Sennacherib.

—*J. Kenneth Kuntz*

HIERON I OF SYRACUSE

ALSO KNOWN AS: Hiero
BORN: date and place unknown
DIED: 466 B.C.E.; Catana, Sicily
RELATED CIVILIZATIONS: Classical Greece, Carthage, Etruscans
MAJOR ROLE/POSITION: Tyrant of Syracuse

Life. Hieron I (HI-uh-rahn) of Syracuse first appears in the historical record when his brother, Gelon of Syracuse, conquered the city of Gela and assigned its governance to him. After conquering Syracuse in 485 B.C.E., Gelon created a strong tyranny in eastern Sicily. However, he fell ill in 478 B.C.E. and passed his authority to Hieron. To guarantee the transition, Hieron plotted against a third brother, Polyzelus, by sending him into a dangerous battle. Learning of the scheme, Polyzelus fled to his father-in-law, Theron of Acragas, and convinced him to prepare for war. Ambassadors, however, diffused the situation.

Hieron demonstrated Syracuse's military power in 474 B.C.E. by decisively defeating an Etruscan naval force near Cumae. He later removed the inhabitants of Naxos and Catana (refounded as Aetna) and transplanted ten thousand colonists, earning a reputation for ruthlessness. He displayed his competitiveness in the Pythian and Olympic Games, triumphing in horse and chariot races in 476, 470, and 468 B.C.E. He commissioned the poets Pindar and Bacchylides to write commemorative odes. As a patron of the arts, Hieron sheltered the elderly poet Simonides. Further, Aeschylus gave a performance of his play, *Persai* (472 B.C.E.; *The Persians*, 1777), at court. The philosopher Xenophanes also visited Sicily. Xenophon, the historian, related a fictitious conversation about tyranny between Hieron and Simonides.

Influence. The creation of a strong state helped prevent Etruscan and Carthaginian domination of the western Mediterranean.

ADDITIONAL RESOURCES
Diodorus, Siculus. *Diodorus of Sicily in Twelve Volumes*. Vol. 11. Translated by C. H. Oldfather et al. Cambridge, Mass.: Harvard University Press, 1992.
Sammartino, Peter, and William Robert. *Sicily: An Informal History*. London: Associated University Press, 1992.

SEE ALSO: Aeschylus; Bacchylides; Etruscans; Gelon of Syracuse; Greece, Classical; Olympic Games; Pindar; Simonides; Theron of Acragas; Xenophanes; Xenophon.

—*Todd William Ewing*

HIERON II OF SYRACUSE

BORN: c. 305 B.C.E.; place unknown
DIED: c. 215 B.C.E.; place unknown
RELATED CIVILIZATIONS: Republican Rome,
Hellenistic Greece, Carthage
MAJOR ROLE/POSITION: Statesman

Life. Ruthless but magnanimous, ambitious but generous, a warrior with a love of mathematics, poetry, and sculpture, Hieron II (HI-uh-rahn) of Syracuse is one of the least known but most remarkable figures of Mediterranean antiquity. After gaining control of the Syracusan army, Hieron set out to rule Syracuse independently of the two great powers of the day—Carthage and Rome. He began by ridding his army of mutinous mercenaries. He led the army to battle, then pulled back the citizens and let the mercenaries be slaughtered. He organized a new army out of his grateful countrymen, who raised him from military captain to the undisputed kingship of Syracuse.

Although originally friendly to Carthage, Hieron shrewdly switched alliances when he realized that Rome would become the region's most important power. Although he remained steadfastly allied with Rome during the First and Second Punic Wars (264-247 B.C.E., 218-201 B.C.E.), he secretly aided neighboring cities (including even Carthage) in an attempt to prevent Rome from completely dominating the Mediterranean. Called to Rome to explain his actions, Hieron responded by bringing 200,000 bushels of corn for the people, which won their hearts and forced the Roman senate to send him home unscathed.

During his long reign, Hieron fortified, enriched, and beautified Syracuse, making it into one of the great city-states of the ancient Mediterranean. To improve his city's defenses, he persuaded Archimedes to turn from pure geometry to mechanics, out of which came the famous mathematician's system of pulleys and levers as well as his discovery of how to weigh objects using water displacement.

Influence. Although Hieron is almost forgotten today, his alliance with Rome was critical to that city's ultimate triumph over Carthage. For that reason, he has played a significant role in some of the most important accounts of Rome, including those of Polybius, Livy, Plutarch, Justin, and Niccolò Machiavelli.

ADDITIONAL RESOURCES

Hoyos, B. D. *Unplanned Wars: The Origins of the First and Second Punic Wars.* Berlin: Walter de Gruyter, 1998.

Kincaid, C. A. *Successors of Alexander the Great.* Chicago: Argonaut, 1969.

SEE ALSO: Alexander the Great; Carthage; Greece, Hellenistic and Roman; Punic Wars; Rome, Republican.

—Jeffrey Sikkenga

HILARY OF POITIERS, SAINT

BORN: c. 315 C.E.; Poitiers, Gaul
DIED: c. 367 C.E.; Poitiers, Gaul
RELATED CIVILIZATION: Imperial Rome
MAJOR ROLE/POSITION: Bishop, theologian

Life. A well-educated pagan who was converted to Christianity by reading the Scriptures, Saint Hilary of Poitiers (HIHL-uh-ree of pwah-TYAY) was to become the most prominent Latin theologian of his age, with a record of uncompromising opposition to Arianism. Banished to Phrygia by order of Constantius II after he declined to condemn Saint Athanasius of Alexandria, the bishop studied the Greek theologians and continued his spirited defense of the divinity of Jesus Christ in the East before he was allowed to return home. Hilary's works include a full doctrinal study of the Trinity in twelve books, controversial writings, commentaries on the Gospel of Matthew and the Psalms, and three hymns.

Influence. Hilary was one of the first to introduce the treasures of Greek theology to the Latin West, and his observations on the Trinity influenced such important subsequent Latin churchmen as Saint Augustine and Saint Thomas Aquinas. He is also supposed to have introduced the practice of singing hymns to the West after he witnessed in exile their powerful effect in spreading Arianism, although the hymns he himself wrote are incomplete. He was named a doctor of the church in 1851 by Pope Pius IX. His feast day is January 13, and the spring term at Oxford University is named for him.

ADDITIONAL RESOURCES

Barnes, T. "Hilary of Poitiers on His Exile." *Vigiliae Christianae* 46 (1992): 129-140.
Hilary, Saint, Bishop of Poitiers, and Lionel R. Wickham. *Hilary of Poitiers, Conflicts of Conscience and Law in the Fourth Century Church.* Liverpool, England: Liverpool University Press, 1997.
Williams, D. "A Reassessment of the Early Career and Exile of Hilary of Poitiers." *Journal of Ecclesiastical History* 42 (1991): 202-217.

SEE ALSO: Arianism; Athanasius of Alexander, Saint; Augustine, Saint; Christianity; Constantius I-III.

—*Carl P. E. Springer*

HIMIKO

ALSO KNOWN AS: Pimiko
BORN: third century C.E.; place unknown
DIED: after 238 C.E.; place unknown
RELATED CIVILIZATIONS: Yamatai, Japan
MAJOR ROLE/POSITION: Queen, shaman

Life. Knowledge of Himiko (HEE-mee-koh), a female ruler of the early Japanese political federation known as Yamatai, comes from the Chinese chronicle *Wei Zhi* (297 C.E.). Warring chieftains named Himiko their sovereign, most likely because of her mastery of the "way of the demons," a form of shamanism. After becoming queen, Himiko was sequestered in a palace served by one thousand female slaves and a single male attendant. She was assisted by her younger brother, who dealt with political and administrative matters. Himiko entered into tributary relations with the Wei (Chinese) emperor. After she gave him ten slaves and two bolts of cloth, the Wei emperor titled her the "Wa ruler friendly to the Wei" and sent her a golden seal with a purple cord, textiles, and bronze mirrors. The *Wei Zhi* abruptly announces Himiko's death and reports that an earthen mound was built on her grave site and that one hundred servants followed her in death. The location of this site has eluded archaeologists.

Influence. In the third century C.E., Japan was a heterogeneous group of communities in contact with China. The perceived efficacy of Himiko's shamanism and the tributary relations she established with the Wei enabled her family to achieve political ascendancy.

ADDITIONAL RESOURCES

Mulhern, C. *Heroic with Grace: Legendary Women of Japan.* Armonk, N.Y.: M. E. Sharpe, 1991.
Tsunoda, R., et al. *Sources of Japanese Tradition.* New York: Columbia University Press, 1958.

SEE ALSO: China; Japan; Wei Dynasty.

—*Linda L. Johnson*

HINDUISM

DATE: beginning in c. 200 B.C.E.
LOCALE: South Asia, India
RELATED CIVILIZATIONS: India, Southeast Asia
SIGNIFICANCE: Hinduism is one of the five largest religions in the world, and it has had a major influence on the art, architecture, and beliefs of southern Asia from India through Cambodia to Indonesia.

Although Vedism, an early form of Hinduism, existed from as early as 1500 B.C.E., Hinduism did not emerge in its classic configuration—with its emphasis on nonviolence, pilgrimages, and the celebration of multiple gods—until circa 200 B.C.E. Three primary ways to practice Hinduism developed: the way of deeds, the way of knowledge, and the way of devotion. Although each led to a different way of worship, each emphasized the limitations on physical desires as a precondition to entering Nirvana.

The way of deeds built on the existing idea of karma, which said that the way a person led his or her life would determine the individual's chance for deliverance through reincarnation. It also built on the traditional Indian beliefs in *ahiṁsā* (nonviolence) and dharma (good conduct). Various sets of laws of correct behavior were developed. The most famous of these is the *Manusmṛti* (probably compiled 200 B.C.E.-200 C.E.; *The Laws of Manu*, 1886). These codes defined the rituals that a faithful Hindu should carry out to live the way of deeds successfully.

Knowledge was another path that could lead to spiritual fulfillment. According to this path, ignorance is the cause of evil and suffering for humans, and the awareness of the union with the Brahmā is the desired spiritual state. The knowledge of having reached the union with Brahmā indicates that one has escaped the wheel of life. This intellectual approach to salvation was more important among the priests and the elite.

The path followed by the common people to spiritual fulfillment has been the way of devotion. This means devoting the self to one of the manifestations of god such as Śiva or Vishnu (Viṣṇu), performing *puja* or worship rituals at their shrines, embarking on pilgrimages, and engaging in other acts of worship. The god can aid the devotee in his or her quest for deliverance from this life. The *Bhagavadgītā* (c. 200 B.C.E.-200 C.E.; *The Bhagavad Gita*, 1785), one of the classics of Hindu religious literature, is one of the early expressions of the way of devotion, and it teaches that devotion is the only sure way to gain salvation.

Important among the many gods of Hinduism are the remote creator god Brahmā and two popular gods, Śiva and Vishnu. Brahmā is godliness, and the other gods are manifestations of that godliness. Both Śiva and Vishnu have a complex of other gods associated with them.

Śiva, the Destroyer, is the most popular god in classic Hinduism, and it is his greatness and power that give him the potential to destroy. Śiva evolved from the Vedic god Rudra, who was originally associated with the healing powers of the medicinal herbs in the mountains. Later Śiva actually took on the identity with all forms of life, including vegetable, animal, and human, and especially with the concept of life creation, meaning sexual energy. The representation of Śiva in popular shrines is the lingam, a phallic-shaped black stone. The lingam is set in the yoni, which is a round flat stone that represents Pārvatī, the consort of Śiva. These symbols of life are placed at the center of shrines dedicated to Śiva, and they are decorated with substances that represent life such as milk and flowers.

This figure contains the three important Hindu gods: Brahmā, Vishnu, and Śiva. (North Wind Picture Archives)

Śiva's life energy is also shown in dance, and he is known as the dancing god. He is frequently portrayed in a dancing pose with four arms whirling gracefully and one leg lifted in the air in movement. In spite of Śiva's association with life, he is also the patron of ascetics and holy men. This side of Śiva draws from his power as the destroyer because he can control or negate the desires of the flesh to permit his spiritual being to express itself. Therefore, Śiva has followers who are devoted to both the celebration of life and to asceticism.

Pārvatī is an important goddess and has many manifestations in the different regions of India. She may be the great mother, the gracious and kind one, or the unapproachable one. In northeastern India in the area of

Bengal, people are devoted to Pārvatī as the great mother, and that devotion has developed into Śaktism or the adoration of the godliness of female qualities. Pārvatī is Mother Earth, and she represents the life-giving qualities of the earth.

Śiva and Pārvatī's son, Ganesha (Gaṇeśa), is the elephant-headed god who is one of the most popular of the Indian pantheon. Ganesha is called the Remover of Obstacles because he has the strength of the elephant, and because of that strength, he can virtually guarantee success to any venture. Therefore, many people are his devotees. Another god figure associated with Śiva is Nandi, the white bull, who is Śiva's mount. Naga, the cobra, is also associated with Śiva and represents fertility and strength. Shrines to Śiva usually include images of Ganesha, Nandi, and Naga.

The other great god complex is focused around Vishnu, the Preserver. Vishnu is the god of home and family values, and he represents stability and order. He is the god of love, and when he sees that good is endangered, he uses all his powers to preserve it. In contrast to Śiva, who has contradictory characteristics, Vishnu is always benevolent. Vishnu has come down to earth at critical times in the past to reveal truth or to save the world or legendary figures. Vishnu's appearances on earth are called avatars (incarnation in human form),

and there have been nine throughout history. The tenth avatar of Vishnu is said to be Kalki, a saving figure with a flaming sword who will come on a white horse to destroy evil and to rescue the faithful. That final saving avatar of Vishnu will be the culmination of history for the devotees of Vishnu.

ADDITIONAL RESOURCES

Embree, Ainslie T. *Sources of Indian Tradition*. 2d ed. New York: Columbia University Press, 1988.

Kinsley, David R. *Hinduism: A Cultural Perspective*. 2d ed. Englewood Cliffs, N. J.: Prentice Hall, 1993.

Noss, David S., and John B. Noss. *A History of the World's Religions*. 9th ed. New York: Macmillan College Publishing, 1994.

Smith, Huston. *The World's Religions: Our Great Wisdom Traditions*. San Francisco: HarperSanFrancisco, 1991.

SEE ALSO: *Bhagavadgītā*; India; Vedism.

—*Ronald J. Duncan*

HIPPARCHUS

BORN: 190 B.C.E.; Bithynia, Asia Minor (later İznik, Turkey)
DIED: after 127 B.C.E.; possibly Rhodes
RELATED CIVILIZATION: Hellenistic Greece
MAJOR ROLE/POSITION: Astronomer

Life. According to ancient sources, Hipparchus (hih-PAHR-kuhs) worked most of his life in Bithynia, although he was in Rhodes near the end of his life. Only one of his minor works, *Ton Aratou kai Eudoxou* (on Aratus and Eudoxus), survives, so what is known of him comes largely from later astronomers, especially Ptolemy. Hipparchus's main contributions were in mathematics and astronomy. In mathematics, he contributed to the development of trigonometry through a table of chords useful for astronomy. He also introduced into Greece the practice of dividing the circle into 360 degrees.

The Greek astronomer Hipparchus at Alexandria. (North Wind Picture Archives)

Best known for his work in astronomy, Hipparchus made careful observations of the lengths of both the sidereal and tropical solar years, which enabled him to calculate the length of the year accurately. He also discovered the precession of equinoxes. Additionally, he improved on the estimations of the sizes of the Sun and the Moon from Earth and of their distances from Earth, and he helped develop the system of epicycles and equants to account for the motions of both the Moon and (to him) the Sun. Ptolemy would later extend this method to explain the behavior of the planets. Finally, Hipparchus created a star chart of 850 stars cataloged according to six magnitudes of brightness.

Influence. Through his work in spherical trigonometry and his careful observational practices, Hipparchus transformed Greek astronomy from a largely speculative science into a predictive one.

ADDITIONAL RESOURCES

Calinger, Ronald. *A Contextual History of Mathematics.* Englewood Cliffs, N.J.: Prentice-Hall, 1999.

Dreyer, J. L. E. *A History of Astronomy from Thales to Kepler.* New York: Dover Press, 1953.

Toomer, G. L., trans. *Ptolemy's Almagest.* London: Duckworth, 1984. Reprint. Princeton, N.J.: Princeton University Press, 1998.

SEE ALSO: Greece, Hellenistic and Roman; Ptolemy; Science.

—Terry R. Morris

HIPPIAS OF ATHENS

BORN: c. 570 B.C.E.; Athens, Greece
DIED: 490 B.C.E.; Lemnos
RELATED CIVILIZATIONS: Classical Greece, Athens, Persia
MAJOR ROLE/POSITION: Political leader

Life. A son of the tyrant Pisistratus, Hippias (HIHP-ee-uhs) of Athens inherited the tyranny upon his father's death in 527 B.C.E., apparently establishing a joint rule with his brother Hipparchus. He continued his father's policies for Athenian development, and his administration was mild and perhaps even popular until 516 B.C.E., when an attempted assassination resulted in his brother's death. His regime became harsher, and the exiled Alcmaeonid family, led by Cleisthenes of Athens, managed to convince the Spartans to overthrow the tyranny. Hippias's allied Thessalian cavalry defeated a small Spartan force at Phaleron, possibly in 511 B.C.E., but in 510 B.C.E., a much larger Spartan army drove them off and Hippias capitulated, leaving Athens for Sigeum (Yenişehir). After the failure of King Cleomenes' invasion of Attica, Hippias appealed to the Persian court at Sardis, which adopted the restoration of the tyranny as its official policy toward Athens. Hippias was consequently with the Persian expedition to Marathon in 490 B.C.E., but an increasingly democratic Athens had no interest in the old tyrant. He found no support and no coup in his favor and accompanied the defeated Persian army back to Asia, dying on the way.

Influence. To Hippias fell the sad lot of being a historical relic, a figure whose most important role was to succumb to Cleisthenes and the forces that would ultimately shape a powerful and democratic Athens.

ADDITIONAL RESOURCES

Burn, A. R. *Persia and the Greeks: The Defense of the West, 546-478 B.C.* Stanford, Calif.: Stanford University Press, 1984.

Herodotus. *The Histories.* Translated by Robin Waterfield. New York: Oxford University Press, 1998.

SEE ALSO: Athens; Cleisthenes of Athens; Greece, Classical; Marathon, Battle of; Persia; Pisistratus.

—Richard M. Berthold

HIPPOCRATES

ALSO KNOWN AS: Hippocrates of Cos
BORN: c. 460 B.C.E.; Cos, Greece
DIED: c. 370 B.C.E.; Larissa, Thessaly
RELATED CIVILIZATION: Classical Greece
MAJOR ROLE/POSITION: Physician

Life. Hippocrates (hihp-AHK-ruh-teez) is frequently referred to as the "father of Western medicine." He lived at a time when intellectuals were beginning to question the magical and supernatural explanations for the ways of nature. He is credited with using a rational, scientific approach to the study of medicine, and in his writings, he emphasized the importance of experimental research and the classifying of observations. In works attributed to him, Hippocrates argued that diseases were not punishments sent by the gods; rather they had natural causes that brought about disturbances in the function of the organism. He also noted that diet, occupation, and climate were important factors in causing disease and that physicians should use natural treatments to cure disease.

Hippocrates is also credited with establishing a code of conduct for physicians. The Hippocratic Oath, while not written by him, is a lasting legacy to his philosophical contribution to medicine. This code, which emphasizes the importance of ethical conduct, has been followed by doctors and health professionals for more than two thousand years.

Influence. Although it is difficult to determine what Hippocrates actually wrote, he is the eminent representative of a new stage of development in the field of medicine. His teachings were scientific and focused on the natural basis for diseases and treatment. In addition, the Hippocratic Oath remains the modern-day standard for behavior in the field of medicine.

Hippocrates. (Library of Congress)

ADDITIONAL RESOURCES

Longrigg, James. *Greek Medicine from the Heroic to the Hellenistic Age.* New York: Routledge, 1998.

Polter, Paul. *Hippocrates.* Cambridge, Mass.: Harvard University Press, 1995.

SEE ALSO: Greece, Classical; Medicine and health.

—*William V. Moore*

HISTIAEUS OF MILETUS

BORN: mid-sixth century B.C.E.; place unknown
DIED: 493 B.C.E.; Sardis, Asia Minor
RELATED CIVILIZATION: Persia
MAJOR ROLE/POSITION: Tyrant of Miletus

Life. The Greek historian Herodotus portrayed Histiaeus (hihs-tuh-EE-uhs) of Miletus, the son of Lysagoras, as the selfish, slavish instigator of his kinsman Aristagoras's failed Ionian Revolt of 499-494 C.E.

During Persian king Darius the Great's Scythian expedition (c. 513 C.E.), Histiaeus saved the king by convincing tyrants in other cities not to destroy a bridge the king needed on his return trip. A grateful Darius gave him Thracian Myrcinus on the Strymon River but grew distrustful and summoned him to Susa, where he became a virtual prisoner. Deterred and detained, Histiaeus fooled Darius into restoring him to the coast by first ordering his son-in-law Aristagoras, Miletus's new ruler, to revolt and then promising Darius that he could subdue the rebels.

Histiaeus headed for the coast but instead of working with the local satrap and joining in the decisive sea battle at Lade, in which the Greek forces were destroyed, he pirated merchant ships at Byzantium. After the revolt was over, he plundered the coast and mainland until Harpagus and Artaphernes impaled and beheaded him.

Influence. Despite Histiaeus's efforts to stop it, the Ionian Revolt spread from Cyprus to the Black Sea and lasted for six years. It won help from Athens, Eretria, and the Persians themselves. The rebels burned Sardis, produced their own coinage, and created a "common-wealth" of Ionians. They also seized control of Black Sea shipping, deposed tyrants, and reformed the Ionian government after the war. This revolt inspired a Greek tragedy by Phrynichus. Histiaeus may have tried to build his own Greco-Persian western empire on Lydia, Caria, and the Hellespont with all the great islands.

ADDITIONAL RESOURCES

Burn, A. R. *Persia and the Greeks: The Defense of the West, 546-478* B.C. Stanford, Calif.: Stanford University Press, 1984.

Huxley, G. L. *The Early Ionians*. New York: Barnes & Noble, 1972.

SEE ALSO: Darius the Great; Greece, Classical; Hecataeus of Miletus; Ionian Revolt; Persia.

—O. Kimball Armayor

HITTITES

DATE: c. 2000-1100 B.C.E.

LOCALE: Central and eastern Anatolia, northwest Syria

SIGNIFICANCE: The Hittites were a major polity in Anatolia during the Late Bronze Age, rivaling New Kingdom Egypt in power. Hittite is the earliest attested Indo-European language.

An understanding of Hittite history and culture can be derived from thousands of cuneiform texts coming primarily from Hattusas (modern Bogazköy, Turkey), the Hittite capital. The name "Hittite" comes from the Hittite name for central Anatolia, Hatti. Although it is not known when and from where the first Indo-European ancestors of the Hittites entered Anatolia, individuals with Hittite-like names occur in the Old Assyrian texts from Anatolian trade centers (c. 1920-1740 B.C.E.). One king mentioned in the Assyrian texts was a certain Anittas who ruled from Kushshar, a city that the early Hittite kings claimed as their city of origin. Anittas (who was probably a Hittite) claims to have destroyed Hattusas, although it became the seat of power of the Hittite kings for more than five centuries (c. 1700-1180 B.C.E.). The Hittite kings did not, however, claim descent from Anittas.

Beginning with Hattusilis I, approximately fifteen kings are known to have ruled from Hattusas in the Old Kingdom (c. 1750-1600 B.C.E.). The Hittite state was formed through expansion in this period. During the reign of Hattusilis I (r. c. 1650-c. 1620 B.C.E.), the Hittites expanded into northern Syria and west into the land of Arzawa. Mursilis I (c. 1600 B.C.E.) raided the city of Babylon (c. 1595 B.C.E.) and ended the First Dynasty of Babylon. However, the Hittites were unable to expand into Mesopotamia, and Hittite control of eastern territories seems to have collapsed soon thereafter.

Hittite influence in western Asia Minor and northern Syria was reasserted in the period of the New Kingdom by Tudhaliyas II (r. c. 1420-1370 B.C.E.). The greatest expansion took place during the reign of Suppiluliumas I (r. c. 1380-1346 B.C.E.) and his immediate successors. The Hittites conquered the powerful Hurrian state of Mitanni, controlled all of Syria north of Damascus, and fought with the Egyptians in Syro-Palestine. Hattusilis III (r. c. 1286-c. 1265 B.C.E.) made a treaty with Rameses II and gave him a Hittite princess in marriage. This treaty stayed in effect until the fall of Hittite power in 1180 B.C.E. However, due to a number of factors, Hittite power began to decline during the reigns of the next three monarchs, Tudhaliyas IV, Arnuwandas III, and Suppiluliumas II. The rising power of Assyria in northern Iraq severely truncated Hittite power in Syria. Ahhiyawa (possibly the Hittite term for the Achaeans), a powerful kingdom to the west, threatened Hittite power in western Anatolia. The Hittites also had serious troubles with the rival Hittite kingdom of Tarhuntassha in the south.

What is not certain, however, is what brought about the fall of the Hittite capital, Hattusas. Invaders from the west, usually identified with the Sea Peoples in Egyptian sources, may have been the catalyst for its end. Contrary to popular scholarly tradition, Hittite power did not end with the fall of Hattusas; successor dynasties continued at Tarhuntassha and southeast at Carchemish on the Upper Euphrates. Smaller neo-Hittite states continued in southeast Anatolia and Syria for at least the next five hundred years (c. 700 B.C.E.). These states were often in conflict with rival Aramean dynasties. Both Aramean and neo-Hittite states were absorbed into the Assyrian world state. Passages from II Samuel and I-II Kings that mention the Hittites most likely refer to the neo-Hittite states of Syria.

Language and writing. Hittite shares a number of linguistic features with Luwian, another Indo-European language of Anatolia, and distantly resembles other ancient Indo-European tongues, including Sanskrit and Mycenaean Greek. Furthermore, the Hittites and other Anatolian Indo-European peoples adopted much of their vocabulary from the indigenous Anatolians. These were primarily terms for social status and certain professions, such as priests and artisans.

The Hittite language was written for nearly five centuries (c. 1650-1180 B.C.E.) in the cuneiform script developed in southern Mesopotamia. The Hittites borrowed the script either from the Assyrian trade colonies or from the Old Babylonian script used in Syria at Tell Meskene/Emar and elsewhere. The Hittites modified the cuneiform system by giving new phonetic values to certain signs. The Hittite kings also employed a hieroglyphic script to write a dialect of Luwian.

Social and political structures. At the pinnacle of Hittite society sat the king, who, unlike Egyptian monarchs, was not considered divine during his lifetime. However, the king was believed to become a god at death. Not only was there an official cult for the spirits of deceased kings, but also they were pictorially represented with headgear similar to those of Hittite deities. The king was considered the appointed regent for the gods and was responsible for the welfare of the people. He was also considered a priest (and often depicted in reliefs as such) and thus was considered sacred and constantly went through a series of purification rituals. He was even brought back from distant campaigns to preside over important religious festivals. The Hittite king also presided as the supreme judge over the land and thus heard many of the most important cases concerning capital crimes.

Although the Hittite queen's position is not as well known as that of the king, she was given great responsibility. She often was depicted seated next to her husband in royal iconography and was usually considered the high priestess of the land, thus controlling a great amount of the temple wealth. The queen mother also exercised great authority. For example, Puduhepa, wife of Hattusilis III, corresponded independently with Rameses II of Egypt and made policy concerning a number of the Syrian vassals of the Hittites.

Hittite princes (the male descendants of Hittite kings) were often depicted on rock reliefs. The king usually designated his eldest son as crown prince, although that decision was changed on a number of occasions. Hattusilis I replaced one son with another, and later replaced him with a grandson. Princes held important positions such as governors of major provincial cities and were even installed as hereditary kings in some regions. There was also a ruling class derived from the blood relatives of the king. They were employed as high officials in the kingdom and were considered the king's advisers. They also acted as regents for child kings.

Hittite law distinguished between the freeborn and the slave, although most were not exempt from some form of compulsory duty. Free persons were able to buy and sell, enter into contracts, change their residence, and marry and divorce. Hittite slaves were commodities that could be bought and sold. Runaway slaves were returned to their master, even if they had crossed national boundaries. However, slaves could be married to free persons, although if the marriage was dissolved, those children who remained with the slave parent were considered slaves. If a slave took a woman for a wife, she condescended to his social level as long as they were married. It is apparent from these laws that a Hittite slave could have his own wealth with which to pay the bride price. If the bride's parents paid the bride price, they relinquished the right to redeem their daughter.

Thus, the legal system recognized the rights and responsibilities of slaves. In fact, district governors were ordered not to pay less attention to cases concerning slaves and others less fortunate. A slave paid half the amount of a free person as reparation for his crimes and only received half the reparation. Slaves, however, suffered corporal punishment, including the loss of their noses and ears, for a series of offenses. If the slave committed a crime that required payment, it was paid by his master. If the master refused, the slave was given over to the injured party. Some slaves (both male and female) were literate. Debt slavery also existed in Hittite Anatolia.

Law and statecraft. The Hittite law code is a collection of about two hundred edicts compiled in cuneiform at Hattusas, the Hittite capital in Anatolia about 1650 B.C.E. (although there are references to earlier pre-Hittite laws). In addition, there is an abridged version written three centuries later that contains some modifications. The laws were divided into two series; the first hundred after the words "if a man" and the second hundred after the words "if a vine." This is not code in the strict sense of the word because not every type of legal case is represented. It is in fact a collection of cases that were originally precedents, not unlike other ancient Near Eastern law codes.

In the archives from Hattusas, there is an extensive collection of treaty documents that describe Hittite relations with vassal states and other international powers. These documents, literary in nature, are structured with six major sections: the speaker's introduction, a historical prologue, stipulations, a statement concerning the document, divine witnesses, and a list of curses for recalcitrance and blessings for compliance.

Religion. The city of Hattusas may have contained as many as twenty temples, as well as a "temple city" in the upper city. It also appears that every city and town in the Hittite realm had at least one temple. Temple personnel included chief priests (usually of royal descent), religious technicians, and a plethora of persons employed for the service of the temple. Hittite myths show influence from indigenous Anatolian (Telepinu, the vanishing god), Hurrian-Mesopotamian (song of Kumarbi, and song of Ullikimmi), and West Semitic traditions (Elkunirsha). There does not appear to be any reliance on Indo-European mythical traditions. There are many Hittite documents concerning their religious cult, calendars, seasonal festivals, and magical rituals.

Material culture. The Hittite diet consisted in part of several cereals and a large variety of fruits and vegetables (beans, chick peas, lentils, cucumbers, onions, leeks, and garlic). Wine and raisins were produced from vineyards, and at least three varieties of beer (and "beer-honey") were known. Meat, lard, butter, and cheeses were derived from such livestock as cattle, sheep, goats, and pigs.

The Hittites had a certain level of town planning for their cities, with relatively straight streets (covered with coarse gravel) that contained small channels in the center. Private houses were usually constructed of mudbrick and contained a courtyard at the front of the residence. Some houses were built with a second story. Although the Hittites did not invent iron technology, they used it for luxury items, and reserved the use of bronze for military purposes.

ADDITIONAL RESOURCES

Bryce, Trevor. *The Kingdom of the Hittites*. New York: Oxford University Press, 1998.

Gurney, O. R. *The Hittites*. Rev. ed. London: Folio Society, 1999.

_____. *Some Aspects of Hittite Religion*. Oxford, England: Oxford University Press, 1976.

Hoffner, H. A., Jr. "Histories and Historians of the Ancient Near East: The Hittites." *Orientalia* 49 (1980): 283-332.

_____. *Hittite Myths*. Atlanta: Scholars Press, 1990.

_____. *The Laws of the Hittites: A Critical Edition*. Leiden, Netherlands: E. J. Brill, 1997.

Macqueen, J. G. *The Hittites and Their Contemporaries in Asia Minor*. 2d ed. London: Thames and Hudson, 1986.

SEE ALSO: Assyria; Babylonia; Hattusilis I; Hurrians; Mitanni; Rameses II; Suppiluliumas I.

—Mark W. Chavalas

HOHOKAM CULTURE

DATE: 1-700 C.E.

LOCALE: American Southwest, present-day Arizona

SIGNIFICANCE: These sedentary farming people are best known for the canal systems they used to support their crops in a desert environment.

The Hohokam (hoh-HOH-kuhm) people flourished in the Sonoran desert in the American Southwest. Their origins remain uncertain. Some scholars believe that they arose from hunter-gatherers who moved to the area from nearby mountains around 1 C.E. However, some archaeologists argue that the Hohokam migrated from present-day Mexico. They base their claims on cultural similarities between the Hohokam and groups living to the south.

The Hohokam inhabited an area of some 25,000 square miles (65,000 square kilometers). They depended on the waters from rivers such as the Salt and the Gila to grow crops including corn, beans, squash, cotton, and tobacco. They used many farming techniques, including floodwater and dry farming, a technique that used rainfall and river runoff to water fields. The Hohokam eventually constructed an extensive network of irrigation canals to support their farms. Scholars do not agree as to when the canal building started, but it became an important component of Hohokam life, contributing to population growth after 600 C.E. For animal foodstuffs, the Hohokam relied upon the rich riparian (river) environment, which yielded rabbits, deer, and antelope.

Hohokam villages were located near sources of water. Early houses were small and square and made from brush and branches covered with clay. They were often built in a pit about one foot (thirty centimeters) deep. Although construction materials remained consistent over time, Hohokam houses gradually became larger. However, the number of small houses has led scholars to conclude that the Hohokam often lived in nuclear family units. The houses were usually built around a central plaza.

Most information regarding the Hohokam has been gleaned from artifacts. Early pottery was plain brown, but after 500 C.E., the Hohokam began decorating their pots. They also crafted clay figurines. Tools were crafted from stone. The presence of shell and turquoise in Hohokam sites indicates that they traded with other groups, but the extent and importance of that trade remains unknown.

After 700 C.E. The Hohokam went into decline sometime after 1400 C.E. Some scholars have referred to the disappearance of the Hohokam. However, present-day Native Americans in the region, the Akimel O'odham, claim to be descendants of the Hohokam. Many archaeologists argue that rather than vanishing, the Hohokam people turned to less complex forms of social organization. Reasons offered for this apparent shift in behavior have included earthquakes, devastating floods, epidemic disease, and soil salinization, which may have reduced the fertility of the fields. Each of these reasons has had its supporters and critics.

ADDITIONAL RESOURCES

Crown, Patricia L., and W. James Judge. *Chaco and Hohokam Prehistoric Regional Systems in the American Southwest*. Santa Fe, N.Mex.: School of American Research Press, 1991.

Johnson, Jolene K. *Hohokam Ecology: The Ancient Desert People and Their Environment*. Washington, D.C.: National Park Service, 1997.

Krech, Shepard, III. *The Ecological Indian Myth and History*. New York: W. W. Norton, 1999.

SEE ALSO: Southwest peoples.

—*Thomas Clarkin*

HOMER

BORN: early ninth century B.C.E.; possibly Ionia, Asia Minor
DIED: late ninth century B.C.E.; Greece
RELATED CIVILIZATION: Archaic Greece
MAJOR ROLE/POSITION: Bard

Life. Very little is known about the author of the *Iliad* (c. 800 B.C.E.; English translation, 1616) and the *Odyssey* (c. 800 B.C.E.; English translation, 1616). The ancient Greeks attributed both to Homer, a bard who probably lived late in the ninth century B.C.E. Both long-standing tradition and linguistic analysis of the two epics indicate that their author was a native of Ionia

in western Asia Minor. A number of cities claimed to be Homer's birthplace, but he was probably a native either of the coastal city Smyrna, now Izmir in Turkey, or of nearby Chios, an island in the eastern Aegean Sea. Homer was said to be blind, like the bard Demodocus in the *Odyssey*, and to have earned a meager living by performing at one court after another. Supposedly he died and was buried on the Aegean island Ios.

Those scholars who believe that Homer was responsible for shaping the two great epics admit that he must have begun either with incomplete narratives that had been handed down in the oral tradition or with a number of songs, some of which could have dated back almost as far as the central historical event in both poems, the fall of Troy in 1250 B.C.E. However, Homer was no mere editor; he provided the unifying vision that is essential to the creation of great art. Moreover, even though excerpts from the epics were recited long after his time, the fact that the text changed very little indicates that Homer had his poems preserved in written form, perhaps by dictating them to a scribe.

Various theories have been advanced to explain the fact that the two works are very dissimilar in tone and outlook. One was that the *Iliad* was written in Homer's youth and the *Odyssey*, in his later years; another, that the two poems had two different authors. Nineteenth century scholars debating the "Homeric question" concluded that each epic was produced by a group of writers. At the end of the twentieth century, that idea still had many adherents, but there was new evidence that the two epics were the work of one genius, thus demonstrating once again that tradition is often quite reliable.

Influence. Homer established the epic as a genre in Western literature and set the standards by which later works would be judged. Moreover, the values reflected in the *Iliad* and the *Odyssey* not only shaped Greek culture but also persisted into the Roman era and influenced the Renaissance. Allusions to Homer so permeate Western literature and his ideas are so basic to Western thought that his epics are ranked as two of the most important poems ever written, as well as two of the finest.

Homer. (Library of Congress)

ADDITIONAL RESOURCES
Beye, Charles Rowan. *Ancient Epic Poetry.* Ithaca, N.Y.: Cornell University Press, 1993.
King, Katherine Callen, ed. *Homer.* New York: Garland, 1994.

Nagy, Gregory. *Homeric Questions.* Austin: University of Texas Press, 1996.
Rutherford, R. B. *Homer.* Oxford, England: Oxford University Press, 1996.

SEE ALSO: Eudocia; Greece, Archaic; Livius Andronicus, Lucius; Tibullus, Albius.

—*Rosemary M. Canfield Reisman*

HORACE

ALSO KNOWN AS: Quintus Horatius Flaccus
BORN: December 8, 65 B.C.E.; Venusia (later Venosa, Italy)
DIED: November 27, 8 B.C.E.; Rome
RELATED CIVILIZATION: Imperial Rome
MAJOR ROLE/POSITION: Poet, satirist

Life. Born of poor parents in southern Italy, Horace (HOHR-uhs) studied in Rome and later in Athens. Having lost his family property in the civil strife after the assassination of Julius Caesar, he worked as a civil servant in Rome. In 38 B.C.E., his early poetry brought him to the attention of Gaius Maecenas, adviser to the future emperor Augustus. With official support and encouragement, Horace became a leading literary figure of the day, publishing the *Epodes* (c. 30 B.C.E.; English translation, 1793) and the *Satires* (c. 30 B.C.E.; English translation, 1712). The first three books of *Odes* (c. 23 B.C.E.; English translation, 1793) appeared in 23 B.C.E., with a fourth written later at the request of Augustus. Horace

Horace. (Kim Kurnizki)

also wrote verse letters and a work of literary criticism called *Ars poetica* (n.d.; *Art of Poetry*, 1709). He disliked the fast pace of the city and often retired to his small farm at Tibur outside Rome.

Influence. During his lifetime, Horace reinterpreted earlier Greek and Latin literary works for his contemporaries, fashioning them to reflect the cultural, political, and social tastes of Augustan Rome. Known and appreciated throughout the Middle Ages and beyond, the poet's works have been read, translated, and imitated since their creation.

ADDITIONAL RESOURCES

Armstrong, D. *Horace.* New Haven, Conn.: Yale University Press, 1989.

Fraenkel, E. *Horace.* Oxford, England: Clarendon Press, 1957.

Rudd, Niall, trans. *Horace 2000, a Celebration: Essays for the Bimillennium.* Ann Arbor: University of Michigan Press, 1993.

Zanker, P. *The Power of Images in the Age of Augustus.* Ann Arbor: University of Michigan Press, 1988.

SEE ALSO: Augustus; Caesar, Julius; Languages and literature; Rome, Imperial; Rome, Republican.

—*John M. McMahon*

HORTENSIA

FLOURISHED: last half of first century B.C.E.
RELATED CIVILIZATION: Republican Rome
MAJOR ROLE/POSITION: Wealthy Roman woman speaker

Life. Daughter of Quintus Hortensius Hortalus, the foremost jurist at Rome in the generation preceding Cicero, Hortensia (hohr-TEHN-see-uh) was probably the wife of Quintus Servilius Caepio, who died in 67 B.C.E. In 42 B.C.E., during the Roman civil war following Julius Caesar's assassination, the triumvirs (Marc Antony, Marcus Aemilius Lepidus, and Octavian) placed Hortensia's name on a list of fourteen hundred wealthy women ordered to provide a valuation of their property for tax purposes. The historian Appian, writing nearly two centuries later, reports that some of the targeted women rushed to the Roman Forum to protest and chose Hortensia to speak for them. Appian records her speech as arguing that the women already deprived of male relatives would be reduced to penury and that they should not have to pay taxes without a voice in making policy. In addition, they would contribute to a war against a foreign enemy but not to the conduct of a civil war. Appian's Greek version of what would have been a Latin speech may be a literary exercise composed by a later rhetor; nevertheless, references to it by Quintilian and Valerius Maximus give some support to its authenticity.

Influence. Hortensia is notable as the only Roman woman documented as speaking publicly in the Forum.

ADDITIONAL RESOURCES

Appian. *Appian's Roman History.* Vol. 4. Translated by Horace White. Cambridge, Mass.: Harvard University Press, 1972.

Munzer, F. *Roman Aristocratic Parties and Families.* Translated by T. Ridley. Baltimore: Johns Hopkins University Press, 1999.

SEE ALSO: Antony, Marc; Appian; Augustus; Quintilian; Triumvirate; Valerius Maximus.

—Janet B. Davis

HOSEA

FLOURISHED: eighth century B.C.E.; Israel
RELATED CIVILIZATIONS: Israel, Judah, Assyria, Egypt
MAJOR ROLE/POSITION: Prophet

Life. Hosea lived during and after the reign of the Israelite king Jeroboam II (r. 786-746 B.C.E.). Little is known of his personal life except his disastrous marriage, which became for him an enacted prophecy of the relationship between God and his people. Hosea's wife, Gomer, was unfaithful (perhaps even a cult prostitute); Hosea's prophecies speak of Israel's unfaithfulness to God. Although the language of prostitution and adultery had always been traditional terms for spiritual unfaithfulness, Hosea extended such language to parallel the Baal fertility rites of God as husband and father.

Hosea had three children by Gomer, all of whom he named symbolically to stress God's judgment over Israel. Later prophecies continued to emphasize punishment, especially at the hands of the Assyrians—a fate that came to pass after Jeroboam's death, with the fall of the capital Samaria in 722 B.C.E. It is uncertain whether Hosea lived to see this. Certainly, his writings must have been taken for safekeeping to the southern kingdom of Judah, where they became incorporated into the twelve books of the minor prophets. They stand first there, though chronologically Amos probably precedes Hosea.

Influence. Hosea's prophecies are viewed by Jews as revealing the many-sidedness of God's relationship with his chosen people: not only his judgment but also his yearning love, his desire to bless, and his promise to restore them after their dispersion.

ADDITIONAL RESOURCES
Craigie, Peter C. *The Old Testament: Its Background, Growth and Content.* Nashville, Tenn.: Abingdon Press, 1986.
Davies, Garham. *Hosea.* Sheffield, England: Sheffield Academic Press, 1998.
Sweeney, Marvin A. *The Twelve Prophets.* Collegeville, Minn.: Liturgical Press, 2000.

SEE ALSO: Assyria; Bible: Jewish; Egypt, Pharaonic; Israel; Judaism.

—David Barratt

HUACA DE LA LUNA

DATE: c. 100-700 C.E.
LOCALE: Cerro Blanco site, Moche Valley, Peru
RELATED CIVILIZATION: Moche culture
SIGNIFICANCE: This temple complex, along with Huaca del Sol, served as a key civic-ceremonial center.

The Huaca de la Luna (WAH-kah deh lah LEW-nah; temple of the Moon) complex, together with Huaca del Sol (temple of the Sun), made up the civic-ceremonial core of the Cerro Blanco site, the capital of the Moche Valley-based kingdom. Once perceived as a royal palace, the complex probably served mainly religious and funerary functions.

Despite earlier and later occupations, Huaca de la Luna reached preeminence between about 300 and 600 C.E. The complex stands more than 82 feet (25 meters) tall at the base of a small mountain and consists of a series of platforms, enclosures, chambers, and ramps in a quadrangular ground plan measuring 951 by 689 feet (290 by 210 meters).

The complex developed through multiple construction stages, both renovations after destructive El Niño rains and periodic ceremonial undertakings. Wall segments with adobe bricks bearing "maker's marks" suggest labor contributions from different corporate groups under Moche control. New construction phases built over older architecture and included elite tombs as parts of fill.

Human sacrifice was practiced: One enclosure yielded multiple skeletons of mature males, probably captive warriors, that revealed indications of disabling trauma, slashed throats, and deliberate mutilation. The ceremonial activities articulated vividly in a series of spectacular polychrome relief murals adorning interior courts and chambers stress Moche divinities, rulership ideology, ritual warfare, and sacrifice.

ADDITIONAL RESOURCES

Bawden, Garth. *The Moche.* Cambridge, England: Blackwell, 1996.

Donnan, Christopher B. *Moche Occupation of the Santa Valley, Peru.* Berkeley: University of California Press, 1973.

SEE ALSO: Huaca del Sol; Moche culture.

—*George F. Lau*

HUACA DEL SOL

DATE: 200 B.C.E.-700 C.E.
LOCALE: Andes, north coastal Peru
RELATED CIVILIZATIONS: Moche, Chimubegan
SIGNIFICANCE: The temple is the largest adobe structure of the pre-Columbian Americas.

Where the Moche River empties into the Pacific Ocean are two sites. One, the Huaca de la Luna (temple of the Moon), sits on the edge of a burial ground. The other, the Huaca del Sol (WAH-kah dehl sohl; temple of the Sun) sits across from it. Scholars speculate that these temples were used for solar or lunar worship or calculation, but no evidence exists to confirm these or any other speculations as to the function of these structures.

The Huaca del Sol is the largest adobe structure in the Americas. It is a stepped pyramid, but structural details are lacking partly because of sea erosion. A second, smaller pyramid appears to top the summit, along with a small upper tier. Further damage was done by Spanish conquistadores, who diverted the local river to flow through the temple and flush it of its gold. Also

flushed was much of the history of the people who built this marvelous monument.

The Moche culture built the Huaca del Sol. They lived on the desolate deserted north coast of Peru from the first through the eighth centuries C.E. They were one of the largest pre-Columbian civilizations in the Americas. For unknown reasons, perhaps major changes in the climate, another group, the Chimubegan, eventually began to dominate the area, and the Moche people disappeared until modern times.

ADDITIONAL RESOURCES

Bawden, Garth. *The Moche.* Cambridge, England: Blackwell, 1996.

Benson, Elizabeth P. *The Mochica: A Culture of Peru.* New York: Praeger, 1972.

Donnan, Christopher B. *Moche Occupation of the Santa Valley, Peru.* Berkeley: University of California Press, 1973.

SEE ALSO: Huaca de la Luna; Moche culture.

—*Michael W. Simpson*

HUAINANZI

ALSO KNOWN AS: Wade-Giles *Huai-nan-tzu*; *Huai Nan Hong Lie*
AUTHORSHIP: Liu An (c. 179-122 B.C.E.) and his subjects
DATE: second century B.C.E.
LOCALE: Anhui
RELATED CIVILIZATION: China
SIGNIFICANCE: One of the early works that shaped the philosophical tradition of Daoism.

Huainanzi (HEWAHI-nan-zih) is also known as *Huai Nan Hong Lie*; *hong lie* means "great and bright," implying that this work expounds the great and bright Dao. It consists of twenty-one "inner chapters" that discuss the Dao and thirty-three "outer chapters" that are miscellaneous comments. Only the inner chapters remain. *Huainanzi*, an encyclopedia-like work, is the first written after the Qin Dynasty (221-206 B.C.E.) that organizes various schools of thought, including Confucianism, Moism, Legalism, and the theory of yin-yang, under Daoist principles. It occupies a prominent place in the Chinese history of aesthetics. It also documents early Chinese myths and fairy tales, and hence, it helps preserve Chinese mythology.

ADDITIONAL RESOURCES

Ames, Roger T. *The Art of Rulership: A Study in Ancient Chinese Political Thought*. Albany: State University of New York Press, 1994.

Cleary, Thomas. *The Book of Leadership and Strategy: Lessons of the Chinese Masters*. New York: Random House, 1992.

Lau, D. C., and Roger T. Ames. *Yuan Dao: Tracing Dao to Its Source*. New York: Ballantine Books, 1998.

Major, John S. *Heaven and Earth in Early Han Thought: Chapters Three, Four and Five of the Huainanzi*. Albany: State University of New York Press, 1993.

Roth, Harold David. *The Textual History of the Huainan tzu*. Ann Arbor, Mich.: Association for Asian Studies, 1992.

SEE ALSO: China; Confucianism; Daoism; Legalists.

—*Zhaolu Lu*

HUANGDI

ALSO KNOWN AS: *Wade-Giles* Shen Yen Huang-ti; the Yellow Emperor
BORN: 2704 B.C.E.; place unknown
DIED: date and place unknown
RELATED CIVILIZATION: China
MAJOR ROLE/POSITION: Tribe leader

Life. The Chinese people often declare themselves to be the descendants of Huangdi (HEWAHNG-dee), a half-real, half-legendary personage. Huangdi was the son of Shao-dian, and he got the name Huangdi, which means "yellow emperor," because he was regarded to have the virtues of the earth, whose soil is yellow. He ruled an area stretching east to the sea, west to present-day Gansu Province in China, south to the Yangtze River, and north to present-day Shanxi and Hebei Provinces. He married Leizu, who gave birth to twenty-five sons. The legends say that Huangdi died when he was 110 years old. He was buried in Qiao Shan in Shanxi Province.

Huangdi lived in a period of constant tribal wars. Being a tribe leader, he strove to improve the virtues of his people, to strengthen the army, and to unify the tribes. His major enemy was Chiyou, the leader of the Jiuli tribe. Although Huangdi suffered several defeats at first, he finally defeated and killed Chiyou at Zhuolu in Hebei Province. After the defeat of Chiyou, he won the respect of all tribes on the central plain and became their acknowledged leader.

Influence. Because of his unification of tribes on the central plain, Huangd7i is credited with founding the Chinese nation. He is also credited with many inventions and discoveries such as silkworm raising, boats, carts, south-pointing chariots, writing, music, and mathematics.

ADDITIONAL RESOURCE

Ko, Yuan. *Dragons and Dynasties: An Introduction to Chinese Mythology*. New York: Penguin Books, 1993.

SEE ALSO: China.

—*Yiwei Zheng*

Hui Shi

Also known as: *Wade-Giles* Hui Shih
Flourished: c. 315 B.C.E.?
Locale: Pre-Imperial state of Wei
Related civilization: China
Major role/position: Rhetorician

Life. The rhetorician Hui Shi (WAY-shee) is known only from caricatures by his rivals; his dates and his doctrines are difficult to determine. He probably advocated a peace policy at several fourth century B.C.E. courts, and among his devices of persuasion was probably a destructive analysis of his opponents' statements. He is denounced by both the philosophers Xunzi and Zhuangzi as blinded by propositional logic from perceiving reality; his peace policy and logical precision both link him to the Mician movement (a Confucian school). Paradoxes attributed to him by Xunzi involve abolishing relative differences ("Heaven and Earth are on the same level") and collapsing relative time frames ("eggs have feathers").

Influence. Some paradoxes later associated with Hui Shi by Zhuangzi echo those of Zeno. Enough such echoes exist to suggest Chinese contact with Greek thought after Alexander the Great's conquest and Hellenization of Bactria (329-327 B.C.E.). The opposition of Zhuangzi and Hui Shi may ultimately symbolize a clash between Indian- and Greek-inspired strands of Chinese thought: between intuition and reason.

ADDITIONAL RESOURCE

Hansen, Chad. *A Daoist Theory of Chinese Thought.* New York: Oxford University Press, 1992.

SEE ALSO: China; Daoism; Xunzi; *Zhuangzi.*
—*E. Bruce Brooks*

Huiyuan

Also known as: *Wade-Giles* Hui-yüan; Jia (family name)
Born: 334 C.E.; Yanmen, Shanxi, China
Died: 416 C.E.; Lushan, China
Related civilization: China
Major role/position: Buddhist monk

Life. At the age of thirteen, Huiyuan's (HWEE-yew-AHN) uncle took him to visit Luoyang city, where he studied and mastered the *Liujing* (Six Classics; the books of the *Wujing*, or Five Classics, plus a lost book on music). He was especially well versed in the works of Laozi and Zhuangzi. When he was twenty-one years old, Huiyuan went to Heng Shan to visit the famous Buddhist master Dao An (314-385 C.E.) and was then converted to Buddhism. He began lecturing on Buddhist scriptures when he was twenty-four. Sometime between 377 and 381 C.E., Huiyuan left his master and moved to Lushan (in modern Jiangxi Province). He then lived in seclusion in the temple called Dong Lin Si for the rest of his life. During his remaining thirty-five to forty years, Huiyuan sent his disciples to search for Buddhist scriptures, which he translated into Chinese. He also corresponded with Kumārajīva and other famous Buddhists in China.

Influence. Huiyuan was very much responsible for the dissemination of Buddhism in southern China and for the Chinese interpretation of the Buddhist doctrine of *prajna*, or transcendental wisdom. He was believed to be the founder of the Buddhist sect called Jing Tu (Pure Land).

ADDITIONAL RESOURCES

Lai, Whalen. *Tao-sheng's Theory of Sudden Enlightenment Re-examined: Interaction with Seng-chao, Hui-kuan, Kumarajiva, and Hui-yuan.* Honolulu: University of Hawaii Press, 1987.

Tanaka, Kenneth Kenichi. *The Dawn of Chinese: Pure Land Buddhist Doctrine.* Albany: State University of New York Press, 1990.

Tsukamoto, Zenryu. *A History of Early Chinese Buddhism: From Its Introduction to the Death of Hui-yüan.* Translated by Leon Hurvitz. New York: Kodansha International, 1985.

SEE ALSO: Buddhism; China; Laozi; Wujing; *Zhuangzi.*
—*Zhaolu Lu*

HUNS

DATE: c. 300-600 C.E.
LOCALE: East-central Europe
RELATED CIVILIZATION: Avars
SIGNIFICANCE: Westward Hunnic migrations from Central Asia drove the Germans across borders of the Roman Empire, thereby altering the demographic composition of the West.

The Huns originated in Turkestan and are believed by some scholars to correspond to the Xiongnu, against whom the Han Dynasty in China constructed the first parts of the Great Wall. The Huns migrated westward along the Eurasian steppe toward Europe in the first and second centuries C.E. Mounted on durable horses, the Huns practiced tactics of evasion rooted in age-old hunting techniques. The general low level of Hunnic technology can be contrasted with their highly effective short reflex bow. The bow was employed to pepper their opponents with arrows at a distance, weakening them to be pulled down by lance or lasso. Roman authors reported that the Huns practiced ritual facial mutilations to cultivate a ferocious image and wore silks and

This engraving depicts the Huns' arrival in Europe. (North Wind Picture Archives)

linens purchased by barter. Hunnic warlords fought primarily to acquire plunder for distribution among the members of their tribes.

Under their greatest leader Attila (c. 406?-453 C.E.), the Huns extended their influence from the Caspian Sea to the Rhine River but were checked at the Battle of Châlons by Roman and German forces in 451 C.E. After Attila's death, the Huns were decisively defeated and dispersed by former Germanic subjects at Nedao in 454 C.E. All that remains of the group is the geographical name of Hungary.

ADDITIONAL RESOURCES

Gordon, C. D. *The Age of Attila*. New York: Dorset Press, 1992.

Maenchen-Helfen, J. Otto. *The World of the Huns*. Berkeley: University of California Press, 1973.

SEE ALSO: Attila; Châlons, Battle of; China; Germany; Rome, Imperial; Xiongnu.

—*William E. Watson*

HURRIANS

DATE: c. 2300-1600 B.C.E.

LOCALE: Northern Mesopotamia, present-day Syria and northern Iraq

SIGNIFICANCE: In the third millennium B.C.E., the Hurrians developed a series of states in Upper Mesopotamia that resulted in the great kingdom of Mitanni in the mid-second millennium B.C.E.

The origins of the Hurrians (HOOR-ee-uhnz) are shrouded in obscurity. They are first described in Sumero-Akkadian sources as inhabiting the land of Subartu, a term used primarily to describe upper Mesopotamia (the Khābūr and Balīkh River Basins in Syria as well as the Tigris River Basin in northern Iraq). Although the earliest attestation of the term Subartu dates to about 2400 B.C.E., evidence of Hurrian occupation of the area does not appear until the reign of the Sargonic king Naram-Sin (c. 2200 B.C.E.), when sources begin to cite names of Hurrian places, chieftains, and individual prisoners of war. Because the Hurrian language is similar to the later Urartian tongue, it is presumed that the Hurrians immigrated to the area some time before this from the north, possibly from the Transcaucasian region in Armenia. At any rate, by 2200 B.C.E., north Mesopotamia was thoroughly Hurrianized, with well-established Hurrian states that continued until the rise of the powerful Hurrian-based kingdom of Mitanni (c. 1600 B.C.E.).

The earliest historical text relating to a Hurrian monarch (a bronze tablet now in the Louvre) mentions Atalshen, king of Urkesh and Nawar (c. 2200 B.C.E.). The city of Urkesh is also mentioned in the earliest known document in the Hurrian language, a building inscription of Tish-atal, king of Urkesh (c. 2100 B.C.E.).

Archaeological work in the Khābūr region has revealed a number of Hurrian sites, including Tell Chuera (which shows evidence of the large stone architecture typical of many of the northern Syrian centers and a clearly defined upper and lower citadel), Tell Beydar (which has a major defense system, an upper and lower citadel, and evidence of nearly 150 tablets contemporary with Early Dynastic texts in southern Mesopotamia and coastal Syria), Tell ʿAtij (apparently a trading post), and Tell Brak (which exhibited a large number of Akkadian public structures).

The best known of the sites in this region is Tell Mozan, later identified as Urkesh, known from Mesopotamian historical texts and from later Hurrian mythological texts. The city had a large city wall and one of the largest bent-axis temple structures in this period. The first stratified epigraphic remains in the Khābūr plains of Syria have been found here and have helped identify the ancient name of the site. Seal imprints with the name "Tupkish, King of Urkesh" have been found, along with the name of Queen Uqnitum and her many retainers. It has even been suggested that a Hurrian scribal equivalent to Semitic Ebla may have existed in this region.

ADDITIONAL RESOURCES

Buccellati, G., and M. Kelly-Buccellati. *Urkesh and the Hurrians*. Malibu, Calif.: Undena, 1998.

Gelb, I. J. *Hurrians and Subarians*. Chicago: Oriental Institute Publications, 1944.

Speiser, E. "The Hurrian Participation in the Civilization of Mesopotamia, Syria, and Palestine." *Cahiers du Histoire Mondiale* 1 (1953-1954): 311-327.

Weiss, H., ed. *The Origins of Cities in Dry-Farming Syria and Mesopotamia in the Third Millennium* B.C. Guilford, Conn.: Four Quarters, 1986.

Wilhelm, G. *The Hurrians.* Warminster, England: Aris & Phillips, 1989.

SEE ALSO: Hittites; Mitanni; Sumerians.

—*Mark W. Chavalas*

HUSAYN

ALSO KNOWN AS: al-Ḥusayn ibn ʿAlī; Hussain; Hossein

BORN: 626 C.E.; Medina, Arabia (later in South Arabia)

DIED: 680 C.E.; Karbalāʾ, Iraq

RELATED CIVILIZATION: Arabia

MAJOR ROLE/POSITION: Political and religious leader

Life. Ḥusayn (KOOS-in) was the son of Fāṭima, daughter of the Prophet Muḥammad and founder of Islam, and ʿAlī ibn Abī Ṭālib, the Prophet's son-in-law and cousin. Tensions over leadership of the new faith had been mounting from the time of the Prophet's death. Many gave allegiance to the Prophet's family; they became known as the Party of ʿAlī or Shīʿite.

Ultimately the struggle concerning the line of succession for the leader of Islam culminated in a battle that took place on October 20, 680 C.E., at Karbalāʾ on the bank of the Euphrates River in what became Iraq. The partisans supporting the lineal descent of Ḥusayn faced the opposing forces, some four thousand strong, of the house of Umayyad under the command of al-Ḥurr ibn Yazīd al Tamini. With fewer than one hundred family members and followers, Ḥusayn was slain while kneeling in prayer on the battlefield. His head was severed and taken to the Umayyad capital at Damascus and presented to the Caliph Yazīd I. After the martyrdom, Karbalāʾ became an important place of pilgrimage for Shīʿite Muslims. Shaykh al Mufīd records a firsthand account of the events in the life of al-Ḥusayn in the *Kitāb al-Irshād* (eleventh century C.E.; *Kitāb al-Irshād: The Book of Guidance Into the Lives of the Twelve Imams*, 1981).

Influence. Ḥusayn's death and the battle at Karbalāʾ had immediate and major religious and historical significance. It was the martyrdom that spearheaded a revolution in the early Islam; Shīʿism was transformed from a political party into a religious sect. The Shīʿite branch of Islam continues to be influential in modern-day Iran, Afghanistan, Pakistan, and parts of Iraq.

ADDITIONAL RESOURCES

Halm, Heinz. *Shiism.* Edinburgh: Edinburgh University Press, 1991.

Lewis, Bernard. *The World of Islam: Faith, People, Culture.* London: Thames and Hudson, 1976.

Momen, Moojan. *An Introduction to Shi'i Islam: The History and Doctrines of Twelver Shi'sim.* New Haven, Conn.: Yale University Press, 1985.

SEE ALSO: Islam; Muḥammad; Umayyad Dynasty.

—*Katherine Anne Harper*

HYDASPES, BATTLE OF

DATE: spring, 326 B.C.E.

LOCALE: Hydaspes (Jhelum) River, Punjab region of present northeast Pakistan and northwest India

RELATED CIVILIZATIONS: Macedonia, India, Classical Greece

SIGNIFICANCE: Alexander the Great's victory over the Indian raja Porus gave him control of the Punjab.

Background. While staying at Taxila, Alexander the Great discovered that Porus, who reigned over Pauravas, east of the Hydaspes (hi-DAS-peez), did not intend to submit to him, so he marched against him.

Action. Both armies faced each other on opposite sides of the fast-flowing river. Porus's large corps of eighty-five elephants was a major problem for Alex-

The defeat of Porus at the Battle of Hydaspes. (Library of Congress)

ander's cavalry. Alexander tricked Porus several times into thinking he was attempting to cross the river until the Indian ruler relaxed his guard. Leaving his marshal Craterus with the army in the main camp, Alexander decided on a surprise dawn attack about 17 miles (27 kilometers) upstream, which was detected. Alexander's force reached what it thought was the opposite bank, but it was a small island. They struggled in chin-high water to the opposite bank proper, where they managed to defeat an Indian force before Porus arrived, with his elephants before him. Alexander deployed his cavalry against Porus's wings, while his infantry wounded the elephants so as to trample the Indians underfoot, and Craterus crossed the river with the main army. The Indian army was routed; Alexander rewarded Porus's gallantry by restoring the region to his rule.

Consequences. The battle was the high point of Alexander's Indian campaign; his continued march to the Hyphasis (Beas) River led to a mutiny.

ADDITIONAL RESOURCES

Bosworth, A. B. *Conquest and Empire: The Reign of Alexander the Great.* Cambridge, England: Cambridge University Press, 1988.
Dodge, Theodore Ayrault. *Alexander.* London: Greenhill Books, 1993.

SEE ALSO: Alexander the Great; Greece, Classical; Macedonia.

—Ian Worthington

HYGINUS

ALSO KNOWN AS: Hyginus Gromaticus
FLOURISHED: first century C.E.; place unknown
RELATED CIVILIZATION: Imperial Rome
MAJOR ROLE/POSITION: Land surveyor, author

Life. Nothing is known of Hyginus's (huh-JI-nuhs) life except that he served under the emperor Trajan. Along with his contemporary Sextus Julius Frontinus, he was the most accomplished land surveyor of his time. His surviving works include *Constitutio limitum* (first century C.E.), *De condicionibus agrorum* (first century C.E.), *De generibus controversiarum* (first century C.E.), *De limitibus* (first century C.E.), and perhaps *De munitionibus castrorum* (first century C.E., authorship disputed). He is not to be confused with the Palatine librarian Gaius Julius Hyginus, freedman of the emperor Augustus; Saint Hyginus, pope from c. 136 to c. 140 C.E.; or Hyginus the mythographer, author of *Genealogiae* (also known as *Fabulae*, probably second century C.E.).

Influence. Surveyors in ancient Rome were honored professionals. They were called either *agrimensores* ("field measurers") or *gromatici*, after the *groma*, one of their main instruments. Techniques established by ancient Roman surveyors were part of the practical science of surveying throughout the medieval era and into the Renaissance. In the nineteenth and early twentieth centuries, the works of the *agrimensores* aroused considerable interest among European classical scholars and philologists such as Friedrich Blume, Karl Lachmann, Theodor Mommsen, Barthold Georg Niebuhr, Adolf Rudorff, and Carl Thulin.

ADDITIONAL RESOURCES
Dilke, Oswald Ashton Wentworth. "Insights in the Corpus Agrimensorum into Surveying Methods and Mapping." In *Die römische Feldmesskunst*, edited by Okko Behrends and Luigi Capogrossi Colognesi. Göttingen, Germany: Vandenhoeck & Ruprecht, 1992.
_____. *The Roman Land Surveyors: An Introduction to the Agrimensores*. New York: Barnes & Noble, 1971.

SEE ALSO: Rome, Imperial; Science; Trajan.
—*Eric v.d. Luft*

HYGINUS, GAIUS JULIUS

ALSO KNOWN AS: Julius Hyginus
BORN: first century B.C.E.; probably Spain or Alexandria, Egypt
DIED: first century B.C.E. or first century C.E.; place unknown
RELATED CIVILIZATION: Imperial Rome
MAJOR ROLE/POSITION: Librarian, author

Life. Little is known of Gaius Julius Hyginus's (GAY-uhs JEWL-yuhs huh-JI-nuhs) life. He is usually called a Spaniard, but some authorities say he was born in Alexandria. He is not to be confused with the second century surveyor Hyginus, Saint Hyginus, pope from c. 136 to c. 140 C.E., or Hyginus the mythographer, author of *Genealogiae* (also known as *Fabulae*, probably second century C.E.). Brought to Rome as either a slave or a prisoner of war, he was freed by the emperor Augustus. In Rome, he may have studied under Lucius Cornelius Alexander Polyhistor. He was first the teacher and later the friend of Ovid. Augustus placed Hyginus in charge of the greater of the two public libraries he founded, the Palatine Library. Hyginus wrote much and was widely respected as an author, a critic, and an editor, but none of his works survives.

Influence. As the Palatine librarian, Hyginus was responsible for collecting, compiling, transmitting, and preserving the finest Latin literature, including the works of Vergil. His lost commentary on Vergil was cited by Aulus Gellius and contributed toward establishing the importance of Vergil for the ages.

ADDITIONAL RESOURCES
Richardson, Ernest Cushing. *The Beginnings of Libraries*. Hamden, Conn.: Archon, 1963.

Rose, H. J. *A Handbook of Latin Literature from the Earliest Times to the Death of St. Augustine.* Wauconda, Ill.: Bolchazy-Carducci, 1996.

Thompson, James Westfall. *Ancient Libraries.* London: Archon, 1962.

See also: Alexander Polyhistor, Lucius Cornelius; Augustus; Gellius, Aulus; Ovid; Rome, Imperial; Vergil.

—*Eric v.d. Luft*

Hyksos

Date: c. 1664-c. 1555 b.c.e.

Locale: Egypt

Significance: The Hyksos ruled Egypt for more than one hundred years, gradually assimilating Egyptian culture.

The term "Hyksos" (HIHK-sohs) derives from an Egyptian term translated "rulers of foreign countries" and refers to a group who established a line of non-native rulers that controlled portions of Egypt in the Second Intermediate Period of Egyptian history.

Manetho, an Egyptian who wrote in the third century b.c.e., described the Hyksos as an invading horde of Asiatics who despoiled Egypt and established a tyrannical rule over the country from their delta enclave at Avaris. Although elements of Manetho's version may be based in historical events, an examination of the evidence suggests a more complex picture. Both archaeological evidence and certain personal names of the period identify the Hyksos as Semitic peoples, predominantly Amorites, who came from Palestine. The Egyptians called such people "Asiatics"; numbers of Asiatics, usually in small groups, had peaceably migrated into the Egyptian delta over the centuries preceding the Hyksos era. These Asiatics became an established part of the Egyptian population by the time of the powerful Twelfth Egyptian Dynasty (1991-1786 b.c.e.).

By the close of the Twelfth Dynasty, centralized control over the land had collapsed and Egypt entered an era of fragmentation (the Second Intermediate Period, Thirteenth through Seventeenth Dynasties) with competing dynasties emerging in various parts of the land. In the northeastern delta of Egypt, a line of Hyksos kings established themselves at Avaris (modern Tell ed-Dabʿa). Whether this was a result of centuries of infiltration or a new influx of Asiatics from Palestine who united with the preexisting Asiatic population of the delta remains a debated point. What is clear is that the Fifteenth Dynasty of Egypt (c. 1664-c. 1555 b.c.e.) were Asiatics known to the native Egyptians as Hyksos; they controlled not only the delta but also other sections of Egypt as far south as Gebelein and exercised some authority over the native rulers in Thebes (Seventeenth Dynasty). Ancient lists record the names of six kings of the Fifteenth Dynasty. Khayan and Apophis, two names found in widely scattered contexts even outside Egypt, must have been great kings of this dynasty whose influence extended over much Egypt. Manetho's Sixteenth Dynasty, sometimes referred to as the lesser Hyksos kings, probably refers to Asiatic lords who served the Hyksos kings at Avaris.

A resurgent Seventeenth Dynasty based in Thebes drove out the Hyksos in the mid-sixteenth century. Kamose and Ahmose I led Egyptian forces against Hyksos strongholds, finally taking Avaris by siege. Ahmose pursued the Hyksos into southern Palestine, where he besieged the Hyksos base at Sharuhen. Ahmose's actions broke the power of the Hyksos in Egypt and signaled a new era of Egyptian power commencing with the Eighteenth Dynasty, founded by Ahmose.

The Hyksos kings readily assimilated Egyptian culture and in most respects presented themselves as native kings. For example, Hyksos kings adopted traditional Egyptian royal titles, including the name of the god Re, and supported Egyptian learning as suggested by the Rhind Mathmatical Papyrus inscribed under Apophis I. The god Seth was given prominence among the Hyksos kings, a god whose ambivalence in Egyptian theology as an opponent of Osiris and Horus may have permitted an assimilation to Seth of foreign elements at home with the Hyksos. Hyksos names include Asiatic divine names including Anat. Recent excavations at sites in the eastern delta (Tell ed-Dabʿa, Tell el-Maskhuta) have yielded more clues to their native culture. Human burials accompanied with donkeys, certain weapons, a style of scarabs, and temple styles found at these sites provide strong links with Middle Bronze Age II culture (c. 1850–c. 1550 B.C.E.) found in Palestine.

ADDITIONAL RESOURCES

Redford, Donald B. *Egypt, Canaan, and Israel in Ancient Times.* Princeton, N.J.: Princeton University Press, 1992.

Seters, J. van. *The Hyksos: A New Investigation.* New Haven, Conn.: Yale University Press, 1966.

Trigger, B. G., et al. *Ancient Egypt: A Social History.* Cambridge, Mass.: Cambridge University Press, 1983.

SEE ALSO: Egypt, Pharaonic.

—*Thomas Vester Brisco*

HYPATIA

BORN: c. 370 C.E.; Alexandria, Egypt
DIED: March, 415 C.E., Alexandria, Egypt
RELATED CIVILIZATIONS: Roman Egypt, Imperial Rome
MAJOR ROLE/POSITION: Mathematician, philosopher

Life. Hypatia (hi-PAY-shee-uh) was the daughter of Theon, a distinguished professor of mathematics at the Alexandria university whose goal was to raise, in Hypatia, the perfect human being. Hypatia studied with the finest teachers, including Plutarch in Athens, and coauthored a treatise on Euclid with her father. Mathematically, she is remembered for her work in algebra and conic sections. She is known to have invented several mechanical devices, including an astrolabe, a planesphere for astronomical studies, and an aerometer for distilling water and measuring its properties. She was equally renowned as a philosopher of the Neoplatonic school. Beautiful and intelligent, she was a popular teacher at the university and received many offers of marriage (all refused).

Hypatia became entangled in a power struggle between the "pagan" Orestes, prefect of Alexandria, and the Alexandrian patriarch, Cyril. Neoplatonism, with its scientific rationalism, ran counter to the mysticism of Christianity, and Hypatia, a good friend of Orestes, became a target of political and religious reprisals. On her way to classes one morning, she was pulled from her chariot by a mob, mauled, and dragged to a church where her hair was torn out and her skin scraped from her bones before she was burned to death.

Influence. Hypatia is the first well-known woman in the history of mathematics. Because of her reputed beauty and dramatic death, her life was widely romanticized later.

ADDITIONAL RESOURCES

Dzielska, Maria. *Hypatia of Alexandria.* Cambridge, Mass.: Harvard University Press, 1996.

Osen, Lynn M. *Women in Mathematics.* Cambridge, Mass: MIT Press, 1995.

Yount, Lisa. *A to Z of Women in Science and Math.* New York: Facts on File, 1999.

SEE ALSO: Christianity; Cyril of Alexandria, Saint; Egypt, Ptolemaic and Roman; Euclid; Greece, Hellenistic and Roman; Plutarch.

—*Robert R. Jones*

— *I* —

IAMBLICHUS OF SYRIA

BORN: early first century C.E.; Syria
DIED: c. 180 C.E.; place unknown
RELATED CIVILIZATIONS: Syria, Roman Greece, Imperial Rome
MAJOR ROLE/POSITION: Writer

Life. The little known about Iamblichus (i-AM-blih-kuhs) of Syria comes from Saint Photius, a ninth century Byzantine scholar whose *Bibliotheca* (after 867 C.E.; only selections exist in English translation) includes a summary of his lost novel, the *Babyloniaca* (165-180 C.E., also known as *A Babylonian Tale* and *The Story of Sinonis and Rhodanes*). The evidence from Photius suggests that Iamblichus was most likely a Syrian who spoke the language of Babylon and was familiar with its culture. Photius records Iamblichus's claim that he had a Greek education as well as references to Roman emperors and military operations that place the composition of the *Babyloniaca* between 165 and 180 C.E.

Like other early Greek novels, *A Babylonian Tale* is a romance featuring lovers who must face perils, hardships, and separation before being reunited in a happy ending. In this case, the beautiful Sinonis and her be-loved Rhodanes must flee for their lives when Sinonis refuses to marry the king of Babylon. Pursued by his agents, they are in constant danger from sorcerers, robbers, and others until, in the end, Rhodanes becomes king and they are free to live and love without fear.

Influence. Although it survives only in the summary of Photius and fragments preserved in the *Suda* (twelfth century C.E.), a Byzantine encyclopedia, Iamblichus's work is an important source for the early history of the novel.

ADDITIONAL RESOURCES
Hägg, T. *The Novel in Antiquity.* Berkeley: University of California Press, 1983.
Reardon, B. P. *Collected Ancient Greek Novels.* Berkeley: University of California Press, 1989.
Stephens, S. A., and J. J. Winkler. *Ancient Greek Novels: The Fragments.* Princeton, N.J.: Princeton University Press, 1995.

SEE ALSO: Greece, Roman; Languages and literature; Rome, Imperial.

—Bradley P. Nystrom

IBYCUS

BORN: mid-sixth century B.C.E.; Rhegium, southern Italy
DIED: date and place unknown
RELATED CIVILIZATION: Classical Greece
MAJOR ROLE/POSITION: Poet

Life. Ibycus (IHB-ih-kuhs) is reported to have left Rhegium after refusing to become a tyrant and, like other poets of his era, wandered about the Greek world. He is said to have spent considerable time in Samos with the tyrant Polycrates of Samos. Perhaps he is most famous for the fabulous story of his death. When attacked by robbers, he called on a flock of cranes to avenge him. Later, in a theater at Corinth, one of the robbers saw a crane and declared that it was one of the avengers of Ibycus, thus revealing his criminality.

Ibycus began his career as a lyricist with narratives about the sack of Troy, the Calydonian boar hunt, and other mythological topics. He was noted in antiquity for his erotic poems, which show a wonderful talent at revealing his emotions, especially his lovesick longings. Most of the seven books of his verses were choral poems in a variety of meters.

Influence. Ibycus, included in the Alexandrian canon of nine lyric poets, was considered to be the most passionate of all poets and one particularly subject to the charms of youth. His innovation of passionate choral love lyrics was highly individualistic, and he seems therefore not to have influenced later poets.

ADDITIONAL RESOURCES
Barron, J. P. "Ibycus: To Polycrates." *Bulletin of the Institute of Classical Studies* 16 (1969): 119-149.

Podlecki, Anthony J. *The Early Greek Poets and Their Times*. Vancouver: University of British Columbia Press, 1984.

SEE ALSO: Greece, Classical; Languages and literature; Polycrates of Samos; Troy.

—James A. Arieti

ICTINUS

ALSO KNOWN AS: Iktinos
FLOURISHED: fifth century B.C.E.
RELATED CIVILIZATIONS: Classical Greece, Athens
MAJOR ROLE/POSITION: Architect

Life. Very little is known about the life of Ictinus (ihk-TI-nuhs), an architect who worked in Athens during the time of Pericles (c. 495-429 B.C.E.). Ancient sources attribute three buildings to him. The first is the Parthenon on the Athenian Acropolis (447-432 B.C.E.), which Ictinus designed together with the architect Callicrates, under the general direction of the sculptor Phidias. The second is the great Telesterion, or Hall of Mysteries, at Eleusis (c. 430 B.C.E.). Ictinus was one of a series of architects associated with this frequently modified building. The third is the temple of Apollo at Bassae in Arcadia, where Ictinus is the only recorded architect. Ictinus also wrote a treatise (now lost), with a certain Carpion, about the design of the Parthenon—a work that probably addressed the revolutionary mathematical concepts underlying its design.

Influence. Because of its monumental scale and many refinements as well as the innovative use of the Doric and Ionic orders and the remarkable design of the interior space, the Parthenon of Ictinus and Callicrates has inspired architects, artists, poets, and travelers since Roman times.

ADDITIONAL RESOURCES
Cooper, Frederick A. *The Architecture*. Vol. 1. in *The Temple of Apollo Bassitas*. Princeton, N.J.: American School of Classical Studies at Athens, 1992.
Dinsmoor, Anastasia N. "Iktinos." In *The Dictionary of Art*. New York: Macmillan, 1996.
Winter, Frederick E. "Tradition and Innovation in Doric Design III: The Work of Iktinos." *American Journal of Archaeology* 84 (1980): 399-416.

SEE ALSO: Art and architecture; Callicrates; Eleusian mysteries; Greece, Classical; Parthenon; Pericles; Phidias.

—Ann M. Nicgorski

IGNATIUS OF ANTIOCH

BORN: c. 30 C.E.; apparently Syria
DIED: December 20, 107 C.E.; Rome
RELATED CIVILIZATIONS: Levantine, Imperial Rome
MAJOR ROLE/POSITION: Religious figure

Life. Little is known of the life and ministry of Ignatius (ihg-NAY-shee-uhs), bishop of Antioch in Syria, until the period immediately preceding his martyrdom under Trajan. In the custody of ten soldiers, Ignatius was taken to Rome, where, according to tradition, he was thrown to wild beasts in the Colosseum. He considered martyrdom a privilege and urged the Roman Christians not to interfere.

The legacy of Ignatius lies in a series of seven letters he wrote on the way to Rome. Six were addressed to churches, Rome among them; the seventh was written to Polycarp, a fellow bishop, who himself would be martyred forty years later. The letters, which significantly helped shape the early second century Church, also provide a window on its organization.

Influence. In an era when Christian congregations were typically led by a college of bishops (overseers) or elders functioning as a pastoral team, Ignatius advocated a single monarchical bishop in each church with authority to deal with heresy and schism. Under this arrangement, elders constituted a second tier of leadership and deacons a third. "Do nothing related to the church without the bishop," he urged. The system he championed soon became normative in the Church. Ignatius was the first to speak of "the Catholic Church."

ADDITIONAL RESOURCES

Eusebius of Caesarea. *The Church History: A New Translation with Commentary*. Translated by Paul M.

Maier. Grand Rapids, Mich.: Kregel, 1999.

Grant, R. M. *Ignatius of Antioch*. Camden, N.J.: Nelson, 1966.

Roberts, Alexander, and James Donaldson, eds. *The Ante-Nicene Fathers*. Grand Rapids, Mich.: Eerdmans, 1956.

SEE ALSO: Christianity; Rome, Imperial; Trajan.

—Robert Black

ILAṄKŌ AṬIKAḶ

ALSO KNOWN AS: Ilangovatikal
FLOURISHED: third to the fourth century C.E.;
　Maturai, India
RELATED CIVILIZATION: India (Tamil)
MAJOR ROLE/POSITION: Prince, poet

Life. Ilaṅkō Aṭikaḷ (ee-LAHN-koh ah-TEE-kahl; prince ascetic), a contemporary of the poet Cātanār, probably the younger brother of the Cēra king Cenkuttuvan, is the author of the famous Tamil epic *Cilappatikāram* (c. 450 C.E.; *The Śilappadikāram*, 1939). Written as three books, *Cilappatikāram* is set in the capitals of the three Tamil kingdoms: Pukār (Cōḷa capital), Maturai (Pāṇṭiya capital), and Vañci (Cēra capital). It is the story of Kōvalan and his wife, the virtuous Kaṇṇaki. The epic is a realistic portrayal of Kōvalan's love for the courtesan Mātavi, his consequent ruin and exile in Maturai, his unjust execution by the Pāṇṭiya ruler for alleged theft of the queen's anklet, Kaṇṇaki's outrage, anger, and the burning of Maturai, and the remorse and death of the king and queen.

Although the first two books of the epic narrate this story, the third describes Cenkuttuvan's victorious expedition to the north to bring Himalayan stone for an idol of Kaṇṇaki, the goddess of chastity (*pattiṇi*).

Ilaṅkō Aṭikaḷ's epic is a synthesis of Caṅkam and Sanskrit poetic styles and is a documentation of the people of the Tamil country, their religious beliefs, music and dance, and lifestyles, and their interaction with foreigners such as Greeks and Arabs.

ADDITIONAL RESOURCES

Hart, George L. *The Poems of Ancient Tamil: Their Milieu and Their Sanskrit Counterparts*. Berkeley: University of California Press, 1975.

Parthasarathy, R. *The Tale of an Anklet: An Epic of South India [and] The Cilappatikaram of Ilanko Atikal*. New York: Columbia University Press, 1993.

SEE ALSO: Cātanār; India.

—Salli Vargis

IMHOTEP

FLOURISHED: twenty-seventh century B.C.E.;
　Memphis, Egypt
RELATED CIVILIZATION: Pharaonic Egypt
MAJOR ROLE/POSITION: Court official, physician,
　architect

Life. Imhotep (ihm-HOH-tehp) served under King Djoser (r. c. 2687-2668 B.C.E.) during Egypt's Third Dynasty. He held major civic/religious offices and is the first recorded architect. He designed Djoser's funer-

ary complex at Saqqara, the necropolis located across the Nile from Memphis.

Earlier royal tombs consisted of single, flat-topped, slant-walled, mud-brick structures (mastabas) that covered underground burial vaults. Imhotep placed six mastabas of diminishing size on top of one another, forming the first known step pyramid. He substituted limestone blocks for mud bricks, thus creating the first monumental stone building (204 feet, or 62 meters, high).

The Saqqara site encompassed more than Djoser's tomb. It included a funerary temple and replicas of palaces and chapels within a rectangular enclosure where the king performed royal functions in the afterlife. Imhotep's name was inscribed on the base of Djoser's statue near the entrance to this vast complex.

Influence. Imhotep was one of the few nonroyal persons to be deified as a god of wisdom and medicine. His legacy as a scholar extended to the Greco-Roman world. Numerous bronze statues depicted him seated with papyrus rolls. His temples in Greece became centers of medical knowledge.

Imhotep's architectural revolution laid the basis for new traditions in royal tomb design. Later architects enlarged the size of Imhotep's blocks and filled in the mastaba steps to form the smooth sloping sides of monumental stone pyramids.

ADDITIONAL RESOURCES

Roth, Leland. *Understanding Architecture*. New York: HarperCollins, 1993.

Stierlin, Henri. *The Pharohs' Master Builders*. Paris: Éditions Pierre Terrail, 1995.

SEE ALSO: Egypt, Pharaonic; Pyramids and the Sphinx.

—*Cassandra Lee Tellier*

Imhotep. (Library of Congress)

INDIA

DATE: 8000 B.C.E.-700 C.E.

LOCALE: Subcontinent of South Asia

SIGNIFICANCE: From Ancient India emerged three major religions—Hinduism, Buddhism, and Jainism—as well as a wealth of literature, art, music, and dance.

The Indian subcontinent forms a cohesive territorial mass, protected by the lofty peaks of the Himalayas in the north, surrounded by the Arabian Sea, the Bay of Bengal, and the Indian Ocean on the west, east, and south respectively. Because of the Himalayas, invasion of ancient India was sporadic, accomplished by small numbers of people hardy enough to venture through the mountain passes. This ensured the continuity of Indian civilization and the survival of its basic culture and religious traditions throughout history. Those who migrated, invaded, or sought refuge in India eventually as-

similated into the mainstream while retaining parts of their distinctive cultures.

The early civilizations emerged along the banks of vast rivers such as the Indus and the Ganges, drawing from them water for consumption and irrigation as well as food and using them to navigate. The great oceans surrounding India enabled travelers and explorers to reach the country. Their presence ensured a lively cosmopolitanism and an openness to outside influences, characteristics that enriched the mainstream culture. Indians also traveled extensively, carrying their way of life to the islands of South and Southeast Asia and establishing outposts of Indian culture that still prevail in those societies.

India has always been prey to the vagaries of the monsoon, an air current that in summer blows from the sea to the land, bringing rainfall and bountiful crops. In the winter, the monsoon brings cool dry winds as it blows seaward from the land. The seasonal cycles of nature guided the activities of the people, and even in modern times, rural Indians are as close to these seasonal shifts of weather as were their ancestors millennia ago.

History. Knowledge of ancient India is gleaned from the work of archaeologists, from the study of ancient Indian writings, especially religious texts, and from the writings of foreigners who visited India. The chronology of Indian history provides particular challenges to any historian, for it is difficult to determine many dates with precision.

The history of ancient India evolves and changes continuously because archaeology is daily providing new clues to the mysteries of the past. Ancient India has provided grist for the mills of British imperial writers and Indian nationalists, each group seeking to transplant its own political agenda—justifying foreign rule or validating national aspirations—onto a study of ancient India. The student has therefore to be cautious about all sources and strive to be as objective as possible. Ancient Indian history is a work in progress, the story being rewritten as each generation draws inspiration from this era and seeks to find meaning in the present by reference to the distant past.

Archaeologists are daily pushing back the dates of the first emergence of humans in India, and different dates for the Paleolithic, Mesolithic, and Neolithic eras and beyond make it difficult to create an accurate historical time line. A profusion of artifacts discovered all over the country point to the probability of people at various stages of development coexisting in the subcontinent. Hence, sophisticated literate urbanites enjoyed all the amenities of city dwelling, while in other regions, forest dwellers endured a more primitive existence.

Indus Valley civilization (c. 3500-1700 B.C.E.). The civilization that emerged in western India along the banks of various rivers including the Indus was remarkable in that it exhibited the first signs in the ancient world of advanced concepts of town planning. This civilization extended over an area far greater than ancient Egypt. Large cities like Mohenjo-Daro and Harappā served as commercial and manufacturing centers, ex-

INDIAN KINGDOMS AND EMPIRES, 400 B.C.E.-500 C.E.

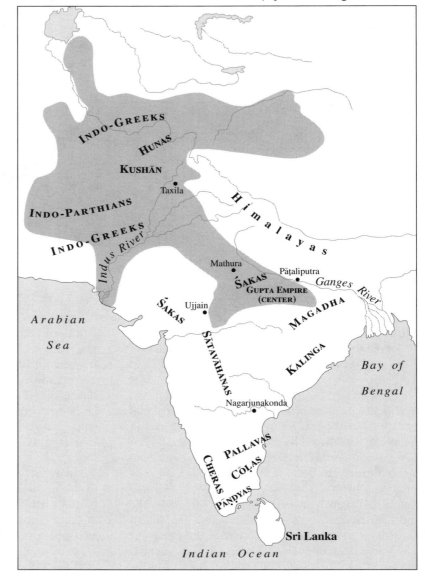

changing goods with a number of neighboring civilizations.

These Indus Valley cities were mainly constructed of baked brick, with multistory houses laid out at regular intervals, vast public citadels, granaries, and shopping and recreation areas. The houses were designed to provide maximum comfort and privacy and were evenly spaced along wide streets. The architectural style of houses—rooms surrounding an indoor courtyard—was similar to that used in modern India, and houses featured indoor bathrooms. This civilization is noted for its elaborate plumbing system. Pipes carried waste to outside drains that were connected to a central drainage system running down the main streets. The drains, covered with stones, provided easy access for regular cleaning. Chutes carried garbage from the homes to outside receptacles. Historians assume that such an elaborate system was serviced by a corps of municipal employees who cleaned the drains and removed the garbage.

That this society valued creature comforts is evidenced by the vast array of jewelry, toys, art objects, gambling dice, and other luxuries found by archaeologists. People wore cotton garments. Carved and engraved seals of stone may have been used to identify goods sent abroad. A profusion of writing on many objects testifies to a high literacy rate. The Indus script has yet to be satisfactorily deciphered, although there have been many attempts by scholars. A standardized system of weights and measures facilitated commerce.

The demise of this civilization continues to puzzle historians, who have surmised that the peace-loving people of this advanced culture were massacred by primitive immigrant hordes. Others theorize that an environmental disaster such as a drought or flood may have forced the people to move east to re-create their civilization in frontier areas of India that were then covered by forests.

Aryans and Dravidians. These two groups may well be the most prominent founders of Indian civilization. Their origins are shrouded in mystery, and historians have speculated about the probable homeland of both peoples. Theories abound about possible conflict between them, and about the impetus this provided to the spreading of civilization to the south of India. The Dravidians, who emerged as a leading political and cultural force in south India, were skilled in manufacturing and architecture, expert in maritime pursuits such as shipbuilding, trade, and commerce, and given to exploration of surrounding countries.

The emergence of the Aryans in Indian history has sparked a contentious debate among historians. In the first part of the twentieth century in Germany, Adolf Hitler and the Nazis identified with the ancient Aryans and politicized this ancient people to justify genocide against Jews, Gypsies, and numerous other groups, partly because they were not Aryan. Hitler's fascist assumptions are now dismissed as myth and false, and the Aryans, their name formerly demeaned by association with modern genocide, have now reverted to their role as creators of significant aspects of ancient Indian civilization. However, controversy still surrounds the Aryans, specifically regarding their emergence in India, the location of their original homeland, whether they can be classified as a racial group, whether they felt and exercised notions of racial purity, and their alleged role in the demise of the Indus Valley civilization. No decisive answers have been found.

The ancient Aryans appear in Indian history about 1500-1000 B.C.E. They are perceived as initially nomadic and pastoral with a developed tribal structure that eventually developed into an agricultural, stable social system that was both rural and urban. Historians have not definitively decided whether the Aryans were foreign invaders or whether their homeland was always India. The issue is fiercely debated. Their contribution to Indian society is, however, not as contentious. The Aryans were notable for their keen sense of organization. From the amalgam of rituals and religious traditions existing among many peoples of India, the Aryans formulated the cohesive, if vast, body of philosophic thought later called Hinduism—the religion of the majority of modern India's more than one billion people.

Hinduism. Hinduism is essentially a religion of personal experience in which salvation of each individual is governed by his or her actions, thoughts, and words. The aim of life is to seek the truth, and Hindus believe that there are innumerable routes to achieve that end. Therefore, all forms of thought must be tolerated, and none should be derided. Hindus do not convert others and would regard such action as inappropriate. There is one supreme divine power, but all manifestations of life share the magic of divinity and must therefore be respected. Hinduism appeals to the most mystic of philosophers but is equally alluring to those who prefer an established convention of ritual and worship. Although there are many sacred books such as the Vedas, there is no one work that must be accepted by all believers. Some Hindus believe that life consists of a cycle of birth and rebirth and that reincarnation occurs until the

Hinduism has remained an important religion in India. This woodcut depicts people paying homage to the god Śiva. (North Wind Picture Archives)

terests to understand the meaning and purpose of life; the pilgrim in the winter of life prepares to merge his soul into the universal concept and to become one with the divine and is beyond attachment to human matters.

Caste system. The ancient social system of caste, associated with Hinduism, is often assumed to be unique to India, but a comparison with Western Europe provides some interesting similarities. The four major divisions are priests (Brahmans), administrators and princes (Kṣatriya), traders and merchants (Vaiśya), and laborers (Śūdra). This corresponds almost precisely with the divisions of society in medieval Europe.

Caste in India is thought to have originally been a deliberate division of society based on occupation. The tribes that were taming the wilderness and building villages, towns, and ultimately cities felt the need to ensure that all the necessary occupations were filled in frontier societies. Hence the requirement for priests who also taught children, military men who governed and protected the people, traders to supply goods, and peasants and laborers to perform the physical work of planting and building. Initially, there was freedom to move between castes and to marry across caste lines. The children of such marriages formed new subcastes and several thousand subcastes exist to this day. It is important to remember that intellect, not wealth, was the ultimate social divide in ancient India. In the modern world, wealth determines status in most societies, especially in the West. The richest members of ancient Indian society were the Vaiśya—the traders—yet they were the third caste in ranking.

Caste groups provided a variety of services to their members, training the young in various trades as well as the rituals and traditions of the religion, providing troops to the ruler during war, supporting widows and orphans, lending money to entrepreneurial members, and providing advice to the king or chief. India also developed an elaborate system of craft and trade guilds that participated in somewhat similar activities.

particular soul—called a divine spark—learns the ultimate lessons of life. Eventually, all divine sparks are saved, none are consigned to eternal damnation. A Hindu prayer states: "Lead me from the unreal to the real. Lead me from darkness to light. Lead me from death to immortality."

Human life is divided into four stages akin to the four seasons, to facilitate the learning experience. The student in the spring of life absorbs all the knowledge that society has to offer; the householder, enjoying the summer of life, learns the joys and limitations of material life, marriage, and family; the retired person, experiencing the autumn of life, resumes his philosophic in-

Political instability and warfare caused by invasions from the north rigidified the caste system into a closed form of segregation that discriminated against outsiders. However, many of the invaders who assimilated into Indian society adopted both Hinduism and caste. The Brahmans, the highest caste, have been accused by historians of attempting to solidify their own superior status by devising endless regulations that separated the castes and forbade intermarriage and even dining together. It is not entirely clear when caste shifted from an occupational status to one based on birth. When that change became widespread, people could not change their caste, although they might change their occupation. For example, a Brahman could work as a cook.

Most horrifying of all was the plight of those who could not be included into caste because their occupations, such as cleaning sewers, rendered them outside the pale of this system. Eventually, over the centuries, such persons were deemed "untouchable," and this discriminatory status was removed constitutionally only when India became free of British rule in 1947. All caste discrimination has been constitutionally outlawed in modern India.

Buddhism. During the sixth century B.C.E.—the era of the philosopher Confucius in China and the lawgiver Solon in Greece—Siddhārtha Gautama, the founder of Buddhism, was born a prince (c. 566 B.C.E.) and heir-apparent to the throne in a kingdom in northern India. He lived a life of luxury in the city of Kapilavastu, married, became a father, and appeared destined for a royal life. However, a keen humanitarian and introspective nature propelled him to wonder about the reason for human suffering. He renounced his princely existence, adopted a life of poverty, and embarked on a quest for enlightenment. After years of search, he finally found an answer and thereafter preached and taught Indians until his death (c. 486 B.C.E.).

Siddhārtha acquired the title of Buddha—the Enlightened One—and taught his followers that human life, subject to constant change, consists of a measure of suffering that is caused by craving and desire for pleasure. This source of unhappiness can be made to cease by following the Eightfold Path, which consists of right views, right resolve, right speech, right action, right work, right effort, right mindfulness, and right concentration. The path is best followed by choosing the Middle Way, neither ascetic nor self-indulgent, devoted to the spiritual journey of achieving Nirvana or a state of liberation, peace, and joy. This gentle philosophy enjoyed immediate and extensive success in ancient In-

dia, particularly as it ignored the segregation of the caste system.

Buddhism became a serious challenge to the entrenched orthodoxy of Brahman priests, and the latter engaged Buddhist monks in spirited debates to woo public support. The adoption of Buddhist thinking by prominent Indian emperors such as Aśoka boosted the popularity of this philosophy in India and eventually over much of Asia.

Jainism. Although it is not as well known to non-Indians as Hinduism and Buddhism, the religion of Jainism has endured since ancient times and enjoys strong support and loyalty among its adherents. Founded by Vardhamāna (c. sixth century to 527 or 467 B.C.E.), Jainism also arose during the sixth century B.C.E. and enjoyed considerable success among the emerging mercantile and trading classes of urban India. Jainism stresses the Three Jewels—right faith, right knowledge, and right conduct—and preaches the value of nonviolence as the central core of its thought.

Hinduism, Buddhism, and Jainism have bequeathed a rich cultural tradition in philosophical writings, art, sculpture, dance, drama, and music. Indian literature, mathematics, and science (for example, astronomy, botany, medicine, and ecology) have all benefited from the emphasis on intellectual pursuits encouraged by these religious traditions.

Mauryan Dynasty. The political unification of an area extending beyond the boundaries of present-day India was first undertaken during the Mauryan era (c. 321-185 B.C.E.). Chandragupta Maurya, assisted by the very able scholar Kauṭilya, founded the Mauryan Empire and provided India with administrative unification, a complex system of bureaucratic control, a unified legal and judicial system, and an effective form of taxation. The ample funds garnered were used to build an elaborate network of roads and bridges, encourage manufacturing, boost the production of mines, and maintain one of the largest armies in the ancient world. Mauryan rulers encouraged domestic and foreign trade, facilitated the travel of tourists across India, funded educational and religious institutions, built hospitals for people and animals, and passed laws to preserve various species of birds and animals.

This dynasty, so remarkably modern in the scope of its activities, also engaged in extensive diplomatic and commercial dealings with a variety of foreign countries. It gave India its greatest emperor, Aśoka (r. c. 265-238 B.C.E.), who propagated the idea of nonviolence and made it a principle of his government. Aśoka's aim to provide a moral foundation for government and an ethical justification for its actions has inspired generations of Indian admirers.

Gupta Dynasty. The vicissitudes of political instability, foreign invasion, and civil conflict tended to erode the unity of the subcontinent achieved by the Mauryan emperors. However, unification remained a goal, and when this goal combined with the energy and power of great rulers, significant empires arose on Indian soil. Although the Gupta Empire (c. 320-540 C.E.) did not achieve the complete unification of India, its cultural achievements were so significant that many historians regard this period as India's golden age. A veritable outpouring of literary works on every conceivable subject form the great legacy of this ancient dynasty.

One of the greatest rulers of this dynasty was Chandragupta II (r. c. 380-415 C.E.), who combined the princely pursuit of military expansion with a keen emphasis on efficient administration, religious toleration, economic betterment, and cultural development. Under the Guptas, Indian art, music, science, literature, and all intellectual pursuits flowered. Elegant poetry was written in Sanskrit, the language of intellectuals and of the literate. Kālidāsa (c. 340-c. 400 C.E.), the greatest dramatist of ancient India, has frequently been compared to playwright William Shakespeare because of the vividness of his descriptions and the sheer beauty of his poetry. Kālidāsa's plays bring Gupta India to life.

The later Gupta rulers faced a severe threat from Huna invaders, tempted by the wealth of India. The Gupta Dynasty that had so enriched Indian civilization succumbed about two centuries after its foundation to a combination of external and internal pressures.

Post-Gupta Ancient India. Harṣa (r. c. 606-c. 647) sought to re-create the Gupta Empire territorially but ruled mainly in the north. He was noted for his liberality and royal patronage to educational and religious institutions. He was a poet and dramatist. He patronized both Hinduism and Buddhism and was a just and mild ruler. However, he left no heir, and his empire fell apart soon after his death.

Although India was frequently prey to foreign invasions, the overwhelming influence of the ancient Hindu-Buddhist-Jain religious and cultural tradition has survived intact. Despite enduring periods of political instability, India's people have exhibited remarkable cultural resilience. Ancient India was the cradle of some of the best aspects of Indian tradition, the emphasis on tolerance, the principle of nonviolence, and the devotion to intellectual and cultural pursuits.

ADDITIONAL RESOURCES

Feuerstein, Georg, et al. *In Search of the Cradle of Civilization*. Wheaton, Ill.: Quest Books, 1995.

Liu, Xinru. *Ancient India and Ancient China*. Oxford, England: Oxford University Press, 1999.

Thapar, Romila. *A History of India*. Vol. 1. London: Penguin, 1990.

Wolpert, Stanley. *A New History of India*. New York: Oxford University Press, 2000.

SEE ALSO: Aśoka; Buddha; Buddhism; Chandragupta Maurya; Gupta emperors; Harṣa; Hinduism; Indus Valley civilization; Jainism; Kālidāsa; Kauṭilya; Mauryan Dynasty; Vedism.

—*Ranee K. L. Panjabi*

INDIAN TEMPLE ARCHITECTURE

DATE: third century B.C.E.-seventh century C.E.
LOCALE: India
RELATED CIVILIZATION: India
SIGNIFICANCE: The profoundly elegant and beautifully decorated Indian temples have served as models and as the inspiration for religious architecture in most regions of Asia.

The temple is the most visible and significant aspect of Indian architecture in that it represents the values of the culture. It is a living place of worship and the residence of the deity. Indian temple builders of all periods created some of the most impressive and original religious structures in the world. The temple is thought of as a *tirtha*, or place where spiritual transformation and release take place.

Defining and adorning sacred space with architectural forms has a long history on the subcontinent, but little is known about the earliest phase because the first structures were made of impermanent materials such as wood and brick. It was not until the time of the Buddhist king Aśoka that creation of permanent architecture in stone began. The earliest monuments are rock-cut caves in the Barabar Hills of Bihār state. Particularly important is the Lomas Ṛṣi cave, with its elaborate decoration surrounding the door that imitates contemporary, indigenous, freestanding wooden architecture. Timbers and bolts, although of no practical purpose, were precisely imitated in stone. Lomas Ṛṣi is the first surviving example of the characteristic ogee, or bentwood arch, a ubiquitous element in all Indian architecture.

It was during the Śuṅga Dynasty (185-72 B.C.E.) that Buddhist religious architecture was established. Many sites were located along the major trade routes and were probably funded by Buddhist merchants. For example, the Western Ghats of Maharashtra is home to Buddhist establishments at Bhaja and Pitalkhora. At both sites, excavations into the rock included great apsidal halls or *caityas* (sanctuaries) and adjoining *vihāras* (monasteries). Care was taken to render the ogee and interior rafters as they would occur in wooden buildings. Stone latticework, false balconies, and semidivine beings decorate the *caityas*' exterior. The monastic quarters have elaborate sculpted displays that introduce repetitions of the ogee, latticework, guardian sculptures, and auspicious symbols.

Also important among the Buddhist sacred architectural monuments were the decorated stupas housing the relics of important Buddhist teachers. The typical stupa is a hemispherical dome resting on a solid drum, surrounded by a balustrade. The stupa at Bharhut with its richly ornamented railing was an early example of the stupa type that was developed further in the later Great Stupa at Sanchi, the elaborate stupas of the southern Andhradesha school, the host of stupas in the Gandhāran region raised during the Kushān period, the Buddhist monuments of Central Asia, and ultimately, the lofty pagodas of the Far East.

It was the very powerful and influential Gupta Dynasty of north India that encouraged Hindu experimentation in stone. Through the dynasty's direct patronage, temple builders of the fifth century C.E. developed the components for freestanding structural stone temples. The basic elements included a *maṇḍapa* (porch or assembly hall), a *garbha gṛha* (cella) that housed the image or symbol of the deity, a *śikhara* (spire) symbolizing the mountain abode of the deity, an *āmalaka* (crowning, decorative member on the spire), and a covered pathway for circumambulation and, eventually, the integration of sculpture. The earliest of the freestanding temples is the very small, flat-roofed Temple

17 at Sanchi (fifth century C.E.). Within a century, as seen in the Dashavatara temple at Deogarh (c. 525 C.E.), the northern style Hindu temple with its decorated pyramidal tower, icon panels allocated to particular places on temple walls, and elaborate rich decoration had evolved fully. It is clear that temple construction from that point on was based on a precise system of proportions and correlated measurements. It was during the Gupta period that the Mahābodhi temple at Bodhgaya was constructed over the original structure raised by Aśoka. The temple as it stands in modern times with its massive pyramidal tower is the product of several renovations of later centuries, and thus, the original Gupta structure is not fully known.

Located to the south of the Gupta kingdom was the Vākāṭaka Dynasty. The Vākāṭakas had political ties with the Guptas, and therefore, the artistic currents from the north were very influential; there are strong affinities between Gupta and Vākāṭaka art. Under the patronage of King Hariṣeṇa, twenty-four Buddhist caves at Ajanta were excavated side by side in the cliff above a river. Dating to the last quarter of the fifth century C.E. are two large *caityas* and twenty-two *vihāras*, most of which include chapels with images of important Mahāyāna deities. The Ajanta caves are famous for their robust yet delicately rendered sculptures, elaborate architectural ornamentation, and the spectacular paintings that are the sole surviving examples of Indian painting of this early period.

The great creative activity that was begun by Hariṣeṇa was continued by the dynasty's successors in the region. The Kalacuri Dynasty took control of the western Deccan in the sixth century C.E. A powerful artistic and religious force, their artisans introduced new elements into cave-temple planning. The Kalacuris excavated some of the most memorable cave temples in India, dedicated to the Pāśupati sect of Śiva. Particularly stunning is the colossal Śiva temple on Elephanta Island in Mumbai harbor. The rather plain exterior of the cave hardly prepares visitors for the grand scale of the majestically decorated interior. Gigantic in scale, the pillars with their bulbous cushion capitals, the huge sculpted relief panels, and mighty guardians flanking entrances to the cella imbue the viewer with a deep awareness of the meaning of the sacred. Equally impressive are the Kalacuri cave temples at Ellora that house many of India's most magnificent religious icons. The sculptors realized in the images a perfect balance between the earthly and the divine, the sensual and the spiritual.

The western Cālukyas located in Mysore state in the south began an active campaign of constructing religious monuments in stone soon after they came to power. The earliest examples date to the sixth century C.E.; they include four caves located at their capital at Badami and the Ravaṇa Phadi cave at nearby Aihole. The caves, excavated under royal auspices, all demonstrate highly evolved iconographical programs combined with splendid craftsmanship. The early Cālukyan sculptural and architectural styles reveal close links with the Kalacuri artistic productions farther to the north.

It was the very dynamic and inventive Pallava Dynasty of Tamil Nādu in south India that experimented with stone architecture and created the distinctive southern style architecture, or the so-called Dravida style. King Mahendravarman I (r. c. 600-630) was the first Pallava to excavate a cave temple in the region. The temple at Mandagapattu was carved in extremely hard granite, a fact noted with pride in an inscription. Dedicated to the Hindu triad of deities, Brahmā, Vishnu (Viṣṇu), and Śiva, it consisted of a pillared verandah (*maṇḍapa*) and a cella at the rear. The successful completion of the cave encouraged the king to undertake nine other excavations, most located in the region surrounding the capital city at Kanchipuram.

Mahendravarman I's successors continued the traditions of rock-cut temples. Narasiṃhavarman I (630-668 C.E.) was an outstanding patron and innovator. At the seaport city called Mahabalipuram, he had his artisans sculpt monolithic temples from boulders located near the shore. Called the Rathas, the exquisite temples serve as astonishing examples of the various types of southern style constructions. The largest of these, the Dharmarāja Ratha, has the characteristic tiered roof with each story being separated by a balustrade consisting of miniature shrines, the typical lion-based pillars, the massive and embellished octagonal crowning stone on top, and superb icons in the slender southern figural style. The Rathas were the first great southern freestanding temples.

Those grand builders of Indian temples and the craftspeople who decorated the walls belonged to guilds that carefully worked out the designs and methods of construction while working in collaboration with the priests. Together they determined the forms and styles of the temples that eventually were set down in canons called the Śilpa-śāstra and the Āgamas, in which every last detail was codified for posterity.

ADDITIONAL RESOURCES

Huntington, Susan L. *The Art of Ancient India*. New York: Weatherhill, 1985.

Meister, Michael, ed. *Encyclopaedia of Indian Temple Architecture*. Philadelphia: University of Pennsylvania, 1983.

SEE ALSO: Aśoka; Buddhism; Gupta emperors; Hinduism; Kushān Dynasty; Mahābodhi temple; Mahendravarman I; Pallava Dynasty; Śuṅga Dynasty; Vākāṭaka Dynasty.

—Katherine Anne Harper

INDUS VALLEY CIVILIZATION

ALSO KNOWN AS: Harappān civilization
DATE: c. 3500-1700 B.C.E.
LOCALE: Northwest India, Pakistan
RELATED CIVILIZATION: India
SIGNIFICANCE: First great culture of the Indian subcontinent.

An excavation conducted at Mohenjo-Daro by Sir John Marshall in the 1920's revealed the first of several ancient cities located along the Indus River that were part of the Indian subcontinent's first civilization. Later surveys and excavations revealed the scope of the culture that extended from Baluchistan in the west to the Rājasthāni desert in the east and from the foothills of the Himalayas in the north to the Gulf of Kutch in the south. Large cities with populations of several thousand people, townships, and villages were linked by rivers and sea and overland routes. An extensive, complex web of settlements supported an economy that was based on agriculture, various industries, and trade.

The cities of the mature phase (c. 2700-1800 B.C.E.) were constructed on the grid system and oriented to the cardinal directions. The cities had extensive sewer systems made from terra-cotta conduits and buildings that were constructed of bricks all of precise and uniform measures. The enterprising inhabitants of the Indus region traded with other distant cultures, and Indus relics have been found in cities of the ancient Near East and in settlements along the Persian Gulf. In order to keep track of trade goods, systems of precise weights and measures, counting, and writing were devised. The Indus script has been found inscribed on thousands of steatite seals; many of the inscriptions are thought to establish ownership. The writing, however, has yet to be convincingly deciphered. In addition to trading agricultural products and possibly woven fabrics, the Indus inhabitants manufactured and traded beads and jewelry made from terra-cotta and various stones, shells, and metals.

The religion of the Indus inhabitants is still difficult to determine. In the earlier Neolithic settlements, burials with a few grave goods were standard. In the later periods, most often the bodies were cremated and the fragments interred in burial urns. There is a noticeable lack of burial objects, and therefore, that rich source of information on religious beliefs is not available. Thus far, no buildings at any of the sites can be identified as having a specific religious use. In the cities, larger structures were located on an acropolis or area raised high above the general population. It has yet to be determined if these buildings were for secular or sacred use. One structure at Mohenjo-Daro called the Great Bath may have been used for ritual purposes. Numerous terra-cotta figurines of Mother Goddesses found in homes provide evidence of some animistic religious notions.

The Indus cities were abandoned in the second millennium, possibly circa 1800-1700 B.C.E. Various theories concerning the abandonment in the region have included the continual flooding of the Indus River, tectonic shifts caused by earthquakes and resulting in the drying of the water resources, and invasion by outsiders, notably the Aryans. Currently, all the theories are being reevaluated.

Identification of the original Indus inhabitants has yet to be determined. The initial excavators and most scholars believe that they were related to India's Dravidian populations, early inhabitants of the subcontinent who migrated southward to their present home in south India.

ADDITIONAL RESOURCES

Kenoyer, Jonathan Mark. *Ancient Cities of the Indus Valley Civilization.* Karachi, Pakistan: Oxford University Press and the American Institute of Pakistan Studies, 1998.

Possehl, Gregory L. *Harappan Civilization.* Warminster, England: ARIS & Phillips and the American Institute of Indian Studies, 1982.

SEE ALSO: India.

—Katherine Anne Harper

ION OF CHIOS

BORN: c. 480 B.C.E.; Island of Chios, Greece
DIED: before 422 B.C.E., probably in Athens
RELATED CIVILIZATION: Classical Greece
MAJOR ROLE/POSITION: Dramatist, poet, writer of memoirs

Life. Ion (yawn of KI-ahs) lived on Chios and in Athens, visiting elsewhere. He seems to have been a supporter of Athens during its wars with Sparta, favoring the conciliatory conservative politician Cimon and disliking the democratic Pericles for boastfulness and pride. As a resident alien, he competed about ten times against native Athenians in fields of tragedy, comedy, and dithyrambic choruses. It was said that after winning in both tragedy and dithyramb, he gave a measure of free wine to all Athenian citizens. After his death, Aristophanes in his comedy *Eirēnē* (421 B.C.E.; *Peace,* 1837) showed Athens' gratitude by punning that Ion had become the immortal morning star, Aoion. A later

critic said his dramas were polished but lacked fire. Like his other writings, the plays are lost.

Influence. Ion is best remembered for brief, vivid recollections of great Athenian personalities: Sophocles, Aeschylus, Cimon, Pericles, Archelaus, Socrates, perhaps Themistocles. Plutarch, who quotes Ion's sketches in his *Bioi paralleloi* (c. 105-115 C.E.; *Parallel Lives,* 1579), twits him for a theatrical need to give serious matters a comic ending but appreciated how Ion described an individual's appearance and character in situations blending culture with humor. Though slight, they were among the earliest Western attempts at biography. In his works, which were famous for an overwhelming variety of format, Ion undoubtedly presented new models for later authors to imitate and perfect.

ADDITIONAL RESOURCES

Benediktson, D. Thomas. *Literature and the Visual

Arts in Ancient Greece and Rome. Norman: University of Oklahoma Press, 2000.

Dover, K. J. "Ion of Chios." *The Greeks and Their Legacy*. New York: Blackwell, 1988.

West, M. L. "Ion of Chios." *Bulletin of the Institute for Classical Studies of the University of London* 32 (1885): 71-78.

SEE ALSO: Aristophanes; Athens; Cimon; Greece, Classical; Pericles; Plutarch; Socrates; Sophocles.

—*Robert D. Cromey*

IONIAN REVOLT

DATE: 499-494 B.C.E.
LOCALE: East Greek Ionia, coastal Asia Minor
RELATED CIVILIZATIONS: Achaemenian Dynasty, Persia, Archaic and Classical Greece
SIGNIFICANCE: The unsuccessful revolt of the Ionian cities set the stage for the Persian invasion of Greece, known as the Greco-Persian Wars.

Background. The major Greek cities of Asia Minor had been subject to Persia since circa 546/545 B.C.E., when Cyrus the Great (r. 558-530 B.C.E.) conquered the region. Persian sovereignty was administered by local Greek tyrants in cooperation with high-ranking Persian officials. According to Herodotus's account of the matter, *Historiai herodotou* (c. 424 B.C.E.; *The History*, 1709), the Ionian Revolt was essentially driven by the private ambitions of two such Greek figures: Histiaeus, tyrant of Miletus, and his nephew and son-in-law, Aristagoras, ruling in his absence at the time.

Action. The failed collaborative attack on the island of Naxos, spearheaded by Aristagoras in alliance with Persia, left Aristagoras in perilous straits and led him, in turn, to opt for rebellion. The revolt began with the Ionian seizure of the Persian fleet that had returned from Naxos. Aristagoras accordingly renounced his tyranny in favor of popular government and sparked a trend to expel the Greek tyrants ruling in the service of Persia. Support from mainland Greece was minimal and ephemeral. Athens provided twenty ships and Eritrea five. These allies, however, withdrew their support im-

mediately after the burning of Sardis (498 B.C.E.), under the threat of Persian revenge. The Ionian fleet encouraged widespread rebellion, demonstrating that political conditions were ripe, yet the Greeks were unable to withstand the Persian counteroffensive. Cyprus was recovered in a major land battle (497 B.C.E.). Three Persian armies that had mobilized from the east systematically reclaimed insurgent territory, until the Greek fleet was crushed off Miletus at Lade (494 B.C.E.).

Consequences. The Persian reconquest of Ionia, culminating in the sack of Miletus (494 B.C.E.), marked the eclipse of East Greek Ionia as a cultural, political, and economic force. Persia instated local popular governments in the subdued Ionian cites and reassessed the tribute imposed on these cities. Persia set its sights on the conquest of Greece.

ADDITIONAL RESOURCES

Burn, A. R. *Persia and the Greeks: The Defense of the West, 546-478 B.C.* Stanford, Calif.: Stanford University Press, 1984.

Green, Peter. *The Greco-Persian Wars*. Berkeley: University of California Press, 1996.

Murray, O. *Cambridge Ancient History*. Vol. 4. Cambridge, England: Cambridge University Press, 1988.

SEE ALSO: Achaemenian Dynasty; Greco-Persian Wars; Greece, Archaic; Greece, Classical; Herodotus; Persia.

—*Zoe A. Pappas*

IPIUTAK

DATE: 100-700 C.E.
LOCALE: Arctic Alaska
RELATED CIVILIZATION: Prehistoric Inuit, or Eskimo
SIGNIFICANCE: This Arctic culture produced superb art similar to that of the Siberians.

The Ipiutak culture site at Point Hope is a village of several hundred houses and numerous burials that was excavated by Helge Larson and F. G. Rainey in 1939. The site produced abundant evidence of ivory artifacts carved in a spectacular curvilinear style showing walrus, bears, wolves, birds, and fantastic creatures that resembled art from northeast Asia. Elements of the Arctic survival kit including snow goggles, needle cases with fine needles for making skin clothing, arrowheads, harpoons, salmon spears, and other tools indicate a full adaptation to the rich faunal resources and cold climate of the Arctic. Superb craftsmanship in flaked stone as well as ivory is evident. A rich social life is indicated by labrets (lip ornaments) and items of personal adornment, and ceremonialism is demonstrated by an ivory mask. Wooden artifacts including parts for sleds have been found at other sites. Houses were semisubterranean and typically between thirteen and sixteen feet (four and five meters) square with a fireplace and sleeping platforms. Ipiutak is generally considered to be a late phase of the Norton tradition and one of the ancestors of the historic Inuit.

ADDITIONAL RESOURCES

Damas, David, ed. *Arctic.* Vol. 5 in *Handbook of North American Indians.* Washington D.C.: Smithsonian Institution, 1984.

Larsen, H. E., and Froelich Rainey. "Ipiutak and the Arctic Whale Hunting Culture." *Anthropological Papers of the American Museum of Natural History* 42 (1948).

Rainey, Froelich G. *The Ipiutak Culture.* Reading, Mass.: Addison-Wesley, 1972.

SEE ALSO: American Paleo-Arctic tradition; Arctic Small Tool tradition; Kachemak tradition; Norton tradition; Subarctic peoples.

—Roy L. Carlson

IRELAND

DATE: 3000 B.C.E.-700 C.E.
LOCALE: Island in the North Atlantic, west of England
SIGNIFICANCE: Between 3000 B.C.E. and 700 C.E., Ireland evolved from a primitive society to a leader in art and scholarship among the civilizations of Europe.

Twenty thousand years ago, what is now Ireland was covered with glaciers. The earliest traces of humans in Ireland indicate that people arrived from the Continent about 6800 B.C.E. At that time, the passage between Ireland and Britain was narrower, so adventurers could row across more easily than in modern times. It is not surprising that the earliest evidence of humans on the island was concentrated around Antrim, in northeastern Ireland. The closest passage was probably between Ireland and what is now Scotland, and Antrim was rich in flint, the implement used for making hunting implements in the Mesolithic Age. The population was small but relatively stable for the next three thousand years and lived a nomadic life, eating fish and any wild game they could capture.

By 3500 B.C.E., Neolithic immigrants had arrived in Ireland, and the population spread northwest to Derry, south to Down and Dublin, and west to Roscommon and Sligo. Ireland's first farmers used new implements—polished stone axes and flint arrowheads—and kept oxen and sheep. They cleared some of the trees that had grown after the glaciers retreated and planted barley and wheat. They did not build houses but used pits as shelters.

The ancient Irish left an impressive series of megalithic (large stone) passage tombs, the most famous of which are Newgrange, Knowth, and Dowth in the Brú na Bóinne (Boyne Valley) in County Meath northwest of Dublin. A passage grave consists of a central stone tomb, used for communal burials, inside a large oval or round structure. The interior can be entered only through a narrow passageway lined by stone slabs. The passageway at Newgrange is almost 21 yards (19 meters) long. Many of the surrounding kerbstones and interior stones are decorated with intricately carved designs. Newgrange has been dated circa 3200 B.C.E., five centuries before the Egyptian pyramids were built. The massive passage graves are evidence of a well-organized society, with considerable knowledge of astronomy, agriculture, and engineering. The stones in the tomb at Newgrange are thought to weigh a total of 200,000 tons (181,400 metric tons), and much of the material was transported to the site from the Wicklow mountains, 80 miles (129 kilometers) away. The tomb was laid out so that the rising Sun of the winter solstice travels the distance of the entrance passageway, lighting up the central chamber. Furthermore, it was designed so that the rains drained out, and it has remained dry inside for more than five thousand years.

Beaker people. The next group of immigrants to Ireland from the Continent were known as the Beaker people. It is thought that they were early horsemen, which may explain how they dispersed so quickly across Europe. Around 2100 B.C.E., they settled in Brú na Bóinne, where the megalithic tombs had been constructed; the tombs, however, had by now been overgrown. The Beaker people were known for their decorated pottery, some of which they deposited in the graves of their dead. The Beaker people were sophisticated farmers and raised domesticated animals. Although familiar with bronze, they still made most of their tools and implements of flint. They collected gold from the rivers and used it to make ornaments and decorative items. Some early Bronze Age mines were found intact in the nineteenth century C.E., when the peat bogs that covered them for several millennia were cut up for fuel. The mines have been dated at 1500 B.C.E., plus or minus 120 years.

In County Antrim and Rathlin Island, the ancient Irish produced stone axes made of an unusual speckled stone that were traded not only to neighboring settlements but also south to Dublin and even across the ocean to the south of England. Thus, Ireland was in the export business five thousand years ago.

Cooking sites that appear to have been from the eighteenth century B.C.E. have been found in Ballyvourney and Killeens, both in County Cork. These sites are known as Fulacht Fian or Fulacht Fiadh—"cooking site of the Fianna," or "cooking site of meat." A site consisted of two pits: a wedge-shaped trough, into which water seeped from the surrounding bog, and a larger dry, stone-lined pit dug on higher ground nearby. In the larger pit, a fire heated layers of stones; these were thrown into the water of the smaller trough with wooden shovels, bringing the water to a boil in a short time. Meat wrapped in straw was immersed in the boiling water, and more stones were added as needed to keep the water boiling. Bones found at these sites indicate that beef, pigs, sheep, and goats were the primary meats, although horses apparently were eaten occasionally.

Celts. While Ireland was still in the Bronze Age, iron was coming into common use in Europe. Iron-using tribes led by wealthy chiefs came into power in Europe, speaking a language that was the precursor of modern Irish Gaelic. The tall, pale-skinned barbarians—called Keltoi by the Greeks—had distinctive dress, language, and lifestyles. The Celts dispersed widely—to Spain and Asia Minor was well as into England and Ireland. The Celts came to Ireland from the Continent to Ireland's west coast and from northern Britain to the northeast of Ireland. Although the Celts

A gathering of Irish chieftans. (North Wind Picture Archives)

did not have an advanced written language, they prized education and were skilled in art, music, and poetry. However, they were also fierce warriors. By 150 B.C.E., they were firmly established in Ireland and had displaced the island's historical inhabitants. By the fifth century C.E., at which time modern Irish history can be said to have begun, the whole island shared a common culture and the Gaelic language.

Religion. The pagan Celts worshiped a number of gods and goddesses. The deities had specific territories with which they were associated and also had specific, often contradictory roles. For example, Macha was a goddess of both crops and war, believed to live at Emain Macha, now called Navan Fort. Áine was a benevolent fertility goddess who could shape-shift into an old hag who brought bad luck to people who defied her; she was thought to live in an island in Lough (Lake) Gar in County Limerick.

By the fifth century C.E., there were Christians in Ireland, but the displacement of the pagans by Christians was minimal until a young man named Patrick was captured in an Irish raid on Roman Britain. After several years of slavery in western Ireland, he escaped back to Britain, studied for the priesthood, and returned to Ireland as a missionary. He not only converted many Irish but also set up Ireland's first monasteries. These monasteries became important both to the religious life of the island and as centers of learning.

Language and scholarship. The pagan Celts' only written language was the cumbersome twenty-character Ogham alphabet, a system of lines and bars varying in number and position. It was useful only for short inscriptions, not for transmitting literature. The advent of Christianity brought the use of Latin, and one of the main monastic occupations was the study and transcription of sacred scriptures and classical writings. Irish and Latin cultures were most eloquently combined in the illuminated manuscripts of the Irish monasteries, of which the most outstanding remaining example is the Book of Kells. The scholarly life of the monasteries was disrupted in the late eighth century

C.E. when the Vikings began invading Ireland, stealing the monasteries' gold and silver treasures and destroying their holy books.

Government and law. By the eighth century C.E., Celtic Ireland had become an agricultural society of nearly half a million inhabitants. The island was divided into five regions, called "fifths": Ulster in the north, Connacht in the west, Munster in the south, Leinster on the east coast, and the smallest province, Meath, between Ulster and Leinster. The fifths contained some 150 *tuatha*, or small kingdoms. A king had two main functions: to lead his people in war and to preside over the *óenach*—a public meeting at which business was transacted, games were played, and horse races were enjoyed. There were three social classes: the unfree (slaves, laborers, and some entertainers), freemen, and nobles. One's rank was not fixed at birth; it could go up or down if one's wealth, level of learning, or ability to practice a trade changed. The *tuatha* were the basic political unit; the social unit was the *fine*, the family unit consisting of all relatives in the male line of descent for five generations. One's legal rights were dependent on one's membership in the *fine*, and the relationships and rights of the *fine* were codified in an elaborate system.

ADDITIONAL RESOURCES

Fry, Peter, and Fiona Somerset Fry. *A History of Ireland.* New York: Barnes & Noble, 1993.

Moody, T. W., and F. X. Martin, eds. *The Course of Irish History.* Rev. and enlarged edition. Dublin, Ireland: Mercier Press, 1994.

Scherman, Katherine. *The Flowering of Ireland: Saints, Scholars, and Kings.* Boston: Little, Brown and Company, 1981.

What Life Was Like: Among Druids and High Kings. Richmond, Va.: Time-Life Books, 1998

SEE ALSO: Beaker people; Celts; Christianity; Patrick, Saint.

—Irene Struthers Rush

IRENAEUS, SAINT

BORN: 120-140 C.E.; probably Smyrna, Asia Minor
DIED: c. 202 C.E.; Lugdunum, Gaul (later Lyons, France)
RELATED CIVILIZATIONS: Gaul, Imperial Rome
MAJOR ROLE/POSITION: Religious figure

Life. Details of the life of Saint Irenaeus (i-ree-NEE-uhs) are sparse. In his youth, he sat under the teaching of Polycarp, bishop of Smyrna and associate of the Apostle John. Irenaeus studied in Rome before traveling to South Gaul, where he became a presbyter in

Lyons before the outbreak of persecution under Marcus Aurelius. On returning from a mission to Rome, he found himself the successor of the martyred Pothinus as bishop of Lyons. A late and uncertain tradition claims martyrdom for Irenaeus during a second wave of persecution, this one initiated by Lucius Septimius Severus.

Influence. Irenaeus was the first theologian of importance in the postapostolic church. In his five-volume work *Adversus haereses* (c. 180 C.E.; *Against Heresies*, 1868), he attacked Gnosticism not only as a theologian but also as a pastor, fearing its effect on his flock. To support his arguments for orthodoxy, Irenaeus stressed the authority of Scripture as the repository of apostolic teachings and gave significant support to the New Testament canon in formation, in opposition to Gnostic belief in a secret oral tradition of the apostles. As a corollary, he asserted a form of apostolic succession, but one that emphasized the continuity of the apostolic message more than an actual unbroken line of episcopal ordinations.

The centerpiece of Irenaeus's theology is the recapitulation of all things in Christ, a development (in some ways, an overdevelopment) of Saint Paul's doctrine of Christ as the Second Adam.

ADDITIONAL RESOURCES

Grant, Robert McQueen. *Irenaeus of Lyons*. New York: Routledge, 1997.

Hitchcock, F. R. M. *Irenaeus of Lugdunum*. Cambridge, England: Cambridge University Press, 1914.

Lawson, J. *The Biblical Theology of St. Irenaeus*. London: Epworth, 1948.

SEE ALSO: Christianity; Marcus Aurelius; Paul, Saint; Rome, Imperial.

—Robert Black

ISAEUS

BORN: c. 420 B.C.E.; possibly Chalcis, Euboea
DIED: 350-340 B.C.E.; possibly Athens, Greece
RELATED CIVILIZATION: Classical Greece
MAJOR ROLE/POSITION: Orator

Life. Ancient sources believed Isaeus (i-SEE-uhs) to be from Chalcis in the Chalcidice or Athens; probably he was born in Chalcis and moved to Athens, where he lived as a resident alien (metic). This move must have predated 392 B.C.E. because Isaeus studied under Isocrates, who opened his school in Athens in that year. Isaeus did not take part in political life (further support for his metic status because only Athenian citizens could engage in politics) but instead pursued a career writing speeches for other people. He specialized in inheritance cases and had an expert knowledge of Athenian law. He also taught the art of speechwriting. Among his pupils was a youthful Demosthenes, and all sources testify to Isaeus's influence on him.

Isaeus is credited with either sixty-four or fifty speeches, but only twelve have survived. His oratorical ability was considered great enough for him to be included in the canon of the ten Attic orators. Although his style is concise like that of his predecessor Lysias, he is not able to portray the individual characteristics of his speakers as well.

Influence. Isaeus taught Demosthenes (regarded as the greatest of Attic orators) and is also a major source for Athenian law, especially the laws of inheritance.

ADDITIONAL RESOURCES

Kamen, Deborah. *Isaeus' Orations 2 and 6*. Bryn Mawr, Pa.: Bryn Mawr College, 2000.

Kennedy, G. *The Art of Persuasion in Greece*. Princeton, N.J.: Princeton University Press, 1963.

Wyse, W. *The Speeches of Isaeus*. Cambridge, England: Cambridge University Press, 1904.

SEE ALSO: Demosthenes; Government and law; Greece, Classical; Isocrates; Lysias.

—Ian Worthington

ISAIAH

BORN: c. 760 B.C.E.; Jerusalem, Judah
DIED: c. 701-680 B.C.E.; probably Jerusalem, Judah
RELATED CIVILIZATIONS: Israel, Judah, Assyria, Egypt, Babylon
MAJOR ROLE/POSITION: Religious leader

Life. Isaiah, a prophet of the Old Testament, served an extremely long period of time, extending over the reigns of four kings of Judah, from Uzziah to Hezekiah. Because of his influential social status, Isaiah took an active and sometimes central part in the course of religious and political events during one of the most turbulent periods in the history of Jerusalem. The book of Isaiah relates his relations with the senior members of the royal house and his free access to the palace, indicating that he belonged to the Jerusalem aristocracy. In the face of the expanding Assyrian Empire, he counseled a passive political and military response, encouraging more faith in God, improved moral leadership, and increased spiritual tenacity of the Israelites. Although Isaiah supported King Hezekiah, he objected to the attempts to forge alliances with Egypt and Babylon as a wedge against Assyria.

Isaiah wrote numerous prophecies about the coming of the Messiah, Jesus Christ, and is quoted more than any other prophet in the New Testament. Probably the best known chapter of the book of Isaiah, chapter 53, describes the life and ministry of Jesus Christ with surprising accuracy.

Influence. Isaiah bore a strong, fervent testimony of Jesus Christ and his mission to humankind, prophesied concerning future times unlike any other biblical writer, and strongly influenced the religious and political history of Israel.

ADDITIONAL RESOURCES
Berrigan, Daniel. *Isaiah*. Minneapolis, Minn.: Fortress Press, 1996.
Crowther, Duane S. *How to Understand the Book of Isaiah*. Bountiful, Utah: Horizon, 1998.

SEE ALSO: Assyria; Bible: Jewish; Egypt, Pharaonic; Hezekiah; Israel; Jesus Christ.

—*Alvin K. Benson*

Isaiah. (Library of Congress)

ISIDORE OF SEVILLE, SAINT

ALSO KNOWN AS: Isidorus Hispalensis
BORN: c 560 C.E.; Cartagena or Seville, Spain
DIED: April 4, 636 C.E.; Seville
RELATED CIVILIZATIONS: Spain, Rome
MAJOR ROLE/POSITION: Encyclopedist, theologian, Church leader

Life. Held to be the most learned man of his age, Saint Isidore of Seville, canonized in 1598, was educated in the Cathedral School of Seville where he mastered Latin, Greek, and Hebrew. He received further training under the supervision of his brother Leander, whom Isidore succeeded as archbishop of Seville in circa 600 C.E. In his role as archbishop, he exerted leadership at the Second Council of Seville (619 C.E.) and the Fourth National Council of Toledo (633 C.E.), the latter of which was important for its promotion of the unification of the Spanish church and state and tolerance of the Jews.

Perhaps Isidore's most significant contribution was his literary production. His most well-known work, *Etymologiae* (seventh century C.E.; partial translation in *An Encyclopedia of the Dark Ages*, 1912; commonly known as *Etymologies*), is divided into twenty books and was an attempt to compile all the existing knowledge of his time. The books cover such topics as rhetoric, medicine, law, theology, linguistics, natural science, and law.

Influence. *Etymologies* was used as a textbook throughout the Middle Ages in many educational institutions. It was reproduced and reprinted for nearly one thousand years. Many works of classical antiquity might not have otherwise survived had they not been included. His *Historia de Regibus Gothorum, Wandalorum, et Suevorum* (c. 624 C.E.; *History of the Reigns of the Goths, Vandals, and Suevi*, 1966) still remains important in studying the early history of Spain.

ADDITIONAL RESOURCES
Brehaut, Ernest. *An Encyclopedist of the Dark Ages: Isidore of Seville.* 1912. Reprint. New York: B. Franklin Reprints, 1971
Macfarlane, Katherine Nell. *Isidore of Seville on the Pagan Gods.* Philadelphia: American Philosophical Society, 1980.

SEE ALSO: Christianity; Spain.

—*Donald E. Cellini*

ISIS, CULT OF

DATE: c. 2400 B.C.E.-551 C.E.
LOCALE: Egypt
RELATED CIVILIZATIONS: Pharaonic Egypt, Hellenistic Greece, Imperial Rome
SIGNIFICANCE: The Egyptian cult of Isis, which promised eternal life, spread to the Greco-Roman world, where it linked central Rome and its provinces. It also influenced early Christianity.

Isis (I-sihs) was among the most important deities of ancient Egypt. Her name derived from *aset* or *eset*, meaning "throne." She was the daughter of Geb and Nut (Earth and Sky), the wife and sister of Osiris, and the mother of Horus.

Isis was described in the *Pyramid Texts* (c. 2350-2100 B.C.E.; English translation, 1924) as the principal mourner for her husband, Osiris, who had been murdered by their brother Seth. Later narratives, many preserved by Plutarch, described how Isis reunited Osiris's dismembered body and revived him so he could take his place as ruler of the underworld. Isis protected her infant son Horus until the boy was old enough to avenge his father's death and ascend the celestial throne of Egypt.

Isis developed a great following. She was associated with other deities, but her powers were believed to transcend them. She was the exemplary wife and mother, the healer, the bestower of fertility and prosperity, the patroness of the dead, and the great magician. Even the flooding of the Nile was attributed to her. By the Ptolemaic period (beginning 305 B.C.E.), Isis was foremost among Egyptian goddesses. Her cult spread to Greece, the Aegean islands, and coastal cites in Asia Minor. After the Roman conquest of Egypt (30 B.C.E.), the cult of Isis was transported throughout the Roman world. Followers came from all social levels despite periodic attempts at repression.

Although little is known of the mysteries of initiation and specific rites, there were priests, regular observances, and ceremonies. Aretalogies (reports of Isis's miracles) were recorded in her many temples. The most important of these was on the island of Philae in Upper Egypt. Isis was exalted in a world that honored many deities. She assumed many roles and appeared in many forms. She was called *myrionymos*, "the one with 10,000 names." A Latin inscription described her as "the one who is all." Unlike other gods, she promised eternal life and possessed power to control destiny. For many of her faithful, she was the only deity.

After Constantine the Great declared Christianity a state religion, other religions were soon prohibited. The cult of Isis was the last to survive. The Blemmyes of Nubia had a treaty with Rome guaranteeing them access to the temple of Isis at Philae. It was not until 551 C.E. that this site was closed by Justinian I. It was Egypt's last functioning temple.

Although the temples were closed, the cult of Isis remained influential. The figure of Isis was identified with that of the Virgin Mary. Images of the Virgin and child can be compared with those of Isis and the infant Horus. It has been speculated that veneration of the Virgin Mary was a direct response to the cult of Isis.

ADDITIONAL RESOURCES
Lesko, Barbara. *The Goddesses of Egypt.* Norman: University of Oklahoma Press, 1999.
Takacs, Sarolta. *Isis and Sarapis in the Roman World.* New York: E. J. Brill, 1995.

SEE ALSO: Christianity; Constantine the Great; Egypt, Pharaonic; Greece, Hellenistic and Roman; Justinian I; Mary; Nubia; Plutarch; Rome, Imperial.

—*Cassandra Lee Tellier*

ISLAM

DATE: beginning in 622 C.E.
LOCALE: Western Asia and North Africa
RELATED CIVILIZATIONS: Byzantium, Persia
SIGNIFICANCE: One of the world's three major monotheistic religions originating in the Near East, Islam shares some common principles and historical contacts with Christianity and Judaism.

Many centuries before the mission of the Prophet Muḥammad (c. 570-632 C.E.), Syria and Mesopotamia (later Iraq) were important seats of trade, culture, and politics. These two areas affected the different faiths and civilizations in the interior of the Arabian Peninsula, largely through trading relations that, in biblical times, were associated with the frankincense route from Yemen. Rare commodities found their way from what the Romans called Arabia Felix ("well-blessed" or "happy"Arabia), and valuable goods from the east, principally from India and China, created prosperous commercial dealings for Syria and Mesopotamia. Historically, these areas were often dominated by powerful imperial overlords who vied for control over the cities at the ends of the trade routes such as Damascus or the ancient cities located where the Tigris and Euphrates Rivers flow closest to each other (a site that later became Baghdad).

In the centuries that followed the rise of Christianity in historical Palestine, the two imperial overlords who rivaled each other across the vast extent of desert separating Syria and Mesopotamia were the Roman and the Sāsānian Empires. During this time, at least one Arab state, that of the Nabataeans in Petra, dealt with the Romans as trade intermediaries in southern Syria. Later, just before the rise of Islam in Arabia, two other less developed Arab tribal states, the Ghassānids in Syria and the Lakhmids in Mesopotamia, served similar intermediary functions, approaching auxiliary status for the Roman and Persian Empires, respectively.

Meanwhile, in Mecca, the Umayyad and Hāshimi clans of the Arab Quraysh tribe vied with each other for both the prestige and material gain associated with control over caravans carrying goods from the Red Sea to Syria. The Meccan system involved an entire network of special trade relations, including the principle of *ḥaram*, which forbade intertribal hostilities on Meccan territory. Mecca's bid to influence Arab tribal life was reinforced by declaring the "black stone" (eventually adopted as a monotheistic symbol by Islam) as a focal point for the then polytheistic ceremonies of tribes visiting Mecca for trade.

The Meccan Islamic community. The Prophet Muḥammad was a Hāshimite. An orphan, he lived under the guardianship of his influential uncle Abū Ṭālib, who may have helped sponsor his early career as a merchant. Probably Muḥammad went with caravans as far as the trade terminus in Syria and had contact there with Christians and Jews. According to Islamic history, around 611 C.E., Muḥammad received revelations from

Pictured in this 1850's woodcut is the temple of Mecca. A pilgrimage to Mecca once in a Muslim's lifetime is one of the main principles of the faith. (North Wind Picture Archives)

God, which Allāh commanded him to recite. The name of Islam's holy scripture, the Qurʾān, derives from the Arabic root for recitation.

The Qurʾān urged believers to acknowledge the oneness of God and to follow all precepts laid down in the Qurʾān, including belief in a day of judgment. The Qurʾān also refers to "people of the book," Christians and Jews who believed in earlier prophets and possessed monotheistic scriptures. Islam argues, however, that earlier monotheists had fallen away from the essence of God's message and that Muḥammad's revelation represented the "seal of the prophets."

Muḥammad's prophethood passed through several phases. Reactions to the Qurʾān, especially its rejection of the religious and social practices of the Meccans, brought threats of persecution. Prominent opponents of Muḥammad came from the Umayyad clan heads. In the year 622 C.E., year one of the Muslim calendar, a handful of believers followed Muḥammad on the flight (*hijrah*) to nearby Medina, where other tribes helped him in return for his arbitration of local disputes. These helpers (*ansar*) spawned other alliances, increasing the community of believers until Muḥammad was able to bring pressure, including military might, against the Meccans. He returned to Mecca a scant year or so be-

fore his death to assume control of a united Islamic community, which had been joined by the former rival clan of the Umayyads.

The first caliphs. The early decades following Muḥammad's death in 632 C.E. saw two major developments that would affect Islamic civilization for many centuries: emergence of the caliphs (from *khalīfah*, successor to the Prophet) and the start of a military conquest that would eventually stretch to India to the east and the Straits of Gibraltar to the west.

Original perceptions of the role of the caliphs emphasized the political importance of having a recognized leader over the community of believers. Religious functions initiated by the Prophet were not transmitted to the caliphs but formed the corpus of ritual obligations to be practiced by all believers. These centered on the Pillars of the Faith, including prayer, fasting during Ramaḍān, alms giving, and pilgrimage at least once in the believer's lifetime to Mecca. Tradition has it that the principal, if highly theoretical, function of the caliph was to "command the good and prevent evil."

Muslims distinguish between a first line of almost literally personal successors to the Prophet, referred to as the "rightly guided," and the beginnings of the first dynastic line of Umayyad caliphs in the conquered capital of Damascus from about 661 C.E. until their defeat by the ʿAbbāsids in 751 C.E.

The "rightly guided" caliphs to 661 C.E. included Abū Bakr, ʿUmar ibn al-Khaṭṭāb, ʿUthmān ibn ʿAffān, and ʿAlī ibn Abī Ṭālib. The main role of Muḥammad's close confidant Abū Bakr seems to have been to maintain unity among the disparate tribes that had sworn loyalty to Muḥammad under the common banner of Islam. ʿUmar ibn al-Khaṭṭāb not only began expanding the Islamic empire by defeating Byzantine forces in Syria and Persian forces in Iraq but also forged some of the earliest traceable governing institutions supervised by the caliphate. These included a systematic listing of warriors for the faith (the *diwan*) and modes of taxation to be applied to peoples under Islamic rule. Distinctions were made between those who converted and those who retained their original monotheistic religions. Nonconverts (*dhimmis*) paid a special head tax.

Caliph ʿUthmān was a member of the Umayyad clan but apparently was less affected by a sense of clan loyalty than an idealistic sense of his responsibility to lead the Muslims. When ʿUthmān was assassinated, however, a call for vengeance came from Umayyad governor of Syria Muʿāwiyah I and others who assumed the new caliph, Muḥammad's cousin (and son-in-law) ʿAlī ibn Abī Ṭālib, would punish the guilty parties. When ʿAlī was challenged by forces supporting Muʿāwiyah on the field at Ṣiffīn in 657 C.E., differences were solved temporarily by arbitration, not war. Nonetheless, the first religious schism in Islam occurred just after the conflict at Ṣiffīn, when a faction with clear egalitarian tendencies, the Khārijites, or seceders, denied that either side was sufficiently meritorious to claim succession to Muḥammad's leadership. Later, when ʿAlī was killed by a Khārijite assassin in 661 C.E., Muʿāwiyah became caliph. His descendants ruled what became a hereditary caliphate based in Damascus until 750 C.E.

Although the Umayyad caliphate continued to spread Islam through military expansion at a vigorous rate, it faced a number of uprisings from within. Certainly supporters of what became known as the *ahl al bayt* ("people of the house of the Prophet") constantly challenged the Damascus caliphate in the name of ʿAlī and his two martyred sons, Ḥusayn and Hassan. Key Islamic cities in Iraq, especially Basra and Al-Kufa, rose up several times in denunciation of both the Umayyads and the Arab tribal-dominated ruling elite. Other rebellions, including conservative supporters of a disappointed Meccan "aristocracy," also had to be forcefully suppressed.

Most historians agree that the Islamic community experienced social and religious as well as political stability only from the mid-ninth century onward. This was caused in part by the replacement of the Umayyads by the longer-lived hereditary ʿAbbāsid caliphate. Mainly, however, stabilization would come when the ʿAbbāsids evolved more effective modes of administration over widespread conquered territory (by means of a bureaucratic network run by *wazirs*, or first ministers under the caliphs). The ʿAbbāsids also viewed Sunni Islamic law as providing universalist precepts in Islam and used the law to manage the large Muslim empire.

ADDITIONAL RESOURCES

Esposito, John, ed. *Oxford History of Islam*. Oxford, England: Oxford University Press, 1999.

Murata, Sachiko, and William Chittick. *The Vision of Islam*. New York: Paragon House, 1994.

SEE ALSO: Abū Bakr; ʿAlī ibn Abī Ṭālib; Arabia; Muḥammad; Qurʾān; ʿUmar ibn al-Khaṭṭāb, ʿUthmān ibn ʿAffān.

—*Byron D. Cannon*

ISOCRATES

BORN: 436 B.C.E.; Athens, Greece
DIED: 338 B.C.E.; Athens, Greece
RELATED CIVILIZATIONS: Classical Greece, Athens
MAJOR ROLE/POSITION: Teacher, philosopher

Life. Isocrates (i-SAHK-ruh-teez) studied under such luminaries as Protagoras, Prodicus, Gorgias, and Tisias, and joined the circle of Socrates. Isocrates wanted to play an important role in Athenian politics, but stage fright and a weak voice precluded his participation. As a result, his writings were meant to be read and are considered to be the earliest political pamphlets known. Through these pamphlets, Isocrates espoused a brand of Hellenism that would unite all Greeks together in revenge against Persia.

In 390 B.C.E., Isocrates established the first permanent institution of liberal arts, preceding Plato's Academy by a few years. Alumni from Isocrates' academy were among the greatest statesmen, historians, writers, and orators of the day. Cicero and Demosthenes used Isocrates' work as a model, and through their work, Isocrates shaped generations of rhetorical practice.

Relatively late in his life, Isocrates married the daughter of Hippias, a Sophist. He died in 338 B.C.E., starving himself to death at the age of ninety-eight after hearing the news of Philip II's victory over Athens in the Battle of Chaeronea.

Influence. Isocrates was the first of a series of great teachers who equated rhetoric and education. His method of teaching students to speak well on noble subjects became the standard of excellence for rhetorical education in Europe until the Renaissance.

ADDITIONAL RESOURCES

Golden, James L., Goodwin F. Berquist, and William E. Coleman. *The Rhetoric of Western Thought*. 5th ed. Dubuque, Iowa: Kendall/Hunt, 1993.

Grube, G. M. A. *The Greek and Roman Critics*. London: Methuen, 1965.

Isocrates. *Isocrates I*. Translated by David C. Mirhady and Yun Lee Too. Austin: University of Texas Press, 2000.

SEE ALSO: Chaeronea, Battle of; Demosthenes; Gorgias; Greco-Persian Wars; Greece, Classical; Philip II; Philosophy; Plato; Protagoras; Socrates.

—*B. Keith Murphy*

ISRAEL

DATE: c. 1000 B.C.E.-c. 100 C.E.
LOCALE: Southeastern end of the Mediterranean
SIGNIFICANCE: This civilization produced the literature and concepts that became the foundation for monotheistic religions and much of Western culture.

Technically, the term "Israel" refers to a state that existed in the southern Levant from about 1000 B.C.E. until about 722 B.C.E. In addition, however, the term is commonly used to refer to the group of people who emerged in the early Iron Age in Canaan and whose descendants made up the political state. Sometimes it is also used to refer to residents of the state of Judah, which was formed at the division of the earlier United Monarchy (c. 1000-922 B.C.E.). Judah existed until 587 or 586 B.C.E., when it was destroyed by the Babylonian Empire. After that time, "Israel" referred to those who traced their ancestry back to the states of Israel or Judah. Some Christian communities have used the term to refer to themselves in a theological sense.

History. Although the Hebrew Bible contains accounts of ancestors of the Israelites such as the patriarchs Abraham, Isaac, and Jacob and stories of a miraculous escape from slavery in Egypt, properly speaking "Israel" first emerges on the stage of history with the mention by the Egyptian pharaoh Merneptah that he had destroyed "Israel" on a campaign into Canaan in about 1226 B.C.E. Several theories concerning the appearance of Israel in the highlands of Canaan in the early Iron Age have been advanced. Although the biblical record, especially the book of Joshua, claims that the Israelites invaded from outside, the results of archaeological investigation indicate that the culture of "Israel" was closely related to that of the Canaanite population.

Biblical tradition contends that the first king of Israel, Saul, came to power in response to pressure from the Philistines. He was followed by two kings, David and Solomon, who established a centralized state centered in the capital of Jerusalem. Little direct historical evidence for this period exists, although recent discoveries have found slightly later inscriptions that mention "the house (dynasty) of David."

The primary source for historical information on the monarchical period is the Hebrew Bible, a source composed well after the events it describes. It also relates events through the lens of a particular theological viewpoint. After the death of Solomon brought an end to the United Monarchy, the states of Israel in the north and Judah in the south came into existence. Although they drew on common traditions, these states developed somewhat different political and cultural institutions.

The northern state of Israel tended to be more powerful economically and militarily, partly because it lay astride trade routes connecting the major power centers of the day. At times, Israel was able to play a significant role in the affairs of the region. For example, King Ahab of Israel was part of a coalition that stopped the Assyrian advance to the south at the Battle of Karkar (Qarqar) in 853 B.C.E. Eventually, Israel succumbed to pressure from Assyria and was annexed into the empire in circa 721 B.C.E. Many of its inhabitants were taken into exile (the Ten Lost Tribes), and others managed to flee, some to the sister state of Judah.

Judah occupied a more isolated area and had fewer natural resources. This resulted in a generally weaker position relative to the political powers of the day. Its ruling dynasty, claiming descent from the line of David, provided a more stable, if not always as able, leadership. During the kingship of Hezekiah in 715-701 B.C.E., Judah nearly met the same fate as its northern neighbor after an attempt at independence from the dominant Assyrians. Miraculously, Jerusalem and Hezekiah were able to survive. Jerusalem finally fell to the Babylonians more than a century later in 598 B.C.E. and again in 587 or 586 B.C.E. At this time, the capital and its temple were destroyed, and the state ceased to exist. Many Judahites were exiled into the Babylonian Empire.

The fall of the Babylonians to the Persians under the leadership of Cyrus the Great allowed the return of exiles to Jerusalem circa 538 B.C.E. The difficult economic situation of the returning exiles was exacerbated by the opposition of those in the area who had not been in exile. The community traces its foundation to the work of the priest Ezra and the governor Nehemiah who, with Persian support, were able to reestablish the political stability of the area and also rebuild the temple that had been destroyed.

The Persian Empire was eventually supplanted by that of the Greeks under Alexander the Great and his followers. With the division of Alexander's empire upon his death, Jerusalem was caught between the Ptolemaic and Seleucid empires. About 200 B.C.E., the area now called Judaea passed under Seleucid control. Attempts by Antiochus IV Epiphanes to force a common Greek culture on the lands of his realm spawned a revolt (168-143 B.C.E.) led by the Maccabee family, the most famous member of which was Judas. This revolt

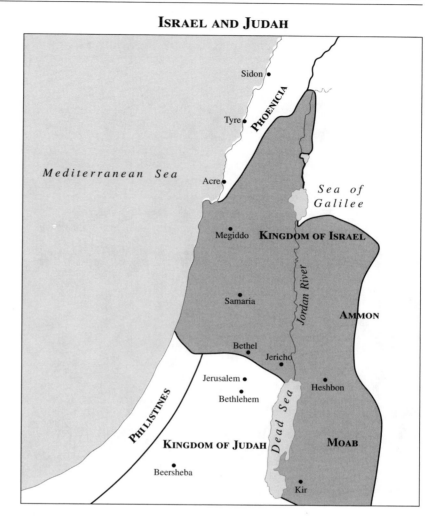

ISRAEL AND JUDAH

ended with a measure of success and established the Hasmonean Dynasty (c. 143-37 B.C.E.). Part of this revolt is remembered in the festival of Hanukkah.

Later tensions within the community led to civil conflict in which the Romans intervened in 63 B.C.E. The Romans ruled the area by a variety of methods. Probably the most important client king was Herod the Great. He is especially noted for his building programs. Remains of his rebuilding of the Jewish temple in Jerusalem, his harbor at Caesarea, and many other building projects are still standing.

The tensions evident within the Jewish community under Greek and Roman rule finally broke out in 66 C.E. in a revolt sparked by the Zealots. Rome methodically put down the rebellion, capturing Jerusalem and the temple in 70 C.E. and reducing the last stronghold at

This engraving depicts Israelites becoming slaves in Babylon. (North Wind Picture Archives)

ical crops included wheat, barley, grapes (wine), and olives (oil).

The basic social and economic unit was the extended family, households consisting of three or four generations. Most of the population lived in rural and village settings. Wealth was primarily held in the form of arable land, which was considered inalienable from the family unit under normal circumstances. The gradual development of an economy based on trade put this traditional system (and the family and clan units on which it was based) under considerable stress, a situation reflected within the prophetic literature of the Hebrew Bible.

Trade was a significant element of the economy, particularly in those areas that were situated along trade routes running between Egypt and Mesopotamia (affecting Israel more than Judah). Trade networks that included alliances with surrounding nations such as the Phoenicians were part of the policy of dynasties such as the Omride Dynasty of Israel. These trade relations were often marked with marriages between royal houses to cement the alliances. The control of trade was probably a more direct source of wealth than exploitation of natural resources. The control of these trade routes was also the goal of the competing superpowers.

Masada in 73 C.E. The urge for independence flared again from 132-135 C.E. under the leadership of Bar Kokhba, who led a disastrous revolt. At this time, Jerusalem was razed and rebuilt as a Roman city. The political state of Israel ceased to exist until modern times.

Economics. The climate of Israel is typical of the Mediterranean, with hot, dry summers and wet winters. The area was more heavily forested in ancient times. The mountainous nature of much of the land encouraged small land holdings with larger fields in the intermountain valleys and in the foothills. The mountainous areas were exploited through the development of terraces, which are still in use. The economy was dominated by dry farming and small animal husbandry. Typ-

Architecture. Construction materials were determined by the nature of the environment, mud-brick being used in the plains and stone in mountainous regions. The most common house form throughout the monarchical period was the "four-room house"—three rooms arranged around a courtyard that functioned as a food preparation area, among other uses. The side rooms most likely extended to a second story.

No remains of the most famous building—the temple that tradition ascribes to King Solomon—have been preserved. The design of this temple with surrounding courtyards seems to have been based on traditions found to the north of Israelite territory. A temple was essentially the "house" of the god. Although in the biblical tradition, this is the only "legitimate" temple, it is clear that other temples existed during the monarchical period.

Religion and ritual. Evidence both from within the Hebrew Bible and from nonbiblical inscriptions indicates that the religion of Israel followed the polytheistic traditions of the previous Canaanite period throughout much of the monarchical period. In the postexilic period, the religion developed a monotheistic belief that came to dominate the practice and sacred writings of the nation. The primary deity worshiped was Yahweh. He seems to have been originally a storm and warrior deity who later assumed the attributes of El, the older Canaanite deity, as the head of the gods and a creator.

Ritual practices included animal sacrifices at a temple, at least until the destruction of the temple of Jerusalem in 70 C.E. The yearly calendar revolved around the agricultural year with festivals marking the primary harvests. Rituals in the temples were carried out by hereditary priests. Other rituals were centered in the home.

Another important religious figure in the culture was the prophet. The prophet acted as a messenger of God, announcing the will of the deity to the king and the people. At times, prophets were closely associated with the power structures of the day. They also acted as a check on the uncontrolled use of power by kings. Throughout the biblical period, the ethic of the community emphasized care for the rights and well-being of "the poor, the widow, and the orphan." This was a primary responsibility of the king during the monarchial period. In the postexilic period, many of the functions of the king were taken over by the High Priest.

Especially in the exilic period, various rituals came to mark the identity of those considering themselves to be Jews. These rituals included observance of the Sabbath, the practice of circumcision, and the observance of laws concerning purity, especially concerning aspects of diet. These practices became codified after the first century C.E. with the work of rabbis now found in the Talmud.

Calendars and chronology. The "day" began at sunset. For example, the Sabbath day of rest lasted from Friday evening until Saturday evening. Months were calculated in relation to the cycles of the Moon. The annual calendar as exemplified in the inscription of the Gezer calendar was based on the agricultural cycle. The new year probably began in the fall of the year, although

there may have been a change to spring dating during the exile. Official dating related to the years of reign of a particular king.

Death and burial. Reflecting the importance of the extended family within the social structure, the predominant method of burial was in "family" tombs, often cut into the rock. A strong tradition within the culture saw death in old age as the natural end of life, but premature death was to be mourned. Not until late in the period and with the increasing importance of the individual did belief in life after death develop. This superseded the conception of the underworld (Sheol) as a shadowy, gravelike minimal existence.

Writing systems. Relatively little written material survives from Israel in this period. Literacy was confined primarily to the elite, a fact that must be considered when evaluating surviving written evidence. Although some ostraca (fragments of pottery and the like containing inscriptions) survive from the monarchical period, monumental inscriptions are not known. The presence of bullae, clay impressed with the seal of an official, indicates that most records were written on papyrus, which has not survived. The major preserved written material is found in the Hebrew Bible.

Language and literature. During the monarchical period, the common language was a dialect of Hebrew (differing slightly in Israel and Judah). After the exile, a shift occurred to Aramaic as the most widely spoken language. During and after the Hellenistic period, many people also spoke Greek. This led to the translation of the Hebrew Bible into Greek, a version known as the Septuagint.

The Hebrew Bible is a collection of a variety of books composed over a long period of time, taking its final form only in the last centuries before the common era. The first five books (or Torah) are traditionally designated the Five Books of Moses, although this is a rather late designation. Scholars believe these to have been written by several authors over a period from the United Monarchy until a final edition in the exilic or postexilic period. These books relate traditions ranging from the beginning of the world to the period shortly before entry into the land of Canaan. Traditions of the historical development of the monarchy are related in the books of Joshua, Judges, 1 and 2 Samuel, and 1 and 2 Kings. These books are composed by a group of authors designated by scholars as the Deuteronomists (because they are also primarily responsible for the book of Deuteronomy in the Torah). The viewpoint of these authors (a stress on moral behavior, the special election of the people by their god, the gift by Yahweh of the land, the worship of Yahweh only and centralization of that worship at the temple in Jerusalem) came to dominate the literature of the entire Bible, although it seems that this group was a minority viewpoint until the exile. It was this same group that began the collection of prophetic writings that were consistent with their viewpoints. This collection eventually came to include writings attributed to Isaiah, Jeremiah, and Ezekiel and twelve smaller prophetic collections.

Other writings in the Hebrew Bible include a collection of hymns related to worship (Psalms), philosophical ruminations (Job, Proverbs, Koheleth), a collection of love poetry (Song of Songs), and later historical writing (1 and 2 Chronicles, Ezra, Nehemiah). Another body of literature that may be found in the Apocrypha of some Bibles was produced in the last centuries before the common era.

One of the most important bodies of writings discovered is designated the Dead Sea Scrolls. These documents, discovered in the 1940's and 1950's, include the oldest substantial copies of the books of the Hebrew Bible and sectarian documents related to a group within the Jewish community known as the Essenes. These documents provide a valuable insight into the culture just before the revolts against Rome.

Education and training. Although there undoubtedly were means of education and training, particularly for those in government service, there is little evidence for schools during most of this period. The common means of training seems to have been apprenticeship, sons often following in the occupation of their fathers.

Women's life. The written materials that are available to study the role of women in the society are typically quite androcentric. This makes any complex analysis difficult. Archaeological and anthropological studies have begun to illuminate the role of gender within this society. Individual women at times became prominent on the historical scene and in the literature, but these examples tend to be noteworthy precisely because they are exceptional.

ADDITIONAL RESOURCES

Ahlström, Gösta. *The History of Ancient Palestine from the Paleolithic to Alexander's Conquest*. Minneapolis, Minn.: Fortress Press, 1993.

Davies, W. D., and Louis Finkelstein, eds. *The Cambridge History of Judaism*. 2 vols. Cambridge, England: Cambridge University Press, 1984.

Millar, Fergus. *The Roman Near East 31* B.C.E.-A.D. *337*. Cambridge, Mass.: Harvard University Press, 1993.

Perdue, Leo G., Joseph Blenkinsopp, John J. Collins, and Carol Meyers. *Families in Ancient Israel*. Louisville, Ky.: Westminster John Knox Press, 1997.

SEE ALSO: Ahab; Alexander the Great; Assyria; Babylonia; Bar Kokhba; Bible: Jewish; Canaanites; Cyrus the Great; David; Dead Sea Scrolls; Essenes; Exodus; Ezekiel; Ezra; Greece, Hellenistic and Roman; Hezekiah; Isaiah; Jerusalem, temple of; Jewish diaspora; Judaism; Maccabees; Masada, Battle of; Persia; Phoenicia; Rome, Imperial; Saul; Seleucid Dynasty; Septuagint; Solomon; Zealots.

—*Robert D. Haak*

ISSUS, BATTLE OF

DATE: November, 333 B.C.E.
LOCALE: Plain on the coast of the Gulf of İskenderun in modern Turkey
RELATED CIVILIZATION: Classical Greece
SIGNIFICANCE: This battle marked a transition from Alexander the Great's liberation of Anatolia to his campaign in the east.

Background. After his victory at Granicus (334 B.C.E.), Alexander the Great of Macedonia campaigned through Anatolia. He needed the coast of Syria-Phoenicia to ensure a connection with mainland Greece,

threatened by the Persian fleet, and as a starting ground for his eastern campaign.

Action. Trying to take advantage of the Cilician terrain, Persian Darius III laid a trap in the mountain pass that Alexander was going to take. Alexander, delayed by bad weather, became aware of Darius's position and forced him into battle near the Gulf of Issus (IH-suhs). Both sides, divided by the Pinarus River, had cavalry on the flanks and prolonged lines of infantry in the center.

The gradually widening phalanx of Alexander drove back the left half of the Persian forces. The Persian cavalry and Greek mercenaries on the right pressed on the

Alexander the Great (far left) defeats Darius III (in chariot) at the Battle of Issus. (Library of Congress)

left flank of Alexander's forces and almost cut them in two. Sensing the danger, Alexander broke through the lines of heavy Persian infantry and personally encountered Darius. The latter retreated followed by the rest of the Persian army. The Macedonians pursued them until nightfall and got hold of the Persian treasury and several members of the royal family.

Consequences. The victory, which gave Alexander the title "king of Asia," was followed by his Egyptian campaign (332-331 B.C.E.) and the final defeat of Darius at Gaugamela (331 B.C.E.).

ADDITIONAL RESOURCES

Bosworth, A. B. *Conquest and Empire: The Reign of Alexander the Great.* Cambridge, England: Cambridge University Press, 1988.

Dodge, Theodore Ayrault. *Alexander.* London: Greenhill Books, 1993.

SEE ALSO: Alexander the Great; Darius III; Gaugamela, Battle of; Granicus, Battle of; Greece, Classical.

—Sviatoslav Dmitriev

— J —

JAINISM

DATE: beginning in sixth century B.C.E.
LOCALE: India
RELATED CIVILIZATION: India
SIGNIFICANCE: One of the three ancient religions of India.

Jainism (JI-nih-zuhm) is one of the world's oldest religions; its roots go back before recorded history. Followers of Jainism are known as Ajainaor, or the followers of Jinas. The ancient teachers whose wisdom and spiritual evolution are most revered are known as Tirthankaras, or "builders of the ford." Their teachings lead humans across the endless cycle of rebirth to ultimate spiritual release.

In Jain philosophy, time consists of infinite millennia that come and go in cycles of several million years. In the current cycle, twenty-four Tirthankaras have appeared. Vardhamāna, the twenty-fourth Tirthankara, was the last to appear. Vardhamāna (Mahāvīra), whose name means "the most courageous one," lived some time between circa 599 and 527 B.C.E. He was a contemporary of Siddhārtha Gautama, who would come to be known as the Buddha.

According to most accounts, Vardhamāna was a highborn member of the warrior caste who renounced the world when he was thirty years old to pursue life as an ascetic. He achieved enlightenment after twelve years of spiritual pursuit. His teachings were eventually documented and disseminated by his twelve disciples.

The key principles of Jainism include *ahimsā*, karma, *anekāntvād*, *apirigraham*, and *satya*. *Ahimsā* is the principle of nonviolence with the corollary practice of compassion for all living beings, while karma involves the notion that all actions produce consequences.

The doctrine of *anekāntvādis*, or the limitations of human perspectives, is embodied in the story of the three blind men's erroneous ideas about the appearance of the elephant. Each comes up with an erroneous concept of the animal based on his own limited contact with a single part of the elephant.

Through the principle of *apirigraham*, Jainism stresses that greed and the desire for material possessions entangles and limits humans. Conversely, the absence of such a desire frees humans not only in this world but also from the endless cycle of birth, suffering, and death. The expression of one's removal from materialism is to be found in *satya*, or a renunciation of secular life.

In Jain culture, lay persons do not inflict harm on any form of life and are thus generally vegetarians. They are also expected to abstain from acts of violence and avoid any form of work or activities where the destruction of life may occur.

Without practicing the rigorous asceticism of nuns and monks, lay persons are nevertheless enjoined to live by vows known as the *anuvratas* or lesser vows, which closely parallel the so-called greater vows taken by the nuns and monks. They observe the so-called Three Jewels or *ratna traya*, which include right perception (*samyagdarśana*), right knowledge (*samyag-jñāna*), and right conduct (*samyagcāritra*). These practices, along with religious tolerance, ethical purity, cultivating harmony between the self and one's environment, and spiritual serenity, ultimately ensure the path to *mokṣa*, or total liberation from the endless cycles of birth, suffering, and death.

ADDITIONAL RESOURCES

Cort, John, ed. *Open Boundaries: Jain Communities in Indian History.* New York: State University of New York Series, Hindu Studies, 1998.

Dundas, Paul. *The Jains.* New York: Routledge, 1992.

Jain, Surender K., ed. *Glimpses of Jainism.* Delhi, India: Motilal Banarsidass, 1997.

Jaini, Padmanabh S., and Robert Goldman. *Gender and Salvation: Jaina Debates on the Spiritual Liberation of Women.* Berkeley: University of California Press, 1991.

Laidlaw, James. *Riches and Renunciation: Religion, Economy, and Society Among the Jains.* Oxford, England: Oxford Studies in Social and Cultural Anthropology, 1996.

Natubhai Shah. *Jainism: The World of Conquerors.* Sussex, England: Sussex Academic Press, 1998.

Sahoo, Ananda Chandra. *Jaina Religion and Art.* Delhi, India: Agam Kala Prakashan, 1994.

SEE ALSO: Buddhism; Hinduism; India; Vardhamāna.
—*Patricia Lin*

JAMES THE APOSTLE

ALSO KNOWN AS: Saint James
BORN: first century C.E.; Galilee
DIED: c. 62 C.E., Jerusalem
RELATED CIVILIZATIONS: Israel, Imperial Rome
MAJOR ROLE/POSITION: Religious leader

Life. James is an English form of Jacob, and there are three men in the New Testament with that popular Hebrew name. Two of them, identified as the son of Zebedee and the son of Alphaeus, were among the twelve disciples, or students, of Jesus Christ. The third, identified as the brother of Jesus, was one of the first apostles, or envoys, to continue the message of Jesus after his crucifixion (c. 30 C.E.).

When Jesus began preaching, his family was alarmed and tried to take him home. James was probably one of the brothers that Jesus then spurned. However, he reported that Jesus appeared to him after the crucifixion, and he soon joined the followers in Jerusalem, where he became a "pillar" of the early Church.

The historian Josephus reported that James the Apostle was martyred around 62 C.E.; tradition holds that his followers left Jerusalem before the Roman army stormed the city in 67 C.E.

Influence. James taught strict observance of Jewish laws as well as the poverty and good works extolled in the epistle that bears his name. He came into conflict with Saint Paul, who taught freedom from the law. Especially in Europe, his message was largely obliterated after the destruction of Jerusalem.

ADDITIONAL RESOURCES

Eisenman, Robert H. *James, the Brother of Jesus: The Key to Unlocking the Secrets of Early Christianity and the Dead Sea Scrolls.* New York: Viking, 1997.
Painter, John. *Just James: The Brother of Jesus in History and Tradition.* Columbia: University of South Carolina Press, 1997.

SEE ALSO: Christianity; Jesus Christ; Paul, Saint.
—*Thomas Willard*

JAPAN

DATE: 8000 B.C.E.-710 C.E.
LOCALE: Archipelago consisting of four main islands (and several thousand smaller ones) off the east coast of the Asian mainland
SIGNIFICANCE: This critical period saw the rise and development of the Japanese nation and the establishment of the imperial line. Buddhism was introduced in 552 C.E., and a major governmental reform in 645 C.E. led to the creation of the medieval Japanese states.

Japanese archaeologists divide the earliest part of Japanese history into four periods: the Paleolithic (preceramic) period, the Jōmon (cord-marked pottery) period, the Yayoi period, and the Kofun (burial mound) period. Underlying this chronology, however, are two basic problems: First, who are the Japanese, and where did they come from? Second, how do the Japanese or "proto-Japanese" relate to the Ainu, a group of people who have resided in Japan since about 7500 B.C.E. but differ racially, culturally, and linguistically from modern Japanese in significant ways?

Paleolithic Japan (before 10,000 B.C.E.). The Japanese islands have probably been occupied by humans for at least 30,000 years, if not longer. However, 10,000 years ago, Paleolithic Japan was a cooler place, and the sea level was 125 feet (38 meters) lower; therefore, some of the archaeological evidence of the earliest inhabitants is submerged. These hunters and gatherers, who had an extensive stone-tool inventory, most likely came to southern Japan through present-day Korea or to northern Japan from eastern Siberia, though there is abundant evidence of land connections to Asia at this time throughout the islands. It appears that the complete physical separation of the Japanese islands occurred only as recently as 18,000 to 12,000 years ago.

Jōmon period (c. 10,000-c. 300 B.C.E.). Starting about 13,000 years ago, when the Japanese climate began to warm, beautiful local pottery traditions—characterized by complex impressions made by twisted cords or sticks on the outside of pots before baking—abruptly appeared at various locales. Such ceramics eventually became commonplace throughout the islands. The Jōmon people (named for this distinctive "cord-marked" ceramic style) were probably the direct descendants of the people of the previous Paleolithic traditions. They were very successful at hunting, fishing, and gathering, and because of the numerous rivers and rugged coastlines, they were largely sedentary. Shell mounds all over the islands indicate how extensively the ocean and rivers were exploited by Jōmon people. The Jōmon pottery eventually came to show distinctive regional styles, suggesting the existence of rather well-defined cultural groups and local folk traditions.

Yayoi (c. 300 B.C.E.-c. 300 C.E.). About two thousand years ago, a distinct break occurred in the archaeological record. In Kyūshū, the southernmost main island of Japan, bronze from the Korean peninsula and a newer style of earthenware pottery appeared, and iron smelting was developed. These changes characterize the Yayoi period, named after the district in modern Tokyo where certain artifacts were first discovered. The Yayoi period also saw the beginning of Japanese-style intensive irrigated wet-rice cultivation, which became the main means of subsistence for almost everyone on the islands. This agrarian rice-based economy—with basically the same kind of farming practices—would persist until Japan's westernization in the late nineteenth century.

However, controversy surrounds the origins of this culture. The Yayoi people may have come from overseas and replaced the earlier Jōmon people (as evidenced by the presence of many new technologies from abroad). For many years, Japanese archaeologists have assumed this to be true, with the implication being that the Jōmon people are the ancestors of modern Ainu, and modern Japanese are the descendants of those who migrated from the Asian mainland during the Yayoi and Kofun periods. However, a majority of archaeologists feel that the record probably indicates a gradual but direct continuity from Jōmon people to early, but historically identifiable, Japanese, with any migration from the mainland blending in with the local cultures. In either case, by the end of the Yayoi period, certain institutional structures were in place—a division of labor, the accumulation of prestige and luxury goods by particular individuals, and the rise of complex political organizations—which created a more stratified society, allowing for the development of a full-fledged Japanese state in the Kofun period.

Kofun period (c. 300 C.E.-710 C.E.). The Kofun period is characterized by the appearance of massive keyhole-shaped burial mounds (*kofun*), which probably required the labor of hundreds (or even thousands) of people for many years to construct. These tombs were built for the deceased members of the ruling class

JAPANESE EMPERORS FROM THE HISTORICAL, YAMATO, AND NARA PERIODS, 539-794 C.E.

Historical Period, 539-645 C.E.	
Kimmei	539-571
Bidatsu	572-585
Yōmei	585-587
Sushun	587-592
Suiko	592-628
Jomei	629-641
Kōgyoku	642-645
Yamato Period, 645-710 C.E.	
Kōtoku	645-654
Saimei	655-661
Tenji	662-671
Kōbun	671-672
Kemmu	673-686
Jitō	690-697
Mommu	697-707
Gemmei	707-714
Nara Period, 710-794 C.E.	
Genshō	715-724
Shōmu	724-749
Kōken	749-758
Junnin	758-764
Shōtoku	764-770
Kōnin	770-781

and could cover seventy acres (twenty-eight hectare) and be as high as 500 feet (152 meters). The earliest *kofun* tumuli are found in the heartland of Japanese traditional culture, the western Kinai region of Ōsaka, Kyōto, and Nara.

The Japanese imperial system apparently began at this time, with most emperors having large *kofun* mound tombs made for them. Ōjin Tennō, perhaps the first historical emperor, reigned in the late fourth to early fifth centuries C.E. (though he was said to be preceded by fourteen legendary sovereigns who were thought to be direct descendants of Amaterasu Ōmikami, the Sun goddess and progenitor of the Japanese people). The first Japanese state, the Yamato, probably appeared in this area during the Kofun period (though some argue for an origin on the southern island of Kyūshū). Eventually Kofun period culture and burial mounds stretched from as far south as Kyūshū to as far north as modern Tokyo.

Government and law. It is not clear exactly when the Yamato state was first established, but certainly it was in existence by the fourth century C.E. Chinese and Korean chronicles speak of a recognizable Japanese kingdom, the Yamatai (though it is not clear if this was actually the Yamato state). At this time, Japan and the states of the Asian mainland initiated their first extensive political, cultural, and economic contacts. Early Japanese leaders borrowed many mainland administrative techniques, which contributed to the rise of centralized Yamato hegemony. One technique was to incorporate local chiefs and political units established in Yayoi times into the new nation-state. Prestige goods from abroad, such as Chinese bronze mirrors, became symbols of power; elaborate titles and ranks were given to leaders of the new aristocratic clans (*uji*) who administered subordinate serflike groups of peasants (*be*).

The Yamato court underwent a major change in the mid-seventh century when the *uji-be* system was vastly modified to give the imperial household more authority, culminating in a series of edicts issued by Emperor Kōtoku called the Taika ("great change") Reforms (645 to 649 C.E.). The intent was to limit the power of the *uji* chiefdom-families, who were becoming increasingly independent, especially in the eastern plains far from the center of government. In an effort to ensure centralized control over the land and the people, a census was conducted, household registries were required, and a unified tax code was imposed. A Chinese-style civil service system was established with bureaucrats being appointed on the basis of merit rather than heredity, and the Chinese calender was adopted. Local village governments were implemented, and restrictions were placed on the size of *kofun* mounds and the number of people employed in building them. These restrictions were an attempt to undermine the rank system that gave the local aristocrats much of their legitimacy and symbolic power.

Religion and ritual. The indigenous religion of Japan, Shintō (literally "the way of the gods"), is a complex elaboration and institutionalization of nature and ancestor worship. Local deities abound, and natural forces and entities—the Sun, Moon, major mountains, wind, trees, and rivers—are all thought to possess supernatural powers. Japanese mythology and origin myths are simply articulated Shintō doctrines. In theory, the living emperor is not only the chief political leader of the nation but also its head Shintō priest. Archaeological evidence strongly suggests that both the Yayoi and Kofun peoples—and perhaps the Jōmon people as well—practiced at least incipient forms of Shintō. For example, rituals such as making offerings of food to the ancestors and the gods, common forms of modern Shintō worship, were extensively practiced; items found in burials and Kofun tombs all have Shintō significance. Religious activity was grounded in the local community, centering on agriculture, just as in modern Shintō.

However, in 587 C.E., the empress Suiko, under the guidance of regent Prince Shōtoku, one of the major founders of the early Japanese state, recognized Buddhism, first imported from China and Korea in 552 C.E., as an official religion. This was partly for political reasons; by advocating the adoption of Buddhism and its rituals, the prince and the Soga clan hoped to consolidate their power against their rivals. Because of this radical religious change and its corresponding political developments, Japanese historians have traditionally referred to the end of the Kofun period as the Asuka period (593-710 C.E.). By the end of the seventh century C.E., about half a dozen Buddhist sects were flourishing in Japan; with them came major transformations in philosophy and ritual. For example, as the Buddhist custom of cremation gained acceptance, many aristocrats now devoted more attention to temple building rather than elaborate tumulus construction. However, Buddhism never replaced the Shintō religion; instead, these religions incorporated elements from each other and began a coexistence that is maintained in modern Japan.

Architecture and city planning. Before the sixth century C.E., the center of imperial power shifted with each emperor. After the Taika Reforms in the mid-seventh century C.E., a permanent capital was established near what later became Nara. This city was laid out with perpendicular street-grids following the model of Chinese capitals. The style of Buddhist temples influenced much public and elite architecture. Roof tiles and drainage ditches replaced the thatched wooden houses found in the earlier times.

Language. Linguists believe that the Japanese language is related to Korean, some of the native languages of eastern Siberia and Manchuria, and possibly distantly to Mongolian, Turkish, and other Altaic languages. However, they do not know when the Japanese language reached the islands nor who spoke it. Hypothetical reconstructions of vocabulary and syntax suggest that proto-Japanese speakers moved to the southern island of Kyūshū about 2500 B.C.E. and developed the language there with little outside contact; people on the main island of Honshū presumably spoke some version of the Ainu language. Later, around two thousand years ago, Japanese-speakers expanded northward up Honshū and southward throughout the Ryūkyū Islands. Of course, this is all speculation, but in any event, by the late Yayoi and early Kofun periods, there is little doubt that the Yamato state was a Japanese-speaking polity.

Writing systems and literature. Though Japanese was spoken by the masses in Kofun times, the business of government was not always conducted in that language. Before the Japanese borrowed the ideographic characters from China around 600 C.E., they had no writing system. Because the structures of the two languages are quite different, it was very hard to use these characters to write Japanese. One solution was simply to do all writing of import in Chinese. Therefore, although educated Japanese could enjoy the Chinese classics, the first great masterpieces of Japanese literature did not appear until the start of the eighth century. The very end of the Kofun and the start of the medieval Nara period (710-794 C.E.) saw the compilation of the government-sponsored histories of the Yamato state, the *Kojiki* (712 C.E.; *Records of Ancient Matters*, 1883) and the *Nihon shoki* (compiled 720 C.E.; *Nihongi: Chronicles of Japan from the Earliest Times to* A.D. *697*, 1896), which chronicled the events of the Kofun period and the mythological past. All other earlier works, such as *Tennōki* (620 C.E.; "record of the emperors"), solicited by Prince Shōtoku and other members of the Soga family in an attempt to justify their authority over the aristocratic *uji* clans, have not survived.

Visual arts. The most typical artwork of the Kofun period was the *haniwa* ("clay ring") figurines that were often placed on the outside of burial mounds. These hollow, unglazed earthenware sculptures ranged anywhere from a foot and a half to five feet (roughly one-half to four meters) in height. Typical *haniwa* shapes included people, houses, and weapons, but one of the most common subjects was the saddled horse. The depiction of a horse helped support the very controversial horse-rider hypothesis, which held that the proto-Japanese state was established by a group of nomadic warriors from northern Asia who invaded the islands on horseback around 400 C.E. and made themselves rulers. Regardless of the correctness of this theory—most archaeologists see little evidence for it, though some historians like the way it corresponds to the chronologies given in the ancient chronicles—the *haniwa* do seem to have a military or protective function of guarding the outside of the burial mounds; no *haniwa* appear to have been placed inside a burial chamber with the deceased.

Women's life. The status of women in early Japan was rather high, especially compared with the institutionalized patriarchy of later medieval Japan when Confucian ethics and Buddhist doctrines became commonplace. For example, of the fifteen historical (non-legendary) emperors of the Kofun period, five were women. Also, shamanism was an important part of Yamato court life before the Taika Reforms, and many shamans and mediums were female. Stories of the time tell of the accomplishments of many marvelous women, both historical and legendary, such as Himiko (the queen and head priest of the Yamatai state described in the Chinese historical accounts of the late third century C.E.), Jingū (an empress credited with many military exploits c. 400 C.E.), and Japan's principal deity, Amaterasu Ōmikami, the Sun goddess. In addition, early Yayoi and Kofun peoples apparently practiced *muko-irikon* (a matrilocal residence pattern), in which the husband went to live with the wife's family. The importance, even dominance, of women in traditional farm families continued in many rural areas and has been documented by anthropologists even up through the twentieth century.

Current views. The developments in the Yayoi and Kofun periods determined the direction that the new Japanese state was to take for the next millennia. The rest of Japanese history is, in a sense, just an elaboration of the cultural, political, and social accomplishments of that time. For example, the Japanese imperial line, the longest-running hereditary royal institution in the world, was established during Yamato times, and has lasted until the present. However, this period is important for other reasons as well. As mentioned, there are still a number of unanswered questions from this era, especially regarding Japanese linguistic and ethnic origins. *Nihonjin-ron* (literally, "the theory of Japaneseness") is the subject of many debates in Japan. The study of Japanese archaeology and the development of the first Japanese state, then, is of tremendous interest to both Japanese scholars and laypersons. Notions of Japanese identity and sense of self are closely tied to the study of these early times, the most important periods in Japanese history.

ADDITIONAL RESOURCES

Aikens, C. Melvin, and Takayasu Higuchi. *Prehistory of Japan*. San Diego, Calif.: Academic Press, 1982.

Barnes, Gina. *Protohistoric Yamato*. Ann Arbor: University of Michigan Center for Japanese Studies, 1988.

_____. *The Rise of Civilization in East Asia: The Archaeology of China, Korea, and Japan.* New York: Thames and Hudson, 1998.

Brown, Delmer, ed. *Ancient Japan.* Vol. 1 in *The Cambridge History of Japan.* Cambridge, England: Cambridge University Press, 1988.

Hane, Mikiso. *Premodern Japan: A Historical Survey.* Boulder, Colo.: Westview, 1991.

Kidder, J. Edward. *Japan Before Buddhism.* New York: Praeger, 1966.

Pearson, Richard, ed. *Windows on the Japanese Past: Studies in Archaeology and Prehistory.* Ann Arbor: University of Michigan Center for Japanese Studies, 1986.

SEE ALSO: Ainu; *Haniwa*; Himiko; Jimmu Tennō; Jingū; Jōmon; Kofun period; *Nihon shoki*; Ōjin Tennō; Shintō; Shōtoku Taishi; Yamato court; Yayoi culture.

—*James Stanlaw*

JĀTAKAS

AUTHORSHIP: According to tradition, narrated by the Buddha (Siddhārtha Gautama)
DATE: fifth-fourth centuries B.C.E.
LOCALE: North India
RELATED CIVILIZATION: India
SIGNIFICANCE: The *Jātakas* are a fundamental part of the earliest Buddhist literature.

The *Jātakas* (JAW-tah-kahs; translated into English as *Buddhist Birth-Stories*, 1925) are a collection of fables and stories that relate the previous lives of Śākyamuni, the historical Buddha, while he was still a bodhisattva or a future buddha. The term *jātaka* means "relating to birth" in the Pāli language. The tales are part of the earliest Buddhist literature and are scattered in various parts of the sacred Pāli canon. They can be found in the *Chulla Vagga*, *Sūtra Piṭaka*, *Cariyā Piṭaka*, and *Vinaya Piṭaka*. Both the *Sūtra Piṭaka* and *Vinaya Piṭaka* are believed to predate the Council of Vesālī (c. 383 B.C.E.). Buddhist tradition asserts that the historical Buddha himself narrated the tales. Each story tells of a previous incarnation of the Buddha and his experiences in that former birth. He took various forms, both human and nonhuman, in his many incarnations.

The charming Jātaka stories are simple expositions of the Buddhist conception of the law of karma, or the unbroken chain of cause and effect that binds all existence together. Based on the theory that everyone has passed through many existences, karmic law asserts that every volitional act brings about a certain result. When motivated by greed, hatred, or delusion, an individual plants the seed of suffering; when acts are motivated by compassion and wisdom, then the karmic conditions for happiness and peace are sown. The acts of each existence will determine the degree of suffering or

joy experienced in a future life. The moral of each story demonstrates that there is a direct link to every past action for better or worse, and thus it serves as an admonition against self-serving or malicious conduct and intention. The hearer of the *Jātakas* should be able to understand that what has been suffered on earth is not the result of mere chance.

Ordinary mortals do not remember their former existences; however, enlightened beings have the gift of recalling former lives. A buddha is supposed to know every existence through which he has passed. Altogether, there are 547 tales; each conveys a moral lesson by recounting acts of self-sacrifice and compassion performed by the incarnated bodhisattva that led to his final birth as the Buddha. According to the Buddhist theory of evolution, it takes thousands of lives to evolve into a perfected soul. Buddhist teachers used the *Jātakas* as a proselytizing and didactic force. Although the stories are full of gentleness and humor, they nonetheless have very powerful educational value and moral content. They were composed for the social and moral awakening of those who heard them. Their extreme popularity and effectiveness as teaching devices is confirmed by their constant representations on Buddhist monuments of all periods and throughout the Buddhist world.

ADDITIONAL RESOURCES

Grey, Leslie. *A Concordance of Buddhist Birth Stories.* Oxford, England: Pali Text Society, 2000.

Jones, John Garrett. *Tales and Teachings of the Buddha: The Jataka Stories in Relation to the Pali Canon.* Boston: G. Allen & Unwin, 1979.

SEE ALSO: Buddha; Buddhism.

—*Katherine Anne Harper*

JAVA

DATE: 1-700 C.E.
LOCALE: Republic of Indonesia
RELATED CIVILIZATIONS: India, mainland Southeast Asia, Śrivijaya
SIGNIFICANCE: Java is perhaps the most densely populated area in Southeast Asia. A rich island civilization, its legacy is superceded only by its direct heir, Angkor.

The Javanese call themselves Wong Djawa or Tijang Djawa, derived from the Sanskrit word *yawa*, meaning barley. Although predominantly Muslim in modern times, the Javanese previously were Hindus and Buddhists, with some animists and ancestor worshipers. The early Javanese had established trade with China from about the second century B.C.E. Between 1 and 300 C.E., Hinduism and Buddhism reached Java and other parts of Southeast Asia from India. By 300 C.E., Indian traders, Brahman priests, and Buddhist monks were observed in various Southeast Asian kingdoms.

Around the sixth century C.E., this process resulted in a synthesis of Hinduism, Buddhism, and native Javanese culture that remains intact in modern times in Bali. Elsewhere, the only evidence of this synthesis are the reliefs and architectural and epigrammatic remains of monuments and temples. Temples dedicated to the Hindu divinities of Vishnu (Viṣṇu), Śiva, and Brahmā reflect not only the worldview of their builders but also the diversity of traditions that coexisted. Likewise various representational depictions of Buddha's life in both Mahāyāna and Theravāda (Hīnayāna) traditions address cultural pluralism. In central Java, Hindu Prambanan, a temple built in the eighth century C.E., and Borabodur, the largest Buddhist monument on record, stood almost side by side as contemporaries.

The five hundred years of Java's history before Borabodur (Shailendra Dynasty, about 750-850 C.E.) remains speculative. Most scholars agree that before the influx of Indian culture, the political integration of Javanese kingdoms and chiefdoms was at a lower level than it was afterward. In the seventh century C.E., the maritime kingdom of Śrivijaya in Sumatra island, west of Java, rose to power and was able to impose hegemony over at least half of mainland Southeast Asia and Java.

Unlike Sumatra's maritime kingdom, Javanese states were inland kingdoms, based on wet-rice cultivation, a cultural complex that involves hydraulic engineering of terraces and canals, the plow, and the water buffalo. Wet-rice cultivation provided the source of tributes to many chiefs and kings and of food supply for large populations. Ecological studies of Java suggest an environment that is fairly consistent and sufficient and that allows for relative isolation. Therefore, Hinduism's impact on the preexisting cultures of Java was more political than economic, moving Java toward greater consolidation and centralization of authority and power. In Java and other classical cultures of Southeast Asia, this led to the development of the notion of divine kingship. Brahmanic tradition created a ruler's court that became the center of the kingdom, residence of administrative functionaries, storehouse of wealth, and site of the military establishment. The center (court) and outlying villages were linked by a pyramidal structure of varying levels of aristocrats and functionaries.

ADDITIONAL RESOURCES

Geertz, Clifford. *Agricultural Involution: The Processes of Ecological Change in Indonesia.* Berkeley: University of California Press, 1971.

Legge, J. D. *Indonesia.* Englewood Cliffs, N.J.: Prentice Hall, 1964.

Osborne, Milton. *Southeast Asia: An Introductory History.* Sydney: George Allen and Unwin, 1980.

SEE ALSO: Buddhism; Hinduism; India.

—E. P. Flores-Meiser

JEHU

BORN: ninth century B.C.E.; Israel
DIED: c. 815 B.C.E.; Israel
RELATED CIVILIZATIONS: Israel, Assyria
MAJOR ROLE/POSITION: King of Israel

Life. Jehu (JEE-hyew) was one of the kings of the northern kingdom of Israel after it had separated from the southern kingdom of Judah. According to 2 Kings 9-10 in the Bible, he was a military commander who acquired the throne by overthrowing Joram, the last king of the Omride Dynasty, known for its acceptance of the pagan fertility god Baal, especially during the rule of Ahab and his queen Jezebel. When Joram was wounded in battle, he retired to Jezreel. Prophets of the Israelite god Yahweh seized this opportunity to anoint the military commander Jehu as king to restore Yahwism and rid the country of Baal worship. Driving to Jezreel with proverbial speed, Jehu assassinated Joram, exterminated the surviving members of the Omride family, killed the despised Jezebel, and slaughtered the Baal worshipers of the kingdom. The Bible is silent about Jehu's reign, but he is depicted on the famous Assyrian monument known as the Black Obelisk paying tribute to Shalmaneser III.

Influence. The prophet Hosea (fl. eighth century B.C.E.) looked back on Jehu's revolt as shameful, proclaiming that Yahweh would punish his dynasty for the bloody event.

ADDITIONAL RESOURCES
Miller, J. M., and J. H. Hayes. *A History of Ancient Israel and Judah*. Philadelphia: Westminster, 1986.
Shanks, Hershel, ed. *Ancient Israel*. Rev. and enlarged ed. Upper Saddle River, N.J.: Prentice Hall and the Biblical Archaeology Society, 1999.

SEE ALSO: Ahab; Assyria; Bible: Jewish; Israel; Hosea; Jezebel.

—*James H. Pace*

JEREMIAH

BORN: c. 645 B.C.E.; Anathoth, Judaea
DIED: after 587 or 586 B.C.E.; Egypt
RELATED CIVILIZATIONS: Judah, Israel, Babylon
MAJOR ROLE/POSITION: Religious figure

Life. Jeremiah's prophetic ministry in Judah spanned forty years, from 627 to 587 or 586 B.C.E. The substance of that ministry is contained in the biblical book that bears his name. In spite of indifference to his message and attacks against his person, he consistently challenged the citizens of Judah to renounce the idolatry of Baalism and to return to their religious roots.

Jeremiah's contemporaries assumed that their morality was irrelevant to their safety and the security of the country. However, Jeremiah denounced this belief, suggesting that God, in response to the wickedness of Judah's immorality, would summon the Babylonians against Judah and its capital, Jerusalem. In 587 or 586 B.C.E., the Babylonians set fire to the city of Jerusalem.

After the collapse of Judah, a contingent of Jews fled to Egypt, taking Jeremiah with them. He may have lived there until his death.

Jeremiah. (Library of Congress)

Influence. In his letter to the exiles in Babylon, Jeremiah affirmed that the Jews, though denied the external expressions of temple ritual, could now discover the moral and spiritual dynamics of an inward faith. The vitality of this faith is the essence of Jeremiah's "new covenant" message in 31:31-34. This text is the longest Old Testament text quoted by the New Testament (Hebrews 8:8-12).

ADDITIONAL RESOURCES

Holladay, William L. *Jeremiah*. 2 vols. Philadelphia: Fortress Press, 1989.

Perdue, Leo G., and Brian W. Kovacs, eds. *A Prophet to the Nations: Essays in Jeremiah Studies*. Winona Lake, Ind.: Eisenbrauns, 1984.

SEE ALSO: Babylon; Israel; Judaism.

—*Mark J. Mangano*

JEROBOAM I

ALSO KNOWN AS: Jeroboam ben Nebat
BORN: tenth century B.C.E.; Palestine
DIED: c. 910 B.C.E.; Palestine
RELATED CIVILIZATIONS: Israel, Judah, Syria
MAJOR ROLE/POSITION: King

Life. Jeroboam I (jehr-uh-BOH-uhm) became the king of Israel around 925 B.C.E. Literary material in the Hebrew Bible is primarily in 1 Kings 11-15 and 2 Chronicles 10 and 13. Jeroboam appears as an official in the royal administration of King Solomon in charge of a conscripted labor force. The prophet Ahijah chooses him to replace Solomon. Solomon tries to arrest Jeroboam, but he escapes to Egypt, returning to Israel after Solomon's death.

After Jeroboam is anointed king of Israel, he embarks on several building projects. He rebuilds Shechem and Penuel and religious centers at Dan and Bethel with statues of golden calves or bulls. He offers sacrifice at the altar and appoints non-Levitical priests. Upon his death, his son becomes king of Israel.

Influence. He is portrayed as the archetype of evil by the Deuteronomist editors of the book of Kings. Scholars understand the sins as the establishment of non-Levitical priests, the establishment of religious centers as rivals to Jerusalem, the making of the golden calves, and the worship of Yahweh contrary to the norm of the Deuteronomist editors.

ADDITIONAL RESOURCES

Ahlström, G. *The History of Ancient Palestine*. Minneapolis, Minn.: Fortress Press, 1993.

Toews, W. *Monarchy and Religious Institutions in Israel Under Jeroboam I*. Atlanta, Ga.: Scholars Press, 1993.

SEE ALSO: Bible: Jewish; Egypt, Pharaonic; Israel; Judaism; Solomon.

—*Roger W. Anderson, Jr.*

JEROME, SAINT

ALSO KNOWN AS: Eusebius Hieronymus
BORN: 331-347 C.E.; Dalmatia (later Croatia)
DIED: probably 420 C.E.; Bethlehem, Palestine
RELATED CIVILIZATION: Imperial Rome
MAJOR ROLE/POSITION: Religious figure

Life. Saint Jerome received a superlative education in Rome, where one of his teachers was the celebrated Donatus. His religious vocation began in Trier and took him off to the Syrian desert, where he lived as a hermit. Priestly ordination followed in Antioch, which

Jerome then left for Constantinople. On moving back to Rome, he became secretary to Pope Damasus and spiritual director of a group of aristocratic women whose interests centered on the ascetic life and the study of Scripture. However, in 385 C.E., the hostility provoked by his waspish attacks on the mores of the capital obliged him to abandon it for Bethlehem, where he spent the rest of his days as the head of a monastery financed by his friend Saint Paul. Throughout his life, Jerome was engaged in prolific literary activity, including biblical translations and commentar-

Saint Jerome. (North Wind Picture Archives)

ies, hagiography, propaganda for celibacy, rebuttals of heretics such as Pelagius, and an extensive correspondence remarkable for both vividness of content and stylistic finesse.

Influence. Jerome's Latin version of the Bible, the Vulgate Bible, was the most important single work of the entire Middle Ages, and his zeal for asceticism was largely responsible for the premium that the Catholic Church placed on the celibate life.

ADDITIONAL RESOURCES

Kelly, J. N. D. *Jerome: His Life, Writings, and Controversies.* Reprint. Peabody, Mass.: Hendrickson, 1998.

Sparks, H. F. D. "Jerome as Biblical Scholar." In *Cambridge History of the Bible*. Vol. 1. New York: Cambridge University Press, 1975.

SEE ALSO: Christianity; Donatus, Aelius; Rome, Imperial.

—Neil Adkin

JERUSALEM, TEMPLE OF

DATE: c. 966 B.C.E.-70 C.E.

LOCALE: Central hill country, Israel

RELATED CIVILIZATION: Israel

SIGNIFICANCE: The temple of Jerusalem was the dwelling place of Yahweh, Israel's god, and was the center of Jewish religion for more than one thousand years.

King Solomon built the first Jewish temple in Jerusalem between 966 and 959 B.C.E. He built it on a previously unoccupied hill north of the city of David. It was about 100 feet (30 meters) long, 30 feet (9 meters) wide, and 50 feet (15 meters) tall,

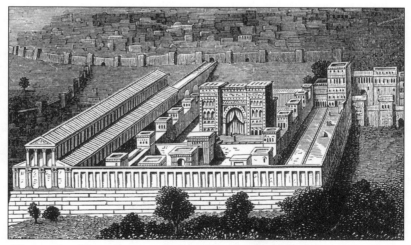

The temple of Jerusalem as rebuilt by Herod. (North Wind Picture Archives)

built of white limestone and cedar, and lavishly decorated with gold. Sacrifices and religious ceremonies were held there as prescribed in the Hebrew scriptures. The first temple was destroyed in 587 or 586 B.C.E. when Nebuchadnezzar II of Babylon sacked Jerusalem.

Jews returning from captivity in Babylon built the second temple. Built on the foundations of the earlier temple, it was completed in 516 B.C.E. In 168 B.C.E., the Seleucid king Antiochus IV Epiphanes looted the temple and placed an idol in it, sparking the Maccabean revolt.

The second temple was completely refurbished by Herod the Great between 20 and 18 B.C.E. This magnificent edifice was destroyed by Titus and the Roman legions in 70 C.E. The Dome of the Rock was built on the surviving Herodian platform in 691 C.E.

ADDITIONAL RESOURCES

Backhouse, Robert. *The Kregel Pictorial Guide to the Temple*. Grand Rapids, Mich.: Kregel Publications, 1996.

Bahat, Dan, with Chaim T. Rubinstein. *The Illustrated Atlas of Jerusalem*. New York: Simon and Schuster, 1990.

Shanks, Hershel. *Jerusalem: An Archaeological Biography*. New York: Random House, 1995.

SEE ALSO: Babylonia; Herodian Dynasty; Israel; Maccabees; Nebuchadnezzar II; Seleucid Dynasty; Solomon; Titus.

—Kriston J. Udd

JESUS CHRIST

ALSO KNOWN AS: Jesus
BORN: c. 6 B.C.E.; Bethlehem, Judaea
DIED: c. 30 C.E.; Jerusalem
RELATED CIVILIZATION: Imperial Rome
MAJOR ROLE/POSITION: Religious leader

Life. Most of the information on the life of Jesus Christ comes from the Gospels by Mark, Matthew, Luke, and John in the New Testament, although Tacitus does describe his execution in his *Ab excessu divi Augusti* (c. 116 C.E., also known as *Annales*; *Annals*, 1598). According to the tradition, Jesus Christ's public ministry began when John the Baptist proclaimed him as the long-awaited Messiah. This news, along with Jesus's "signs and wonders," generated a sizable following. This created suspicion and then envy among the Jewish leadership. Their opposition grew when Jesus made claims to be divine. These claims may have led Judas, one of Jesus's twelve disciples, to help the Jewish authorities arrest Jesus. In an unprecedented trial, they found Jesus guilty of blasphemy and wanted him crucified. Pontius Pilate, the Roman governor, had to approve capital punishment. He publicly washed his hands, signifying that he would not accept ultimate responsibility for Jesus's death.

The Roman soldiers flogged Jesus, mocked him, beat him, had him carry the cross-piece to the execution site, and crucified him. The Jewish leaders also mocked Jesus. When Jesus died, a wealthy follower placed the body in a new tomb. According to his followers, Jesus rose from the dead, appeared to hundreds of them, and then ascended into heaven.

Influence. Jesus's followers evangelized throughout the Roman Empire and eventually the world. They preached Christ's message of love and promise of eternal life. Christians believe sinful humans can live forever with God because Jesus's death atoned for their sins.

ADDITIONAL RESOURCES

Fredricksen, Paula. *From Jesus to Christ: The Origins of the New Testament Images of Christ*. 2d ed. New Haven, Conn.: Yale University Press, 2000.

_____. *Jesus of Nazareth, King of the Jews: A Jewish Life and the Emergence of Christianity*. New York: Alfred A. Knopf, 1999.

The New Testament: The Authorized or King James Version of 1611. With an introduction by John Drury. New York: Alfred A. Knopf, 1998.

Porter, J. R. *Jesus Christ: The Jesus of History, the Christ of Faith*. New York: Oxford University Press, 1999.

Tacitus, Cornelius. *The Annals of Imperial Rome*. Translated by Michael Grant. Rev. ed. Reprint. New York: Barnes & Noble, 1993.

SEE ALSO: Bible: New Testament; Christianity; Tacitus.

—Emerson Thomas McMullen

Jesus Christ. (Library of Congress)

JEWISH DIASPORA

DATE: 722 B.C.E.-700 C.E.
LOCALE: Mediterranean Basin and Mesopotamia
RELATED CIVILIZATIONS: Greece, Rome, Persia,
Egypt

The Greek term "diaspora" means scattering. The Jewish diaspora began when Israel's capital, Samaria, was sacked in 722 B.C.E., and prisoners were deported to Assyria. The Babylonians carried other Jews to Mesopotamia after they conquered Jerusalem in 587 or 586 B.C.E. Some returned when the Persian king Cyrus the Great allowed them circa 530 B.C.E., but large Jewish communities remained in Mesopotamia for centuries. Other Jews fled to Egypt when Jerusalem fell. They established themselves around the island of Elephantine in the Nile and even built a temple there. When Alexandria was established circa 300 B.C.E., many Jews settled there, eventually becoming approximately one-third of the city's population. More Jews were driven out of Judaea after the failed revolts against Rome in 66-73 C.E. and 132-135 C.E.

Diaspora Jews usually were allowed to live some-what separately from the general population, observing their own dietary restrictions, paying a tax to support the Jerusalem temple, and handling their own legal affairs. Their customs, such as circumcision and Sabbath observance, were regarded as peculiar by most Greeks and Romans. They could not however, avoid some degree of assimilation with whoever lived around them. Alexandrian Jews, for example, took to using the Greek language to such an extent that they had to have their scriptures translated into Greek by 200 B.C.E.

ADDITIONAL RESOURCES

Barclay, J. M. G. *Jews in the Mediterranean Diaspora: From Alexander the Great to Trajan, 323* B.C.E.-*117* C.E. Berkeley: University of California Press, 1996.
Rutgers, L. V. *The Hidden Heritage of Diaspora Judaism.* Leuven, Netherlands: Uitgevrij Peeters, 1998.

SEE ALSO: Assyria; Babylonia; Cyrus the Great; Egypt, Pharaonic; Greece, Hellenic and Roman; Jerusalem, temple of; Judaism; Persia; Rome, Imperial.
—*Albert A. Bell, Jr.*

JIMMU TENNŌ

ALSO KNOWN AS: Kamu Yamato Iware Biko
BORN: second century C.E. (legendary date 711
    B.C.E.); place unknown
DIED: third century C.E. (legendary date 584 B.C.E.);
    place unknown
RELATED CIVILIZATIONS: Korea, China
MAJOR ROLE/POSITION: First emperor of Japan,
    military leader

Life. According to Japanese chronicles such as the
Nihon shoki (compiled 720 C.E.; *Nihongi: Chronicles
of Japan from the Earliest Times to* A.D. *697*, 1896),
Jimmu successfully coalesced sufficient communities
in Kyūshū to create a fighting force that defeated all
others in his drive to take control of the largest plain, the
Kinai, at the head of the Inland Sea on Honshū. After
three years of fighting, Jimmu was crowned emperor at
Kashiwara no Miya. Shōtoku Taishi, regent in 600 C.E.,
claimed this coronation to have taken place in 660
B.C.E. according to a Chinese calendar cycle. Jimmu
then settled in the Yamato plain, the most fertile soil in
Japan. From this base, Jimmu and his successors

moved to rule and control as much of Japan as they were
able during the succeeding Yamato court period.

Influence. In mythology, Jimmu Tennō (jeem-moo
tehn-NOH), the first emperor of Japan, was the direct
descendant of the Sun goddess, Amaterasu Ōmikami,
and all Japanese were descended from other gods on the
Heavenly Plain. The concept of the divinity of the emperor, part of the Shintō religion, continued until January 1, 1946, when the Showa Emperor (then known as
Hirohito) disclaimed the divinity of the imperial line,
which traced itself back to Jimmu.

ADDITIONAL RESOURCES
Hall, John W. *Japan: From Prehistory to Modern
    Times.* Ann Arbor: University of Michigan Press,
    1991.
Sansom, George B. *Japan: A Short Cultural History.*
    Stanford, Calif.: Stanford University Press, 1952.

SEE ALSO: Japan; *Nihon shoki*; Shintō; Shōtoku Taishi;
Yamato court.
                    —Edwin L. Neville, Jr.

JINGŪ

ALSO KNOWN AS: Jingō; full name, Jingū Kōgō
BORN: early fourth century C.E.?; place unknown
DIED: late fourth century C.E.?; place unknown
RELATED CIVILIZATIONS: Japan, Korea
MAJOR ROLE/POSITION: Ruler, military leader

Life. In the traditional Japanese chronicle *Nihon
shoki* (compiled 720 C.E.; *Nihongi: Chronicles of Japan
from the Earliest Times to* A.D. *697*, 1896), Jingū (jehn-
goo) is listed as the *kōgō*, or consort, of Chūai, the legendary fourteenth emperor, and as the mother of his
more historical successor, Ōjin Tennō. Although the
traditional date of Ōjin's birth is 201 C.E., his reign is
more reliably dated to the late fourth and early fifth centuries C.E. The lifetime of Ōjin's mother, then, must be
dated earlier in the fourth century C.E. However, many
scholars believe that the details of Jingū's life are historically inaccurate at best and pure legend at worst.
    The *Nihongi* records that Jingū was the daughter of

Okinaga no Sukune and Princess Katsuragi no Taka-
nuka. After the death of Chūai in a war against Kyūshū,
Jingū is said to have successfully completed her husband's military campaign and then led one of her own
against the Korean kingdom of Silla. In order for her to
accomplish these tasks, her pregnancy was said to have
continued for three years, with Ōjin being born after
her success in Korea. Jingū ruled Japan for sixty-nine
years. Only at her death did her son Ōjin succeed to the
imperial throne.

Influence. Jingū is worshiped as a Shintō deity to-
gether with the goddess Hime-gami and Jingū's son
Ōjin, deified as Hachiman. As such, she is a symbol of
Japanese unity.

ADDITIONAL RESOURCES
Jackson-Laufer, Guida M. "Jingo-kogo." In *Women
    Who Ruled: A Biographical Encyclopedia.* New
    York: Barnes and Noble, 1998.

Koreans submit to Empress Jingū. (North Wind Picture Archives)

Nihongi: Chronicles of Japan from the Earliest Times to A.D. *697.* Translated by W. G. Aston. 1896. Reprint. Bristol, England: Oxford University Press, 1997.

SEE ALSO: Japan; Korea; *Nihon shoki*; Ōjin Tennō; Yamato court.

—*Thomas J. Sienkewicz*

JOHANAN BEN ZAKKAI

ALSO KNOWN AS: Yohanan ben Zakkai
BORN: c. 1 C.E.; Judaea
DIED: c. 80 C.E.; Beror Heil, west of Jerusalem, Judaea
RELATED CIVILIZATIONS: Israel, Imperial Rome
MAJOR ROLE/POSITION: Rabbi, founder of school at Jamnia

Life. Johanan ben Zakkai (joh-HAN-uhn behn ZAK-ay-i) was a student of the famous Hillel. Little is known of his early years although he taught several decades in the Galilee where his best known pupil was Hanina ben Dosa.

Johanan was a vocal opponent of the First Jewish Revolt against Rome (66-73 C.E.). Escaping from Jerusalem, he set up a rabbinic academy at Jamnia on the Mediterranean coast, which was instrumental in setting the course of future Judaism. Previously, Judaism was known for its diversity of expression, but Pharisaic Judaism became dominant. Johanan helped shaped a Judaism without a priesthood and temple (destroyed in 70 C.E.) and set the standards for synagogue worship.

Numerous legends embellish Johanan's life: that he escaped from Jerusalem in a coffin, that he met the Roman general Vespasian and prophesied the latter's destiny as Roman emperor, and that Vespasian himself granted Johanan's request to establish the Jamnia school. Scholars continue to debate the accuracy of these legends as they work to piece together details of his life.

Influence. Johanan and his school at Jamnia were instrumental in the survival of Judaism following the Roman destruction of Jerusalem.

ADDITIONAL RESOURCES
Neusner, Jacob. *A Life of Yohanan ben Zakkai: c. 1-80*

C.E. Vol. 6 in *Studia Post-Biblica*. Leiden, Netherlands: E. J. Brill, 1970.
Porton, Gary. "Yohanan ben Zakkai." In *Anchor Bible Dictionary*. Vol. 6. New York: Doubleday, 1996.

SEE ALSO: Israel; Jerusalem, temple of; Judaism; Rome, Imperial; Vespasian.

—Fred Strickert

JOHN CHRYSOSTOM, SAINT

BORN: c. 347 C.E.; Antioch, Syria
DIED: September 14, 407; Comana, Helenopontus
RELATED CIVILIZATION: Byzantine Empire
MAJOR ROLE/POSITION: Church leader, theologian

Life. Born into a wealthy Antiochene family, John Chrysostom (KRIHS-uhs-tuhm) received an education typical of his time, emphasizing Greek philosophy and rhetoric. He was baptized at age eighteen and, after the death of his mother, lived as an ascetic for about eight years (c. 373-c. 381 C.E.). The harsh regimen harmed his health, and he returned to Antioch, where he was ordained a priest. His talent as a preacher earned him the title Chrysostom ("Golden Mouth"). His reputation caused him to be chosen in 398 C.E. as patriarch of Constantinople, a position he did not want. His efforts for the poor were admired, but his condemnation of the lax morals of that great city earned him the hatred of the empress Aelia Eudoxia, who took his criticism personally. In 404 C.E., Chrysostom was exiled. Already in

poor health, he died during a forced march from one place of exile to another.

Influence. Chrysostom's preaching and his exposition of biblical passages, especially from the New Testament, earned him a place among the doctors of the Church. Some of his sermons against Jewish influences in the Church, however, perpetuated the anti-Semitism that tended to crop up in fourth century C.E. thought.

ADDITIONAL RESOURCES
Kelly, J. N. D. *Golden Mouth: The Story of John Chrysostom—Ascetic, Preacher, Bishop*. London: Duckworth, 1995.
Young, F. M. "John Chrysostom." *Expository Times* 109 (November, 1997): 38-41.

SEE ALSO: Byzantine Empire; Christianity; Constantinople; Eudoxia, Aelia; Judaism.

—Albert A. Bell, Jr.

JOHN THE BAPTIST, SAINT

BORN: c. 7 B.C.E.; Judaea
DIED: c. 27 C.E.; Samaria
RELATED CIVILIZATION: Near East
MAJOR ROLE/POSITION: Religious figure

Life. John the Baptist was born to Zechariah, a priest in the line of Abijah, and Elizabeth, a daughter of Aaron and a cousin to Mary, mother of Jesus Christ. According to the Christian faith, John was the last great Jewish prophet, preparing people for the coming of Christ.

Before his public ministry began, John lived an austere life as an anchorite in the desert. When he emerged, he baptized, in the River Jordan, people who wished to repent their sins and live a righteous life in preparation for God's final harsh judgment. Among those John baptized was Jesus Christ.

John's strong and attractive personality won him many followers. He was known as "the Baptist" during his own lifetime as he traveled throughout the lower valley of the River Jordan on his religious mission.

Saint John the Baptist. (Library of Congress)

However, John did make an enemy of Herod Antipas, who ruled Galilee and the central area of Transjordan; John preached against Herod's marriage to a near relative (which was against Jewish law). Herod had John imprisoned, and he was later executed.

Influence. The Roman Catholic Church considers John a martyr for the faith. His feast day is celebrated on August 29.

ADDITIONAL RESOURCES
Bergeaud, Jean. *Saint John the Baptist.* New York: Macmillan, 1963.
Kazmierski, Carl R. *John the Baptist.* Collegeville, Minn.: Liturgical Press, 1996.
Kraeling, Carl H. *John the Baptist.* New York: Scribner, 1951.

SEE ALSO: Christianity; Jesus Christ; Judaism.
—*Patricia E. Sweeney*

JOHN THE EVANGELIST, SAINT

ALSO KNOWN AS: John the Apostle
BORN: c. 10 C.E.; probably Capernaum
DIED: c. 100 C.E.; Ephesus
RELATED CIVILIZATIONS: Imperial Rome, Jerusalem
MAJOR ROLE/POSITION: Christian apostle, writer

Life. The synoptic gospels describe Saint John the Evangelist, son of Zebedee, as a fisherman who heeded the call to follow Jesus of Nazareth. John, along with his own brother James and the brothers Peter and Andrew, became one of a core group among the disciples who eyewitnessed significant events including the raising of Jairus's young daughter, the transfiguration, and Jesus's Gethsemane prayer.

The Gospel according to John refers to him only as "the beloved disciple" and emphasizes his role at the Last Supper and as witness to the crucifixion and to the empty tomb on Easter morning. Often depicted as the

Saint John the Evangelist. (North Wind Picture Archives)

youngest disciple, he seems to have outlived the others, spawning a rumor that he might never die.

Entrusted with the care of Jesus's own mother, he provided leadership for several decades in Jerusalem. He is credited with writing the gospel in Ephesus before his death either of old age or under the persecution of Domitian. The Ephesus Johannine community led by "John the elder" continued to write several letters and Revelation.

Influence. The Gospel of John is often considered the loftiest in language and theology; the soaring eagle became its symbol. The early Christological debates re-lied heavily on its formulations, although the Gnostic heresy also claimed it.

ADDITIONAL RESOURCES

Brown, Raymond E. *The Gospel According to John.* 2 vols. Garden City, N.Y.: Doubleday, 1970.
Culpepper, H. Alan. *John, the Son of Zebedee.* Minneapolis: Fortress, 2000.

SEE ALSO: Christianity; Gnosticism; Jesus Christ; Mary.

—Fred Strickert

JŌMON

DATE: c. 8000-300 B.C.E.
LOCALE: From the Ryūkyū Islands to northern Japan
SIGNIFICANCE: Named for a characteristic type of pottery, Jōmon is Japan's oldest historical period

Beginning about 18,000 B.C.E., the warming climate and rising sea water began to separate a land mass from the Asian continent along the Tsugaru Strait in the north and the Korean Channel in the west. By 10,000 B.C.E., the detached lands came to form island chains that would constitute the modern Japanese archipelago. At about this time, a new culture characterized by the use of pottery with rope patterns emerged, thereby creating the term Jōmon (JOW-mown; literally "rope patterns").

Current archaeological excavation of Jōmon village sites such as Sannai Maruyama in Aomori, northern Japan, which had a population of five hundred or more, seems to disprove the long-held assumption that the Jōmon people were nomadic. In addition to hunting small animals and gathering plants, fruit, and nuts for their primary livelihood, they engaged in highly skilled fishing, tool making, and extensive trading with part-ners across the surrounding waters. Toward the end of the period, limited farming of grain was started in some regions of western Japan where natural food sources were less abundant than in other areas. Total Jōmon population during the peak period has been estimated at 260,000, and the average lifespan was about thirty years.

Jōmon society was basically egalitarian with no sign of class differences in housing and burial custom, but remnants of massive nonresidential constructions and elaborately ornate figurines indicate religious practices and central roles played by priests and sorcerers in Jōmon community life.

ADDITIONAL RESOURCES

Barnett, William, and John W. Hoopes. *The Emergence of Pottery.* Washington, D.C.: Smithsonian Institution Press, 1995.
Kenrick, Douglas M. *Jomon of Japan.* New York: Kegan Paul International, 1995.

SEE ALSO: Ainu; Japan; Kofun period; Yayoi culture.

—Kumiko Takahara

JORDANES

FLOURISHED: sixth century C.E.
RELATED CIVILIZATIONS: Goths, Byzantine Empire, Imperial Rome
MAJOR ROLE/POSITION: Bishop, writer

Life. Jordanes (johr-DAY-neez) was a bishop and writer during the reign of the emperor Justinian I and probably lived in the capital, Constantinople. He published two books of history dedicated to Pope Vigilius.

The first, the *Romana* (c. 550 C.E.), was a summary of Roman history from a Christian perspective and was cribbed together from various other chronicles. The second book, the *Getica* (c. 551 C.E.; *The Origin and Deeds of the Goths*, 1908), was a history of the Gothic tribes who had overthrown the Roman Empire in the West and who were fighting the emperor in both Spain and Italy. The material in the *Getica* was, as Jordanes tells us, largely taken from the lost *Historia Gothica* of Roman statesman Cassiodorus, who was intimately familiar with the Ostrogoths of Italy. Jordanes did, however, add certain material from various Greek and Latin writers absent from the *Historia Gothica*.

Influence. Although Jordanes' Latin grammar was rather poor and the *Romana* is quite uninteresting, the *Getica* is of tremendous importance because it is one of the very few sources for the legends, myths, and early history of the Gothic tribes. Outside it, only a few notices in Roman histories describe what the Goths did, and no trace remains of what the Goths themselves had to say.

ADDITIONAL RESOURCES
Goffart, Walter. *Narrators of Barbarian History*. Princeton, N.J.: Princeton University Press, 1988.
Wolfram, Herwig. *History of the Goths*. Berkeley: University of California Press, 1988.

SEE ALSO: Cassiodorus; Christianity; Goths; Justinian I; Rome, Imperial.

—David Langdon Nelson

JOSEPHUS, FLAVIUS

ALSO KNOWN AS: Joseph ben Matthias
BORN: c. 37 C.E.; Jerusalem, Palestine
DIED: c. 100 C.E.; probably Rome
RELATED CIVILIZATIONS: Imperial Rome, Judaea
MAJOR ROLE/POSITION: Historian, military leader

Life. Born into a distinguished Jewish family of priests, Flavius Josephus (FLAY-vee-uhs joh-SEE-fuhs) was educated by outstanding scholars of the day. Although opposed to the Jewish uprising against Roman rule, he nevertheless served as commander of Jewish forces at Galilee. When the Romans captured the fortress of Jotapata, he infuriated Jewish Zealots when he surrendered rather than commit suicide. As prisoner in Rome, he won the favor of Emperor Vespasian and took his family name, Flavius. In 70 C.E., he returned to Palestine with Roman troops in a futile attempt to stop the rebellion. He then lived in Rome under imperial patronage, where he devoted the rest of his life to historical and literary writings.

In his first work, *Bellum Judaium* (75-79 C.E.; *History of the Jewish War*, 1773), Josephus tried to convince Jews of the Diaspora that continued resistance to Rome was doomed to failure. His second work, *Antiquitates Judaicae* (93 C.E.; *The Antiquities of the Jews*, 1773), traces the history of the Hebrew people from their earliest legends until the great revolt against the Romans. The work included his *Vita* (*Life*), which

Flavius Josephus. (Library of Congress)

was an autobiographical defense of his conduct in Galilee. Finally, *Contra Apionem* (n.d.; *Against Apion*, 1821) praised Jewish culture and answered anti-Semitic accusations.

Influence. Josephus provides the best account of the Jewish war against Rome, and his works include important information about Jewish history and culture during the period that Christianity emerged. Like most ancient historians, Josephus often embellished his stories and did not always strive for factual accuracy.

ADDITIONAL RESOURCES
Feldman, Louis. *Josephus's Interpretation of the Bible*. Berkeley: University of California Press, 1998.
Rajak, Tessa. *Josephus: The Historian and His Society*. Philadelphia: Fortress Press, 1984.

SEE ALSO: Christianity; Jewish diaspora; Judaism; Rome, Imperial; Vespasian.

—Thomas T. Lewis

JOSIAH

BORN: c. 648 B.C.E.; place unknown
DIED: 609 B.C.E.; Megiddo, Palestine
RELATED CIVILIZATION: Judah
MAJOR ROLE/POSITION: King of Judah

Life. The son of the assassinated monarch Amon, eight-year-old Josiah (joh-SI-uh) was appointed king of Judah in 640/639 B.C.E. Inspired either by his own religious impulses or by the discovery in 622 B.C.E. of an early version of the book of Deuteronomy, Josiah promulgated a purging of alien religious features from the Judaean cult. Such a religious reformation was not without political ramifications: The purge doubtless included the removal of Assyrian cultic objects and was concomitant with the dissolution of the Assyrian Empire. Josiah, killed at Megiddo by Pharaoh Neco II in 609 B.C.E., was buried in Jerusalem.

Influence. The influence of Josiah's reformation remains debatable, the biblical descriptions notwithstanding, because the accounts are tendentious. His efforts to centralize the cult were, evidently, not entirely successful. Josiah failed to achieve national independence: During his reign, Assyrian hegemony over Judah increasingly gave way to Egyptian influence; expansion of Judaean holdings appears limited only to the environs of Bethel. Nevertheless, of all the kings, only Josiah is unreservedly praised for his unique commitment to the law of Moses. Indeed, Josiah's idealized portrayal as the faithful king in the Deuteronomist history has led scholars to conclude that the work was most likely first redacted during Josiah's reign.

ADDITIONAL RESOURCES
Cross, Frank Moore. *Canaanite Myth and Hebrew Epic*. Cambridge, Mass.: Harvard University Press, 1973.

Josiah. (North Wind Picture Archives)

Miller, J. Maxwell, and John H. Hayes. *A History of Ancient Israel and Judah*. Philadelphia: Westminster Press, 1986.
Sweeney, Marvin. *King Josiah of Judah*. New York: Oxford University Press, 2000.

SEE ALSO: Assyria; Egypt, Pharaonic; Israel; Judaism.

—Walter C. Bouzard, Jr.

JUBA I OF NUMIDIA

BORN: c. 85 B.C.E.; place unknown

DIED: April, 46 B.C.E.; near Thapsus (now in Tunisia)

RELATED CIVILIZATIONS: Numidia, Republican Rome

MAJOR ROLE/POSITION: Political and military leader

Life. Juba I (JEW-buh) of Numidia, the last of a long line of Numidian kings, was the son of Hiempsal II. As a young man, he was his father's agent in Rome. In 63 B.C.E., he was publicly assaulted by Julius Caesar when the latter was supporting a rival claimaint to the Numidian throne.

Sometime between 62 and 50 B.C.E., Juba became king of Numidia, although Rome did not confirm his rule until 49 B.C.E. His cultural debt to Rome was strong, and he put his coinage onto the Roman standard, adopted Latin titulature, and initiated an elaborate Romanized building program. As Rome degenerated into civil war, Juba gravitated toward Pompey the Great. After the Battle of Pharsalus, Africa and Numidia became a major refugee center for Pompeians. Caesar landed in Africa in late 46 B.C.E., and within a few months, the Pompeians and Juba were defeated. Juba fled to his royal city of Zama with the Roman officer Marcus Petreius. Refused entry, they withdrew to a country estate and, after an elaborate banquet, killed each other, an event that became a moral paradigm. Caesar returned to Italy with Juba's infant son, who became Juba II of Mauretania.

Influence. Juba I is a fine example of the Romanization of a prominent personality and his culture on

Juba I. (North Wind Picture Archives)

the fringe of the Roman world. He played an important, although tragic, part in the Roman civil war.

ADDITIONAL RESOURCES

Braund, David. *Rome and the Friendly King: The Character of the Client Kingship.* New York: St. Martin's Press, 1984.

Fage, J. D. *A History of Africa.* New York: Routledge, 1995.

SEE ALSO: Africa, North; Caesar, Julius; Juba II of Mauretania; Pharsalus, Battle of; Pompey the Great; Rome, Republican.

—*Duane W. Roller*

JUBA II OF MAURETANIA

BORN: c. 50 B.C.E.; Numidia

DIED: c. 24 C.E.; place unknown

RELATED CIVILIZATION: Early Imperial Rome

MAJOR ROLE/POSITION: Scholar, political and military leader

Life. Juba II (JEW-buh) of Mauretania, brought to Rome in 46 B.C.E. by Julius Caesar after the suicide of his father, Juba I of Numidia, was raised in the

household of Octavia and married Cleopatra Selene, the daughter of Marc Antony and Cleopatra VII. As a young man, he achieved fame as a scholar, writing on the history of Rome, linguistics, the theater, and painting. In 25 B.C.E., Augustus placed him on the throne of Mauretania, where he ruled until his death in 24 C.E., functioning as the implementer of Augustan policy in northwest Africa. He continued his scholarship, exploring his kingdom and beyond, and

Juba II. (North Wind Picture Archives)

writing the definitive work on North Africa.

In 2 B.C.E., Juba became an adviser to Gaius Caesar on his journey to Arabia and Armenia. Traveling with the expedition, he wrote *On Arabia* (now lost), which examined the Arabian peninsula, the Red Sea regions, and the routes to India. Around 3 C.E., he returned home and made preparations for his son Ptolemy of Mauretania to succeed him, spending his last years in political and scholarly retirement.

Influence. In addition to being a major example of a king allied to Rome who brought Romanization to his territory, Juba II was one of the outstanding scholars of his era. The fragments of his works provide important information both about the early history of Rome and the southern extent of the known world, from West Africa to India.

ADDITIONAL RESOURCES

Braund, David. *Rome and the Friendly King: The Character of the Client Kingship.* New York: St. Martin's Press, 1984.

Fage, J. D. *A History of Africa.* New York: Routledge, 1995.

SEE ALSO: Africa, North; Antony, Marc; Augustus; Caesar, Julius; Cleopatra VII; Juba I of Numidia; Rome, Imperial.

—Duane W. Roller

JUDAISM

DATE: 1000 B.C.E.-700 C.E.
LOCALE: Middle East
RELATED CIVILIZATIONS: Egypt, Mesopotamia, Greece, Rome, Byzantium
SIGNIFICANCE: Judaism, the religion and culture of the Jews, originated in Palestine and spread throughout the ancient Middle East.

Judaism, derived from Hebrew *yehudah,* or Judah, one of the twelve sons of the patriarch Jacob and the eponymous ancestor of the tribe of Judah, is the religion and culture of the Jewish people. Its defining belief is the existence of one and only one god, the god of Israel. The Jewish people viewed themselves as standing in a special relationship with this god, whom they called Yahweh. The relationship was defined by the terms of a covenant. Keeping the terms of the covenant, as defined by the divine law called Torah, would result in corpo-rate blessing. The Written Torah is found in the Hebrew scriptures (the Old Testament of the Christian Bible), primarily its first five books, which are traditionally attributed to Moses.

Israelite religion (1000-587 or 586 B.C.E.). The religion of Israel during the period of monarchy and political independence traces its origins to Yahweh's relationship with the ancestors (Abraham and Sarah, Isaac and Rebekah, Jacob, Rachel, and Leah). The exodus of the Hebrews from Egypt under the leadership of Moses is the beginning of Israel's nationhood. The revelation of the covenant at Mount Sinai mediated by Moses became the national constitution and ultimately the foundation of Judaism. However, the term Judaism is properly applied only after the destruction of Jerusalem and the first (or Solomonic) temple in 587 B.C.E. because the tribe of Judah was the sole identifiable survivor of Israel's wars.

The Torah of Moses regulated the religious and civic life of the nation and was supplemented by the apparatus and priesthood of the Jerusalem temple beginning with the reign of Solomon (r. 961-921 B.C.E.). With the separation of Israel from Judah at Solomon's death, Israel in the north of Palestine (the Ten Tribes) struggled to establish stable leadership, while Judah in the south was dominated by the Davidic royal line supported by the Jerusalem priesthood. Prophets such as Elijah, Amos, and Jeremiah challenged these structures largely on the basis of the ideals of the Mosaic Torah. The prophets interpreted the triumph of Assyria over Israel in 722 B.C.E. and Babylonia over Judah in 587 or 586 B.C.E. as the divine punishment warranted by the terms of the covenant.

Early Judaism (587 or 586 B.C.E.-70 C.E.). The Judaean elite, including priests, royal administrators, and craftsmen, were exiled to Babylonia, where they established refugee communities; other Judaeans fled to Egypt and elsewhere. These diaspora communities retained a connection to their traditions yet reshaped them for managing life in exile within first the Babylonian, then the Persian, and later the Greco-Roman empires. No longer able to rely on land and temple to define Judaic identity, rules regulating food (*kashrut*) and the Sabbath, as well as the ritual of circumcision that marks covenant membership, took on new significance. The exilic priestly leadership was instrumental in shaping Israelite narrative and legal traditions into the canonical text of the Torah enshrined in the Pentateuch (the first five books of the Hebrew Bible). Back in Jerusalem, the temple of Solomon was rebuilt, though it was much less impressive.

Late in the fifth century B.C.E., Ezra imposed the governance of Torah upon the Jews living in Palestine; some had returned from abroad, and some had never left. Alexander the Great conquered Palestine in 332 B.C.E., and thereafter Greek culture penetrated the area. After the Greeks, the Seleucid Dynasty gained control of Palestine in 200 B.C.E., and pressure to forsake the distinctive ways of Judaism and adopt Hellenistic modes of thought and culture dramatically increased.

Although some Jews welcomed assimilation, others, led by Judas the Maccabee, resisted. Soon they established Jewish independence from Greek domination governed by the Hasmoneans, the dynasty of the family of Judas. The Pharisees, pietists who championed a constructive interpretation of Torah, came to have influence through their support of the Maccabean revolt. Other factions within Judaism, representing different applications of the tradition, also emerged around this time, including the Zealots who were militantly messianic in outlook, and the Essenes who were ascetic and apocalyptic. The Dead Sea Scrolls, discovered near Khirbat Qumran, appear to derive from them. After the transition to Roman rule in 63 B.C.E., the Sadducees, a Jewish priestly elite, cooperated with the Roman provincial government in managing the Jewish affairs of Palestine. In origin, Christianity was also a Judaic movement, one that identified Jesus of Nazareth as the Jewish messiah come to establish the kingdom of God.

Rabbinic Judaism (70-700 C.E.). The failure of the First Jewish Revolt against the Roman occupation (66-73 C.E.) resulted in the destruction of Jerusalem, including the second temple. This demise of the traditional structures of Judaism, along with Roman imperial domination, forced the search for new forms of religious expression and identity. The Pharisaic tradition emerged as the most adaptable expression of Judaism. Under the sponsorship of Pharisaic rabbis, the Hebrew scriptures were canonized. With the collapse of the Second Jewish Revolt (132-135 C.E.), moderate rabbinic leadership provided an ideology and approach to religious practice that did not depend on the traditional priesthood, the Jerusalem temple, or Jewish political independence.

Judah the Prince, a second century C.E. rabbi, edited the collection of rabbinic interpretations of Torah called the Mishnah, also known as the Oral Torah, that became the standard legal code within Judaism. The Mishnah was organized by topic and was supplemented by later additions called the Toseftah by the Tannaim, rabbis of the Mishnaic period. During the third and fourth centuries C.E., rabbinic interpretations of biblical texts, called Midrashim, were compiled as commentary on the Hebrew text. This corpus was designed to regulate life within the Jewish community, including diet, hygiene, family life, civil affairs, religious festivals, and agriculture. Mishnah continued to define community practice, and further generations of rabbinic scholars, now called the Amoraim, reinterpreted and reapplied earlier legal rulings. These were collected into two Talmuds, one the work of rabbis in Jerusalem, the other the work of those in Babylon. After Palestinian Judaism lost its influence, the Babylonian Talmud, edited finally in the seventh century, became the judicial standard for much of Judaism.

ADDITIONAL RESOURCES
Cohen, Shaye J. D. *From the Maccabees to the Mishnah*. Philadelphia: Westminster Press, 1987.

De Lange, Nicholas. *Judaism*. New York: Oxford University Press, 1986.

Johnson, Paul. *A History of the Jews*. 1987. Reprint. Lonon: Phoenix, 2001.

SEE ALSO: Alexander the Great; Amos; Assyria; Babylonia; Bible: Jewish; David; Dead Sea Scrolls; Egypt, Pharaonic; Elijah; Exodus; Greece, Hellenistic and Roman; Israel; Jeremiah; Jerusalem, temple of; Jesus Christ; Jewish diaspora; Maccabees; Moses; Persia; Rome, Imperial; Seleucid Dynasty; Solomon; Talmud; Zealots.

—*Barry L. Bandstra*

JUGURTHA

ALSO KNOWN AS: Iugurtha
BORN: c. 160 B.C.E.; Numidia
DIED: 104 B.C.E.; Rome
RELATED CIVILIZATIONS: Numidia, Republican Rome
MAJOR ROLE/POSITION: King of Numidia, military leader

Life. Jugurtha (joo-GUR-thuh) was the adopted son of the Numidian king Micipsa. Following Micipsa's death, in 118 B.C.E., the Numidian monarchy was equally divided among Jugurtha, Hiempsal, and Adherbal (Micipsa's natural sons). Jugurtha murdered Hiempsal soon afterward and forced Adherbal to flee to Rome. The Roman senate mediated an uneasy and short-lived truce between the brothers. In 112 B.C.E., Jugurtha besieged Adherbal in Cirta, murdered him, and massacred the inhabitants, including the city's Italian residents. This brought the wrath of Rome.

The Jugurthine War began in 111 B.C.E. The Roman army pursued Jugurtha across North Africa but was unable to defeat him decisively. Jugurtha had an ally in his father-in-law, Bocchus I, king of Mauretania.

In 107 B.C.E., consul Gaius Marius and quaestor Lucius Cornelius Sulla were sent to Numidia to defeat Jugurtha. Two years later, Sulla convinced Bocchus it was in his best interest to betray Jugurtha and ally with Rome. Bocchus delivered Jugurtha in chains to the Romans. They sent him to Rome to be executed, but he died in prison.

Influence. Jugurtha became a symbol of African independence from Roman intervention. His war sparked a long-running rivalry between Marius and Sulla that eventually led to a bloody and violent Roman civil war.

ADDITIONAL RESOURCES

Raven, Susan. *Rome in Africa*. 3d ed. New York: Routledge, 1993.

Sallust. *The Jugurthine War/The Conspiracy of Catiline*. Translated by S. A. Handford. New York: Penguin Books, 1963.

SEE ALSO: Africa, North; Marius, Gaius; Rome, Republican; Sulla, Lucius Cornelius.

—*J. S. Costa*

JULIA (DAUGHTER OF AUGUSTUS)

ALSO KNOWN AS: Julia, daughter of Augustus
BORN: 39 B.C.E.; Rome
DIED: 14 C.E.; Rhegium (later Reggio di Calabria, Italy)
RELATED CIVILIZATION: Imperial Rome
MAJOR ROLE/POSITION: Daughter of Augustus

Life. Julia was the only daughter of Augustus and his first wife, Scribonia. Julia's first husband, Marcus Claudius Marcellus, died when Julia was sixteen. Two years later, Augustus forced her to marry Marcus Vipsanius Agrippa, who was old enough to be her father. They had five children—Gaius Julius Caesar, Lucius Julius Caesar, Julia, Agrippina the Elder, and Agrippa Julius Caesar (Postumus), born during Julia's exile. After the death of Agrippa, Augustus requested that Tiberius divorce his wife and marry Julia. They had one child who died in infancy.

The education of Julia, supervised by Augustus, included instruction in spinning and weaving. She was forbidden to say or do anything without her father's permission. Augustus once scolded Lucius Vinicius as being ill mannered for visiting Julia at Baiae without getting the emperor's consent.

Augustus, preferring Julia's sons to Tiberius, adopted and trained them in the business of government, which led Tiberius to suddenly withdraw from state affairs. Historian Suetonius, however, claims that Tiberius's motive was his intense dislike for Julia, whom he dared not charge with adultery or divorce on any other grounds. When Augustus discovered that Julia had been adulterous, he banished her in 2 B.C.E. to the island of Pandateria. Five years later, he transferred her to the city of Rhegium. One of her lovers, Iullus Antonius, was executed for adultery and four senators were also banished. Julia's mother, Scribonia, accompanied her daughter into exile.

Once Tiberius came to power, he disposed of Agrippa Postumus by ordering his assassination and refused to confirm Augustus's decree, which had confined Julia to Rhegium. Instead, he restricted her to a single house where he forbade visitors, and there Julia wasted away by slow starvation and died in 14 C.E.

Influence. Augustus used his daughter Julia as a pawn in his dynastic policies. Widowed at the age of sixteen and forced into several unhappy marriages, Julia looked for happiness elsewhere. Augustus's harsh treatment of Julia reflects his domestic policies, known as the *lex* Julia, in which he attempted to legislate Roman morality according to traditional values. Julia, like other Roman women, refused to be an instrument of her father's policies.

ADDITIONAL RESOURCES

Suetonius. *Augustus*. Translated by Robert Graves. New York: Penguin, 1980.

Wells, Colin M. *The Roman Empire*. Cambridge, Mass.: Harvard University Press, 1995.

SEE ALSO: Agrippa, Marcus Vipsanius; Agrippina the Elder; Augustus; Rome, Imperial; Scribonia; Suetonius; Tiberius.

—Brigitte Hees

JULIA (DAUGHTER OF JULIUS CAESAR)

ALSO KNOWN AS: Julia, daughter of Julius Caesar
BORN: 79 B.C.E.; place unknown
DIED: 54 B.C.E.; place unknown
RELATED CIVILIZATION: Republican Rome
MAJOR ROLE/POSITION: Daughter of Julius Caesar

Life. History records a few sparse facts about Julius Caesar's only daughter. Julia was born of his first marriage, to Cornelia (Lucius Cornelius Cinna's daughter), when he was in his early twenties. During Lucius Cornelius Sulla's reign of terror, Caesar at some risk had defied the dictator's order to marry Cornelia, so presumably he loved her.

In 59 B.C.E., while Caesar was consul, he broke Julia's previous betrothal and arranged for her to marry Pompey the Great. The moralist Cato the Censor had denounced such arrangements as "prostitution," but matches made for political advantage were not new to Roman patricians, and the marriage seems to have been happy. It brought renewed collaboration between Caesar and Pompey, pulling away the latter from senatorial interests.

Julia died in childbirth five years later; her newborn child lived only a few days. Plutarch says both Caesar and Pompey were "much afflicted" by her death. Against the tribunes' opposition, Julia's funeral and burial were conducted on the field of Mars. Several years later, Caesar sponsored public games and festivals in her honor, celebrating his victories in Africa.

Influence. Julia's life is significant because of its "what ifs." Had she lived longer as Pompey's wife, the First Triumvirate might have endured. If she had borne surviving children, Julius Caesar probably would not have made Octavian his heir. The Roman Republic's transformation into empire would have occurred differently, with consequences for later Western history.

ADDITIONAL RESOURCES

Plutarch. *Plutarch's Lives: The Dryden Translation, Edited with Notes by Arthur Hugh Clough*. New York: Modern Library, 2001.

Suetonius. *The Twelve Caesars*. Translated by Robert Graves. London: Viking Press, 2000.

SEE ALSO: Augustus; Caesar, Julius; Cato the Censor; Plutarch; Pompey the Great; Sulla, Lucius Cornelius; Triumvirate.

—Emily Alward

JULIA DOMNA

ALSO KNOWN AS: Augusta
BORN: c. 167 C.E.; Emesa, Syria
DIED: 217 C.E.; Antioch, Asia Minor
RELATED CIVILIZATION: Imperial Rome
MAJOR ROLE/POSITION: Imperial wife

Life. In 187 C.E., Julia Domna, the daughter of Julius Bassianus, chief priest of the Sun god Elagabalus, married Lucius Septimius Severus, emperor 193-211 C.E. Severus sought her as his second wife because her horoscope predicted that she would marry a king. She bore two sons: Caracalla (Marcus Aurelius Antoninus) in 188 C.E. and Publius Septimius Geta in 189 C.E. Geta, her favorite, was murdered by his brother in 212 C.E., but she continued to support Caracalla politically during his reign.

Julia Domna was a handsome woman. Her numerous surviving portraits depict her in a recognizable coiffure, wearing the *stola* and *palla* of the Roman matron, highlighting her role as the wife of an emperor and mother of sons. She was also a literary patron, supporting Galen, the medical author, and Flavius Philostratus, the philosopher.

In 217 C.E., Macrinus, the prefect of the Praetorian Guard, ordered Julia Domna out of Antioch after he murdered her son Caracalla. Julia Domna, too ill with breast cancer to be moved, starved herself to death.

Influence. Julia Domna is renowned as the most politically significant woman of the Severan period. Her influence secured the power of later emperors Elagabalus (Aurelius Antonius Marcus) and Marcus Aurelius Severus Alexander.

ADDITIONAL RESOURCES
Hemelrijk, Emily A. *Matrona Docta: Educated Women in the Roman Elite from Cornelia to Julia Domna.* New York: Routledge, 1999.
Kleiner, Diana E., and Susan B. Matheson, eds. *I, Claudia: Women in Ancient Rome.* New Haven, Conn.: Yale University Art Gallery, 1996.
Turton, Godfrey. *The Syrian Princesses.* London: Cassel, 1974.

SEE ALSO: Caracalla; Galen; Philostratus, Flavius; Rome, Imperial; Septimius Severus, Lucius.
—Christina A. Salowey

JULIA MAMAEA

ALSO KNOWN AS: Julia Avita Mamaea
BORN: second century C.E.; Syria
DIED: 235 C.E.; Germany
RELATED CIVILIZATION: Imperial Rome
MAJOR ROLE/POSITION: Mother of Marcus Aurelius Severus Alexander

Life. Julia Domna's (JEWL-yuh DAHM-nuh) marriage to Lucius Septimius Severus began a forty-year dynasty of Syrian women who held great influence over the Roman Empire. Julia Domna's sister Julia Maesa continued the dynasty, then Maesa's daughters Julia Soaemias and Julia Mamaea. When the bizarre behavior of Soaemias's son, Elagabalus, repulsed the Roman people, Maesa urged Elagabalus to adopt his cousin, Gessius Bassianus Alexianus, the son of Mamaea and Gessius Marcianus. Because Gessius, now known as Marcus Aurelius Severus Alexander, became the favorite of the Romans, Elagabalus tried

to have him killed. At Maesa and Mamaea's urging, the Praetorian Guard executed Elagabalus and Soaemias.

Severus Alexander succeeded Elagabalus, but because he was only fourteen, the power rested in Mamaea's hands. She strengthened the senate, and it supported her social and educational reforms. When Severus Alexander and Mamaea went to Gaul in 234 C.E. to lead troops against the Germans and arranged a bargain for peace, Maximinus Thrax led the Pannonian legions in revolt, killing both Severus and Mamaea and bringing an end to the Severan Dynasty.

Influence. Julia Mamaea tried to reestablish the authority of the senate and to work for the good of the people throughout the empire.

ADDITIONAL RESOURCES
Birley, A. *Septimius Severus: The African Emperor.* New Haven, Conn.: Yale University Press, 1988.

Grant, M. *The Roman Emperors: A Biographical Guide to the Rulers of Imperial Rome, 31* B.C.-A.D. *476.* New York: Charles Scribner's Sons, 1985.

SEE ALSO: Julia Domna; Rome, Imperial; Septimus Severus, Lucius.

—*T. Davina McClain*

JULIAN THE APOSTATE

ALSO KNOWN AS: Flavius Claudius Julianus
BORN: 331 C.E.; Constantinople
DIED: June 26 or 27, 363 C.E.; Ctesiphon, Mesopotamia
RELATED CIVILIZATION: Imperial Rome
MAJOR ROLE/POSITION: Roman emperor

Life. Julian was a nephew of Constantine the Great. Raised as a Christian, he had early inclinations toward Hellenic religion (paganism). His education introduced him to Neoplatonism. He was made Caesar by his cousin Constantius II in 355 C.E. As Caesar, Julian carried out successful campaigns against the Allemanni and Franks in Gaul. He was proclaimed emperor (Augustus) by his troops about 359 C.E. at Paris. When Constantius died en route to offer battle against Julian's forces, Julian attained the throne in 361 C.E. In 362 C.E., Julian advanced east against the Persians. After limited success, he was mortally wounded in a skirmish early in 363 C.E.

Julian's reign was characterized by his efforts to stem the growth of Christianity. He attempted to sever Christianity from its Greco-Roman intellectual heritage by prohibiting Christians from teaching the "pagan" classics, and he attempted to undermine Christianity's claims to supercede Judaism by trying to rebuild the Jewish temple in Jerusalem. Julian also created a hierarchical empire-wide network of pagan priests to rival the well-organized Christian system. Among Julian's writings are fragments of his anti-Christian polemic *Against the Galileans* (translation 1913), and two prose hymns, which espouse a Neoplatonic view of the traditional gods as offspring and agents of the Supreme One or Good.

Influence. Although Julian's efforts to restrict Christianity failed, he remained an inspiration to Late Antique pagans, who dated their calendar from his reign.

ADDITIONAL RESOURCES
Bowersock, G. *Julian the Apostate.* Cambridge, Mass.: Harvard University Press, 1978.
Smith, R. *Julian's Gods.* New York: Routledge, 1995.

SEE ALSO: Allemanni; Christianity; Constantine the Great; Constantius I-III; Franks; Jerusalem, temple of; Rome, Imperial.

—*Michael B. Hornum*

JUNIUS BRUTUS, LUCIUS

BORN: sixth century B.C.E.; Rome
DIED: c. 508 B.C.E.; Rome
RELATED CIVILIZATION: Prerepublican Rome
MAJOR ROLE/POSITION: Consul

Life. According to the historian Livy, as a young man Lucius Junius Brutus (LEW-shee-uhs JEWN-yuhs BREW-tuhs) watched the tyrannical Roman king Lucius Tarquinius Superbus kill his male relatives and take his possessions. To save himself and wait for the right time to act, he pretended to be slow-witted, *brutus* in Latin.

One day, Brutus happened to be present when the king's sons posed a question to the Oracle at Delphi about who would next rule Rome. When Brutus heard the answer, "he who kisses his mother first," he pretended to fall on the ground and touched his lips to the earth, the mother of all.

A few months later, Brutus was present when Lucretia committed suicide after naming Sextus Tarquinius, Superbus's youngest son, as her rapist. Brutus stepped forward to lead the people in expelling the royal family. For his heroism, he was elected one of the first consuls of Rome in 509 B.C.E.

While Brutus was consul, his own sons plotted to return the Tarquins to power in Rome. When they were exposed, Brutus had to preside over their execution.

Brutus died in battle, killed by Arruns, one of Superbus's sons. The women of Rome mourned him for a year as an avenger of a woman's honor because he began his revolution to avenge the rape of Lucretia.

Influence. Since the beginning of the Roman Republic, the name Brutus has signified democracy and liberation in opposition to tyranny and oppression.

ADDITIONAL RESOURCE

Livy. *The Rise of Rome.* Translated by T. J. Luce. Oxford, England: Oxford University Press, 1999.

SEE ALSO: Livy; Lucretia; Rome, Prerepublican.
—*T. Davina McClain*

JUSTIN MARTYR, SAINT

BORN: c. 105 C.E.; Samaria, Palestine
DIED: c. 165 C.E.; Rome
RELATED CIVILIZATION: Imperial Rome
MAJOR ROLE/POSITION: Christian apologist, theologian

Life. Saint Justin Martyr was born to a Roman family residing in Samaria. He was educated in various philosophies, especially Platonism, which always informed his work but did not bring satisfaction. This he found in the study of Judaic and Christian writings, which convinced Justin that the messianic prophecies of the Hebrew texts pointed to Jesus Christ. He probably converted following a seaside debate with a mysterious old man at Ephesus and after seeing Christians martyred for their faith. Sometime after 135 C.E. and through the reign of Antoninus Pius (r. 138-161 C.E.), he openly taught the Christian faith in the capital. He was martyred early in the reign of Marcus Aurelius (r. 161-180 C.E.).

Of the writings that survive, his *First Apology* (c. 155 C.E.; English translation, 1861) includes a strong plea for justice addressed to Antoninus. In this work, he explains Christian worship, doctrine, and morals to convince his reader of Christian loyalty and integrity. However, also central to this work is his claim that Hebrew prophecy and Greek philosophy, both informed by the divine Logos (the Word), pointed to the coming of Christ. Through this argument, he helped to establish the early Christian theme that this faith was superior to Greek philosophy and was the culmination of Judaic tradition. In Justin's mind, only those who were possessed by demons failed to realize these truths. His *Sec-*

ond Apology (c. 161 C.E.; English translation, 1861) included further complaints of injustice along with an essay on the meaning of suffering, and his *Dialogue with Trypho* (c. 135 C.E.; English translation, 1861) focused entirely on his argument that Christianity was the true Israel.

Influence. Justin represented the height of second century C.E. Christian apologetics as well as an important milestone in Christian theology and attacks on heresy. His writings were certainly influential among Christian communities and may have affected non-Christian readers such as the Roman philosopher Celsus.

ADDITIONAL RESOURCES

Barnard, L. *Justin Martyr: His Life and Thought.* Cambridge, England: Cambridge University Press, 1967.

Chadwick, Henry. *Early Christian Thought and Classical Tradition.* New York: Clarendon Press, 1984.

Goodenough, E. *The Theology of Justin Martyr: An Investigation into the Conceptions of Early Christian Literature and Its Hellenistic and Judaic Influences.* Amsterdam, Netherlands: Philo Press, 1968.

Grant, R. *Greek Apologists of the Second Century.* Philadelphia, Pa.: Westminster, 1988.

Osborn, E. *Justin Martyr.* Tübingen, Germany: Mohr, 1973.

SEE ALSO: Antoninus Pius; Christianity; Jesus Christ; Judaism; Marcus Aurelius; Rome, Imperial.
—*Kenneth R. Calvert*

JUSTINIAN I

BORN: 483 C.E.; Macedonia
DIED: 565 C.E.; Constantinople
RELATED CIVILIZATIONS: Imperial Rome,
    Byzantine Empire
MAJOR ROLE/POSITION: Emperor

Life. Justinian I ruled the Eastern Roman Empire, with his empress Theodora, as it was evolving into the Byzantine Empire. During Justinian's reign, the culture of his empire was becoming less Roman and increasingly Eastern, although Latin remained the official language. The Western Empire had seen its borders invaded by Germanic forces. Justinian's goal, never accomplished, was to unify the Roman Empire.

Although Justinian was not without military victories, his greater accomplishment was the codification of the laws. He created a commission to survey the old law codes, remove what was obsolete, and resolve inconsistencies. The *Digesta* (533 C.E., also known as *Pandectae*; *The Digest of Justinian*, 1920), the product of three years of the commission's work, was followed by the *Institutiones* (533 C.E.; *Justinian's Institutes*, 1915), a legal textbook. The following year produced the *Codex Iustinianus* (529, 534 C.E.; English translation, 1915; better known as *Justinian's Codification*), a second edition of a collection of imperial edicts going back to around 120 C.E. first published in 529 C.E. Together they have been known as the *Corpus Juris Civilis* since the sixteenth century.

Influence. Although Justinian did not restore the Roman Empire, he did codify its law. The rediscovery of the code of Justinian in the late eleventh century C.E. in Bologna, Italy, influenced the development of the civil law of medieval Europe. The influence was not uniform; it varied with locale.

Justinian I. (Hulton Archive)

ADDITIONAL RESOURCES

Evans, J. A. S. *The Age of Justinian: The Circumstances of Imperial Power.* New York: Routledge, 1996.
Lawson, F. H. *A Common Lawyer Looks at the Civil Law.* Ann Arbor: University of Michigan Law School, 1953.

SEE ALSO: Byzantine Empire; Justinian's codes; Rome, Imperial; Theodora.

—*Patricia A. Behlar*

JUSTINIAN'S CODES

ALSO KNOWN AS: *Corpus Juris Civilis* (three works)
AUTHORSHIP: Compiled by Tribonian
DATE: 528-535 C.E.
LOCALE: Byzantium
RELATED CIVILIZATIONS: Byzantine Empire,
    Imperial Rome

SIGNIFICANCE: Justinian I collected the written laws and commentaries of the Roman Empire and arranged them in a digest and code.

As emperor of the Eastern Roman Empire (r. 527-565 C.E.), Justinian I succeeded in achieving two goals. He was able to reconquer large portions of the Western Empire and create a systematic legal system using hundreds of years of Roman legal writings.

In 529 C.E., Justinian created a committee headed by his trusted adviser Tribonian. A new code was published in 529 C.E. but quickly became outdated. Justinian's second effort, the *Digesta* (533 C.E., also known as *Pandectae*; *The Digest of Justinian*, 1920), condensed and interpreted the writings of Roman legal luminaries including Ulpian, Paul, Papinian, and Gaius. Tribonian's committee carefully read and categorized the writings based on their subject matter. Because many of the previous commentaries were discarded by the committee, the digest's commentaries were considered the authoritative analysis of the law. Citing other commentaries was considered a punishable offense.

With a new code and set of commentaries in place, Tribonian published the *Institutiones* (533 C.E.; *Justinian's Institutes*, 1915), a legal textbook for law students. The institutes served as the third part of the *Corpus Juris Civilis*, which included the digest and a second edition of the code published in 529 C.E., known as *Codex Iustinianus* (529, 534 C.E.; English translation, 1915; better known as *Justinian's Codification*). The *Corpus Juris Civilis* served as the basis of the legal system for the Eastern Empire. Its rediscovery in the eleventh century C.E. revitalized the civil legal system in Europe.

ADDITIONAL RESOURCES

Evans, J. A. S. *The Age of Justinian: The Circumstances of Imperial Power.* New York: Routledge, 1996.

Justinian. *The Digest of Roman Law.* Translated by C. F. Kolbert. New York: Penguin Books, 1979.

Moorhead, John. *Justinian.* New York: Longman, 1994.

SEE ALSO: Byzantine Empire; Justinian I; Rome, Imperial.

—Douglas Clouatre

JUVENAL

ALSO KNOWN AS: Decimus Junius Juvenalis
BORN: c. 60 C.E.; Aquinum
DIED: c. 130 C.E.; place unknown
RELATED CIVILIZATION: Imperial Rome
MAJOR ROLE/POSITION: Poet, satirist

Life. Little concrete information exists on the life of Juvenal (JEW-vuhn-uhl), and most of it ultimately comes from his poems. The persona in his poems is that of a disgruntled Roman, probably of the equestrian class, who views the pervasive changes in his society with bitter disdain. In contrast to earlier Roman satire, the hallmark of Juvenal's work is *indignatio* (anger), and his style is highly rhetorical and bombastic. The collection of satires *Saturae* (100-127 C.E.; *Satires*, 1693) consists of sixteen poems divided into five books. His targets are varied, including women, foreigners (particularly Greeks), debased aristocrats, stingy patrons, and effeminates. The poems provide a fascinating, if biased, look into the life and manners of the Roman elite in the early empire.

Influence. Juvenal's satires have often been popular, and in the Middle Ages, he was revered as a moralist. He had a vast influence on later European satirists, especially the Italian poet Ludovico Ariosto, the English poet John Dryden, and English writer Samuel Johnson. Juvenal inspired a long tradition of neo-Latin satire as well.

ADDITIONAL RESOURCES

Anderson, W. S. *Essays on Roman Satire.* Princeton, N.J.: Princeton University Press, 1982.

Braund, S. H. *Roman Satirists and Their Masks.* Bristol, England: Bristol Classical Press, 1996.

Coffey, M. *Roman Satire.* Bristol, England: Bristol Classical Press, 1989.

Rudd, Niall, trans. *Themes in Roman Satire.* Norman: University of Oklahoma Press, 1986.

SEE ALSO: Languages and literature; Lucilius, Gaius (satirist); Rome, Imperial.

—Christopher Nappa

— K —

KACHEMAK TRADITION

DATE: 1500 B.C.E.-700 C.E.
LOCALE: Gulf of Alaska region
RELATED CIVILIZATIONS: Northwest Coast cultures, Arctic cultures
SIGNIFICANCE: These subarctic maritime people, who used bone, ivory, stone, and shell to create tools and objects, were succeeded by the Athapaskan culture.

This long cultural tradition began with a maritime-adapted people who used fishhooks, stone oil lamps, labrets (lip ornaments), and simple toggling harpoons and made both flaked and ground stone tools. The sites around Kachemak (kah-chee-mahk) Bay were originally investigated by Frederica DeLaguna in the early 1930's. Through time, the tradition became more elaborate, with an increase in the numbers of wealth objects. Pendants, figurines, labrets, beads, and decorative pins were fashioned from bone, ivory, jet, shell, and soft red stone. Heavy lamps sculptured with figures of humans and sea mammals also occur. Slate was ground to make barbed points and daggers. Ritualism is indicated by trophy heads, artifacts of human bone, and artificial eyes found in the skulls of human burials. In the upper and middle Cook Inlet region, the Kachemak tradition was succeeded by Athapaskan culture in the late prehistoric period, whereas on the outer coast, it continued and probably evolved into the Pacific Eskimo.

ADDITIONAL RESOURCES

Damas, David, ed. *Arctic*. Vol. 5 in *Handbook of North American Indians*. Washington, D.C.: Smithsonian Institution, 1984.

DeLaguna, Frederica. *The Archaeology of Cook Inlet, Alaska*. Philadelphia: University of Pennsylvania Press, 1934.

McCartney, Allen P., Hiroaki Okada, Atsuko Okada, and William Workman, eds. *Arctic Anthropology: North Pacific and Bering Sea Maritime Societies, the Archaeology of Prehistoric and Early Historic Coastal Peoples*. Madison: University of Wisconsin Press, 1998.

SEE ALSO: American Paleo-Arctic tradition; Arctic Small Tool tradition; Ipiutak; Subarctic peoples.

—*Roy L. Carlson*

KADESH, BATTLE OF

DATE: c. 1275 B.C.E.
LOCALE: Kadesh (Qadesh), on the Orontes River in western Syria, north of Damascus
RELATED CIVILIZATIONS: Hittite Empire, New Kingdom Egypt
SIGNIFICANCE: The battle defined the spheres of influence for the expanding Hittite and Egyptian Empires in Syria and the Levant.

Background. Both Egypt and the Hittites were expanding into Syria. Egypt's Rameses II organized a major campaign to capture the strategically located city of Kadesh, which was blocking further Egyptian expansion, and the Hittite ruler, Muwatallis, prepared to meet him there.

Action. As Egyptian forces approached Kadesh, they were falsely led to believe the Hittite army had withdrawn. Unaware of the waiting Hittite army, Rameses led the first of four divisions to camp northwest of Kadesh. As the second division approached the camp, a massed force of Hittite chariotry struck its right flank. The ambushed Egyptians broke and fled toward the main camp while the pursuing Hittites descended on the unprepared encampment and broke through its eastern shield wall. Rameses rallied his troops to hold until his third division could arrive, but it was the unexpected arrival of a highly trained Egyptian youth corps that turned the battle. The Egyptians pushed the Hittite troops back across the Orontes. The following morning, Muwatallis proposed a truce, which Rameses accepted.

Consequences. Although Muwatallis and Rameses both claimed victory, the battle was indecisive because the political boundaries remained unchanged: Both armies were mauled, the Egyptians withdrew, and Kadesh remained a Hittite ally.

ADDITIONAL RESOURCES
Gardiner, Alan. *The Kadesh Inscriptions of Ramesses II*. London: Oxford University Press, 1960.

Gurney, O. R. *The Hittites*. New York: Penguin Books, 1990.

SEE ALSO: Egypt, Pharaonic; Hittites; Muwatallis; Rameses II.

—*Sondra Jones*

KALEB

ALSO KNOWN AS: Ella Asbeha; Ellesbaan; Hellesthaios
BORN: late fifth century C.E.; place unknown
DIED: c. 535 C.E.; place unknown
RELATED CIVILIZATION: Axum
MAJOR ROLE/POSITION: King

Life. Kaleb served as the ruler of the Ethiopian kingdom of Axum at the apogee of its power in the early sixth century C.E. Although he appears in many contemporary Byzantine texts, notably Cosmas Indicopleustes' *Topographia christiana* (sixth century C.E.; *The Christian Topography of Cosmas*, 1897) and Procopius's "Persian War" in *Polemon* (after 549 C.E.; *History of the Warres*, 1653), and in several Ethiopian inscriptions and hagiographic texts, the details of his life and reign remain vague. He figures prominently in the Ethiopian chronicle *Kebre Nagast* (fourteenth century C.E.; *The Glory of Kings*, 1995).

Known in these texts under a wide variety of names, Kaleb's most famous action was his defeat of the Ḥimyarite kingdom of Yemen in 525 C.E. In order to curry favor with the Sāsānian Persians, who were hostile to the Byzantine Empire, the Jewish Ḥimyarite ruler Dhu Nuwas persecuted the Christians living within his realm, massacring large numbers of them at Najran in 523 C.E. The Axumites, who converted to Christianity during the fourth century C.E., took the opportunity to reclaim their former influence in southern Arabia and strengthen their loose political alignment with Byzantium. Kaleb led the Axumite force across the Red Sea to victory over the Ḥimyarite army. Both Ethiopian and Greek sources maintain that Kaleb abdicated before his death and became a monk.

Influence. The Catholic and Ethiopian churches canonized Kaleb after his death. His successful invasion of Yemen played an important role in the formation of later Ethiopian historical traditions.

ADDITIONAL RESOURCES
Fowden, G. *Empire to Commonwealth*. Princeton, N.J.: Princeton University Press, 1993.
Trimingham, J. *Christianity Among the Arabs in Pre-Islamic Times*. London: Longman, 1979.

SEE ALSO: Africa, East and South; Azum; Byzantine Empire; Christianity; Ethiopia; Judaism; Sāsānian Empire.

—*Ian Janssen*

KĀLIDĀSA

BORN: c. 340 C.E.; west central India
DIED: c. 400 C.E.; west central India
RELATED CIVILIZATIONS: Gupta Empire, India
MAJOR ROLE/POSITION: Poet, dramatist

Life. Kālidāsa (KAHL-ee-DAHS-uh) lived during the reign of Chandragupta II (r. c. 380-413), though Indian tradition often places him during the reign of Vikramāditya I of the first century B.C.E. His name, meaning "servant of Kali," identifies him as a devotee of Śiva, and a great deal of his poetry recounts tales of the legends of Śiva and praise for the city of Ujjain, with which Kālidāsa is associated.

Kālidāsa's major works are in the form of epic poetry, including the *Kumārasambhava* (traditionally c. 60 B.C.E., probably c. 380 C.E.; *The Birth of the War-God*, 1879), which retells the birth of Kumāra and Śiva's love for Pārvatī, and the *Raghuvaṃśa* (traditionally c. 50 B.C.E., probably c. 390 C.E.; *The Dynasty of Raghu*, 1872-1895), regarding the life of Rāma; lyric poetry, including the elegy *Meghadūta* (traditionally c. 65 B.C.E., probably c. 375 C.E.; *The Cloud Messenger*, 1813); and drama, including the *Mālavikāgnimitra* (traditionally c. 70 B.C.E., probably c. 370 C.E.; English translation, 1875), the *Vikramorvaśīya* (traditionally c. 56 B.C.E., probably c. 384 C.E.; *Vikrama and Urvaśī*, 1851), and the *Abhijñānaśākuntala* (traditionally c. 45 B.C.E., probably c. 395 C.E.; *Śakuntalā: Or, The Lost Ring*, 1789), all tales of love. Kālidāsa's poetry is widely regarded as achieving the highest levels in description and expression of emotion of all classical Indian literature.

Influence. Kālidāsa was one of the first Sanskrit writers to receive the attention of Europeans and remains the chief exemplar of Sanskrit culture, particularly of the Gupta era of Indian civilization. English and German scholarship in the field of Sanskrit and classical Indian culture was sparked by Sir William Jones's translation, published in 1789, of the *Abhijñānaśākuntala*.

ADDITIONAL RESOURCES

Ingalls, Daniel H. H. *Sanskrit Poetry: From Vidyakara's Treasury*. Cambridge, Mass.: Harvard University Press, 1968.

Kalidasa. *The Complete Works of Kalidasa*. Translated by Chandra Rajan. New Delhi, India: Sahitya Akademi, 1997.

Miller, Barbara Stoler, ed. *Theater of Memory: The Plays of Kalidasa*. New York: Columbia University Press, 1984.

SEE ALSO: Ashvaghosa; Bhartṛhari; India.

—Dennis C. Chowenhill

KALITTOKAI

AUTHORSHIP: Kapilar, Naltuvanar, Marutanilanakanar, Uruttiran, and others
DATE: fourth century C.E.
LOCALE: Maturai, India
RELATED CIVILIZATION: India (Tamil)
SIGNIFICANCE: This anthology of secular poems is part of the larger anthology *Eṭṭūtokai*.

Kalittokai (*Kalittokai in English*, 1999) is a later collection of Caṅkam literature and consists of 150 love poems in the *kali* meter of the *akam* (internal) genre. The characters, themes, and meter differ from the earlier anthologies of the period. Although there are references to kings, poets, chieftains, and events from other collections, this anthology mentions only Pāṇṭiya kings. *Kalittokai* (kah-lee-TOH-ka-i) depicts the five basic situations of love in the five regions (*aintinai*) common to Caṅkam literature. This anthology is divided into five parts. The first part relates to *pālai* (arid), the second to *kuriñci* (mountain), the third to *marutam* (lowland), the fourth to *mullai* (forest), and the fifth to *neytal*

(seashore). Successful love is the dominant theme in this collection, but fourteen poems deal with mismatched love (*peruntinai*) and unrequited love (*kaikkilai*). *Kalittokai* offers a vivid folk-style interpretation of human relationships, which is different from the classical style used in the early Caṅkam poems. *Kalittokai* belongs to the transitionary stage between bardic and *bhakti* poems.

ADDITIONAL RESOURCES

Marr, John Ralston. *The Eight Anthologies*. Madras, India: Institute of Asian Studies, 1985.

Murugan, V. *Kalittokai in English*. Chennai, India: Institute of Asian Studies, 1999.

Ramanujam, A. K. *Poems of Love and War: From the Eight Anthologies and the Ten Songs of Classical Tamil*. New York: Columbia University Press, 1985.

SEE ALSO: *Aiṅkururnūru*; Caṅkam; India; *Kuruntokai*; *Paripāṭal*; *Patirruppattu*.

—Salli Vargis

KANIṢKA

ALSO KNOWN AS: Kanishka
BORN: first century C.E.; probably west-central Asia
DIED: c. 102 C.E.; probably northern India
RELATED CIVILIZATIONS: Kushān Dynasty, India
MAJOR ROLE/POSITION: Emperor

Life. The dates of Kaniṣka (kuh-NIHSH-kuh) and the Kushān Dynasty are very uncertain. Until new evidence surfaces, the accepted dates of his reign are circa 78 C.E.-102 C.E., which agrees with the Indian Śaka system of dating. Estimates of his year of accession, however, range from 58 B.C.E. to 288 C.E. He was the most famous ruler of the Kushān Dynasty, formed by Kujūla Kadphises I (r. 25-50 C.E.) from a union of five Yuezhi tribes in Bactria. Buddhist literature states that he emanated from a royal family of Bahalaka in Tokharistan and was a direct descendant of Vima Kadphises (r. 50-78 C.E.), considered by the Chinese to be the first conqueror of India.

He succeeded Vima to the throne in 78 C.E. and within three years created an empire that included Uzbekistan and Tazikistan in Central Asia; Gandhāra or eastern Afghanistan; Bactria; the Chinese-controlled regions of Kashgar, Khotan, and Yarkand; Kashmir, Sind, and Bahāwalpur in the Punjab; and the United Provinces of northern India east to Benares and south to the Vindhya Mountains. From his capital at Puruṣapura in modern Peshāwar, he reigned for about twenty-four years, personally supervising the building of the new cites of Kaniṣkapur in Kashmir and Sirsukh in Taxila.

Under his guidance, art in various forms developed prolifically and merged with the traditions of Indian culture. The cities of Puruṣapura, Mathurā, Sārnāth, and Amarāvāti were adorned with buildings and artistic sculpture. Gandhāra art, a blend of Greek and Indian Buddhist themes, developed, flourished, and was supported by wealthy patrons.

At his court resided not only Chinese princes who were held as hostages but also great scholars who played leading roles in the intellectual activities of his age. Among these were the poet and philosopher Ashvaghosa, philosopher Nāgārjuna, Buddhist teachers Pārśva and Vasumitra, politician and minister Māthara, and court physician Caraka, author of the *Caraka-saṃhitā* (first or second century C.E.; English translation, 1949) and founder of the Ayurvedic medicine widely practiced in India.

Although Kaniṣka was a devout liberal Buddhist, he also practiced a religious eclecticism, tolerated diverse religious practices in his empire, and introduced a divergent pantheon that reflected Zoroastrian, Buddhist, Brahmanical, and Greek deities. He witnessed the spread of Buddhism to Central and East Asia, erected great stupas over relics of the Buddha and, on the advice of Pārśva, convened the Fourth Buddhist Council at Taxila attended by Vasumitra, Ashvaghosa, and others. A great proponent of the Northern School of Buddhism, Mahāyāna, he is viewed by Buddhists as one of their greatest patrons. After twenty-four years of ruling, Kaniṣka died about 102 C.E. and was succeeded by Vāśiśka.

Influence. Although of Turkish origin, Kaniṣka was a full-fledged Indian who took a deep and active interest in Indian culture. In the world of Buddhism, he is considered one of the greatest monarchs of ancient India, second only to Aśoka, third emperor of the Mauryan Dynasty.

ADDITIONAL RESOURCES

Elliot, Sir Charles. *Hinduism and Buddhism.* 3 vols. London: Routledge and Kegan Paul, 1954.

Majumdar, R. C., ed. *The History and Culture of the Indian People: The Age of Imperial Unity.* Vol. 2. Bombay: Bharatiya Vidya Bhavan, 1968.

Matrceta. *Invitation to Enlightenment: Letter to the Great King Kaniṣka.* Translated by Michael Hahn. Berkeley, Calif.: Dharma, 1999.

SEE ALSO: Ashvaghosa; Buddhism; Gandhāra art; Hinduism; India; Kushān Dynasty; Mauryan Dynasty; Yuezhi culture; Zoroastrianism.

—George J. Hoynacki

Karaikkal Ammaiyar

Also known as: Punithavathi
Flourished: sixth century C.E., India
Related civilization: Dravidian
Major role/position: Twenty-fifth of the sixty-three Śaivite Nāyānmars

Life. Even as a child, Karaikkal Ammaiyar (kah-RAHI-kahl a-MAHI-yahr) daughter of the chief of Karaikkal, a village on the southeastern coast of India, was a devotee of Śiva. She was married to Paramatattan, a wealthy merchant. According to legend, one day a client gave Paramatattan two mangoes, one of which Karaikkal Ammaiyar gave away to a Śaivite ascetic. When Paramatattan asked her for the mango, she prayed to Lord Śiva, and a deliciously ripe mango appeared in her hand. Alarmed at her divine powers, Paramatattan abandoned her, thus releasing her from the bondage of marriage. Upon her request, Śiva miraculously replaced her beautiful body with only a skeletal frame, so she could pursue her life as an ascetic without any hindrance.

Influence. The fervent outpouring of devotional love songs composed by Karaikkal Ammaiyar and other Nāyānmars gave birth to the Bhakti Movement in India. Among the numerous songs she composed, the most noted ones are *Arpudhathiruvandhati*, a song in praise of the lotus feet of Śiva, and *Irattaimanimalaiandhathi*, one hundred songs with alternate songs being the same type of poem. More than fourteen hundred years after her death, devotees continue to celebrate her life, throwing ripe mangoes in the air as the deity is taken in procession.

ADDITIONAL RESOURCES
Arunachalam, M. *Women Saints of Tamil Nadu.* Bombay, India: Bharatiya Vidya Bhavan, 1970.
Peterson, Indira Viswanathan. *Poems to Siva: The Hymns of the Tamil Saints.* Princeton Library of Asian Translations. Princeton, N.J.: Princeton University Press, 1989.
Sasivalli, S. *Karaikkal Ammaiyar.* Madras, India: International Institute of Tamil Studies, 1984.

See also: Hinduism; India.

—*Kokila Ravi*

Karasuk culture

Date: 1250-700 B.C.E.
Locale: South Siberia, Mongolia, Kazakhstan
Related civilizations: Kelteminar, Afanasievo, Andronovo
Significance: The Karasuk culture was the principal society responsible for the development of nomadism in the Eurasian steppes.

Karasuk (kah-rah-suhk) culture chronology spans the Bronze and early Iron Ages. Their obscure origins are traced to the Karasuk River, a tributary of the Yenisey, and the culture spread throughout southern Siberia and Kazakhstan. The Karasuk, Andronovo, and Afanasievo cultures together indicate the movement of Indo-Europeans eastward across Siberia to Xinjiang.

Their grave sites contained stone slab facings and fences, and corpses faced south, with bowls of food nearby. Cremation was practiced in some areas. Near the end of the first millennium, the Karasuk of Siberia engaged in metallurgy, working in bronze. They also practiced raising stock , especially goats, and had some knowledge of farming. Their clay pottery included spheric-bottomed and high-necked vessels, and their ceramics in general reveal ties to the earlier Andronovo culture. They had more copper tools, rings, and pendants than the Andronovo, and by the ninth century B.C.E., they had tools of bronze. Sword-length daggers with hollow handles and animal heads were typical weapons found in these grave sites.

The Karasuk were linked with China, with Transbaikal and Cisbaikal regions to the east, and with the Caucasus to the west. During the period 1000-800 B.C.E., population growth was hampered by competition for pasture lands from the steppe nomads and for irrigation networks by the settled societies to the south. Their Tagar successors in the Minusinsk Basin were genetically linked to the Karasuk, as the latter were to the Andronovo.

ADDITIONAL RESOURCES

Dani, A. H., and V. M. Masson, eds. *The Dawn of Civilization: Earliest Times to 700* B.C. In Vol. 1 of *History of Civilizations of Central Asia*. Paris: UNESCO, 1992.

Davis-Kimball, Jeannine, Vladimir A. Bashilov, and Leonid T. Yablonsky. *Nomads of the Eurasian Steppes in the Early Iron Age*. Berkeley, Calif.: Zinat Press, 1995.

SEE ALSO: Afanasievo culture; Andronovo culture; China; Kelteminar culture.

—John D. Windhausen

KASKA

ALSO KNOWN AS: Kashku; Kirrukaska
DATE: 1600-1100 B.C.E.
LOCALE: Eastern Europe, Turkey
RELATED CIVILIZATIONS: Hittite Empire, Mycenaean Greece
SIGNIFICANCE: The Kaska are thought to have destroyed the Greeks and Hittites.

The Kaska (KAHS-kuh) were an ancient people who lived in northern Anatolia (modern Turkey). The term Kirrukaska (*kirru*, blond, and *kaska*, head) reveals that these people were noted for their blond hair and blue eyes. It is thought that the Kaska were a subgroup of a larger aggregate group known as the Sherdana, who originated in North Africa and eventually migrated via extensive sea voyaging to settle the Black Sea area, Scandinavia, and the northern Atlantic islands of Britain, Ireland, and Iceland as well as the northern Anatolian territory of the Kaska.

The Kaska were known as a fierce tribal people who did not settle in cities. The mighty Hittite Empire immediately to the south repeatedly attempted to conquer the Kaska from 1600 B.C.E. to about 1193 B.C.E., but the Kaska's expertise in guerrilla warfare made them impossible to defeat using the customary tactics of the day. The eventual destruction of the Hittite Empire was attributed to the Kaska. It is also thought that the Kaska may have joined with other Sherdana tribes as well as a group of Berbers and survivors of the breakup of the Cretan civilization in a loose confederation known as the Sea Peoples.

The Sea Peoples were collectively thought to be responsible for the destruction of virtually all the Greek city-states (such as Mycenae and Pylos) as well as the Hittite Empire by 1200 B.C.E. Descendants of the original Kaska are still seen in northern Turkey, where they are known as Circassian Turks.

ADDITIONAL RESOURCES

Sanders, N. K. *The Sea Peoples: Warriors of the Ancient Mediterranean*. London: Thames and Hudson, 1985.

Stillman, N., and N. Talus. *Armies and Enemies of the Ancient Near East 3000* B.C. Wilshire, England: Wargames Research Group, 1984.

Yadin, Y. *The Art of Warfare in Biblical Lands in the Light of Archaeological Discovery*. London: Weidenfeld & Nicolson, 1963.

SEE ALSO: Greece, Mycenaean; Hittites.

—Michael W. Simpson

KASSITES

DATE: c. 1595-1160 B.C.E.
LOCALE: Central and southern Mesopotamia, present-day Iraq
SIGNIFICANCE: The Kassites ruled Babylonia for a longer period than any other dynasty.

The Kassites, who were originally from the Zagros Mountains in the east, took advantage of the power vacuum left by the Hittite raid of 1595 B.C.E., which ended the First Dynasty of Babylon. They occupied central and southern Mesopotamia and adopted Babylonian culture. A few of their words have been identified as Indo-European loanwords.

Although a list of thirty-six Kassite kings exists, the first two centuries of the Kassites' history is obscure. Most informative is the Assyrian Synchronous History, which is quite anti-Kassite in its bias. Especially illuminating are the Akkadian letters found at Amarna in Egypt in 1897, which include letters between the Kassite kings and the pharaohs Amenhotep III and Akhenaton (Amenhotep IV). These describe the exchange of gifts and the sending of brides to the Egyptian court. Seals belonging to the Kassite king Burnaburiash II (c. 1360-c.1333 B.C.E.) have been discovered in Thebes in Greece.

The eighteenth Kassite king, Kurigalzu I (c. 1400-c. 1375 B.C.E.), built a new capital at Dur Kurigalzu (Aqar-Quf) which now boasts the tallest standing zig-gurat, some 170 feet (52 meters) high. The Kassite Dynasty was destroyed by an Elamite raid in 1160 B.C.E.

ADDITIONAL RESOURCES

Moran, W. L. *The Amarna Letters*. Baltimore: Johns Hopkins University Press, 1992.
Saggs, H. W. F. *The Greatness That Was Babylon*. New York: New American Library, 1968.

SEE ALSO: Akhenaton; Assyria; Babylonia.

—*Edwin Yamauchi*

KAUṬILYA

ALSO KNOWN AS: Viṣṇugupta; Cāṇakya
FLOURISHED: unknown, possibly first century C.E.; India
RELATED CIVILIZATION: India
MAJOR ROLE/POSITION: Statesman

Life. Kauṭilya (koh-TEEL-yah) is generally regarded as the author of a famous Sanskrit treatise on *nīti-śāstra*, or practical statecraft, entitled the *Artha-śāstra* (dates vary, third century B.C.E.-third century C.E.; *Treatise on the Good*, 1961). However, historical evidence does not provide a sure date or provenance for this text, nor for its author. The *Treatise on the Good* was a manual widely read in the Indian Middle Ages, as shown by numerous citations in later works on politics. The text, in mixed verse and prose, seems to consist of several historical layers and therefore is most likely of composite authorship, the name Viṣṇugupta perhaps referring to the latest compiler.

In later legends and literature, a minister of Emperor Chandragupta Maurya (r. c. 321-c. 297 B.C.E.) named Kauṭilya ("the crooked one") appears; he is said to have been instrumental in establishing the Mauryan Empire in India.

Influence. The *Treatise on the Good* had considerable influence on political thought in India. Also, many legends are recounted of Cāṇakya or Kauṭilya, and he is sometimes compared, though perhaps not accurately, to Europe's Niccolò Machiavelli. The playwright Viśākhadatta (fourth century C.E. or later), in his memorable work *Mudrārākṣasa* (possibly fourth century C.E. or later; *Mudraraksasam*, 1900), portrays Kauṭilya as an effective and powerful, though deceitful, politician.

ADDITIONAL RESOURCES

Kauṭilya. *The Arthaśāstra*. Translated by L. N. Rangarajan. New York: Penguin, 1992.
Scharfe, Hartmut. *Investigations in Kautalya's Manual of Political Science*. 2d ed. Wiesbaden, Germany: Harrassowitz, 1993.

SEE ALSO: Chandragupta Maurya; India; Mauryan Dynasty; Viśākhadatta.

—*Burt Thorp*

KELTEMINAR CULTURE

DATE: 5000-3000 B.C.E.
LOCALE: Central Asia south of the Aral Sea
RELATED CIVILIZATIONS: Afanasievo, Andronovo, Karasuk
SIGNIFICANCE: The Kelteminar culture was the first extended settled civilization in the western part of Central Asia.

Discovered in 1939 by Soviet archaeologist S. P. Tolstov along the eastern bank of the Amu Dar'ya River in Khorezm, the Kelteminar (kehl-TEH-mee-nahr) culture extended south of the Aral Sea throughout the Akcha Darya Delta and into western Siberia. It was named after an abandoned canal in Khwārizm where the initial discoveries were made.

In the fifth millennium, incised pottery and pottery made from shells were first produced south of the Aral Sea. Clay pottery, round and pointed on the bottom, was decorated with drawings and stamped designs. Shells were used both in making pots and for adornments. The population engaged in fishing, hunting, and food gathering. This was a prehistoric society devoid of domesticated animals and farming, in contrast to the Jeitun society to the south. Kelteminar people lived in oval-shaped frame homes, often seasonal, with about 100 to 120 residents to a village. Grave sites reveal artifacts of flint and quartz that were inserted into wooden or bone handles. Arrowheads were in abundance.

The Kelteminar society maintained some contacts with the agricultural communities of the southern Jeitun and Anau cultures and with the neolithic communities to the north in the Ural and lower Ob River regions.

ADDITIONAL RESOURCES

Dani, A. H., and V. M. Masson, eds. *The Dawn of Civilization: Earliest Times to 700 B.C.* In Vol. 1 of *History of Civilizations of Central Asia.* Paris: UNESCO, 1992.

Davis-Kimball, Jeannine, Vladimir A. Bashilov, and Leonid T. Yablonsky. *Nomads of the Eurasian Steppes in the Early Iron Age.* Berkeley, Calif.: Zinat Press, 1995.

Levine, Marsha, Yuri Rassamakin, Aleksandr Kislenko, and Nataliya Tatarintseva, with an introduction by Colin Renfrew. *Late Prehistoric Exploitation of the Eurasian Steppe.* Cambridge, England: McDonald Institute for Archaeological Research, 1999.

SEE ALSO: Afanasievo culture; Andronovo culture; Karasuk culture.

—*John D. Windhausen*

KERMA

ALSO KNOWN AS: Karmah
DATE: 2400-1570 B.C.E.
LOCALE: Upper Nile, Kerma Basin, Nubia, and the Sudan
RELATED CIVILIZATIONS: Egypt, Kush, Meroe
SIGNIFICANCE: The city of Kerma was the foundation on which the Kushite state was built and on which the Nubian engagement and subsequent conquest of the Egyptian empire was based.

Early Egyptian interactions along the length and breadth of the Nile River promoted the formation of trading blocs and alliances that evolved into centers of commerce and trade. During the course of the Second Intermediate period (1650-1550 B.C.E.), these economic and political interactions played a role in determining the nature and extent of the Egyptian impact on Nubia. Early intrusions into Nubia spurred the creation of Egyptian and Nubian fortresses, administrative centers, and commercial depots that resulted in some of the earliest developments in the Kushite or Nubian state centered at Kerma (kahr-MUH) in the period from 2400 to 1570 B.C.E. During periods of expansion by the Egyptian state, Kushite developments appear to have waned, whereas during periods of Egyptian withdrawal or decline, Kushite fortunes soared. By the sixteenth

century B.C.E., the kingdom of Kerma had attained the climax of its development. Although Kerma was heavily influenced by Egypt, its non-Egyptian, or black African, cultural character and identity persisted.

History. Although the peoples of Nubia and Egypt evolved in tandem, and modern studies argue that Egyptian culture may have evolved from Nubian roots, the archaeological evidence indicates that the peoples of the city and state of Kerma and the Kerma Basin passed through three primary phases of development. These include Early Kerma (2400-2000 B.C.E.), Middle Kerma (2000-1668 B.C.E.), and Late Kerma (1668-1570 B.C.E.). During the period extending from 2400 to 1570 B.C.E., Kerma evolved into the powerful kingdom of Kush (Napata), or Kash, as the Egyptians knew it.

In the Early period, Kerma saw the development of satellite centers and cities—replete with defensive walls and ditches—that covered areas encompassing between 22 and 62 acres (9 and 25 hectares). Much of this pattern appears to coincide with the Egyptian advance on and withdrawal from the region of Lower Nubia. By the Middle Kerma period, Kush had become a powerful political entity that was recognized as such for the first time by the Egyptians. An intensive pattern of trade between Egypt and Kush ultimately served to promote the expansion of Egyptian influence among the peoples of the Kerma Basin and beyond. Finally, during the Late Kerma period, the full-scale Egyptianization of the Kushites resulted from the acculturation of the Nubian elite, the presence of Egyptian colonists and settlers who were incorporated into the kingdom of Kush, the wholesale adoption of Egyptian dynastic symbols and rituals, and the militaristic Kushite domination of those regions formerly held by the Egyptians.

In many aspects, the Kushites adopted artistic and cultural influences from dynastic Egypt and those Egyptian colonists who continued to reside in the kingdom of Kush and the Kerma Basin after the withdrawal of the Egyptian state. These Egyptians were at first accepted and embraced by the Kushites. However, in time, although Nubia and Egypt jointly administered and managed the former Egyptian provinces of Lower Nubia then under Kushite rule, the Kushites eventually sought the removal of the Egyptian managerial elite and the installation of an indigenous Kushite bureaucracy.

Ultimately, the Kerma-based Kushite civilization persisted as a formidable political and commercial entity for a span of some one thousand years. For centuries thereafter, Kushite civilization endured periods of austerity, warfare, and transformation. It flourished in times of commercial expansion in new cities and within and beyond subsequent Kushite political capitals located at the sites of Napata and later Meroe. Therefore, the Nubian and Kushite traditions begun within the Kerma Basin in 2400 B.C.E. persisted in one form or another until the decline and final collapse of Kushite civilization in 200 C.E.

Death and burial. Kerma was one of the earliest paramount centers and settlements of the Kushites. The massive settlement at Kerma was excavated during the course of several field seasons by archaeologist George Andrew Reisner in 1913-1916. As the result of his focus on the excavation of monumental tumuli, or the burial mounds and chambers of Kerma, Reisner concluded that the funerary ceremonies of the elite involved the sacrifice of captives. In one such burial mound, Reisner recovered the remains of 322 individuals who were purportedly sacrificed as retainers for the person entombed at the heart of the burial mound. The presence of so many sacrificial victims and the energy and resource expenditures represented by the effort required to construct burial mounds on such a massive scale—several of which measured more than 299 feet (91 meters) in diameter—indicate the existence of a highly centralized political authority and ultimately

provide some of the best current evidence for the existence of the first major black African state or polity of sub-Saharan Africa.

Architecture. In addition to its reputation as a massive burial ground consisting of several thousand burials, the city of Kerma incorporated a sophisticated complex of indigenous African architecture of third millennium B.C.E. origins. Aspects of this architectural tradition were inspired by foreign prototypes of Egyptian origin. The monumental *deffufa*, or Egyptian-influenced solid mud-brick towers of Kerma, provide indications of the commercial and defensive underpinnings of Kerma's indigenous architectural and social developments. The Western Deffufa of Kerma measures approximately 89 by 179 feet (27 by 52 meters) at its base, rises to a present-day (eroded) height of 62 feet (19 meters), and incorporates 29-foot-thick (9 meter-thick) mud-brick walls.

Current views. The size of the Western Deffufa, coupled with the recovery of some five hundred mud seals of Egyptian character associated with it, has led archaeologist Graham Connah to argue that this structure was a "watchtower associated with the Nile trade." Excavations in the vicinity of the Western Deffufa reveal evidence of a large fortified city with origins in the third millennium B.C.E. This supports the theory that Kerma was in fact the earliest urbanized, politically centralized, ancient state or polity of sub-Saharan or black Africa.

ADDITIONAL RESOURCES

Connah, Graham. *African Civilizations: Precolonial Cities and States in Tropical Africa, an Archaeological Perspective.* Reprint. Cambridge, England: Cambridge University Press, 1994.

Davidson, Basil. *African Kingdoms.* New York: Time-Life Books, 1971.

O'Connor, David. *Ancient Nubia: Egypt's Rival in Africa.* Philadelphia: University Museum, University of Pennsylvania, 1993.

Phillipson, David W. *African Archaeology.* Cambridge, England: Cambridge University Press, 1992.

Vogel, Joseph O., ed. *Encyclopedia of Precolonial Africa: Archaeology, History, Languages, Cultures, and Environments.* Walnut Creek, Calif.: AltaMira Press, 1997.

SEE ALSO: Africa, East and South; Egypt, Pharaonic; Napata and Meroe; Nubia.

—Ruben G. Mendoza

KHOIKHOI

ALSO KNOWN AS: Khoikhoin; Hottentots (pejorative)
DATE: 500 B.C.E.-700 C.E.
LOCALE: South Africa, Botswana, and Namibia
RELATED CIVILIZATION: South Africa
SIGNIFICANCE: This pastoralist herding culture of southern Africa was part of the larger aboriginal Khoisan group.

The Khoikhoi (KOY-koy) were a people defined in part by their pastoral lifestyle, in part by their morphologic differences from their darker-skinned neighbors, and in part by their linguistic differences from the Bantu speakers who lived next to them. Their name, derived from one of their own languages, means something like "the real people." They are grouped together with the hunter-gatherer San under the name Khoisan. Major Khoikhoi subgroups known in historic times include the Namaqua, Gouriqua, Attaqua, and Gamtoos.

The origins of the Khoikhoi have been a matter of great speculation since the arrival of the Dutch in the seventeenth century because of their relatively lighter skin color and distinctive "click" language. During the 1700's, scholars suggested a variety of origins for the Khoikhoi: They were Jews who fled from Asia sometime after the biblical flood; they were descendants of shipwrecked children; or they were migrants from a northern homeland. Scholars have since discarded these ideas in favor of a hypothesis that the Khoikhoi, like the San, were indigenous inhabitants of southern Africa, descended from stone tool-using aborigines.

Some modern anthropologists believe that the Khoikhoi were originally hunter-gatherers, like the San, who adopted herding technology after exposure to immigrant farming cultures from the lakes region of East Africa. Others now think that the Khoikhoi developed pastoralism independently of outside influences. Still others, such as historian Richard Elphick, believe that the Khoikhoi migrated with their stock from an area north of the Kalahari Desert in modern Namibia

sometime around the second century C.E. Some archaeological finds support Elphick's interpretation, showing that domesticated small stock moved south to the western coast of South Africa sometime between 200 and 400 C.E.

Whether the Khoikhoi adopted a pastoral lifestyle from other peoples or developed it independently, they quickly came to use the possession of cattle or sheep or goats as a means of social distinction. The need for pasture for their stock brought them into direct competition with the San, who relied on the same environment for their livelihood as did the Khoikhoi pastoralists. This led to conflict between the two groups: In historic times, for instance, records show that San hunters stalked or stole Khoikhoi cattle. Eventually, however, some Khoikhoi and San developed an interdependent economic relationship—San helped care for the stock and provided extra food through hunting and gathering in exchange for a few cattle to start a herd of their own. After the arrival of the Dutch in 1652, this relationship was common between Khoikhoi and San, and Europeans adopted it as well. Khoikhoi cattle helped maintain the original colony at Cape Town for many years.

ADDITIONAL RESOURCES

Boonzaier, Emile, Penny Berens, Candy Malherbe, and Andy Smith. *The Cape Herders: A History of the Khoikhoi of Southern Africa*. Athens: Ohio University Press, 1996.

Clark, J. Desmond, and Steven A. Brandt, eds. *From Hunters to Farmers: The Causes and Consequences of Food Production in Africa*. Berkeley: University of California Press, 1984.

Inskeep, R. R. *The Peopling of Southern Africa*. New York: Harper & Row, 1979.

SEE ALSO: Africa, East and South; Eastern African Microlithic/Khoisan peoples; Khoisan.

—Kenneth R. Shepherd

KHOISAN

DATE: 8000 B.C.E.-700 C.E.
LOCALE: South Africa, Namibia, and Botswana
RELATED CIVILIZATION: South Africa
SIGNIFICANCE: These historic hunter-gatherers and pastoralists of South Africa include the groups known as Khoikhoi, San, and the subgroups !Kung, and Soaqua.

"Khoisan" is the collective name for the indigenous hunter-gatherers and pastoralists of Southern Africa. Khoisan differ from their Bantu-speaking neighbors not only in their language families (they speak a series of tongues known collectively as the "click" languages), but also through their relatively light skin color and their shorter stature. Khoisan dominated the southern part of the continent from at least 15,000 years ago up to the arrival of the Bantu population during the African Iron Age. They maintained a Stone Age technology up into historic times and were the first population contacted by Europeans at the time of their arrival in the fifteenth century.

Khoisan are divided into two major groups: the San (formerly known as Bushmen), who lived in small nomadic groups, were rather short and gracile, and developed a hunter-gatherer lifestyle; and the Khoikhoi (formerly known as Hottentots), who lived in larger groups, were slightly taller and more robust, and developed a herding culture based on native cattle. The two groups show extensive linguistic as well as serological and morphological differences, although there has been extensive intermarriage between the two in historic times.

Subfossil evidence suggests that the San were among the oldest indigenous peoples of southern Africa. Remains showing San characteristics have been dated to the late Stone Age, from about 20,000 years ago. Excavations at prominent San sites, such as rock shelters, show that these groups lived in the same places for thousands of years. They moved back and forth between inland sites in summer and coastal sites in winter, living off the abundance of the environment. Coastal sites such as Kasteelberg in the western Cape show that San groups (and possibly Khoikhoi as well) preyed extensively on seal populations and on local shellfish, while the inland sites probably relied on local vegetation and small animals.

The San were among the first groups of South Africans encountered by European settlers, and anthropologists suggest that some of the supposed differences between them and the Khoikhoi may have actually been European misunderstandings about their culture. Dutch writers, for instance, differentiated between the groups near the seacoast (whom they called *strandlopers*) and groups in the interior, even though these may have been elements of the same culture. Scholars also believe that mixing between the San and Khoikhoi through marriage may have existed in ancient times, but it has become much more commonplace in the modern era. San clientage, a relationship defined by interdependence between individual San and other groups—Europeans as well as Khoikhoi—has an equally ancient history.

Khoisan were classified as colored under the apartheid system of government in South Africa and have begun to reassert elements of their aboriginal cultures since the free elections of the 1990's.

ADDITIONAL RESOURCES

Boonzaier, Emile, Penny Berens, Candy Malherbe, and Andy Smith. *The Cape Herders: A History of the Khoikhoi of Southern Africa.* Athens: Ohio University Press, 1996.

Clark, J. Desmond, and Steven A. Brandt, eds. *From Hunters to Farmers: The Causes and Consequences of Food Production in Africa.* Berkeley: University of California Press, 1984.

Inskeep, R. R. *The Peopling of Southern Africa.* New York: Harper & Row, 1979.

SEE ALSO: Africa, East and South; Khoikhoi.

—Kenneth R. Shepherd

KING'S PEACE

ALSO KNOWN AS: Peace of Antalcidas
DATE: 386 B.C.E.
LOCALE: Mainland Greece and Asia Minor
RELATED CIVILIZATIONS: Persia, Classical Greece
SIGNIFICANCE: The King's Peace ended the Corinthian War (395-386 B.C.E.) and made Sparta master of Greece.

The Corinthian War pitted the Spartans against a coalition of Greek city-states supported by Persia and led by Athens, Thebes, and Corinth. Peace negotiations in 392 B.C.E. failed, and indecisive fighting continued for several years.

The tide turned in 387 B.C.E. when the Persian king Artaxerxes II transferred his support to Sparta. The Spartan fleet threatened to cut off grain imports to Athens, which was compelled to accept a treaty promulgated by Artaxerxes and negotiated by the Spartan Antalcidas. This treaty granted autonomy to all Greek states except for Cyprus, Clazomenae, and the cities of Asia Minor, which were to belong to Persia. Athens lost its overseas holdings but kept the islands of Lemnos (Límnos), Imbros (Gökçeada), and Skyros (Skíros). Thebes lost supremacy in Boeotia. Representatives convened at Sparta and ratified the treaty in 386 B.C.E.

Although the Spartans had abandoned the Greeks of Asia Minor, they now controlled mainland Greece. Under the pretense of enforcing the King's Peace, they imposed their will on other cities, until the Thebans defeated them at Leuctra in 371 B.C.E.

ADDITIONAL RESOURCES

Badian, E. "The King's Peace." In *Georgica: Greek Studies in Honour of George Cawkwell*, edited by Michael Flower and Mark Toher. London: University of London, Institute of Classical Studies, 1991.

Hamilton, Charles D. *Agesilaus and the Failure of Spartan Hegemony.* Ithaca, N.Y.: Cornell University Press, 1991.

SEE ALSO: Agesilaus II of Sparta; Corinthian War; Greece, Classical; Leuctra, Battle of; Persia.

—James P. Sickinger

KITOI CULTURE

DATE: c. 3000-2900 B.C.E.
LOCALE: Central Asia, present-day Russia
RELATED CIVILIZATIONS: Mongolia, Russia
SIGNIFICANCE: The Kitoi culture was one of the first to carve stone sculptures of the human face.

The Kitoi (KEE-toy) was a Mongoloid culture that was in existence before the second millennium B.C.E. This Neolithic culture followed the Serovo and preceded the Glazkovo cultures in the regions east and north of Lake Baikal. Members of this culture also lived in the taiga (coniferous forest) and tundra areas of Siberia.

Much of modern knowledge of the Kitoi culture comes from the material found in graves in areas around Lake Baikal as well as in the Angara, Selenga, and upper Lena River valleys. This grave material indicates that the members of the culture had more developed tools than did people in the Serovo culture. What is more, the large number of fishhooks found in the graves suggests that the Kitoi people engaged in fishing rather than hunting. They lived in small, seminomadic communities made up of houses that were partially subterranean. They did not engage in farming and their only domesticated animal was the dog. During this culture, sculptures of human faces on stones and stone rings began to appear. Nephrite (a type of jade) and copper objects were first fashioned during this cultural period. The members of the culture made pottery and engaged in stone polishing.

ADDITIONAL RESOURCES

Murowchick, Robert, and Ariana Klepace, eds. *China: Ancient Culture, Modern Land.* Norman, Oklahoma: University of Oklahoma Press, 1995.

Sasson, Jack, ed. *Civilizations of the Ancient Near East.* New York: Charles Scribner's Sons, 1995.

SEE ALSO: Mongolia.

—Annita Marie Ward

KOFUN PERIOD

DATE: 300-seventh century C.E.
LOCALE: Japan
RELATED CIVILIZATION: Japan
SIGNIFICANCE: During this period, a central government formed in Japan and made contact with neighboring Korea and China, gradually importing aspects of their cultures, including Buddhism and a writing system.

The Kofun (KOH-foon) period gets its name from the large burial mounds (*kofun*, or tumuli) that were built during this time. The Kofun period began with the first keyhole-shaped burial mounds in 300 C.E. and ended in the seventh century. During this period, which is known largely through Nara period Japanese writings and contemporary Korean and Chinese records, the Yamato government formed and forged links with China and Korea. The Japanese imported a number of ideas and concepts, including Buddhism and pottery technology from Korea and bureaucratic and writing systems from China.

The Kofun period can be divided into three parts—early, middle, and late—by the shape and construction of the tombs. In the early Kofun period (c. 300-c. 400 C.E.), the mounds were square, round, or keyhole shaped and were most commonly in the Kinai (Kansai) region, where the first centralized government started in Yamato. Most of the tombs in the Kinai area are believed to be tombs for members of the imperial family. At first, tombs were built around existing hilltops but were gradually moved to flat surfaces around the middle Kofun period. The funerary goods included bronze mirrors, weapons, jewelry, and farming tools made of iron.

Cultivation of rice in paddies, which began in the Yayoi period (c. 300 B.C.E.-c. 300 C.E.), flourished during the Kofun period, partly because of water-management techniques imported from Korea. The construction of reservoirs and irrigation canals required civic planning, coordination, and the mobilization of large numbers of people. This level of societal organization and concentration of power is reflected in the large number of burial mounds (more than ten thousand) built during this period.

The size of tombs, especially the ones in the Kinai area of Japan, became greater during the middle Kofun period (c. 400-c. 500 C.E.). The largest existing mound tomb from this period, that believed to be of Emperor Nintoku, is some 486 meters (531 yards) long, 305 meters (333 yards) wide, and 35 meters (38 yards) high. The second largest tomb is that of Emperor Ōjin, Nintoku's predecessor. The introduction of equestrian culture and metallurgy from China and Sue ware pottery techniques from Korea is reflected in the mound's funerary goods, which include harness and Sue ware. In addition to pit-shaft stone burial chambers, horizontal-style stone burial chambers were introduced in some parts of Japan. *Haniwa* clay figures—often simple cylinders but also animals, people, buildings, and weapons—began to appear in mounds. Their origin and purpose are unknown.

During the late Kofun period (c. 500-seventh century C.E.), the horizontal-style tombs replaced the keyhole-shaped mounds around the Kinai region, and the size of tombs became smaller throughout Japan. Funerary goods included more personal items. After the arrival of Buddhism in 552 C.E. (which favored cremation) and the adoption of many cultural and political practices from Korea and China, the practice of building tombs decreased, ceasing by the seventh century. Instead of tombs, the imperial family turned to constructing Buddhist temples. The Soga family, of which Shōtoku Taishi was a member, worked to centralize power, creating reforms that were carried out largely from 645 to 710 C.E., after its fall from power and before the capital was located in Nara.

The dwellings of the Kofun period were typically square pits, with sides of about 3 to 10 meters (3 to 11 yards), large supporting posts, and thatched roofs, built in clusters. Central hearths were replaced by clay ovens (Korean technology) in the fifth century. Inside these dwellings, archaeologists have found indigenous Haji ware pots, iron knives and sickles, and stones believed to have been used as weaving weights.

ADDITIONAL RESOURCES

Barnes, Gina Lee. *Protohistoric Yamato: Archaeology of the First Japanese State.* Ann Arbor: University of Michigan Press, 1988.

Brown, Delmer, ed. *Ancient Japan.* Vol. 1 in *The Cambridge History of Japan.* Cambridge, England: Cambridge University Press, 1988.

Imamura, Keiji. *Prehistoric Japan.* Honolulu: University of Hawaii Press, 1996.

Miki, Fumio. *Haniwa.* Translated and adapted by Gina Lee Barnes. New York: Weatherhill, 1974.

Nihongi: Chronicles of Japan from the Earliest Times to A.D. *697*. Translated by W.G. Aston. 1896. Reprint. Bristol, England: Oxford University Press, 1997.

SEE ALSO: Buddhism; China; *Gigaku*; *Haniwa*; Japan; Korea; *Nihon shoki*; Nintoku, Ōjin; Shōtoku Taishi; Yamato court; Yayoi culture.

—Hiroko Johnson

KOGURYŎ STYLE

DATE: dynasty traditionally founded 37 B.C.E., destroyed 668 C.E.
LOCALE: Manchuria and northern Korea
RELATED CIVILIZATION: Korea
SIGNIFICANCE: The warlike Koguryŏ Dynasty produced fortresses and tumuli in a distinctive style.

The Iron Age Koguryŏ (koh-goor-yoh) kingdom, located near the middle reaches of the Aprok and Hun Rivers, emerged before the common era from a confederation of five feudal chiefs of warlike peoples related to Ye, Mac, or Ye-Mac. The Koguryŏ Dynasty ruled a land of horse-riding pastoralists and dry farmers renowned for bravery, toughness, and their prowess in hunting, archery, wrestling, and the martial art called *subāk*.

Constant warfare with surrounding peoples forced the Koguryŏ Dynasty to construct more than one hundred mountain fortresses. Typically, fortresses were enclosed on three sides by high mountain walls or cliffs and fronted on the fourth by a large stone wall. This pattern is also called the *korobong* style.

The Koguryŏ buried their elite in tumuli decorated with beautiful painted murals depicting earthly pursuits, abstract designs, and Daoist hermits with supernatural powers. They also constructed Jucksukchong, large, square-based, often pyramidally shaped, stone tomb mounds that ranged from 98 to 197 feet (30 to 60 meters) per side and reached heights of 66 to 98 feet (20 to 30 meters).

The Koguryŏ Dynasty was destroyed in 668 C.E. by the allied forces of the Chinese Tang (618-907 C.E.) and Korean Silla (57 B.C.E.-935 C.E.) Dynasties.

ADDITIONAL RESOURCES
Choi, Moo-Jang. *Koguryo Archaeology I, II*. Seoul, Korea: Minumsa, 1995.
Nho, Tae-Don. *The Study of Koguryo History*. Seoul, Korea: Sagyejul, 1999.

SEE ALSO: Kofun period; Korea.

—G-Young Gang

KOREA

DATE: 3000 B.C.E.-700 C.E.
LOCALE: Korean peninsula and Manchuria
SIGNIFICANCE: The land that later became Korea and Manchuria was populated by peoples who accepted foreign, mainly Chinese, cultural and technological innovations and successfully adapted them to suit their own needs.

The Korean Neolithic Age (6000-1000 B.C.E.) begins with the appearance of pottery and polished stone artifacts. Chulmun pottery, a brownish-gray ware decorated with engraved oblique lines, appears about 3000 B.C.E. Chulmun pottery occurs in lake and shoreline sites, although during the later Neolithic period, it also appears inland, suggesting subsistence changes.

At the beginning of the Korean Bronze Age (1000-300 B.C.E.), Mumun pottery, a reddish-brown plain ware, appears in association with bronze artifacts. Bronze metallurgy was quickly absorbed into the existing technology. Soon Korean styles, including mandolin-shaped Bipa daggers and Danyuchomun mirrors decorated with coarse lines and knobbed backs, appear. These styles, found only in Manchuria and Korea, have no Chinese prototypes. During this period, the Choson chiefdom arose, eventually controlling territory from Lioning in southwestern Manchuria to the Taedong River Basin in northwest Korea. Similar polities appear around it sometime thereafter.

The Korean Iron Age (300 B.C.E.-300 C.E.) begins with the arrival of iron metallurgy from China. The late Bronze Age and the early Iron Age are not clearly distinguishable archaeologically. Munum pottery persists until circa 100 B.C.E., and Korean bronze metallurgy reaches its apogee in the early Iron Age with the production of elegant Sehyung daggers and Semun bronze mirrors with delicate line designs. The Late Iron Age (100 B.C.E.-300 C.E.) is called the Proto-Three Kingdom period. The period's characteristic pottery is the gray and bluish-gray Kimhae ware made using cloth-covered paddles.

During this period, the Chinese Han destroyed Choson and established four military dependencies (108 B.C.E.-313 C.E.) in its territory. Afterward, iron metallurgy and Chinese Han culture were spread widely throughout Korea by the Han and by refugees from Choson. Meanwhile, tribes and chiefdoms in the hitherto politically undeveloped south coalesced into three confederacies, the Ma-Han, Pyun-Han, and Jin-Han. By the late 200's C.E., the Paekche became the dominant chiefdom within the Ma-Han, unified that confederacy, and began expanding toward the confederation of five chiefdoms known as Koguryŏ. At the same time, the Saro chiefdom (called Silla after 500 C.E.) came to dominate the Jin-Han confederation.

During the Three Kingdoms period (300-668 C.E.), the Koguryŏ, Paekche, and Silla Dynasties transformed their respective polities into kingdoms. Between 346 and 375 C.E., the Paekche gained supremacy over Kaya chiefdoms of the Pyun-Han confederation in south-central Korea and then conquered the southwest part of Koguryŏ territory. In 391 C.E., the Koguryŏ effectively countered the Paekche, expelled the four Han military dependencies from the peninsula, took Manchuria, and began an expansion into the south. Eventually they moved their capital from Jian near the middle reaches of Aprok River southward to P'yongyang near the Taedong River. Faced with internal troubles, the Paekche could not check Koguryŏ's southward expansion and, in 475 C.E., were forced to cede the Han River Basin to them. This was a key strategic loss as control of the Han Basin gave direct access to China by sea.

In the face of this, the Paekche moved their capital from Hansung southward to Ungjin and reorganized politically. This proved successful as in 551 C.E., the Paekche, allied with Silla, recovered the Han Basin. However, in 553 C.E., Silla defeated the Paekche and drove them from Han. Then, in 660 C.E., Silla, in concert with Chinese Tang allies, destroyed the Paekche.

The Koguryŏ, who had faced deep internal unrest and constant attack by their many enemies following their earlier defeat by the Paekche, were totally defeated in 668 C.E. by the allied forces of the Silla and the Chinese Tang Dynasties. This defeat completed the unification of three formerly independent kingdoms under Silla and initiated the Unified Silla period (668-935 C.E.). During this time, refugees from Koguryŏ established Parhae at Jilin in Manchuria in 698 C.E. and gained control of land north to the Taedong River.

Agriculture and animal husbandry. The transformation from food collection to production occurred in Korea during the late Neolithic period. In association with food production, stone hoes, picks, and plows appeared, and sickles made of either stone or animal teeth were used. The major cultigen in this period is Decan grass, cultivated by slash-and-burn dry farming. Dogs and pigs are the earliest domesticated animals. As farming became more important, Chinese millet, foxtail millet, sorghum, beans, and barley were cultivated. Sometime before about 600 B.C.E., wet-rice agriculture from the Yellow River Basin in China was introduced onto the peninsula.

During the subsequent Bronze Age, horses and oxen appear, and the inventory of farming implements increases. Semilunar stone grain harvesting knives and grooved stone adzes for felling trees and plowing were also introduced from China. After the introduction of iron metallurgy, many farming implements were made of iron. Iron Age farmers raised domesticated chickens, depended on animals for plowing, and cultivated fruit trees such as chestnut, pear, and peach trees. Irrigation reservoirs were first constructed during the Proto-Three Kingdom period by the peoples of the three Hans. Irrigation works on a grand scale were built by the Paekche and Silla, and the cultivation of wet rice has been central to Korean agriculture ever since. Plowing rice paddys with oxen became common, and new seed plants were developed after 500 C.E.

Death and burial. During the Neolithic period, no single, distinctive type of burial form predominated in Korea. In the Bronze Age, however, stone cists and megalithic stone dolmen, called *goindol*, appear. Although the former type is found in Manchuria, Mongolia, and near Lake Baikal, the latter is known only from the Korean peninsula and the Lioning region in Manchuria. To entomb the powerful elite there, thousands of dolmen were built all over the peninsula. Dolmen, which occur in clusters ranging from a few dozen to hundreds, fall into a northern and southern type. Burials in the north were made both above and below ground and then covered with stone slabs 16 to 23 feet (5 to 7 meters) long and about 1.5 to 3 feet (0.5 to 1 meter) high. Burials of the southern type were always placed under the ground beneath the dolmen.

By 100 B.C.E., *goindol* were no longer erected. In their place, stone-lined tombs and proto-stone mound tombs were used. Stone-lined tombs commonly contain Sehyung daggers and many other bronze artifacts that reflect the elite status of their occupants. The major burial type in the Koguryŏ kingdom from the Iron Age to the Proto-Three Kingdom period was the large stone mound tomb, or Jucksukchong. Jucksukchong occur in many types and sizes. Their construction reached its climax during the Three Kingdom period when large, square-based, often pyramidally shaped, stone mound tombs were built to heights of 66 to 98 feet (20 to 30 meters) and 98 to 197 feet (30 to 60 meters) in length.

After the Koguryŏ capital was moved from Jian to P'yongyang (427 C.E.), stone mound tomb construction ceased and earth mound tombs with interior stone chambers entered through stone passageways became popular. In southern Korea south to the Han River, the major early Iron Age burial type is the wooden coffin tomb. Large coffin jars appear only in the Youngsan River Basin sometime later. In Silla, at the end of the Proto-Three Kingdom period, stone mound tombs with interior wooden chambers were built. During the mid-500's C.E., earth mound tombs with interior stone chambers entered through stone passageways were constructed in Silla. This tomb type appeared earlier in Paekche during the late 300's C.E. With the spread of this type of burial, stone mound tombs with interior wooden chambers disappeared. The earth mound tomb with stone chamber was constructed for family burial. Since the late Bronze Age, stone-lined tombs have been used by ordinary people on the peninsula. In general, stone chambers with an entrance passage within an earth mound tomb appeared among the Three Kingdoms during times of strong government when the dynasties were expanding their sovereign powers.

Performing arts. Ancient Chinese writings accord the peoples of the Korean peninsula with great skill in singing and dancing, particularly in group dances connected with worship of celestial dieties. Dancing is commonly depicted in mural paintings in burial tumuli. String music was highly developed.

Religion and ritual. During the Neolithic period, the most important deity appears to have been a powerful and benevolent Sun god. The origin myths that survive to the present all relate either to the Sun or to some celestial beings, suggesting that peoples of the Choson chiefdom, the three Hans and Three Kingdoms were Sun worshipers. Shamanism was probably always important. In the Bronze Age, its presence is attested to by the widespread occurrence of such common shamanistic implements as bronze mirrors, bronze bells, and bronze blocks. The chief of the Choson was called Tangun-Wanggum (literally, shaman-chief). However, political and religious authority began to separate during the Proto-Three Kingdom period. Among the three Han, the Chungun, or shaman, directed ceremonies worshiping the celestial gods but were not considered political leaders. As agriculture became increasingly important during the Proto-Three Kingdom period, autumn harvest rituals of thanksgiving offered to the Sun became widespread.

Buddhism was introduced from China during the Three Kingdoms period. It was accepted at Koguryŏ in 372 C.E., at Paekche in 384 C.E., and at Silla only in 535 C.E. Because Buddhism strengthens sovereign power by offering spiritual consolidation, it was spread under the auspices of the royal families of these kingdoms. Confucianism was also introduced from China slightly before the Three Kingdom period. The Confucian emphasis on social and moral order made it popular with the ruling elites in Korea. Daoism, on the other hand, incorporated elements of Korean folk religion such as mountain worship and beliefs in hermits with supernatural power.

Education and training. There was no formal educational system before the Three Kingdom Period. At that time, the spread of Confucianism fostered the growth of formal teaching and learning. The first formal educational institution, Taehak, was founded at the capital of Koguryŏ in 372 C.E. and later Kyungdang for teaching local young men archery and academic subjects. It is not known whether Paekche had similar educational institutions, although Confucian teachers, called Paksa, were present there from the mid-300's C.E. There was no formal Confucian education at Silla. There, the Wharangdo system was used to instill loyalty to king and country and obedience and respect for parents and elders in boys of the noble class.

Settlements and social structure. Neolithic peoples in Korea practiced a mixed subsistence that combined limited gardening with hunting and gathering. The numerous Neolithic archaeological sites located near lakes and rivers suggests a dependence on fishing as well. Neolithic houses were built in round or square pits nearly 20 feet (6 meters) long and 23-28 inches (60-70 centimeters) deep. A hearth for heating and cooking was located in the center of the pit house.

During the Bronze Age, sites became larger and were located inland on low hills. Both the new location and the increased size of these sites probably reflect the greater contribution of agriculture to subsistence. Bronze Age pit houses were rectangular in shape. As houses became larger, the depth of their pits decreased. During this period, wars between neighboring tribes and chiefdoms increased in frequency and intensity. The construction of dolmen burial tombs indicates that society had become socially stratified.

Although pit houses were still built during the Iron Age, wooden houses built at ground level came into wide use. The traditional Korean house-floor heating system, called *ondol*, appears first in the Iron Age. The development and widespread use of iron tools increased both the efficiency of agricultural production and the frequency and deadliness of warfare. However, this new technology does not seem to have diminished the need, present since Neolithic period, for human power in agriculture. As a result, communal living and work patterns continued to be important. The basic Korean folk customs and laws regarding murder, theft, and adultery were probably established during the Iron Age.

In the Three Kingdom period, long-distance trade widened to include regions as far away as India and remote parts of East Asia. Both the fine arts and the art of war flourished, and the Chinese legal system was imported into Korea. Finally, with the first appearance of writing, the history of Three Kingdoms is recorded.

ADDITIONAL RESOURCES
Hong, Wontack. *Paekche of Korea and the Origin of Yamato Japan*. Seoul, Korea: Kudara International, 1994.

Portal, Jane. *Korea: Art and Archaeology*. London: British Museum, 2000.

Pratt, Keith L., Richard Rutt, and James Hoare. *Korea: A Historical and Cultural Dictionary*. Richmond, Surrey, England: Curzon Press, 1999.

Rees, David. *Korea: An Illustrated History, from Ancient Times to 1945*. New York: Hippocrene Books, 2001.

SEE ALSO: China; Han Dynasty; Koguryo style; Pak Hyokkose.

—G-Young Gang

KURUNTOKAI

AUTHORSHIP: Compiled by Parikko, works of 205 poets
DATE: between first and fifth centuries C.E.
LOCALE: Ancient Tamil Nādu
RELATED CIVILIZATIONS: Pre-Aryan Dravidian civilization, India
SIGNIFICANCE: This anthology of short poems is part of the larger anthology *Eṭṭutokai*.

Kuruntokai (*Kuruntokai*, 1976) is part of the Caṅkam anthology *Eṭṭūtokai*, which along with the collection *Pattuppāṭṭu* forms the core of the Caṅkam classics, the earliest known Tamil poetry collection. Ascribed to 205 bards and compiled by Parikko, *Kuruntokai* (kew-REWN-toh-kahi) contains 401 stanzas or 40 songs in the *akaval* meter, four-foot lines with a difference in rhyme. The poems range from four to eight lines, except for numbers 307 and 391, which have nine lines. Artistically sophisticated, each of these poems is self-contained, classically perfect, yet fresh and spontaneous. The collection begins with an invocation to Lord Murukan by Peruntevanar.

Love is the subject matter of these poems, which fall in the *akam* (internal) category of Caṅkam poetry. *Kuruntokai* explores various facets of love in a charming manner. Human passions occupy only a few lines of these poems, but the rich description of landscapes and natural setting appropriate for the depiction of these passions occupies center stage. *Akam* literature in general and *Kuruntokai* in particular contain the most exquisite natural descriptions that can be found in Tamil literature. Although apt metaphors and similes abound in the collection, historical allusions are also numerous. Some of the phrases and ideas appearing in *Kuruntokai* recur later in *Tirukuṟaḷ* (third or fourth century C.E.; English translation, 1987) and *Cilappatikāram* (c. 450 C.E.; *The Śilappadikāram*, 1939). According to tradition, elaborate commentaries on *Eṭṭūtokai* were written by scholars Peraciriyar and Naccinarkiniyar, but neither is extant.

ADDITIONAL RESOURCES
Ramanujam, A. K. *The Interior Landscape: Love Poems from a Classical Tamil Anthology*. Delhi, India: Oxford University Press, 1994.
Varadarajan, M. *The Treatment of Nature in Sangam Literature*. Madras, India: South India Saiva Sidhantha Works Publishing Society, 1969.

SEE ALSO: *Aiṅkururnūru*; Caṅkam; Iḷaṅkō Aṭikaḷ; India; *Kalittokai*; *Kuruntokai*; *Paripāṭal*, *Patirruppattu*; Tiruvaḷḷuvar.

—*Kokila Ravi*

KUSHĀN DYNASTY

ALSO KNOWN AS: Kuṣāna Dynasty
DATE: second century B.C.E. to c. 300 C.E.
LOCALE: Central Asia, Pakistan, Afghanistan, north India
RELATED CIVILIZATION: India
SIGNIFICANCE: Dynasty responsible for the spread of Buddhism from India to Central Asia and China.

The Kushāns (koo-SHAHN) were originally a Turkish tribe called the Yuezhi, who originally inhabited the border region of northwestern China. In the middle of the second century B.C.E., they migrated westward into the Oxus region of Central Asia. By the first century B.C.E., the first Kushān king, Kujūla Kadphises I, consolidated rule in Bactria with the capital at Taxila (modern Peshāwar). His successor, Vima Kadphises, extended Kushān authority into India and perhaps as far as the Gangetic Plain by the mid-first century C.E.

It was under King Kaniṣka (c. 78-102), the third in line, that the kingdom reached its greatest height. When their kingdom became rich from trade, the Kushāns adopted the Roman gold standard. It was during the reign of Kaniṣka that the Fourth Buddhist Council was held in Kashmir; this council gave rise to the salvific Mahāyāna Buddhism that later flourished in Central and East Asia and was responsible for deification of the historical Buddha Śākyamuni (Siddhārtha Gautama).

Although there is no record of traditional Kushān art from the early centuries in Central Asia, the Kushāns became great patrons in the lands they conquered, where two distinct schools produced rich works that influenced subsequent art on the subcontinent, Central Asia, and China. The Gandhāra school (later in Pakistan) was characterized by its hybridized Greco-Roman and Parthian inspiration in the treatment of Buddhist subjects. Sculpture of the Mathurā school (fifty miles, or about eighty kilometers, south of Delhi) created lithe and robust Buddhist, Jain, and Hindu figures wearing exuberant ornamentation and transparent drapery. It was during the reign of Kaniṣka that images of the historical Buddha and other bodhisattvas may have been first created.

ADDITIONAL RESOURCES
Czuma, Stanislaw J., and Rekha Morris. *Kushan Sculpture: Images From Early India*. Cleveland, Ohio: The Cleveland Museum, 1985.
Rosenfield, John M. *The Dynastic Arts of the Kushans*. Berkeley: University of California, 1967.
Thakur, Manoj K. *India in the Age of Kanishka*. Delhi, India: Worldview Publication, 1999.

SEE ALSO: Ashvaghosa; Buddha; Buddhism; Gandhāra art; Hinduism; India; Indian temple architecture; Jainism; Kaniṣka; *Tipiṭaka*; Yuezhi culture.

—*Katherine Anne Harper*

— L —

La Florida pyramid

Date: constructed 1800-1600 B.C.E.
Locale: Andes, Lima
Related civilizations: La Florida, Guañape, Chira-Villa
Significance: La Florida pyramid represents the emergence of a distinctive Peruvian cultural tradition characterized by impressive public and ceremonial constructions.

Built between 1800 and 1600 B.C.E., La Florida (lah floh-REE-dah) pyramid was a public ceremonial center in the city of Lima that required seven million days to construct. Along with early large temples and ceremonial centers of the north-central region of Peru, La Florida pyramid represents the earliest buildings known in the Americas. The presence of La Florida affirms that civilization in Peru first developed in this region. Considered the most prominent accomplishment of the Initial Period (1800-800 B.C.E.), La Florida was used as a worshiping platform by the different communities responsible for its existence and coincided with the expansion of village life. Similar to many great architectural achievements of this epoch, the construction of La Florida pyramid consisted of several stages. It evolved from the abandoned Río Seco pyramids, but unlike other prominent structures, the pyramid did not serve as a place of residence. Excavations in 1962 by the Museo Nacional de Antropología y Arqueología unearthed subsidiary platforms and buildings at the foot of the pyramid but did not reveal any evidence of habitation. The pyramid consisted of contiguous walls composed of angular fieldstones, which were covered with clay plaster.

ADDITIONAL RESOURCES

Davies, Nigel. *The Ancient Kingdoms of Peru*. London: Penguin Books, 1997.
Lanning, Edward P. *Peru Before the Incas*. Englewood Cliffs, N.J.: Prentice-Hall, 1967.

SEE ALSO: Andes, central; Andes, south; Lima culture.
—*Michael J. McGrath*

La Tène culture

Date: c. 500-400 B.C.E.
Locale: Lake Neuchâtel, Switzerland
Related civilization: Celts
Significance: Ushered in the Second Iron Age and an industrial revolution that reshaped European civilizations.

Materials from around 500 B.C.E. reveal a shift in art styles, introducing a true Celtic culture. Some examples were found in later Hallstatt burials, but it was first recognized at La Tène (lah-TEHN; "the shallows") on Lake Neuchâtel. During the severe winter of 1853-1854, the lake level dropped to reveal ancient wood pilings. F. Keller dredged the area and discovered utensils and weapons, and from the 1880's to the early 1900's, more than twenty-five hundred items with distinctive curvilinear designs were discovered. The site gave its name to the Second Iron Age in Europe, from 500 B.C.E. through Roman times.

This culture clearly evolved from Hallstatt, with identical conical helmets and oval shields found at sites from both periods. Hallstatt duck and solar symbols continued, as did wagon burials of chieftains—although in two-wheeled (not four-wheeled) chariots. At places such as Manching in southern Germany, hill forts evolved into urban centers with industries in copper, iron, glass, amber, pottery, textiles, and the minting of coins.

The Second Iron Age of La Tène laid the foundation of northern European civilization. Various succeeding Celtic peoples are jointly credited with an industrial revolution that produced horseshoes, iron-rimmed wheels, standardized tools, soap, the rotary flour mill, a harvester on wheels, and an iron plow that could open heavier and more fertile soils for cultivation.

ADDITIONAL RESOURCES
Collis, John. *Defended Sites of the Late La Tène in Central and Western Europe*. Oxford, England: British Archaeological Reports, 1975.

Hill, J. D., and C. G. Cumberpatch. *Different Iron Ages: Studies on the Iron Age in Temperate Europe*. Oxford, England: Tempus Reparatum, 1995.

SEE ALSO: Celts; Hallstatt culture; Neolithic Age Europe.

—*Thomas J. Sienkewicz*

LABARNAS I

ALSO KNOWN AS: Labernash
FLOURISHED: seventeenth century B.C.E.
RELATED CIVILIZATION: Hittite
MAJOR ROLE/POSITION: King

Life. Labarnas I (LAB-ur-nas; r. c. 1680-c.1650 B.C.E.) is considered by historians to be the first king of the Hittites and the founder of the Old Hittite Kingdom. Although in an offering list from Hattusas (modern Bogazköy, Turkey), some earlier members of the royal family are mentioned, it is not certain whether these actually ruled as kings.

No original inscription from the time of Labarnas I has survived; therefore, knowledge about him and his reign comes from an edict of the later king Telipinus, which begins with a summary account of previous rulers that places Labarnas I at the top of the list. According to this document, Labarnas I was a victorious king and able to keep the region between Central Anatolia and the Mediterranean Sea under military and political control. In Hittite times, this area was called the Lower Land. The cities Hupisna (*Greek* Kybistra or Cybistra),

Tuwanuwa (*Greek* Tyana), Nenassa (*Greek* Nanessos?), Landa, Zallara, Purushanda, and Lusna (*Greek* Lystra?) were being governed by his sons. It seems that during Labarnas I's reign, the land of the Hittites was still small, but the state was well established.

A certain Tawannannas is known as the queen of Labarnas I, but no information is available about the members of their family. Labarnas I was succeeded by Labarnas II with his throne name Hattusilis I, who apparently was no blood relation to his predecessor.

Influence. Labarnas I founded the Old Hittite Kingdom, and the later rulers of the Hittites bear the name of Labarnas I as a royal title.

ADDITIONAL RESOURCES
Bryce, Trevor. *The Kingdom of the Hittites*. Oxford, England: Clarendon Press, 1998.
Gurney, Oliver R. *The Hittites*. 2d ed. London: Penguin Books, 1990.

SEE ALSO: Anatolia; Hattusilis I; Hittites; Telipinus.

—*Oguz Soysal*

LACTANTIUS, LUCIUS CAELIUS FIRMIANUS

BORN: c. 240 C.E.; North Africa
DIED: c. 320 C.E.; Augusta Treverorum (later Trier, Germany)
RELATED CIVILIZATION: Imperial Rome
MAJOR ROLE/POSITION: Christian teacher, apologist

Life. Lucius Caelius Firmianus Lactantius (lew-SHEE-uhs SEE-lee-uhs fur-mee-AN-uhs lak-TAN-shee-uhs), having studied with rhetoric teacher Arnobius, received an imperial summons to teach rhetoric at the court of Diocletian in Nicomedia. He may have converted to Christianity while in Bithynia. He therefore

lost his position at the start of the Great Persecution (303-313 C.E.) and eventually (305 C.E.) moved west, where he began writing the works for which he is known. In 317 C.E., he began tutoring Crispus, the oldest of Constantine the Great's sons, in Augusta Treverorum. He may have died there but not before dedicating a revised edition of the *Divinae institutiones* (303-313 C.E.; *Divine Institutes*, 1964) to Constantine, whom he had known since their days together in Nicomedia.

Of Lactantius's numerous works, the two most important are the *Divine Institutes*, a work in seven books intended to encapsulate all of Christian apologetics and to thereby refute all the opponents of Christianity in all ages, and *De mortibus persecutorum* (317-318 C.E.; *On the Deaths of the Persecutors*, 1933), a shrill political pamphlet that describes the divine punishment of the emperors who had persecuted Christians. It is also an extraordinarily important historical source for the period of the Great Persecution.

Influence. Because of the classical elegance of his Latin, Lactantius in the Renaissance became known as the "Christian Cicero." As a Christian thinker and theologian, he was overshadowed by others, but he is important as a prolific writer and as a vocal opponent of paganism.

ADDITIONAL RESOURCES

Digeser, Elizabeth DePalma. *The Making of a Christian Empire: Lactantius and Rome.* Ithaca, N.Y.: Cornell University Press, 2000.

Ogilvie, R. M. *The Library of Lactantius.* Oxford, England: Clarendon Press, 1978.

SEE ALSO: Christianity; Constantine the Great; Diocletian; Rome, Imperial.

—*Mark Gustafson*

LANGOBARDS

ALSO KNOWN AS: Lombards
DATE: first century-700 C.E.
LOCALE: Lower Saxony, Bohemia, Pannonia, Italy
SIGNIFICANCE: After descending into the Italian peninsula in the later sixth century C.E., the Langobards dominated Italy until Carolingian victories isolated them in the southern Duchy of Benevento in the early ninth century C.E.

The Langobards were a tribal branch of the Germanic peoples, whose origins seem to have been in the southern Scandinavian regions and along the lower Elbe. They were identified by Romans such as Tacitus and Strabo as part of the Suebi peoples. Their name derives from their distinctive "long beards," though they also were known as Winnili.

Their early history is barely distinguishable from that of other tribes in Germania. Marcomanni and Roman invasions of the later second century C.E. upset the tribe's stability, and many migrated south along the Elbe into Moravia and Bohemia (by 470-520 C.E.). They developed a strong kingdom along the Danube and moved into Pannonia in the 520's C.E. They shielded Byzantium's northern provinces during the Gothic Wars, and Langobard units served with Narses and Belisarius. From the later 560's C.E., Langobards (perhaps 150,000) moved into Italy, filling a power vacuum caused by the Gothic Wars. Their dukes quickly established themselves in northern cities and adapted to Roman conditions and customs. Byzantine attempts to defeat and remove the Langobards in 576 C.E. (with Frankish allies) and 590 C.E. failed. Battles with Byzantine armies continued into the seventh century C.E., by the end of which the emperors held only the Exarchate and the region around Otranto.

Langobard society was patriarchal and aristocratic, using a *wergeld* scale that recognized several levels of freemen, half-free men (*aldii*), and slaves. The *fara*, or clan, was the basic social unit, though these lost political significance as kings gained power and authority during the seventh century C.E. The Italian Regnum Lombardorum had capitals in Verona, Milan, and finally Pavia (from the 620's C.E.). Kings were aided by notaries, a chancellor, noble judges, and a cellarer. Locally, dukes and *gastaldi* (royally appointed, nonhereditary), *sculdahis* (local judges), and other officials maintained order among natives and newcomers. Langobard laws were first codified and written down (in Latin) under King Rothari in 643 C.E., and evolution of the code continued until after the Carolingian invasion (755 C.E.). Urban artisans and professionals (for example, notaries) were organized into Roman-style guilds. Although both Langobard coins and copies of imperial issues circulated, trade was localized and generally in kind.

Pagan Langobards were first converted to Arianism in the later fourth century C.E. but turned to Catholicism as they interacted with Byzantium and moved into Italy. King Authari's Catholic queen Theodelinda (married 589 C.E.) accelerated the process, especially at court. By about 700 C.E., the process was completed. Kings founded and endowed monasteries in Italy, including the Celtic Bobbio (614 C.E.).

Not surprisingly, Langobards had little effect on Italian architecture, and native Langobard artifacts show influences from the Byzantines, Celts, and Anglo-Saxons.

Christianity affected burial practices, as cremation and provision of grave goods eventually ceased, leaving modern archaeologists very little with which to work; the principal literary source is the late eighth century Paul the Deacon.

ADDITIONAL RESOURCES

Christie, Neil. *The Lombards*. Malden, Mass.: Blackwell Publishers, 1998.

Fisher Drew, Katherine. *The Lombard Laws*. Philadelphia: University of Pennsylvania Press, 1973.

Kiszely, I. *The Anthropology of the Lombards*. 2 vols. British Archaeological Reports, International Series 61. Oxford, England: Oxford University Press, 1979.

Paul the Deacon. *History of the Lombards*. Philadelphia: University of Pennsylvania Press, 1973.

Wickham, Chris. *Early Medieval Italy*. Totowa, N. J.: Barnes and Noble, 1981.

SEE ALSO: Angles, Saxons, Jutes; Arianism; Belisarius; Byzantine Empire; Celts; Christianity; Germany; Goths; Merovingian Dynasty; Narses (Byzantine military leader); Rome, Imperial; Strabo; Tacitus.

—Joseph P. Byrne

LAOS

DATE: c. 1000 B.C.E.-c. 700 C.E.

LOCALE: Southeast Asia, north and east of modern Thailand, west of modern Vietnam

SIGNIFICANCE: The region of Laos was home to one of the earliest civilizations in Southeast Asia. During the centuries immediately before and after the beginning of the common era, the land now known as Laos became home to one of the major groups of Tai people in Southeast Asia.

Most historians agree that Laos did not exist as a nation until about 1350 C.E., when the Lao king Fa Ngum united the territories now known as Laos in the kingdom of Lan Xang. Nevertheless, the history of the land and the people is far older than Laotian political history. The earliest civilization in the land now known as Laos developed on the Plain of Jars some time in the first half of the first millennium B.C.E. This civilization is referred to as the Megalithic culture, after the upright stone slabs and the huge stone burial jars that give the plain its name. The slabs, which marked underground burial chambers, were products of the first phase of Megalithic culture. In addition to bodies, the burial chambers contained bronze artifacts and hand-thrown pottery.

The second phase of the Megalithic culture lasted from about 500 B.C.E. until the first century C.E. The people of this second phase cremated their dead and placed the ashes, along with bronze ornaments and glass beads, in massive jars, which were carved with iron tools. Aside from these remains, there are few clues to the identity of these early inhabitants of Laos, but archaeologists believe that the people of the Megalithic culture engaged in trade in salt and iron throughout the areas of northeastern Thailand, southern China, and northern Vietnam.

The Lao people are part of a linguistic group known as the Tai (frequently written as T'ai), which also includes the Thai and various ethnic minority groups spread throughout Southeast Asia. The Tai peoples are generally believed to have lived in antiquity in southern China, in the region of the provinces of Yunnan and Guangxi. As the Han Chinese extended their power southward, the Tai people began moving down into Laos, Thailand, and northern Vietnam. This migration was gradual and probably extended over the course of the first millennium of the common era. References to the Lao people occur in Chinese and Vietnamese writings during this period.

The southward movement brought the Lao and other Tai peoples into contact with established principalities, notably those of Funan and Champa, which had been in contact with India and had been greatly influenced by Indian religious and political culture. From these earlier Southeast Asian civilizations, the Lao began to adopt many of the Indian customs and traditions that became part of Lao society.

ADDITIONAL RESOURCES

Coedès, Georges. *The Indianized States of Southeast Asia*. Honolulu: East-West Center Press, 1968.

Stuart-Fox, Martin. *A History of Laos*. Cambridge, England: Cambridge University Press, 1997.

SEE ALSO: China; Funan; Han Dynasty; India; Tai; Vietnam.

—Carl L. Bankston III

LAOZI

ALSO KNOWN AS: *Wade-Giles* Lao-tzu; Li Er; Lao Dan (*Wade-Giles* Lao-tan)
BORN: 604 B.C.E.; Quren, state of Chu, China
DIED: sixth century B.C.E.; place unknown
RELATED CIVILIZATION: China
MAJOR ROLE/POSITION: Philosopher, religious figure

Life. Little is known of the life of Laozi (LAOOD-zew), whose name literally means "the Old Master." According to the first history of ancient China, Sima Qian's *Shiji* (first century B.C.E.; *Records of the Grand Historian of China*, 1960, rev. ed. 1993), Laozi was named Li Er and was posthumously honored as Dan. Sima Qian also states that Laozi was a curator of the archive in the capital of Zhou and that Confucius once visited him for lessons on rituals. It is believed that before Laozi retired, he wrote the Daoist text the *Dao De Jing* (possibly sixth century B.C.E., probably compiled late third century B.C.E.; *The Speculations on Metaphysics, Polity, and Morality of "the Old Philosopher, Lau-Tsze,"* 1868; better known as the *Dao De Jing*).

Laozi's *Dao De Jing* is the canon of both philosophical and religious Daoism. The word *dao* literally means "road" or "way." In Daoism, it refers to the source and principle of everything in the universe. The Dao cannot be defined in a positive manner: It is not anything concrete, tangible, or fixed, although it is at work in everything. The *Dao De Jing* describes the Dao with such words as "soft," "quiet," and "empty" and emphasizes yin rather than yang. Its doctrine of reversal states that, if pressed hard, everything will turn to its opposite. Its attitude toward life and the world is best summarized in the doctrine of *wu-wei*, or the principle of noncontention. According to the *Dao De Jing*, *wu-wei* is to be waterlike, to follow the flow of nature and not to oppose it. Waterlike people are reserved, flexible, and willing to go to low places, yet they always find ways to demonstrate their strength and accomplish their goals.

The *Dao De Jing* embraces a laissez-faire political philosophy. It promotes a small state and discourages the use of force. Its moral philosophy is directly opposed to that of Confucianism. Although Confucianism believes in rebuilding social order by strengthening the moral code, the *Dao De Jing* minimizes the role of the moral code. Instead, it encourages a low-key approach by reducing people's desires. It advocates unity and harmony between humanity and nature and discourages the human tendency to separate from nature. It is arguably one of the most original environmentally friendly philosophies. Religious Daoism believes that being close to nature is the best way to have a long healthy life.

Influence. As the founder of the philosophical tradition of Daoism as well as religious Daoism, Laozi's influence on the Chinese civilization is enormous. Historically, Daoism has complemented Confucianism. Along with Buddhism, these belief systems have been the backbone of Chinese culture.

ADDITIONAL RESOURCES

Chan, Wing-tsit, trans. *The Way of Lao Tzu*. New York: Bobbs-Merrill, 1963.

LaFargue, Michael. *The Tao of the Tao Te Ching*. Albany: State University of New York Press, 1992.

SEE ALSO: China; Confucianism; Daoism.

—Chenyang Li

Laozi. (North Wind Picture Archives)

Latin League and War

Date: 493-c. 340 B.C.E. (league); 340-338 B.C.E. (war)
Related civilization: Republican Rome
Significance: Rome's cooperation with and takeover of this league was the instrument by which Rome came to control Italy.

The Latin League was a group of central Italian cities cooperating in military endeavors shortly after the Roman Republic was established in 509 B.C.E. Rome was a member of this league, which extended to its members basic civic rights concerning commerce, intermarriage, and emigration between member cities. Member cities met annually on the Alban Mountain and conducted the Latin Games; there, they considered their differences, celebrated their unity, and planned military campaigns. Successful military campaigns usually resulted in the establishment of colonies on captured land. The colonists were veterans from the combined army. These colonies then became full members of the league.

The combined manpower reserve of Rome and the Latins was the most important element in Roman military success during the republic. However, this success seemed to accrue disproportionately to Rome, and by 340 B.C.E., the league dissolved in war among the members. The result was the emergence of Rome as the unambiguous hegemon at the conclusion of the war in 338 B.C.E. Afterward, the Latin festival was conducted under strict Roman supervision, and Rome demanded troops and resources on a more consistent basis than had previously been possible. This enforced cooperation marked an important threshold in Rome's rise to power: Rome became able to field consistently larger armies than ever before. Nevertheless, the basic structure of the league changed little for another 150 years, so that individual cities continued to maintain considerable internal autonomy.

ADDITIONAL RESOURCES

Cornell, T. J. *The Beginnings of Rome*. London: Routledge, 1994
Salmon, E. T. *The Making of Roman Italy*. Ithaca, N.Y.: Cornell University Press, 1982.

See also: Rome, Prerepublican.

—Randall S. Howarth

Laurel culture

Date: 200 B.C.E.-700 C.E.
Locale: From eastern Quebec across northern Ontario and central and southeastern Manitoba to east-central Saskatchewan in Canada; northern Michigan and Minnesota in the United States
Significance: Despite a paucity of food sources, the Laurel culture thrived on the Canadian Shield by exploiting natural waterways. They developed into a fairly complex Woodland culture that practiced mound burials and produced exotic ceramics.

Dwelling among lakes and east-west-flowing rivers, the Laurel people relied on water-based mobility to secure sustenance in a region in which food was often in short supply. Moose, beaver, and fish were widely eaten, and archaeological excavations in Minnesota have revealed pits dug for the preparation of wild rice.

During the warm season, Laurel people lived in base camps located near major bodies of water, which supplied the inhabitants with fish and provided transportation to hunting and foraging grounds. These camps were probably divided into small family units, each of which would go to its own hunting area during the cold months. Among artifacts found at Laurel sites are various ornaments and tools made of local copper, bone harpoons, and beaver-tooth knives and awls. Laurel ceramics were distinctive, bearing various decorative devices achieved by incision or impression.

The earthen burial mound culture to the south evidently spread to the Laurel people, as such interments were made at large seasonal camps. Before burial, the brains and marrow of the long bones were often removed and red ocher placed in the grave. Although artifacts were rarely included in the graves, offerings (such as stone projectile points and smoking pipes) were placed in the mound fill as burials were added.

ADDITIONAL RESOURCES

Stoltman, J. B. *The Laurel Culture in Minnesota*. Minnesota Prehistoric Archaeology Series. Saint Paul: Minnesota Historical Society, 1973.

Sturtevant, William C., ed. *Plateau*. Vol. 12 in *Handbook of North American Indians*. Washington, D.C.: Smithsonian Institution Press, 1998.

Wright, J. V. *The Laurel Tradition and the Middle Woodland Period*. Ottawa: National Museum of Canada, 1967.

SEE ALSO: Adena culture; Middle Woodland tradition.

—*Jeremiah R. Taylor*

LEGALISTS

DATE: fourth century-second century B.C.E.
LOCALE: China
RELATED CIVILIZATIONS: Qin Dynasty, China
SIGNIFICANCE: Legalists informed and guided the government of the Qin Dynasty and the transitional era leading up to it and were revived as a resource by Communist China.

The Legalists advocated an approach to law and administrative methods in government that was extremely influential during the era preceding the Qin Dynasty (221-206 B.C.E.). Legalism (*fajia*) is not a formal philosophy and lacks a chief text espousing it, but it is one of the six schools of Chinese philosophy in Sima Tan's first century B.C.E. classification scheme. The primary texts expressing the ideals of Legalism are the *Guanzi* (fourth century B.C.E.; selections translated in *Economic Dialogues in Ancient China*, 1954; complete translation *Guanzi*, 1985), the *Shangjun shu* (also known as *Shangzi*; compiled 359-338 B.C.E.; *The Book of Lord Shang*, 1928), and the *Han Feizi* (latter half of third century B.C.E.; *The Complete Works of Han Fei Tzu: A Classic of Chinese Legalism*, 1939-1959, 2 volumes; commonly known as *Han Feizi*), all named after the individuals most associated with these texts' authorship.

Legalism emphasizes the importance of three principles: *shih*, the position or power necessary to regulate government and enforce law; *shu*, administrative techniques; and *fa*, law. In contrast to Confucianism, which extols the virtues (such as benevolence) of a great leader, Legalism insists that good government, which is necessary to the welfare of the people, depends on consistent standards and laws, particularly exemplars and measurements. In the Qin Dynasty, measurements were standardized, laws were enforced consistently (and harshly) across classes, and the characters used to write Chinese were made uniform.

To counter the privileges and discretionary powers that Confucianism granted to rulers, Legalists insisted on publishing laws that regulated the behavior of individuals and the practices of agriculture and commerce and specified the punishments for misbehavior. The belief behind this was that people are neither naturally good (as Mencius had claimed) nor bad (Xunzi's claim) but shaped by rewards and punishments, which would motivate individuals to be virtuous. Legalists regarded the failures of past governments as caused not so much by bad ideology as by the natural effects of an increasing population: As there were exponentially more individuals to rule and more diversity among them, what was needed was the unifying effect of strong law. Therefore, the authority of antiquity, another Confucian ideal, was no longer paramount, nor was the maintenance of a class of scholars. In accordance with the advice of Han Fei (d. 233 B.C.E.), the principal advocate of Legalism, intellectuals were distrusted and books from antiquity burned.

Legalism was denounced by Emperor Wudi (r. 140-87 B.C.E.) of the Han Dynasty as Confucianism regained popularity, but the ideas of the Legalists regarding law and standardization remained influential in Chinese government.

ADDITIONAL RESOURCES

Creel, H. G. *Chinese Thought from Confucius to Mao Tse-tung*. New York: New American Library, 1960.

De Bary, Theodore, and Irene Bloom. *From Earliest Times to 1600*. Vol. 1 in *Sources of Chinese Tradition*. 2d ed. New York: Columbia University Press, 1999.

Graham, A. C. *Disputers of the Tao: Philosophical Argument in Ancient China*. La Salle, Ill.: Open Court, 1989.

SEE ALSO: China; Confucianism; Han Dynasty; *Han Feizi*; Mencius; Qin Dynasty; Wudi; Xunzi.

—*Dennis C. Chowenhill*

LEO I (EMPEROR)

ALSO KNOWN AS: Leo the Butcher
BORN: c. 400 C.E.; Dacia
DIED: 474 C.E.; place unknown
RELATED CIVILIZATIONS: Imperial Rome,
    Byzantine Empire, Germany
MAJOR ROLE/POSITION: Eastern Byzantine emperor

Life. Leo I spent most of his life in the military. When the Eastern emperor Marcian died in 457 C.E., the military leader Aspar, a German, was instrumental in having Leo crowned as emperor because he felt that he could easily control Leo. The patriarch Anatolios crowned Leo as emperor, the first known case of imperial coronation by a patriarch. During his reign, Leo dealt with natural disasters, religious disputes, foreign conflicts, and Aspar's considerable influence at court. By marrying his daughter to the future emperor Zeno, an Isaurian, Leo was able to counteract Aspar's influence, and in 471 C.E., Aspar was murdered. In 474 C.E., Leo died and was succeeded by his grandson Leo II.

Influence. Leo's reign was a mixed success for the Eastern Empire. Although his foreign campaigns were costly to the treasury, his removal of Germanic control from the imperial court was necessary for the East's independent survival.

ADDITIONAL RESOURCES

Bury, J. B. *History of the Later Roman Empire: From the Death of Theodosius I to the Death of Justinian.* New York: Dover, 1978.

Jones, A. H. M. *The Later Roman Empire, 284-602.* Norman: University of Oklahoma Press, 1964. Reprint. Baltimore: Johns Hopkins University Press, 1986.

Treadgold, Warren. *A History of Byzantine State and Society.* Stanford, Calif.: Stanford University Press, 1997.

SEE ALSO: Alani; Byzantine Empire; Germany; Rome, Imperial.

—*R. Scott Moore*

LEO I, SAINT

ALSO KNOWN AS: Leo the Great; Pope Leo I
BORN: late fourth century C.E.; possibly Tuscany
DIED: November 10, 461 C.E.; Rome
RELATED CIVILIZATION: Imperial Rome
MAJOR ROLE/POSITION: Pope/Bishop of Rome,
    writer

Life. Leo I, bishop of Rome from 440 to 461 C.E., vigorously defined and expanded the power of the papacy. He was a bridge between the fading power of the Roman Empire and the emerging world of the early Middle Ages and western Christendom. Under Leo, the Christian Church filled the vacuum left by Rome. Consequently, the papacy gradually became the dominant spiritual and cultural force in Western Europe.

Little is known of his early life. His educational background was thoroughly Latin. During his early career, he became an ecclesiastical diplomat representing the theological and political interests of several popes.

In 440 C.E., Leo was elected the forty-seventh bishop of Rome. He firmly asserted papal authority in many controversies including various heretical disputes. His

Tome (449 C.E.; English translation, 1923), adopted by the Council of Chalcedon in 451 C.E., remains the orthodox position regarding the nature of Jesus Christ. His surviving writings include numerous sermons and more than a hundred personal letters in which he offered guidance on matters of doctrine, liturgy, and personal behavior. Traditionally, his personal intervention with Attila in 452 C.E. is believed to have saved Rome from being sacked by the Huns. Leo died in 461 C.E. and was buried in St. Peter's Basilica.

Influence. Leo enhanced the power of the papacy, and many historians regard Leo as the founder of the modern papacy.

ADDITIONAL RESOURCE

Scaff, Philip, and Henry Wace. *Leo the Great and Gregory the Great.* Volume 12, second series, in *Nicene and Post-Nicene Fathers.* Peabody, Mass.: Hendrickson, 1994.

SEE ALSO: Attila; Chalcedon, Council of; Christianity; Huns; Rome, Imperial.

—*Steve O'Bryan*

LEONIDAS

BORN: c. 510 B.C.E.; Sparta, Greece
DIED: August 20, 480 B.C.E.; Thermopylae, Thessaly, Greece
RELATED CIVILIZATION: Persia
MAJOR ROLE/POSITION: King of Sparta

Life. Leonidas (lee-AHN-id-uhs), king of Sparta, belonged to the senior of two royal families in Sparta and married Gorgo, the daughter of his tragic half brother Cleomenes. Leonidas is best remembered for his self-sacrifice at the Battle of Thermopylae, 480 B.C.E., described by Greek historian Herodotus.

Leonidas (upper left) died during the Battle of Thermopylae. (North Wind Picture Archives)

While Sparta and its allies celebrated Carneian and Olympic festivals, the Spartans sent Leonidas with three hundred men to rally central Greece against the Persians in Malis. Persian leader Xerxes I waited four days, then attacked for two as the Greeks fought off vastly superior numbers. That night the Malian traitor Ephialtes told Xerxes of the Anopaea mountain track that led to Thermopylae and directed Hydarnes's troops around the mountain, brushing aside the thousand Phocians Leonidas had posted there.

Warned of Hydarnes's descent and remembering the Delphi's prophecy that either Sparta would fall to the Persians or a Heraclid king would die, Leonidas did not waver and, despite being surrounded, fought to the end with his own three hundred Spartans and volunteer Thespians as the Thebans surrendered.

Influence. Leonidas's valor was not fatalistic. He had been ordered to delay Xerxes and inspire the Greeks. However, he ran out of time because the Phocians ran away. He could not inspire the Greeks by retreating as the Phocians had or by surrendering as the Thebans had. Therefore, to fulfill his mission, he fought on until his death.

ADDITIONAL RESOURCES

Burn, A. R. *Persia and the Greeks: The Defense of the West, 546-478* B.C. Stanford, Calif.: Stanford University Press, 1984.

Green, Peter. *The Greco-Persian Wars.* Berkeley: University of California Press, 1996.

Grundy, G. B. *The Great Persian War.* London: John Murray, 1901.

SEE ALSO: Delphi; Greco-Persian Wars; Greece, Classical; Herodotus; Persia; Thermopylae, Battle of.

—*O. Kimball Armayor*

LEUCIPPUS

FLOURISHED: fifth century B.C.E.
RELATED CIVILIZATION: Classical Greece
MAJOR ROLE/POSITION: Philosopher

Life. Almost nothing is known with certainty about the life of Leucippus (lew-SIHP-uhs), who is believed to have proposed the atomic hypothesis between 440 and 430 B.C.E. He was probably born in Miletus and spent part of his life in Abdera, where he was the teacher of Democritus, who elaborated on Leucippus's hypothesis. He also may have traveled to Elea, where he met the philosopher Zeno of Elea. The later Greek atomist Epicurus claimed that Leucippus never existed, possibly out of jealousy. Aristotle and Theophrastus both refer to him in their writings as the founder of atomism.

Influence. Leucippus's own statement of the atomic hypothesis appeared in a work entitled *The Great World System*, which has not survived. He is also known to have written *On the Mind*, of which only a fragment remains. He is considered to be the originator of the terms and concepts of the atomic theory as expounded by Democritus. The atomic theory was incorporated by Epicurus and his disciples into the Epicurean philosophy, which saw no room for supernatural influences or an immortal soul in a world composed entirely of "atoms and the void." Epicurean literature was suppressed by Catholic Church authorities but would reappear in the Renaissance.

ADDITIONAL RESOURCES

Bailey, Cyril. *The Greek Atomists and Epicuris*. New York: Russell and Russell, 1964.

McKirahan, Richard D., Jr. *Philosophy Before Socrates*. New York: Hackett, 1994.

SEE ALSO: Aristotle; Democritus; Epicurus; Greece, Classical; Theophrastus; Zeno of Elea.

—*Donald R. Franceschetti*

LEUCTRA, BATTLE OF

DATE: Summer, 371 B.C.E.
LOCALE: Southwestern Boeotia
RELATED CIVILIZATION: Classical Greece
SIGNIFICANCE: Theban destruction of Spartan military supremacy.

Background. From 400 until 371 B.C.E., Sparta strove to create an empire in Greece and opposed the unification of Boeotian cities. The Theban Epaminondas defied Sparta at the peace conference of 371, insisting on the right of the Boeotian Confederacy to exist. In retaliation, King Agesilaus II of Sparta ordered his army to attack Thebes.

Action. Under King Cleombrotus, the Spartan and allied army marched from Phocis into western Boeotia, continuing along the southern coast to neutralize the Boeotian navy. Cleombrotus's route gave Epaminondas time to block him at the small, narrow plain of Leuctra (LEWK-trah). Cleombrotus deployed his army of some 11,000 troops in two wings with the Spartans on the right. To the north, Epaminondas surprised the Spartans with some innovations. He massed his Theban contingent fifty shields deep on the left in a formation that jutted forward from his main line. He ordered his Boeotian confederates on his right to advance more slowly than he and to march in an oblique formation. Pelopidas, his subordinate officer, led the elite Sacred Band as his cutting edge. The cavalry of both armies took an unusual position in front of their phalanxes.

Cleombrotus opened the battle by ordering his cavalry to attack and by shifting the Spartans to the right to outflank Epaminondas. A gap opened in his line through which streamed his defeated cavalry. Pelopidas charged immediately, pinning the Spartans until Epaminondas brought the main force to bear. Cleombrotus was killed and the Spartan army broken.

Consequences. By destroying the Spartan army, Epaminondas ended Spartan ascendancy in Greece and created the Theban hegemony.

ADDITIONAL RESOURCES

Brewer, Paul. *Warfare in the Ancient World*. Austin, Tex.: Raintree Steck-Vaughn, 1999.

Buckler, J. *The Theban Hegemony, 371-362* B.C.E.

Cambridge, Mass.: Harvard University Press, 1980.
Lazenby, J. F. *The Spartan Army.* Warminster: Aris and Phillips, 1985.

SEE ALSO: Agesilaus II of Sparta; Epaminondas; Greece, Classical; King's Peace.

—John Buckler

LEYDEN PLATE

DATE: 320 C.E.
LOCALE: Petén area of Guatemala
RELATED CIVILIZATION: Maya
SIGNIFICANCE: One of the earliest dated Maya artifacts.

Discovered in 1864 near Puerto Barrios, Guatemala, the Leyden (LID-uhn) plate is a two-sided jade object, 8.5 inches (21.6 centimeters) long by 3 inches (7.6 centimeters) wide. The plaque contains inscriptions in the Maya hieroglyphic writing script on one side and a drawing representing a prisoner of war on the flip side. The prisoner's resemblance to such figures found on monuments in Tikal, along with this great city state's emblem glyph, leads some scholars to conclude that it was part of a collection of looted objects taken from the tomb of a Tikal ruler.

Inscriptions include a recorded date using the Maya long count system. The total of the five numbers—8, 14, 13, 1, 12, whose placement represents ascending levels of multiples of 20—comes to 1,253,912 days or 3,433.1 years. When the Maya zero year corresponding to 3113 B.C.E. in the modern Western calendar is subtracted from this long count date, the result is 320 C.E. This date makes the Leyden plate one of the oldest dated artifacts from this pre-Columbian civilization.

ADDITIONAL RESOURCES

Macri, Martha J., and Anabel Ford. *The Language of Maya Hieroglyphs.* San Francisco: Pre-Columbian Art Research Institute, 1997.
Morley, Frances, and Sylvanus G. Morley. *The Age and Provenance of the Leyden Plate.* New York: Johnson Reprint, 1970.
Morley, Sylvanus G. *The Ancient Maya.* 4th ed. Stanford, Calif.: Stanford University Press, 1987.

SEE ALSO: Altar de Sacrificios; Copán; Maya; Tikal.

—David A. Crain

LIANGZHU CULTURE

DATE: 3400-2100 B.C.E.
LOCALE: Southern Jiangsu and northern Zhejiang provinces of China
RELATED CIVILIZATION: China
SIGNIFICANCE: One of the earliest cultures to engage in Sun worship.

The Liangzhu (LEEAHNG-jew; *Wade-Giles* Liang-chu) culture was a Neolithic culture whose pottery shapes partly evolved from the Ma-Chia-pong culture. Pots were mainly wheel-made gray ware with a black skin, produced by oxidized firing. Although there was some oxidized firing of red ware, this type of pottery was much less common than the gray ware.

Members of the culture made long-necked *gui* pitchers, but the culture is more generally recognized for its jade jewelry, including pendants, bracelets in animal forms, and mask decorations. Two interesting artifacts of the culture that are often found in graves from the Liangzhu period are *bi* disks and *cong* tubes. The perforated *bi* disks, which may have originally been a symbol of either heaven or the Sun, became a symbol for heaven during later Chinese civilizations. Anthropologists are unable to determine the function of *cong* tubes, which had square exteriors and cylindrical hollow centers; they may have been symbols of the earth or may have been astronomical instruments.

The Liangzhu was a farming culture that developed a triangular-shaped shale plow for use in the wet soil of the area. Farmers must have raised silkworms, as woven silk from the last part of the Liangzhu period has been found. Tools utilized both *gui* and *zhang* blades.

ADDITIONAL RESOURCES
Loewe, Michael, and Edward L. Shaughnessy, eds. *The Cambridge History of Ancient China from the Origins of Civilization to 221* B.C.E. Cambridge, England: Cambridge University Press, 1999.

Murowchick, Robert E., and Araiana Klepac, eds. *China: Ancient Culture, Modern Land.* Norman: University of Oklahoma Press, 1995.

SEE ALSO: China.

—*Annita Marie Ward*

LICINIUS, VALERIUS LICINIANUS

BORN: mid-third century C.E.; Upper Moesia
DIED: 325 C.E.; Thessalonica, Macedonia (modern Thessaloníki, Greece)
RELATED CIVILIZATION: Imperial Rome
MAJOR ROLE/POSITION: Military leader, co-emperor

Life. Before becoming involved in imperial politics and the problem of succession, Valerius Licinianus Licinius (vuh-LEHR-ee-uhs li-sihn-ee-AN-uhs li-SIHN-ee-uhs) served in the Roman army, rising in rank to become second to Gaius Galerius Valerius Maximinianus (Maximinus), who named him co-emperor. Licinius ruled over the Danubian provinces, Illyricum, and other Western Roman territory. A capable military leader, Licinius defeated his rival Maximinus to rule as co-emperor with Constantine the Great from 308 to 324 C.E. despite periods of hostilities between the co-emperors. Actual fighting broke out in 316 C.E. Licinius was partially defeated. He lost some of his territory but was able to have his son Licinius II named as successor along with the sons of Constantine the Great. War between the co-emperors broke out again in 322 and continued until 324 C.E. Licinius suffered two serious defeats at Adrianople and Chrysopolis that destroyed his ability to field any more troops. He was captured by Constantine the Great and executed in 325 C.E. His successor, Licinius II, was executed in 327 C.E.

Influence. Licinius probably subscribed to the Edict of Toleration promulgated by Galerius in 311 C.E. This edict granted official toleration to all religions, including Christianity. However, as Licinius's opponent Constantine the Great became openly favorable to the Christians, Licinius began to persecute them. Despite being defeated by Constantine, Licinius was a skillful military commander and a capable provincial administrator, particularly in tax matters.

ADDITIONAL RESOURCES
Barnes, Timothy D. *Constantine and Eusebius.* Cambridge, Mass.: Harvard University Press, 1981.
Frend, W. H. C. *The Rise of Christianity.* Philadelphia: Fortress Press, 1985.

SEE ALSO: Christianity; Constantine the Great; Galerius Valerius Maximianus, Gaius; Rome, Imperial.

—*Victoria Erhart*

LICINIUS LUCULLUS, LUCIUS

BORN: c. 117 B.C.E.; place unknown
DIED: c. 56 B.C.E.; Rome
RELATED CIVILIZATION: Republican Rome
MAJOR ROLE/POSITION: Military leader

Life. Descended from the consular families of the Licinii Luculli and the Metelli, Lucius Licinius Lucullus (lew-SHEE-uhs li-SIHN-ee-uhs lew-KUHL-uhs) was related to the dictator Lucius Cornelius Sulla by marriage. He began his career in 88 B.C.E. as military tribune under Sulla in the first Marian-Sullan civil war and followed Sulla to the East, serving as quaestor and legate in the First Mithradatic War (89-84 B.C.E.). He impressed a fleet for Sulla from Crete, Cyrene, Cyprus, Rhodes, Cos, Cnidus, and Colophon, but in 85 B.C.E., his loyalty to Sulla led him to refuse assistance to Fimbria, then besieging Mithradates VI Eupator in Pitane. As a result, Mithradates escaped, and ultimately Rome fought two more wars to defeat Mithradates. Upon the outbreak of the Third Mithradatic War (75-65 B.C.E.), Lucullus, then consul, used his connections to obtain the command against Mithradates. Lucullus spent the next eight years in bitter, difficult fighting in Pontus and Armenia. In the end, after angering both the Roman bankers (he curtailed indemnity from the Asian cities from the first war) and his own troops (by his rigid discipline and unceasing demands), Lucullus was stripped of the command, which was given to Pompey the Great, who then quickly ended the war and conquered the East.

Upon his return to Rome, Lucullus's last years were given to political affairs—defending lawsuits over his conduct in the East, fighting three years to obtain a triumph, and obstructing the policies of Pompey at all turns. He retired to his luxurious villa and gardens in 58 B.C.E., where he gained notoriety for his luxurious lifestyle, and died there, probably a victim of Alzheimer's disease, in early 56 B.C.E.

Influence. Ultimately, despite his victories in the East, Lucullus's legacy revolves around his obstruction of the policies of Pompey, which, combined with the support of the Optimates in the senate, drove Pompey into secret alliances for control of the state with Julius Caesar, Marcus Licinius Crassus, and Titus Annius Milo, a situation that ultimately led to Pompey's civil war with Caesar and the destruction of the Roman Republic.

ADDITIONAL RESOURCES
Arkenberg, Jerome S. "Licinii Murenae, Terentii Varrones, and Varrones Murenae: A Prosopographical Study of Three Roman Families." *Historia* 42:3 (1993): 326-351.
Greenhalgh, Peter. *Pompey: The Roman Alexander.* Columbia: University of Missouri Press, 1981.
Gruen, Erich S. *The Last Generation of the Roman Republic.* Los Angeles: University of California Press, 1974.
Keaveney, Arthur. *Lucullus: A Life.* London: Routledge, 1992.

SEE ALSO: Caesar, Julius; Crassus, Marcus Licinius; Mithradates VI Eupator; Pompey the Great; Rome, Republican; Sulla, Lucius Cornelius.

—*Jerome S. Arkenberg*

LIMA CULTURE

DATE: 200 B.C.E.-600 C.E.
LOCALE: Central Andes
SIGNIFICANCE: A highly developed civilization, the Lima culture represented a classic pre-Inca culture.

The Lima culture was in the central coast region of Peru: Pachacamac, Maranga, Pucllana, Culebras, and Cajamarquilla. Its valley regions—Chancay, Chillón, Rimac, and Lurín—had fortresses and fortified settlements. Drawings of warriors, battle scenes, and trophy heads were obsessions of coastal artists. The Lima culture developed advanced forms of technology, art, and social organization. The two most salient features of the Lima culture are its architecture and pottery, both of which have provided archaeologists with valuable information. The principal characteristic of the architecture was the use of adobe bricks to construct pyramids. The pottery was white, red, and black and was decorated with interlocking fish and serpents. The largest population center of the Lima culture was Maranga, located in the Rimac valley. Maranga covered 370 acres (149 hectares), and its largest monumental platform was Huaca San Marcos, which measured at its base 985 by 395 feet (300 by 120 meters) and stood 98 feet (30 meters) high. The structure was surrounded by rooms and walled enclosures, one of which measured 109 acres (44 hectares) and may have served as a residence for Maranga's upper class.

ADDITIONAL RESOURCES
Lanning, Edward P. *Peru Before the Incas.* Englewood Cliffs, N.J.: Prentice-Hall, 1967.
Von Hagen, Adriana, and Craig Morris. *The Cities of the Ancient Andes.* London: Thames and Hudson, 1998.

SEE ALSO: Andes, central; Andes, south.

—*Michael J. McGrath*

LINEAR B

DATE: used c. 1400-c. 1230 B.C.E.
LOCALE: Mycenae
RELATED CIVILIZATION: Mycenaean Greece

The form of writing developed by the Mycenaean Greeks is known as Linear B from the simple outline shape of its signs. It was derived from an earlier, as yet undeciphered, script employed in the Minoan culture of Crete, termed Linear A. Linear B is syllabic, with ninety signs representing syllables composed of a pure vowel or a consonant plus a vowel. Other signs are pictograms, and a third component consists of units designating numbers, weights, and measures. Discovered in early twentieth century excavations, the script was not easily or quickly learned. Collaboration by British architect and decoder Michael Ventris and British philologist John Chadwick led to its being deciphered as a form of Greek in 1952.

The function of the script was defined by accounting needs within each kingdom; it apparently served no other uses. Scribes recorded information about such matters as personnel, livestock, agricultural produce, and land ownership on clay tablets, many very small and containing information about a single item. The tablets were unbaked, evidently to be discarded at the end of the year. They were preserved only through the fires that destroyed the palace centers where they were produced. The disappearance of the script after the destruction, along with the meagerness of the finds and absence of Linear B communications in archives of other contemporary civilizations, implies a limited scribal literacy, not deeply rooted in the civilization.

ADDITIONAL RESOURCES

Chadwick, John. *The Decipherment of Linear B*. New York: Cambridge University Press, 1992.

_____. *Reading the Past: Linear B and Related Scripts*. Berkeley: University of California Press, 1997.

Miller, D. Gary. *Ancient Scripts and Phonological Knowledge*. Philadelphia: J. Benjamins, 1994.

SEE ALSO: Crete; Greece, Mycenaean; Languages and literature; Writing systems.

—*Carol G. Thomas*

LING LUN

BORN: c. 2700 B.C.E.; place unknown
DIED: c. 2600 B.C.E.; place unknown
RELATED CIVILIZATION: China
MAJOR ROLE/POSITION: Court official

Life. Ling Lun (LIHNG-lewn) is mentioned in Chinese literary tradition as an official in the court of the mythological Huangdi, the Yellow Emperor. Although the existence of either person has not been verified by archaeological evidence, the ancient Chinese classical texts include them near the very beginning of recorded history. They could be thought of as representing a period of transition from nomadic hunting-and-gathering societies to agricultural cities in Neolithic China.

According to the *Lüshi Chunqiu* (compiled third century B.C.E.; commonly known in English as *Lord Lü's Spring and Autumn*), an ancient compendium of natural philosophy, Ling Lun was ordered by Huangdi to establish the central pitch to which the nation's music would be tuned. He traveled west to a valley north of the Tibetan Himalayas and selected stalks of bamboo of equal thickness. He chose a length of 3.9 inches (9.9 centimeters), and the pitch produced by blowing into this pipe became the standard pitch. Starting with this note, he observed the singing of six male and six female phoenixes (mythical birds that symbolized the harmony of marriage) and chose the lengths of eleven other bamboo pipes, added to the first, to reflect the birds' beautiful voices. In this way, the cosmic male-female duality (yang and yin) was represented in a division of the octave into twelve parts.

Influence. When Ling Lun returned, he cast bronze bells to these pitches, and all of the ceremonial instruments were tuned to these frequencies, thus ensuring that the emperor's reign united earth and heaven and beginning a fascination with tuning that was inherited by China's future rulers.

ADDITIONAL RESOURCES

Liang, Mingyue. *Music of the Billion*. New York: Heinrichshofen, 1985.

Loewe, Michael, and Edward L. Shaughnessy, eds. *The Cambridge History of Ancient China from the Origins of Civilization to 221 B.C.E.* Cambridge, England: Cambridge University Press, 1999.

Needham, Joseph. *Science and Civilization in Ancient China*. Vol. 4. Cambridge, England: Cambridge University Press, 1962.

SEE ALSO: China; Huangdi.

—*John E. Myers*

Liu Xie

Also known as: *Wade-Giles* Liu Hsieh; Huidi
Born: c. 465 C.E.; Ju County, Shandong
Died: c. 532 C.E.; place unknown
Related civilization: China
Major role/position: Monk, critic

Life. A voracious reader from a poor family, Liu Xie (lee-EW SHEE-eh) studied Buddhism from Sengyou (445-518 C.E.) in Dinglin Temple and spent much of his early years rectifying Buddhist scriptures with his teacher. His learning was soon recognized by two influential people: Shenyue, a philologist who first theorized the Chinese tonic system and its applications in verse, and Xiaodong, prince of Emperor Wudi of Liang (502-577 C.E.). Liu Xie was assigned a privileged position enabling him to attend the imperial court and became the prince's messenger and edict draftsman. In his later years, Liu Xie chose to become a monk and adopted the Buddhist name Huidi (wisdom of the earth).

Liu Xie's magnum opus *Wenxin Diaolong* (sixth century C.E.; *The Literary Mind and the Carving of Dragons*, 1959) contained fifty essays of literary criticism divided into four parts: the source of literary inspiration (Daoism), literary genres, style, and the postlude. These essays discredit the practice of clinging obstinately to formal definitions of beauty followed by earlier writers, emphasize the unity of content and form, and propose six criteria for literary criticism.

Influence. Liu Xie's book presented a system of literary theory and criticism and showed how Daoism and Buddhism influenced literary scholarship.

ADDITIONAL RESOURCES

Cai, Zong-qi. *A Chinese Literary Mind*. Stanford, Calif.: Stanford University Press, 2000.
Liu Hsieh. *The Literary Mind and the Carving of Dragons*. Translated by Vincent Yu-chung Shih. New York: Columbia University Press, 1959.

See also: Buddhism; China; Daoism.

—*Charles Xingzhong Li*

Liu Yiqing

Also known as: *Wade-Giles* Liu I-ch'ing
Born: 403 C.E.; Xuzhou, Jiangsu, China
Died: 444 C.E.; China
Related civilization: China
Major role/position: Aristocrat, novelist

Life. A kinsman of Emperor Wendi (r. 424-453 C.E.) of Song and king of Linchuan in Jiangxi, Liu Yiqing (lee-EW YEE-ching) was an aide-de-camp to the emperor, imperial decree announcer, commander in chief, and concurrently governor of Yanzhou in Shandong, with the privilege of constructing his own mansion and appointing his own subordinates.

Historians credit Liu Yiqing with distinctive literary attainments. He liked recruiting literati, understandably so, because he was living in an age of unconventionality when orthodox Confucianism gradually yielded to Daoism. This philosophical transition was reflected in his influential novel *Shishuo Xinyu* (fifth century C.E.; new sayings of the world). Its eight volumes were divided into thirty-six chapters, including chapters on moral integrity, discourse, government affairs, and literature. This novel contained anecdotes regarding the aristocrats from the end of the Han Dynasty (220 C.E.) to the Eastern Jin Dynasty (420 C.E.), reflected on their life and thoughts, and presented satirical accounts of their lordly, luxurious, loose behaviors and the vogue of *qingtan* (idle, metaphysical discourse).

The novel was annotated with more than four hundred references by Liu Xiaobiao (462-521 C.E.), a noted writer of the Liang Dynasty (520-557 C.E.), but only some of the annotations have survived. What survived is the three-volume edition of the original work reorganized by Yanshu (991-1055 C.E.), a famous Ci poet (one who wrote poetry to certain tunes) of the Northern Song Dynasty (960-1127 C.E.).

Influence. *Shishuo Xinyu* pioneered the genre of the sketchbook, invited many later novels of its kind, and offered rare information on the ancient Chinese aristocracy.

ADDITIONAL RESOURCES
Dudbridge, Glen. *Lost Books of Medieval China*. London: British Library, 2000.

Qian, Nanxiu. *Spirit and Self in Medieval China*. Honolulu: University of Hawai'i Press, 2001.

SEE ALSO: China; Daoism; Han Dynasty; Wendi.
—*Charles Xingzhong Li*

LIVIA DRUSILLA

ALSO KNOWN AS: Julia Augusta
BORN: January 30, 58 B.C.E.; place unknown
DIED: 29 C.E.; Rome
RELATED CIVILIZATION: Imperial Rome
MAJOR ROLE/POSITION: Wife of Caesar Augustus

Life. Livia Drusilla (LIHV-ee-uh drew-SIHL-uh) was born into the prestigious Claudius and Livius Drusus families of Rome. Although married to the older Tiberius Claudius Nero, a divorce was arranged so that she could marry the upcoming triumvir Octavian (who in turn divorced Scribonia), who needed connections with the aristocracy of Rome.

Although married for fifty-two years (38 B.C.E.-14 C.E.), Augustus and Livia had no children of their own. However, the Julio-Claudian dynasty emerged through the children of Livia's first marriage, Tiberius (emperor from 14-37 C.E.) and Drusus Julius Caesar (whose son was Claudius and grandsons Caligula and Nero).

Upon the death of Augustus in 14 C.E., Livia was adopted into the Julian clan and given the title Augusta.

Extremely popular, she was depicted on coins and statues, and cities were named in her honor. She held power behind the scenes during the reign of Tiberius until her death in 29 C.E. Out of jealousy, many spread rumors against her, yet without basis.

Influence. Livia was the model of the ideal Roman woman, combining domestic and public spheres. Noted for her devotion, virtue, and simplicity of lifestyle, she was actively involved in the affairs of state.

ADDITIONAL RESOURCES
Bartman, Elizabeth. *Portraits of Livia: Imaging the Imperial Woman in Augustan Rome*. Cambridge, England: Cambridge University Press, 1999.
Purcell, N. "Livia and the Womanhood of Rome." *Proceedings of the Cambridge Philological Society,* 1986, pp. 78-105.

SEE ALSO: Augustus; Caligula; Nero; Scribonia; Tiberius.

—*Fred Strickert*

LIVIUS ANDRONICUS, LUCIUS

BORN: c. 284 B.C.E.; Tarentum
DIED: c. 204 B.C.E.; place unknown
RELATED CIVILIZATIONS: Hellenistic Greece, Republican Rome
MAJOR ROLE/POSITION: Author

Life. Lucius Livius Andronicus (lew-SHEE-uhs LIHV-ee-uhs an-druh-NI-kuhs) was a Greek who was most likely brought to Rome after the capture of Tarentum in 272 B.C.E. After being freed, he took the name of his master, Livius Salinator. Livius became a schoolteacher and translated Homer's *Odyssey* (c. 800 B.C.E.; English translation, 1616) into Latin as a textbook for his students. This was the first literary use of

Latin. In this work, he used the Saturnian meter as opposed to the Greek dactylic hexameter. He was asked to compose and act in the first Latin comedy and the first Latin tragedy for the Ludi Romani of 240 B.C.E. His plays were translations from Greek originals. In 207 B.C.E., Livius composed a hymn to drive out the evil omens during the Second Punic War (218-201 B.C.E.). Only fragments of his works remain.

Influence. Often referred to as the "father of Latin literature," Livius introduced Greek themes and forms to Latin literature. Because of his poetic successes, actors and playwrights were permitted to meet on the Aventine hill at the temple of Minerva. Livius's works were used in schools at least until Horace's time.

ADDITIONAL RESOURCES

Hadas, M. *A History of Latin Literature.* New York: Columbia University Press, 1952.

Hornblower, S., and A. Spawforth, eds. *The Oxford Classical Dictionary.* 3d ed. Oxford, England: Oxford University Press, 1996.

Warmington, E. H. *Remains of Old Latin.* Cambridge, Mass.: Harvard University Press, 1993.

SEE ALSO: Greece, Hellenistic and Roman; Homer; Rome, Republican.

—Sherwin D. Little

LIVY

ALSO KNOWN AS: Titus Livius
BORN: 59 B.C.E.; Patavium (later Padua), Italy
DIED: 17 C.E.; Patavium (later Padua), Italy
RELATED CIVILIZATION: Imperial Rome
MAJOR ROLE/POSITION: Historian

Life. A provincial free of cynicism, Livy (LIHV-ee) held a fervent, patriotic belief that virtue was the foundation of Roman greatness. This sentimental admiration for the past gained him entrance into the literary circle fostered by the emperor Augustus. In keeping with imperial ambitions, Livy worked to fashion a monumental history that was worthy of Rome's glorious achievements. The result, *Ab urbe condita libre* (c. 26 B.C.E.-15 C.E.; *The History of Rome,* 1600), contained 142 books that chronicled Roman history from 753 to 9 B.C.E. Thirty-five books survive. Books 1-10 record remembrances beginning at the legendary foundation of Rome and ending with the Third Samnite War. Books 21-45 cover the period from the Second Punic War through the wars of the early second century to 167 B.C.E. Unlike previous historians, Livy was not a man of action. He held no public position and worked largely in isolation, compiling and organizing the personali-

ties, morals, and means through which the Roman people came to be.

Influence. Livy was the greatest of the annalistic historians, perfecting the rhetorical, year-by-year chronicles that were Roman history. His early books became the prose epic of Rome, ranking him with Vergil as the creator of Roman identity. Very popular in his own time, Livy was essential reading during the Renaissance. However, his uncritical use of sources damages his reputation today.

ADDITIONAL RESOURCES

Chaplin, Jane D. *Livy's Exemplary History.* New York: Oxford University Press, 2000.

Luce, T. J. *Livy: The Composition of His History.* Princeton, N.J.: Princeton University Press, 1977.

Walsh, P. G. *Livy: His Historical Aims and Methods.* Cambridge, England: Cambridge University Press, 1961.

SEE ALSO: Languages and literature; Punic Wars; Rome, Imperial; Vergil.

—Ronald J. Weber

LOCARNO BEACH

DATE: 1500-400 B.C.E.
LOCALE: Fraser River Delta and Gulf Islands, British Columbia, Canada, and Strait of Juan de Fuca, Washington state
RELATED CIVILIZATIONS: Saint Mungo phase, Marpole phase, Northwest Coast cultures
SIGNIFICANCE: The Locarno Beach phase, marked by highly developed art, social rank, and maritime subsistence, led to the Marpole phase.

The Locarno Beach (loh-KAHR-noh) phase site in Vancouver was first excavated by archaeologist C. E. Borden

in 1949. Other sites with components of this phase have since been found. The preceding Saint Mungo phase has the beginnings of cultural complexes found in more detail in Locarno Beach. Small antler carvings showing birds, animals, humans, and mythical creatures provide a wealth of information about beliefs in spirit power and reincarnation. Miniature masks indicate transformation beliefs and the presence of masked dancers. The portrayal of ribs and backbones on these carvings suggests shamanic curing practices. Wedges made of antler, chisels of hardened bone, and adze blades of nephrite indicate woodworking and the probable manufacture of dugout canoes and plank houses. Fishing and sea mammal hunting implements, including parts for spear-throwers, are found. Social status was indicated by wearing ornamental lip plugs called labrets. Daggers made of slate suggest warfare. The succeeding Marpole phase is only slightly different.

ADDITIONAL RESOURCES

Carlson, Roy L. "Sacred Sites on the Northwest Coast of North America." In *Bog Bodies, Sacred Sites, and Wetland Archaeology*. Exeter, England: University of Exeter, 1999.

Croes, Dale R. *The Hoko River Archaeological Site Complex*. Pullman: Washington State University Press, 1995.

SEE ALSO: Marpole phase; Saint Mungo phase.

—*Roy L. Carlson*

LONGINUS

FLOURISHED: first century C.E.

RELATED CIVILIZATIONS: Roman Greece, Imperial Rome

MAJOR ROLE/POSITION: Literary critic

Life. Nothing is known with certainty about Longinus (lohn-JI-nuhs). He most likely lived in the first century C.E. and wrote *Peri Hypsous* (first century C.E.; *On the Sublime*, 1739) during the reign of Nero (r. 54-68). A substantial part of Longinus's *On the Sublime* has been lost. Still, the treatise, Platonic in its rhetoric and Aristotelian in its logic, is perhaps the finest example of literary criticism produced in antiquity. The author is writing to rebut the literary views of Caecilius of Caleacte and, by discussing a parallel set of authors, both demolishes those views and explains to those in public life how to move the souls of their hearers through language. Longinus bases his aesthetic theory on his sense of human dignity, which he places in the faculty of speech and in the human responses to grand natural phenomena—such as volcanoes and oceans—and their authentic artistic evocations.

Influence. Longinus seems to have had no influence in antiquity, as he is nowhere cited. After the translation into French by Nicolas Boileau in 1674, Longinus enjoyed a great vogue in Europe, which reached its zenith in the eighteenth century, when his terminology, insight, and viewpoint became such a part and parcel of both critics and their readers that in the nineteenth century he was simply subsumed. His influence continued to operate in this beneath-the-surface way in the twentieth century.

ADDITIONAL RESOURCES

Benediktson, D. Thomas. *Literature and the Visual Arts in Ancient Greece and Rome*. Norman: University of Oklahoma Press, 2000.

Longinus. *On the Sublime*. Translated with commentary by James A. Arieti and John M. Crosset. New York: Edwin Mellen Press, 1985.

Tate, Allen. *Longinus and the New Criticism: Essays of Four Decades*. Chicago: Swallow Press, 1968.

SEE ALSO: Greece, Hellenistic and Roman; Languages and literature; Rome, Imperial.

—*James A. Arieti*

LONGSHAN CULTURE

DATE: 5000-1900 B.C.E.

LOCALE: Northern Shandong Province and southward along the eastern seaboard to Zhejiang Province

RELATED CIVILIZATION: Neolithic China

SIGNIFICANCE: As early as the fifth millennium B.C.E. in Jiangsu Province, this culture coexisted with the Yangshao culture in the central plains region.

Evidence of the Longshan (LOHNG-shan; *Wade-Giles* Lungshan) culture was first discovered in 1931, at Chengziyai in northwest Shandong Province. It had long been mistakenly referred to as the Black Pottery culture because of the type of pottery found at the site; the Black Pottery culture is now recognized as the late phase of the Longshan culture. This culture occupies an area from part of Hebei Province across Shandong Province and southward into Zhejiang Province. It is believed to have arisen in the fifth millennium B.C.E. in northern Jiangsu Province and southern Shandong Province.

Initially the ceramics of the Longshan regions were red, evolving into gray and black ware. The vessels are burnished and sometimes incised or ridged. The vast majority have legs or stems as support. The Longshan culture introduced the fast-turning potter's wheel to the history of ceramics and discovered the technique of controlled firing.

From about 3000 B.C.E., the Longshan people were rice farmers who lived in timber houses near the water; they had domesticated the pig and water buffalo. The weather was much warmer in northern China than it be-

came in modern times, and there were alligators, elephants, and deer to hunt. Their tools and weapons were made of wood, bone, and stone.

ADDITIONAL RESOURCES

Loewe, Michael, and Edward L. Shaughnessy, eds. *The Cambridge History of Ancient China from the Origins of Civilization to 221 B.C.E.* Cambridge, England: Cambridge University Press, 1999.

Shangraw, Clarence F. *Origins of Chinese Ceramics.* New York: China Institute in America, 1978.

SEE ALSO: Black Pottery culture; China; Yangshao culture.

—*Juliana Y. Yuan*

LONGUS

FLOURISHED: second or third century C.E.
RELATED CIVILIZATION: Imperial Rome
MAJOR ROLE/POSITION: Pastoral novelist

Life. Longus (LAHNG-uhs), about whose life nothing is known, is the author of *Daphnis and Chloe* (English translation, 1916), a Greek prose work dated to the late second or early third century C.E. It belongs to a genre (*erotici graeci*) typified by stories of young lovers who endure separation, supernatural occurrences, and unexpected hardships before being reunited.

Set on the island Lesbos, the work consists of four books. The principal characters are foundlings who experience their own romantic awakenings even as they encounter numerous obstacles. The plot includes kidnapping, war, divine intervention, and romantic interludes. Longus's writing excels in lush description and a vivid natural imagery reminiscent of contemporary visual arts.

Influence. In tone and style, *Daphnis and Chloe* draws upon the pastoral poetry of Theocritus of Syracuse, while echoing numerous Greek authors such as Homer and Thucydides. Like other works of Greek

prose fiction, it is generally thought to have had a wide circulation. The work survived in manuscript form into the Renaissance, when it was first translated into French and other languages. The tale has since inspired a great number of artistic works, including Joseph-Maurice Ravel's famous ballet.

ADDITIONAL RESOURCES

Barber, G. *Daphnis and Chloe: The Markets and Metamorphoses of an Unknown Bestseller.* London: British Library, 1989.

Hunter, R. L. *A Study of "Daphnis and Chloe."* New York: Cambridge University Press, 1983.

MacQueen, B. D. *Myth, Rhetoric, and Fiction: A Reading of Longus's Daphnis and Chloe.* Lincoln: University of Nebraska Press, 1990.

Turner, P. *Daphnis and Chloe.* New York: Penguin, 1989.

SEE ALSO: Homer; Languages and literature; Rome, Imperial; Theocritus of Syracuse; Thucydides.

—*John M. McMahon*

LÜ BUWEI

ALSO KNOWN AS: *Wade-Giles* Lü Pu-wei
BORN: date and place unknown
DIED: 235 B.C.E.; Szechwan Province, China
LOCALE: China
RELATED CIVILIZATIONS: Zhou Dynasty, China
MAJOR ROLE/POSITION: Prime minister

Life. Under the hostage-exchange system prevalent during the Warring States period (475-221 B.C.E.), a prince from the state of Qin with disputed claims to the right of succession took his residency in the court of neighboring Zhao. There he was befriended by Lü Buwei (loo bew-WAY), reputed to be the richest man in

China. Lü traveled to Qin to plead on his guest's behalf. Once put on the throne, in 250 B.C.E., the grateful Qin monarch quickly installed his Zhao benefactor as his prime minister. However, the king owed Lü more than his throne: During his stay in Zhao as a prince, he had been given Lü's favorite concubine as wife. The timing of the birth of the Qin monarch's child would give rise to the speculation that he was not the child's real father. He died in 247 C.E., and the following year, the concubine's child formally succeeded to the throne at age thirteen, with Lü serving as regent and prime minister.

However, Lü was not able to hold on to his power long enough to see the full glory of his many splendid achievements in the service of Qin, as a military strategist, builder of canals, and patron of culture. Lü's reckless sexual indiscretions with his former concubine, now queen dowager, had become an intolerable embarrassment for the young monarch. In 237 C.E., Lü was stripped of his position and banished; two years later, he committed suicide, reportedly in anticipation of a death sentence from the man he had trained to be king.

Influence. Although he did not live to see the birth of China's unified empire, Lü Buwei was very much one of its architects. Though an outsider, and a merchant by background, Lü served Qin as prime minister for thirteen years during its critical period of growth and change.

ADDITIONAL RESOURCES

Needham, Joseph. *Introductory Orientations.* Vol. 1 in *Science and Civilisation in China.* Cambridge, England: Cambridge University Press, 1954.

Sima Qian. *Historical Records.* Translated by Raymond Dawson. Oxford, England: Oxford University Press, 1994.

Twitchett, Denis, and Frederick W. Mote, eds. *Cambridge History of China.* Cambridge, England: Cambridge University Press, 1998.

SEE ALSO: China; Qin Dynasty.

—Sugwon Kang

LU JI

ALSO KNOWN AS: *Wade-Giles* Lu Chi; Lu Shiheng
BORN: 261 C.E.; kingdom of Wu (Shanghai)
DIED: 303 C.E.; China
RELATED CIVILIZATION: China
MAJOR ROLE/POSITION: Prose writer, critic

Life. Lu Ji (lew JEE) was from a military family of the kingdom of Wu (222-280 C.E.). His grandfather was a founder of Wu, his father a commander, and he himself a young general. After Wu was subjugated by Western Jin (265-316 C.E.), Lu Ji turned to literary studies and in 290 C.E. relocated to Luoyang, the Jin capital, with his younger brother Lu Yun. Their literary talents created a furor, and they were soon known as the "two Lu's." There Lu Ji became an adviser to the prime minister and commander in chief of Hebei, but he was framed and executed by Sima Ying, king of Chengdu, when Lu Ji was a defeated rear general of Ying's punitive expedition against the king of Changsha.

Lu Ji's *pianwen* (rhythmical prose) was marked with rich parallelism and rhapsodic diction, as in *Diao Weiwudi Wen* (third century C.E.; in memory of Emperor Wudi of kingdom Wei) and *Bianwang Lun* (third century C.E.; on the capitulation debate). More influential was his *Wen Fu* (third century C.E.; *The Art of Letters*, 1951). Written in the *fu* form (prose interspersed with verse), this treatise discusses the methods of composing *fu* poetry, criticizes the vogue of imitation of the great masters, and encourages originality in creative writing. His original works did not survive, but *Lu Shiheng Ji* (writings of Lu Shiheng), collected by later scholars, is extant.

Influence. Lu Ji's *pianwen* enriched literary parallelism, and his *The Art of Letters* secured a place in history for early literary criticism.

ADDITIONAL RESOURCES

Hamill, Sam, trans. *The Art of Writing: Lu Chi's Wen Fu.* Minneapolis, Minn.: Milkweed, 1991.

Watson, Burton. *Early Chinese Literature.* New York: Columbia University Press, 1972.

SEE ALSO: China; Sima Xiangru; Wudi.

—Charles Xingzhong Li

LUCAN

ALSO KNOWN AS: Marcus Annaeus Lucanus
BORN: 39 C.E.; Corduba (later Córdoba), Spain
DIED: 65 C.E.; Rome
RELATED CIVILIZATION: Imperial Rome
MAJOR ROLE/POSITION: Epic poet

Life. Lucan (LEW-kan) was the grandson of Seneca the Elder and the nephew of the Stoic philosopher and tragedian Seneca the Younger. He was educated in Rome. His poetic talent was recognized early by the emperor Nero, who honored him by making him a quaestor at an early age. However, this patronage ended when Nero, who also considered himself a poet, became jealous of Lucan's poetic skill. Lucan joined the Pisonian conspiracy, which plotted to overthrow Nero. When the plot was discovered, Nero compelled Lucan to commit suicide.

Lucan's only surviving work is the *Bellum Civile* (n.d.; *The Civil Wars*, 1914). This epic poem narrates the civil wars beginning with Julius Caesar's march across the Rubicon and concluding with his stay in Alexandria (49-48 C.E.). This epic was left incomplete when Lucan committed suicide. Romans in the first century C.E. criticized Lucan's poem because it did not contain standard epic conventions such as an epic hero or the gods. His style was judged more rhetorical than poetic.

Influence. Although later Roman epic poets turned to Vergil for their inspiration, Lucan was popular in the Middle Ages and among the Romantic poets.

ADDITIONAL RESOURCES

Ahl, F. M. *Lucan: An Introduction*. Ithaca, N.Y.: Cornell University Press, 1976.

Bartsch, Shadi. *Ideology in Cold Blood: A Reading of Lucan's Civil War*. Cambridge, Mass.: Harvard University Press, 1997.

Johnson, W. R. *Momentary Monsters: Lucan and His Heroes*. Ithaca, N.Y.: Cornell University Press, 1987.

Masters, J. *Poetry and Civil War in Lucan's "Bellum Civile."* Cambridge, England: Cambridge University Press, 1992.

Morford, M. P. O. *The Poet Lucan: Studies in Rhetorical Epic*. Oxford, England: Oxford University Press, 1967.

SEE ALSO: Caesar, Julius; Nero; Rome, Imperial; Seneca the Elder; Seneca the Younger; Vergil.

—*Emily E. Batinski*

LUCIAN

BORN: c. 120 C.E.; Samosata, Syria
DIED: c. 180 C.E.; probably Egypt
RELATED CIVILIZATIONS: Roman Greece, Imperial Rome
MAJOR ROLE/POSITION: Sophist, satirist

Life. Lucian (LEW-shen) grew up in the Roman province of Syria, during the reign of the emperor Hadrian. After being apprenticed to a sculptor, he became a student of rhetoric, at which he excelled. Earning his living as a traveling speaker, he delighted audiences with his satirical dialogs and parodies of the Greek literary and philosophical tradition.

Lucian belongs to the Greek intellectual movement known as the Second Sophistic (first to third centuries

Lucian. (Library of Congress)

C.E.), whose models were the writers of Classical Athens. His writings are pervaded by cynicism, and he pokes fun at human gullibility and the pointless pursuit of wealth and power.

Eighty works survive, ranging from rhetorical exercises through a series of satirical dialogs, *Theōn dialogoi* (*Dialogues of the Gods*, 1684), to longer biographies of philosophers (*Nigrinus*) and religious charlatans (*Peregrinus*). Of particular interest are a treatise, *Pōs dei historian sungraphein* (*History as It Should Be Written*, 1684), and *Hermotimus*, which subjects Stoic philosophy to ironic scrutiny. His most celebrated work is *Alēthōn diēgēmatōn* (*A True History*, 1634), a parodic fantastic voyage to the Moon and the underworld, in which "nothing is true."

Influence. Lucian remained popular through the Renaissance, and his *A True History* became the model for the fantastic journeys of Gulliver, Baron Munchausen, and Jules Verne.

ADDITIONAL RESOURCES

Georgiadou, A., and D. H. J. Larmour. *Lucian's Science Fiction Novel: True Histories.* Leiden, Netherlands: E. J. Brill, 1998.

Jones, C. P. *Culture and Society in Lucian.* Cambridge, Mass.: Harvard University Press, 1986.

Macleod, M. D. *Lucian: A Selection.* Warminster, England: Aris & Phillips, 1991.

Marsh, D. *Lucian and the Latins.* Ann Arbor: University of Michigan Press, 1998.

SEE ALSO: Hadrian; Greece, Hellenistic and Roman; Languages and literature; Rome, Imperial; Second Sophistic.

—*David H. J. Larmour*

LUCILIUS, GAIUS (POET)

ALSO KNOWN AS: Lucilius Junior
BORN: first century C.E.; Campania, Italy
DIED: first century C.E.; place unknown
RELATED CIVILIZATION: Imperial Rome
MAJOR ROLE/POSITION: Poet, philosopher, politician

Life. This Gaius Lucilius (GAY-uhs loo-SIHL-ee-uhs), not to be confused with the satirist Gaius Lucilius (first century B.C.E.), is best known as the friend of Seneca the Younger. Because of his literary talent, political skill, and carefully cultivated friendships with prominent Romans, he rose from obscurity to knight of Rome (*eques Romanus*). He showed courage and won honor by remaining loyal to the memory of Gnaeus Cornelius Lentulus Gaetulicus, who was executed by Caligula. He held several procuratorships (provincial administrative positions) under the reigns of Claudius and Nero.

The Stoic Seneca addressed *Quaestiones naturales* (c. 62-64; *Natural Questions*, 1614), *Ad Lucilium epistulae morales* (pb. 1917-1925; moral epistles), and *De providentia* (c. 63-64; *On Providence*, 1614) to Lucilius, whose own philosophical leanings are unclear. He was certainly an Epicurean as a young man, as Seneca frequently based expositions of Stoicism on his questions or promptings. He may have converted to Stoicism later. He wrote much in both prose and poetry, but except for a few lines of verse quoted by Seneca, none of his works survives.

Influence. Directly, Lucilius influenced only Seneca, but since Seneca's own influence in philosophy and drama remains considerable into the twenty-first century, it can be said that, through Seneca, the influence of Lucilius remains considerable.

ADDITIONAL RESOURCES

Griffin, Miriam T. *Seneca: A Philosopher in Politics.* Oxford, England: Clarendon, 1976.

Sørensen, Villy. *Seneca: The Humanist at the Court of Nero.* Chicago: University of Chicago Press, 1984.

SEE ALSO: Caligula; Claudius; Nero; Rome, Imperial; Seneca the Younger.

—*Eric v.d. Luft*

LUCILIUS, GAIUS (SATIRIST)

ALSO KNOWN AS: Lucilius
BORN: c. 180 B.C.E.; Suessa Aurunca, Campania, Italy
DIED: c. 102 B.C.E.; Neapolis (now Naples), Italy
RELATED CIVILIZATION: Republican Rome
MAJOR ROLE/POSITION: Roman satirist

Life. Gaius Lucilius (GAY-uhs loo-SIHL-ee-uhs) was a member of a prominent family, which included a brother who was a senator and a sister who was the grandmother of Pompey the Great. Lucilius himself was a landowner who never sought political office. He served under Scipio Aemilianus during the siege of Numantia in 134-133 B.C.E. and started publishing in 131 B.C.E. He became a member of Scipio Aemilianus's literary circle. His works were published in three separate collections (c. 125, c. 120, and c. 108 B.C.E., only fragments remain) that were later collected into one group. His satires were often autobiographical, with topics such as his own life and friends, travel, and public and private morality. He was outspoken and critical, mentioning enemies by name.

Influence. Considered the founder of satire, a purely Roman form of literature, Lucilius established dactylic hexameter as the standard meter for Latin satire. He was a great influence on later Latin satirists, especially Horace, whose Satire I.5, journey to Brundisium, in *Satires* (35 B.C.E., 30 B.C.E.; English translation, 1567), is based on one of Lucilius's satires (Book 3). Horace is critical of Lucilius's use of coarse language, sounding like Old Comedy. The later satirists, Juvenal and Aulus Persius Flaccus, considered him the creator of the genre.

ADDITIONAL RESOURCES
Gruen, Erich S. *Culture and National Identity in Republican Rome.* Ithaca, N.Y.: Cornell University Press, 1994.
Hadas, M. *A History of Latin Literature.* New York: Columbia University Press, 1952.
Hornblower, S., and A. Spawforth, eds. *The Oxford Classical Dictionary.* 3d ed. Oxford, England: Oxford University Press, 1996.

SEE ALSO: Horace; Juvenal; Rome, Republican; Scipio Aemilianus.

—*Sherwin D. Little*

LUCRETIA

BORN: sixth century B.C.E.; place unknown
DIED: c. 509 B.C.E.; Collatia
RELATED CIVILIZATION: Prerepublican Rome
MAJOR ROLE/POSITION: Wife, legendary role model

Life. According to the Roman historian Livy, during an argument among Roman nobles, Lucius Tarquinius Collatinus challenged his companions to surprise their wives and discover whose was best. Although they found the other wives socializing, they found Collatinus's wife, Lucretia (loo-KREE-sha), spinning wool. All hailed Lucretia's obvious excellence, but one, Sextus Tarquinius (the son of King Lucius Tarquinius Superbus), was overcome with lust for her. Sextus secretly returned a few days later, and Lucretia welcomed him because he was her husband's kinsman. That night, he tried to seduce Lucretia and threatened her with death if she rejected him. When that failed, he threatened to place a dead slave in her bed next to her body and say that he caught them together. At this, Lucretia submitted, but after Sextus left, she sent for her father and husband. When they arrived, Lucretia told them that Sextus had raped her and demanded that they avenge her. She then declared she must die to prevent any woman from pretending to have been attacked and living immorally. Her words, actions, and suicide spurred Lucius Junius Brutus, a friend who accompanied Collatinus, to call for the expulsion of the king and an end to the monarchy in Rome.

Influence. Throughout Roman history and into the Renaissance, Lucretia represented wifely virtue for her devotion to the home and her determination to control her reputation even after her death.

ADDITIONAL RESOURCES
Donaldson, I. *The Rapes of Lucretia.* Oxford, England: Oxford University Press, 1978.
Livy. *The Rise of Rome.* Translated by T. J. Luce. Oxford, England: Oxford University Press, 1999.

SEE ALSO: Junius Brutus, Lucius; Livy; Rome, Prerepublican.

—*T. Davina McClain*

LUCRETIUS

ALSO KNOWN AS: Titus Lucretius Carus
BORN: c. 98 B.C.E.; probably Rome
DIED: October 15, 55 B.C.E.; Rome
RELATED CIVILIZATION: Republican Rome
MAJOR ROLE/POSITION: Poet, philosopher

Life. Almost nothing is known about Lucretius (loo-KREE-shuhs). What little is known is contradictory and largely mythical, apart from the fact that he was a Roman poet who composed in epic Latin verse the monumental poem *De rerum natura* (c. 60 B.C.E.; *On the Nature of Things*, 1682). This explained the entire philosophical system of Epicurus, whom Lucretius praises as a savior rescuing humankind from superstition and fear, especially fear of death and divine anger. Cicero praised the poem, which still survives, as a work of art and genius.

Influence. *On the Nature of Things* is the most important and extensive treatise on Epicurean philosophy to survive, thanks largely to the brilliant poetic talent of Lucretius. It had a significant impact in the ancient world (particularly on Vergil) both as poetry and as phi-losophy. Rediscovered in 1417, it had an enormous influence on Renaissance rationalism and the scientific revolution. Among other things, it gave the idea of the social contract to English philosopher Thomas Hobbes and French philosopher Jean-Jacques Rousseau and of atomism to French scientist and philosopher Pierre Gassendi and British scientist Robert Boyle.

ADDITIONAL RESOURCES
Clay, D. *Lucretius and Epicurus*. Ithaca, N.Y.: Cornell University Press, 1983.
Hadzits, G. *Lucretius and His Influence*. New York: Cooper Square, 1963.
Minyard, D. *Lucretius and the Late Republic*. Leiden, Netherlands: E. J. Brill, 1985.
Sedley, D. *Lucretius and the Transformation of Greek Wisdom*. New York: Cambridge, 1998.
West, D. *The Imagery and Poetry of Lucretius*. Norman: University of Oklahoma Press, 1994.

SEE ALSO: Epicurus; Rome, Republican; Vergil.
—*Richard C. Carrier*

LUWIANS

DATE: c. 1400-700 B.C.E.
LOCALE: Anatolia and Syria
SIGNIFICANCE: The Luwians represent the diffusion of Hittite culture throughout Anatolia and form a possible bridge to later civilizations.

The Luwians were a people closely related to the Hittites and, like them, spoke a language now classified as Indo-European. Their identity is largely linguistic rather than political; many examples of the Luwian language, written in hieroglyphic script, survive. The Luwians are primarily associated with the western area of Anatolia (often termed Arzawa in Hittite sources) closest to the Aegean Sea but are also known to have spread across southern Anatolia and even into Syria in the centuries following the collapse of the Hittite state. This raises the question of whether the Luwians were indeed ethnically separate from the Hittites or were Hittites who survived independently of the state apparatus at Hattusas. Arzawa and other Luwian principalities were under the sway of the Hittite realm from about 1400 to 1250 B.C.E. but otherwise were semi-independent. The Arzawa Luwians may have influenced the emerging civilizations of the Lydians and Phrygians and, much more certainly, the Anatolian culture of Lycia. Due to their geographical closeness to the Greek-speaking world, the Luwians are prominent in speculations attempting to link the Hittite world to the Trojan War and the world of the Homeric epics.

ADDITIONAL RESOURCES
Bryce, Trevor. *The Kingdom of the Hittites*. New York: Oxford University Press, 1998.
Gurney, O. R. *The Hittites*. New York: Penguin Books, 1990.
Wood, Michael. *In Search of the Trojan War*. Berkeley: University of California Press, 1998.

SEE ALSO: Hittites; Homer; Lycia; Lydia; Phrygia; Troy.
—*Nicholas Birns*

LYCIA

DATE: 1200 B.C.E.-700 C.E.
LOCALE: On the southwestern coast of modern Turkey in ancient Asia Minor
RELATED CIVILIZATIONS: Lukka, Lycia, Classical and Hellenistic Greece, Rome
SIGNIFICANCE: Important seafaring group that provided trade goods for ancients traveling between Egypt, the Levant, and Greece.

Greek tradition suggests that Lycia (LIH-shya) derives its name from a Greek source. Historian Herodotus reports that the people of the region took their name from Lycus, who fled to the region from Athens. Mythographer Antonius Liberalis and poet Ovid relate that the goddess Leto named the region Lycia, or "Wolf Land," after the wolves that guided her to water when she needed to wash her newly born children. The region more likely takes its name from the Lukka, who immigrated to the area during the Late Bronze Age. Greeks accepted this name as that of the indigenous people at least as early as the composition of Homer's *Iliad* (c. 800 B.C.E.; English translation, 1616), which describes the Lycians as Trojan allies.

Lycia's rugged geography never supported a large population, but the steep mountains and narrow valleys had large forests and fertile fields. Towns in the interior based their economy on agriculture; coastal towns relied on sea trade. Because of the emphasis on seafaring and trade, the largest Lycian cities grew up on the coast or along major rivers. Throughout its history, Lycia exported timber, chalk, wine, fruit, grain, fish, dye, and goats' hair for rope making.

The early period. Egyptian records mention Lukkans as a Hittite ally in the conflict between Rameses II and the Hittites in the thirteenth century B.C.E. It is likely that the Lukkans are the Lukki sea raiders who plundered Cyprus and Egypt at this time. They also are listed in the group of the Sea Peoples who raided Egypt during Pharaoh Merneptah's reign (c. 1208 B.C.E.).

Herodotus presents the first documented history of Lycia. In the mid-sixth century B.C.E., the Achaemenian Persian general Harpagus won the surrender of all major Lycian cities. The Persians imposed economic and political order on the Lycians, required an annual tribute payment, and encouraged the development of a Lycian dynasty in the main city of Xanthus. This dynasty extended its power throughout western and central Lycia until the early fourth century B.C.E.

The Lycians sided with the Persian king Xerxes I against the Greeks in the early fifth century B.C.E. After the Greek victory in 479 B.C.E., the Lycians declared peace with Athens but had only a nominal presence in its Delian League. In 430 B.C.E., Athens sent a general, Melesandros, to Lycia, supposedly to recover annual tribute for the league. A more plausible reason for this visit to Lycia was to secure the coast for Athenian naval forces and ships bringing Egyptian grain to Athens during the Peloponnesian War.

Historian Arrian relates that Alexander the Great secured Lycia in 334-333 B.C.E. in order to deny naval bases to the Persians. After this, Greek settlers migrated to Lycia with increasing frequency and quickly Hellenized the region. The greatest remains of the Lycian culture are rock-cut tombs with temple and house facades (c. late fifth to fourth centuries B.C.E.). Many of these bear inscriptions in Lycian, but by the end of the fourth century B.C.E., the Lycian language had ceased to exist in a written form. Good examples of Lycian tombs survive at Myra, on Lycia's southeastern coast.

After Alexander's death in 323 B.C.E., Lycia passed back and forth between competing Hellenistic powers until the end of the third century B.C.E., when the Seleucid ruler Antiochus the Great seized Lycia. The Lycians sided with Antiochus in the ensuing war with Rome and its allies. When the Romans defeated Antiochus, they gave Rhodes control of Lycia.

The Roman period. In 167 B.C.E., the Romans declared Lycia independent. The Lycian League, formed sometime in the third century B.C.E. but unable to exercise power, governed Lycia during its time of independence. Delegates from the region's major cities formed an assembly that made decisions about war, foreign policy, and taxes; conferred honors on individuals; and settled disputes between individuals and member cities.

In 43 C.E., the Roman emperor Claudius annexed Lycia as a province. Now a part of the Roman Empire, Lycia ceased to have a role in foreign affairs. The Lycian League declined in power and became a mere intermediary between Lycian cities and Rome. By the second century C.E., Lycia was heavily Romanized, with a developed provincial nobility and emperor cult, Roman structures such as baths, and Roman entertainments such as gladiatorial combats and wild beast hunts.

Christianity began to take hold in Lycia as early as the second century C.E. Many Lycian towns supported more than one church, and the fifth century saw the establishment of monasteries throughout the region. Saint Nicholas, bishop of Myra in the fourth century, is well known for his dispersal of gifts to the needy. He is also patron saint of children, thereby earning him the nickname "Father Christmas."

During the Roman period, Lycia continued to provide anchorages and trade goods to merchants and sea travelers. The political and economic turbulence of the third century C.E. negatively affected Lycia's prosperity. With the return of peace in the fourth century, however, Lycia rapidly recovered. The region maintained a position of security until the breakout of bubonic plague in 541 C.E.

During the seventh century, the Byzantine Empire established naval bases on the Lycian coast to defend against attacking Arab forces. In 655 C.E., the Arabs crushed the Byzantine navy off Lycia's eastern coast. The Byzantines briefly regained control of the region in the ninth century but eventually lost it to the Turks.

ADDITIONAL RESOURCES

Bryce, T. R. *The Lycians in Literary and Epigraphic Sources.* Copenhagen: Museum Tusculanum Press, 1986.

Foss, Clive. "Lycia in History." In *The Fort at Dereagzi and Other Material Remains in Its Vicinity: From Antiquity to the Middle Ages*, edited by James Morganstern. Tübingen, Germany: Ernst Wasmuth, 1993.

Jones, A. H. M. "Lycia." In *The Cities of the Eastern Roman Provinces.* Oxford, England: Clarendon Press, 1937.

Keen, Antony G. *Dynastic Lycia.* Leiden, Netherlands: Brill, 1998.

Magie, David. "Lycia: Federation and Province." *Roman Rule in Asia Minor.* Princeton, N.J.: Princeton University Press, 1950.

SEE ALSO: Alexander the Great; Antiochus the Great; Athens; Byzantine Empire; Greece, Classical; Greece, Hellenistic; Herodotus; Homer; Rome, Imperial; Xerxes I.

—*Mary G. Tindle*

LYCURGUS OF SPARTA

FLOURISHED: probably between the ninth and seventh centuries B.C.E.
RELATED CIVILIZATIONS: Dorian Crete, Sparta, Archaic Greece
MAJOR ROLE/POSITION: Statesman

Life. Lycurgus (li-KUR-guhs) of Sparta is traditionally credited with all the Spartan institutions of political stability and military success. The Spartans built a shrine for him when he died.

Lycurgus's *eunomia* ("good order") was probably not the work of a single person but rather an accretion. It was both precursor and aftermath to the Spartan enslavement of Messenia. According to the Spartan junior royal house of the Eurypontids, the Spartans began experiencing success in wars with Eurypontid king Charillos' Eurotas River Valley conquest in the first Olympiad of 776 B.C.E. and Eurypontid king Theopompus's victory in Messenia because of new brigading and army discipline. Lycurgus's *eunomia* came from the *eunomus* ("good law") of the previous generation's Eurypontid king, with Lycurgus acting as a notable Spartan Delphi-consultant.

However, the senior royal house of Agiads made Lycurgus one of their own and enshrined him as the

Lycurgus of Sparta. (North Wind Picture Archives)

guardian of underage king Leobotes. Lycurgus brought Cretan military and political institutions to Sparta and had responsibility for all Spartan law.

Influence. A great statesman, Lycurgus brokered a great social contract so practical that all subsequent Spartan peculiarities were attributed to him. Ionian proto-historians working on Spartan king lists and chronology could not reconcile two conflicting family traditions, each of which took credit for him. Later historians could not reconcile either one with real life.

ADDITIONAL RESOURCES

Forrest, W. G. *A History of Sparta*. London: Bristol Classics, 1995.

Murray, Oswyn. *Early Greece*. London: Fontana Press, 1980.

SEE ALSO: Greece, Archaic.

—*O. Kimball Armayor*

LYDIA

DATE: 700-500 B.C.E.
LOCALE: Western Asia Minor
RELATED CIVILIZATION: Archaic Greece
SIGNIFICANCE: For a time, this non-Greek kingdom dominated Asia Minor through its military power and location on the trade routes between the Aegean coast and the Anatolian interior.

The kingdom of Lydia spread east from the Aegean Sea to the Hermus (Gediz) and Caÿster River Valleys in western Asia Minor (Anatolia). Its neighbors to the north, east, and south were Mysia, Phrygia, and Caria, respectively. Lydia was noted for the gold and silver deposits found in its rivers and its location on the trade routes between the coastal cities of Smyrna and Ephesus and the interior of Anatolia. Lydia's civilization was shaped by Greek, Anatolian, and Persian cultures.

Lydia rose to power under the Mermnad, a family of rulers who reigned from the mid-600's to 550 B.C.E. Their founder was Gyges, who ruled from about 640 to about 645 B.C.E. The kingdom reached its peak during the reign of Alyattes, who extended his rule into Ionia. Alyattes' son, King Croesus (r. c. 550-546 B.C.E.) was to be the last Mermnad ruler. Croesus brought the Greek coastal cities (such as Miletus) under his control but maintained friendly relations with them by forming alliances with them. Croesus used his vast wealth to rebuild shrines at Ephesus and made pilgrimages to the famous Greek shrine at Delphi. At his royal capital of Sardis, Croesus impressed visitors with his hospitality and wealth. "To be as rich as Croesus" became a popular phrase in myth.

Croesus's wealth was based on the electrum deposits found in the rivers that flowed through Lydia. Electrum is a natural alloy of gold and silver and can also contain copper, iron, and other metals. Around 635 B.C.E., the Lydians began to mint coins—they were the first people to do so—and used them in their trade with other peoples. Lydian coins, with their distinctive lion-bull image, became famous throughout the Greek world, and their invention was soon copied by Greek cities. The Lydians were a commercial people who traded with peoples on the coast and the interior. They were the first people to establish permanent retail shops in Sardis.

Militarily, the Lydians possessed a formidable cavalry and had knowledge of siege techniques. Both enabled them to hold sway over lesser powers. In addition, Sardis was a well-fortified city. Despite these advantages, the Lydians were unable to resist the might of the Persian Empire and its ruler, Cyrus the Great. The Persians swept over the Lydian kingdom in 546 B.C.E., occupied its capital of Sardis, and overthrew Croesus. The Lydian king had allied himself with Egypt and Syria in anticipation of a Persian advance. Sparta also promised military aid. However, Croesus's plans were futile. According to historian Herodotus, the defeated Lydian king threw himself on a funeral pyre. The Persians eventually made Lydia an outpost of their empire. Although Lydia never regained its independence, the Lydians managed nevertheless to maintain their cultural identity. The Lydians spoke an Indo-European language, had an alphabet, and invented the so-called Lydian mode in music.

Persian dominance over Lydia ended with the arrival of Alexander the Great. Alexander swept into Lydia in 334 B.C.E. en route to his conquest of the Persian Empire and Asia. After Alexander's death, Lydia became a province of the Seleucid Empire (from 280 B.C.E.), with Sardis as a royal capital. For a brief period, Lydia was absorbed by the kingdom of Pergamum. In 189 B.C.E., following the Roman defeat of the Seleucid ruler Antiochus the Great at the Battle of Magnesia ad Sipylum,

Lydia became part of the Roman Empire. It was part of the Roman province of Asia until Emperor Diocletian (r. 284-305 C.E.) made it a separate province. In early Christian times, Sardis was one of the seven churches in Asia.

ADDITIONAL RESOURCES

Akurgal, Ekrem. *Ancient Civilizations and Ruins of Turkey.* Istanbul: Haset Kitabevi, 1985.

Bean, George. *Aegean Turkey.* New York: F. A. Praeger, 1966.

Freely, John. *The Aegean Coast of Turkey.* Istanbul: Redhouse Press, 1996.

Hanfmann, G. M. A. *Sardis from Prehistoric to Roman Times.* Cambridge, Mass.: Harvard University Press, 1983.

Pedley, John Griffiths. *Sardis in the Age of Croesus.* Norman: University of Oklahoma Press, 1968.

Seton, Lloyd. *Ancient Turkey.* Berkeley: University of California Press, 1989.

SEE ALSO: Alexander the Great; Antiochus the Great; Croesus; Cyrus the Great; Diocletian; Greece, Archaic; Gyges; Herodotus; Persia; Rome, Imperial; Seleucid Dynasty.

—*Adriane Ruggiero*

LYSANDER OF SPARTA

BORN: late fifth century B.C.E.; place unknown
DIED: 395 B.C.E.; Haliartus, Boeotia
RELATED CIVILIZATIONS: Persia, Athens, Sparta
MAJOR ROLE/POSITION: Soldier and statesman

Lysander of Sparta. (Hulton Archive)

Life. A friend of Agesilaus II of Sparta from the junior royal family, Lysander (li-SAN-dur) of Sparta won the Battle of Notion in 407 B.C.E. with the support of Persian Cyrus the Younger, resulting in Alcibiades' second exile from Athens. Then he built an international oligarchy, subverted his successor Callicratidas, who was lost and drowned off the Arginusae Islands in 406 B.C.E., and aimed at the whole Aegean.

In 405 B.C.E., Lysander, supported by Cyrus the Younger's wealth, destroyed the Athenian navy at Aegospotami in the Hellespont, starved Athens into submission, and installed Spartan commandants (*harmosts*) and ten-man oligarchies (*decarchies*) everywhere he could.

In spring, 404 B.C.E., Lysander as *harmost* established the Thirty Tyrants and ruled Athens until king Pausanias of the senior royal family recalled him in 403 B.C.E., restored Athenian democracy, and changed Lysander's hated governance elsewhere.

In 401 B.C.E., Lysander supported Cyrus the Younger's revolt against Artaxerxes II until Cyrus was killed at Cynaxa. He then made Agesilaus king, to lead another war against Artaxerxes II in 396 B.C.E. Agesilaus despatched him to the Hellespont to counsel another Persian revolt and then back to Sparta to attack Persia's ally Thebes. He was killed in 395 B.C.E. trying to coordinate with Pausanias, who was exiled for bad faith and bad timing.

Influence. Lysander won the Peloponnesian War (431-404 B.C.E.) and tried to build an elective Spartan monarchy and a maritime empire governed by his friends.

ADDITIONAL RESOURCES
Forrest, W. G. *A History of Sparta*. London: Bristol Classics, 1995.
Rood, Tim. *Thucydides*. New York: Clarendon Press, 1998.

SEE ALSO: Aegospotami, Battle of; Agesilaus II of Sparta; Alcibiades of Athens; Athens; Pausanias of Sparta; Peloponnesian Wars; Persia; Thirty Tyrants.

—*O. Kimball Armayor*

LYSIAS

BORN: c. 445 B.C.E.; Athens, Greece
DIED: c. 380 B.C.E.; Athens, Greece
RELATED CIVILIZATIONS: Athens, Syracuse, Classical Greece
MAJOR ROLE/POSITION: Speechwriter

Life. Pericles persuaded Cephalus, the father of Lysias (LIHS-ee-as), to leave his home in Syracuse and settle in Athens, where Lysias was born. At the age of fifteen, Lysias joined the Athenian colony of Thurii. During his stay in Italy, he reportedly learned oratory from the Syracusan Teisias, who was one of the first to expound theories on the art of rhetoric. After anti-Athenian disturbances in Thurii, Lysias returned to Athens and helped manage his family's shield factory.

In 404 B.C.E., the Thirty Tyrants seized control of Athens. They arrested Lysias along with his brother Polemarchus and seized their property. Polemarchus was executed, but Lysias escaped and furnished the democratic exiles with mercenaries, weapons, and money. After the restoration of the Athenian democ-racy in 403 B.C.E., a motion to grant Lysias citizenship failed, and he lived the rest of his life as a resident alien, supporting himself by writing speeches for others to deliver in court and before the assembly.

Influence. A corpus of thirty-five speeches attributed to Lysias survives, displaying the simple Attic style of everyday language, for which he is famous and which Julius Caesar adopted. From a speech on the murder of an adulterer to one in which Lysias recounts the plight of his family, his work gives us a unique glimpse into Athens after the Peloponnesian War.

ADDITIONAL RESOURCES
Todd, S. C., trans. *Lysias*. Austin: University of Texas Press, 2000.
Usher, S. *Greek Oratory: Tradition and Originality*. New York: Oxford University Press, 1999.

SEE ALSO: Athens; Greece, Classical; Thirty Tyrants.

—*Andrew Wolpert*

LYSIMACHUS

BORN: c. 361 B.C.E.; Pella, Macedonia
DIED: 281 B.C.E.; Corupedium, Lydia, Asia Minor
RELATED CIVILIZATION: Hellenistic Greece
MAJOR ROLE/POSITION: King

Life. Lysimachus (li-SIHM-uh-kuhs) was one of Alexander the Great's generals, and after Alexander's death he was allotted Thrace and probably the western shore of the Black Sea. Having defeated the local tyrant Seuthes (322 B.C.E.), put down the resistance of Thracian cities (313 B.C.E.), and founded Lysimacheia (309 B.C.E.), in 305 B.C.E., he assumed the royal title. Fearful of Demetrius Poliorcetes' successes in Greece, Lysimachus, after forging an alliance with Cassander and Seleucus I, invaded Anatolia, which was controlled by Demetrius's father, Antigonus I Monophthalmos. In the ensuing Battle of Ipsus (301 B.C.E.), Lysimachus and Seleucus defeated Antigonus and Demetrius.

After taking over all western Anatolia north of the Taurus Mountains, Lysimachus married Ptolemy I Soter's daughter, Arsinoë. By 285 B.C.E., Lysimachus occupied Macedonia and Thessaly. His realm stretched from Epirus to the Taurus. At the instigation of Arsinoë, he killed Agathocles (283 B.C.E.), his son from a previous marriage and the heir-apparent. This murder alienated his followers, who welcomed the intrusion of Seleucus, during which Lysimachus was defeated and killed in the Battle at Corupedium (281 B.C.E.). His Asian realm went to the Seleucids, and his European possessions slipped into anarchy.

Influence. Lysimachus's life exemplifies the period of the Diadochi, when an empire could be built and lost in a lifetime with the help of personal ability and luck. His rule, often considered rapacious, is unlikely to have differed from those of other Diadochi.

ADDITIONAL RESOURCES

Lund, Helen S. *Lysimachus: A Study in Early Hellenistic Kingship*. New York: Routledge, 1992.

Müller, Ludvig. *Lysimachus, King of Thrace*. New York: F. S. Knobloch, 1966.

SEE ALSO: Alexander the Great; Cassander; Demetrius Poliorcetes; Diadochi; Greece, Hellenistic and Roman; Ptolemaic Dynasty; Seleucid Dynasty; Seleucus I.

　　　　　　　　　　　　　　　—*Sviatoslav Dmitriev*

LYSIPPUS

ALSO KNOWN AS: Lysippos
BORN: c. 390 B.C.E.; Sicyon, Greece
DIED: c. 300 B.C.E.; place unknown
RELATED CIVILIZATION: Classical Greece
MAJOR ROLE/POSITION: Sculptor

Life. Credited with being the greatest sculptor of the Sicyon artistic school, Lysippus (li-SIHP-uhs) had a prolific career. Beginning as a bronzesmith, he probably concentrated in that medium. Inscribed statue bases and ancient literary references define his range: deities, athletes, heroes, and animals. His skill of truth in portraiture led Alexander the Great to appoint Lysippus as his court sculptor.

Despite the exceptional quality and number of his works, no originals remain, although some attributions have been suggested from Roman copies. Perhaps his most famous statue was a youth scraping himself, associated with the *Apoxyomenos* (*Body-Scraper*) in the Vatican Museum. A marble statue of the athlete Agias in Delphi may be a contemporary copy of a Lysippan bronze from Pharsalus. Other famous works included many of Heracles, who in one rested after his labors and in another imbibed wine as a tabletop decoration. His celebrated allegorical statue *Kairos* (*Opportunity*) showed the youth as elusive and ephemeral.

Influence. Lysippus formed a large workshop whose students probably carried on his preference for sculpting the human form not as it existed but as it appeared to the eye, resulting in a small head, long legs, and a slim body. His finesse in fine detail, imparting greater naturalism to his figures, was well known.

ADDITIONAL RESOURCES

Edwards, C. "Lysippos." In *Personal Styles in Greek Sculpture*, edited by O. Palagia and J. J. Pollitt. Cambridge, England: Cambridge University Press, 1996.

Johnson, F. P. *Lysippos*. Durham, N.C.: Duke University Press, 1927.

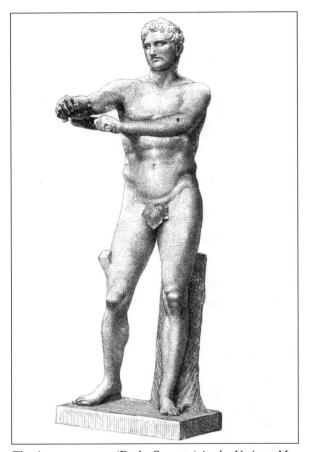

The Apoxyomenos (Body-Scraper) *in the Vatican Museum is a reproduction of one of Lysippus's works.* (North Wind Picture Archives)

Stewart, A. *Greek Sculpture*. New Haven, Conn.: Yale University Press, 1990.

SEE ALSO: Alexander the Great; Art and architecture; Greece, Classical.

　　　　　　　　　　　　　　　—*Nancy Serwint*

— M —

MACCABEES

DATE: c. 168-c. 100 B.C.E.
LOCALE: Palestine
RELATED CIVILIZATION: Israel
SIGNIFICANCE: The Maccabees recaptured Jerusalem from the Seleucids and ruled Judaea as an independent territory until the end of the second century B.C.E.

The name Maccabee (MAC-ah-bee), Hebrew for "hammer," was bestowed upon Judas, the third son of a Jewish Hasmonaean family, and subsequently upon his father Mattathias and four brothers John, Simon, Eleazar, and Jonathan. Judas successfully united Jewish rebels in a revolt begun by Mattathias in 168 B.C.E. against Antiochus IV Epiphanes, the Hellenistic Seleucid ruler who had abolished Jewish religious practice and converted the temple in Jerusalem for pagan worship. After being driven to the hills, Judas led Jewish armies against Antiochus until they had recaptured Jerusalem and reinstated traditional worship in the temple, the event celebrated during Hanukkah.

Judas assumed the role of religious, political, and military leader and made efforts to recapture Jewish territory until his death in 160 B.C.E. His brother Jonathan was subsequently named high priest, although he was not the correct hereditary candidate, and continued solidification of the Judaean state. Simon ascended in 142 B.C.E. and established Judaea as an independent territory. After Simon's assassination in 134 B.C.E., his son John Hyrcanus came to power and ruled until 104 B.C.E. Although Judaea was conquered by Rome later in the first century B.C.E., the Maccabees guaranteed the survival of Jewish culture and religion, which had faced extinction before the revolt.

ADDITIONAL RESOURCES

Bickerman, Elias. *The Maccabees: An Account of Their History from the Beginnings to the Fall of the House of the Hasmoneans.* New York: Shocken Books, 1947.
Cohen, Shaye. *From the Maccabees to the Mishnah.* Philadelphia: Westminster John Knox Press, 1995.

SEE ALSO: Jerusalem, temple of; Judaism; Rome, Imperial; Seleucid Dynasty.

—*John Grady Powell*

MACEDONIA

DATE: 700 B.C.E.-700 C.E.
LOCALE: Greek peninsula
SIGNIFICANCE: Ancient kingdom in the northeast corner of the Greek peninsula that established control over Greece in the fourth century B.C.E. and conquered an Asian empire extending from Egypt to India.

The origins and language of the Macedonian people are obscure. The ruling dynasty claimed to be Greek, professing descent from mythical Heracles through the royal house of Argos. Scholars heatedly debate whether Macedonians were distant relatives of the Greek people, speaking a distinctive dialect, or were of unrelated stock.

History. The first king of Macedonia, Perdiccas I (c. 650 B.C.E.), led a tribe of shepherds calling themselves Macedonians from the mountainous territory around Pieria and Olympus to the fertile plain below. Little is known concerning Macedonia's first five kings. The sixth king, Amyntas I (d. 498? B.C.E.), resisted attempts by the expanding Persian Empire to control Macedonia. His son, Alexander I (r. 497?-c. 454 B.C.E.), was forced to submit and become a Persian vassal; however, he secretly aided the Greek defense against Persian forces.

Macedonia in the fifth century B.C.E. was weak and unable to oppose the major Greek powers effectively. When Athens expanded its empire to the northern coast

Macedonian leader Philip II is assassinated. (North Wind Picture Archives)

of the Aegean, Macedonia offered little resistance until the reign of Perdiccas II (r. c. 450-c. 413 B.C.E.). Perdiccas alternated between inciting rebellions in Athenian client cities and allying with Athens against his own Balkan enemies. King Archelaus (r. c. 413-399 B.C.E.) yearned for Greek approval. Although he invited leading Greek artists to his capital Pella—where the playwright Euripides spent his last years—and aided Athens after its defeat in the Peloponnesian War (431-404 B.C.E.), Athenians considered Archelaus a shifty, untrustworthy barbarian.

Under Philip II (r. 359-336 B.C.E.), Macedonia became the greatest power in the Greek peninsula. He reorganized his army, providing new weapons and drilling his men in the use of the phalanx formation. No army could stand against Philip; he conquered his Balkan neighbors as far north as the Danube River and es-tablished control of the Greek city-states by defeating the combined might of Athens and Thebes at the Battle of Chaeronea in 338 B.C.E. Philip's power and wealth attracted historians, philosophers, writers, and artists to his capital, and Pella rivaled Athens as a center of Greek culture.

After Philip's assassination, his son Alexander the Great (r. 336-323 B.C.E.) carried out the invasion of Asia that Philip had planned. The Macedonian army thoroughly defeated the Persian forces, and Alexander conquered an empire stretching from the Libyan Desert in the west to the banks of the Indus River in the east. After Alexander's death, his generals divided the empire into rival Hellenistic kingdoms and contended with each other for supremacy.

Although frequently challenged by federations and leagues of Greek city-states, Macedonia remained the dominant power in Greece. In 280 and 279 B.C.E., successive invasions by large numbers of Gauls nearly destroyed the Macedonian army and devastated the countryside. Bringing an army from Asia Minor in 277 B.C.E., Antigonus II Gonatas defeated a band of Gauls. He became king and founded the Antigonid Dynasty, which ruled until the Roman conquest of Macedonia.

Macedonian kings opposed Roman expansion into the Balkans and supported Carthage during the Punic Wars (264-146 B.C.E.), thereby winning the enmity of Rome. After defeating the Macedonian army in 167 B.C.E., Rome abolished the monarchy and partitioned the country into four client republics. In 146 B.C.E., Rome turned Macedonia into a Roman province.

When the Roman Empire divided in 395 C.E., Macedonia lay within the eastern half, which became the Byzantine Empire. By then, most of the population had converted to Christianity. In the sixth and seventh centuries C.E., Slavic peoples, speaking a dialect related to Bulgarian, invaded Macedonia and displaced many of the Greek-speaking inhabitants.

War and weapons. Macedonia was at war, or under the threat of war, throughout its history. All kings maintained a standing army, and the country lived on an almost permanent war footing. Philip II armed his men with 16-foot (5-meter) pikes, counterweighted at their butt ends so that they balanced with 12 feet (4 meters) of their length extending in front of the weapons' holders. Philip drilled his soldiers to charge in phalanx formation—as an eight-man-deep rectangle or as a sixteen-man-deep wedge. Each soldier held his pike with both hands and thrust with his full weight forward. In this configuration, the leading pikemen were protected by four protruding pike points and had a reach of 12 feet (4 meters) with their own pikes. Other armies carried spears of 7 feet (2 meters) or less; therefore, Philip's phalanxes struck opponents before they could employ their own weapons. Combined with cavalry, whose mobility both Philip and Alexander the Great wielded to great effect, the Macedonian infantry was nearly invincible until it faced the Roman legion.

Government and law. The king of Macedonia held absolute power, limited only by the strength of tradition. He served as the country's religious leader, sacrificing daily to the appropriate deities and presiding over numerous festivals and ceremonies. There was no fixed rule of succession; the Macedonians who made up the royal infantry and cavalry met as an assembly to chose the next king. However, from Perdiccas I (c. 650) to the death of Alexander the Great's son, Alexander IV, in

about 310 B.C.E., only male descendants of the Argead Dynasty—whose claimed descent from Zeus through Heracles gave them a semisacred aura—were selected to rule. The king, as supreme commander of the armed forces, led his forces into battle. He owned all mineral deposits and timber in the kingdom as well as all conquered land, which he disposed of as he saw fit. Royal revenues, including land taxes and harbor dues, were huge, but equally large were the expenses of arming and maintaining the state's land and naval forces, as well as the costs of its royal court. To citizens of Greek city-states, the all-powerful Macedonian kings seemed barbaric relics of archaic times, justifying the Greeks' contempt for Macedonia.

Religion and ritual. Macedonians shared the common religious features of the Greek world and worshiped its twelve Olympic gods. The cult of Zeus and places of devotion such as Mount Olympus were especially popular, and Heracles, the reputed ancestor of the royal family, received much admiration. Mystery cults, which promised life after death, were also widespread. By the fourth century C.E., however, most Macedonians had converted to Christianity.

Economics. The major occupations of the Macedonian people were herding, farming, and logging. The country was self-sufficient in foodstuffs and in good years might even export some food. The major export, however, was lumber. Logs that could be shaped into ship's timbers were highly valued; after disastrous naval battles, Greek city-states turned to Macedonia for timber to rebuild their fleets. The expansion of Macedonia brought gold and silver mines under the control of the kings, who issued coinage and used profits to support the army and court.

Agriculture and animal husbandry. Early Macedonians were originally shepherds, pasturing their sheep and goats in the high meadows surrounding Mount Olympus and the Pierian range during the summer and moving to lower ground during the winter. After they expanded into the lowlands and coastal areas, Macedonians raised grains and other foodstuffs.

Settlements and social structure. By the fourth century B.C.E., the majority of the population were peasant farmers living in small villages near their farmland. Other than the capital and a few ports, cities were modest settlements serving an agricultural and herding hinterland. Macedonian cities had local governmental structures modeled after those of Greece. Unlike the sovereign assemblies or oligarchies of Greece, however, all local authorities were subject to the overriding authority of the king. Also, unlike Greek cities whose economies depended on slave labor, workers in Macedonian cities were free subjects of the king. The largely peasant population was a rich source of recruits for the Macedonian infantry. Wealthier residents who could afford to own horses provided cavalry for the army.

Language and literature. Literate Macedonians admired Greek culture and were familiar with Greek texts. They revered the Homeric epics—the warrior ethos of the *Iliad* (c. 800 B.C.E.; English translation, 1616) particularly appealed to a warrior nation—and they were aware of current Athenian playwrights and poets. The language Macedonians spoke in the seventh century B.C.E. seems beyond recovery; it could have been a unique dialect of Greek or a Balkan language related to Illyrian or Thracian. By the time of Philip II and Alexander, however, the spoken language was the common Greek tongue, and Alexander and his successors spread the Greek language and literature throughout their Asian and African territories.

Current views. Questions concerning the ethnic origins of the Macedonians have occasioned furious debates. Greek nationalists and most Greek scholars claim, often passionately, that Macedonia was always Greek. Slavic authors, living in the Republic of Macedonia (formerly part of Yugoslavia), vigorously insist that ancient Macedonians were never Greek; extremists argue they were actually Slavs. More neutral scholars are divided; many believe Macedonians were Greek, but others think the evidence is too ambiguous to permit certainty.

ADDITIONAL RESOURCES

Borza, Eugene M. *In the Shadow of Olympus: The Emergence of Macedon*. Princeton, N.J.: Princeton University Press, 1990.

Errington, R. Malcolm. *A History of Macedonia*. Berkeley: University of California Press, 1990.

Hammond, Nicholas G. L. *The Miracle That Was Macedonia*. New York: St. Martin's Press, 1991.

_____. *Philip of Macedon*. Baltimore: Johns Hopkins University Press, 1994.

SEE ALSO: Alexander the Great; Antigonid Dynasty; Athens; Chaeronea, Battle of; Gaugamela, Battle of; Gauls; Granicus, Battle of; Greece, Classical; Hydaspes, Battle of; Olympias; Peloponnesian War; Philip II; Philip V; Punic Wars; Rome, Republican.

—Milton Berman

MACROBIUS, AURELIUS THEODOSIUS

FLOURISHED: fifth century C.E.; Rome
RELATED CIVILIZATION: Imperial Rome
MAJOR ROLE/POSITION: Author

Life. It is unclear to which late, imperial Macrobius (ma-KROH-bee-uhs) the three literary works surviving under this name should be attributed. The author, however, appears to have been an aristocrat and public official during the first half of the fifth century C.E. who was well acquainted with the leading men of his day. A work that compares Greek and Latin verbs survives in part. Aurelius Theodosius Macrobius's only complete work to survive, *Comentarii in Somnium Scipionis* (n.d.; *Commentary on the Dream of Scipio*, 1952), is a commentary on Cicero's *Somnium Scipionis* ("Dream of Scipio"), part of *De Republica* (n.d.; English translation, 1948), which is an important source for the history of Neoplatonic thought. Macrobius's most important work is the *Saturnalia* (n.d.; English translation, 1969), antiquity's last surviving example of "sympotic" literature. The work presents (fictitious) conversations conducted by leading pagan figures on the evening before, as well as during the days of, Rome's great pagan festival, the *Saturnalia*. The first evening's discussion is devoted to law and grammar. Morning and evening sessions on subsequent days are devoted to set topics, including such fare as pagan religion (Christianity is ignored), the calendar, jokes, eating, and drinking as well as history, philosophy, and literature.

Influence. Macrobius was not widely read during the Middle Ages, received much greater attention during the Renaissance, and in modern times attracts attention mainly for his preservation of fragments from earlier authors.

ADDITIONAL RESOURCES

Cameron, A. "The Date and Identity of Macrobius." *Journal of Roman Studies* 56 (1966): 25-38.

Davies, P. V. *The Saturnalia*. New York: Columbia University Press, 1969.

Stahl, W. H. *Commentary on the Dream of Scipio*. New York: Columbia University Press, 1952.

SEE ALSO: Cicero; Languages and literature; Philosophy; Rome, Imperial.

—*Hans-Friedrich Mueller*

MADAGASCAR

DATE: 500 B.C.E.-700 C.E.
LOCALE: Off the eastern coast of southern Africa
SIGNIFICANCE: Furthest western extent of the Indonesian/Polynesian migration.

Because Madagascar (ma-da-GAS-kar) was originally settled by preliterate peoples, no written history of the first colonization of Madagascar exists, and Madagascar's prehistory must be reconstructed primarily from archaeological data.

Although it lies not far from the eastern coast of Africa, humanity's original home, Madagascar was settled relatively late in human history, probably between 500 and 700 C.E. Therefore, Madagascar retained a unique ecology, with many species that had survived nowhere else, such as a wide variety of lemurs, early primates that had been replaced by the more robust and adaptable monkeys elsewhere.

Small bands of hunter-gatherers may have made their way into Madagascar earlier, but they apparently had relatively little impact on the land. The elusive Mikea people, who follow a way of life strongly reminiscent of the San (formerly known as Bushmen) of the Kalahari Desert, may represent the descendants of such an early population. However, some anthropologists claim that other evidence groups the Mikea clearly with the rest of the Malagasy and that the similarities of their culture to that of the Kalahari San are simply a matter of form following function.

The main population group of Madagascar, the Malagasy, is a light-skinned people akin to the Malay and Polynesians. Their language is clearly a member of the same large family of languages as those of Indonesia and the Pacific Islands. Their terraced fields, in which they raise rice, are similar to those of Indonesia. The canoes of the Vezo, a Malagasy people who have retained an orientation to the sea, are strongly reminiscent of the outrigger canoes with which the Polynesians colonized the scattered islands of the Pacific.

The exact route by which the proto-Malagasy arrived in Madagascar is a subject of historical debate.

Some historians theorize a direct route across the Indian Ocean, and modern experimenters have sailed a replica outrigger canoe along the relevant currents. However, the absence of human occupation on intervening islands such as Mauritus and Reunion before European discovery in the sixteenth century is evidence against this theory. Most historians hold that the proto-Malagasy came along the northern fringe of the Indian Ocean, following the coastline of Asia and Africa.

When they first arrived in the area, these early settlers planted colonies on the mainland of Africa as well as on the island of Madagascar itself. They brought with them a number of traditional Asian foods, including coconuts, breadfruit, yams, bananas, and taro. Rice was not a part of the first settlement, although when it did arrive, it would become very important in Malagasy culture and the basis of many traditional sayings.

The original Malagasy settlers of Madagascar are known as the *Tompon-tany*, the lords of the land. As they settled, they drove inland from west to east, changing the environment and causing mass extinctions of the Madagascar megafauna. Several species of giant lemurs and giant tortoises were made extinct, as was the largest bird ever known. This was the elephant bird, *Aepyornis maximus*, about 8 feet (2.5 meters) tall and weighing about 660 pounds (300 kilograms). It is remembered in the native language as *vorombe*, literally "big bird." Whole eggs can still be found when heavy rains scour them from the streambeds, although the embryos within them are, of course, long dead.

On Madagascar, the Malagasy developed a distinctive culture that combined African and Indonesian culture. Their rectangular houses with the doors on the western side are clearly derived from Indonesian dwellings, as is the symbolic importance of the various sides and corners. Nowhere on Madagascar does one find the round hut that is so common on the African mainland. The Malagasy attached strong importance to the cardinal directions and always would give directions in terms of north, west, east, and south, rather than left or right. This may have been a holdover from the needs of navigation across the trackless ocean.

Their religious tradition of ancestor worship, centered around family tombs, appears to have been derived from mainland Africa, as does the importance of cattle. The Malagasy traditionally spoke to their ancestors as if living and saw them as continuing to play an important part in the society of the living. Many Malagasy regarded the ancestors, the *razana*, as the source of both economic and moral welfare. One of the most important elements of ancestor worship has been the *famadihana*, the annual ceremony of opening the family tomb and rewrapping the bones of the ancestors. Although cattle were very important to traditional Malagasy culture, they were not sacred, as they were in India. However, much like the mainland African pastoralists, the Malagasy rarely slaughtered cattle to eat. Instead, cattle were considered to be a representation of wealth and generally slaughtered only as a part of a religious ceremony.

Although most Malagasy adopted a primarily terrestrial way of life, the Vezo retained a tradition oriented to the sea. Those who captured sea turtles would follow an elaborate ritual reminiscent of their landbound neighbors' cattle sacrifices in order to liberate the turtles' spirits before eating the meat. Dolphins that washed ashore were buried in shrouds in a human cemetery and treated like the people's own kin.

ADDITIONAL RESOURCES

Heale, Jay. *Madagascar*. New York: Marshall Cavendish, 1998.

Lanting, Frans. *A World Out of Time: Madagascar*. New York: Aperature Foundation, 1990.

Madagascar: Society and History. Durham, N.C.: Carolina Academic Press, 1986.

Oluonye, Mary N. *Madagascar*. Minneapolis, Minn.: Carolrhoda Books, 2000.

SEE ALSO: Africa, East and South; Malay; Polynesia.
　　　　　　　　　　　　　—*Leigh Husband Kimmel*

MAECENAS, GAIUS

ALSO KNOWN AS: Gaius Maecenas Cilnius

BORN: c. 70 B.C.E.; Arretium (modern Arezzo) in northern Italy

DIED: 8 B.C.E.; Rome

RELATED CIVILIZATIONS: Republican and Imperial Rome

MAJOR ROLE/POSITION: Political adviser and diplomat, patron of literature

Life. Gaius Maecenas (GI-uhs mih-SEE-nuhs) claimed derivation from ancient Etruscan nobility and was a very wealthy member of the Roman equestrian class. A confidant and adviser of Augustus, he aided in the arrangement of the future emperor's first marriage and was with him at the Battle of Philippi. Instrumental in negotiations with Marc Antony during the Triumvirate, he was later entrusted with management of affairs in Italy in the emperor's absence.

Maecenas pursued a sybaritic style of life in a mansion with splendid gardens on the Esquiline hill. He was an aficionado of poetry and dabbled in both verse and prose but made his greatest contribution to letters as the patron of Vergil and Horace. Because his financial support freed the poets to devote themselves fully to their art, they expressed their gratitude through dedicatory references, for example, in the first of Horace's *Odes* (23 B.C.E.; 13 B.C.E.; English translation, 1621). Because he served as the intermediary between the poets and Augustus, he has been seen as a kind of minister of propaganda.

Influence. Maecenas was an archetype of the patron of the arts, forerunner of the Medicis or the Guggenheims. His benefactions helped make possible such masterworks as Horace's *Odes* and *Epodes* (c. 30 B.C.E.; English translation, 1638) and Vergil's *Georgics* (c. 37-29 B.C.E.; English translation, 1589) and *Aeneid* (c. 29-19 B.C.E.; English translation, 1553).

ADDITIONAL RESOURCES

Gold, Barbara, ed. *Literary and Artistic Patronage in Ancient Rome*. Austin: University of Texas Press, 1982.

Syme, Ronald. *The Roman Revolution*. Oxford, England: Clarendon Press, 1939.

SEE ALSO: Antony, Marc; Augustus; Horace; Philippi, Battle of; Rome, Imperial; Rome, Republican; Vergil.
　　　　　　　　　　　　　—*James P. Holoka*

MAGNA GRAECIA

DATE: 700 B.C.E.-700 C.E.
LOCALE: Southern Italy
RELATED CIVILIZATIONS: Rome, Greece
SIGNIFICANCE: This is the area where Roman and Greek cultures first came into conflict and merged.

The term Magna Graecia (MAG-nuh GREE-shuh) generally refers to the coastal regions of Italy from the heel of the Italian peninsula clockwise to just north of the Bay of Naples, wherein a significant cluster of Greek-founded cities prospered before and into the Roman period. Some of the more prominent of these colonies were Tarentum (Taranto), Croton (Crotone), Paestum, Naples, and Cumae, but dozens of other cities are known, many of which have been at least partially excavated. The term can also be taken more generally to denote the Greek world outside mainland Greece. Mainland Greeks established colonies around the Mediterranean and Black Seas, mostly in the eighth through sixth centuries B.C.E. Most of these colonies were located where trading entrepôts had already been established. Mycenaean remains at some of these sites confirm the existence of long-established trade ties between Greece and Italy. The most significant of the colonizers of Italy were the Achaeans, a confederation of small cities in the northwest part of the Peloponnese. The Spartans had one Italian colony, although it gradually gained preeminence over many of the others.

The colonies in Italy, like all Greek colonies, tended to retain loose political and economic ties to their mother cities. The result was twofold. The petty particularism of intercity rivalries and suspicion common to mainland Greece became an embedded feature of Magna Graecia as well. On the other hand, these ties to mainland Greece also provided an important conduit for Greek influence and commerce between the Greek and Italian worlds. For example, Greek-style vases are regular features in all sorts of non-Greek settings, especially in Etruria. The cities farthest southeast, such as Tarentum and Heraclea, tended to retain their distinctive Greek character the longest. The cities farther northwest around the Bay of Naples exhibited a more obvious cultural fusion with the Italian cultures with which they actively interacted. Pompeii is the most famous example of this process. Naples is an important exception to this rule, as it retained the use of the Greek language well into the Imperial Roman period.

Generally speaking, textual evidence for the history of this region is filtered through the experience of the Romans whose domination of Magna Graecia began in the last years of the fourth century B.C.E. The archaeological record and anecdotal references in the ancient sources are the main resources for the period preceding the Romans.

The colonies. Tarentum, located at the northeast corner of the Gulf of Tarentum, was the lone Spartan foundation and is traditionally dated to 706 B.C.E. Initially unimportant, it eventually gained prominence at the expense of its neighbors in the middle and late 400's B.C.E., gradually becoming the most important city in the southern gulf. Tarentum's rise to prominence was largely at the expense of Croton, a colony of the Achaeans (c. 710 B.C.E.). Croton, located in the toe of the Italian boot, was the most powerful city in the area and well positioned geographically to dominate intercourse with Sicily and eastern Italy. It was this geographic advantage that prompted Dionysius I the Elder of Syracuse to seize the city in 379 B.C.E., after which it never regained its former prominence.

Paestum, located thirty-five miles (fifty-six kilometers) southeast of Naples, was a colony of Sybaris, itself a colony of the Achaeans. Founded about 600 B.C.E., it was originally named Poseidonia. It quickly became prominent in trade with the Etruscans to the north. Some of the best surviving examples of Greek temple architecture from the sixth and fifth centuries B.C.E. are located within the original walls of the city along with many other significant remains. Paestum became a Roman colony in 273 B.C.E.

Cumae, founded in 740 B.C.E. by Euboean colonists, was the first of the Greek colonies on the Italian mainland. Located about ten miles (sixteen kilometers) northwest of Naples, it became the mother city of a whole series of other colonies, including Naples itself. The history of Cumae intersected early on with that of Rome. Aristodemus, the tyrant of Cumae, defeated an Etruscan army near Rome in 505 B.C.E. that probably included Roman elements. By 338 B.C.E., Cumae had become a staunch ally of the Romans after having cooperated with them in their war with their Latin allies. Thereafter, Cumae remained a significant city until long after the Western Roman Empire collapsed. Naples, founded by Cumae about 600 B.C.E., had eclipsed its mother city in influence by the late 400's B.C.E., after which it became the most important city in the area. Naples had become an ally of the Romans by 326 B.C.E.

and retained independent status for another two hundred years.

One of the most intriguing figures of Magna Graecia was Pythagoras. Born in Samos, Pythagoras migrated to Croton about 530 B.C.E. and became a dominant intellectual figure there in science and religion. Much is ascribed to him personally, but it is likely that his disciples developed many of the ideas attributed to him. The ancients ascribe the first discussion concerning the transmigration of the soul to Pythagoras. These ideas were very important to the development of Plato's ideas more than one hundred years later. Pythagoras's followers developed a semisecret society in his name that featured secret initiation rites and dietary restrictions. Pythagoras seems to have become a cult figure during his own lifetime as well as the ancient paragon of the wise old sage. Pythagoras's forays into science were related to his interest in religion, as were the works of the other Pre-Socratic philosophers. He discovered the well-known geometric theorem that bears his name, as well as mathematical relationships in musical harmonics.

Contact with Rome. Roman interaction with Magna Graecia coincides with some important thresholds in Roman history. The first paved Roman road was built in 312 B.C.E. to Capua and extended to Brundusium (Brindisi) by 244 B.C.E. The first Roman silver coinage was struck not in Rome but in Magna Graecia—probably Naples, about 325 B.C.E.—and should be associated with a treaty struck between Rome and Naples at about the same time. The Romans were interested in Naples' fleet of ships. From the Greek point of view, this alliance with the Romans was consistent with the policy of the southern Italian Greeks to make alliances with powerful outsiders to counter local threats rather than to develop and maintain citizen militias. Rome's involvement with Naples and Roman expansion into south-central Italy eventually alarmed Tarentum, the theretofore dominant city in the very south of Italy. This is the background to Tarentum's invitation to Pyrrhus, king of Epirus, to defend southern Italy from Roman expansion. This invitation backfired when Pyrrhus was unable to counter Rome's enormous manpower reserves. After a series of indecisive battles with the Romans, Pyrrhus was forced to withdraw from Italy, leaving his erstwhile clients to submit to Roman terms.

The challenge from Pyrrhus was the last real obstacle Rome faced in organizing the southern peninsula under its control. Surprisingly, the Romans exercised a light hand in the settlement and did not attempt to rule the Greeks directly. Nevertheless, at least some of the Greek cities of southern Italy maintained ambivalent feelings concerning Roman hegemony. When Hannibal invaded Italy in the late 200's B.C.E., some of these cities offered him aid and comfort. This assistance accounts for Hannibal's long stay in southern Italy and, of course, a much more onerous settlement with the Romans after Hannibal's hurried departure in 203 B.C.E. The Romans confiscated significant portions of land in the south and settled it with Roman and allied veterans and replaced the political independence of the Greek cities with Roman control. Some of these Greek cities disappeared altogether after this date, but it is difficult to know exactly what happened to them.

Since the 300's B.C.E., a significant cultural fusion of the Greeks with indigenous Italian peoples had been taking place. This fusion was hastened by the new Roman settlers such that the distinctive Greek character of Magna Graecia was mostly diluted after 200 B.C.E. Even so, southern Italy remained a culture apart from central and northern Italy. The rugged geography of southern Italy was clearly a factor. It provided refuge for rebellious elements late in Rome's war with its Italian allies in the 90's and 80's B.C.E. and for the slave army of Spartacus in the 70's B.C.E. Little is known of the history of Magna Graecia apart from what concerned the Roman Empire for the next few centuries.

After the Western Roman Empire collapsed in the fifth and sixth centuries C.E., Magna Graecia remained divorced from Roman control until the 1800's C.E. The Byzantine emperor Justinian I's abortive attempt to recover Italy from the barbarians in the 500's C.E. resulted in a Byzantine enclave in the south that remained well into the Middle Ages. Nevertheless, this control was always limited to the coastal cities. Magna Graecia became a zone of opportunity for bandits and invaders for centuries thereafter.

ADDITIONAL RESOURCES

Fredericksen, M. *Campania*. London: Routledge, 1984.

Pugliese Carratelli, Giovanni. *The Western Greeks*. London: Thames and Hudson, 1996.

Ridgway, D. *The First Western Greeks*. New York: Cambridge University Press, 1992.

SEE ALSO: Byzantine Empire; Dionysius I the Elder of Syracuse; Greece, Archaic; Hannibal; Plato; Pythagoras; Rome, Prerepublican; Spartacus.

—*Randall S. Howarth*

MAGNESIA AD SIPYLUM, BATTLE OF

DATE: 190 B.C.E.
LOCALE: Magnesia, western Asia Minor northeast of Smyrna
RELATED CIVILIZATIONS: Seleucid Syria, Roman Republic
SIGNIFICANCE: Rome's victory over Antiochus the Great ended Seleucid power in Asia Minor, thereafter exposing the subcontinent to Roman imperial domination.

Background. Antiochus the Great, having formed an alliance with the Aetolian League and Sparta, sought to expand his power in the eastern Mediterranean by invading Greece in 192 B.C.E. This action alarmed Rome, whose legions decisively checked the Seleucid king's expansion at Thermopylae two years later. Antiochus's defeat was soon followed by a Roman invasion of Asia Minor.

Action. At Magnesia ad Sipylum (mag-NEE-zhuh ad SIH-pih-luhm), Antiochus the Great assembled his army of 70,000 near the Hermus River. He placed the infantry in the center, interspersed with war elephants, and stationed sizable formations of cavalry on both flanks and to the front. The Roman force of 30,000, under the command of Gaius Domitius, was deployed on the left against the river, with contingents of cavalry positioned to the right of this main legionary formation. As the legions attacked Antiochus's center, Syrian cavalry penetrated the Roman line and momentarily endangered the Roman left flank. Almost simultaneously, an intense charge by Roman cavalry broke the enemy's left. Under the pressure of this combined Roman assault, Syrian resistance collapsed. In the ensuing rout, 50,000 Syrians were killed or captured.

Consequences. Rome's victory at Magnesia ad Sipylum ended Seleucid power in Asia Minor and forced Antiochus the Great to relinquish all territories northwest of the Taurus Mountains to Rhodes, Pergamum, and Rome's Greek allies in Asia Minor.

ADDITIONAL RESOURCES
Green, Peter. *Alexander to Actium: The Historical Evolution of the Hellenistic Age.* Reprint. Berkeley: University of California Press, 1993.
Liddell Hart, B. H. *Scipio Africanus: Greater than Napoleon.* Cambridge, Mass.: Da Capo Press, 1994.

SEE ALSO: Antiochus the Great; Greece, Hellenistic; Rome, Republican; Seleucid Dynasty.

—*Donathan Taylor*

MAHĀBHĀRATA

AUTHORSHIP: Composite; attributed to the legendary Vyāsa
DATE: 400 B.C.E.-200 C.E., present form by c. 400 C.E.
LOCALE: India
RELATED CIVILIZATION: India
SIGNIFICANCE: This monumental poem records early Indian political, ethical, mythological, and philosophical thought and is considered a religious scripture in Hinduism.

Called the "great epic of India," the *Mahābhārata* (mah-HAW-BAW-rah-tah) is composed in Sanskrit, the chief classical and sacred language of ancient India, and is probably the longest single literary work extant in any language. In its shortest version, the poem consists of more than 74,000 stanzas, divided into sections of varying length. Certain features—most prominent the use of formulaic repetitions with slight variations—suggest an origin in ancient oral tradition. Extant, however, are two main manuscript traditions, associated with north and south India. The title *Mahābhārata* is taken to mean "the narrative of the great war of the Bhāratas," the latter a dynasty of northern India that gives India its official name, Bharat. The epic's central narrative records in great detail a succession dispute between two branches of this dynasty and the resultant war, said to involve most of the ruling families of known India. A large part of the poem describes in copious detail a violent eighteen-day battle that ends with the tragic deaths of most participants. The historicity of this war and the poem's political details have proved difficult to confirm.

The *Mahābhārata* displays features known from national epics elsewhere: genealogies and tales of ancestors; descriptions of the youth and adventures of important heroes; embassies, debates, and parleys before the decisive battle; the involvement of deities and related mythological digressions; descriptions of weapons and battle tactics; and taunts and the issuing of challenges. Religious episodes, such as legends of saints and the description of pilgrimage sites, occur frequently.

In some of its sections, such as one narrating a great cattle raid, the *Mahābhārata* describes a culture like that of other archaic Indo-Europeans—nomadic cattle herders. However, the text also refers to city-dwellers and slash-and-burn agriculturalists. The poem's complex overlay of diverse features has led historical scholars to posit a composite authorship, stretching over centuries and carried out in different locales. Such a theory would account for the many long sections that interrupt the story with religious and philosophical teachings, most notably the Śānti Parvan (first or second century C.E.), more than 15,000 stanzas in length. These didactic sections, however, are filled with narratives, anecdotes, and parables meant to illustrate the teachings.

This is a traditional mode of religious instruction in India—a mixture of storytelling and sermon.

Krishna (Kṛṣṇa) figures both as a human player in the epic, the friend of the great hero Arjuna, and as an important deity. It is Krishna who relates the most famous episode of the *Mahābhārata*, the *Bhagavadgītā* (c. 200 B.C.E. -200 C.E.; *The Bhagavad Gita*, 1785).

ADDITIONAL RESOURCES

Brockington, John. *The Sanskrit Epics*. Leiden: E. J. Brill, 1998.
Buitenen, J. A. B. van, trans. *The Mahābhārata*. 3 vols. Chicago: University of Chicago Press, 1973-1978.
Hiltebeitel, Alf. *Rethinking India's Oral and Classical Epics*. Chicago: University of Chicago Press, 1999.
Sharma, Arvind, ed. *Essays on the Mahābhārata*. Leiden: E. J. Brill, 1991.

SEE ALSO: *Bhagavadgītā*; Hinduism; India.
—*Burt Thorp*

MAHĀBODHI TEMPLE

DATE: 300 B.C.E.- 600 C.E.
LOCALE: Bodh Gayā, India
RELATED CIVILIZATION: India
SIGNIFICANCE: This temple was built at the place where the Buddha attained enlightenment and is a major pilgrimage site for Buddhists.

The Mahābodhi (mah-HAW-BOH-dee) temple is the main structure of Bodh Gayā, where the Buddha attained enlightenment. Aśoka is credited with the construction of a structure around the Bodhi tree, under which the Buddha reached enlightenment. A first century B.C.E. relief sculpture from Bharhut showing a two-story structure built around the Bodhi tree and the Vajrasana (the Diamond seat) is probably the earliest pictorial evidence for the temple. The Chinese pilgrim Faxian (early fifth century C.E.) reported a stupa built at the place of enlightenment. Another Chinese pilgrim, Xuanzang (seventh century C.E.), saw a structure with a 160-foot (49-meter) tower beside the Bodhi tree. Sometime after the twelfth century C.E., the temple fell into neglect. Burmese missions were sent to restore the structure in 1875 and 1880. In conjunction with the second Burmese mission, J. D. Beglar

The Mahābodhi temple. (© Eye Ubiquitous/Corbis)

restored the structure, primarily based upon an eleventh century C.E. miniature model of the temple. The Mahābodhi temple, along with the Bodhi tree and the Vajrasana, is a major pilgrimage site for Buddhists.

ADDITIONAL RESOURCES

Barua, Dipak K. *Bodh Gaya Temple: Its History.* Buddha Gaya, India: Buddha Gaya Temple Management Committee, 1981.

Cunningham, Alexander. *Mahābodhi.* New Delhi, India: Munshiram Manoharlal Publishers, 1998.

Leoshko, Janice, ed. *Bodh Gaya: The Site of Enlightenment.* Bombay, India: Marg, 1988.

SEE ALSO: Aśoka; Buddha; Buddhism; Faxian; India; Xuanzang.

—Albert T. Watanabe

MAHENDRAVARMAN I

ALSO KNOWN AS: Mahendravikramavarman; Cettakāri; Cittrakārapulli
BORN: date and place unknown
DIED: c. 630 C.E.; place unknown
RELATED CIVILIZATION: South India
MAJOR ROLE/POSITION: King and playwright

Life. One of the kings of the Pallava Dynasty of south India, Mahendravarman (mah-HEHN-drah VAHR-mahn) I ruled from his capital at Kānchipuram from about 600 to 630 C.E. During his reign, a long-drawn-out conflict began with the Cālukyas, his western neighbors. The war was to shape politics in south India for several generations.

He was a Jain in his early life and later converted to Hinduism, embracing the god Śiva as his patron deity. He was the patron of a number of excavated rock-cave temples dedicated to Śiva at Tiruchipalli and Mahābalipuram. As a Śaivite convert, he did much to support the resurgence of Hinduism in south India after a long period of the religion's being eclipsed by the popularity of Jainism and Buddhism. In his inscriptions, the king refers to himself as Cettakāri (temple builder), and in that respect, he was a pioneer in the creation of stone architecture in south India. Another of his names, Chittrakārapulli (tiger among painters), attests to his ability as an artist. Mahendravarman I was known as a great patron of all the arts; he was known also as a famous musician who wrote a treatise on music.

The Pallava king is best remembered as a writer of plays, two of which survive: *Mattavilāsaprahasana* (seventh century C.E.; English translation, 1974), literally, "the sport of the intoxicated," and *Bhagavadajjukam* (seventh century C.E.; *Bhagavaddajjuka prahasana*, 1978), literally, "the saint and the prostitute." Mahendravarman demonstrates in his plays knowledge of various religious beliefs and schools of thought as well as a spirited sense of humor. Both plays are lively, one-act farces written in Sanskrit. The writer indulges in witty frolic as a way to criticize in lighter vein the hypocrisy of some contemporary religious practices.

Influence. Mahendravarman I greatly influenced the future course of politics and religion in south India. In particular, his patronage of stone architecture created the foundations for the south Indian style of architecture and art.

ADDITIONAL RESOURCES

Lockwood, Michael. *Mamallapuram and the Pallavas.* Madras, India: The Christian Literature Society, 1982.

Lockwood, Michael, and A. Vishnu Bhat, trans. *Mattavilasa Prahasana (The Farce of Drunken Sport).* Madras, India: The Christian Literature Society, 1981.

Poulose, K. G. *Bhagavadajjukam in Kutiyattam: The Hermit and the Harlot.* Delhi, India: New Bharatiya Book Corporation, 2000.

SEE ALSO: Hinduism; India; Indian temple architecture; Pallava Dynasty.

—Katherine Anne Harper

MAKOURIA

ALSO KNOWN AS: Makhorae; Makuria; Maqurra
DATE: fifth-eighth centuries C.E.
LOCALE: Upper Nubia
SIGNIFICANCE: The Nubian Christian kingdom of Makouria endured for a thousand years until the fourteenth century C.E.

After the fourth century C.E. decline of Kush, the area between Aswan and the confluence of the Niles was divided into three kingdoms: Nobatia in the north, Alwa in the south, and Makouria (mah-KEW-ree-ah) in the center. Makouria was previously unknown, and its subjects cannot be easily identified with an earlier political entity. Known to Arab traders as al-Muqurra, it was located between the Nile River's Third and Fifth Cataracts. Its capital, Dongola, was situated on the east bank. Its location was exceptionally favorable for agriculture and trade, and it emerged as a political power of Nubia.

The post-Meroitic history of Upper Nubia is fragmentary. The stele of King Ezana provides one of the few literary references to the period between the downfall of Kush and the advent of Christianity. When the Axumite king arrived in Nubia in 350 C.E., the Noba, former subjects of Meroe, had taken possession of large areas of the Meroitic steppe lands. Some of these people later are designated as the Tanqasi culture, named after a major site of their mound grave groupings. Although their origins are obscure, Makouria's early rulers may have been those buried beneath the mounds at Tanqasi. The sixth century *Ecclesiastical History* by John of Ephesus (fragmentary work, part 3 translated as *The Third Part of the Ecclesiastical History of John, Bishop of Ephesus*, 1860) provides reliable political information; Makouria was then a recognized, independent kingdom.

In 540 C.E., the Byzantine emperor Justinian I closed the temple of Isis at Philae. Christian missionaries were dispatched to Nubia, where the new religion was readily accepted by rulers and subjects. Motives were political as well as religious: Rival kings chose rival sectarian affiliations. The contemporary historian John of Biclarum documents Makouria's conversion to the Diophysite faith in about 570 C.E.; John of Ephesus notes that the ruler of Nobatia, Makouria's rival, had adopted the Monophysite sect of Christianity.

Makourian-Nobatian rivalries did not last, as the two kingdoms merged into a single confederation sometime in the seventh century. This united kingdom, ruled by the king of Makouria, maintained its capital at Dongola. It now extended from Aswan to the vicinity of the Fifth Cataract. Although the reasons for this unification remain unclear, the combined kingdom existed peacefully for six hundred years.

After the Arab invasion of Egypt in 639 C.E., raiders traveled up the Nile and attacked Makouria. (Their records do not mention Nobatia, which already had been absorbed.) They laid siege to Dongola, destroying the cathedral. Attacks and counterattacks ensued, with heavy casualties on both sides.

In 652 C.E., the king of Makouria and Egypt's Muslim rulers reached an agreement commonly known as the Baqt, which is believed to have determined Muslim-Nubian relations for the next six centuries. It institutionalized economic relations and guaranteed the sovereignty of Makouria, a non-Muslim kingdom, an event without precedent in early Islamic history. With this mutual agreement of nonaggression, Nubia was left in peace and the Arabs had a stable frontier. Until the fourteenth century C.E., an indigenous Nubian culture was able to develop.

ADDITIONAL RESOURCES

Davies, W. V., ed. *Egypt and Africa: Nubia from Prehistory to Islam*. London: The British Museum Press, 1991.
Shinnie, P. L. *Ancient Nubia*. New York: Kegan Paul International, 1996.

SEE ALSO: Alwa; Axum; Christianity; Ezana; Islam; Justinian I; Napata and Meroe; Nobatae; Nubia.

—Cassandra Lee Tellier

MALALAS, JOHN

BORN: c. 490 C.E.; Antioch, Syria
DIED: c. 578 C.E.; Constantinople
RELATED CIVILIZATION: Byzantine Empire
MAJOR ROLE/POSITION: Historian

Life. John Malalas (muh-LAY-las) wrote the Greek *Chronographia* (n.d.; *The Chronicle of John Malalas*, 1986), a chronicle of world history in eighteen volumes covering the period from creation to 563 C.E. His aims were to make accessible to common people an account of the course of sacred Christian history from Adam to the present and to provide a summary of political events under the current and recent emperors. Malalas had access to the city archives of Antioch because of his mid-level job in the imperial bureaucracy. Some time before the sack of Antioch by the Sāsānians in 540 C.E., Malalas moved to Constantinople. He continued his chronicle down through much of the reign of Emperor Justinian I (r. 527-565 C.E.). Malalas's chronicle seeks to give a year-by-year account of interesting political or religious events, natural disasters, military hostilities, and occurrences he thought would be interesting to his readers. Malalas recorded a wide variety of events without trying to draw connections between them.

Influence. Despite the loose and seemingly disorganized arrangement of his material, Malalas's chronicle is important because of the numerous citations of now lost historical works that are included verbatim in the text. Also important is Malalas's use of oral sources in accounts of events during his own time period. Malalas's chronicle was used as an authoritative source by later historians well into the Middle Ages.

ADDITIONAL RESOURCES

Jeffreys, Elizabeth. *Studies in John Malalas.* Sydney: Australian Association for Byzantine Studies, 1990.
Jeffreys, Elizabeth, Michael Jeffreys, and Roger Scott. *The Chronicle of John Malalas.* Melbourne: Australian Association for Byzantine Studies, 1986.

SEE ALSO: Byzantine Empire; Justinian I; Languages and literature.

—*Victoria Erhart*

MALAY

DATE: 8000 B.C.E.-700 C.E.
LOCALE: Malaysia and Southeast Asia
SIGNIFICANCE: Malayan sites, both mainland and insular, exhibit an indigenous culture influenced by other areas in Asia and Southeast Asia.

Over time, the term "Malay" (muh-LAY) has conjured up various connotations and usages in the context of world history. Once forming the half of a former linguistic family, Malayo-Polynesian (now called Austronesian), Malay was also used to denote a phenotype. This phenotype is characterized by a light brown skin color, medium to short stature, black and straight or wavy hair, and broad cheekbones. Distinct from the classical Mongoloid phenotype associated with populations in north China, Manchuria, and Siberia, the Indonesian-Malay phenotype is also known to physical anthropologists as that of the generalized Mongoloids. Being Malay also meant the trusteeship to the source of Southeast Asian spices or being a Muslim in Southeast Asia. Colonial and postcolonial partition relegated the term to the inhabitants of peninsular Malaya, if not the entire republic. The geographical consolidation of the republic makes Malaysia both mainland and insular Southeast Asia, and it embodies the respective cultural traditions of both.

Entrance into the Neolithic Age is indicated by three criteria: the presence of pecked or ground stone adzes, pottery, and horticulture. Although the Chinese influence on Southeast Asian cultural history is still acknowledged, greater recognition is being made of the creative and independent contribution of Southeast Asia to its own cultural history. Horticulture probably began around 1100 B.C.E. on the mainland, and by 800 B.C.E., the Neolithic Age was established in the Malay region. The sequence of cultural development was not uniform, however, varying with the site and locale. Also, the familiar cultural sequencing that accompanies events such as the start of agriculture or metalworking often does not apply in this area.

The late phase of the Hoabinhian tradition (c. 13,000-c. 5000/4000 B.C.E.) continued into the Neolithic period. Hoabinhian stone tools, mostly of the late phase and some bearing similarity to those in northern Vietnam, have been found at more than sixteen sites in Malaya. Cord-marked pottery, pounding and grinding stones, bone tools, burials, and red ochre are frequent finds. However, many sites in Malaya have no stratigraphic sequence, so interpretations of development must be based on comparisons of information from neighboring cultures with that from local sites. In Malaya, the Neolithic Age was characterized by the domestication of indigenous tubers, breadfruit and other fruit trees, fowl, and pigs, undoubtedly supplemented by hunting, gathering, and fishing.

Domestication of rice followed later; the earliest dates given are 4000-3300 B.C.E. for China and 3500 B.C.E. for Thailand. Rice cultivation was noted at Thailand's Non Nok Tha site, judged to be Neolithic, although bronze had begun to be used. (The appearance of metal generally signals the end of the Neolithic period.) Modest by comparison, the Malayan Ban Kao culture (c. 3000-c. 900 B.C.E.), derived from various sites, gives rise to some puzzling interpretations. No metal was reported, and Ban Kao pottery differs from Non Nok Tha's and appears to be connected with the Chinese Longshan tradition. The main Ban Kao site dates later than Non Nok Tha.

The Ban Kao site produced bark-cloth beaters, spindle whorls, and fishing equipment. Bark-cloth beaters are Austronesian innovations; their use on the prehistoric mainland is limited to southern Vietnam and Malaya. Both areas are Austronesian settlements, the result of Austronesian expansion from insular Southeast Asia around 4000 B.C.E. This expansion continued until around 1000 B.C.E., as people migrated eastward into the Philippines, Indonesia, Hawaii, and New Zealand, and westward into Madagascar, spreading Southeast Asian culture as they traveled.

The following metal age, beginning about 1000 B.C.E., was rich, with various sites producing fine bronze and bronze-and-iron objects such as plowshares, axes, spearheads, fishhooks, ornaments, and bronze drums. Between 100 B.C.E. and 100 C.E., the projected start of Indianization in the Malay region, megalithic structures were constructed. In the following centuries, various states and empires arose in the region, with Malay chiefdoms often playing the role of vassals or weaker allies.

ADDITIONAL RESOURCES

Bellwood, Peter. *Man's Conquest of the Pacific*. New York: Oxford University Press, 1979.

Beri, K. K. *History and Culture of South-East Asia: Ancient and Medieval*. New Delhi, India: Sterling Publishers, 1994.

Sorensen, P. "Neolithic Cultures of Thailand (and North Malaysia) and Their Lungshanoid Relationships." In *Early Chinese Art and Its Possible Influence in the Pacific Basin*, edited by N. Barnard. New York: Intercultural Arts Press, 1972.

SEE ALSO: China; Java; Laos; Mon-Khmer; Vietnam.

—*E. P. Flores-Meiser*

MANDE

ALSO KNOWN AS: Mali
DATE: c. 4000 B.C.E.-700 C.E.
LOCALE: Sub-Saharan West Africa
RELATED CIVILIZATION: West Africa
SIGNIFICANCE: A family of languages spoken by various cultures in the modern West African countries of Burkina Faso, Mali, Senegal, Gambia, Guinea, Sierra Leone, Liberia, Ivory Coast, and Ghana.

The Mande language family includes Maninka, Bamana, Dyula, Khasonka, Kuranko, Vai, Kono, and Ligbi. The Mande language first developed along the Niger River on the border of Guinea and Mali.

Proto-Mande speakers lived during the Neolithic period, as indicated by words that dealt with food production. The date of origin for the Proto-Mande language, 5000 B.C.E., corresponds to the beginnings of Neolithic settlements in this area. Trade between Berbers in North Africa, beginning about 2000 B.C.E., led to development of Mande kingdoms between 1000 B.C.E. and 600 C.E.

Mande society consisted of two divisions: The

Horonw were agriculturalists and made up the rulers, soldiers, and commoners. The Nyamakalaw controlled the life force, Nyama, and acted as contacts with the spirit world. They carved masks and figures and made costumes for use in rituals performed by the Horonw to control Nyama. Nyamakalaw also were the blacksmiths because the working of iron manipulates Nyama. This duality can be traced to the Mande creation stories in which the blacksmith/carver is often the first person on earth and therefore possesses special powers.

ADDITIONAL RESOURCES

Gillon, Werner. *A Short History of African Art*. New York: Facts On File, 1984.

Hodges, Carleton, ed. *Papers on the Manding*. Bloomington: University of Indiana, 1971.

Mukhtar, Muhammad Jamal al-Din, ed. *Ancient Civilizations of Africa*. London: Heinemann, 1992.

SEE ALSO: Africa, West; Berbers; Niger-Congo.

—*William L. Hommel*

MANICHAEANISM

DATE: c. 230-800 C.E.

LOCALE: Beginning in Mesopotamia, this religious movement spread to north Africa in the west and to China in the east.

RELATED CIVILIZATIONS: Persia, Mesopotamia, India

SIGNIFICANCE: Manichaeanism (ma-NIH-kee-uh-nih-zuhm) challenged Christianity and left a dualistic legacy for the Middle Ages.

Mani (c. 216-276 C.E.) was born in Mesopotamia to parents who belonged to the Persian Arsacids. He claimed that he received his first revelation from his celestial twin at the age of twelve. According to the *Cologne Mani Codex* (third century C.E.; English translation, 1979), Mani's family belonged to the Jewish-Christian Elchasaite sect.

Upon his second revelation at the age of twenty-four, Mani rejected the water baptisms of this sect and preached instead salvation by *gnosis* (revealed knowledge). Mani proclaimed his gospel in Mesopotamia, Persia, and India and enjoyed the patronage of Shāpūr I (r. 240-272 C.E.) but then was killed by Bahrām I.

Mani taught that there were two independent principles, light and darkness. In the first epoch, the Great God (Zurvan) lived apart in the realm of light, while Ahriman lived in the realm of darkness. In the second epoch, Primal Man (Ohrmizd) was defeated by the prince of darkness. An envoy, the Living Spirit, liberated Primal Man, who made the physical universe from the bodies of the sons of darkness. The powers of darkness created Adam and Eve and sought to retain in their descendants the particles of light. Christ was sent to enlighten people with *gnosis* and to liberate the particles of light that they unknowingly possess.

Manichaeans were divided into the elite *electi* and the laymen, known as *auditores*, or "hearers." The elect abstained from marriage and from eating meat. The auditors harvested fruits and vegetables, which contained particles of light. When the elect ate the produce, they would liberate the light by burping so that they could ascend into the Milky Way.

The earliest canonical texts were written in Syriac and Middle Persian. Later Manichaean texts include fourth and fifth century C.E. Coptic manuscripts such as the *Kephalaia* (*The Kephalaia of the Teacher*, 1995). A large corpus of Manichaean manuscripts have been found at Turfan in Turkestan (northwest China), dating to the eighth and ninth centuries. These are in Middle Persian, Sogdian, Chinese, and Uighur.

In Mani's lifetime, his teachings reached Palestine and Egypt. Despite the harsh edict against Mani and his followers in 297 C.E. by the emperor Diocletian, who labeled them subversive, the movement continued to flourish. Saint Augustine was for nine years (373-382 C.E.) a Manichaean *auditor*. After his dramatic conversion to Christianity, Saint Augustine wrote influential anti-Manichaean refutations.

Later dualistic movements such as the Paulicians in Armenia (seventh to twelfth centuries), the Bogomils in Serbia (eleventh to twelfth centuries), and the Albigenses (or Cathari) in northern Italy and southern France (twelfth to thirteenth centuries) were labeled "Manichaean" for their similar views.

ADDITIONAL RESOURCES
Klimkeit, Hans J. *Gnosis on the Silk Road.* San Francisco: HarperSanFrancisco, 1993.
Lieu, S. N. C. *Manichaeism in the Later Roman Empire and Medieval China.* Tübingen: J. C. B. Mohr, 1992.
Rudolph, Kurt. *Gnosis.* San Francisco: HarperSanFrancisco, 1987.
Runciman, Steven. *The Medieval Manichee.* Cambridge, England: Cambridge University Press, 1955.

SEE ALSO: Augustine, Saint; Christianity; Diocletian; Persia; Shāpūr I.

—*Edwin Yamauchi*

MANILIUS, MARCUS

FLOURISHED: first century C.E.; place unknown
RELATED CIVILIZATION: Imperial Rome
MAJOR ROLE/POSITION: Poet, astrologer

Life. Marcus Manilius (MAHR-kuhs ma-NIHL-ee-uhs) wrote a long didactic poem in five books, the *Astronomica* (n.d.; English translation, 1977), a treatise on astrology. Nothing is known about his life. Scholars surmise from his zodiacal allusion in Book 4 of the *Astronomica* to the ascension of Tiberius (14 C.E.) that he outlived Augustus. His name was probably Marcus Manilius, but other forms are possible. He may have been Roman. He knew the works of Vergil, Livy, and Cicero, and he specifically opposed the poet Lucretius, but since his apparent knowledge of Greek literature was broader, he may have been Greek. His idiosyncratic Latin diction suggests that he may have been from Asia Minor.

Influence. The *Astronomica* found favor among the Roman Stoics. In the first century, Juvenal, Lucan, Seneca the Younger, and Gaius Valerius Flaccus all referred to it. In the fourth century, Julius Firmicus Maternus derived much of Book 8 of his *Mathesis* (c. 335 C.E.; English translation, 1975) from Book 5 of the *Astronomica*. In the sixteenth century, Julius Caesar Scaliger compared Manilius favorably to Ovid. Johann Wolfgang von Goethe knew the *Astronomica* well and was more impressed with its style than with its astrological speculation.

ADDITIONAL RESOURCES
Manilius. *Astronomica.* Edited by G. P. Goold. Cambridge, Mass.: Harvard University Press, 1992.
Neugebauer, Otto. *Astronomy and History.* New York: Springer, 1983.
_____. *A History of Ancient Mathematical Astronomy.* New York: Springer, 1975.

SEE ALSO: Cicero; Juvenal; Livy; Lucan; Lucretius; Seneca the Younger; Tiberius; Valerius Flaccus, Gaius; Vergil.

—*Eric v.d. Luft*

MANTINEA, BATTLES OF

DATE: 418, 362, 207 B.C.E.
LOCALE: Central Arcadia
RELATED CIVILIZATIONS: Classical and Hellenistic Greece
SIGNIFICANCE: Mantinea was the center of struggles for domination of the central Peloponnese.

Background. The geographical position of the large Arcadian plain dominated by Mantinea (man-TIH-nee-uh) in the north and Tegea in the south gave it strategical importance to anyone wishing to apply military pressure to Sparta, Argos, or Achaea (Akhaïa).

The battle of 418 B.C.E. began with Agis II of Sparta marching on Mantinea to crush its alliance with Athens and Argos. Agis devastated the land until his enemies confronted him. He then drew up his line, with his Spartans on his right and his allies on the left. Against him stood the Mantineans, with their own members on their right and their allies on their left. Owing to the disobedience of two officers, a gap opened in the Spartan line into which the Mantineans poured. Agis, however, routed those opposite him, defeated the enemy, and ended their threat to Sparta.

In 362 B.C.E., the Thebans and their allies under Epaminondas confronted Mantinea, Sparta, and Athens south of their earlier battle. Epaminondas led his army in an oblique march against the Spartan line, which he easily broke, but was killed early in the battle. Fighting stopped, and the battle resulted immediately in stalemate and eventually in general peace.

The conflict of 207 B.C.E. pitted Philopoemen and his Achaeans with some mercenaries against the Spartan Machanidas and his mercenaries. Machanidas made the unusual move of interspersing catapults along his line. Philopoemen attacked immediately, but in confused fighting, Machanidas repulsed his mercenaries. When he failed to pursue them, Philopoemen wheeled against the Spartans, decisively defeating them and killing Machanidas.

Consequences. Each battle temporarily furthered the victor's political goals but was ultimately indecisive. Even the peace gained in 362 B.C.E. was short-lived.

ADDITIONAL RESOURCES

Brewer, Paul. *Warfare in the Ancient World.* Austin, Tex.: Raintree/Steck-Vaughn, 1999.

Buckler, J. *The Theban Hegemony, 371-362 B.C.E.* Cambridge, Mass.: Harvard University Press, 1980.

Hanson, Victor Davis. *The Wars of the Ancient Greeks.* London: Cassell, 1999.

Pritchett, W. K. *Studies in Ancient Greek Topography.* Vol. 2. Berkeley: University of California Press, 1969.

SEE ALSO: Alcibiades of Athens; Epaminondas; Greece, Classical.

—*John Buckler*

MAO SHAN REVELATIONS

DATE: received 367-370 C.E.

LOCALE: Southern China, near Nanjing

RELATED CIVILIZATION: China

SIGNIFICANCE: The influence of the Mao Shan texts, one of the most systematic and influential Daoist meditation traditions, can still be seen in modern Chinese religion.

The Mao Shan texts were revealed in southern China during a time of cultural ferment to members of the old local elite, a group whose political and religious status was being undermined by the arrival of northern aristocratic refugees. These inspired texts incorporated elements drawn from northern Celestial Masters of Daoism and Buddhism and from indigenous southern shamanism and were supposedly dictated by Daoist immortals to Yang Xi, a retainer for a prominent local family, between 367 and 370 C.E. The texts, notable for their literary quality, reveal ways to reach "supreme purity," a higher heaven than any known in the northern Daoist traditions.

Although the Mao Shan texts appear to incorporate ritual practices, messianic elements, and cosmological theories drawn from other traditions, their emphasis on solitary meditative visualizations as the highest method for achieving salvation is quite distinctive. The texts became so prestigious that many well-written forgeries were sold by outsiders eager to profit from the popularity of the Mao Shan manuscripts.

By the fifth century C.E., high officials and even emperors showed interest in Mao Shan teachings. The tradition was extraordinarily popular in the Tang Dynasty (618-907 C.E.), but over time, many of its essential elements were absorbed by other Daoist movements.

ADDITIONAL RESOURCE

Robinet, Isabella. *Taoist Meditation: The Mao-Shan Tradition of Great Purity.* Albany: State University of New York Press, 1993.

SEE ALSO: Buddhism; China; Daoism.

—*Scott Lowe*

MARATHON, BATTLE OF

DATE: September, 490 B.C.E.
LOCALE: Plain of Marathon, 20 miles (32 kilometers) northeast of Athens, Greece
RELATED CIVILIZATIONS: Classical Greece, Persia
SIGNIFICANCE: Greece defeated the invading Persians, which enabled the Classical Greek influences of philosophy, politics, and education to evolve.

Background. Ionian Greek cities on the coast of Asia Minor revolted against Persia. The Persian leader Darius the Great invaded the city-state of Athens as punishment for supporting Ionia.

Action. Some 10,000 Athenian and 1,000 Plataean soldiers attacked 20,000 Persians shortly after they landed from the Bay of Marathon. The Greek commander Miltiades the Younger ordered an immediate attack so that afterward they could defend Athens from a second invading Persian force.

Miltiades strategically allowed the Persians to push back the weaker center of his line. Greek soldiers on the ends attacked forward and completed a "double envelopment"; both Persian wings were pushed backward and inward on themselves. The Persians panicked and retreated to their ships, suffering 6,400 casualties to only 192 Greek casualties. The Greeks quickly marched to Athens and scared away the second Persian force.

Consequences. Defeating the invading Persians saved the evolving Classical Greek ideals of civilization from suppression under Persia. The Persians, defeated, returned home.

ADDITIONAL RESOURCES
Creasy, E. S. *Fifteen Decisive Battles of the World.* New York: Dorset Press, 1987.
Green, Peter. *The Greco-Persian Wars.* Berkeley: University of California Press, 1996.

SEE ALSO: Athens; Greco-Persian Wars; Greece, Classical; Miltiades the Younger; Persia.

—Alan P. Peterson

The Battle of Marathon was a decisive victory for the Greeks. (North Wind Picture Archives)

MARCUS AURELIUS

ALSO KNOWN AS: Marcus Aurelius Verus; Marcus Aurelius Antoninus
BORN: April 26, 121 C.E.; Rome
DIED: March 17, 180 C.E.; Sirmium, Pannonia, or Vindobona (modern Vienna)
RELATED CIVILIZATION: Imperial Rome
MAJOR ROLE/POSITION: Emperor

Life. In 161 C.E., Marcus Aurelius (MAHR-kuhs ah-REEL-yuhs) succeeded his adoptive father Antoninus Pius as emperor and requested that the Roman senate name his adoptive brother Lucius Verus co-emperor. They were immediately confronted with a Parthian invasion in the East. Verus drove back the Parthians, but his troops brought back the plague, which decimated Rome's frontier armies and civilian population.

Verus died in 169 C.E., and from 167 C.E. until his death, Aurelius was almost continuously directing military campaigns against invading Germans and Sarmatians along the Danube frontier. His forces eventually drove back these invaders and attacked them in their territories north of the Danube. Aurelius stabilized the frontiers by permitting some Germans to settle in plague-devastated provinces.

Although he spent much of his reign at war, Marcus Aurelius was essentially a man of peace and a Stoic philosopher who recorded his personal thoughts on life and public service in his famous *Tōn eis heauton* (c. 171-180 C.E.; *Meditations*, 1634). Despite his basic benevolence, he showed no tolerance for the Christians, whom he regarded as nonconformists who posed a serious threat to the Roman Empire.

Influence. Marcus Aurelius was the last of the "five good emperors" who ruled the Roman Empire at its height. He was a highly learned and moral individual who provided effective leadership during a time of crisis and change in the empire.

Marcus Aurelius. (Library of Congress)

ADDITIONAL RESOURCES
Birley, Anthony. *Marcus Aurelius: A Biography.* New Haven, Conn.: Yale University Press, 1987.
Marcus Aurelius. *Meditations.* Translated by Maxwell Staniforth. Harmondsworth, England: Penguin Books, 1964.

SEE ALSO: Antoninus Pius; Christianity; Germany; Parthia; Rome, Imperial; Sarmatians.

—*Thomas I. Crimando*

MARCUS AURELIUS'S COLUMN

DATE: c. 180-192 C.E.
LOCALE: Rome, Italy
RELATED CIVILIZATION: Imperial Rome
SIGNIFICANCE: Commemorates the campaigns of Marcus Aurelius against the Germans and Sarmatians.

The column of Marcus Aurelius, commissioned by his son, Lucius Aurelius Commodus, shortly after the emperor's death in 180 C.E., contains 116 scenes on a helical frieze depicting two German campaigns of Marcus Aurelius, the *bellum Germanicum* (172-173 C.E.) and the *bellum Sarmaticum* (174-175 C.E.). This impressive 300-foot-high (91-meter-high) column celebrated the achievements of the deified Marcus Aurelius and the strength of Roman arms.

Modeled after the column of Trajan, the column of Marcus Aurelius depicts various aspects of war, such as marching, sacrifices to the gods, and actual combat. However, several differences in Marcus Aurelius's column reflect upon the increasing instability of the Roman Empire as well as Commodus's own notion of the emperor. In the "Rain Miracle" scene, a personification of rain showers down on the battlefield, confounding the enemy and rejuvenating the Romans. Although the scene reveals the gods' favor of the Romans, it is somewhat tragic because, unlike Trajan's invincible army, Marcus Aurelius's men needed divine intervention during combat. Commodus perhaps reveals his own belief in the emperor as a living god by the frontal placements of Marcus Aurelius above the crowds, usually on a high podium, unlike Trajan who is depicted as the first among equals.

ADDITIONAL RESOURCES
Birley, Anthony. *Marcus Aurelius: A Biography*. New Haven, Conn.: Yale University Press, 1987.
Kleiner, Diana E. E. *Roman Sculpture*. New Haven, Conn.: Yale University Press, 1992.

SEE ALSO: Art and architecture; Germany; Marcus Aurelius; Rome, Imperial; Sarmatians; Trajan.
—*Elizabeth A. Gardiner*

MARITIME ARCHAIC

DATE: c. 6000-1100 B.C.E.
LOCALE: Eastern Canadian maritime provinces
RELATED CIVILIZATION: Algonquian
SIGNIFICANCE: This early group of hunter-gatherers centered around the Gulf of Saint Lawrence following the end of the Pleistocene era eventually became the Algonquian.

When the term "archaic" is applied to Native American cultures, it refers to the cultures that arose following the last Ice Age. The Maritime Archaic culture was part of a larger group generally referred to as Eastern Woodland Archaic and closely related to the Laurentian Archaic group to the northwest. They inhabited the areas surrounding the Gulf of Saint Lawrence, primarily in present-day Newfoundland, New Brunswick, and Northeastern Quebec.

These people can almost certainly be identified with a culture whose remains were among the earliest found in North America, called the Red Paint people because of the preponderance of red, iron-based dyes found in elaborate burial sites. Also found in these sites are well-developed spear points and primitive farming implements. The existence of these sites suggests that the Archaic cultures had at least the beginnings of a sense of territoriality, but by and large, they followed migratory game with the seasons. The Maritime Archaic people also relied on the sea for a great deal of their sustenance, especially for shellfish. The Maritime Archaic people eventually became the Algonquian, who have inhabited eastern Canada and the northeastern United States during historical times.

ADDITIONAL RESOURCES
Snow, Dean. *The Archaeology of North America*. New York: Viking Press, 1976.
Trigger, Bruce G., and Wilcomb E. Washburn, eds. *North America*. Vol. 1 in *The Cambridge History of the Native Peoples of the Americas*. New York: Cambridge University Press, 1996.

SEE ALSO: Archaic North American culture; Archaic tradition, northern; Middle Woodland traditions.
—*Marc Goldstein*

MARIUS, GAIUS

BORN: 157 B.C.E.; Cereatae. Near Arpinum, Latium
(later Arpino, Italy)
DIED: January 13, 86 B.C.E.; Rome
RELATED CIVILIZATION: Republican Rome
MAJOR ROLE/POSITION: Military leader

Life. Born to a modest farming family, Gaius Marius
(GI-uhs MEHR-ee-uhs) joined the army at age twenty-
one. In 134 B.C.E., he fought in his first campaign, in
Numantia.

In 107 B.C.E., Marius was elected consul for the first
of what would be an unprecedented seven terms. He
took command of the Jugurthine War in Numidia,
achieving a final victory when quaestor Lucius
Cornelius Sulla captured Jugurtha. When Marius took
credit for the capture, a bitter feud began that resulted in
a bloody civil war.

Marius distinguished himself in battle in Gaul
against the Teutones in 102 B.C.E. and the Cimbri in 101
B.C.E. A violent confrontation with Sulla was delayed
by the outbreak of the Social War in 91 B.C.E. Following
the defeat of the allies, a violent struggle ensued between Marius's and Sulla's supporters, during which a
defeated Marius died of disease.

Influence. Marius reorganized and reformed the
Roman army. He eliminated the property requirement,
instituted high fitness and training standards, rewarded
his soldiers with land upon their retirement, and improved weapon design. Marius's reforms created client
armies whose generals relied on soldiers' loyalty to further their political aims. He demonstrated how political
success first required military success.

Gaius Marius. (Library of Congress)

ADDITIONAL RESOURCES

Keppie, Lawrence. *The Making of the Roman Army.*
New York: Barnes and Noble, 1994.

Kildahl, Phillip A. *Caius Marius.* Twayne's Rulers and
Statesmen of the World Series 7. New York:
Twayne, 1968.

Plutarch. *Fall of the Roman Republic.* Translated by
Rex Warner. New York: Penguin Books, 1972.

SEE ALSO: Gauls; Jugurtha; Rome, Republican; Sulla,
Lucius Cornelius.

—*J. S. Costa*

MAROBODUUS

BORN: date and place unknown
DIED: c. 36-37 C.E.; Ravenna, Italy
RELATED CIVILIZATIONS: Germany, Bohemia
MAJOR ROLE/POSITION: Military and political
leader

Life. Maroboduus (muh-RAHB-uhd-uhs), a member of Germanic tribal nobility, spent some of his formative years at the court of Emperor Augustus (r. 27
B.C.E.-14 C.E.), where he received a typical Roman edu-

cation. Maroboduus also served some time in the Ro-
man army. After the Germanic tribes had been pacified
by Nero Claudius Drusus in 9 B.C.E., the Romans aided
Maroboduus in his rise to power. He built and trained a
large army and began to subjugate other tribes in central
Europe. In 6 C.E., Rome had to send Tiberius with
twelve legions against him. Shortly before the armies of
Rome and Maroboduus would have met and battled in
Bohemia, Illyricum rose in revolt against Rome.
Tiberius and his legions were needed there. Tiberius

and Maroboduus came to terms. Maroboduus was officially recognized as king of the Marcomanni tribes in Germany.

Arminius, leader of the Cherusci in Germany, rose up against Rome and massacred Publius Quinctilius Varus and his three Roman legions in 9 C.E. Threatened by Arminius, Maroboduus had to call for help from Rome in 17 C.E. Instead, Rome helped to overthrow Maroboduus and put its own man in his place. Maroboduus was granted refuge in Ravenna, Italy, where he spent the last eighteen years of his life.

Influence. Maroboduus proved to be a remarkably talented leader, who led his people into Bohemia and away from the Roman sphere of influence in Germany.

ADDITIONAL RESOURCES
Bunson, Matthew. *A Dictionary of the Roman Empire.* New York: Oxford University Press, 1995.
Tacitus, Cornelius. *The Annals of Imperial Rome.* Translated by Michael Grant. Rev. ed. New York: Barnes & Noble, 1993.

SEE ALSO: Arminius; Augustus; Germany; Rome, Imperial; Tiberius; Quinctilius Varus, Publius.

—Victoria Erhart

MARPOLE PHASE

DATE: 500 B.C.E.-700 C.E.
LOCALE: Fraser Delta and Strait of Georgia, British Columbia, Canada, and Puget Sound, Washington state
RELATED CIVILIZATIONS: Locarno Beach phase, Saint Mungo phase, Northwest Coast cultures
SIGNIFICANCE: This phase represents an early climax in Northwest Coast social and cultural complexity.

Marpole is the best-known phase of Northwest Coast prehistoric cultures because of the many excavated sites. The main site is a deep, multiacre shell midden at Marpole in Vancouver that is now covered with buildings. It was excavated in the early 1900's, the 1930's, and the 1950's. Other Marpole phase sites in the Gulf Islands were excavated from the 1960's through the 1990's. Marpole culture evolved from the earlier Locarno Beach phase. The Marpole people used woodworking tools—wedges, chisels, adzes, and stone spool-shaped hand mauls. They also fished and hunted using the commonly found harpoon heads and points used on spears. Stone bowls depicting a seated human figure with ribs were probably used by the shaman in curing illness. The bow and arrow was used beginning about 500 C.E. Both lip plugs (labrets) and artificial head deformation are found in Marpole phase sites, indicating a complex ranked society. Slavery was probably practiced. The Marpole people existed until about 1500.

ADDITIONAL RESOURCES
Burley, David. *Marpole: Anthropological Reconstructions of a Prehistoric Northwest Coast Culture Type.* Burnaby, B.C.: Department of Archaeology, Simon Fraser University, 1980.
Mitchell, Donald. "Prehistory of the Coasts of Southern British Columbia and Northern Washington." In *Northwest Coast,* edited by Wayne Suttles. Vol. 7 in *Handbook of North American Indians.* Washington, D.C.: Smithsonian Institution Press, 1990.

SEE ALSO: Locarno Beach; Saint Mungo phase.

—Roy L. Carlson

MARTIAL

ALSO KNOWN AS: Marcus Valerius Martialis
BORN: March 1, 38-41 C.E.; Bilbilis, Hispania (Spain)
DIED: c. 130 C.E.; Hispania (Spain)
RELATED CIVILIZATION: Imperial Rome
MAJOR ROLE/POSITION: Epigrammatist, humorist

Life. Martial (MAHR-shall) came to Rome as a young man and gained attention by publishing a pamphlet, *Epigrammaton liber* (80 C.E.; *On the Spectacles,* 1980), celebrating both the grand opening of the Flavian Amphitheater and the glory of the Flavian family, who became his patrons. Martial is best known for his twelve books of epigrams, which he published over the next twenty years before retiring to his hometown.

Martial's fifteen hundred epigrams are mostly short, satirical in nature, and characterized by a "point" at the end, usually made by the last word of the poem. Martial's subject matter is daily life in Rome. He is a realist, a hater of pretense, eager to expose hypocrisy, and willing to name names. Martial describes without moralizing. His humor may be cruel and even vicious, but he understands people perfectly.

Criticism of Martial focuses on the obscenity that colors about one-fifth of his epigrams. Another objection has been his admiration of the despotic emperor Domitian; however, Martial could hardly afford to offend the ruler who had supported him. Less pardonable is Martial's obvious hatred of women, another recurrent theme.

Influence. Martial crystallized the epigram as a literary form and is sometimes called "the father of the epigram."

ADDITIONAL RESOURCES

Coffey, M. *Roman Satire.* Bristol: Bristol Classical Press, 1989.

Sullivan, J. *Martial: The Unexpected Classic.* Cambridge, England: Cambridge University Press, 1991.

SEE ALSO: Catullus; Frontinus, Sextus Julius; Phaedrus; Quintilian; Rome, Imperial.

—*Andrew Adams*

MARY

ALSO KNOWN AS: Virgin Mary; Saint Mary
FLOURISHED: first century C.E.
RELATED CIVILIZATION: Imperial Rome
MAJOR ROLE/POSITION: Religious figure

Life. The only source of information about Mary is the Christian Bible, which centers on her role as mother of Jesus and does not provide a full biographical account. According to the Christian tradition, an angel told Mary that she would supernaturally bear Jesus Christ, the prophesied Messiah. When she became pregnant, an angel told Joseph, her betrothed, not to abandon Mary because her conception was by the Holy Spirit. So Joseph married her but had no sexual relations with her.

Augustus ordered everyone to his hometown for a census. Mary and Joseph left Nazareth for Bethlehem, where she gave birth to Jesus in a stable. A host of angels appeared to shepherds pasturing their flocks and told them that the Messiah, the savior, had been born in Bethlehem. They went to see Jesus and then spread the word of his birth.

After Jesus was circumcised, Mary and Joseph traveled to Jerusalem for purification rites, to consecrate Jesus, and to offer a sacrifice for him. While there, they received prophetic mes-

Mary. (Library of Congress)

sages—one was that a sword would pierce Mary's heart. This prophecy came true thirty-three years later when Mary watched Jesus be crucified. However, her grief turned to joy when Jesus rose from the grave a few days later.

Influence. Mary's obedience and humility have been examples to Christians down through the ages. As the mother of Jesus, she is an object of veneration in the Christian Church and a favorite subject in art.

ADDITIONAL RESOURCES

Michelis, Denis. *The Virgin Mary.* Brookline, Mass.: Holy Cross Orthodox Press, 1994.

The New Testament: The Authorized or King James Version of 1611. Introduction by John Drury. New York: Alfred A. Knopf, 1998.

SEE ALSO: Christianity; Jesus Christ.

—*Emerson Thomas McMullen*

MASADA, BATTLE OF

DATE: 73 C.E.

LOCALE: Israel

SIGNIFICANCE: The defeat of the Zealot Jews by the Romans at the Battle of Masada marked the end of the Jewish revolt against Roman rule of Judaea.

Background. The mountaintop fortress of Masada (mah-SAW-duh) was built by Herod the Great, one of the most powerful kings in the Eastern Roman Empire. Ten years after Herod's death (4 B.C.E.), Judaea came under the direct control of Rome. The Jews were unwilling to accept Roman rule and Roman suppression of Jewish life. As a result, riots gave way to increased violence, and in 66 C.E., a full-scale revolt broke out. The leaders of the revolt were the Zealots, an extremist Jewish sect.

Action. During the revolt, the Zealots seized the fortress of Masada from its Roman occupiers. Situated on a rugged mass of rock about thirteen hundred feet (roughly four hundred meters) above the western shore of the Dead Sea, Masada was nearly impregnable and posed a special challenge to the Roman Tenth legion that besieged it. The Zealot force of nearly one thousand was able to use bathhouses, aqueducts, and thick siege walls. A snakelike path led up the mountain, and rocks and boulders provided perfect spots for the Zealots to hide behind during attacks. Vastly outnumbered, the Zealots were able to withstand the Roman siege for three years. In the end however, the fifteen-thousand-strong Roman army was able to defeat the Zealots through a combination of catapults and battering rams. The Zealot leader Elazar ben Yair decided that all the Jewish defenders should commit suicide rather than accept defeat and a life of slavery. The Zealots obeyed; the men proceeded to kill their wives and children and then one another. Only two women and five children survived, after hiding themselves. They told their story to Flavius Josephus, who then recorded it for posterity in his history of the First Jewish Revolt.

Consequences. The fall of Masada and the destruction of Jerusalem and the temple marked the dispersal of the Jews from Judaea. In the late twentieth century, Masada became widely known through the excavations carried out by archaeologist Yigael Yadin. He uncovered ritual baths and a synagogue used by the defenders as well as twenty-five skeletons of men, women, and children.

ADDITIONAL RESOURCES

Josephus, Flavius. *The History of the Jewish War.* Translated by Henry St. John Thackeray et al. Cambridge, Mass.: Harvard University Press, 1999.

Williamson, G. A. *The World of Josephus.* Boston: Little, Brown, 1964.

Yadin, Yigael. *Masada.* New York: Welcom Rain, 1998.

SEE ALSO: Herodian Dynasty; Jerusalem, temple of; Judaism; Rome, Imperial; Zealots.

—*Adriane Ruggiero*

MAURYAN DYNASTY

DATE: c. 321-185 B.C.E.
LOCALE: India, Pakistan, Afghanistan
RELATED CIVILIZATION: India
SIGNIFICANCE: The first empire of the Indian subcontinent.

Chandragupta Maurya in about 321 B.C.E. founded the Mauryan Dynasty. He began by overthrowing the unjust Nanda ruler of Magadha. Then, from his capital at Pāṭaliputra, he began extending his authority to create an empire that eventually embraced all lands north of the Vindhya Mountains and extended from sea to sea. To govern his wealthy empire, he created a powerful centralized bureaucracy. He and his chief minister, Kauṭilya, established a model of governance that persisted well into the modern era in India. Most of what is known of Chandragupta Maurya comes from a Greek ambassador named Megasthenes, who wrote a treatise about his long stay in India.

The third ruler, Aśoka (r. c. 265-238 B.C.E.), became the most famous of the Mauryan line. Through prolonged warfare, he extended the empire until it covered nearly the whole subcontinent of India. Eventually sickened by bloodshed and full of remorse for having caused great suffering, Aśoka converted to Buddhism. Throughout his remaining years, he promoted the Buddhist religion and morality. Declaring that all subjects were his children, he encouraged all to eschew any form of killing, the eating of meat, and any cruel conduct toward living things. Aśoka recorded his declarations in some forty-four edicts carved on stone pillars and the faces of rocks located throughout his empire. In the edicts, he encourages his subjects to promote tolerance, mutual respect, self-control, kindness, and truthfulness.

THE KINGS OF THE MAURYAN DYNASTY

King	Reign
Chandragupta	c. 321-301 B.C.E.
Bindusāra	301-269
Aśoka	265-238
Kunala	232-225
Daśaratha	232-225
Samprati	225-215
Salisuka	215-202
Devavarman	202-195
Satadhanvan	195-187
Bṛhadratha	187-185

ADDITIONAL RESOURCES

Dikshitar, V. R. *The Mauryan Polity.* Delhi, India: Motilal Banarsidass, 1993.

Nilakanta Sastri, K. A., ed. *Age of the Nandas and Mauryas.* Delhi, India: Motilal Banarsidass, 1988.

SEE ALSO: Aśoka; Chandragupta Maurya; India; Kauṭilya.

—*Katherine Anne Harper*

MAUSOLUS

BORN: date unknown; Caria
DIED: 353/352 B.C.E.; Caria
RELATED CIVILIZATIONS: Classical Greece, Persia
MAJOR ROLE/POSITION: Satrap

Life. Mausolus (maw-SOH-luhs) was a Persian satrap of Caria in southwest Asia Minor, where he ruled from 377/376 B.C.E. until his death in 353/352 B.C.E. Keen to increase his own power, his friendly relations with Persia were soured by his being one of the leaders in the Great Revolt of the Satraps in 362 B.C.E., although he deserted the cause and hence was not punished by the Persian king. This allowed Mausolus to continue his imperialistic policy, encroaching on the territories of Lycia and Ionia and also moving his capital from Mylasa to Halicarnassus, where he built a great fortress and married his sister Artemisia II.

In 356 B.C.E., Mausolus supported the revolt of Rhodes, Byzantium, Chios, and Cos against Athens in the Social War, and a few years later, he annexed Rhodes and Cos. He may even have engineered the Social War, as he could not expand his power on land because of the Persian king's settlement after the Satraps' revolt and could only turn to the islands. Mausolus was a patron of the arts and literature but is perhaps best remembered for his tomb. The mausoleum, made of white marble and measuring 100 by 127 feet (30 by 39 meters) and 134 feet (41 meters) high, was completed after his death.

Influence. As well as being the source of the word "mausoleum," Mausolus may be credited with spreading Greek culture in inland Asia Minor long before Alexander the Great.

ADDITIONAL RESOURCES

Hornblower, S. *Mausolus*. Oxford, England: Oxford University Press, 1982.

Sealey, R. *Demosthenes and His Time*. Oxford, England: Oxford University Press, 1982.

SEE ALSO: Artemisia II; Greece, Classical; Persia.
—Ian Worthington

MAXENTIUS

ALSO KNOWN AS: Marcus Aurelius Valerius Maxentius
BORN: c. 283 C.E.; place unknown
DIED: October 28, 312 C.E.; Milvian Bridge, near Rome
RELATED CIVILIZATION: Imperial Rome
MAJOR ROLE/POSITION: Usurper, Roman emperor

Life. Maxentius (mak-SEHN-shee-uhs), son of Maximian and Eutropia, was married to the daughter of Gaius Galerius Valerius Maximianus. Upon the abdication of Maximian and Diocletian in 305 C.E., he was passed over in favor of better candidates. While he was residing in Rome, events swept Maxentius into prominence. On October 28, 306 C.E., a revolt broke out in Rome, and most officials went over to Maxentius. First Italy and then Africa proclaimed their allegiance to him. Flavius Valerius Severus marched on Rome, but his troops deserted to their old emperor Maximian. In order to avoid further embarrassment, Severus made peace with Maxentius and confirmed him as emperor.

After the murder of Maximian in 310 C.E., Maxentius successfully invaded Africa and brought it under his control. Emboldened by his successes, Maxentius declared war on Constantine the Great. The latter had

received dispatches from Rome begging him to intervene against the tyrant. After victories at Turin and Verona, Constantine drove Maxentius toward Rome. The decisive battle was fought in 312 C.E. at the Saxa Rubra where Maxentius's army was broken and driven toward the Tiber. As Maxentius's army fled across the Milvian Bridge, the bridge broke beneath them, and many were drowned in the river. Maxentius was among the victims. Constantine became master of the West.

Influence. The defeat of Maxentius ended the tetrarchic system of Diocletian. It also led to the acceptance of Christianity as a religion of equal standing within the bounds of the Roman Empire.

ADDITIONAL RESOURCES

Alföldi, Andreas. *The Conversion of Constantine and Pagan Rome*. New York: Oxford University Press, 1998.

Burckhardt, W. *The Age of Constantine the Great*. New York: Dorset Press, 1989.

SEE ALSO: Christianity; Constantine the Great; Diocletian; Galerius Valerius Maximianus, Gaius; Maximian; Milvian Bridge, Battle of; Rome, Imperial.
—Martin C. J. Miller

MAXIMIAN

ALSO KNOWN AS: Marcus Aurelius Valerius Maximianus
BORN: c. 250 C.E.; Sirmium, Pannonia Inferior
DIED: 310 C.E.; Massilia (later Marseille, France)
RELATED CIVILIZATION: Imperial Rome
MAJOR ROLE/POSITION: Roman emperor

Life. A career soldier, Maximian (mak-SIHM-ee-an) was a comrade-in-arms of Diocletian. In 285 C.E., Diocletian appointed his old friend to the rank of Caesar to rule over the Roman West. In 293 C.E., Maximian was elevated to Augustus and Diocletian's coruler in a four-person imperial college called the

Tetrarchy. Maximian campaigned against foreign invaders in Gaul, Germany, Spain, and North Africa. After celebrating a triumph in Rome, he began building the famous baths of Diocletian in 299 C.E. A few years later, in 303 C.E., Diocletian joined Maximian in Rome, where they celebrated a joint triumph, the twentieth anniversary of their reign, and enacted the Great Persecution, a state-sponsored pogrom against Christians.

In 305 C.E., Diocletian abdicated from the emperorship and compelled Maximian to follow him. Restless in retirement, Maximian returned to politics in 307 C.E., joining his son Maxentius in a civil war against the legitimate augusti, Flavius Valerius Severus and Gaius Galerius Valerius Maximianus. Failing to depose his own son, Maxentius, Maximian allied himself with Constantine the Great in Gaul and later attempted to subvert his erstwhile benefactor. He was captured in Massilia and forced to commit suicide in 310 C.E.

Influence. Maximian's political vicissitude pointed to the instability of the tetrarchy without the guidance of Diocletian's strong personality.

ADDITIONAL RESOURCES

Barnes, Timothy D. *Constantine and Eusebius*. Cambridge, Mass.: Harvard University Press, 1981.
Corcoran, S. *Empire of the Tetrarchs*. Oxford, England: Oxford University Press, 1996.

SEE ALSO: Africa, North; Christianity; Constantine the Great; Diocletian; Galerius Valerius Maximianus, Gaius; Gauls; Germany; Maxentius; Rome, Imperial; Spain.

—*Byron J. Nakamura*

MAYA

DATE: 1000 B.C.E.-900 C.E.
LOCALE: Guatemala, Belize, Yucatán peninsula of Mexico, western Honduras, El Salvador
SIGNIFICANCE: The Maya civilization was marked by the rise of competing city-states, often at war with one another, centralized under the capital of Tikal, Guatemala, and is identified by temples and palaces with monuments providing historical information.

History. Although evidence indicates that people lived in Central America after the retreat of the Pleistocene glaciers, the first traces of Maya culture date from about 1000 B.C.E. during the Middle Preclassic period (1000-300 B.C.E.) with the introduction of pottery. The earliest Maya were farmers living in small villages, as evidenced by an oval house platform with post molds at Cuello and ceramics from Cuello, Santa Rita Corozal, Colha, and other sites in Belize.

The Late Preclassic period (300 B.C.E.-300 C.E.) marked the rise of cultural complexity as seen in temples with stuccoed and painted facades, built by the common Maya folk at the instructions of the emerging Maya rulers. The site of Cerros, Belize, emerged as an important Late Preclassic community, with a core consisting of temples and other elite buildings and a larger area of dispersed small households beyond. The Late Preclassic also is noted for the development of long-distance trade for elite items, such as jade and obsidian, that were commissioned by the ruling elite, used during their lifetimes, and often buried with them or as offerings and dedications to building construction or termination rituals. Stucco masks on temple facades are similar to developments at the same time at other Maya communities, notably Tikal, Uaxactun, and Dzibilchaltún, and point to long-distance communication among emerging elites that may actually have fostered the development of the Classic civilization.

The Classic period (300-900 C.E.) is defined as the time when the Maya erected stelae, carved monuments with dates, in the Maya long count. The earliest dated stela is 292 C.E. at Tikal, and the last dated stela is 889 C.E. at Caracol. The stelae are stone slabs, each with a depiction of an important Maya person, often a ruler, on one side and hieroglyphic writing and dates on the other side. The stelae were erected in front of temples and palaces in the central areas of Classic period cities for public viewing and recounted significant events in a ruler's life, notably, birth, marriage, accession to the throne, battles won, and death.

The height of the Maya civilization was during the Late Classic period (600-900 C.E.), when building efforts, population, and artistic endeavors reached their peaks. The high population densities in cities increasingly taxed the Maya farmers, who provided labor to construct the Maya temples and palaces and food for the city folk.

ANCIENT MESOAMERICAN CITIES AND AREAS

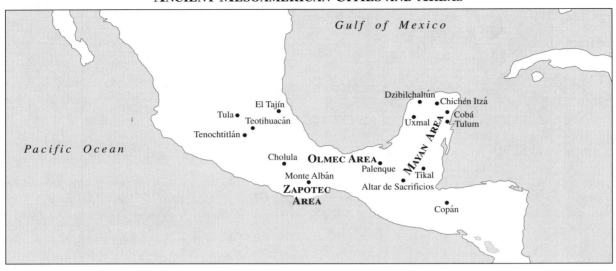

The collapse of the Classic Maya civilization by 900 C.E. was precipitated by overpopulation and ecological disasters brought on by extensive clearing of the rainforest and overuse of the land for agriculture. Certainly, warfare between regions was endemic during the Late Classic period. Although a few cities, such as Lamanai in Belize, continued during the subsequent Postclassic period (900-1500 C.E.), the center of power moved to the northern Maya lowlands of the Yucatán peninsula, and the Maya living in the southern Maya lowlands returned to their rural farming way of life.

Architecture and city planning. The basic unit of Maya architecture was the *plazuela* (plaza group), consisting of several buildings around a central plaza. The *plazuela* was the basis for household architecture as well as that of the temples and palaces in the city cores. Consequently, the urban character of Maya cities was dispersed. The main plaza of a city consisted of a temple along one or two sides, with palaces or elite administrative buildings along the other two sides, with a ball court nearby. The temple consisted of a large, rubble-filled platform with a small room on top, and often a decorative architectural extension termed a "roof comb" that further elevated the temple.

Agriculture and animal husbandry. The Maya developed systems of agriculture to suit the varied environments and the increasing population. Although slash-and-burn agriculture was carried out, hill slopes were terraced, canals were dug in swamps to create drained field or raised field agriculture, and people had kitchen gardens and practiced tree cropping. Traces of agricultural activity, together with preserved plant food remains from Cerros, Colha, Cuello, Copán, Wild Cane Cay, and Frenchman's Cay, reveal that the Maya ate corn and beans and tree crops such as native palms and forest fruits. With few domesticated animals—dog, muscovy duck, and stingless bee—the Maya relied on wild animals for meat, including fish at coastal sites and deer and peccary inland.

Calendars and chronology. The Maya had two calendar systems based on multiples of twenty that intersected every fifty-two years. The beginning of the Maya calendar corresponds to the year 3113 B.C.E. in the Christian calendar. Archaeologists develop chronologies of the Maya by reference to the dated stelae and also from study of the changing styles of pottery vessels from excavations. Generally, polychrome pottery is typical of the Classic period, whereas carved or incised decoration is typical of the Postclassic period.

Death and burial. The Maya had no separate cemeteries but instead buried people under the floors and in the construction fill of residences and temples. The royal Maya were interred in stone tombs in temples that had been the focus of their rituals and political lives. This tradition reflects the importance the Maya placed on ancestry and lineage membership. Pottery vessels, obsidian and chert artifacts, shell, carved bone, and various perishable items were placed as grave offerings, the number and level of craftsmanship reflecting the deceased's social standing.

Government and law. The Classic Maya were ruled by the kings of royal Maya dynasties, whose word was law. The Maya rulers in each region were supported in part by subsistence farmers who owed labor and paid a food tax to them. The royal Maya family lived in the cities, along with craft specialists producing finely made goods for the royal Maya, artisans working on a variety of building, plastering, and craft works, and a few bureaucrats associated with the Maya royalty.

Medicine and health. Human skeletal studies indicate the Maya were relatively healthy, although some studies indicate the common Maya were shorter and had less access to imported foods such as seafood.

Navigation and transportation. Boat models recovered from Altun Ha, Moho Cay, and Orlando's Jewfish, as well as incised depictions of canoes on bones from a burial in Temple 1 at Tikal, indicate the Maya had boats and paddles, but there is no evidence of sails. Their settlement of offshore islands also indicates the use of boats. Overland transportation was by trails and *sacbes* (limestone causeways). Human porters, sometimes slaves, were used to carry goods.

Religion and ritual. The Maya had a pantheon of gods, but the Maya king was the most important ritual figure. Fasting, bloodletting, and vision quest were carried out by the royal Maya at important state events, notably accession to the throne, marriage, the birth of a child, and death. The public display of royal Maya bloodletting, with a stingray spine, rope, or obsidian blade piercing the tongue, penis, ear, or other soft body part, is recorded on stelae and other carvings and on Maya pottery vessels.

Science and technology. The Maya had a complex mathematical system involving the advanced concept of zero as well as a complicated calendrical system. Technologically, the Maya had no domesticated draft animals and did not use the wheel, either for transportation or in the production of pottery vessels, which were produced by hand using the coil technique. The Maya were sophisticated craftspeople whose skill was reflected in their pottery and chert stone tools and also in their organization and construction of temples and palaces.

Settlements and social structure. Maya settlement patterns reveal a hierarchical social structure. Each geographic region had a capital with towns and villages

The pyramid of Kukulkan at Chichén Itzá in the Yucatán Peninsula, Mexico. (Corbis)

located around it, owing political and economic allegiance to that city. Trade, as well as fairs and religious events, was focused on the city.

Sports and entertainment. Ball courts are a feature of Maya cities but not of smaller communities. Located at the city center, the ball game was an important political event, with the cost of losing sometimes being death. The game was played with a rubber ball, and the players had elaborate gear. Depictions of the ball game in progress can be seen in carvings at the ball court at Chichén Itzá. The ritual significance of the ball game is tied to the origin myth of the Maya hero twins recorded in the *Popul Vuh*, a historic text.

Trade and commerce. Although most of the everyday goods and resources were obtained from nearby locations, obsidian, jade, exotic pottery, marine resources, and mercury were obtained from distant areas by the elite and were displayed as status symbols. Some exotics, such as obsidian, a volcanic rock used to make sharp-edged blades, were traded even to the common Maya. Trading ports along the Caribbean include Wild Cane Cay and Cozumel.

Visual and performing arts. The Maya displayed art publicly, from stone or stuccoed masks on temple facades and the brightly colored temples and other public architecture to murals at Bonampak and cave paintings. Multicolored painted pottery was typical of the Classic period, with ritual and historic themes of figures depicted on Late Classic vases, many of which had hieroglyphic writing. Fancy pottery was used in public feasting and ritual ceremonies of the royal Maya, with vessels for chocolate, tamales, and other foods depicted on pottery. Figures were also depicted in relief and sometimes as at Copán, in the round, on stelae, which, along with the hieroglyphs, were historical documents and public statements by the elite Maya. There are artistic depictions of dancers and musicians on pottery vessels and actual musical vessels from Pacbitun and other Maya sites.

War and weapons. By the Late Classic, warfare was endemic among the lowland Maya, with Maya kings competing for control of neighboring cities. The downfall of cities was recorded on stelae at the conquering city. One by one, the Late Classic cities fell, and by 900 C.E., the southern lowland cities were abandoned.

Women's life. Royal Maya women had power, sometimes by virtue of a marriage alliance with another city or as the mother of a king. They are often depicted in high art involved in rituals and ceremonies. Grave offerings were associated with women of all ranks, re-

flecting their lineage's rank. Although analogies between modern or sixteenth century Maya women and the Classic civilization may be questioned, there are artistic depictions showing women involved in a variety of tasks, including weaving and grinding corn.

Writing systems. The Classic Maya had a hieroglyphic writing system that is preserved on stelae and other carved monuments, on pottery vessels, and on some stone carvings. The writing was used to record historical information about the royal Maya and to describe important rituals, but was not about commerce and only incidentally about astronomy and mathematics, as used in the calendars. The ability to read and write was evidently limited to the upper class, as hieroglyphics at some smaller communities were decorative but not real glyphs, indicating that the medium was the message.

Current views. Old views of the empty ceremonial center supported by rural slash-and-burn farmers have been replaced by new views of densely populated cities supported by more intensive agriculture. Reasons for the collapse of the civilization still focus on ecological and demographic problems, but the roles of warfare and climate change are now considered. Once considered a peaceful people focusing on astronomy and mathematics, the Maya as revealed through the decipherment of the hieroglyphs were shown to be a bellicose people. Current examination of the nature of craft specialization and trade of salt, obsidian, chert, and other materials will enhance knowledge of Classic Maya society and economy.

ADDITIONAL RESOURCES

Coe, Michael. *The Maya*. New York: Thames and Hudson, 1993.

Fash, William. *Scribes, Warriors, and Kings*. New York: Thames and Hudson, 1991.

Harrison, Peter. *The Lords of Tikal*. New York: Thames and Hudson, 1999.

McAnany, Patricia, and Barry Isaac, eds. *Prehistoric Maya Economies of Belize*. Research in Economic Anthropology, Supplement 4. Greenwich, Conn.: JAI Press, 1989.

Schele, Linda, and David Freidel. *A Forest of Kings*. New York: William Morrow, 1990.

SEE ALSO: Altar de Sacrificios; Ball game, Mesoamerican; Chichén Itzá; Cobá; Copán; Olmecs; Palenque; Pyramid of the Moon; Tikal.

—Heather I. McKillop

MELA, POMPONIUS

FLOURISHED: c. 44 C.E.; place unknown
RELATED CIVILIZATION: Imperial Rome
MAJOR ROLE/POSITION: Historian, geographer

Life. Nothing is known of Pomponius Mela (pahm-POH-nee-uhs MEE-luh) except what he says and what may be inferred from his only surviving book, *De chorographia* (also known as *De situ terrarum orbis*, 43 or 44 C.E.; *The Cosmographer, Concerninge the Situation of the World*, 1585). He boasts of his native region and his hometown Tingentera in the Roman province of Baetica, Spain. The location of Tingentera is uncertain. It was near the Pillars of Hercules (Strait of Gibraltar) and may be the Julia Traducta attested on coins. He praises Claudius's conquest of Britain, promoting the emperor's imminent triumph. The expectant air suggests that Pomponius was writing at Rome, perhaps to win imperial patronage. Like other Spanish-born Roman writers, Pomponius had migrated to the capital. The book was published between August, 43 C.E. (Claudius's departure for the front) and February, 44 C.E. (his triumph at Rome). A generation later, Pomponius was named as a source for nine books of Pliny the Elder's *Naturalis historia* (77 C.E.; *Natural History*, 1938-1963). Pomponius treats the coastal region of the known world without regard to the continental interiors. The book is cast as a coasting voyage, beginning and ending on the North African side of the Pillars of Hercules, skirting the Mediterranean coasts of Africa, Asia, and Europe, and then the outer coasts of Europe, Asia, and Africa. Pomponius was unoriginal. Even his one apparent novelty, the Nile's underground bed, probably is owed to the same source as the underground beds of the Po, Ister, and Alpheus.

Influence. Pomponius's work provides a view of the Roman world during his time. Scholars disagree about whether Pomponius meant the book to stand alone or be followed by a more comprehensive work; recent opinion inclines to the first view.

ADDITIONAL RESOURCES
Elton, Charles Isaac. *Origins of English History*. London: B. Quaritch, 1890.
Mela, Pomponius. *Pomponius Mela's Description of the World*. Translated by F. E. Romer. Ann Arbor: University of Michigan Press, 1998.

SEE ALSO: Britain; Claudius; Pliny the Elder; Rome, Imperial.

—F. E. Romer

MELANESIA

DATE: 8000 B.C.E.-700 C.E.
LOCALE: Oceania, Pacific Islands
SIGNIFICANCE: Melanesians, many of whom came from Southeast Asia, created a rich material culture marked by oceangoing canoes and art work.

Melanesia (meh-lah-NEE-zhuh) is the great arc of mountainous islands situated north and east of Australia and south of the equator. These islands form chains in the western Pacific from Fiji to New Guinea and consist of the Fiji group, New Caledonia, Vanuatu, and the Solomons. The modern islands contain an enormous range of cultures, peoples, languages (some nine hundred language groups), and geographical features. The name comes from Greek *melas*, "black," and *nesos*, "island," because inhabitants are predominantly dark-skinned. Melanesians are distinguished from the peoples of Micronesia to the north and of Polynesia to the east by such racial and cultural characteristics as woolly black hair, nearly black skin, and medium stature.

History. Anthropologists believe present-day Melanesians descended from Asian migrants who traveled by way of the islands of Indonesia some 33,000 years ago, when a lowered sea level may have resulted in land bridges and narrow straits. For centuries, traders from Southeast Asia and outlying islands undoubtedly sailed to western Melanesia. The Melanesians represent the earliest islands to be settled in Oceania. When the Europeans arrived in Melanesia in the sixteenth century, they found Melanesian societies to be Neolithic in nature, in that they used a technology based on stones, bones, and shells and cultivated tubers and tree fruits of largely Southeast Asian origin.

The social organization of the Melanesians before the arrival of Europeans was based primarily on kinship but did not exhibit class distinctions. Family ties were determined by descent through either a male or female lineage, though occasionally a vague mythological character constituted the common ancestor. Marriages were arranged by elders seeking to strengthen alliances and benefit from the transfer of property to the bride's family. Men of conspicuous wealth or who were strong leaders might take several wives. Leadership of the community fell to men who exhibited outstanding physical strength, considerable wealth, or proven qualities of leadership. The position was not hereditary except, it is believed, among the inhabitants of Fiji.

Feuds between neighboring communities were perpetuated by raids, thievery, and insults—real or imaginary—to important people. There were times when the disputes erupted into cannibalism or all-out war. Serious social upheavals were prevented only by the economic interdependence of the people and strong ties of kinship.

The settlement of Fiji exhibits a fusion of racial elements because of its later settlement. The first people to arrive there were light-skinned, broad-nosed Polynesians speaking an Austronesian language. They originated in insular Southeast Asia and gradually migrated east past already settled Melanesian islands. The discovery of distinctive pottery, decorated in horizontal geometric bands (Lapita pottery) and dating from around 1290 B.C.E., indicates these migrants had reached Fiji by about 1500 B.C.E. or earlier. Dark-skinned Melanesians arrived no earlier than 500 B.C.E., bringing with them their distinct pottery traditions. The fusion of these primordial peoples gave rise to modern Fijians.

Their hierarchical social structure came from that of the Polynesians, in which status and descent passed through the male line with power concentrated in the chief. The hereditary chiefs possessed the *mana* (spiritual energy) of an ancestral spirit. However, the son of a woman belonging to a chief could lay claim to the property of his mother's brothers. This possibility, combined with polygamy, kept society in a state of constant turmoil. The feudal aristocracy joined in confederations that extended their influence through war. Treachery and cannibalism were inseparable from these struggles; women were taken as trophies or exchanged to form alliances. Much of the blame for barbarism attributed to the early Melanesians, especially on Fiji, falls on the native aristocracy. To humiliate their enemies, a chieftain might take the polished skull of a defeated enemy and use it as a drinking vessel. Some chiefs apparently took delight in cooking and consuming body parts as their agonized victims looked on. Men were buried alive to support the wooden posts of new houses. War canoes were launched over the living bodies of young girls, and the widows of chiefs were strangled to accompany their husbands in the spirit world.

Material culture and economy. The feudal islanders were guardians of one of the highest material cultures of the Pacific. They built great oceangoing double canoes nearly 100 feet (30 meters) long. The dugout canoe with a single outrigger is an ancient mode of transport used by the Melanesians from earliest times. They developed variations in the basic design, such as the use of board siding, posts at prow and stern, and fabricated sails. Double hulls fitted with sails were produced for major trading voyages. The feudal islanders' houses were large, decorated solid-thatched houses. Elsewhere the Melanesian house types varied from simple circular huts of wood and fibers to large communal dwellings.

The prosperous early Melanesians engaged in a variety of economic pursuits: agriculture, hunting, fishing (where feasible), gathering of wild plant products, and limited trade by bartering.

Arts. Elaborate art forms are found everywhere in Melanesian settlements. The people expressed themselves in painting, pottery, sculpture, and carved materials. Forms of personal ornamentation such as body painting, masks, and ornaments, as well as totems, amulets, and clubhouse carvings, were used to display religious and ceremonial symbolism. The media used include stone, clay, wood, vegetable, bark, shells, hair, and feathers. They enjoyed such typical patterns as stylized representations of birds, fish, animals, and the human form. Their abstract geometrical designs were usually derived from these subjects.

Melanesian music and dance consisted of songs to celebrate both legendary and current events. These often had spiritual significance. Drums, gongs, rattles, reed pipes, and ceremonial weapons were used with group dancing and choral singing. Solo instrumental performance was rare.

Food. The food of the Melanesians was traditionally derived from agriculture and fishing supplemented by hunting and gathering. Most of their dietary starch came from tuberous roots: taro in wet lowlands, with yams more common in areas of seasonal rainfall. The poorer soils produced cassava, and the cooler uplands provided sweet potatoes. These starchy roots were wrapped in edible leaves for roasting or baking. The starchy pith of the wild sago palm remains a staple food of the swamplands of western Melanesia. They also ate coconuts, bananas, and breadfruit. Fish provided protein for coastal inhabitants; those inland ate chicken and pork. A dried coconut meat called copra was valued and exported.

Recreation for the ancient Melanesians often consisted of the "sing-sing," during which they sang and danced for hours or even days. For refreshment, especially in Fiji and Vanuatu, they drank kava, made from a hot, peppery root. Farther west, the islanders chewed areca nuts wrapped in betel leaves, which made the teeth turn red.

Religion. The religious beliefs and customs of the Melanesians were as varied and diverse as were their languages and social structures. Individual communities attached themselves to specific sets of spirits that were associated with particular kinship lines in order to be separate from the spirits of other groups. Sometimes an individual person would assert individuality by adhering to a discrete spirit. Myths, songs, and dances were passed down orally for generations (even centuries), explaining the origins of land forms and cultural features based on the powers of supernatural beings. Religious societies for men only had clubhouses in which elaborate initiation ceremonies were held as well as regular ceremonial worship. The initiations involved lengthy, physically exhausting dances and singing.

Masks and headdresses were worn during these ceremonies.

The community's moral code was enforced by fear of malevolent spirits, especially ghosts of the departed, and supported by theories of illness and death. Special professional functionaries, spirit mediums or oracles, rendered supernatural interpretations of local events. If successful, they could wield irresistible power over their followers. Sorcery, magic, and taboos made these practices more intimidating.

Observers have noted that throughout Melanesia traditional religions seemed to stress means of gaining wealth as much as freedom from physical harm.

ADDITIONAL RESOURCES

Allen, Michael, ed. *Vanuatu: Politics, Economics and Ritual in Island Melanesia.* New York: Academic Press, 1982.

Hays, Terence E. *Oceania.* Vol. 2 in *Encyclopedia of World Cultures.* Boston: G. K. Hall, 1991.

Oliver, Douglas. *Native Cultures of the Pacific Islands.* Honolulu: University of Hawaii Press, 1989.

Trompf, G. W. *Melanesian Religion.* Cambridge, England: Cambridge University Press, 1991.

SEE ALSO: Micronesia; Polynesia; Sea Peoples.

—*John M. Bullard*

MELEAGER OF GADARA

ALSO KNOWN AS: Meleagros
BORN: c. 140 B.C.E.; Gadara, Syria
DIED: c. 70 B.C.E.; Isle of Cos, Greece
RELATED CIVILIZATIONS: Hellenistic and Roman Greece
MAJOR ROLE/POSITION: Poet, philosopher, anthologist

Life. The son of Eucrates, a Hellenistic Galilean, Meleager (mehl-ee-AY-gur) of Gadara lived in Tyre during his youth and early adulthood. He was fluent in Greek, Syrian, and Phoenician. In his early career, he composed *Charites* ("the graces," now lost), Menippean satires on popular philosophical themes. His philosophy may have been Cynic, but because all his philosophical works are lost, his leanings cannot be ascertained.

Meleager was one of the earliest Greek epigrammatists. He adapted the epigrams of Asclepiades and Callimachus of Cyrene and paid homage to Antipater of Sidon. As an older man, on Cos, he compiled *Stephanos* (c. 90-80 B.C.E.; *Fifty Poems*, 1890; best known as *Garland*), an anthology of epigrams. Its original scope and composition cannot be determined because, in the tenth century, Constantine Cephalas incorporated it into the *Anthologia Hellēnikē* (collected in the late ninth century C.E., revised and augmented in the late tenth century C.E.; *The Greek Anthology*, 1916, also known as *Palatine Anthology*). About 130 of Meleager's own epigrams survive. A specialist in erotic poetry, his diction is emotional but his prosody is controlled.

Influence. Meleager's *Garland* determined to a large extent the content of *The Garland* of Philip of

Thessalonica (Thessaloníki), inspired Greek poets throughout the classical and Byzantine eras, and affected such diverse poets as the Roman Catullus, the Englishman Robert Herrick, and the American Ezra Pound.

ADDITIONAL RESOURCES
Cameron, Alan. *The Greek Anthology from Meleager to Planudes*. Oxford, England: Clarendon Press, 1993.

Fowler, Barbara Hughes. *The Hellenistic Aesthetic*. Madison: University of Wisconsin Press, 1989.
Webster, T. B. L. *Hellenistic Poetry and Art*. New York: Barnes & Noble, 1964.

SEE ALSO: Callimachus of Cyrene; Catullus; Greece, Hellenistic and Roman; Languages and literature; Philosophy.

—*Eric v.d. Luft*

MENANDER (GRECO-BACTRIAN KING)

ALSO KNOWN AS: Milinda
BORN: c. 210 B.C.E.; Kalasi near Alexandria, probably Alexandria-in-Caucaso (modern Begram, Afghanistan)
DIED: 135 B.C.E.; Bactria
RELATED CIVILIZATIONS: Greece, India
MAJOR ROLE/POSITION: King

Life. Menander (meh-NAN-dur) was one of the most important of the Greco-Bactrian kings. He is the only Indo-Greek king to be named in classical Indian sources. He is best known as the Milinda of the *Milinda-pañha* (first century B.C.E., some material added later, date uncertain; *The Questions of King Milinda*, 1890-1894), a Buddhist work in the form of a dialogue between Milinda and the Buddhist sage Nāgasena. His early career is obscure.

He rose to the kingship circa 155 B.C.E. His kingdom covered much of present-day Afghanistan and Pakistan. According to the historian Strabo, Apollodorus of Artemita reported that Menander advanced beyond the Hypanis (modern Gharra, a tributary of the Indus River) as far as the Imaus (either the Yamuna or Sun rivers). Indian sources describe a Greek advance into India at this time. Patañjali (fl. c. 140 B.C.E.) in his *Mahābhāṣya* (second century B.C.E.; English translation, 1856) cites references to the Greek conquest of Sāketa (Ayodhyā) and Madhyamikā. Kālidāsa in his play *Mālavikāgnimitra* (traditionally c. 70 B.C.E., probably c. 370 C.E.; English translation, 1875) refers to the defeat of Greek forces at the Indus River by Vasumitra during the reign of his grandfather Puṣyamitra (d. 148 B.C.E.). The *Yuga Purāna* (n.d.; *The Yuga Purana*, 1986) in the *Gārgi Saṁhitā* (n.d.; a work on astrology), describes the Greek advance into India, culminating in the capture of Pāṭaliputra (Patna).

Menander, however, was unable to consolidate his conquests and left India without annexing any territory. The *Milinda-pañha* reports that Menander withdrew from the world and left his kingdom to his son. However, Plutarch in *Ethika* (after c. 100 C.E.; *Moralia*, 1603) says that Menander died in camp and that his ashes were equally divided among the cities of his kingdom, where monuments were dedicated to him. Plutarch's account is reminiscent of descriptions of the dispersal of the Buddha's remains. At the time of his death, Agathocleia, his wife (probably the daughter of king Agathocles), served as regent for Strato, their son, who was not of age to assume the kingship. The coins of Menander were bilingual (in Greek and Kharoshti). Pallas was most frequently on the reverse. His titles were "soter" (savior) and "dikaios" (just).

Influence. With Menander, the influence of the Greco-Bactrian kings reached its zenith. His successors were unable to stay in power. In the century after Menander's death, more than twenty rulers are recorded. By the middle of the first century B.C.E., the Yuezhi-Kushān, Saka, and Scytho-Parthian ethnic groups had taken over the region. In addition to his exploits, Menander's fame is assured in the portrayal of Milinda in the *Milinda-pañha*.

ADDITIONAL RESOURCES
Menander. *Menander*. Edited by David R. Slavitt. Philadelphia: University of Pennsylvania Press, 1998.
Narain, A. K. *Cambridge Ancient History*. Vol. 8. Cambridge, England: Cambridge University Press, 1989.

SEE ALSO: Bactria; Buddhism; Greece, Hellenistic and Roman; India; Yuezhi culture.

—*Albert T. Watanabe*

MENANDER (PLAYWRIGHT)

BORN: c. 342 B.C.E.; Athens, Greece
DIED: c. 292 B.C.E.; Piraeus, Greece
RELATED CIVILIZATION: Hellenistic Greece
MAJOR ROLE/POSITION: Comic playwright

Life. Menander (meh-NAN-dur) came of age in Athens just as the democracy fell. He reportedly belonged to the circle of Demetrius Phalereus, who ruled Athens for Macedonia from 317 to 307 B.C.E. In thirty years, Menander wrote more than one hundred plays, winning in dramatic competition eight times. His plays set the standard for refined domestic "situation" comedies. Although he was extremely popular in antiquity, his writings were lost for centuries until some were recovered at the beginning of the twentieth century. Only *Dyskolos* (317 B.C.E.; *The Bad-Tempered Man*, 1921, also known as *The Grouch*) survives complete, but it is not as good as his reputation. Better are the nearly complete *Samia* (321-316 B.C.E.; *The Girl from Samos*, 1909) and partial *Epitrepontes* (after 304 B.C.E.; *The Arbitration*, 1909), which display the complex plots and subtle characters that are Menander's hallmark. Menander writes smooth, witty Greek that lends itself easily to being quoted for philosophical maxims.

Influence. Menander became the model for virtually all situation comedy in the Western tradition, primarily through the Roman adaptations of his plays by Plautus and Terence. The comedies of the English playwright William Shakespeare and the French playwright Molière and even modern television situation comedies ultimately go back to Menander's legacy. Famous quotes of Menander were popular in antiquity in their own right, and he is the only pagan author to be quoted in the New Testament.

ADDITIONAL RESOURCES

Miller, Norma. *Menander: Plays and Fragments*. New York: Penguin, 1987.
Walton, J. M., and P. D. Arnott. *Menander and the Making of Comedy*. Westport, Conn.: Greenwood, 1996.
Webster, T. B. L. *Introduction to Menander*. Manchester, England: University of Manchester Press, 1974.

SEE ALSO: Athens; Demetrius Phalereus; Greece, Hellenistic; Macedonia; Performing arts; Plautus; Terence.
—*Wilfred E. Major*

The playwright Menander. (North Wind Picture Archives)

MENCIUS

ALSO KNOWN AS: originally Mengke (*Wade-Giles* Mengk'o); Mengzi (*Wade-Giles* Meng-tzu)
BORN: c. 372 B.C.E.; Zou, China
DIED: c. 289 B.C.E.; China
RELATED CIVILIZATIONS: China, Zhou Dynasty
MAJOR ROLE/POSITION: Government minister, philosopher

Life. The primary sources for information regarding the life of Mencius (MEHN-shee-uhs) are the book *Menzi* (first transcribed in the early third century B.C.E.; English translation in *The Confucian Classics*, 1861; commonly known as *Mencius*), the *Han Shi Waizhuan* (second century B.C.E.; *Han Shih Wai Chuan*, 1952), and the *Shiji* (first century B.C.E.; *Records of the Grand Historian of China*, 1960) of Sima Qian. Legend identifies Mencius as from the Meng family of the state of Lu. Historian Sima Qian claims that Mencius came from Zou, a state bordering Lu in Shandong.

Mencius studied with followers of Confucius's grandson, Zi Si, and eventually found himself among the class of philosophers in China who were maintained as councilors, with no official responsibilities for government. Like others of this class, Mencius traveled from state to state seeking an agreeable position.

Though details about the sequence of Mencius's travels conflict among historical accounts, it is generally agreed that he spent a good deal of this time in the states of Liang and Qi. According to Sima Qian, Mencius visited the Jixia Academy (founded by King Wei of Qi in the fourth century B.C.E.), presumably to debate with other philosophers who gathered there, and was eventually made a minister in the state of Qi.

Influence. The *Mencius* came to be regarded as one of the four classics during the Song Dynasty (960-1279 C.E.), and from this time onward, it has been regarded as a major expression of many of the ideals of Confucianism.

ADDITIONAL RESOURCES

Hinton, David, trans. *Mencius*. Washington, D.C.: Counterpoint Press, 1998.
Lau, D. C., trans. *Mencius*. New York: Penguin Books, 1970.
Shun, Kwong-Loi. *Mencius and Early Chinese Thought*. Stanford, Calif.: Stanford University Press, 1997.

SEE ALSO: China; Confucianism; Sima Qian; Zi Si.
—*Dennis C. Chowenhill*

MENELAUS OF ALEXANDRIA

ALSO KNOWN AS: Menelaos
BORN: c. 70 C.E.; Alexandria, Egypt?
DIED: c. 130 C.E.; place unknown
RELATED CIVILIZATIONS: Hellenistic and Roman Greece, Egypt, Imperial Rome
MAJOR ROLE/POSITION: Mathematician, astronomer

Life. Menelaus (mehn-el-AY-uhs) of Alexandria invented the geometry of spheres, in which concentric arcs are analogous to lines in the geometry of planes. Little is known of his life except that he lived for a time in Alexandria and for a time in Rome. Mathematician Ptolemy reported that Menelaus observed the proximity of the star Beta Scorpii to the Moon in 98 C.E. Plutarch reported his conversation with a certain Lucius about the angles of incidence of reflected light. Mathematical commentator Pappus of Alexandria

and Neoplatonist philosopher Proclus both mentioned him. Only his book on spherical geometry, *Sphaerica* (first century C.E.; English translation, 1936), survives, but he is supposed to have also written books on mechanics, optics, basic geometry, and astronomy. The original Greek text of *Sphaerica* has been lost. The content has been preserved through an Arabic translation.

Influence. The Menelaus theorem was an important advance in both planar and spherical trigonometry and remains applicable in astronomy. In its most basic form, it says that for any triangle ABC, if AXB, AYC, BCZ, and XYZ are each lines, then $(AX/XB) = (AY/YC) \cdot (CZ/BZ)$. Menelaus's most immediate and significant effect was on another Alexandrian mathematician and astronomer, Ptolemy, who lived about a generation later.

ADDITIONAL RESOURCES

Brunschwig, Jacques, and G. E. R. Lloyd. *Greek Thought: A Guide to Classical Knowledge.* Cambridge, Mass.: Harvard University Press, 2000.

Gow, James. *A Short History of Greek Mathematics.* New York: Chelsea, 1968.

Heath, Thomas Little. *A History of Greek Mathematics.* New York: Dover, 1981.

Neugebauer, Otto. *A History of Ancient Mathematical Astronomy.* Berlin: Springer, 1975.

SEE ALSO: Greece, Hellenistic and Roman; Plutarch; Ptolemy; Rome, Imperial.

—*Eric v.d. Luft*

MENIPPUS OF GADARA

FLOURISHED: third century B.C.E.; Gadara, Palestine (later Umm Qays, Jordan)
RELATED CIVILIZATIONS: Hellenistic Greece, Imperial Rome
MAJOR ROLE/POSITION: Satirist

Life. Menippus (meh-NIHP-uhs) of Gadara was born a slave in Sinope, a city on the southern shore of the Black Sea associated with the Cynic philosopher Diogenes of Sinope and the comic poet Diphilus. Diogenes Laertius reports that Menippus bought his freedom, acquired huge riches through money lending, became a citizen of Thebes, lost his fortune, and finally committed suicide in grief at the loss.

Menippus was known for his serious-comic writing, in which he mingled humor with philosophical reflections. Though none of his writings remain, his work was imitated through the 150 books of *Saturae Menippeae* (probably 81-67 B.C.E.; *Menippean Satires*, 1985) adapted by the Roman Marcus Terentius Varro (116-27 B.C.E.), of which some surviving fragments give an idea of the original. The satires of the Sophist Lucian perhaps also give an idea of the kind of writing Menippus produced, in which he alternated poetry and prose. Menippus's works, like iambic poetry generally, included criticisms of people, places, and things.

Influence. Menippus's innovation of mingling prose and poetry in the same work has been imitated ever since, famously in Boethius's *De consolatione philosophiae* (n.d.; *Consolation of Philosophy*, 1973) and, in the English Renaissance, in Sir Philip Sidney's *Arcadia* (1590). The term "Menippean" has come to refer to this technique.

ADDITIONAL RESOURCES

Hall, Jennifer: *Lucian's Satire.* New York: Arno Press, 1981.

Matton, Sylvain. "Menippus in Antiquity and the Renaissance." In *The Cynics*, edited by R. Bracht Branham and Marie-Odile Goulet-Cazé. Berkeley: University of California Press, 1996.

SEE ALSO: Boethius; Diogenes of Sinope; Greece, Hellenistic and Roman; Lucian; Rome, Imperial; Varro, Marcus Terentius.

—*James A. Arieti*

MERENPTAH

ALSO KNOWN AS: Merneptah
BORN: early to mid-thirteenth century B.C.E.; place unknown
DIED: 1204? B.C.E.; place unknown
RELATED CIVILIZATION: Pharaonic Egypt
MAJOR ROLE/POSITION: Pharaoh

Life. Merenptah (MEHR-ep-tah), the thirteenth son of Rameses II, was advanced in age when he ascended to the throne after his father's long reign. The major event of his ten-year reign was a war with the Libyans in Merenptah's fifth year. Inscriptions at the temple of Amun at Karnak name elements of the Aegean Sea Peoples among the Libyans' allies. Merenptah's great victory stele records a hymn commemorating victory over the Libyans. An account of a campaign to Palestine was added to this stele. Of particular interest is the statement, "Israel is laid waste, his seed is not." This is the earliest mention of Israel in a contemporary source and the only one in Egyptian records.

Merenptah. (North Wind Picture Archives)

Merenptah's tomb in the Valley of the Kings contained four nested sarcophagi. Merenptah's mummy was not found therein, nor in the cache of royal mummies discovered in 1881. This caused speculation that he was the pharaoh of the Exodus, drowned and lost in the Red Sea. His body, however, was found in a later cache of royal mummies in 1898.

Influence. Merenptah was the last great pharaoh of the Nineteenth Dynasty; his reign was followed by dynastic uncertainty and weak rulers. His victory stele remains important in research concerning the emergence of Israel. A series of scenes on a wall at Karnak, formerly attributed to Rameses II, have been correlated with the Israel passage on the victory stele and reassigned to Merenptah.

ADDITIONAL RESOURCES

Clayton, P. *Chronicle of the Pharaohs*. London: Thames and Hudson, 1994.

Redford, D. *Egypt, Israel and Canaan in Ancient Times*. Princeton, N.J.: Princeton University Press, 1992.

SEE ALSO: Egypt, Prepharaonic; Israel; Rameses II.
          —Daniel C. Browning, Jr.

KINGS OF THE MEROVINGIAN DYNASTY

King	Reign
Merovech	447-458 C.E.
Childeric I	458-481
Clovis I	481-511
Childebert I	511-558
Chlotar I	558-562
Charibert	562-566
Sigebert I	562-575
Chilperic I	566-584
Chlotar II	584-628
Dagobert I	628-637
Clovis II	637-655
Chlotar III	655-668
Childeric II	668-674
Dagobert II	674-678
Theuderic III	674-691
Clovis III	391-395
Childebert II	695-711
Dagobert III	711-716
Chilperic II	716-721
Theuderic IV	721-737
Childeric III	743-751

MEROVINGIAN DYNASTY

DATE: 450-751 C.E.

LOCALE: France and western Germany

SIGNIFICANCE: The most powerful and stable kingdom after the barbarian invasions of the Roman Empire.

The first Merovingian was Merovech or Meroveus, a semilegendary figure whose name means "born of the sea." This dynasty was probably descended, in fact, from the most successful war leaders of the Salian Franks. These kings considered their territory to be property, and it was natural for them to divide it up among their sons. Clovis (r. 481-511 C.E.) was the most formidable Merovingian king, uniting all the Frankish territories of the Rhineland. He had converted to Catholic Christianity, which would ensure contact between the Frankish kingdom and the Byzantine Empire through the sharing of this faith.

On his death, according to custom, Clovis willed his kingdom to be divided among his four sons. They fell to fighting, but by 558 C.E., Chlotar I had reunited the kingdom. He died three years later, and again the kingdom was divided among four sons. Not until 613 C.E. was the kingdom once more intact under Chlotar II. His son, Dagobert I, was the last true king of all the Franks. After his death, during the continual fraternal wars, power was usurped by ministers of the court called Mayors of the Palace. The last Merovingian was Childeric III, who was deposed by Pepin the Short, the Mayor of the Palace, in 751 C.E. This established the Carolingian Dynasty.

ADDITIONAL RESOURCES

James, Edward. *The Franks*. Oxford, England: Blackwell, 1991.

Thorpe, Lewis, trans. *Gregory of Tours: The History of the Franks*. Harmondsworth, England: Penguin, 1982.

Wood, Ian. *The Merovingian Kingdoms, 450-751*. London: Longman, 1994.

SEE ALSO: Byzantine Empire; Christianity; Chlotar I; Clovis; Franks.

—Brian Hancock

MESSALLINA, VALERIA

ALSO KNOWN AS: Messalina
BORN: c. 20 C.E.; probably Rome
DIED: 48 C.E.; Rome
RELATED CIVILIZATION: Imperial Rome
MAJOR ROLE/POSITION: Empress

Life. Valeria Messallina (vuh-LIHR-ee-uh mehs-uh-LI-nuh) was the great-granddaughter of Augustus, the first emperor of Rome. She married the emperor Claudius in 38 or 39 C.E. They had two children, Claudia Octavia (future wife of the emperor Nero) and Britannicus (executed by Nero after Claudius's death). Messallina worked actively to secure her own position and the eventual succession of her son. In 48 C.E., she entered into an illicit marriage with Gaius Silius, a Roman aristocrat and consul-designate. Messallina may have been part of a plot to make Silius emperor or simply may have been attempting to gain the support of a powerful aristocratic faction by marrying one of its prominent members. Claudius soon learned of Messallina's treason, and although Claudius failed to act decisively, his secretary Narcissus arranged for the execution of Silius and Messallina.

Influence. For ancient authors such as Tacitus and Juvenal, Messallina served as an example of unrestrained sexual license, a woman who lacked all self-control or modesty and abused her position as empress to satisfy her desires.

Valeria Messallina. (Library of Congress)

ADDITIONAL RESOURCES

Joshel, Sandra R. "Female Desire and the Discourse of Empire: Tacitus' Messalina." *Signs: Journal of Women in Culture and Society* 21, no. 1 (1995): 50-82.

Juvenal. *The Satires*. Translated by Niall Rudd. New York: Clarendon Press, 1999.

Levick, B. M. *Claudius*. London: B. T. Batsford, 1990.

Tacitus, Cornelius. *The Annals of Imperial Rome*. Translated by Michael Grant. Rev. ed. New York: Barnes & Noble, 1993.

SEE ALSO: Augustus; Claudius; Juvenal; Nero; Rome, Imperial; Tacitus.

—Shawn A. Ross

MESSENIAN WARS

DATE: late eighth to mid-seventh century B.C.E.

LOCALE: Messenia, in southwestern Greece

RELATED CIVILIZATIONS: Messenia, Sparta, Archaic Greece

SIGNIFICANCE: Conquest of Messenia provided the Spartans with valuable land and slave labor, contributing to Sparta's dominant position in Greece from the seventh to the fourth century B.C.E.

Background. Land hunger drove the Spartans to conquer their fertile western neighbor, Messenia.

Action. Sparta fought two major wars to subdue Messenia, a neighboring region in the southwestern Peloponnese. During the First Messenian War (third quarter of the eighth century B.C.E.), Sparta subjugated much of Messenia and enslaved its inhabitants, who became known as helots. Two generations later, the helots revolted at a moment of Spartan weakness (early 660's B.C.E.), precipitating the Second Messenian War. Sparta spent twenty years ruthlessly suppressing this rebellion and afterward oppressed the Messenians with renewed vigor. In each war, Spartan victory depended on seizure of the stronghold of Ithome in central Messenia.

Consequences. Victory in the Messenian Wars enabled Sparta to dominate Messenia for more than three hundred years. The Messenians posed a constant threat of rebellion, which the Spartans greatly feared. The Spartans maintained their position by brute force and terror, necessitating an intensively militarized state. Many Messenians fled slavery, producing a Messenian diaspora of exiles.

ADDITIONAL RESOURCES

Cartledge, P. *Sparta and Lakonia: A Regional History*. Boston: Routledge and Kegan Paul, 1979.

Hanson, Victor Davis. *The Wars of the Ancient Greeks*. London: Cassell, 1999.

Oliva, P. *Sparta and Her Social Problems*. Amsterdam, Netherlands: Hakkert, 1971.

Pausanias. *Guide to Greece*. Vol. 2. Translated by Peter Levi. New York: Penguin, 1979.

SEE ALSO: Greece, Archaic.

—Shawn A. Ross

MICROBLADE TRADITION, NORTHWEST

DATE: 9000 B.C.E.-1200 C.E.

LOCALE: Alaska panhandle, Yukon, British Columbia, Washington state

RELATED CIVILIZATIONS: Diuktai culture, Denali complex

SIGNIFICANCE: A technological tradition indicating a historic relationship between early Alaskan, northwest North American, and Siberian cultures.

Archaeological sites belonging to this tradition contain assemblages of small, parallel-sided, stone flakes called microblades and the nodules of stone from which these flakes were detached. Microblades are typical artifacts of both northern Eurasian and arctic North American prehistoric cultures. They were used as insets in the sides of bone or antler points to form cutting edges and in wooden handles to make knives. This method of making such tools began about 30,000 years ago in north China and is found later between 18,000 and 10,000 years ago in Siberia in the Diuktai culture. From there, it spread to the Denali complex in central Alaska and, by 9,000 years ago, was found in British

Columbia. Somewhat later, it spread as far south as the Columbia River. This way of making artifacts is quite different from that used by most other native North American peoples and is thought to have been introduced into Alaska by the ancestors of NaDene speakers, from whom it spread to their neighbors.

ADDITIONAL RESOURCES
Carlson, Roy L. "Cultural Antecedents." In *Northwest Coast*, edited by Wayne Suttles. Vol. 7 in *Handbook*

of North American Indians. Washington, D.C.: Smithsonian Institution Press, 1990.
_____. *Early Human Occupation in British Columbia*. Vancouver: University of British Columbia Press, 1996.

SEE ALSO: American Paleo-Arctic tradition; Archaic North American culture; Arctic Small Tool tradition; Subarctic peoples.

—Roy L. Carlson

MICRONESIA

DATE: 8000 B.C.E.-700 C.E.
LOCALE: Islands of the west Pacific Ocean, east of the Philippines
SIGNIFICANCE: Micronesia has provided anthropologists and historians a rich "laboratory" for the study of humankind and the intriguing migrations in world history.

Micronesia (mi-kroh-NEE-zhuh) is the group of 2,500 volcanic and small atoll islands that make up the western section of Oceania; the other two groups are Polynesia and Melanesia. Micronesia lies in the tropical western part of the Pacific Ocean, extending some 3,000 miles (4,800 kilometers) from east to west and some 1,000 miles (1,600 kilometers) from north to south. The total area of the islands is no more than 1,100 square miles (2,850 square kilometers), of which Guam accounts for 207 square miles (537 square kilometers). It is not unusual to find smaller islands less than 1 square mile (2.5 square kilometers) in size. Micronesian islands are either low (atoll) or high (volcanic), a characteristic that partially provides the basis for cultural distinctions. Among the main island groupings for Micronesia are the Palaus, Marianas, Carolines, Marshalls, and Gilberts. What is known about Micronesia has been pieced together from ethnography, ethnolinguistics, ethnohistory, and some spotty archaeology, providing more information for recent than early history.

Cultural formation. Scholars have determined that western and eastern Micronesia followed different developmental paths. Western Micronesia (Palau, Marianas, and possibly Yap) was settled directly by immigrants from Indonesia or the Philippines, presumably since Neolithic times if not earlier. Eastern Micro-

nesia and Polynesia were probably settled by immigrants from a region in eastern Melanesia distinguished by the Lapita culture. Micronesia and Polynesia may have had a direct connection with Japan based on the type of fishing gear commonly found. Contact among Micronesian islands leading to cultural borrowing is presumed, notwithstanding periodic connection with Polynesia. The reason for this division between east and west is that the languages of western Micronesia have been traced linguistically to Indonesia and the Philippines, and the eastern Micronesian languages have been traced to New Hebrides Island in Melanesia. All belong to the Austronesian (formerly Malayo-Polynesian) linguistic family. Eight intergrading, often mutually unintelligible, linguistic groups have been recognized: the Chamorros of the Mariana Islands, Palauans, Yapese, eastern Carolines, western Carolines, southwestern Micronesian islands, the Marshallese, and the Gilbertese.

Archaeological artifacts. Early excavations in Micronesia date to the 1930's and have continued sporadically to the twenty-first century. Materials salvaged include limited stone adzes, widespread shell fishhooks, and pottery. Universal use of shell throughout Micronesian history makes it difficult to date earlier tools. Skeletal evidence of pigs, dogs, and fowl is unevenly distributed. The dating sequence provided by ceramic artifacts—which exists only for western Micronesia— places the earliest date at 1800 B.C.E. Megalithic stone monuments, ruined pavements, walls, house platforms, and occasional stone carvings of human faces have similarly been found. Sites of extensive stonework and coral rubble such as those in Yap, Palau, and Ponape point to the development of societies with complex sociopolitical integration that could be called chiefdoms and states. These structures have been interpreted as having been associated with elaborate priesthoods and ceremonials, aristocratic chiefs and noble kings, and even empires. Money objects of various forms—shells, large stones, and glass beads—attest to the existence of complex trading networks. However, this part of Micronesian cultural history belongs to the more recent ages and has continued into historic times.

Origin and cultural theories. Scholars have long held the view that Micronesia was populated directly from insular Southeast Asia to the west or via intervening New Guinea to the east. However, no early stone tools of insular Southeast Asian origin have yet been found. The few simple, untanged, oval or lenticular stone adzes that have been found point to a Melanesian origin. In insular Southeast Asia, the stone flake (Tabonian) industry that separates it from mainland Southeast Asia is estimated at 30,000 B.C.E., lasting until 9000 B.C.E. This tradition was succeeded by a flake-blade industry often coterminous with the beginnings of ceramic industries and enriched by later metal traditions. The chronology of cultural traditions in all Southeast Asia and Oceania varies in detail from place to place. The keeping of dogs, associated with Micronesian cultural history, is the result of multiple migrations and invasions from the outside as well as the creative adaptations undertaken by the migrants after arrival.

Current theories on the origins of Micronesians are based on linguistic theories. The traceable homeland of the Austronesian languages before their expansion into Oceania and even mainland Southeast Asia is insular Southeast Asia itself, in particular the islands of Taiwan, the Philippines, and Indonesia. These Austronesians carried with them the Neolithic complex of horticulture, pig and fowl domestication, burial practices, and pottery in various combinations. Among the plants associated with subsistence in the Pacific are tubers, breadfruit, bananas, coconut, and later rice. Both Micronesia and Polynesia formed a tuber/tree cultivation complex, and Melanesians depended mainly on tuber production.

The linguistic explosion and expansion of the Austronesian speakers probably took place between 5000 B.C.E. and 3000 B.C.E., using at first land bridges and later watercraft. Some of these migrations must have been undertaken by small family groups and later may have involved more organized, large colonizing expeditions. Conceivably, laps of these journeys extended many centuries and over distances of thousands of

miles from their embarking points. Population transfer due to severe winds has been known to occur in modern-day Micronesia and could be entertained as a possible means of migration. By about 1500 B.C.E., the closer islands of Polynesia were settled, providing for further expansion beyond. The same was true for Micronesia.

The earliest pottery date provided by the Marianas Red shards is circa 1755 B.C.E. Marianas Red shards bear resemblance to Philippine shards found in a cave in Masbate Island, dated at 1000 B.C.E. but estimated to have been started somewhere in central Philippines at least by 1500 B.C.E. The Marianas Red ware is thin and red-slipped, usually plain, and a few reconstructed vessels seem to have had flat bases and carinations. Some have lime-filled decoration in rows of stamped circles, lines, and zigzags reminiscent of dentate stamping. Association of these shards with shell artifacts at this time zone is not yet conclusive. Other Marianas Red artifacts date much later, about 100 B.C.E. Marianas Red was replaced by plain, unslipped ceramic after 700 B.C.E. and is said to bear no resemblance to the Lapita ceramic culture. Lapita pottery has been estimated to have reached Melanesia from insular Southeast Asia around 1500 B.C.E., about the time the Marianas were being colonized from the west.

By 800 C.E., the Marianas Red pottery culture was eclipsed by the Latte phase of Marianas and western Micronesian cultures. However, pottery production continued until modern times. Considered among the most remarkable examples of stone architecture in Oceania, the Latte consists of two parallel rows of upright coral or volcanic rocks slotted at the top and set on with generally hemispherical capstones. Used as platforms and status markers for houses and other buildings, the rows are usually set 13 feet (4 meters) apart and vary in length with the longest having been reported at 72 feet (22 meters) long.

To the east, atoll Nukuoro is the only island to have received archaeological attention. Radiocarbon dates point to first settlement between the mid-1500's and 1300 B.C.E., with continual occupation thereafter. The continuity from prehistory to colonial contact is sometimes demonstrable, as in the case of the Nan Madol ruins in the Carolines first reported in 1835 and later in 1857. Nan Madol is often described as a small town and a ceremonial center covering an area of 0.2 square mile (70 hectares). Although considered historic, Nan Madol represents a sociocultural synthesis that is dynastic in scope, bridging the connection between ancestral and present-day Ponapeans.

Physically, Micronesians are predominantly of Mongoloid phenotype, suggesting close ties to Southeast Asia. However, gene flow from Melanesia is also demonstrable. This Mongoloid strain at the time of Austronesian expansion conceivably would have been already mixed with other earlier groups. The pre-Neolithic Negrito, the Ainoid, and the Veddoid are populations suggested to have predated the Southeast Asian Mongoloids. For now, despite a rich reservoir of ethnographic knowledge, the Micronesian past remains a puzzle, archaeologically and otherwise. Only the Marianas have so far provided some useful evidence.

ADDITIONAL RESOURCES

Bellwood, Peter. *Man's Conquest of the Pacific*. New York: Oxford University Press, 1979.

Spoehr, Alexander. *Marianas Prehistory*. Chicago: Chicago Natural History Museum, 1957.

Wuerch, William L., and Dirk Anthony Ballendorf. *Historical Dictionary of Guam and Micronesia*. Metuchen, N.J.: Scarecrow Press, 1994.

SEE ALSO: Melanesia; Polynesia.

—*E. P. Flores-Meiser*

MIDAS

ALSO KNOWN AS: Mita of Mushki
BORN: 738 B.C.E.; Anatolia
DIED: 696/695 B.C.E.; Anatolia
RELATED CIVILIZATIONS: Assyria, Phrygia
MAJOR ROLE/POSITION: King

Life. Little is known of the historical Midas. He was apparently king of the Phrygians, a Balkan tribe that settled in Anatolia, part of modern Asia Minor, about the eleventh century B.C.E. According to Assyrian writings, local power was granted to Midas of Phrygia about 730 B.C.E. Midas appears to have opened trade in the region during his reign, as the historian Herodotus refers to Phrygia serving as a trading power during this period. Midas submitted his power to Sargon II of Assyria about 709 B.C.E.; Sargon's successor, Sennacherib, occupied the region some years later. Midas may have resisted the occupation, as Assyrian documents refer to fighting with Mita of Mushki almost certainly Midas. The invasion of Phrygia by the

Cimmerians from the west in 700 B.C.E. probably marked the end of Midas's rule. Whether he committed suicide, as described in one version of events, or married a daughter of Agamemnon, a king of the Cimmerians, is unclear.

Influence. Midas is best known as a hero of Greek mythology. According to legend, Midas was granted by Dionysus, god of wine, the "gift" of turning all he touched into gold. The "Midas touch" has come to mean the ability of a person to create wealth.

ADDITIONAL RESOURCES

Brown, Dale. *Anatolia: Cauldron of Cultures*. New York: Time-Life, 1995.

Sasson, Jack, ed. *Civilizations of the Ancient Near East*. New York: Scribner, 1995.

SEE ALSO: Assyria; Herodotus; Phrygia; Sargon II; Sennacherib.

—*Richard Adler*

MIDDLE WOODLAND TRADITION

DATE: 8000 B.C.E.-900 C.E.
LOCALE: North America
RELATED CIVILIZATIONS: Adena culture, Hopewell
SIGNIFICANCE: The Middle Woodland tradition represents a stage of development in Native American civilizations marked by an increase in horticulture, distinctive ceramics, and earthen burial mounds.

First appearing in the field of archaeology in the 1930's, the term "Woodland" has traditionally been applied to cultures in the Southeast, Northeast, Midwest, and the eastern Great Plains that existed between the hunting and gathering Archaic cultures and the later mound-building Mississippian culture. Late twentieth century archaeologists argue that the dates for the Woodland period cannot be so constrained because the nature and timing of natural and cultural processes were not uniform in North America. Certain traits of this culture appeared much earlier than the traditional Woodland starting dates of 2000 or 1000 B.C.E., and in some parts of North America, the West, for example, some Woodland traits never appeared at all. For many archaeologists, the evidence of prehistoric sites suggests a continuity of cultures as opposed to a strict demarcation between them.

In the most basic terms, the Woodland tradition is characterized by three traits: the continuing development of horticulture, the manufacture of distinctive ceramics, and the construction of earthen burial mounds. Many archaeologists point to additional interrelated characteristics, such as a more sedentary lifestyle, the emergence of easily recognizable territorial boundaries, more complex social orders, more intensive exchange of exotic materials, and a growth in populations living in circumscribed territories.

In about 8000 B.C.E., the glaciers made their final retreat, which brought vast environmental and climatic changes over the next several thousand years: a rise in sea levels, a flattening of the gradient of interior streams, a maturation of lakes, a transformation of tundra into grassland prairies and conifer forests into deciduous, and the dying out of the megafauna (the woolly mammoth, outsized bison, giant sloth). With all these changes came an alteration in the ways people lived. Some, especially those who lived in the higher latitudes, continued hunting but for much smaller prey. Those along the coasts became experts at fishing. Still others relied on seasonal harvests of local wild plants, a practice that would eventually lead to the domestication of plant life.

An archaeological site near the Alabama/Tennessee state line demonstrates this early move toward agriculture. At the time, severe winters still ravished this area. The freeze-thaw cycles caused shifts in the rock mass, and torrents of water dug out the long, tubular tunnel known as Russell Cave. Apparently, the first visitors to the cave lived on seasonal wild plants such as nuts, seeds, and berries and game such as deer, gray squirrel, raccoon, rabbit, porcupine, black bear, and the bobcat. Evidence suggests that many of the visitors used the cave as a base camp, leaving in spring to join larger encampments. While in the cave, they transformed what nature had provided into useful tools. Animal skins became clothes, and bones were shaped into awls, needles, and fishhooks. Chert stones were fashioned into grinders and spear points, which at this time were shift-

The mound builders of Hopewell left this engraved ceramic cup. (Hulton Archive)

ing from the earliest Clovis points to corner, basal, and side-notched points. Such artifacts of specialized resource procurement and processing suggest the movement toward what archaeologists term "primary forest efficiency."

At sites along the South Atlantic coast, fiber-tempered plain and decorated ceramics appeared around 2500 B.C.E., probably for use in collecting, preparing, and storing food, a distinctly agricultural characteristic. Some of the most famous of the fiber-tempered ceramics are the Stallings Island ware and the Orangeware from sites in northeast Florida and southeast coastal Georgia. By 1000 B.C.E., the fiber-tempered ceramics had spread throughout much of the Deep South, soon to be replaced by fabric-impressed and, a little later, by cord-marked sand-tempered ceramics, a shift that points to the increase in the cultivation of wild and domesticated seed crops such as sunflower, sumpweed, goosefoot, knotweed, and maygrass.

Although no human burials have been found there, the millions of cubic feet of earth that make up the mounds at the Poverty Point site in Louisiana, constructed between about 1,800 B.C.E. and 500 B.C.E., mark another hallmark of the Woodland tradition that appeared sporadically and then swept across the eastern portion of what is now the United States: burial mounds. For many archaeologists, the Adena and Hopewell cultures are the most visible manifestation of Woodland burial ceremonialism, as well as the growth of a more complex social order. These sites speak also to other Woodland characteristics. At Poverty Point, copper from the Great Lakes was found, along with lead ore from Missouri, soapstone from Alabama and Georgia, and sundry tools from Ohio, Arkansas, Mississippi, Indiana, and Tennessee; at Hopewell sites, mica from the Appalachian Mountains was discovered, along with volcanic glass from Yellowstone, chert from North Dakota, conch shells and sharks' teeth from the Gulf of Mexico, and copper from the Great Lakes. Such exotic artifacts speak to a pattern of long-distance trade. Sedentary village life in a circumscribed territory with a growing population was risky. Deer herds could be killed by severe winters; crops could fail. Clearly, one answer for peoples of the Woodland tradition was to form networks of reciprocal trade.

By 800-900 C.E., village life had changed even more. Villagers no longer looked only to the domestica-tion of local plant life but to a crucial import, maize. Large, flat-topped mounds emerged. The characteristic pottery was tempered with crushed mussel shell. The Woodland gave way to the Mississippian culture.

ADDITIONAL RESOURCES

Anderson, David G., and Kenneth E. Sassaman, eds. *The Paleoindian and Early Archaic Southeast.* Tuscaloosa: University of Alabama Press, 1996.

Jennings, Francis. *The Founders of America: From the Earliest Migrations to the Present.* New York: Norton, 1993.

Niles, Judith. *Native American History: A Chronology of the Vast Achievements of a Culture and Their Links to World Events.* New York: Ballantine Books, 1996.

Thomas, David Hurst. *Exploring Ancient Native America: An Archaeological Guide.* New York: Routledge, 1999.

SEE ALSO: Adena culture; Archaic North American culture; Clovis technological complex; Poverty Point.

—*Anna Dunlap Higgins*

MILAN, EDICT OF

AUTHORSHIP: Constantine the Great (c. 272/285-337 C.E.) and Valerius Licinianus Licinius (d. 325 C.E.)

DATE: 313 C.E.

LOCALE: Milan in northern Italy

RELATED CIVILIZATION: Imperial Rome

SIGNIFICANCE: Ended the Great Persecution and gave religious freedom to Roman citizens and legal status to Christianity.

From early in its existence, Christianity had been regarded as a *religio illicita* (an illicit cult) in the Roman Empire, and the Church had often been persecuted by the authorities. However, in 306 C.E., the Christians gained a champion in Constantine the Great, the new ruler in Britain, Gaul, and Spain. At the beginning of his reign, he ended the persecution and gave Christians the right to renew their worship in his domains. As Constantine broke away from the other emperors and the religious policies of the Second Tetrarchy (306-311 C.E.), he evolved from Olympian polytheism to Solar syncretism in his own beliefs. During his military campaign to conquer Italy from Maxentius in 312 C.E., he prayed to the *Deus Summus* ("highest god") for help and felt that his answer came in the form of divine revelations from the Christian god and divine power from Christian symbols.

Following his religious conversion and Italian victory, he wished to extend imperial patronage and legal protection to Christians in other parts of the Roman world. Valerius Licinianus Licinius (r. 308-324 C.E.) was then ruling the Eastern European imperial provinces and Gaius Galerius Valerius Maximinianus (r. 305-315 C.E.) those in western Asia. Licinius had ceased persecuting Christians in 311 C.E., but Galerius was still persecuting them in late 312 C.E. Therefore, in February of 313 C.E., Constantine summoned Licinius to a conference at Milan in northern Italy. He persuaded his co-emperor to adopt a religious accord that is known as the Edict of Milan. This agreement "granted both to the Christians and to all people the uninhibited right of following the religion which each desires" in order that the *Deus Summus* in the heavenly seat would be benevolent to the emperors and their subjects. It ordered that the Christians be allowed to hold their religious rites without hindrance and that the Church be given back its communal property without delay. It ended with the hope that this new policy would restore civic tranquillity and divine favor to the Roman Empire. After the meeting, Licinius marched east and overthrew Galerius. In June of 313 C.E., he announced the Milan agreement in the form of imperial letters sent to the governors of the Eastern provinces (Christian writers Lucius Caelius Firmianus Lactantius and Eusebius of Caesarea preserved copies). The Edict of Milan established the Christian cult as a *religio licita* in the Roman Empire, Catholic churches as corporate entities within Roman law, and the Christian faithful as a protected group in Roman society.

ADDITIONAL RESOURCES

Anastos, M. V. "The Edict of Milan (313): A Defense of Its Traditional Authorship and Designation." *Revue des Études Byzantines* 25 (1967): 13-41.

Odahl, Charles M. *Constantine and the Christian Empire*. London: Routledge, 2001.

SEE ALSO: Christianity; Constantine the Great; Eusebius of Caesarea; Lactantius, Lucius Caelius Firmianus; Licinius, Valerius Licinianus; Maxentius; Rome, Imperial.

—*Charles M. Odahl*

MILINDA-PAÑHA

AUTHORSHIP: Unknown
DATE: first or second century C.E.
RELATED CIVILIZATIONS: India, Greece
SIGNIFICANCE: The *Milinda-pañha* is one of the more popular Buddhist works. It is also one of the few works in Indian literature that refers to the Greco-Bactrian king Menander, although it probably does not provide much accurate historical information about him.

The *Milinda-pañha* (mih-LIHN-dah PAHN-ha; *The Questions of King Milinda*, 1890-1894) is a Buddhist work in Pāli. It takes the form of a dialogue between the king Milinda (Menander) and the Buddhist sage Nāgasena. The work opens with a description of the past lives of Milinda and Nāgasena. Books II and III, "The Distinguishing Marks" and "The Cutting Off of Perplexity," present a series of questions and answers about the nature of human existence, mental states, rebirth, and Nirvana. Book IV consists of dilemmas, apparent contradictions of Buddhist doctrine that

Nāgasena resolves. In Book V, "A Question Solved by Inference," Nāgasena allegorically describes a City of Righteousness (*dhamma*) and the enlightened inhabitants of the city. Book VI, "Special Qualities of Asceticism," contains a discourse on that subject. The last book (incomplete) consists of similes that exemplify the various qualities of the enlightened. In the end, Milinda gives his kingdom over to his son and withdraws from the world. Similes and analogies pervade much of the work.

ADDITIONAL RESOURCES

Milinda's Questions. Translated by I. B. Horner. Oxford, England: Pali Text Society, 1990.

Norman, K. R. *Pali Literature*. Wiesbaden, Germany: Otto Harrassowitz, 1983.

SEE ALSO: Buddhism; Greece, Hellenistic and Roman; India; Menander (Greco-Bactrian king).

—*Albert T. Watanabe*

MILTIADES THE YOUNGER

BORN: c. 554 B.C.E.; Attica, Greece
DIED: 489 B.C.E.; probably Athens, Greece
RELATED CIVILIZATIONS: Classical Greece, Athens, Persia
MAJOR ROLE/POSITION: Military and political leader

Life. A member of the powerful family of the Philaïdai, Miltiades (mihl-TI-uh-deez) the Younger was elected archon in 524/523 B.C.E. In about 516 B.C.E., the Athenian tyrant Hippias sent him to the Thracian Chersonese to replace his murdered brother, Stesagoras. There Miltiades contracted an alliance with the Thracian king Olorus by marrying his daughter and became a sort of Athenian viceroy in the region. He accompanied the Persian king Darius the Great on his Scythian expedition in about 513 B.C.E. and later reported that he had unsuccessfully urged his fellow Greeks to destroy Darius's bridge cross the Danube. In 493 B.C.E., he was driven from the Chersonese by Persian forces and returned to Athens, where he was unsuccessfully prosecuted by political enemies and subsequently elected general every year until his death. In 490 B.C.E., he urged the Athenians to meet the Persian army at Marathon and is generally recognized as the architect of that spectacular victory. Riding a wave of popularity, he led an expedition against Naxos in 489 B.C.E. but failed to capture the city and was severely wounded. He was subsequently tried for "deceiving the people" and fined fifty talents but died from his wound, leaving the debt to his son, Cimon.

Influence. Miltiades was responsible for the victory at Marathon, which provided the Athenians and other Greeks the boost in morale they needed to resist the invasion of Xerxes I ten years later.

ADDITIONAL RESOURCES

Bott, D. H., ed. *A Nepos Selection: Miltiades, Themistocles, Alcibiades, Atticus.* New York: St. Martin's Press, 1970.

Burn, A. R. *Persia and the Greeks: The Defense of the West, 546-478* B.C. Stanford, Calif.: Stanford University Press, 1984.

Herodotus. *The Histories.* Translated by Robin Waterfield. New York: Oxford University Press, 1998.

Miltiades the Younger. (North Wind Picture Archives)

SEE ALSO: Athens; Cimon; Darius the Great; Greece, Classical; Hippias of Athens; Marathon, Battle of; Persia; Xerxes I.

—*Richard M. Berthold*

MILVIAN BRIDGE, BATTLE OF

ALSO KNOWN AS: Pons Mulvius (Latin)
DATE: October 28, 312 C.E.
LOCALE: North of Rome on a plain above the Milvian Bridge
RELATED CIVILIZATION: Imperial Rome
SIGNIFICANCE: The battle led to the conversion of Constantine the Great to Christianity and the beginning of the Christianization of the Roman Empire.

Background. Between 306 and 312 C.E., the tetrarchic system of cooperating emperors failed as the successors of Diocletian (r. 284-305 C.E.) competed among themselves for domination of the Roman Empire. Con-

stantine the Great (r. 306-337 C.E.) received power as the legitimate emperor over Britain, Gaul, and Spain, and Maxentius (306-312 C.E.) usurped rule in Italy and Africa. After a temporary alliance between them broke down, they went to war in early 312 C.E.

Action. Constantine marched with fewer than 40,000 troops from Gaul to challenge Maxentius, who had 100,000 troops in Italy. After winning several hard battles in the north of the peninsula, Constantine crossed through the Apennines to face Maxentius near Rome. Worried that his enemy had larger forces and that earlier emperors has failed to dislodge him from the capital, Constantine appealed to the *Deus Summus* ("highest god") for help in his time of trial. A vision of a cross of light above the Sun and a dream of Christ carrying Christian symbols inspired Constantine to put the cross and Christogram on his military standards and shields. Jeered by the Roman populace and cheered by a Sibylline oracle, Maxentius left the safety of Rome to fight Constantine on a plain above the Tiber River next to the Milvian Bridge (MIHL-vee-uhn; Pons Mulvius in ancient Latin, Ponte Milvio in modern Italian) on October 28, 312 C.E. Several charges by Constantine and his cavalry won the battle and drove the enemy forces into the river, where the usurper drowned.

Consequences. Constantine believed that the Christian deity had expelled his enemy from the capital and that Christian signs had empowered his army to gain the victory. Therefore, he spent the remaining twenty-five years of his reign patronizing the Catholic Church and promoting the Christian religion in the Roman Empire.

ADDITIONAL RESOURCES
Barnes, T. D. *Athanasius and Constantius: Theology and Politics in the Constantinian Empire.* Cambridge, Mass.: Harvard University Press, 1993.
Odahl, Charles M. *Constantine and the Christian Empire.* London: Routledge, 2001.

SEE ALSO: Christianity; Constantine the Great; Diocletian; Maxentius; Rome, Imperial.
—*Charles M. Odahl*

MIMAJI

ALSO KNOWN AS: Mimashi (Japanese)
FLOURISHED: c. 612 C.E.; place unknown
RELATED CIVILIZATIONS: Korea, China, Japan
MAJOR ROLE/POSITION: Dancer, performer

Life. Little is known of Mimaji's (mih-MAH-jee) life. His background may have been Chinese. Traditionally, he is said to have studied music and dance at the court of Wu in southern China. In 612 C.E., he traveled from the Korean kingdom of Paekche to Japan and introduced *gigaku*, a form of dance drama performed wearing masks, to the Yamato court. With the support of Shōtoku Taishi, the ruler of Japan, Mimaji founded in Sakurai a school for the training of Japanese youth in this dance form, which was incorporated into Buddhist ceremonies and rituals.

Influence. By the Heian period, *gigaku* was beginning to be replaced by a Chinese import, the more solemn form of dance and drama known as *bugaku*. However, it was still performed before commoners at Buddhist temples and influenced their art.

ADDITIONAL RESOURCES
Hong, Wontack. *Paekche of Korea and the Origin of Yamato Japan.* Seoul: Kudara International, 1994.
Ortolani, Benito. *The Japanese Theatre: From Shamanistic Ritual to Contemporary Pluralism.* New York: E. J. Brill, 1990.

SEE ALSO: China; *Gigaku*; Korea; Yamato court.
—*Thomas J. Sienkewicz*

MIMNERMUS

BORN: c. 670-640 B.C.E.; Colophon or Smyrna, Asia Minor
DIED: date and place unknown
RELATED CIVILIZATION: Archaic Greece
MAJOR ROLE/POSITION: Poet, musician

Life. All that has been surmised about Mimnermus (mihm-NUR-muhs) is derived from his poems and

therefore, because of the impossibility of distinguishing life from art, is uncertain. Practicing his art in Colophon, Mimnermus was the first to write love poems in elegiac verse. He set his own poems to flute music and was celebrated for his melancholic melodies. He addresses a set of elegies to a girl named Nanno, who accompanied his recitations on the flute, but she is said to have rejected him. The most important theme in

Mimnermus's surviving poems is the detestation that a man faces because of old age, which renders him sexually unattractive. Among the themes in surviving fragments are various mythological subjects, the joys and pleasures of youth, the founding of Colophon, and a war between Smyrna and Lydia. He refers to an eclipse of the Sun, but it is uncertain whether the eclipse occurred in 648 or 585 B.C.E.

Influence. Mimnermus had a steady following throughout antiquity, and both Greek and Roman poets pay tribute to him. Among his admirers are the Greek poet Callimachus of Cyrene, who praises him for the shortness of his poems, and the Roman poet Propertius, who says that in matters of love, Mimnermus was worthier than Homer.

ADDITIONAL RESOURCES

Allen, A. *The Fragments of Mimnermus: Text and Commentary.* Stuttgart, Germany: F. Steiner, 1993.

Podlecki, Anthony J. *The Early Greek Poets and Their Times.* Vancouver: University of British Columbia Press, 1984.

SEE ALSO: Callimachus of Cyrene; Greece, Archaic; Languages and literature; Propertius.

—*James A. Arieti*

MINUCIUS FELIX, MARCUS

BORN: late second century C.E.; place unknown
DIED: c. 250 C.E.; place unknown
RELATED CIVILIZATIONS: North Africa, Imperial Rome
MAJOR ROLE/POSITION: Christian apologist

Life. Nothing is known of Marcus Minucius Felix (MAHR-kuhs muh-NYEW-shee-uhs FEE-lihks) apart from his apologetic work known as *The Octavius* (English translation, 1898). This Latin text suggests that the author, like Tertullian of Carthage (c. 155/160-after 217 C.E.), was a lawyer and was native to Roman North Africa. Minucius Felix wrote his apologetic work in the form of a conversation between Octavius, a Christian, and Caecilius, a polytheist from Numidia who was converted through this encounter. Writing in the late second or early third century C.E., Minucius Felix attacked Greco-Roman mythology yet offered little insight concerning specific Christian doctrines. He depended on Stoic philosophy far more than Christian scripture in his defense of monotheism and providence. That this work addressed certain moral accusations (such as cannibalism or incest) often found in Roman, anti-Christian polemic suggests that *The Octavius* was a response to the work *On the True Doctrine* (published in Latin 175-181 C.E.; translation 1987), written by the philosopher Celsus (fl. c. 178 C.E.). Of greater certainty is the similarity between *The Octavius* and Tertullian's *Apologeticus* (c. 197 C.E.; *Apology*, 1917). The parallels are so strong, in fact, as to suggest a single author. However, it is more likely that either Tertullian or Minucius Felix used the other's work to write his own defense of the Christian faith.

Influence. *The Octavius* of Minucius Felix represents an early Christian effort to defend and define Christianity in the Latin West. The work is also important for its insight regarding the relationship of early Christianity to the social and religious atmosphere of the Roman Empire.

ADDITIONAL RESOURCE

Baylis, H. J. *Minucius Felix and His Place Among the Early Fathers of the Latin Church.* New York: Macmillan, 1928.

SEE ALSO: Africa, North; Christianity; Rome, Imperial; Tertullian

—*Kenneth R. Calvert*

MITANNI

DATE: c. 1600-1100 B.C.E.

LOCALE: Northern Syria

SIGNIFICANCE: Mitanni was a powerful state in Upper Mesopotamia that transmitted Mesopotamian civilization to Anatolia and the Aegean region.

The kingdom of Mitanni (mih-TA-nee) was a confederation of Hurrian states in Upper Mesopotamia in the late second millennium B.C.E. Its capital was Washukanni, which has not been located for certain but may have been Tell Fakhariyah, located near the headwaters of the Khābūr River in Syria. By at least 1450 B.C.E., Mitanni was the most powerful state in the Tigris-Euphrates region.

Knowledge of Mitanni does not come from palatial archives but from correspondence with neighboring polities, including Egypt, the Hittites, and Mesopotamia, as well as records from Mitanni vassal states, such as Nuzi (northern Iraq), Terqa (on the Syrian Euphrates), and Alalakh (coastal Syria). From these fragmented sources, it is apparent that Mitanni was a political term that was most often used to describe the confederation of Hurrian states and vassals. Each of these vassals had its own king, who was bound to Mitanni by a treaty sworn by oath and sacrifice. Although the state of Mitanni was composed primarily of Hurrians, there was a significant substratum of individuals with Indo-European personal names, as well as West Semitic speaking peoples, Hittites, and Assyrians.

The history of the Mitanni state can be only partially reconstructed. The earliest attested king was Kirta, father of Shuttarna, whose names appear on a seal from Alalakh of Saustatar, a later Mitanni ruler. By 1500 B.C.E. (roughly contemporary with the early New Kingdom of Egypt), it appears that Mitanni had expanded into most of Syria under the reigns of Paratarna and Saustatar. This newly formed confederation was probably opposed by the expansion of Thutmose III of Egypt (r. c. 1504-1450 B.C.E.).

Later Mitanni kings are known primarily through the Amarna letters from Egypt (c. 1411-1350 B.C.E.), in which the Mitanni kings engaged in diplomatic relations with the kings of Egypt. For example, Artatarma I sent his daughter to Egypt to become the wife of Thutmose IV (r. 1420-1411 B.C.E.). The warming of relations between the two states may have been caused by the rise of Assyria in northern Iraq and the Hittites in Anatolia, weakening the Mitanni state. The Mitanni king Tushratta continued to have good relations with Amenhotep III (r. c. 1411-1370 B.C.E.). However, the Mitanni state became somewhat fragmented and suffered defeat from the hands of the Hittite king Suppiluliumas I. Thus, after circa 1350 B.C.E., the Hurrian state of Mitanni ceased to be a major role player in ancient Near Eastern politics. Mitanni continued to be a buffer between the Hittites and Assyria for at least the next two centuries, until the area was absorbed in the Assyrian Empire.

There is, however, more detailed information concerning Hurrian culture in the late second millennium B.C.E. Because of their military and political power and their central location, the Hurrians of Mitanni became the transmitter of Assyro-Babylonian culture and trade to Anatolia, Palestine, and ultimately the Aegean. Versions of Assyro-Babylonian myths and other literature have been found in Hurrian and Hittite literature. Furthermore, elements of the Hurrian Kumarbi myth are found in the later Greek Homeric epics.

ADDITIONAL RESOURCES

Gelb, I. J. *Hurrians and Subarians*. Chicago: Oriental Institute Publications, 1944.

Goetze, A. "On the Chronology of the Second Millennium B.C." *Journal of Cuneiform Studies* 11 (1957): 53-73.

Jankowska, N. B. "Asshur, Mitanni, and Arrapkhe." In *Early Antiquity*, edited by I. M. Biakonoff. Chicago: University of Chicago Press, 1991.

Morrison, M. A., and D. I. Owen et al. *Studies on the Civilization and Culture of Nuzi and the Hurrians*. Winona Lake, Ind.: Eisenbrauns, 1981.

Wilhelm, G. *The Hurrians*. Warminster, England: Aris & Phillips, 1989.

Wiseman, D. *The Alalakh Tablets*. London: The British School of Archaeology in Iraq, 1953.

SEE ALSO: Assyria; Babylonia; Hittites; Hurrians; Suppiluliumas I; Thutmose III.

—*Mark W. Chavalas*

MITHRADATES I

ALSO KNOWN AS: Arsaces IV; Mithridates I
BORN: c. 200 B.C.E.; place unknown
DIED: 138 B.C.E.; place unknown
RELATED CIVILIZATIONS: Hellenistic Greece, Persia
MAJOR ROLE/POSITION: Statesman

Life. The family of Mithradates I (mihth-rah-DAYT-eez), the house of Arsaces, first appeared in history as leaders of the Parni, a confederation of Persian-speaking nomads. Around 260 B.C.E., the Parni entered what later became Turkmenistan and northern Iran. There they came into contact with the Seleucid Greek empire, which had inherited occupied Persia upon the death of Alexander the Great. Initially Seleucid vassals, the Parni settled the frontier province of Parthia, thereby acquiring the name "Parthians." Over the decades, they frequently revolted against their Greek overlords.

Around 171 B.C.E., Mithradates took power just as his Seleucid antagonists were distracted by a mix of internal revolts, dynastic civil wars, and military threats from Rome. Posing as kinsman and liberator of the Persians, he steadily conquered all of Iran, much of Afghanistan, and, by 144 B.C.E., Mesopotamia. Around 140 B.C.E., the Seleucid emperor Demetrius II attempted to recover Iraq but instead was outfoxed, defeated, and captured by the Parthians. His empire secured by this victory, Mithradates assumed the titles of shah and "king of kings" to accentuate his position as restorer of Persia's ancient glories. In his last years, he also created the institutional foundations that established the Parthian state.

Influence. The Parthian empire constructed by Mithradates I would rule Persia for nearly four hundred years (150 B.C.E. to 240 C.E.) and made Persia again a world power.

ADDITIONAL RESOURCES
Wiesehöfer, Josef. *Ancient Persia, from 550 B.C. to 650 A.D.* London: I. B. Tauris, 1996.
Yarshater, Ehsan, ed. *The Cambridge History of Iran.* Vol. 3, part 1. New York: Cambridge University Press, 1993.

SEE ALSO: Arsacid Dynasty; Greece, Hellenistic and Roman; Mithradates II; Parthia; Persia; Seleucid Dynasty.

—Weston F. Cook, Jr.

MITHRADATES II

ALSO KNOWN AS: Mithridates II
BORN: 145 B.C.E.; place unknown
DIED: 87 B.C.E.; place unknown
RELATED CIVILIZATIONS: Parthia, Republican Rome, Hellenistic Greece
MAJOR ROLE/POSITION: King, political and military leader

Life. The son of King Artabanus I, Mithradates II (mihth-rah-DAYT-eez) became king in 124-123 B.C.E., when his father died, while Parthia was under attack from all sides. He reconquered all of Parthia's former provinces and more. By the end of his reign, Parthia spanned from the Euphrates River in the west to the Caspian Sea in the east. He took captive Tigranes the Great, son of the Armenian king, and later placed him on the Armenian throne. He also intervened in the Seleucid civil war in 88 B.C.E.

Mithradates increased the prestige of Parthia by entertaining ambassadors of the Han Dynasty from China and reopening the Silk Road to China. He later concluded a short-lived offensive and defensive alliance with the Roman general Lucius Cornelius Sulla.

He was responsible for several reforms. He divided his kingdom among four satraps and assumed the title "king of kings," consciously imitating the Persian Empire. He also reformed the Parthian army, abandoning Greek tactics and adopting Iranian tactics that emphasized cavalry. The bulk of the Parthian army was divided between the horse archer and the armored *cataphract* (spearmen). These changes led to the Parthian victory over the Romans at Carrhae in 53 B.C.E.

Influence. Mithradates made Parthia one of the world's great powers. He reorganized its government and reformed its army so that it was an even match for Rome.

ADDITIONAL RESOURCES

Colledge, Malcom A. R., ed. *The Parthian Period.* Leiden, Netherlands: E. J. Brill, 1986.

Lerner, J. D. *The Impact of Seleucid Decline on the Eastern Iranian Plateau.* Stuttgart, Germany: F. Steiner, 1999.

SEE ALSO: Carrhae, Battle of; Greece, Hellenistic and Roman; Mithradates I; Parthia; Persia; Rome, Republican; Seleucid Dynasty; Sulla, Lucius Cornelius; Tigranes the Great.

—*James O. Smith*

MITHRADATES VI EUPATOR

ALSO KNOWN AS: Mithradates the Great; Mithrides VI Eupator

BORN: c. 134 B.C.E.; probably Sinope, kingdom of Pontus

DIED: 63 B.C.E.; Panticapaeum, Crimea

RELATED CIVILIZATIONS: Hellenistic Greece, Anatolia

MAJOR ROLE/POSITION: King

Life. Mithradates VI Eupator (mihth-rah-DAYT-eez; r. 120-63 B.C.E.), the last independent Hellenistic monarch to oppose Rome, respected Roman arms and distrusted the senate's word. Between 110 and 90 B.C.E., he built a state centered on his ancestral kingdom of Pontus (northeastern Turkey) and the Hellenized Tauric Chersonese (Crimea). He allied with Greek cities and warlike tribes around the Black Sea and, by marriage, with King Tigranes the Great (r. 95-55 B.C.E.) of Armenia.

Mithradates clashed with rival king and Roman ally Nicomedes III Euergetes of Bithynia (r. 128-94 B.C.E.) over Cappadocia. Provoked into the First Mithradatic War (89-85 B.C.E.), Mithradates overran Asia Minor in 89 B.C.E. in a campaign worthy of Alexander the Great. In 88 B.C.E., his armies entered Greece, and Mithradates ordered the massacre of reputedly 80,000 Romans in

Mithradates VI Eupator (right) killed himself after being defeated by Pompey the Great. (Hulton Archive)

Asia. The king's autocratic manner forfeited him support among his Greek allies. In 86 B.C.E., the proconsul Lucius Cornelius Sulla crushed Pontic armies in Greece, captured Athens, and carried the war to Asia. By the Treaty of Dardanus (85 B.C.E.), Mithradates agreed to an indemnity and withdrew to his kingdom.

The Third Mithradatic War (74-65 B.C.E.), erupted when King Nicomedes IV (r. 94-74 B.C.E.) willed Bithynia to Rome. Mithradates suffered a decisive defeat by Lucius Licinius Lucullus at Cyzicus in 73 B.C.E. Thereafter, Lucullus invaded Pontus. Mithradates fled to Armenia in 70 B.C.E.. He left Pontus for Crimea in 65 B.C.E. and was driven to suicide there in 63 B.C.E.

Influence. Because Mithradates had been hailed a liberator by provincials, the Roman commanders Lucullus and Pompey the Great reformed provincial administration. Ironically, Mithradates' threat cata-pulted Sulla and Pompey to extraordinary commands that spelled the demise of the Roman Republic.

ADDITIONAL RESOURCES

Appian. "The Mithridatic Wars." In *Appian's Roman History II*, translated by Horace White. Cambridge, Mass.: Harvard University Press, 1922.

Plutarch. "Lucullus." In Vol. 2 of *Plutarch's Lives*, translated by B. Perrin. Cambridge, Mass.: Harvard University Press, 1928.

Sherwin-White, A. N. *Roman Foreign Policy in the East, 168 B.C. to A.D. 1.* Norman: University of Oklahoma Press, 1984.

SEE ALSO: Greece, Hellenistic and Roman; Lucullus, Lucius Licinius; Pompey the Great; Rome, Republican; Sulla, Lucius Cornelius.

—Kenneth W. Harl

MITHRISM

DATE: c. 2000 B.C.E.-c. 500 C.E.
LOCALE: Asia Minor, Persia, Europe
RELATED CIVILIZATIONS: Persia, Greece, Imperial Rome
SIGNIFICANCE: This religious tradition, which probably originated in Persia, was associated with Sun worship in ancient Greece and Rome and was the most important rival of early Christianity in Europe.

Mithrism, also known as Mithraism, a religion centered on worship of the god Mithras, seems to have originated in Persia (later Iran). The earliest documents relating to this belief system date from the fourteenth century B.C.E. in Iran and India and indicate that the god had already been worshiped for about two thousand years.

The early history and the rituals of Mithrism are largely unknown, mainly because it was a secret society, and initiates were forbidden to reveal details of its practice. In addition, most of the contemporary reports of Mithrism were composed by early Christians who were trying to abolish paganism and thus must be viewed with some suspicion. In ancient Persia, Mithras was often associated with Ahura Mazda, god of light, and with the Sun. In India, he was associated with Varuṇa, lord of heaven. As the cult spread, it became associated with Sun worship.

Mithrism apparently reached the Roman Empire by way of pirates from Asia Minor. By this time, Mithras was associated both with contractual agreements and social relationships and with victory for the righteous in battle. These associations were extremely appealing to the Romans, and Mithrism quickly spread through the Roman Legions. Nero (r. 54-68 C.E.) often had himself depicted as a Sun god and readily accepted Mithrism in conquered areas, associating himself with the god.

Mithrism was an exclusively male cult into which members were initiated at adolescence. Initiation ceremonies may have involved severe tests, including exposure to heat and cold, scourging, and long fasts, though as these reports were made by Christians, they must be treated with some circumspection. There are also reports of human sacrifice during the ceremonies, but no firm evidence supports these claims. Animal sacrifice was probably involved, especially of bulls, with which Mithras was associated from very early times.

Mithrism was Christianity's main rival. When the Christians came to power, they persecuted adherents of Mithrism but also adopted some of their rituals in an attempt to make the opposing belief less appealing.

Constantine the Great (r. 306-337 C.E.), the first Roman emperor to adopt Christianity, waged a major campaign to wipe out Mithrism. Although the cult probably persisted to some extent for several centuries thereafter, Mithrism, already shrouded in secrecy, had become an enemy of the Roman Empire, and virtually no records exist of the worship of Mithras after Constantine's campaign.

ADDITIONAL RESOURCES

Ferguson, John. *The Religions of the Roman Empire.* Ithaca, N.Y.: Cornell University Press, 1970.
Turcan, Robert. *The Cults of the Roman Empire.* Trans-lated by Antonia Nevill. Cambridge, Mass.: Black-well, 1996.
Vermuseren, M. J. *Mithras, the Secret God.* New York: Barnes & Noble, 1963.

SEE ALSO: Christianity; Constantine the Great; Greece, Classical; Greece, Hellenistic and Roman; Persia; Religion and ritual; Rome, Imperial.

—*Marc Goldstein*

MIXTECS

DATE: 1530 B.C.E.-700 C.E.
LOCALE: Western Oaxaca, Mexico, with emphasis in the Mixteca Alta or highland regions
SIGNIFICANCE: The Mixtec are renowned for exquisite works of art in metal, stone, and ceramics and for developing a writing system that contributed to the Mixteca-Puebla style of northern Mesoamerica.

The term Mixtec refers to both a group of people and the language spoken by modern descendants living in the western Oaxaca. The Mixtec civilization dates back to the Late Classic to Postclassic periods (700-1520 C.E.).

History. The Mixtec civilization began to develop around 1530 B.C.E., when people settled in small villages and adopted agriculture. Their cultural practices and lifestyles were very similar to nearly all Mesoamerican cultures developing in the Formative period (2000-200 B.C.E.).

As these small villages grew in size, people began to organize into different social classes. From these differences rose the Mixtec civilization, which included a formalized state religion and numerous polities controlling networks of cities, towns, and villages. During the Early Classic period (200 B.C.E.-300 C.E.) outside influence came from the Zapotecs living in cities such as Monte Albán in the Valley of Oaxaca, but the predominance of foreign influence shifted to Teotihuacán in the Valley of Mexico after 300 C.E.

After 700 C.E. The Late Classic period (600-900 C.E.) brought the decline of Teotihuacán as well as Maya lowland kingdoms, creating a void in international power. By the Terminal Classic period (900 to 1000 C.E.), Mixtec political and cultural influence had spread throughout western Oaxaca and the surrounding regions, including Puebla and the Valley of Mexico.

Although there may have been some outside influence from the Toltecs during the Terminal Classic period and early in the Postclassic period (1000-1520 C.E.), the Mixtec developed their own traditions. The Mixtec established large sociopolitical and religious centers responsible for governing the region as well as promoting their social, cultural and religious beliefs and practices. The transition to the Postclassic period was not tranquil, and the rise of the Aztec empire in the fifteenth century did affect aspects of Mixtec politics and economics, but their daily life and cultural practices remained much the same. However, the Spanish conquest in the 1500's brought great cultural and political changes to the traditional Mixtec ways of life.

Government. Although the founder of the Mixtec royalty has not been identified, there was an elite lineage from which Mixtec kings descended. Unlike the Aztec Empire, in which government was controlled through a single capital, the Mixtec had multiple kings that ruled polities. These kingdoms were organized in a hierarchical fashion so that in situations requiring centralized control such as invasion from foreigners (such as the Aztecs), the Mixtec kingdoms could join together.

War and weapons. The Mixtecs used warfare to control less powerful kingdoms, to obtain captives for ritual sacrifice ceremonies, and to protect themselves from invading groups. Warfare involved arrows, spears, atlatls (spear-throwers), and wooden swords inlayed with obsidian blades.

Settlements and social structure. The social strata in Mixtec civilization were the noble families, the lesser noble families, the commoners, and the servants and slaves. The kings and the elite families were considered direct descendants of the Mixtec ruling lineage. The priests were also from the noble families and served as oracles who could communicate with the supernatural world. Although priests could never rule a Mixtec city or polity, their supernatural powers provided them great influence over the ruling kings and elite. The commoners composed the bulk of the Mixtec population. Through their daily efforts in agriculture, they supported the elite and priest classes. Servants and slaves had little recognition within the Mixtec social structure.

Architecture and city planning. Mixtec structures were built from cobbles and cut stone and finished with plaster or stucco on rectangular platforms arranged around plazas. The city core of temples, palaces, and plazas was for the king, the priests, and associated elite classes. The Mixtec region was environmentally variable; therefore, most cities were built somewhat haphazardly to exploit the local topography. This contrasts with the gridlike streets and regularly shaped buildings of Teotihuacán or Tula in the Valley of Mexico.

Economics. Agriculture and commoners drove Mixtec economics. Most families produced a surplus, some of which was given to the elite, and the rest could be traded for goods. Commoners also were required by the elite classes to extract from the land valuable resources including gold, jade, chert, limestone, basalt, and possibly obsidian. During the Postclassic period, the Mixtec traded not only among their own kingdoms but also with other cultures living in the region. Most of these goods had to be transported over land by human labor, and ocean or river transport of trade goods using canoes was limited.

Calendars and chronology. The Mixtec calendar systems reflect a sophisticated understanding of time, using at least two different calendars, 260-day and 365-day, with cycles imposed on the interaction of these calendars. The Mixtecs were also aware of the passage of linear time, as noted by the historical records within the codices.

The 260-day calendar was used to plan rituals as well as for divination. The 365-day calendar, similar to the one used by most modern Western cultures, tracked time for secular purposes such as agriculture. It took fifty-two years to cycle to a day with identical dates for the 260-day and 365-day calendar. This was considered to be a very auspicious cycle, much like the turn of the one-hundred year cycles (centuries) of modern Western societies.

Religion and ritual. Mixtec religion created a balance among the supernatural realm, the natural world, and humans. Mixtec deities controlled aspects of nature including the Sun, the rain, and the wind. Many of these deities were associated with concepts of life, death, and fertility. Mixtec deities were not always benevolent and at times acted in direct opposition to human wishes.

Religious rituals were an important responsibility for Mixtecs because they maintained the balance in their universe. The endings and beginnings of important cycles also were associated with rituals: for example, the new fire ceremonies, which symbolized the renewal of the universe. The Mixtec civilization held human sacrifice to be the most important form of ritual offering to the deities and ancestors. There were two basic forms of sacrifice, self-sacrifice and the sacrifice of human victims. In self-sacrifice or bloodletting, people would cut their skin in order to bleed from sacred parts of their bodies, including the tongue, cheek, or genitalia. The ritual sacrifice of human victims involved the extraction of the victim's heart. Generally, these victims were captured warriors and elites from surrounding cities.

Death and burial. Evidence suggests that the Mixtecs mummified some of their elite for the purpose of supernatural consultation, and priests were responsible for communicating with these ancestors. For Mixtec lords and other elite, there was life after death. The burial caves served as portals to netherworlds where they continued their existence devoid of all pain and discomfort. However, commoners were buried beneath their houses. Although ancestor worship did occur among this class, it is not clear whether they believed there was life after death for commoners.

Sports and entertainment. The Mixtecs participated in a ritualized activity known as the ball game. The playing of the ball game was a religious and supernatural event in which the outcome had repercussions on the groups playing the game. In the most important games, played only by elite, one or more members of the losing team would be sacrificed.

Writing systems. The Mixtecs developed a writing system using logographs (pictures that are symbolic of people, places, and actions) to convey important information concerning the religious, political, and cultural beliefs and practices of their elite class. This distinctive writing style is associated with the Mixteca-Puebla style that was adopted by surrounding cultures including the Zapotecs, the Aztecs, and the Quiché Maya. This form of written communication was very important because the iconography and pictures created a lingua franca that could be understood by speakers of many different languages and cultures living in the region.

Language and literature. The Mixtecs created hand-painted manuscripts known as codices, and scholars have analyzed the eight documents that have been recovered. These manuscripts not only record the historical events and genealogy of the elite class but also express important information and symbolism concerning their religious, political, and cultural beliefs and practices. The Mixtec codices are particularly noteworthy because they provide a native perspective on Mixtec civilization and represent the longest continuous genealogical record of kingship recovered in Mesoamerica.

Visual arts. The contribution of the Mixtec artists and priests to the distinctive Mixteca-Puebla style is recognized not only in codices but also in painted murals found in the palaces and temples of their cities. Mixtec artisans created exquisite works of art including

gold jewelry and sculptures, jade carvings, and ceramic vases and vessels in the Mixteca-Puebla style.

Current views. Recent research combines the archaeological record with information found in codices to understand the historical mechanisms of Mixtec kingship. These studies have also revealed more detail on the complex relationship between the Mixtec and other culture groups living in the region and in surrounding territories.

ADDITIONAL RESOURCES

Byland, Bruch, and John Pohl. *The Archaeology of the Mixtec Codices: In the Realm of Eight Deer.* Norman: University of Oklahoma Press, 1994.

Spores, Ronald. *The Mixtecs in Ancient and Colonial Times.* Norman: University of Oklahoma Press, 1984.

Winter, Marcus. *Oaxaca: The Archaeological Record.* Mexico City: Minutiae Mexicana, 1992.

SEE ALSO: Ball game, Mesoamerican; Maya; Zapotecs.

—*Michelle R. Woodward*

MOABITES

DATE: c. 1200-c. 63 B.C.E.
LOCALE: The region immediately east of the Dead Sea
RELATED CIVILIZATIONS: Israel, Egypt, Assyria, Babylonia, Greece, Rome
SIGNIFICANCE: Moab was the neighbor and frequent enemy of Israel.

What is known about Moab is found primarily in the Bible. There the term refers both to a place and to the people who inhabited it. It was a fertile land, famous for grain and livestock production as well as for being the burial place of Moses. References to the Moab in the Bible are extremely derogatory, depicting the nation as originating from an incestuous union and later as opposing the Israelites in their attempt to enter Canaan after the Exodus. Claim to northern Moab was the cause of disputes between the Israelites and the Moabites (MOH-ab-itz). Israel interpreted this animosity theologically, resulting in the denunciation of Moab

throughout the Bible. Remarkably, King David's genealogy is traced to Moab in the book of Ruth.

Outside the Bible, Moab is mentioned in Egyptian and Assyrian texts. A Moabite monument, the famous Mesha inscription, tells how Mesha, king of Moab, drove the Israelites from his territory in the ninth century B.C.E. Moab was defeated consecutively by the Assyrians, Babylonians, and Greeks before being absorbed into the Roman Empire.

ADDITIONAL RESOURCES

Dearman, Andrew, ed. *Studies in the Mesha Inscription and Moab.* Atlanta, Ga.: Scholars Press, 1989.

Hoerth, A. J., G. L. Mattingly, and E. M. Yamauchi, eds. *Peoples of the Old Testament World.* Grand Rapids, Mich.: Baker Books, 1994.

SEE ALSO: Assyria; Babylonia; Bible: Jewish; David; Greece, Classical; Israel; Moses; Rome, Imperial.

—*James H. Pace*

MOCHE CULTURE

ALSO KNOWN AS: Mochica
DATE: 200/100 B.C.E.-600 C.E.
LOCALE: Moche River Valley, Peru
SIGNIFICANCE: Arguably the earliest expansionist state on the north coast of Peru, the Moche civilization featured irrigation agriculture, a state labor tax, and a wealth of information about the culture recorded on painted and molded pottery vessels.

Developing from the earlier Caballo de Muerto and other cultures of the Moche Valley in the preceding Early Horizon period (1000 to 300 B.C.E.) associated with the Chavín civilization, Moche developed during the Early Intermediate period, beginning about 200 B.C.E. The Early Intermediate was a time of regionalism in Peru, with a number of river valley polities including the Moche vying for political supremacy.

The first capital of the Moche civilization was at Cerro Blanco and consisted of two main temples, Huaca del Sol (temple of the Sun) and Huaca de la Luna (temple of the Moon), built of adobe bricks on the banks of the Moche River. Distinctive makers' marks on the bricks indicate the temples were built by village labor parties, a sign of forced labor that marked later civilizations in Peru. The basic pattern of state and empire that were known from the later Chimu and Inca states were set with the Moche. The culture was based on irrigation agriculture and expanded beyond the Moche River Valley to incorporate other river valley states.

The city and culture were devastated by an El Niño event around 550 C.E. that is recorded in the Quelccaya glacier near Cuzco and indicates flooding, erosion, and sand piling on the city. After that event, Cerro Blanco was rebuilt and became more dependent on highland corn and marine resources, turning away from the previous emphasis on irrigation farming. Also recorded in the glacial core is a subsequent drought about 562-594 C.E. that precipitated the abandonment of Cerro Blanco and the relocation of the capital north to Pampa Grande in the Lambeyeque Valley.

One of the most famous Moche sites is Sipan, a temple site where the Peruvian archaeologist Walter Alva excavated an elaborate burial of a Moche warrior-priest. The most well-preserved and sumptuous of elite tombs, the burial includes other individuals buried alongside the warrior-preist, as well as gold, feather, and ceramic offerings, many previously known only from artistic depictions on pottery vessels.

Moche art, known mainly from spouted pottery vessels from burials, consists of four styles. Much of the art consists of stylized scenes representing mythological, shamanistic, or political events that are ren-

Archaeologists examine a small object in this partially excavated tomb of a Moche warrior-priest. (Time and Life)

dered in a two-dimensional painting style, with profile figures. By ethnographic analogy to modern Moche healers, some of the scenes have been interpreted as ritual shamanistic ceremonies. Another group of pottery vessels consists of naturalistic portraits in three dimensions, made by modeling the clay. Many pottery vessels include naturalistic depictions of people, plants, animals, and scenes of everyday life, including a large group of sexually explicit art. Another group of pots display stylized abstract designs.

ADDITIONAL RESOURCES

Donnan, Christopher B. *Moche Art and Iconography.* Los Angeles: University of California Press, 1976.

Moseley, Michael E. *The Incas and Their Ancestors: The Archaeology of Peru.* London: Thames and Hudson, 1992.

SEE ALSO: Chavín de Huántar; Huaca de la Luna; Huaca del Sol; Lima culture; South American Intermediate area.

—Heather I. McKillop

MOGOLLON CULTURE

DATE: 200 B.C.E.-700 C.E.

LOCALE: Present-day southeast Arizona, southwest New Mexico, United States, and northern Sonora and Chihuahua, Mexico

RELATED CIVILIZATIONS: Cochise, Hohokam, Anasazi

SIGNIFICANCE: The Mogollon culture, known for its pottery and pit houses, developed from the earlier Cochise culture and later merged with the Anasazi.

The Mogollon (muh-guh-YOHN) culture, part of early Pueblo cultures, influenced other Southwest cultures and later merged with the Anasazi. Archaeologist Emil Haury named this tradition after the Mogollon Mountains of the central Arizona-New Mexico border. Mogollon culture developed from the earlier Cochise culture and retained many of its traits, including the gathering of seeds, roots, berries, nuts, and insects and the hunting of small game. In addition to gathering and hunting, the Mogollon people grew corn and beans without irrigation, clustered in villages in pit houses, and made coiled pottery. The vast area occupied by people of this cultural tradition can be divided into a northern mountainous region and a southern valley or desert region. These not only represent topographic differences but also differences in cultural history. Distinct subregions or cultural subtraditions identified by archaeologists are Chihuahua, Forestdale, Grasshopper, Jornada, Mimbres, Pine Lawn, Point of Pines, Q Ranch, San Simón, and Upper Little Colorado.

Mogollon tradition is especially known for its pottery and architecture. The early period is identified with predominantly plain, dark-brown pottery. This changed to decorated red on brown and later to red on white.

Finally, under Anasazi influence, the pottery became black on white with geometric and other designs.

Structures commonly identified with this tradition are pit houses. These ranged in shape from circular and oval to square with rounded corners. Pit houses were sunken below the frostline, making them more thermally efficient than aboveground structures. During the Early Pit House period (200-550 C.E.), roundish structures usually measured from 10 to 16 feet (3 to 4.8 meters) in diameter and were excavated to a depth of 2 to 5 feet (0.6 to 1.5 meters). Roofs of poles covered with branches and mud were either umbrella-type with a center post or dome-shaped with beams supported by marginal posts. Early settlements commonly consisted of four to six pit houses with an estimated population of around thirty men, women, and children. Not all pit houses had interior hearths, and some may have served as other than living quarters. Later pit houses usually had central hearths. Household equipment and furnishings included a variety of clay vessels, grass beds, rabbit-fur or bird-feather blankets, plant-fiber scouring pads, fire drills, fire tongs, metates (lower mill stones), and manos (upper mill stones). Some settlements contained larger pit houses, or kivas, which were used for special rituals or ceremonies. Early settlements were commonly located on elevated ground, such as ridges or mesa tops, which overlooked arable land and which probably served a defensive purpose.

During the Late Pit House period (550-1000 C.E.), settlements were located on both high landforms and in valleys close to garden areas. Pit houses became rectangular, and the dead were buried in simple pits outside the dwellings or inside under the floor. At the end of this period, structures changed from pit houses to aboveground pueblo dwellings. The Mogollon culture, as evidenced by dated archaeological sites, continued until 1200 C.E.

ADDITIONAL RESOURCES

Cordell, Linda. *Ancient Pueblo Peoples*. Montreal: St. Remy Press, 1994.

Cordell, Linda, and George Gumerman, eds. *Dynamics of Southwest Prehistory*. Washington, D.C.: Smithsonian Institution Press, 1989.

SEE ALSO: Anasazi; Cochise culture; Hohokam culture.

—*Philip E. Lampe*

MON-KHMER

DATE: c. 2000 B.C.E.-800 C.E.
LOCALE: Mainland Southeast Asia, primarily modern Myanmar and Cambodia
SIGNIFICANCE: Mon-Khmer civilizations helped bring Indian influence into Southeast Asia and to spread the Buddhist religion. Many of the languages in Southeast Asia are derived from the Mon-Khmer family.

The term "Mon-Khmer" (mahn-kuh-MEHR) is usually used to refer to a family of languages spoken primarily in mainland Southeast Asia. These languages include Mon (primarily concentrated in Myanmar, formerly known as Burma), Khmer (also known as Cambodian), Muong, Khasi, Wa, and Vietnamese. Speakers of Mon-Khmer languages intermarried with speakers of other language groups in Southeast Asia, and languages spread across national and tribal groups, so it is difficult to trace the extent to which Mon-Khmer speakers have actually been cultural or genetic descendants of the ancient Mon-Khmer.

The Mon-Khmer people are believed to have migrated into Southeast Asia from southwest China or from the Khasi Hills in northwest India as early as 2000 B.C.E. The Mon, one of the primary subgroups of the Mon-Khmer, followed the Salween River in what is now Myanmar. Among Mon-Khmer groups, the Mon are generally believed to have retained the greatest cultural continuity with the ancient Mon-Khmer. The subgroup that became known as the Khmer migrated farther east into what is now Cambodia (also known as Kampuchea).

The Mon became the first people in Southeast Asia to take up the Buddhist religion. Beginning about the sixth century B.C.E., they created Buddhist kingdoms stretching throughout contemporary southeastern Myanmar and into contemporary Thailand. This early

Buddhist civilization is known as Dvaravati. The people of the Dvaravati civilization maintained contact with India and played a critical part in transmitting Indian culture and religion to other civilizations in Southeast Asia. The Thai, Lao, Khmer, and Burmese languages all use variations of a Mon-Khmer writing system derived from the writing of India.

People thought to have been speakers of the Khmer branch of Mon-Khmer founded the early kingdoms of Funan and Chenla in what is now Cambodia in the first centuries of the common era. Like the Mon, the Khmer were heavily influenced by India, although early Khmer society drew more heavily on Hinduism than on Buddhism. About the third century C.E., the Khmer developed a version of Mon-Khmer writing that became the basis of the Cambodian, Thai, and Lao writing systems. About 790 C.E., a prince of a small Khmer kingdom, who claimed descent from the kings of Funan, took the name Jayavarman II and extended his power over a large part of Cambodia. This was the basis of the influential Angkor civilization, named after the huge temple complex built by the successors of Jayavarman II.

ADDITIONAL RESOURCES

Brown, Robert L. *The Dvaravati Wheels of the Law and the Indianization of Southeast Asia*. New York: E. J. Brill, 1996.

Coedès, George. *The Indianized States of Southeast Asia*. Honolulu: University of Hawaii Press, 1971.

Dumarçay, Jacques, and Michael Smithies. *Cultural Sites of Burma, Thailand, and Cambodia*. New York: Oxford University Press, 1995.

SEE ALSO: Buddhism; China; Funan; Hinduism; India; Laos; Pyu; Vietnam.

—*Carl L. Bankston III*

MONGOLIA

DATE: 2000-700 B.C.E.

LOCALE: Northern Asia between China and Russia with the Gobi Desert in the southeast

SIGNIFICANCE: The predecessors of Genghis Khan founded the first steppe empire and played significant roles in the settling and fortunes of the Americas, Central Asia, China, and Siberia.

The ancestors of Genghis Khan, founder of the Mongol Empire in the 1300's, were among the first modern humans to migrate successfully to some of Earth's harshest lands with their long, cold, and arid winters. His nomadic predecessors (called Mongoloids by scientists) also settled Siberia, traveled across the Bering Strait into the Americas, and navigated across the Pacific Ocean to settle the Pacific Islands and Australia.

The Mongols originated in the region around Lake Baikal, the deepest lake in the world and a natural boundary between Siberia and present-day Mongolia (mahn-GOHL-yuh). Archaeologists have discovered

This Mongolian rider demonstrates the prowess on horses of members of this group. (North Wind Picture Archives)

50,000-year-old hand axes and other stone implements that are the remains of Mongolia's earliest inhabitants, predecessors of the Neanderthal. Stone Age humans were living in the southern Gobi Desert region between 10,000 and 20,000 years ago.

According to *The Secret History of the Mongols*, the official literary account of Genghis Khan's reign, the Mongol people date to an ancient time when heaven mandated that a blue-gray wolf and his wife, a fallow deer, mate. Their son, Batachikan, was the first human ancestor of Genghis Khan. The first nonmythical mention of a people living on the steppe lands north of Chinese civilization dates to the eighth century B.C.E. However, the Chinese sources do not identify the people by name until the third century B.C.E.

The Mongol people did not exist as a political entity until the creation of the Mongol Empire by Genghis Khan in the 1300's. Before the creation of the Mongol Empire, large, loosely organized Mongol, Tungus, and Turkic tribes inhabited the steppes. These tribes were continually at war with other nomadic tribes and sedentary peoples whose civilizations were based on agriculture rather than pastoralism. The ambitions that drove these tribes to war included the desire to achieve military or political superiority and even greater wealth and political influence.

The earliest of the great pastoralist empires in Inner Eurasia, the Xiongnu, existed in this area from 200 to 133 B.C.E. Under the command of Motun, who ruled from 209 to 174 B.C.E., the Xiongnu federation expanded imperial power and wealth to include the Gobi Desert and the rest of Mongolia. The Xiongnu were probably the builders of the first state in Central Asia. They were the first people of the Mongol lands to pose a serious threat to the sedentary peoples of the Chinese kingdoms. The Xiongnu Empire was the first of the many empires to follow that was founded by a great military commander who established a unified kingdom and that later fell apart because of intratribal warfare over wealth and power.

Following a disastrous attempt to conquer the Xiongnu, Han China agreed to treat these barbarians as diplomatic equals and to provide regular gifts to Motun so he would not attack China. Motun financed the growth of his empire through conquests that supplied it with the food, raw materials, and additional soldiers his nomadic people needed. Among Motun's achievements was the creation of a stable relationship between his nomadic tribesmen and the agrarian Chinese Empire.

In 133 B.C.E., the great Han emperor Wudi (r. 141-87 B.C.E.) rebelled at the system of paying tribute to the Huns and waged a relatively successful war to stop the payments. As the power of Motun's successors declined, Mongolia once again became a region of independent tribes engaged in continuous struggles for wealth and power. Some refugees from the Xiongnu Empire migrated west. Historians believe some of these refugees eventually became parts of the troops of Attila, king of the Huns.

During the third and fourth centuries C.E., two barbarian empires—the T'o-pa (386-534 C.E.) and the Juan-Juan (350-555 C.E.)—fought to unite the independent tribes into a powerful and wealthy federation that controlled far-flung territories.

By the mid-sixth century C.E., a federation of predominantly Turkish-speaking tribes from the Altay region expanded the territories once controlled by the Juan-Juan. The Turkish empires that followed fell apart for many of the same reasons that the earlier steppe federations had—strong and successful leadership disappeared, as did the sources of wealth, including the tribute that China paid and the markets and foodstuffs it provided.

The Uighur tribes evolved into the next major steppe power, reigning from 744 to 840 C.E. Their military power, political influence, and wealth exceeded those of predecessor states. The Uighurs helped a disgruntled Tang general, An Lushan, overthrow the Chinese emperor. A grateful new emperor richly rewarded his Uighur allies with gifts, diplomatic recognition, and ready access to Chinese markets.

The Uighur built permanent palaces and fortresses. They also developed their own written language, which many captured tribes, including the Mongols, adopted. Once again, civil warfare and vassal tribal resistance led to a Central Asian empire's disintegration. A confederation of Mongol, Siberian, and Turkic tribes contributed to the decline and fall of the Uighur Empire. The Kirghiz gained control after the Uighur, but they failed to establish their own commercial or military empire and soon fell out of power.

Tribes from Manchuria and people from China attempted to fill the military and political vacuum that developed with the decline of the Kirghiz. During this period, Mongolian replaced the Turkic languages as the dominant language. Mongolia reverted to a land of regional powers unable to threaten north China or control trade along the Silk Road.

Genghis Khan and his successors built the largest

land-based empire ever. That empire ruled much of modern-day China, Korea, the Middle East, and Russia. In some cases, this rule lasted more than one hundred years. The empires of Mongolia thus played a significant role in human history.

ADDITIONAL RESOURCES

Christian, David. *A History of Russia, Central Asia, and Mongolia*. Vol. 1 in *Inner Eurasia from Prehistory to the Mongol Empire*. Oxford, England: Blackwell, 1998.

Derev'anko, Anatoliy P., ed. and comp. *The Paleolithic of Siberia: New Discoveries and Interpretations*. Edited by Demitri B. Shimkin and W. Roger Powers, translated by Inna P. Laricheva. Urbana: University of Illinois Press, 1998.

Fairservis, Walter A., Jr. *Archeology of the Southern Gobi of Mongolia*. Durham, N.C.: Carolina Academic Press, 1993.

Sinor, Denis. *The Cambridge History of Early Inner Asia: From the Earliest Times to the Rise of the Mongols*. Cambridge, England: Cambridge University Press, 1990.

SEE ALSO: Attila; China; Han Dynasty; Huns; Silk Road; Wudi.

—Fred Buchstein

MONOPHYSITISM

DATE: appeared after the Council of Chalcedon, 451 C.E.

LOCALE: Northern Africa

SIGNIFICANCE: A heretical belief of the early Christian Church that taught that Jesus Christ had only one nature, a divine one, rather than two (divine and human), as maintained by the orthodox at the Council of Chalcedon.

The term Monophysitism (muh-NAH-fuh-sit-ih-zuhm) is from the Greek words *monos* meaning one and *physis* meaning nature. Monophysitism was an attempt to solve one of the main theological dilemmas of Christianity: the nature of Christ. If Christ was divine but took human form upon birth, what kind of union was created? The dispute began in the 440's C.E. in Alexandria, the center of Christianity in Egypt. Two patriarchs of Alexandria, Eutyches and Dioscorus, developed teachings that were originally put forth by an early Church father, Saint Cyril of Alexandria. At the Council of Chalcedon in 451 C.E., Dioscorus was deposed by the orthodox clergy, who argued that Christ was "perfect in both deity and humanness; this selfsame one is actually God and actually Man, with a rational soul and a body." In 452 C.E., the emperor Theodosius II forbade the Monophysites to have priests, to assemble, to make wills, or to inherit property. Any priests who disobeyed the imperial edict were banished from the Byzantine Empire.

In Egypt, nearly the entire population sided with Dioscorus and thus remained in heresy, that is, outside the official teachings of the Church. Riots broke out in Alexandria, and the emperor sent in troops to restore order. In 454 C.E., Timothy Aelurus succeeded Dioscorus as patriarch, and soon orthodox bishops were replaced by Monophysite bishops. Emperor Justinian I eventually restored unity to the Church in the 500's C.E., and orthodoxy held sway. The emperors who followed Justinian alternately favored or condemned Monophysitism. By the 600's C.E., the schism, or break, in the Church had hardened, with different regions establishing their own Monophysite churches.

ADDITIONAL RESOURCES

Bondi, Roberta. *Three Monophysite Christologies*. Oxford, England: Oxford University Press, 1976.

Frend, W. H. C. *The Rise of the Monophysite Movement*. London: Cambridge University Press, 1972.

Torrance, Iain R., and Sergius Severus. *Christology After Chalcedon*. Eugene, Ore.: Wipf and Stook, 1998.

SEE ALSO: Byzantine Empire; Chalcedon, Council of; Christianity; Cyril of Alexandria, Saint; Jesus Christ; Justinian I; Rome, Imperial; Theodosius II.

—Adriane Ruggiero

MONTANISM

DATE: c. 156-300 C.E.
LOCALE: Phrygia in Asia Minor, North Africa, Rome
SIGNIFICANCE: Montanists created a schism in the Christian church by offering leadership based on ecstatic and prophetic utterances rather than on episcopal authority.

Preaching the imminent return of Christ and claiming immediate revelations from the Holy Spirit, Montanus and the small sect that gathered around him in the mid-second century C.E. caught the attention of the Christian church. Instead of spiritual renewal, however, the result of Montanism (MAHN-tehn-ih-zm) was, for the most part, controversy and schism.

Montanus, a Phrygian Christian, claimed that the promised Paraclete of John 14 was manifesting himself through prophets and prophetesses—specifically, through Montanus and two female followers, Prisca (or Priscilla) and Maximilla. They believed themselves to be the voices of the Holy Spirit, and the messages they delivered were ringing calls to a more rigorous and committed Christian lifestyle. They endorsed extensive fasting, prohibited second marriages, and maintained that serious sins after baptism were beyond forgiveness. True Christians will not flee persecution, they taught, but will embrace it.

Some in the church were drawn to the fervor of the "new prophecy"; Tertullian, the great North African apologist, joined their ranks in 206 C.E. However, over time their visions, their practice of speaking in tongues, and their claims of direct revelation were seen as spiritual excesses. Although traces of Montanism survived into the sixth century C.E., the movement had long since ceased to influence the Christian Church.

ADDITIONAL RESOURCES

Aune, D. E. *Prophecy in Early Christianity and the Ancient Mediterranean World.* Grand Rapids, Mich.: Eerdmans, 1983.

Eusebius of Caesarea. *The Church History: A New Translation with Commentary.* Translated by Paul M. Maier. Grand Rapids, Mich.: Kregel, 1999.

SEE ALSO: Africa, North; Christianity; Rome, Imperial; Tertullian.

—Robert Black

MONTE ALBÁN

DATE: 500 B.C.E.-700 C.E.
LOCALE: Oaxaca Valley, southern Mexico
RELATED CIVILIZATIONS: Zapotecs, Mixtecs
SIGNIFICANCE: Monte Albán was one of the first civilizations in Mexico and was the largest and most important Zapotec complex.

Monte Albán refers to a hilltop that was artificially flattened and built up to create a city that became the capital of Zapotec society. Monte Albán also refers to the surrounding settlements on nearby hilltops, hillsides, and valleys, all of which pertained to and supported the capital. The Monte Albán hill was unoccupied until about 500 B.C.E.; it may have been chosen by competing Zapotec villages as the site for an administrative center, as it was on neutral territory. Although the hilly area did not possess much water or good soil and was located 1,300 feet (396 meters) above the valley, it offered a key strategic position with a view of the three fingerlike valleys spreading out around it.

As Monte Albán was constructed and settled, the population of the Oaxaca Valley decreased. During Monte Albán period IA (500-300 B.C.E.), Monte Albán's population exceeded five thousand people, at least half of the Oaxaca Valley's population. New villages were formed along the foothills and terraces of the mountain, and by period IC, the population of the Oaxaca Valley had risen to about fifty thousand, the majority of whom lived within 12 miles (20 kilometers) of the capital. The developing state at Monte Albán was distinguished by features such as a centralized government of religiously trained rulers, an administrative hierarchy, a system of exacting tributes from communities and wars toward this purpose, and an organized system of priests and public works based on construction of religious temples and other structures. The civil-ceremonial center on top of Monte Albán, circa period I, included temples and residences for the elite, although the more luxurious palaces that later emerged as housing for rulers did not yet exist. Commoners lived in more modest, adobe-like structures, which were sometimes located behind defensive walls built in this period.

During period I, several novel innovations emerged: the *comal*, a large griddle used for mass-producing tortillas, and irrigation systems. Irrigation was necessary to bring water to the arid piedmont and terraced areas of Monte Albán and involved a system of dams and canals.

The first incidence of literary texts in Mexico dates to period I; this is an important set of large stone slabs now called the *danzantes* (dancers). Placed in the southwest portion of the hilltop, there are four rows, totaling about three hundred slabs. Numbers (bars and dots) and hieroglyphs are carved on the slabs alongside figures depicting sacrificed human victims and captives of war. The numbers are understood, although the text is not: Zapotec writing is still largely undeciphered. The scenes depicted, as well as the monstrous effort required to create the slabs, suggest that Monte Albán was militarily powerful. During this period, the citizens of Monte Albán used calendars, the first to emerge in pre-Hispanic society.

The move into Monte Albán period II (100 B.C.E.-200 C.E.) was gradual. This period was highly dynamic, marked by well-established sociopolitical organization throughout Zapotec society and expansion into neighboring territories. Society functioned by means of commoners who provided labor and farmed crops and raised animals to provide food for the society, as well as monetary payments exacted from villages. Study of period II pottery shards, which incidentally represented the most colorful (red, orange, white, black) pottery to date, shows that the number of communities decreased in comparison to Monte Albán period I, although the cities in Monte Albán II were larger.

Important construction of public buildings flourished during period II, such as the creation of the 980-by-660-foot (300-by-200-meter) Main Plaza on top of Monte Albán. This plaza served as the focus of the hilltop's buildings; the North Platform, temples, tombs, and the like were built on top of the smaller structures built in period I. Another important building of period II was an arrowhead-shaped building now known as Building J, which was oriented in near-perfect alignment with the star Capella. The exterior of the building shows scenes of warfare and conquest of various kings, common themes in Zapotec glyphs at Monte Albán. Important changes in period II were the emergence of large palaces and tombs built for rulers, and the standardization of temples to contain two rooms.

Monte Albán reached its apogee in period III, between 200 and 700 C.E. During the first half of this Classic period, the population expanded, especially in the valley, although the capital of Monte Albán continued to wield power. In period IIIB, geographical expansion slowed greatly, but many new buildings were constructed in the capital. The population reached its maximum size of 115,000 during period III, and Monte Albán stretched over settlements on neighboring ridges and hills as well as valleys. As was the case beginning in period II, new structures on the capital's hilltop were built over old ones, and many of the structures that remain are from period III. The capital contained a main large plaza, temples, palaces, ball courts, platforms, administrative centers, and other buildings, all built on a massive scale. The territory of Monte Albán III was characterized by a highly complex political and social system, an ever-expanding population, and well-developed architecture. Both the pottery and architecture of Monte Albán were distinctively Zapotec.

After 700 C.E. By period IV, 700-950 C.E., the structure of Zapotec society had changed dramatically. In contrast to the highly centralized control of the past, by 700 C.E., administrative control in the territory of Monte Albán had shifted to smaller, autonomous areas, and the capital decreased in population from 16,500 in period III to an estimated 4,000 people. The capital was abandoned to a great extent and left to become ruins, which were later used by the Mixtecs for burial grounds. One theory supposes that the fourteen groups or families who held administrative buildings in the Main Plaza may have relocated to smaller locales away from the capital, forming their own ruling centers. Although period IV is not fully understood, this argument makes sense to the extent that excavations of these new, smaller locales yielded tombs, artifacts, and elite dwellings that are in keeping with the Monte Albán styles.

Monte Albán was eventually encroached upon by the Mixtecs and later the Aztecs. Although it lost its control over the region, elements of Zapotec culture, including language, were maintained.

ADDITIONAL RESOURCES

Flannery, Kent, and Joyce Marcus. *Zapotec Civilization: How Urban Society Evolved in Mexico's Oaxaca Valley.* London: Thames and Hudson, 1996.

Paddock, John, ed. *Ancient Oaxaca: Discoveries in Mexican Archeology and History.* Stanford, Calif.: Stanford University Press, 1966.

Weaver, Muriel Porter. *The Aztecs, Maya, and Their Predecessors: Archeology of Mesoamerica*. 3d ed. San Diego, Calif.: Academic Press, 1993.

SEE ALSO: Mixtecs; Zapotecs.

—*Michelle C. K. McKowen*

MONTUHOTEP I

ALSO KNOWN AS: Nebhepetre; Mentuhotep I
REIGNED: 2061-2011 B.C.E.
RELATED CIVILIZATION: Pharaonic Egypt
MAJOR ROLE/POSITION: King, military leader

Life. A local ruler from the area of Thebes, Montuhotep (mahn-tew-HOH-tehp) I controlled a relatively small area around his capital in Upper Egypt at the beginning of his reign. The rest of the country was ruled by a combination of local princes and a king in northern Egypt with a capital at Heracleopolis, near the Fayum. The first half of Montuhotep I's reign was spent in the conquest of Egypt and the reunification of the country for the first time since the end of the Old Kingdom. He took the title "Uniter of the Two Lands" (Upper and Lower Egypt) to commemorate his success in battle.

His conquest of Lower Egypt allowed him to benefit from the artists and craftspeople who had continued to work in the royal workshops through the First Intermediate Period, and the local style of Thebes was quickly supplanted by that of artists who were imported from Memphis. His most famous monument is a terraced temple and tomb at the site of Deir el-Bahri, on the west bank of Thebes.

Influence. Reunifier of Egypt after the period of unrest known as the First Intermediate Period, Montuhotep I was the founder of the Middle Kingdom. His fifty-year reign is one of the longest in Egyptian history.

ADDITIONAL RESOURCES
Clayton, Peter A. *Chronicle of the Pharaohs*. New York: Thames and Hudson, 1994.
Robins, Gay. *The Art of Ancient Egypt*. Cambridge, Mass.: Harvard University Press, 1997.

SEE ALSO: Egypt, Pharaonic.

—*Sara E. Orel*

MOSCHUS OF SYRACUSE

ALSO KNOWN AS: Moschos
BORN: third or second century B.C.E.; Syracuse, Sicily?
DIED: second century B.C.E.; place unknown
RELATED CIVILIZATION: Hellenistic Greece
MAJOR ROLE/POSITION: Poet

Life. Moschus (MAHS-kuhs) of Syracuse was the middle of the three bucolic poets, between Theocritus of Syracuse and Bion. He probably lived in Alexandria, Egypt, where he studied under Aristarchus of Samothrace. He wrote light verse rather than serious poetry but was influenced by more serious poets, such as Apollonius Rhodius. All his surviving works are in hexameter.

Of Moschus's three short poems anthologized by Greek anthologist Joannes Stobaios in the fifth century C.E., one extols rustic simplicity and the other two are erotic. Two additional short pastoral love poems, "Eros Drapetês" (n.d.; "The Runaway Love," 1651) and "Eros the Plowman" (n.d.; translation, 1651), are attributed to Moschus. His mock epic poem, *Europa* (n.d.; English translation, 1651), is known for its crude humor, suggestive themes, and grotesque imagery. The *Megara* (n.d.), a mournful dialogue between Heracles' wife Megara and mother Alcmene, is believed to have been written by either Moschus or one of his near contemporaries.

Influence. Bucolic, or pastoral, poetry celebrates the country life and its occupations, especially shepherding. It reached its zenith in the poet Vergil's *Eclogues* (43-37 B.C.E.; English translation, 1575, also known as *Bucolics*). All three of the bucolic poets inspired English poets Alexander Pope and William Wordsworth.

ADDITIONAL RESOURCES
Fowler, Barbara Hughes. *The Hellenistic Aesthetic*. Madison: University of Wisconsin Press, 1989.
Webster, T. B. L. *Hellenistic Poetry and Art*. New York: Barnes & Noble, 1964.

SEE ALSO: Apollonius Rhodius; Aristarchus of Samothrace; Greece, Hellenistic and Roman; Languages and literature; Theocritus of Syracuse; Vergil.

—*Eric v.d. Luft*

MOSES

BORN: c. 1300 B.C.E.; near Memphis, Egypt
DIED: c. 1200 B.C.E.; place unknown
RELATED CIVILIZATIONS: Pharaonic Egypt, Near East
MAJOR ROLE/POSITION: Religious leader

Life. Although born an Israelite, Moses was adopted by an Egyptian princess and raised at the royal court.

Moses. (Library of Congress)

Later he identified with his own oppressed people. After killing an Egyptian slave driver, he fled into the land of Midian. There, according to the Bible, God appeared to him in a burning bush and commissioned him to lead the Israelites from Egyptian bondage to freedom in Canaan (Palestine).

Moses returned to Egypt and told the pharaoh (perhaps Rameses II) to "let my people go." After the Israelites experienced a miraculous deliverance at the Reed (traditionally Red) Sea in the Exodus from Egypt, Moses led them to Mount Sinai. There, he became the mediator of the covenant between God and his people. If they would obey the covenant stipulations—including the Ten Commandments—then God would protect and prosper them in Canaan. Moses later guided the Israelites through the Sinai wilderness to the eastern rim of Canaan, where he died.

Influence. Moses stands as the towering figure in Jewish history. The laws he promulgated became the foundation of Judaism. Christianity and Islam also honor him as a prophet of ethical monotheism.

ADDITIONAL RESOURCES
Beegle, Dewey. *Moses, the Servant of Yahweh*. Grand Rapids, Mich.: Eerdmans, 1972.
Coats, George. *Moses: Heroic Man, Man of God*. Sheffield, England: Sheffield Academic Press, 1988.
Kushelevsky, Rella. *Moses and the Angel of Death*. New York: P. Lang, 1995.

SEE ALSO: Bible: Jewish; Canaanites; Egypt, Pharaonic; Exodus; Israel; Judaism.

—*Ronald W. Long*

Mozi

ALSO KNOWN AS: *Wade-Giles* Mo-tzu; Mo Di
  (*Wade-Giles* Mo Ti)
BORN: c. 470 B.C.E.; China
DIED: c. 391 B.C.E.; China
RELATED CIVILIZATION: China
MAJOR ROLE/POSITION: Philosopher, teacher

Life. Few facts are known about the life of Mozi (MOH-tsih), although tradition claims he was from the lower classes and worked as a carpenter. His teachings are preserved in a book, *Mozi* (fifth century B.C.E.; *The Ethical and Political Works of Motse*, 1929; also known as *Mo Tzu: Basic Writings*, 1963), compiled by his disciples. Based on this source, Mozi seems to have been a forceful, pragmatic thinker whose primary concern was to promote an ideal government that would bring the greatest good to the common people of China. In a time of growing religious skepticism, Mozi taught respect for spirit beings. He wanted both rulers and subjects to follow the will of heaven by practicing "universal love" and abstaining from offensive war.

Mozi's ideal society is strongly hierarchical, with all members required to follow the examples of their superiors. Even the emperor is obligated to model himself on heaven. Mozi's followers embraced this authoritarian model, swearing absolute obedience to their leaders.

Influence. For several centuries after Mozi's death, his followers were renowned for their defensive military skills. Tradition claims they often rushed to save besieged cities. Mozi's teachings advanced the development of Chinese logical thought and influenced later Chinese concepts of proper government.

ADDITIONAL RESOURCES

Graham, A. C. *Disputers of the Tao: Philosophical Argument in Ancient China.* La Salle, Ill.: Open Court, 1989.
Lowe, Scott. *Mo Tzu's Religious Blueprint for a Chinese Utopia: The Will and the Way.* Lewiston, N.Y.: The Edwin Mellen Press, 1992.

SEE ALSO: Arabia; China; Daoism.

—*Scott Lowe*

Muʿallaqāt, Al-

AUTHORSHIP: Seven poets, probably compiled by
  Ḥammād ar-Rāwiyah
DATE: eighth century C.E.
LOCALE: Al-Kufa, Iraq
RELATED CIVILIZATIONS: Arabia, the Near East,
  Mesopotamia
SIGNIFICANCE: An important anthology of seven pre-
  Islamic Arabic poems.

The *Al-Muʿallaqāt* (ahl mew-AWL-ah-kaht; *The Seven Golden Odes of Pagan Arabia*, 1903) is a collection of *qasida*, or Arabic odes, dating from al-Jāhilīyah, or the pre-Islamic age, that was probably gathered by Ḥammād ar-Rāwiyah (Ḥammad the Transmitter or Reciter, c. 694–c. 772 C.E.) in Al-Kufa, Iraq. Although the guidelines Ḥammād used to select works for this anthology are uncertain, some think that length was important because these poems are also known as "the seven long poems." The seven poets in this book represent the flower of early Arabic poetry and illustrate fine details of Bedouin life in the sixth century C.E.

The formal *qasida* include references to forsaken love; descriptions of former camp grounds, beloved horses and camels, and trials in the desert; and praise of the poet's prince or patron. The earliest poet represented in *Al-Muʿallaqāt* is Imruʾal-Qays (d. c. 550 C.E.), a member of the ancient royal family of Yemen, who is said to have invented the *qasida* form. Tarafah (fl. sixth century C.E.), a native of Bahrain, settled at the court of ʿAmr ibn Hind in al-Ḥīra and was noted for his satire. Zuhayr ibn Abī-Sulmā Rabīʿa (c. 520–c. 609 C.E.), the son and father of Arabian poets, was a warrior poet who sang about the end of the war of Dāḥis. ʿAmr ibn Kulthūm (fl. sixth century C.E.), celebrates in his poem his patron ʿAmr ibn Hind and his tribe, the Taghlib of Mesopotamia. ʿAntara (fl. sixth century C.E.) was noted for his love for his cousin ʿAbla and later became the hero of a romance. His poem is filled with vivid descriptions of his role in battles during the war of Dāḥis. Al-Ḥārith ibn Ḥilliza of Bakr (fl. sixth century C.E.) attacks the accusers of his patron, and the Banū Bakr. Labīd (d. c. 661 C.E.) was the youngest of the seven, and the only one to convert to Islam. In addition to these standard seven poets, al-Nābigha (fl. c. 600 C.E.), who wrote at courts in Iraq and Syria, and al-Aʿshā (before 570–c. 625 C.E.), a blind poet from Arabia, are sometimes added.

Ḥammād may have referred to the anthology not as *Al-Muʿallaqāt* but as al-Mashhūrāt, or "the famous ones." The term *al-Muʿallaqāt*, or "suspended poems," known only circa 900 C.E., probably is related to the word *ʿilq*, which means "a precious thing," especially one hung in a storeroom or in a conspicuous place. It is possible that this derivation resulted in the tenth century tradition of these poems being written in gold on linen and hung from the Kaʿba in Mecca.

ADDITIONAL RESOURCES

Arberry, A. J. *The Seven Odes of Love*. Cairo, Egypt: American University in Cairo Press, 1997.

O'Grady, Desmond. *The Seven Odes: The First Chapter in Arabic Literature*. New York: Macmillan, 1957.

—*Thomas J. Sienkewicz*

MUḤAMMAD

ALSO KNOWN AS: Abū al-Qāsim Muḥammad ibn ʿAbd Allāh
BORN: c. 570 C.E.; Mecca, Arabia
DIED: June 8, 632 C.E.; Medina, Arabia
RELATED CIVILIZATION: Arabia
MAJOR ROLE/POSITION: Prophet, religious leader

Life. Muḥammad (mew-HAM-muhd), an orphan at the age of six, lived first with his grandfather ʿAbd Al-Muṭṭalib and from age eight with his uncle Abū Ṭālib, whom he accompanied on his trading journeys into Syria. Muḥammad's marriage to Khadījah, a wealthy widow, at the age of twenty-five brought prosperity and seclusion to the home they made at Mount Hira. According to the Qurʾān, he received his first revelation at the age of forty. Khadījah and those very close to him were the first believers. Three years later, he revealed the message to other close relatives, after which he faced strong opposition.

Muḥammad, under the protection of his uncle Abū Ṭālib, continued preaching. His followers, particularly those without protection, were persecuted. He ordered them to take refuge in Abyssinia while he and many others stayed in Mecca. Many, including a few eminent men of Quraysh, were converted. Meccan polytheists initiated a boycott of Banu Hāshim, the Prophet's clan. The believers, for three years, faced many difficulties. Few men of Quraysh attempted to end the boycott.

The death of Abū Ṭālib and Khadījah in 619 C.E. set off bitter attacks from Meccan polytheists. The Prophet's search for supporters and protectors in the nearby town of Ṭāʾif was fruitless. He continued to fight

Muḥammad the Prophet. (Library of Congress)

polytheism in Mecca and the surrounding area until a group of men from Medina offered him a home (622 C.E.) to which he and his followers migrated, an event known as the *hijrah* (flight). This turning point marks the start of the Islamic calendar.

The first major event after the migration was the Battle of Badr (624 C.E.), which ended in a Muslim victory. The Meccans, however, took their revenge the following year at Uhud, where the Prophet was wounded and lost one of his teeth. The Battle of Trench's, the Meccans' siege of Medina (627 C.E.), was the climax of these two battles but was not successful.

On a pilgrimage to Mecca, the Prophet stopped and negotiated a truce, the Treaty of Hudaybiyyah (628 C.E.). This put him on a par with the Meccans and opened the way for further conversions. The breaking of this treaty by the Meccans resulted in the conquest of Mecca (629 C.E.). The Prophet and ten thousand believers entered the city without resistance, then conquered Ṭāʾif and the surrounding area. The Prophet's campaign to Tabuk (630 C.E.), near the Byzantine frontier, in command of a force of thirty thousand, was the climax of his power. He died a few months after having performed his Last Pilgrimage.

Muḥammad's marriages to ʿĀʾishah bint Abī Bakr and a number of other women each served a purpose, mainly to establish ties of affiliation. Had he claimed supernatural powers, he would have been no different from the soothsayers or magicians common at the time. His faith in God and that of his followers and the verses of the Qurʾān distinguished him and were key to his success.

Influence. Having fulfilled his duty as a messenger, Muḥammad saw in his lifetime the fruits of his success. Islam grew to become the foundation of one of the greatest civilizations of the world.

ADDITIONAL RESOURCES

The Encyclopaedia of Islam. Prepared by a number of leading orientalists; edited by an editorial committee consisting of H. A. R. Gibb et al. under the patronage of the International Union of Academies. New ed. Leiden, Netherlands: E. J. Brill, 1960-[2000].

Kennedy, Hugh. *The Prophet and the Age of the Caliphates.* New York: Longman, 1999.

Lings, Martin. *Muhammad.* London: Islamic Text Society, 1991.

SEE ALSO: Abū Bakr; ʿAlī ibn Abī Ṭālib; ʿĀʾishah bint Abī Bakr; Arabia; Islam; Qurʾān; ʿUmar ibn al-Khaṭṭāb, ʿUthmān ibn ʿAffān.

—M. Mehdi Ilhan

MULANSHI

ALSO KNOWN AS: *Wade-Giles Mu-lan shih*
AUTHORSHIP: Unknown
DATE: c. 386-581 C.E.
LOCALE: North China
SIGNIFICANCE: *Mulanshi* represents a high point of development of the ballad as a genre and creates a heroine who best voices the national interest and sentiment during the Northern Dynasties.

Mulanshi (MEW-lahn-shee; *Ballad of Mulan*, 1923) has circulated among the Chinese people for well over a millennium. Historians credit its authorship to the people of the Northern Dynasties (386-588 C.E.), when aggressive northern tribes invaded north China. The ballad is collected in the one-hundred-volume *Yuefushi Ji* (compiled eleventh century C.E.; partial translation; commonly known as *Anthology of Ancient Songs*) com-piled by Guo Maoqian. Mulan is the young heroine of the ballad (on which the 1998 Walt Disney film *Mulan* was based). When her aging father is drafted into the Imperial army to fight against the invading troops of Hu (a general term for the northern and western tribes), Mulan disguises herself as a warrior and takes his place. She undertakes responsibilities that are not traditional for a woman, fights countless battles for ten years, and brings victory to her country and glory to her family. The emperor awards her citations, wealth, and a high office, but Mulan kindly declines them and expresses her unyielding character: "I wish to ride on a winged steed,/ And fly aback to my home." Upon arrival, she "took off her suit of armor,/ And put on her girl's wear," happily returning to normal life.

The ballad has only 330 Chinese characters, but its fast-moving narrative paints a tightly knit plot incorporating seven events, each corresponding to one stanza of short and long lines.

ADDITIONAL RESOURCES
Chang, Wei, and Ch'eng-an Chiang. *The Legend of Mu Lan*. Monterey, Calif.: Victory Press, 1997.

Ts'ai, Cho-chih, Yen-kuang Lu, and Kate Foster. *One Hundred Celebrated Chinese Women*. Singapore: Asiapae Books, 1995.

SEE ALSO: China.

—*Charles Xingzhong Li*

MUMMIUS, LUCIUS

FLOURISHED: second century B.C.E.
RELATED CIVILIZATIONS: Republican Rome, Spain and Hellenistic Greece
MAJOR ROLE/POSITION: Military leader and statesman

Life. As Rome's provincial governor in Spain, Lucius Mummus (LEW-shee-uhs MUHM-ee-uhs) commanded the Republic's forces against the Lusitanians in 153 and 152 B.C.E. Responding to their devastating attack with unforgiving slaughter, he celebrated a triumph on returning to Rome.

As consul in 146 B.C.E., Mummius defeated the Achaean League. Succeeding Quintus Caecilius Metellus Macedonicus as commander at the Isthmus, Mummius crushed Achaea's forces in late summer. His troops then plundered the city of Corinth, where, months earlier, Rome's ambassadors had been threatened with violence. Assisted by a senatorial commission, he organized the affairs of the Greek peninsula, razing Corinth to the ground and attaching other communities that had opposed Rome to the Macedonian province. Attentive to the gods, he also repaired and adorned religious shrines throughout Greece. On returning home in 145 B.C.E., he celebrated his second triumph.

In 142 B.C.E., Mummius served as censor, a magistracy responsible for supervising public morals. His moderation contrasted with the severity of his colleague, the conqueror of Carthage, Scipio Africanus.

Influence. Mummius admired Greek culture, distributing statues, monuments, and paintings from the plunder of Corinth to towns throughout Italy and even in Spain. However, like many Roman philhellenists, he saw no contradiction in making war against contemporary Greek communities.

ADDITIONAL RESOURCE
Green, Peter. *Alexander to Actium: The Historical Evolution of the Hellenistic Age*. Reprint. Berkeley: University of California Press, 1993.

SEE ALSO: Achaean League; Greece, Hellenistic and Roman; Rome, Republican; Scipio Africanus.

—*Denvy A. Bowman*

MUWATALLIS

ALSO KNOWN AS: Muwatallish
BORN: fourteenth century B.C.E.; Anatolia
DIED: 1294 B.C.E.; Hattusas (modern Bogazköy, Turkey)
RELATED CIVILIZATIONS: Hittites, Pharaonic Egypt, Hurrians
MAJOR ROLE/POSITION: Statesman

Life. Muwatallis (mew-wah-TAL-uhs) was the second of four sons of the Hittite king Mursilis II (d. 1306) and ascended the throne upon his father's death. His predecessors had exercised their sway over northern Syria without being challenged by Egypt. However, Pharaoh Rameses II marched his army north to Kadesh on the Orontes River. The Amorite chieftain Benteshina defected to Rameses' side. Muwatallis worked out a stratagem to slow the Egyptian advance. A group of Hittite allies pretending to be deserters seeking sanctuary with Rameses ambushed the pharaoh. The Hittite chariots swept in, bearing two men each and overpowering the Egyptian infantry. Rameses eventually rallied his forces and saved the Egyptians from complete defeat. Benteshina again pledged fealty to the Hittites.

Kadesh was one of the most massive battles of the ancient world and one of the most inconclusive. Although it stemmed the tide of Egyptian conquest in Syria/Palestine, it did not lead to any large-scale Hittite expansion. Muwatallis also warred against the Kaska tribes to the north; much of this fighting was actually led by his brother Hattusilis III, who served as viceroy. Muwatallis wrote or at least publicized prayers to the Hittite Sun god, Ishtanu. Muwatallis was succeeded by his son Urhi-Teshub (Mursilis III), and eventually by Hattusilis III.

Influence. Muwatallis's domestic achievements are overshadowed by his fighting the great Egyptian pharaoh to a draw at Kadesh. This prevented the Egyptians from controlling Syria.

ADDITIONAL RESOURCES
Bryce, Trevor. *The Kingdom of the Hittites*. New York: Oxford University Press, 1998.
Redford, Donald. *Egypt, Canaan, and Israel in Ancient Times*. Princeton, N.J.: Princeton University Press, 1992.

SEE ALSO: Babylonia; Hittites; Kadesh, Battle of; Kaska; Rameses II.

—Nicholas Birns

MYCENAE, PALACE OF

DATE: 1600-1120 B.C.E.
LOCALE: Within the citadel of Mycenae, northeast Argive plain, Peloponnese, Greece
RELATED CIVILIZATION: Mycenaean Greece
SIGNIFICANCE: Mycenaean palaces mirrored both economic viability and political force; the palace at Mycenae was the most spectacular of the palaces.

The palace of Mycenae (mi-SEE-nee), known in legend as the palace of Agamemnon, occupies the center of the citadel at Mycenae, near the southern wall. The walled citadel was constructed atop a highly defensible rocky hill with rugged ravines on the north and south sides.

An early palace on the citadel is presumed to date to about 1600 to 1500 B.C.E.; however, little is known of this structure. The archaeologically visible complex is the later palace, probably constructed between the mid-fourteenth through the mid-thirteenth century B.C.E. The citadel, rising 328 feet (100 meters) over the surrounding plain, is circumscribed by a cyclopean wall of 2,953 feet (900 meters) in length. The wall varies in thickness from 16 to 26 feet (5 to 8 meters), with an average height of 26 feet (8 meters). The principal entrance was through the monumental lion gate, located in the northwest corner of the wall. Cisterns within and beyond the citadel assured a water supply during periods of drought or siege. A wide ramp led from the lion gate to the palace.

The palace complex consisted of structures serving state and residential functions. The design centered around the *megaron*, or throne room. The *megaron* was a rectangular structure, 75 by 38 feet (23 by 11.5 meters). In entering the *megaron* from the front, visitors passed through a courtyard and a covered portico. The room of significance was the nearly square *megaron* chamber, which measured 43 by 38 feet (13 by 11.5 meters). In the center of the *megaron* was a circular hearth more than 11 feet (3.5 meters) in diameter. Four wooden columns supported the roof. The *megaron*'s plastered walls contained at least one fresco depicting warriors, chariots, and elaborately dressed women. The floors consisted of painted stucco with linear motifs. Attached to the *megaron*'s courtyard were one and possibly two small rooms. Another series of rooms lay off two corridors on the north side of the court, possibly serving administrative or residential functions for state officials.

Several building complexes were located to the east of the palace. Of importance is the House of Columns, named for the numerous column bases that remain. This structure has been suggested by George Mylonas, a principal investigator, to have served as the residence of the ruler, or *wanax*. In proximity are a complex of rooms that may have served as manufacturing quarters for luxury items. Other palace rooms and complexes within the citadel served administrative,

The lion gate is at the entrance to the citadel in which the palace of Mycenae is located. (Hulton Archive)

storage, and workshop (textile, ceramic, and gold work) functions.

The economic importance of the palace is manifest in both the redistributive nature of the citadel and the trade networks (particularly for ceramic goods) that were established through the Aegean and Mediterranean Seas. Concentrations of agricultural products (for example cereals, olives, and wool) and manufacturing surpluses most likely served as a power base for the *wanex* and kinsmen.

Devastation either from internal or external forces came to Mycenae near the end of the thirteenth century B.C.E. The palace may have escaped destruction until about 1120 B.C.E., when Mycenaean economic and political power collapsed.

ADDITIONAL RESOURCES

Mylonas, George E. *Mycenae and the Mycenaean Age.* Princeton, N.J.: Princeton University Press, 1966.

Taylor, Lord William. *The Mycenaeans.* Rev. ed. New York: Thames and Hudson 1999.

SEE ALSO: Greece, Mycenaean; Linear B.

—*Rene M. Descartes*

MYRON

ALSO KNOWN AS: Myron of Eleutherae
BORN: c. 490 B.C.E.; Eleutherae, Boeotia, Greece
DIED: c. 430 B.C.E.; Athens, Greece
RELATED CIVILIZATION: Classical Greece
MAJOR ROLE/POSITION: Sculptor

Life. Little is known of Myron's (MI-ron) early life other than that he was born in Boeotia, which lacked the cultural refinement of neighboring Attica but excelled in the athletic contests at both Delphi and Olympia with superb displays of the human body in action. Becoming a pupil of Ageladas (Hageladas), director of a metal-casting school and a master of athletic sculpture, Myron achieved a reputation throughout the Hellenic lands, becoming noted for his statues of athletes, which combined masculinity with grace. No other sculptor in history has rivaled Myron in portraying the male body in action. His best-known work the *Discobolos*, or *Discus Thrower*, of which only marble copies survive, was completed about 450 B.C.E. His *Ladas*, of which no copies survive, showing a runner at the 476 B.C.E. Olym-piad at his moment of victory, was even more admired. Other famous works include *Athena and Marysas* and an incredibly realistic *Heifer*. His only pupil was his son Lycius.

Influence. By radically departing from the rigidity and prescribed format of sixth century B.C.E. Greek sculpture, Myron became a major force responsible for bridging the gap between Archaic Greek sculpture and its full development in the fifth century B.C.E. His emphasis on realism anticipated both Hellenistic and Roman sculpture.

ADDITIONAL RESOURCES

Boardman, John. *Greek Art*. London: Thames and Hudson, 1996.
Gardner, Ernest A. *Six Greek Sculptors*. New York: Ayer, 1977.

SEE ALSO: Art and architecture; Greece, Classical.

—*Nis Petersen*

NAEVIUS, GNAEUS

BORN: c. 270 B.C.E.; Campania, Italy
DIED: c. 199 B.C.E.; North Africa
RELATED CIVILIZATION: Republican Rome
MAJOR ROLE/POSITION: Poet, playwright

Life. Gnaeus Naevius (NEE-uhs NEE-vee-uhs) is believed to have been of Campanian, perhaps specifically of Capuan, origin. He is reported to have participated in the First Punic War and so may have served among the Campanian *socii* (non-Roman nationalities who were allies of the Romans) in the war and taken up residence in Rome at the war's end. At some time during his life, Naevius was imprisoned for attacks on prominent citizens. After his release from prison, he left Rome and died at Utica in North Africa.

He presented his first plays, principally based on Greek models, in 235 B.C.E. He wrote comedy, tragedy, and epics. He invented a new serious dramatic form based on Roman themes, the *praetexta*. He wrote an epic on the First Punic War in the native Saturnian meter rather than in the Greek hexameter.

Influence. Naevius is symbolic of the absorption of the destiny of the entire Italian peninsula into that of Rome; although he came from Campania, he became one of the most nationalistic of Rome's early poets. In his dramas based on Greek models, he inserted native elements. He invented a new serious dramatic form based on Roman themes, and his choice of a theme and meter for his epic indicates his desire to make Latin literature more truly a Roman product. His writings survive only in fragments.

ADDITIONAL RESOURCE
Warmington, E. H. *Remains of Old Latin.* Cambridge, Mass.: Harvard University Press, 1967.

SEE ALSO: Greece, Hellenistic and Roman; Punic Wars; Rome, Republican.

—*C. Wayne Tucker*

NAPATA AND MEROE

DATE: ninth century B.C.E.-fourth century C.E.
LOCALE: Countries along and on both sides of the Nile from Aswan to the confluence of the Blue and White Nile Rivers
RELATED CIVILIZATIONS: Sudanic civilization, Egypt, Rome
SIGNIFICANCE: Napata and Meroe were influential African kingdoms south of Egypt along the Nile.

The important African kingdom of Napata (NA-puh-tuh), often called Kush, took shape in the ninth century B.C.E. The central areas of the kingdom lay along the Dongola Reach along the Nubian stretches of the Nile River. Its capital was the city of Napata, and today that name is given also to the kingdom as a whole.

Egyptian colonial rule, which had crushed Kerma in the sixteenth century B.C.E., had been a pervasive force in the region through the thirteenth century B.C.E. However, by the eleventh century B.C.E., Egyptian rule over the Nubian stretches of the Nile was clearly something of the past, and the older Sudanic cultural traditions of the region soon began to reassert themselves strongly in all realms of life, from pottery manufacture to politics. A century and a half later, Napata began its rise. In 750 B.C.E., under its fourth known king, Piye (Piankhi), Napata launched an invasion of Egypt. In the next several years, Piye, claiming to be the protector of the traditions of Egypt, allied with the priesthood of Amun in Thebes and established his rule over large portions of that country. His successors, remembered as the Twenty-fifth Dynasty, solidly established Napatan rule over all of Egypt. In the 670's and 660's B.C.E., however, Assyrian invasions challenged Napata's control over the country and finally led to the complete withdrawal of Napata authority from Egypt in 655 B.C.E.

After the 650's B.C.E., Napatan history entered an era

of which knowledge is very sketchy. Although the capital of the kingdom, Napata, as well as the royal burial grounds of Nun, lay along the Dongola Reach, the kings had expanded their empire well to the south by then. Their southern territories stretched along the Nile from the Fourth Cataract to as far as the confluence of the Blue and White Nile Rivers. At least one other major city in the kingdom, Meroe (MEHR-oh-wee), appears to have been founded even before the seventh century B.C.E. near where the Atbara River joins the Nile, and there may have been still other early towns in the southern regions yet to be excavated by archaeologists.

Three potentially advantageous features characterized the southern portion of the Napata kingdom. First, because it received a regular yearly rainfall, this region had the potential to support a larger population and a more diversified agricultural base than the restricted belt of irrigated farmlands of the Dongola Reach. Second, the southern provinces early took up ironworking, which many scholars now believe spread there from an independent origin area of iron technology farther south in Africa. Third, the stretches of the Nile around the town of Meroe lay in and near regions in which could be found a number of the products that came to be valued by Levantine and Mediterranean merchants during the last millennium B.C.E. The inhabitants also carried on a much older Sudanic cotton-weaving tradition and soon became important manufacturers and exporters of cotton cloth. The southern areas of the kingdom had, in other words, economic capacities that allowed them to benefit greatly from the commercial trends of the age. The Dongola Reach, in the old heartland of the state, lacked many of these capacities and so became something of an economic backwater by the last three or four centuries B.C.E.

Napatan kingship relocates. Sometime between 640 and 300 B.C.E., the advantages of the southern areas led to a major shift of power in the Napatan state: The capital and the center of government moved south to the city of Meroe. From that point onward, historians called the state by a new name, after its new capital, the kingdom of Meroe. Exactly when this shift took place is uncertain, but it may have happened in the late seventh or early sixth century B.C.E. For a long time after the shift of the political capital, the rulers of Meroe continued to be buried along the Dongola Reach at Nun, in the old royal burial grounds. Not until 324 B.C.E. did the kings and queens begin to be interred at Meroe itself. Napata remained, however, an especially important

and, at times, a relatively autonomous province of the kingdom throughout its later history.

The high period of Meroitic power and influence lay in the centuries between 300 B.C.E. and 100 C.E.. New directions of change in Egypt and the eastern Mediterranean came to play an essential part in the prosperity of Meroe during this period. After the death of Alexander the Great in 323 B.C.E., his conquests, which included Egypt, were divided among his three leading generals. In this division, the rule over Egypt went to Ptolemy I Soter, whose descendants formed the last dynasty of independent ancient Egypt.

Ptolemy and his immediate successors were quick to consolidate their hold over Egypt by molding their rule to fit in with traditional Egyptian views and ideology. At the same time, however, their own roots lay in the Hellenistic world of the eastern Mediterranean, with its wide-ranging cultural and commercial connections. So the Ptolemies from the first were very aware that if they were to maintain and strengthen their political base, they would have to build the commercial strength of their country. For this reason, they welcomed merchant activity. They also subsidized the opening of the Red Sea to seagoing commerce, gaining for the first time a regular Egyptian participation in the new era of trade with northeastern Africa and the Indian Ocean.

Economy and society. The Ptolemaic development of commerce in the Red Sea had the immediate consequence for Meroe of providing regular outlets for Meroitic products. The city of Meroe lay less than 250 miles (400 kilometers) from suitable ports on the Red Sea coast, and very soon a variety of products began to move to these ports from Meroe and its sister towns along the Nile. Some goods, such as iron, were produced in the urban areas, and other items, such as tortoise shell and ostrich feathers, in the hills between Meroe and the Red Sea. Still other products, including gold and ivory, came from areas farther south in the Middle Nile Basin.

The cities of Meroe grew into significant manufacturing centers during these centuries. They produced cotton cloth for the trade. The city of Meroe itself became the leading iron-producing locale in the northern Middle Nile Basin. Its ironworks supplied local needs, military and domestic, and probably also provided iron and iron tools for regional trade with the surrounding peoples of the Middle Nile Basin.

The Meroitic kingdom through most of its history, it is suspected, had a two-sector economy, manifested in two kinds of social structures. It had an urban population located in the towns along the Nile, the most important being the city of Meroe itself. In these cities resided the king and a class of government officials. An indigenous merchant class arose in the towns. In addition, weavers, ironsmiths, potters, masons, and other skilled artisans plied their trades as the Meroitic state built up its thriving economy. Below these strata would have come the servants and laborers, including probably slaves. These working folk would have formed the majority of the society and carried out much of the heavy and menial labor of urban life.

Outside the cities, a different kind of society and economy would have prevailed. Divided into an uncertain number of provinces, rural areas were populated, as they had been for several thousand years, by people with mixed herding and cultivating economies or, in drier areas, by communities relying principally on livestock raising.

In the steppes to the east of the Nile, just south of the Atbara River, the Meroites built and maintained large earthen diversion dams across the beds of seasonal streams. As archaeologists have noted, these engineering works created reservoirs for livestock during the long, nine-month dry season of that area. In addition, the dams allowed recessional irrigation of fields to be practiced. In recessional irrigation farming, farmers planted crops in the wet soils left behind as the water shrank in the dry season. By this means, both the meat and grain supplies available to the urban populations of Meroe along the Nile would have been considerably enhanced.

The kingdom of Meroe had a multiethnic population. The people in towns such as the city of Meroe and probably the people of the Dongola Reach spoke the Meroitic language. In the countryside, though, many different languages of the Nilo-Saharan family were spoken. For instance, in the dry steppe lands immediately west of the Nile lived livestock-herding peoples who spoke Nubian languages. Eastward, on both sides of the road to the Red Sea, lay the country of the most northerly Cushitic people, the Blemmyes, who were probably the same people as the Medjay of the ancient Egyptian records. Their modern-day descendants are the Beja of the Red Sea Hills region.

Religion. Throughout the lands of the Meroitic kingdom and probably earlier in those of the Napatan kingdom, the prevailing belief system remained the basically monotheistic Sudanic religion, with its one Divinity, associated with the sky. Faced with the Egyptian idioms with which religion was cloaked in the Napatan

writings, scholars have often presumed that Egyptian polytheistic religion took hold in the Dongola Reach and in Meroe during its heyday. However, the striking feature of the known Napata written observance of religion is that it most commonly evoked a single Egyptian god, Amun. Apparently the Napata priests used an Egyptian idiom, prestigious because of the earlier experience of Egyptian colonial rule, but they accommodated it to an indigenous conception of spirit—they saw Amun as a particular manifestation of Divinity rather than as a separate god. The lesser extent to which a few other Egyptian gods appear in the Napatan record suggests that they may have been understood as simply other manifestations of Divinity, again a belief in keeping with earlier Sudanic religious ideas.

The same case can be made for religion in the Meroitic kingdom, where again a single notable "god" predominates in the record: Apedemak, symbolized in sculpture by a lion figure. Like the subject peoples of the rural countryside of the kingdom, the people of the cities most likely were adherents of the old Sudanic religion. However, they may have used additional idioms and held subsidiary beliefs influenced by Egyptian religion.

Relatively little is known as yet about the nature of kingship in Napata and Meroe. In overall ideology, the Napatan and Meroitic states most probably were Sudanic sacred states. This conclusion is not certain, because the one archaeological feature especially diagnostic of a Sudanic sacral state, the burial of royal servants along with the king, disappeared along the Nubian stretches of the Nile after the fall of Kerma. The burials of the rulers of Napata and Meroe were nevertheless awe-filled events, surrounded by sacred elements. In Napatan times, there came first a ceremonial voyage of the body up the Nile from Napata to Nun, and at all times, the burial site itself was commemorated by an inscription and a small pyramid, reflective of lingering Egyptian influences. In the Meroitic period in particular, it is clear that the *kandake*, or queen, was also an uncommonly powerful figure. She was often able, as is evident from Greek and Roman documents and from the Meroitic monuments themselves, to act as the full-fledged ruler of the kingdom and in such cases to be buried with full royal ritual. (The modern-day woman's name Candace comes directly from the ancient Meroitic word for "queen.")

Writing and language. The earliest written records of the Napata kingdom were set down in Egyptian, but by the last three centuries B.C.E., the Meroites had begun to write their own language. From that point in time, Meroitic became the written language of government and religion in the kingdom. It is believed most probably to have been a Nilo-Saharan language. Unfortunately, although scholars know the phonetic values of the Meroitic alphabet, they do not know the meanings of most of the words, and so they have not yet properly deciphered the language. That task remains an important scholarly project for the future.

From power to decline. Meroe seems still to have been at the height of its power in the last century B.C.E. and first century C.E. After Rome incorporated Egypt into its empire in 23 B.C.E., Meroe and Rome established their mutual boundary between Philae and the northernmost Meroitic fortress, Ibrim, at the far south of the modern-day country of Egypt. In the first century C.E., Roman envoys traveled to Meroe city. As the story in the biblical book Acts of Philip's meeting with an "Ethiopian" on the road to Gaza shows, Meroites from time to time must have ventured north to visit the Roman Empire as well.

After 100 C.E., Meroe entered a period of extended decline. By the late 340's C.E., when the army of King

Ezana of Axum invaded the region, only small centers of Meroitic authority remained, and Nubian peoples controlled large parts of the former territories of the kingdom. By the fifth century C.E., two or three Nubian kingdoms had taken shape across the former lands of Meroe.

ADDITIONAL RESOURCES

Taylor, John. *Egypt and Nubia*. London: British Museum Press, 1991.

Trigger, Bruce G. *History and Settlement in Lower Nubia*. New Haven, Conn.: Yale University Press, 1965.

Welsby, Derek A. *The Kingdom of Kush: The Napatan and Meroitic Empires*. Princeton, N.J.: Markus Wiener, 1998.

SEE ALSO: Africa, East and South; Alwa; Apedemak; Arkamani; Axum; Beja; Cushites; Egypt, Pharaonic; Egypt, Ptolemaic and Roman; Ezana; Kerma; Makouria; Nobatae; Nubia; Piye.

—*Christopher Ehret*

NĀRĀYAṆA

DATE: coined 1000 B.C.E. or earlier
LOCALE: India
RELATED CIVILIZATION: India

Nārāyaṇa (naw-RAW-yah-nah) is a name applied to Brahmā, Prajāpatī, or Puruṣa, but more frequently to Vishnu (Viṣṇu) or Krishna (Kṛṣṇa). Also, it may have been a deity for the Nara-Nārāyaṇ, an aboriginal seafaring people. It is derived from *nara* (man), the original and eternal man, or from *nāra* (waters), since the primeval ocean was the first *ayana*.

During the period written about in the *Śatapatha Brāhmaṇa* (c. 1000-800 B.C.E.; English translation in *Sacred Books of the East*, 1882), Nārāyaṇa became connected with Vishnu. The *Mahābhārata* (400 B.C.E.-400 C.E., present form by c. 400 C.E.; *The Mahabharata of Krishna-Dwaipayana Vyasa*, 1887-1896) and other texts refer to Nārāyaṇa as an ancient ṛṣi, the son of Dharma, whose task it was to destroy demons. In the epic, Nārāyaṇa as Vishnu is depicted reclining on the serpent Śeṣa and floating on waters. The *Mahābhārata*

also speaks of white people of Śvetadvīpa who worshiped Nārāyaṇa, a thousand-rayed man-god.

During the medieval period, under Muslim influence, Nārāyaṇa became known as Satyapir (*satya*, or true, and *pir*, "saint") and was later known as Satya-Nārāyaṇa, which was a fusion of Hindu and Muslim terms—symbolizing the union of the Muslim and Hindu dieties, Rahim and Rāma, respectively.

ADDITIONAL RESOURCES

Gonda, J. *Visnuism and Sivaism: A Comparison*. New Delhi, India: Munshiram Manoharlal, 1996.

Singh, H. Ranbir. *Influence of Vaishnavism on Literature of East India: Proceedings of a Regional Seminar Held in 1985 Under the Joint Auspices of the Sahitya Akademi*. New Delhi, India: Manipur Sahitya Parishad, 1993.

Zimmer, H. *Myths and Symbols in Indian Art and Civilization*. New York: Harper Torchbooks, 1962.

SEE ALSO: Hinduism; *Mahābhārata*.

—*Arthur W. Helweg*

NARRIṆAI

AUTHORSHIP: 192 early Tamil poets
DATE: first-fourth century C.E.
LOCALE: South India
RELATED CIVILIZATION: South India
SIGNIFICANCE: One of the earliest Caṅkam works, this anthology influenced all later Tamil literature.

The *Narriṇai* (nah-RIH-nahi; English translation in *Poets of the Tamil Anthologies*, 1979) is an early poetical anthology in Tamil, the language of south India; it is the most ancient literary source for recovering the culture of a people speaking a non-Aryan language in South Asia. The work is regarded as having major importance in the field of Caṅkam (Śaṅgam), or classical Tamil, literature. It consists of four hundred love poems written by 192 poets of whom 174 are known by name. The Pāṇḍyan king Paṇṇāḍu Tanda Māṟan Vaḷudi was the patron of the anthology. The poems consist of nine to twelve lines in the *akaval* meter, four-foot lines with a difference in rhyme.

The central theme of all the verses is love. Each of the writers evokes the experience of love and passes it on to the reader. The poems weave a tapestry of human emotions against rich descriptions of mountains, forests, meadows, riverbanks, and seashores. In language that is at times sensuous and full of subtle suggestion, lovers at all times of the day and night and in all seasons meet in joy or languish because of separation. In most of the poems, the course of love does not run smoothly, and the lovers suffer the travail and anguish of love. In all cases, the lovers' feelings are mutual; convention forbade exploration of unrequited love. Both men and women, many of whom are named, contributed the poems. The poems also demonstrate that there was equality between the sexes, at least in the sphere of love.

ADDITIONAL RESOURCE

Subramanian, A. V., trans. *Narrinai (An Anthology of Amour)*. Thanjavur, Tamil Nādu, India: Government of Tamil Nadu, 1989.

SEE ALSO: Caṅkam; India.

—*Katherine Anne Harper*

NARSES (BYZANTINE MILITARY LEADER)

BORN: c. 480 C.E.; Armenia
DIED: 574 C.E.; probably Rome or Constantinople
RELATED CIVILIZATIONS: Imperial Rome, Byzantine Empire
MAJOR ROLE/POSITION: Military leader

Life. Narses' (NAHR-seez) background and exact birth date are in dispute, but it seems clear that he was partially of Armenian ancestry. Narses was a eunuch and spent most of his adult career as a diplomat and courtier. The emperor Justinian I admired his efficiency, though, and noted his command skills when Narses was called on to suppress the Nika Riots in Constantinople in 532 C.E.

Narses became an insurance policy for Justinian in case the successful general Belisarius became too insubordinate. Narses' rivalry with Belisarius contributed to the latter's defeat by the Ostrogoths in 539 C.E. After Belisarius's defeat, Justinian recalled him as the Ostro-

Narses, in his victory over the Goths. (North Wind Picture Archives)

goths successfully resisted the Roman attempt to re-conquer Daly. Narses inflicted two decisive defeats on the Ostrogoths, one at Busta Gallorum, in the summer of 552 C.E., and the other at Mons Lactarius in the same year.

Astonishingly for a man of his age, Narses remained military viceroy of Italy for fifteen more years, during which he cemented Roman control over the peninsula and vanquished Frankish and Slavic incursions. In 567 C.E., however, he was removed by the new emperor, Justin II. Shortly thereafter, the Langobards and their allies invaded Italy. Narses remained in retirement in Italy until he died seven years later.

Influence. Although much of what Narses conquered was lost to the Langobards in the ensuing de-cades, Constantinople ruled parts of Italy until 1071. This was vital in maintaining the links between Italy and the Greek Classical heritage.

ADDITIONAL RESOURCES

Fauber, L. H. *Narses, Hammer of the Goths.* New York: St. Martin's Press, 1990.

Treadgold, Warren. *A History of the Byzantine State and Society.* Stanford, Calif.: Stanford University Press, 1997.

SEE ALSO: Belisarius; Byzantine Empire; Goths; Justinian I; Langobards.

—*Nicholas Birns*

NARSES (SĀSĀNIAN EMPEROR)

ALSO KNOWN AS: Narseh
BORN: date and place unknown
DIED: c. 302 C.E.; place unknown
RELATED CIVILIZATIONS: Sāsānian Persia, Imperial Rome
MAJOR ROLE/POSITION: Emperor, military leader

Life. Narses (NAHR-seez) was a son of Shāpūr I, the second Sāsānian ruler. Nothing is known of his early life and birth. He is mentioned in the trilingual inscription of Shāpūr at Naqsh-e Rostam (c. 262 C.E.) as "the Mazda-worshipping king of India, Sistan, and Turan to the shore of the sea," and a fire altar is dedicated to him. The next mention of him is as "king of the Armenians" in his own bilingual inscription of Paikuli.

Apparently, there was an agreement that the sons of Shāpūr I would succeed him in order of seniority until the last son was dead. However, when Bahrām I died, his son Bahrām II succeeded him. This must have angered Narses because after his succession, Narses erased the name of Bahrām from several rock reliefs. Some nobles must have supported Narses' claim because revolts occurred during the reign of Bahrām II, and when Bahrām III ascended to the throne after the death of his father, various nobles rallied behind Narses, who defeated his enemies and became emperor in 293 C.E.

Narses reversed the religious policy of the Bahrāms, becoming more tolerant of Manichaeans and others. His wars with the Romans ended in defeat, and in a 296 C.E. treaty, he ceded land in Mesopotamia and parts of Armenia to Rome. Because Narses was the last of the sons of Shāpūr to rule, he was able to pass the throne to his son Hormizd II. During Narses' reign, Armenia converted to Christianity, which also began to spread in the Sāsānian Empire.

Influence. Narses determined the future succession to the throne and revived his father's policy of religious tolerance.

ADDITIONAL RESOURCES

Frye, Richard. N. *History of Ancient Iran.* Munich: C. H. Beck, 1984.

Humbach, Helmut, and Prods O. Skjaervo. *The Sassanian Inscription of Paikuli.* Wiesbaden, Germany: Harrasowitz, 1978.

SEE ALSO: Armenia; Christianity; Persia; Rome, Imperial; Sāsānian Empire; Shāpūr I.

—*Richard N. Frye*

NASCA CULTURE

ALSO KNOWN AS: Nazca culture
DATE: c. 100 B.C.E.-600 C.E.
LOCALE: South coast, Peru
SIGNIFICANCE: The Nasca culture is known for its sophisticated pottery and textiles, geoglyphs, and hydraulic engineering.

Despite severe environmental limitations, Nasca (NAHS-kah) peoples flourished along Peru's arid south coast and were distinguished by their arts, distinctive iconography, and engineering achievements.

The Nasca pottery style centered in the Ica and Grande drainages and extended between the Cañete and Acarí Valleys. Slip painting, polishing, thin terracotta wares, and intricate polychrome designs characterize fancy serving vessels, including bowls, jars, bottles, and plates. Elaborate Nasca textiles also were technically sophisticated, employing cotton or camelid fiber and including plain-weave, tapestry, embroidery, and crochet forms.

Borrowing from earlier Paracas traditions, Nasca imagery portrayed naturalistic depictions (flora, fauna, and humans) and mythical representations (zoomorphs and anthropomorphs) emphasizing supernatural divinities and agricultural fertility. Nasca culture also expressed concerns for warfare. Trophy heads and weapons occur as artifacts and as common artistic motifs. Moreover, later sites frequently have a defensive character. Terminal Nasca styles bear striking affinities to Wari culture in the adjoining highlands and denote substantial coast-highland interaction during Wari state formation.

At its apogee, Nasca society operated as a confederation of large chiefdoms sharing in strong sociocultural traditions. Site types include residential settlements (Dos Palmos and Tambo Viejo), towns (Ventanilla), and ceremonial centers (Huaca del Loro, Cahuachi). One of the largest, Cahuachi, covers more than 370 acres (150 hectares) and consists of a series of adobe platform mounds, room complexes, and enclosures. In addition to the ritual architecture, offering caches, and burials, the lack of domestic residences and refuse suggests that Cahuachi reached prominence largely as an empty ceremonial center, in which distinct groups, each associated with its own mound, convened for corporate religious activities. Later Nasca peoples used Cahuachi as a cemetery.

Irrigation agriculture, supplemented by marine resources and hunting, was the economic mainstay. To reclaim land for farming, Nasca peoples engineered sophisticated underground canal-cistern systems (*puquios*) to acquire, transport, and store water efficiently with minimal evaporation.

Although geoglyphs occur elsewhere in the Andes, the Nasca were their most prominent proponents. In the desert plains of Nasca, exposed rocks and sediments develop a dark patina through weathering and oxidation. By moving darker materials away to reveal lighter surfaces underneath, local peoples created giant ground drawings, including straight lines, abstract and geometric figures, and naturalistic images (bird, monkey, and spider). Although some geoglyphs may have astronomical significance, most archaeologists believe they functioned as topographic landmarks and pathways for ritual processions performed in the interest of agricultural fertility and group prosperity. Some geoglyphs extend straight for tens of miles and point to key mountaintops. Many also identify subterranean water sources and geological faults that direct water flow. Because some geoglyphs overlap and because of regional and representational variability, it is likely that the Nasca lines represent the cumulative work of many groups through time without formal planning or organization.

ADDITIONAL REFERENCES

Kroeber, Alfred L., and Donald Collier. *The Archaeology and Pottery of Nazca, Peru.* Walnut Creek, Calif.: AltaMira, 1998.
Silverman, Helaine. *Cahuachi in the Ancient Nasca World.* Iowa City: University of Iowa Press, 1993.

SEE ALSO: Andes, central; Andes, south.

—George F. Lau

NATUFIAN CULTURE

DATE: c. 11,000-8300 B.C.E.
LOCALE: Levant, particularly present-day southern Israel to southern Syria
RELATED CIVILIZATION: Prehistoric Mesopotamia
SIGNIFICANCE: The Natufians were precursors to later Near Eastern agriculturalists, through their technological innovations and evolving patterns of social distinction.

Increasing moisture and a warmer climate between 11,000 and 9000 B.C.E. favored the expansion of wild cereals, legumes, and stands of nut trees in the Levant. The Natufians, transitional between hunting, foraging, and incipient agricultural traditions, developed a technology and settlement pattern characteristic of later agrarians.

The sedentary Natufians intensively gathered wild wheat, barley, other vegetal foods, and nuts. They employed stationary and portable stone mortars as well as pestles, bowls, and sickles. Many Natufian stone tools had been developed by earlier cultures such as the Geometric Kebaran. Depending on locality, their diet included gazelle, ibex, other large and small game, fish, and waterfowl. Their only domesticate was the dog. It remains controversial whether the Natufians initiated cereal cultivation.

Early Natufian settlements on the Mediterranean coast had circular subterranean houses with storage pits for surplus vegetal foods. Later sites in the steppe and desert regions exhibit less substantial dwellings. Communities contained 150 to 250 individuals. Stone and bone art includes abstracts, human and animal motifs, and female figurines.

Substantial information has been obtained from burials placed beneath dwelling floors. Exotic grave goods and other paraphernalia suggest status distinctions. Incipient political centralization in the personage of a chief has been inferred from certain burials.

ADDITIONAL RESOURCES
Bar-Yosef, O., and F. R. Valla, eds. *The Natufian Culture in the Levant.* Ann Arbor, Mich.: International Monographs in Prehistory, 1991.
Henry, Donald O. *From Foraging to Agriculture.* Philadelphia: University of Pennsylvania Press, 1989.

SEE ALSO: Fertile Crescent; Israel.

—*Rene M. Descartes*

NĀṬYA-ŚĀSTRA

AUTHORSHIP: Ascribed to Bharata Muni
DATE: between 200 and 300 C.E.
LOCALE: India
RELATED CIVILIZATIONS:: India
SIGNIFICANCE: The earliest theoretical treatise on drama, music, and dance of ancient India, it set the standard for histrionic art throughout South and Southeast Asia.

Nāṭya-śāstra (NAWT-yah SHAWS-trah; *The Nāṭya-śāstra,* 1950) the oldest treatise on poetic and dramatic expression, is also referred to as *Bharata Nāṭya-śāstra* and is attributed to Bharata Muni, a rhetorician and mythical inventor of drama. It has been hailed as a divinely inspired exhaustive work on Sanskrit dramaturgy. According to legend, Brahmā presented a fifth Veda to all society explaining the nature of dance, drama, music, and poetics (*nāṭya*). Śiva and Pārvatī contributed the dance and Vishnu (Viṣṇu) the four dramatic styles.

It is a prescriptive law book (*śāstra*) expounding rules and regulations on dramaturgy open even to the Śūdra (laborer) caste, which was excluded from Vedic rituals. The encyclopedic work contains thirty-six sections, probably compiled over several centuries, covering acting techniques, costumes and equipment, gestures (*mudras*), facial expressions, bodily postures and cadences (*karanas*), plot, characters and scenery, audience participation, language forms, poetics, meter and sentiments (*rasa*), music and melodies (*rāgas*), elocution, aesthetics, rhetoric and grammar. Dance forms such as *bhāratanāṭyam* of Tamil Nādu, *kathakali* of Kerala, and *kuchipudi* of Andhra Pradesh closely follow its principles. Its influence went beyond north India to Dravidian south India and throughout Sri Lanka and Southeast Asia.

ADDITIONAL RESOURCES
Bharata Muni. *The Natya Saastra of Bharata Muni.* Delhi, India: Sri Satguru Publications, 1996.

Ghosh, Manomohan, trans. *The Natyashastra: A Treatise on Hindu Dramaturgy and Histrionics by Bharata-Muni.* Calcutta, India: Royal Asiatic Society of Bengal, 1950.

Keith, A. Berriedale. *A History of Sanskrit Literature.* London: Oxford University Press, 1966.

SEE ALSO: Bharata Muni; Hinduism; India.
—*George J. Hoynacki*

NEBUCHADNEZZAR II

ALSO KNOWN AS: Nabū-kudurri-uṣur (Akkadian)
BORN: c. 630 B.C.E.; place unknown
DIED: 562 B.C.E.; Babylon
RELATED CIVILIZATIONS: Chaldean Mesopotamia, Hebrew Palestine
MAJOR ROLE/POSITION: King of Babylonia

Life. Next to nothing is known of Nebuchadnezzar II's (nehb-uh-kuh-DREHZ-ur) early life. He did have a great deal of military experience and was leading an army in Syria when he learned of his father's death. He quickly returned to Babylon, where he ascended the throne of Nabopolassar in 605 B.C.E. and ruled the Chaldean kingdom for the next forty-three years.

Nebuchadnezzar's own inscriptions indicate that he actively campaigned against Egypt and Syria; his armies even penetrated Arabia. He attacked Jerusalem in March of 597 B.C.E. and (apparently) again in 587 or 586 B.C.E. According to the Old Testament, he destroyed Solomon's temple and deported the Hebrews into Babylonia, where they remained captives until 538 B.C.E.

In Babylon, Nebuchadnezzar launched several extensive building projects. He constructed a new royal residence, refurbished the temple of his god Marduk (the Esagila) and the ziggurat (temple tower) Etemenanki, and surrounded the city with no fewer than five fortification walls. Historians Diodorus Siculus and Quintus Curtius Rufus assert that he also built the legendary Hanging Gardens of Babylon in honor of his wife (a Median princess) to remind her of her homeland.

Influence. Nebuchadnezzar appears prominently in the book of Daniel, where he is negatively described as having introduced the worship of a new god into Babylonia and as having lived among the beasts of the field for seven years.

Nebuchadnezzar II. (Library of Congress)

ADDITIONAL RESOURCES
Sack, R. H. *Images of Nebuchadnezzar: The Emergence of a Legend.* Cranbury, N.J.: Associated University Press, 1991.

Wiseman, D. J. *Nebuchadrezzar and Babylon.* London: Oxford University Press, 1985.

SEE ALSO: Arabia; Babylonia; Cyaxares; Damascus document; Jerusalem, temple of.

—*Ronald H. Sack*

NEFERTITI

ALSO KNOWN AS: Nofretete
BORN: c. 1366. B.C.E.; Thebes, Egypt
DIED: c. 1336 B.C.E.; probably Egypt
RELATED CIVILIZATION: Pharaonic Egypt
MAJOR ROLE/POSITION: Queen

Life. Three thousand years after her death, Nefertiti (nehf-ehr-TEET-ee) remains a symbol of artistic loveliness, but during her lifetime, she was revered as the queen-consort of the eccentric originator of Egyptian monotheism, the pharaoh Akhenaton. Scholars debate Nefertiti's parentage, with many claiming she was an Aryan Mitanni princess and others asserting she was the daughter of Amenhotep II. Whatever the circumstances of her birth, she married Akhenaton and bore the pharaoh six daughters and possibly two sons. Akhenaton advocated the worship of a single Sun god, Aton. Nefertiti was a devout follower of this cult, and she encouraged her husband in establishing a new capital devoted to the worship of Aton, called Akhetaton (modern Amarna).

After the twelfth year of Ahkenaton's reign, Nefertiti's status changed. According to one theory, she fell from favor and was replaced as queen by one of her daughters, Meritaten. Other theories include her elevation to coregent, perhaps as the mysterious Smenkhkare, to placate her when Akhenaton took his daughter as wife in order to produce a son. Still others suggest she moved to Hataten, a nearby villa, to devote herself to raising their son, Tutankhamen (Tutankhaten), or ran away with her brother-in-law and disappeared from the historical record.

Influence. Despite the confusion surrounding her life, Nefertiti lingers in history as an ardent reformer and symbol of timeless beauty.

ADDITIONAL RESOURCES
Commie, Anne, and Deborah Klezmer. *Women in World History.* Waterford, Conn.: Yorkin Publications, 1997.

Nefertiti. (Library of Congress)

Seibert, Ilse. *Women in the Ancient Near East.* New York: Schram, 1974.

SEE ALSO: Akhenaton; Egypt, Pharaonic; Tutankhamen.

—*Michaela Crawford Reaves*

NEMESIANUS

ALSO KNOWN AS: Marcus Aurelius Olympius
    Nemesianus
BORN: c. 253 C.E.; Carthage, North Africa
DIED: after 283 C.E.; probably Rome
RELATED CIVILIZATION: Imperial Rome
MAJOR ROLE/POSITION: Poet

Life. Nemesianus (neh-mee-zhee-AHN-uhs) was a third century C.E. Roman poet. He is one of the few individuals known as writers during this enigmatic period in Roman literary history. Nemesianus is usually thought to have been a favorite of the emperor Carus and his two sons, Carinus and Numerianus. He is said to have contemplated an epic on their achievements, but no evidence remains of this work. Most of Nemesianus's poetry was in the form of eclogues (nature poems), of which he wrote at least four. His best-known work, *Cynegetica* (c. 283 C.E.; *The Chase*, 1934), is a didactic poem on hunting. About 325 lines of it survive, and scholars have usually considered these lines to be a fragment of the whole work. In 1997, however, in his doctoral dissertation at New York University, David Wondrich suggested that the *Cynegetica* as it exists may well be complete. Nemesianus also reportedly wrote poems on sailing and fishing. Traditionally, scholars have considered Nemesianus unoriginal, but more recent criticism has emphasized his unique response to the challenges of his time.

Influence. Nemesianus's work helped maintain Latin literature until its renaissance in the fourth and fifth centuries C.E. He was known, if not particularly read, throughout the Middle Ages.

ADDITIONAL RESOURCES
Conte, Gian Biagio. *Latin Literature: A History.* Baltimore: Johns Hopkins University Press, 1994.
Williams, Heather J. *The Eclogues and Cynegetica of Nemesianus.* Leiden, Netherlands: E. J. Brill, 1986.

SEE ALSO: Languages and literature; Rome, Imperial.
                                        —*Nicholas Birns*

NEOLITHIC AGE EUROPE

DATE: 8000-3500 B.C.E. in southeastern and 3200-
    1500 B.C.E. in northern Europe
LOCALE: Continental Europe and the British Isles
SIGNIFICANCE: Europeans shifted from exclusive dependence on hunting and fishing to cultivation of plants and domestication of livestock; this facilitated settlement into villages with the use of pottery and ground stone rather than chipped stone artifacts, and in some instances, gave rise to permanent dwellings and monuments.

The Neolithic (New Stone) Age represents the last period of dependence on stone tools before they were replaced by metal implements. This took place in a different way in each locale and was often a subtle transformation of predecessor Mesolithic peoples who in some cases coexisted at "frontiers" and most likely traded with their farming neighbors.

History. The Neolithic Age occurred earliest in southeastern and latest in northwestern Europe, and the transition was most likely somewhat different in each region. In southeastern Europe, the Neolithic transition may have started about 8000 B.C.E., although more probably in most places around 6500 B.C.E. and was most likely derived from Neolithic communities in southwest Asia. Early sites reflect a mobile lifestyle with annual reoccupation of central sites, and buildings and structures slowly became more permanent. By 6000 B.C.E., Neolithic communities extended to the Hungarian plain and northeast to the Carpathians. By 5500 to 4000 B.C.E., smaller sites coalesced into larger tells and in some cases expanded into new zones. Whether this was caused by growing populations or acculturation of Mesolithic peoples is not clear. Copper and gold working were introduced and developed. From 4000 to 3500 B.C.E., tells were abandoned, and the settlements that followed tended to be smaller and dispersed, often situated on defendable hills.

In the central and west Mediterranean, the Neolithic dates to 6000-7000 B.C.E. with the appearance of ditched enclosures in Italy, but again the transformation was slow and gradual. People were mobile and slowly incorporated sheep and cereals. Before 5000 B.C.E., Impressed ware pottery was broadly distributed, and afterward, settlements increased in coastal and inland regions.

The Linear Pottery culture (Linearbandkeramik or LBK) was the first evidence of the Neolithic in central and western Europe (5500 to 5000 B.C.E.) in regions corresponding largely to loess soils or the southern extent of the sandy and clay soils of the north European plain. Some sites are in fertile valleys in lowlands near water and often include woodlands. Settlements appear to be continuously occupied, with timber long houses, intensive gardens, and husbandry, particularly cattle. The Linear Pottery culture seems to have rapidly replaced the indigenous foraging lifestyle, and these peoples may represent colonization by folks from the south or Hungarian plains or may include extensive mixture with the indigenous foraging inhabitants. From 5500 to 4000 B.C.E., settlement was extended to the limits of the loess soils and also fertile soils in Poland. Regional differentiation also occurred, leading to the Rössen and Lengyel cultures.

By 4000 B.C.E., the Neolithic Age spread to much of central and western Europe, including southern Scandinavia, Britain, and Ireland, and appears to be an extension of central European traditions. These northern cultures are regionally differentiated, such as the Beaker people in northern Europe and southern Scandinavia. From 4000 to 2500 B.C.E., systematically laid-out nucleated hamlets and villages, often encircled by fences or palisades, were frequently located near lakes or on the edges of marshes of the Alpine region of Germany, Switzerland, and France. Hunting and fishing supplemented domesticated animals and cereals. The Globular Amphora culture, recognized primarily by its burials, appeared after or alongside the Beaker culture. Later, in Poland and Bohemia, the most likely more mobile Corded Ware culture appeared.

Agriculture and animal husbandry. Neolithic peoples grew wheats (emmer, einkorn, bread, and club), barleys (two- and six-row), legumes (lentils and chickpeas), and sometimes oats and millet. They also collected wild fruits and nuts, hunted wild game, and herded sheep, goats, cows, and pigs. Linear Pottery peoples practiced hoe agriculture in permanent or rotating fields in clearings near their houses. There is later evidence for the use of animals pulling ploughs in the Baden or Pécel culture (c. 4000-3000 B.C.E.) in southeastern Europe and in the middle Neolithic Beaker culture in northern Europe. Animals were also used for wool.

Economy and trade. Neolithic people initially exploited both wild food and domesticates. Dependence on husbandry and cereals increased such that a more stable rural, agrarian existence resulted in some re-

gions. Coastal peoples also fished by net and boat and collected shellfish and land snails.

They traded few pots but many luxury items, including Baltic amber, obsidian, and flint from various mines, copper from the Balkans, gold from perhaps Bulgaria, and the Mediterranean mussel, *Spondylus gaederopus* (used in jewelry). Cattle may have been traded in the late Neolithic Age.

Religion and ritual. Suggestive of religious ritual are structures within settlements on the lower Danube that may represent shrines. At sites in Bulgaria, there are clay plaques carved with rectilinear motifs. In northern Europe, burials near monumental enclosures might indicate ancestor worship.

Death and burial. In early southeastern Europe, burials were rare, occurring in pits in settlements, outside houses, with or often without grave goods. Later people were buried individually between houses or in unoccupied parts of settlements and later, in cemeteries. As for grave goods, male hunting equipment was the most common, along with other evidence of the deceased's status and prestige. Central and western European Neolithic sites exhibit scattered burials in graves or reused pits near houses, and there are also small or large cemeteries that increase in frequency to the north and west. Flexed inhumations are common, although infrequently there are extended burials and cremations. In some cases, there is evidence for flesh removal procedures.

Later, in southern Scandinavia, there are dolmens and earthen barrows in which many grave goods are included with individual inhumations. Long mounds contained either wooden or stone chambers that are either tent-shaped or rectangular, with well-prepared floors. There was often evidence of firing of the wooden chambers.

Community monuments. Two types of monuments coincide with the first domesticates in northern Europe. Many types of enclosures seem to have been the foci of community activity. Circular monuments—whether passage graves, henges, or stone circles—may have provided open arenas for public gatherings. Other monuments were mounds or cairns with the remains of the dead. These structures often exhibit more effort and technology than was put into domestic dwellings. By contrast, the most elaborate architecture in central Europe involved massive long houses used as living quarters.

Settlements and social structure. Settlement mounds in southeastern Europe included an orderly arrangement of houses, shared activities, and nearby burials. In northeastern Bulgaria, sites were organized within borders defined by palisades and ditches and houses tightly packed in the interior. These "villages" were continuously occupied for centuries. In Britain, domestic structures were scarce, and causeway-accessed enclosures and monuments such as henges may also have served as the foci for social interactions.

Linear Pottery culture was characterized by wooden long houses, labor-intensive to build, of tripartite modular form suggesting different foci for families or activities. Construction and orientation were usually consistent, which implies that tradition and meaning were associated with these structures, which perhaps experienced continued use by extended families. Initially there were farmsteads or hamlets and later villages representing larger social units. Enclosures of unknown function, not always associated with settlements, may have been used by larger gatherings.

War and weapons. During the late fourth and early third millennia B.C.E., central European Neolithic sites were more commonly found on defendable hilltops, and elaborate battle-axes appear in tombs. Simpler battle-axes are associated with Lengyel culture.

Visual arts. The Neolithic Age can be partially characterized by flint and stone axes elaborately worked relative to the choice of raw materials and manufacturing techniques, the carving of amber into beads and pendants, and the manufacture of pottery in a variety of styles. Figurines were common, particularly in southeastern Europe.

Calendars. Henges share significant astronomical orientations reminiscent of primitive observatories. For example, early phases of Stonehenge may be calendric.

Women's life. The associated grave goods indicate a division of labor, but reconstruction of activities from grave goods is difficult. In Scandinavia, graves of men are associated with weapons and graves of women with jewelry and also small, polished working axes.

Current views. Initially, the Neolithic Age referred to a chronological phase and a technological innovation, the polished stone ax. Pottery became another marker. Investigators in the 1970's and 1980's defined the Neolithic as a shift to agriculture, a stable mixed farming strategy. This new economic system spread across Europe as peoples colonized or acculturated. This migration model has been replaced by in situ transitions to new sets of social relations, ideas, and interactions with others that took place in different ways and at different times, depending on the settings.

ADDITIONAL RESOURCES

Bradley, Richard. *The Significance of Monuments*. London: Routledge, 1998.

Darvill, Timothy, and Julian Thomas, eds. *Neolithic Houses in Northwest Europe and Beyond, Neolithic Studies Group Seminar Papers 1*. Oxbow Monograph 57. Oxford, England: Oxbow Books, 1996.

Hodder, Ian. *The Domestication of Europe: Structure and Contingency in Neolithic Societies*. Cambridge, Mass.: Basil Blackwell, 1990.

Thomas, Julian. *Understanding the Neolithic*. 2d ed. New York: Routledge, 1999.

Tilley, Christopher Y. *An Ethnography of the Neolithic: Early Prehistoric Societies in Southern Scandinavia*. New York: Cambridge University Press, 1996.

Whittle, Alasdair. *Europe in the Neolithic: The Creation of New Worlds*. New York: Cambridge University Press, 1996.

SEE ALSO: Beaker people; Hallstatt culture; La Tène culture; Stonehenge.

—*Joan C. Stevenson*

NEOPLATONISM

DATE: third-sixth centuries C.E.
LOCALE: Rome and Greece
RELATED CIVILIZATIONS: Roman Greece, Imperial Rome
SIGNIFICANCE: Neoplatonism represented a last attempt of pagan philosophy to combine science and spirituality.

Neoplatonism (nee-oh-PLAY-tehn-ih-zm) refers to the philosophy developed by Plotinus (205-270 C.E.), in which the philosopher addresses the ordering of matter by a nonphysical deity or cosmic mind. Plotinus proposes a theory of emanation in which he posits a deity so transcendent, so beyond being, so beyond anything in human experience or imagination as to be wholly incapable of articulation. It cannot be known except by a "way of removing," by which every attribute that can be thought is removed until only god alone is left. The emanation from the ineffable god or "One" is the Divine Intelligence; from the Divine Intelligence emanates the General Soul. From the General Soul emanates everything else, including matter. The first three—the One, the Divine Intelligence, and the General Soul—constitute a "trinity" of descending hierarchical value.

Neoplatonism also addresses how humans might come into contact with the divine. Because much Neoplatonism deals with this subject, Neoplatonism may be described as both a philosophic and a religious doctrine. However, without an organized structure including worshipers or adherents, institutionalized rituals and observances, or the support of the political authorities, it was not destined to endure, although it influenced subsequent movements in philosophy and literature over the centuries.

ADDITIONAL RESOURCES

O'Meara, Dominic J. *Plotinus: An Introduction to the Enneads*. Oxford, England: Oxford University Press, 1995.

Rist, John M. *Plotinus: The Road to Reality*. Cambridge, England: Cambridge University Press, 1967.

SEE ALSO: Greece, Hellenistic and Roman; Philosophy; Plotinus; Religion and ritual; Rome, Imperial.

—*James A. Arieti*

NEPOS, CORNELIUS

BORN: c. 100 B.C.E.; Northern Italy
DIED: c. 25 B.C.E.; place unknown
RELATED CIVILIZATIONS: Republican and Imperial Rome
MAJOR ROLE/POSITION: Biographer

Life. Cornelius Nepos (kawr-NEEL-yuhs NEE-puhs) was a native of Cisalpine Gaul and dedicated his whole life to literature. There is no record of his holding public office. His book, *De viris illustribus* (c. 34 B.C.E., before 27 B.C.E.; *On Famous Men*, 1853), which survives in part, contains biographical sketches rather than critical history. Originally, it consisted of at least sixteen books: eight pairs, of which one book was on Roman characters and the other on non-Roman characters. The pairs of books included such categories as generals, historians, and kings. The works were designed to praise the subjects and elucidate morals. Of these lives, only twenty-four remain, including the lives of historians Titus Pomponius Atticus and Cato the Censor. There were two editions, one published before the death of Atticus in 34 B.C.E., the second published before 27 B.C.E. His lost works include the three-volume *Chronica*, a universal history, which is referred to in Catullus's dedicatory poem, and *Exempla*, a collection of anecdotes gathered from his historical and scientific research.

Influence. Nepos is the earliest extant Roman biographer. His work was not based on serious research and is marked by omissions and inaccuracies and hasty and careless composition. His simple vocabulary and sentence structure made *On Famous Men* a favorite school book.

ADDITIONAL RESOURCES

Hadas, M. *A History of Latin Literature*. New York: Columbia University Press, 1952.

Hornblower, S., and A. Spawforth, eds. *The Oxford Classical Dictionary*. 3d ed. Oxford, England: Oxford University Press, 1996.

Nepos, Cornelius. *Cornelius Nepos*. Translated by John Carew Rolfe. Cambridge, Mass.: Harvard University Press, 1994.

SEE ALSO: Atticus, Titus Pomponius; Cato the Censor; Rome, Imperial; Rome, Republican.

—*Sherwin D. Little*

NERO

ALSO KNOWN AS: Nero Claudius Caesar
BORN: December 15, 37 C.E.; Antium, Latium (later Anzio, Italy)
DIED: June 9, 68 C.E.; Rome
RELATED CIVILIZATION: Imperial Rome
MAJOR ROLE/POSITION: Emperor

Life. The son of Gnaeus Domitius Ahenobarbus and Agrippina the Younger, Nero (NEE-roh) attained the throne upon the death of his stepfather Claudius in 54 C.E. Though later marked by violence, Nero's early reign was distinguished for moderate, responsible government, largely because of the influence of his tutor Seneca the Younger and praetorian commander Afranius Burrus.

Soon, however, the young emperor's taste for luxury required the imposition of heavy taxation and property

Nero. (Hulton Archive)

confiscation to resupply the dwindling treasury. In 64 C.E., Rome was nearly destroyed by the Great Fire, which many believed Nero himself ignited in order to clear land for his new Domus Aurea (Golden House). The emperor blamed the Christians, which led to the first Great Persecution.

More interested in publicly demonstrating his talents as a poet than in governing, Nero was the victim of two failed senatorial conspiracies, in 65 and 66 C.E. Finally, open rebellion erupted in the provinces, and he was forced to commit suicide in 68 C.E., the last of the Julio-Claudian rulers.

Influence. Nero is the most infamous of Caesars because of his image as a cruel and debauched monarch. He was responsible for many murders, including those of his mother, stepbrother Britannicus, and first two wives, Octavia and Poppaea Sabina. He was, however, a great patron of the arts and Greek culture and, though loathed by the Roman senate, remained popular with the common people.

ADDITIONAL RESOURCES

Scarre, Christopher. *Chronicle of the Roman Emperors.* London: Thames and Hudson, 1995.

Suetonius. *The Twelve Caesars.* Translated by Robert Graves. London: Viking Press, 2000.

SEE ALSO: Agrippina the Younger; Christianity; Claudius; Poppaea Sabina; Rome, Imperial; Seneca the Younger.

—*Kelli E. Stanley*

NERVA, MARCUS COCCEIUS

BORN: c. 30 C.E.; Narnia, Italy
DIED: January 28, 98 C.E.; Rome
RELATED CIVILIZATION: Imperial Rome
MAJOR ROLE/POSITION: Emperor

Life. Marcus Cocceius Nerva (MAHR-kuhs kahk-SEE-yuhs NEHR-vuh) came to power at the age of sixty-one on September 18, 96 C.E., after Domitian's assassination. Related distantly to the Julio-Claudians, he had held the consulship in 71 and 90 C.E. For the conspirators, his age, childlessness, and lack of military connections made him an ideal moderate candidate in a dangerous transitional period. He placated the military

and people with donatives, land distribution programs, and tax reductions.

From a senatorial perspective, Domitian's last years had been a reign of terror. His murder released a wave of fury that condemned the emperor's memory and destroyed his statues and monuments. The military, however, fondly remembered Domitian as a generous paymaster, and in 97 C.E., the Praetorian Guard compelled Nerva to accede to the execution of two principal conspirators.

His authority crippled, Nerva, perhaps again under compulsion, adopted Trajan, the powerful governor of Upper Germany, as his son, coemperor and successor.

This act stabilized the government and prevented a recurrence of civil war. After a sixteen-month reign, Nerva succumbed to a stroke.

Influence. Aside from the forum Nervae (Transitorium), his greatest accomplishment was his stabilizing adoption of Trajan.

ADDITIONAL RESOURCES

Garzetti, Albino. *From Tiberius to the Antonines*. London: Methuen, 1974.

Scarre, Chris. *Chronicle of the Roman Emperors*. London: Thames and Hudson, 1995.

SEE ALSO: Domitian; Rome, Imperial; Trajan.

—*David J. Ladouceur*

NESTORIUS

BORN: c. 381 C.E.; Antioch
DIED: c. 451 C.E.; Panopolis, Egypt
RELATED CIVILIZATION: Byzantine Empire
MAJOR ROLE/POSITION: Religious figure

Life. In 428 C.E., Nestorius (neh-STOHR-ee-uhs) became bishop of Constantinople, a post from which he stirred theological controversy with Cyril, his counterpart in Alexandria. Saint Cyril of Alexandria advocated the term *Theotokos*, or "God-bearer," in reference to the Virgin Mary. The term meant that Jesus Christ's divine nature underwent the human act of birth; hence, Mary was "mother of God." In response, Nestorius advocated the term "Christ-bearer" for Mary, implying that only Christ's human nature underwent birth, not the divine.

The controversy was exacerbated by hot tempers, misunderstandings, and rivalries between Alexandrian and Antiochene schools of theology. The 431 C.E. Council of Ephesus deposed Nestorius, and his writings were later destroyed. Nestorius was driven into exile for his remaining twenty years. While banished, he wrote the *Liber Heraclidis* (fifth century C.E.; *Bazaar of Heracleides*, 1925), a defense of his orthodox intentions. However, belief that Christ's human and divine natures constituted two people under the appearance of one became associated with Nestorius, though this is an exaggeration of his teaching. Nestorius hailed the Council of Chalcedon's declaration in 451 C.E. that Christ was "one person in two natures" as confirmation of his doctrine.

Influence. Nestorius taught that Christ's divinity was shielded from human suffering. Biblical statements about Christ referred distinctly to his divinity or to his humanity. Some twentieth century historians have reevaluated Nestorius's teachings, suspicious of the politics involved in condemning him as a heretic.

ADDITIONAL RESOURCES

Driver, G. R., and L. Hodgson. *Nestorius: The Bazaar of Heracleides*. Oxford, England: Oxford University Press, 1925.

Ferguson, Everett. *Doctrinal Diversity*. New York: Garland, 1999.

Gonzalez, Justo L. *A History of Christian Thought*. Vol 1. Nashville, Tenn.: Abingdon, 1970.

SEE ALSO: Byzantine Empire; Chalcedon, Council of; Christianity; Cyril of Alexandria, Saint; Jesus Christ; Mary.

—*William P. McDonald*

NICAEA, COUNCIL OF

DATE: 325 C.E.
LOCALE: Nicaea (later İznik, Turkey)
RELATED CIVILIZATIONS: Imperial Rome, Byzantine Empire
SIGNIFICANCE: The council condemned Arianism and established the Nicene Creed.

Early Christianity had been struggling to identify the relationships between the figures in the Godhead (what would later become known as the Father, Son, and Holy Spirit) for a couple of centuries. One side tended to emphasize the preeminence of God, making the Son a lesser deity. The other side insisted on equality between the figures, but often blurred the distinctions. Arius, a presbyter in Alexandria, insisted that the Son was not of the same substance as deity (*homoousios*), but rather only a similar substance (*homoiousios*). Deposed for heresy, he rallied many supporters, and the schism threatened the unity of the entire Eastern church. Constantine the Great, recent conqueror of the eastern half of the empire, wanted unity in the church, so he called for a council of bishops to resolve the dispute.

In 325 C.E. at Nicaea (ni-SEE-uh), which means "victory" and demonstrates a desire to bring victory to the dispute, about three hundred bishops of the church met to discuss the theological issues. Saint Athanasius of Alexandria, another presbyter from Alexandria, managed to convince Emperor Constantine that Arius was wrong, and most bishops were unwilling to offend the new and powerful emperor. Thus, the overwhelming majority of the bishops at the council voted in favor of the Nicene Creed, which stated that the Son was of the same substance (*homoousios*) as the Father.

Although Arianism was condemned and the Nicene position became the orthodox position in the church, Arianism continued to plague the church for another half century. This brought a significant amount of trouble to the church, both theologically and politically.

ADDITIONAL RESOURCES

Arnold, Marvin M. *Nicaea and the Nicene Council of A.D. 325*. Washington, Mich.: Arno, 1987.
Dudley, Dean. *History of the First Council of Nice*. New York: ECA Associates, 1990.

SEE ALSO: Arianism; Athanasius of Alexandria, Saint; Christianity; Constantine the Great; Jesus Christ.

—*James B. North*

NICANDER OF COLOPHON

ALSO KNOWN AS: Nikandros
BORN: second or third century B.C.E.; Colophon, Ionia, Turkey
DIED: second century B.C.E.; Alexandria, Egypt?
RELATED CIVILIZATION: Hellenistic Greece
MAJOR ROLE/POSITION: Physician, poet

Life. Almost nothing is known about Nicander (nuh-KAN-dur) of Colophon's life. He wrote on medical topics in verse, mostly hexameter. Two of his books and some scholia survive. *Alexipharmaca* describes many types of poisonings by animals, plants, and inanimate agents and suggests antidotes and other treatments. *Theriaca* deals more specifically with poisonings caused by animal bites, stings, and scratches. Among the titles of Nicander's lost works are *Georgica*, *Melissurgica* (*Bee-Keeping*), *Heteroeumena* (*Metamorphoses*), and *Prognostica*.

As a physician, he followed the empiric school of Philinus of Cos and Serapion of Alexandria. He introduced the medicinal use of the leech. This common method of phlebotomy (bloodletting) persisted into the nineteenth century.

Influence. Nicander affected rhetoric, toxicology, and therapeutics. His reputation as both physician and poet was strong throughout ancient times and was revived in the Renaissance. The first printed editions of *Theriaca* and *Alexipharmaca* appeared jointly in Venice in 1499.

ADDITIONAL RESOURCES

Gow, A. S. F., and A. F. Scholfield, eds. *Nicander of Colophon: Poems and Poetical Fragments*. Cambridge, England: Cambridge University Press, 1953.
Knoefel, Peter K., and Madeline C. Covi. *A Hellenistic Treatise on Poisonous Animals: The "Theriaca" of Nicander of Colophon, a Contribution to the History of Toxicology*. Lewiston, N.Y.: Edwin Mellen, 1991.
White, Heather. *Studies in the Poetry of Nicander*. Amsterdam, Netherlands: Hakkert, 1987.

SEE ALSO: Greece, Hellenistic and Roman; Languages and literature; Science.

—*Eric v.d. Luft*

NICIAS OF ATHENS

ALSO KNOWN AS: Nikias son of Nikeratos
BORN: c. 470 B.C.E.; Athens, Greece
DIED: 413 B.C.E.; Syracuse
RELATED CIVILIZATION: Classical Greece
MAJOR ROLE/POSITION: Statesman and military leader

Life. Nicias (NIHSH-ee-uhs) of Athens gained prominence in Athens during the Archidamian War as a successful general and rival of the aggressive Cleon of Athens. After Cleon's death, he ended the war by negotiating the Peace of Nicias with Sparta in 421 B.C.E. Hostilities soon resumed, however, and at home a strong new opponent, Alcibiades of Athens, appeared.

In 415 B.C.E., Nicias, Alcibiades, and another general, Lamachus, were given command of an expedition to Sicily, one that Nicias considered ill-advised. Alcibiades was soon deposed, and Nicias and Lamachus initially achieved little. However, in 414 B.C.E., they besieged Syracuse, the foremost city in Sicily, almost taking it. Within a year, Lamachus's death, the relief of Syracuse by the Spartan Gylippus, and errors in judgment by the ailing Nicias brought him to the brink of defeat. The ar-rival of reinforcements under Demosthenes led only to further disasters. Nicias, fearing disgrace, resisted withdrawal, only to be defeated and trapped. He surrendered but was executed by the Syracusans.

Influence. Nicias proved unequal to the major political and military crises of his career, contributing greatly to the downfall of Athens in the Peloponnesian War (431-404 B.C.E.). His role in the Sicilian Expedition is remembered, not altogether fairly, as an example of bad generalship.

ADDITIONAL RESOURCES
Powell, Anton. *Athens and Sparta*. New York: Routledge, 1996.
Thucydides. "History of the Peloponnesian War." In *The Landmark Thucydides: A Comprehensive Guide to the Peloponnesian War*, edited by Robert B. Strassler. New York: Free Press, 1996.

SEE ALSO: Archidamian War; Alcibiades of Athens; Cleon of Athens; Greece, Classical; Peloponnesian War.
—*Scott M. Rusch*

NICOLAUS OF DAMASCUS

ALSO KNOWN AS: Nicholas of Damascus
BORN: c. 64 B.C.E.; Damascus
DIED: date unknown; Rome
RELATED CIVILIZATIONS: Hellenistic Jews, Imperial Rome
MAJOR ROLE/POSITION: Historian

Life. Nicolaus of Damascus (NIHK-uh-lahs of duh-MAS-kuhs), the historian and adviser of Herod the Great, was born into a wealthy Damascene family. His father, a high officeholder, was a skilled rhetorician who ensured that his son had an excellent classical education.

Wide travel helped Nicolaus develop a cosmopolitan outlook. By the 30's B.C.E., his scholarly works had begun to attract attention. He accepted Cleopatra VII's invitation to tutor her children by Marc Antony. Probably after the Battle of Actium in 31 B.C.E., he came to the court of Herod, the client king of Judaea and a Hellenistic patron. As Herod's relationship with Augustus flourished, so too did that of Nicolaus. Perhaps to solidify both relationships with Augustus and to propagandize for the emperor in the east, Nicolaus wrote a laudatory biography for Augustus.

He served as a mediator between Augustus and Herod and advised Herod in his conflicts with his sons. His final years, he lived in Rome. His numerous works, among which are a universal history in 144 books and an autobiography, are nonextant or fragmentary.

Influence. The Jewish historian Flavius Josephus, whose works survive, used Nicolaus as his major source for the postbiblical period.

ADDITIONAL RESOURCES
Feldman, Louis H., and Gohei Hata, eds. *Josephus, the Bible and History*. Detroit, Mich.: Wayne State University Press, 1989.
Nicolaus of Damascus. *Life of Augustus*. Bristol, England: Bristol Classical Press, 1984.
Wacholder, Ben Zion. *Nicolaus of Damascus*. Berkeley: University of California Press, 1962.

SEE ALSO: Antony, Marc; Augustus; Cleopatra VII; Josephus, Flavius; Rome, Imperial.
—*David J. Ladouceur*

NICOMACHUS OF GERASA

ALSO KNOWN AS: Nikomachus; Nikomachos; Nicomachos
FLOURISHED: c. 100 C.E.; Gerasa, Arabia Petraea (later Jerash, Jordan)
RELATED CIVILIZATION: Hellenistic Greece
MAJOR ROLE/POSITION: Neo-Pythagorean philosopher, mathematician

Life. Hardly anything is known of Nicomachus of Gerasa (nuh-KAHM-uh-kuhs of JEHR-uh-suh) beyond his surviving works. His *Arithmētikē eisagōgē* (n.d.; *Introduction to Arithmetic*, 1926) is a general textbook that synthesizes the metaphysics of Plato and Pythagoras, emphasizing mathematics. His *Enchiridion harmonikēs* (n.d.; *Handbook of Harmony*, 1967) is also primarily a work of metaphysics. His *Theologoumena arithmetikēs* (n.d.; theology of arithmetic) survives only in fragments and in a summary by the ninth century Byzantine patriarch and scholar Saint Photius. Among Nicomachus's lost works are a biography of Pythagoras, a geometry textbook, and perhaps an encyclopedia.

Influence. Translated into Latin by both Lucius Apuleius and Boethius, *Introduction to Arithmetic* remained popular through the Middle Ages and Renaissance. *Handbook of Harmony* was a key text in both music and astronomy, insofar as it expounded the "harmony of the spheres" theory of planetary motion that Johannes Kepler partially vindicated in his *Harmonice Mundi* (1619; partial translation *Harmonies of the World*, 1952). In the twentieth century, philosophers such as Edward Pols have asserted that the most creative eras in human history are Pythagorean eras, that is, eras when the relationship between metaphysics and mathematics is very close.

ADDITIONAL RESOURCES
Guthrie, Kenneth Sylvan. *The Pythagorean Sourcebook and Library.* Grand Rapids, Mich.: Phanes, 1987.
Levin, Flora Rose. *The Harmonics of Nicomachus and the Pythagorean Tradition.* University Park, Pa.: American Philological Association, 1975.
O'Meara, Dominic J. *Pythagoras Revived: Mathematics and Philosophy in Late Antiquity.* Oxford, England: Clarendon Press, 1989.

SEE ALSO: Apuleius, Lucius; Greece, Hellenistic and Roman; Philosophy; Plato; Pythagoras; Science.

—*Eric v.d. Luft*

NIGER-CONGO

DATE: 8000 B.C.E.-700 C.E.
LOCALE: West Africa
RELATED CIVILIZATIONS: West Africa, Benue-Kwa, Adamawans, Sanaga, Nyong, Bantu
SIGNIFICANCE: Niger-Congo is one of the four major language families that exist in Africa. Approximately three-fourths of all of Africa's languages are part of the Niger-Congo language family, including those of the Bantu subgroup.

The Niger-Congo (NI-jehr-KAHN-goh) language family can be traced back more than 15,000 years in West Africa. The major subdivisions of the Niger-Congo family are Kordofanian, Niger-Congo (Mande-Congo), Mande, Volta-Congo, Atlantic, Gur-Adamawan (North Volta-Congo), and Benue-Kwa.

History. The Holocene era in West Africa provided optimum rain-forest cover and woodland savanna. By 9000 B.C.E., the people of the Niger-Congo culture complex had combined the collection of edible tubers with a fishing economy. The wet era maximized rivers, and this allowed for increased fishing and navigation over a broad area. The enhanced productivity had a major social impact in that it led to the outward expansion of yam farming and fishing communities. By the sixth millennium B.C.E., the elaboration of farming techniques and climatic conditions had led to increased populations. Increased population densities led to the spread of ideas and culture as the Niger-Congo peoples began to spread southward into the rain forest and across the woodland savanna into the Atlantic coast hinterland. In the fourth millennium B.C.E., one major subgroup of Niger-Congo, speakers of Bantu languages, were spreading into the forests of the Congo Basin. By the last millennium B.C.E., the Niger-Congo heritage of planting, religion, and music was rapidly spreading beyond West Africa into eastern and southern Africa.

Agriculture and animal husbandry. From 9000 to 1000 B.C.E., the environment was influenced primarily by climatic shifts. At the beginning of this period,

Niger-Congo communities inhabited the woodland savanna and the fringes of the rain forest. By 5000 B.C.E., an important shift had taken place in that communities had begun affecting their environments through the use of polished stone axes. However, only in the last millennium B.C.E. did human agency and agricultural development come to reshape the environment dramatically.

Around 8000 B.C.E., cultivated yams began to replace wild yams in the diet of Niger-Congo people in the West African woodland savanna. The alternating expansion and retreat of the forest caused by fluctuating rain levels in the Holocene caused the Niger-Congo peoples to become innovative in their techniques of food gathering and production. The encroachment of the rain forests in the Holocene negatively affected the harvesting of wild yams; therefore, people began to plant yams deliberately. In the West African planting tradition, plant cuttings taken from tubers are placed in an opening in the soil, where they are left to mature. This planting method is distinct from seed and grain cultivation. The plant cuttings had to be protected and the land prepared for them to viably develop because dense rain-forest cover blocks out vital sunlight. In addition to cutting back forest cover, forest debris was placed over the soil to protect the soil from the tropical rains that cause extreme leeching and hardening of soils. This protection and preparation evolved into cultivation. In addition to yams, Niger-Congo speakers domesticated okra, oil palms, blackeyed peas, and guinea fowl.

By 6000 B.C.E., goats were being kept and, in the drier areas, cattle also. Between 5500 and 3500 B.C.E., there was an expansion of agriculture and a wave of agricultural innovation. Late in the sixth millennium and early fifth millennium B.C.E., the Niger-Congo peoples were spreading out of southern Nigeria into parts of present-day Cameroon and the Central African Republic. The fertile volcanic soils of this region allowed for increased agricultural production. The novelty of distinct soils and different environments opened the opportunity for innovation.

By the fourth millennium B.C.E., some groups were beginning grain cultivation. In the Volta River Basin, Niger-Congo descendants who spoke Gur languages and produced the Kintampo culture complex were relying heavily on Sudanic grain crops. Some time between 4000 and 3000 B.C.E., Saharo-Sahelian crops such as gourds were being cultivated by Niger-Congo communities that had moved into the drier savanna and grassland areas.

From 3000 to 1000 B.C.E., another group of Niger-Congo descendants, speaking Mande languages, spread through the Niger River Basin, where they cultivated rice. As the wet phase tapered off between about 2600 and 2000 B.C.E., drier open woodland savanna and grasslands expanded, allowing for another phase of agricultural expansion through innovative cultivation techniques.

Economics and trade. Between the sixth and fifth millennia B.C.E., a variety of material products were being manufactured. The items produced include woven mats, baskets, and raffia cloth; pounded bark cloth; and carved-wood boats, figurines, and drums. In addition to handcrafts, fishing and hunting products supplemented the economy, which was partially dependent on the exchanging of regionally produced goods.

Between 3500 and 1000 B.C.E., intraregional trade was conducted in the Niger Delta. Groups including the Ijo traded river and sea products such as fish, salt, and shells in exchange for inland products such as sorghum, livestock, and raw leather. In the third and second millennia B.C.E., the bayous of the Niger Delta plain were dominated by the Bozo fishers and Marka rice growers. After 1000 B.C.E., manufactured goods were more commonly traded in the region.

Technology. The Niger-Congo peoples manufactured Microlithic stone tools, particularly small points. Additionally, bows, arrows, and fishhooks were produced. Stone arrows were used together with poisons for hunting. In the sixth millennium B.C.E., polished stone axes had become an important tool for clearing plots of land for growing yams.

Architecture and city planning. Niger-Congo peoples lived in compact villages of one hundred to two hundred inhabitants. The inhabitants of a village tended to belong to the same matriclan, but people outside the clan were frequently incorporated into a village community. By the seventh millennium B.C.E., villages were organized along a main route of transport. Rectangular-shaped houses with gabled roofs covered with woven palm mats lined a river or lane. The tradition of building along a main thoroughfare was continued by Niger-Congo descendants up to the first millennium B.C.E. In the second half of the last millennium B.C.E., innovations in building based on influence from Sudanic architecture become apparent. The new style was reflected in round houses with conical roofs in compact villages.

Government and social structure. Hereditary clan chiefs served as politico-religious leaders within a single village. The influence of the clan chief extended to intravillage matters pertaining to land allocation, integration of outsiders into the community, adjudicating disputes, presiding over ceremony and ritual, and negotiating intercommunal relations.

Niger-Congo society followed a system of matrilineal descent. The clan, specifically the matriclan, was the unit of social organization. The political base was built upon a matrilocal and uxorilocal system. Bride service, whereby a young male served the parents of his future wife for an average of seven to ten years, facilitated the transition of the incorporation of the man into the woman's mother's village. Children born to a couple belonged to this matriclan.

Women's life. In preagricultural times, the Niger-Congo diet depended on the collection of wild yams, which was the charge of women. As the society was transformed into a more agricultural one, women became the primary cultivators of the domesticated yams.

Language. A sub-branch of Niger-Congo began to emerge between the sixth and fifth millennia B.C.E. as the Atlantic coast was settled. Far-flung communities developed different dialects. One sub-branch was the Benue-Kwa, the ancestral language of modern-day Igbo, Yoruba, and Akan. A second sub-group of Niger-Congo descendants, which developed early on, is the Adamawans. Between the fifth and fourth millennia B.C.E., the southeastern Benue-Kwa were inhabiting the more forested areas in the region of the confluence of the Sanaga and Nyong Rivers in southern Cameroon. In the early fourth millennium B.C.E., the southernmost Benue-Kwa developed into a linguistically distinct group known to scholars as the Proto-Bantu.

Religion and ritual. West African Niger-Congo beliefs in a creator had evolved by the sixth millennium B.C.E. Territorial spirits also played a prominent role in belief. The most important element in the belief system, however, was the ancestors. When respected and venerated, the ancestors would guide their descendants and bless them with good fortune. When neglected, the ancestors would cause ill fortune for the clan.

Medicine and health. Medicine and healing are closely linked to Niger-Congo concepts of good, evil, and balance. Illness and misfortune, in the worldview of the Niger-Congo peoples, were the result of malevolent and envious thoughts on the part of an individual. Hatred and evil were perpetrated by witches, who used medicines and supernatural powers. Only proper diagnosis and prescription by a doctor-diviner could alleviate a witch's malevolent curse.

Performing arts. The Niger-Congo arts encompass the use of carved wooden masks, figurines, and drums in performance. Percussion instruments, particularly drums, were used to create music with varied pitches. Polyrhythmic music accompanied dances, which are distinct because of the multiple body movements that were more important than fancy footwork. Niger-Congo performance is remarkable because it unites economy, ritual, celebration, and entertainment.

ADDITIONAL RESOURCES

Bendor, S. J. *The Niger-Congo Languages.* Lanham, Md.: University Press of America, 1989.

Grimes, B. F. *Ethnologue: Languages of the World.* Dallas: Summer Institute of Linguistics, 1992.

Phillipson, David W. *African Archaeology.* Cambridge, England: Cambridge University Press, 1993.

Vogel, Joseph A., ed. *Encyclopedia of Precolonial Africa: Archaeology, History, Languages, Cultures, and Environments.* Walnut Creek, Calif.: AltaMira Press, 1997.

SEE ALSO: Africa, West; Bantu, Congo Basin; Bantu, Mashariki; Mande.

—*Catherine Cymone Fourshey*

NIHON SHOKI

AUTHORSHIP: compiled by Prince Toneri Shinnou, O no Yasumaro

DATE: compiled 720 C.E.

LOCALE: Japan

RELATED CIVILIZATION: Japan

SIGNIFICANCE: The *Nihon shoki* presents the mythological origin of the Japanese and a chronology of the imperial line, starting with Jimmu, the first emperor of Japan, and ending with the Empress Jitō (686-697 C.E.).

The *Nihon shoki* (nee-HOHN SHOH-kee; *Nihongi: Chronicles of Japan from the Earliest Times to* A.D. *697,* 1896) was a thirty-volume set of books, written in Chinese by the principal compiler, Prince Toneri Shinnou, with the help of O no Yasumaro. The emperor Temmu (r. 672-686) commissioned the work, along with the *Kojiki* (712 C.E.; *Records of Ancient Matters,* 1883), to justify the existence and power of the imperial line. The *Nihon shoki* begins with a story of the creation of the world and links this "time of the gods" to the reign of the first emperor, Jimmu (beginning in 660 B.C.E. according to legend). It claims a divine origin for the emperor, thus providing a rationale for the political authority that the imperial line had retained throughout Japanese history.

Although modern scholars regard much of the *Nihon shoki* as a mythical history, it is the first of six official Japanese histories compiled by imperial order before 887 C.E. The ancient myths and legends in the first part of the work were important resources for the Shintō religion. Later volumes recorded the history of the imperial family and powerful Japanese clans, describing historical events such as meetings between the Japanese and Koreans and the introduction of Buddhism. The *Nihon shoki* and the earlier *Kojiki*, also written in Chinese and with similar content, present valuable information about the early Japanese and their culture. The *Nihon shoki* has been reissued many times. Some of these volumes were *Shoku Nihonji* (797 C.E.) and *Shoku Nihon Kouki* (869 C.E.).

ADDITIONAL RESOURCES

Allan, Tony, Michael Kerrigan, and Tony Phillips. *Realm of the Sun*. Alexandria, Va.: Time/Life Books, 1999.

Davis, F. Hadland, and Evelyn Paul. *Myths and Legends of Japan*. Mineola, N.Y.: Dover, 1992.

Tyler, Rayall, and Robert Boynton. *Japanese Tales*. New York: Pantheon, 1989.

SEE ALSO: Japan; Jimmu Tennō; Shintō; Yamato court.

—*Annita Marie Ward*

NILO-SAHARANS

DATE: beginning 9000-5000 B.C.E.
LOCALE: Central and eastern Africa
SIGNIFICANCE: The Nilo-Saharans created a form of agriculture that they brought into eastern Africa.

Nilo-Saharan peoples invented and spread a distinctive kind of agriculture across the vast Sudan belt of Africa between 9000 and 5000 B.C.E. and also brought that agriculture southward after 3500 into eastern Africa. They were also among the creators of the earliest great states of the African continent. Their modern-day descendants include many well-known societies, from the Maasai of East Africa to the Songay people of Mali in West Africa.

In the ninth millennium B.C.E., two major groupings of people emerged among the ancient Nilo-Saharans. The Northern Sudanians, residing in the southeastern Sahara—then a region of sparse grassland and steppes—were the initiators of the earliest indigenous African agriculture, Sudanic agriculture. Between 9000 and 7500 B.C.E., they participated, along with their eastern neighbors, the Cushitic Afrasan peoples, in domesticating the African variety of wild cattle. Then, around 7500 B.C.E., the Northern Sudanians began to domesticate several indigenous wild plants, most notably cotton and sorghum, both of which came to have worldwide importance. Until about 6500 B.C.E., however, they pursued their agricultural activities in only a few areas.

Through most of the rest of the southern Sahara, a different set of Nilo-Saharan peoples, belonging to the Aquatic tradition, predominated from 9000 to 6500 B.C.E. Along the then numerous rivers and lakes of the region, they pursued a water-based way of life, hunting hippos, fishing extensively, and gathering plant foods. First developed around 9000 B.C.E., the Aquatic livelihood spread rapidly across Africa from the bend of the Niger and the Hoggar Mountains in the west to as far east as the Nile River and Lake Turkana. For more than two thousand years, the Aquatic way of life prospered.

However, beginning around 6500 B.C.E., there ensued a one-thousand-year period of drier climate in which the rivers and lakes shrank, cutting into the food supplies of the Aquatic communities. Taking advantage of this shift of fortune, the Northern Sudanian farmers expanded far and wide across the southern Sahara, absorbing the Aquatic peoples into new societies. From 5500 B.C.E. onward, farming and cattle raising became the dominant means of livelihood all across the regions now called the Sudan and Sahel belts of Africa.

The Nilo-Saharan peoples developed the earliest version of monotheism known. From around the eighth millennium B.C.E., they came to believe in a single Divinity that undergirded existence. The Nilo-Saharan names for this belief are translated with the word "Divinity" rather than "god," because the early Nilo-Saharans understood Divinity as more of a single force or condition of spirit than a discrete being. They symbolized Divinity's power with celestial imagery, associating Divinity especially with rain and lightning. The Northern Sudanians, it is believed, spread this new belief during their periods of agricultural expansion.

Some of the early Nilo-Saharans also developed a potent and long-lived political ideology called Sudanic sacral chiefship. In this ideology, chiefs were deeply sacred persons, and their everyday human functions, such as eating, were hidden from the view of everyone. In several regions, this kind of chiefship evolved fairly soon into a sacral kingship, with the kings ruling over very small kingdoms. Along the middle Nile River, this level of rule arose no later than the fourth millennium B.C.E. In the Air Mountains region of the south-central Sahara, the archaeological evidence places its appearance in the third millennium B.C.E. Along with the rise of sacral kingship came a new custom, the killing and the burying of servants with a dead king, so that they could serve the king in the afterlife as they had in this world.

The ideas of Sudanic sacral kingship had a deep and lasting influence on the development of state institutions in the Sudan and Sahara of Africa. The Kerma kingdom (c. 2400-1570 B.C.E.) along the Nubian stretches of the Nile built its power on this basis, as did the much later kingdoms of Nobatia and Alwa (Alodia), before they adopted Christianity in the sixth century C.E. The fa-

mous later West African empire of Wagadu (c. 300-1200 C.E.), also called Ghana, was founded on these ideas. The Kanem and Borno empires of the central Sudan (800-1900 C.E.) had a Sudanic sacral basis. Most notably, the ancient Egyptians adopted key elements of this same political ideology in their earliest states. Until the Third Dynasty of the Old Kingdom, they followed the very Sudanic practice of burying servants along with the dead pharaohs. Both then and later, the pharaohs, unlike the kings of the nearby ancient Middle East, claimed the sacred status of gods themselves.

ADDITIONAL RESOURCES

Bender, M. L. *Topics in Nilo-Saharan Linguistics*. Hamburg, Germany: Buske, 1989.
Ehret, Christopher. "Nilo-Saharans and the Saharo-Sudanese Neolithic." In *Archaeology of Africa*, edited by Thurston Shaw, Paul Sinclair, Bassey Andah, and Alex Okpoko. New York: Routledge, 1993.

SEE ALSO: Afrasans; Africa, East and South; Alwa; Christianity; Divinity; Ghana; Kerma; Egypt, Pharaonic; Nobatae.

—*Christopher Ehret*

NILOTES

DATE: beginning c. 4000 B.C.E.
LOCALE: East-central Africa in what is now southern Sudan, northern Uganda, and western Kenya
SIGNIFICANCE: Nilotic population movements brought agriculture to the southern Middle Nile Basin and affected the culture and economy of East Africa.

The Nilotes are a widespread grouping of peoples, who have long been key players in the history of the eastern Sudanic regions of Africa and in the northern parts of East Africa. Their early population movements established agriculture all across the southern Middle Nile Basin. After 1000 B.C.E., their expansions farther south reshaped the culture and economy of large parts of East Africa.

The ancestral Nilotic society of around 4000 B.C.E. formed one of the then numerous Nilo-Saharan farming populations of the Sudan belt and southern Sahara. Their lands lay in the open plains east of the White Nile and west of the Blue Nile. They raised cattle, sheep, and goats and cultivated several crops, including sorghum, bulrush millet, and gourds.

A major African rainfall shift in the third millennium B.C.E., from wetter climates to climates much like those of modern times, cleared the way for the first great expansions of Nilotes into new lands to the south. A huge area of formerly inundated country in the southern Middle Nile Basin slowly dried out, gradually opening a vast expanse of new grazing land for the Nilotes' cattle. Between 2500 and 1500 B.C.E., one group, the Western Nilotes, moved directly into those newly opened areas. The Southern and Eastern Nilotes passed still farther south, taking up lands near and just north of the present-day borders of Uganda.

The Western Nilotes encountered a distantly related Nilo-Saharan people, the Koman, who still practiced the old, highly productive Aquatic tradition of gathering and hunting. Absorbing the Koman into their society, the Nilotes evolved a new mixed economy, combining both extensive cattle raising and extensive fishing. It remained a highly successful way of life until modern times.

The Southern Nilotes, in contrast, settled in the later second millennium B.C.E. in the plains southwest of the southern Ethiopian highlands. There they came under strong influences from Cushitic peoples, adopting from them age-grade institutions. In age-grade systems, men pass through a series of life stages ("age grades"), along with other men of their age cohort. Each such grade plays a different role, assigned by established custom, in the governance of the society. Because the age grades recruit men from a large number of local communities, they have the potential to bring thousands of people together in one politically cooperating set of communities. Between 800 B.C.E. and 700 C.E., the Southern Nilotes, because of this advantage in the size of their political groupings, were able to spread farther south into large areas of modern-day central and western Kenya and northern Tanzania, bringing their strong cattle-raising economy with them.

The Western and Eastern Nilotes have additional historical significance. Between 1500 and 1000 B.C.E.,

in the areas between Lake Chad and the southern Nile River, certain as yet unidentified African peoples independently invented ironworking. Between 1000 B.C.E. and 100 C.E. the Western and Eastern Nilotes became important intermediaries in the farther eastward spread of this technology to the neighboring peoples.

ADDITIONAL RESOURCES

Butt, Audrey. *The Nilotes of the Anglo-Egyptian Sudan and Uganda.* London: International Africa Institute, 1970.

Vossen, Rainer. *The Eastern Nilotes.* Berlin: D. Rainer, 1982.

SEE ALSO: Afrasans; Africa, East and South; Nilo-Saharans.

—Christopher Ehret

NINE SAINTS

ALSO KNOWN AS: Tesseatou Kidoussan
DATE: fifth century C.E.
LOCALE: Axum
SIGNIFICANCE: The arrival of the Nine Saints in Axum is symbolic of the divisions in the church under the Byzantine Empire over the nature of Christ.

Throughout the fifth and sixth centuries C.E., theological quarrels that revolved around the nature of Christ as both divine and human created an environment of violence and persecution. Some Christian adherents believed that Jesus Christ had two separate natures. The Monophysites, however, theorized that Christ had one nature that was simultaneously divine and human.

When Pope Leo I declared in an official letter that Christ had two natures, the Monophysite adherents, monks known as the Nine Saints, fled Rome and sought refuge in the eastern kingdom, Axum, which upheld the Monophysite doctrine. Pope Leo's letter was written circa 451 C.E. The arrival of the Nine Saints in Axum took place between 460 and 497 C.E. based on the history *Tarike Nequest.* This document refers to the arrival of the Nine Saints in the reign of Ella Amida IV (r. 475-486 C.E.).

During their residence in Axum, the Nine Saints expanded monastic laws and consolidated the power of

the church. With the assistance of local monks in campaigns of conversion, Christianity spread to new converts among the Beja and Amhara in this era. Support from the political elite helped put in place institutional structures (convents, monasteries, and churches) that supplanted the shrines of local cults throughout Axum and neighboring territories.

ADDITIONAL RESOURCES

Connah, Graham. *African Civilizations: Precolonial Cities and States in Tropical Africa, an Archaeological Perspective.* Reprint. Cambridge, England: Cambridge University Press, 1994.

Hable Selassie, Sergew. *Ancient and Medieval Ethiopian History to 1270.* Addis Ababa: United Printers, 1972.

Meouria, Tekle Tsadik. "Christian Aksum." In *Ancient Civilizations of Africa*, edited by G. Mokhtar. UNESCO General History of Africa 2. Los Angeles: UNESCO, 1981.

SEE ALSO: Africa, East and South; Axum; Beja; Byzantine Empire; Christianity; Ethiopia; Leo I the Great, Pope and Saint.

—Catherine Cymone Fourshey

NINTOKU

BORN: 375 C.E.?; place unknown
DIED: 427 C.E.; place unknown
RELATED CIVILIZATION: Japan
MAJOR ROLE/POSITION: Sixteenth emperor of Japan

Life. Nintoku's father was Ōjin Tennō, the fifteenth emperor of Japan. Although most of what is known about him is based on information found in the *Nihon shoki* (compiled 720 C.E.; *Nihongi: Chronicles of Japan from the Earliest Times to* A.D. *697*, 1896), which is a mixture of myth and history, he is generally regarded as a historical rather than a mythical ruler. According to the *Nihon shoki*, Ōjin Tennō had two sons, Princes Nintoku and Uji. Ōjin wanted Uji to succeed him on the Japanese throne. However, upon Ōjin's death, Uji tried to get Nintoku to become emperor. Nintoku refused, saying that he did not want to fail to respect their dead father's wishes. For three years, the two brothers argued about who would be emperor. Finally, Prince Uji, realizing that his brother would not do as he wanted, killed himself so that Nintoku would have to assume the throne. Upon his brother's death, Nintoku became very distraught, so Uji had to return to life to give his brother comfort and encouragement. Having done that, he died again, and Nintoku became the emperor.

When Nintoku died, in 427 C.E., he was entombed in the largest burial mound (*kofun*) ever built in Japan. Nintoku's tumulus, located in Sakai City in Ōsaka Prefecture, took thousands of workers nearly twenty years to complete. It is some 531 yards (486 meters) long, 333 yards (305 meters) wide, and 38 yards (35 meters) high and was completed in 443 C.E. (The date of completion of the tomb and whether it is Nintoku's have been the subject of debate.) There are three moats around it. More than 11,000 *haniwa* (terra-cotta figures) were on and around Nintoku's tumulus. In the late nineteenth century, a section of the mound slid away, revealing a stone coffin, gold-plated armor, and a sword.

Influence. Throughout history, Nintoku was revered by the Japanese people because he had clarified the role and duty of the Japanese emperor. According to the *Nihon shoki*, after surveying his kingdom from the top of a mountain, Nintoku noted a lack of smoke rising from the rooftops, which meant that his people had no food to cook. To remedy the situation, he abolished forced labor. After three years, prosperity returned to Japan. When Emperor Nintoku again climbed to the top of the mountain, he saw smoke rising and realized that his people had prospered. In a conversation with the empress, he noted his happiness, which she wondered at, considering that their own home had fallen into disrepair. Nintoku explained that the true job of an emperor was to make sure that his people prospered. If the people were prosperous and happy, then so was the emperor; likewise, if the people were poor, then so was the emperor.

ADDITIONAL RESOURCES

Allan, Tony, Michael Kerrigan, and Charles Phillips. *Realm of the Sun*. Alexandria, Va.: Time/Life Books, 1999.

Davis, F. Hadland, and Evelyn Paul. *Myths and Legends of Japan*. Mineola, N.Y.: Dover, 1992.

Tyler, Rayall, and Robert Boynton. *Japanese Tales*. New York: Pantheon, 1989.

Zona, Guy A. *Even Without Trees Give Prosperity to the Mountains: And Other Proverbs of Japan*. New York: Touchstone Books/Simon and Schuster, 1996.

SEE ALSO: Japan; Kofun period; *Nihon shoki*; Ōjin Tennō; Yamato court.

—Annita Marie Ward

NOBATAE

ALSO KNOWN AS: Nobadae
DATE: 500-700 C.E.
LOCALE: Nubian region of the Upper Nile (present-day Republic of Sudan), northeast Africa
RELATED CIVILIZATIONS: Noba, Blemmye
SIGNIFICANCE: The Nobatae were successors to the kingdom of Meroe in Nubia.

The once-powerful kingdom of Meroe began to decline as competition for Roman trade gradually increased with the rival kingdom of Axum in northern Ethiopia. Nomadic people from the west, the Nobatae (nuh-bah-TAH-ay), had gradually moved into the region. They may have been related to a southern tribal society known as the Noba. From the eastern desert came the

Blemmyes (Beja), who had been persistently raiding Roman garrisons in Nubia. Together, the Nobatae and the Blemmyes formed what archaeologists call the Ballana culture, named after the site of an important royal cemetery.

These two Nubian peoples were often at war with one another. For a period in the fifth century C.E., the Nobatae and the Blemmyes found a common cause against attempts by a Christian Egypt to suppress the cult of Isis and convert their temples to churches. However, under the leadership of King Silko, the Nobatae eventually claimed victory over the Blemmye people in the sixth century C.E. A carved representation of Silko on the walls of the temple of Kalabsha shows him being crowned with a headdress bearing Egyptian symbols. Similar crowns unearthed in royal burial sites suggest that the Ballana people still adhered to some of the ancient traditions of Meroe. The architectural traditions of the region had changed, however, and large mound graves, or tumuli, had replaced the pyramid tombs of Meroitic rulers.

The tumuli at Ballana and Qustul, on opposite sides of the Nile near Faras, consist of enormous earthen domes, some measuring more than 200 feet (60 meters) in diameter. The principal royal figure in each tumulus wore an elaborate silver crown and was placed on a wooden bed surrounded by weapons, jewelry, cooking utensils, silver and bronze vessels, and furniture. Within the many brick chambers of the tombs were the bodies of sacrificed soldiers, horses and their grooms, camels, sheep, donkeys, and dogs. Trade with Roman Egypt is evidenced by the number of imported objects such as bronze lamps, glassware, and pottery found in the graves. Although large-scale sculpture was absent by this time, examples of silversmithing, leatherwork, and ivory-inlay work testify to the skills of the local artisans.

By the sixth century C.E., Nubia had become three distinct kingdoms, with the territory of the Nobatae emerging as the kingdom of Nobatia. To its south lay the kingdoms of Makouria and Alwa. Nubia formally adopted Christianity in 543 C.E. with the conversion of the king of Nobatia. Sometime between 650 and 710 C.E., Makouria and Nobatia were united.

ADDITIONAL RESOURCES

Adams, William L. *Nubia: Corridor to Africa*. London: Penguin Books, 1977.

Africa in Antiquity: The Arts of Ancient Nubia and the Sudan. New York: The Brooklyn Museum, 1978.

Taylor, John. *Egypt and Nubia*. London: British Museum Press, 1991.

Trigger, Bruce G. *History and Settlement in Lower Nubia*. New Haven, Conn.: Yale University Press, 1965.

SEE ALSO: Africa, East and South; Axum; Beja; Christianity; Egypt, Ptolemaic and Roman; Napata and Meroe.

—Craig E. Lloyd

NOK CULTURE

DATE: 500 B.C.E.-200 C.E.
LOCALE: Central/North Nigeria, West Africa
RELATED CIVILIZATION: West Africa
SIGNIFICANCE: This culture developed an iron technology and produced highly figurative terra-cotta sculpture before the arrival of either Arabs or Europeans.

The earliest known ironworking community in West Africa is that of the Nok culture, named after a village on the Jos Plateau of northern Nigeria. Field research indicates that the Nok people were farmers who grew crops including grain and oil-bearing seeds. During open-cast tin-mining operations in the 1930's, a number of finely constructed terra-cotta figures as well as iron and stone implements were uncovered. These figures are remarkable for the sensitivity of the sculptors' crafting, which records details of facial expression, hairstyle, and ornamentation. Bodies are often adorned with rings, bracelets, necklaces, anklets, waistbands, and garters.

Though primarily found in broken sections, some of the Nok terra-cotta pieces would have originally formed standing figures measuring about four feet (slightly more than one meter) in height. The attitude of many of the figures indicates that they were made for religious purposes, much like sculpture found in Nigeria in more modern times. Some of the figures are kneeling or genuflecting. The unique and expressive faces on several of the heads suggest that they may have commemorated ancestors much in the way sculptures have been used in many parts of West Africa as recently as the twentieth century. Examples of animal subjects have also been uncovered. Excavations at Taruga, a second site occupied by the same people, have produced remains of iron-smelting furnaces. Slag and the ceramic nozzles used in the smelters for conducting air from bellows to the flames inside have been found.

ADDITIONAL RESOURCES

Connah, Graham. *African Civilizations: Precolonial Cities and States in Africa, an Archaeological Perspective*. Cambridge, England: Cambridge University Press, 1987.

Davidson, Basil. *Africa: History of a Continent*. New York: Macmillan, 1972.

Fagg, Bernard. *Nok Terracottas*. London: Ethnographica, 1990.

SEE ALSO: Africa, West.

—*Craig E. Lloyd*

NONNUS OF PANOPOLIS

ALSO KNOWN AS: Nonnos
BORN: c. 400 C.E.; probably Panopolis (later Akhmīm), Egypt
DIED: c. 470 C.E.; perhaps Alexandria, Egypt
RELATED CIVILIZATIONS: Imperial Rome, Byzantine Empire, Roman Egypt
MAJOR ROLE/POSITION: Poet

Life. Aside from his connection with Panopolis and his approximate dates, nothing is known of the life of Nonnus of Panopolis (NAHN-uhs of puh-NAH-puh-lihs), beyond the fact that he was a prolific poet.

Nonnus's *Dionysiaca* (n.d.; English translation, 1959), an epic poem in forty-eight books, deals with the exploits of Dionysus, god of wine. In this archaizing poem, Nonnus uses the same dactylic hexameter meter as Homer, along with some of Homer's vocabulary and formulas.

Nonnus also wrote *Metaphrasis Evangelii Joannis* (n.d.; *Paraphrase of John*, 1881) in dactylic hexameter. Although it adds various ornamental details, the *Paraphrase of John*, approximately 3,750 lines in length,

fairly accurately reflects the gist of Saint John the Evangelist's gospel.

Influence. Nonnus occupies an important transitional position in literary history, in view of his two narrative poems, one pagan and one Christian. In "Exiles," the modern Greek poet Constantine P. Cavafy includes an imaginative reconstruction of Nonnus as an author who was read and admired at Alexandria in the ninth century C.E.

ADDITIONAL RESOURCES

Hopkinson, Neil, ed. *Studies in the Dionysiaca of Nonnus*. Cambridge, England: Cambridge Philological Society, 1994.

Nonnos. *Dionysiaca*. Translated by W. H. D. Rouse. 3 vols. Rev. ed. Cambridge, Mass.: Harvard University Press, 1984.

SEE ALSO: Byzantine Empire; Egypt, Ptolemaic and Roman; Homer; John the Evangelist, Saint; Rome, Imperial.

—*Edwin D. Floyd*

NORTHERN WEI DYNASTY

ALSO KNOWN AS: Bei Wei
DATE: 386-533 C.E.
LOCALE: North China
RELATED CIVILIZATION: China
SIGNIFICANCE: The rulers of the Northern Wei Dynasty were a nomadic people who adopted Chinese ways in order to rule their empire most effectively.

The Northern Wei (way) Dynasty, the most powerful of northern Chinese dynasties before the reunification of China under the Sui and Tang Dynasties, was founded by Toba tribesmen whose ancestry can be traced to the Xiongnu, a proto-Mongol, or proto-Turkish people. In the late fourth century C.E., the Toba invaded the weak north China states. They named their kingdom Wei after they took over Shanxi Province, and by 439 C.E., they had unified all of north China.

Although the Wei had enormous military power, their nomadic culture was too primitive to prepare them to rule the empire. Partly because of that and partly because they were attracted to the more advanced Chinese culture, the Wei actively pursued a policy of adopting Chinese ways and customs. They relied on Chinese civil servants to administer the agricultural areas, adopted Chinese-style clothing and customs, and made Chinese the official language of the court.

Although the policy of adopting Chinese customs helped the Wei stabilize their regime and develop the economy, it alienated the military from their rulers. The military, composed of tribesmen, still adhered to their nomadic culture. When they were pushed beyond their endurance by the sinicization policy, they rebelled, and in 534 C.E., the Northern Wei toppled. The greatest cultural contribution of the Wei was in Buddhist art.

ADDITIONAL RESOURCES
Fairbank, John. *China: A New History.* Cambridge, Mass.: Belknap Press of Harvard University Press, 1992.
Gernet, Jacques. *A History of Chinese Civilization.* Translated by J. R. Foster and Charles Hartman. New York: Cambridge University Press, 1996.

SEE ALSO: China; Sui Dynasty; Tang Dynasty; Xiongnu.

—*Yiwei Zheng*

NORTON TRADITION

DATE: 500 B.C.E.-700 C.E.
LOCALE: Subarctic North America
RELATED CIVILIZATIONS: Choris culture, Ipiutak culture
SIGNIFICANCE: This widespread tradition shows a high degree of sophistication despite the harsh conditions of the subarctic environment.

The Norton tradition reached from Bristol Bay and the Alaska peninsula, north along the Bering Sea and east all the way to Greenland, and south to the north Pacific coast. It consisted of the Choris, Norton, and Ipiutak cultures. It persisted from 3000 B.C.E. to 1200 C.E. and was well established by 500 B.C.E. It was followed by the cultures that make up the Thule tradition, ancestral to the Ipiutak, whose remains are found at an excavation in the Point Hope area of Alaska, consisting of hundreds of underground houses and a cemetery in which lavish burials were performed. The dig yielded intricate ivory carvings that suggest origins in Siberia. Flaked stone artifacts indicate origins in the Arctic Small Tool tradition, which appeared around 4000 B.C.E., also called the Denbigh Flint complex. The tools are named after another site on Norton Sound.

Norton culture proper can be dated from 2500 B.C.E. to about 1000 C.E. around the Bering Sea. It continued south to the Pacific coast by 600 C.E. and was superseded by the Ipiutak culture. The Norton tradition was ancestral to the Yupik culture as well. The Ipiutak culture lasted from 100 to 700 C.E., and the Yupik began as early as 100 B.C.E. and continued into the present, although neither spread as far to the south.

Possible earlier cultures, also of the Thule tradition, the Okvik and Old Bering Sea, were found all across the Bering Strait, back to coastal Siberia, possibly even originating in the Scythian tradition of Asia. However, authorities differ, and some feel these cultures could have evolved from the Norton, though this view is supported mostly by conjecture. The groups of this tradition differed somewhat in the styles evident in their artifacts, cultural uses and practices in varied environments, evidence of pottery, and whether they depended primarily on hunting, fishing, or a combination of both in shaping their culture.

ADDITIONAL RESOURCES
Dixon, E. James. *Quest for the Origins of the First Americans.* Albuquerque: University of New Mexico Press, 1994.
Giddings, James Louis. *The Archaeology of Cape Denbigh.* Providence, R.I.: Brown University Press, 1964.

SEE ALSO: Ipiutak; Subarctic peoples.

—*Michael W. Simpson*

NUBIA

ALSO KNOWN AS: Kush; Napata

DATE: c. 8000-700 B.C.E.

LOCALE: Nile Valley, south of Egypt to the confluence of the Blue and White Nile Rivers, about 560 miles (900 kilometers) from north to south, west of the Red Sea, east of the Libyan desert

RELATED CIVILIZATIONS: Egypt, Greece, Persian Empire

SIGNIFICANCE: Nubia was a corridor for trade and cultural exchange. Through it flowed Egyptian products and knowledge in textiles, ceramics, metallurgy, weaponry, technology, and agriculture as well as gold and exotic valuables from continental Africa.

The name "Nubia" dates only from the third century C.E. Before that, Nubia was known as the land of Yam, Kush, or Ethiopia. The Old Kingdom (2686-2125 B.C.E.) Egyptians used the name "Wawat" for the river valley between the First and Second Cataracts and "Yam" for the lands beyond, known as "Kush" to the Egyptians from the Middle Kingdom (2055-1650 B.C.E.) onward and also to the Assyrians and the Old Testament, in which the term sometimes included parts of southern Arabia. The Greeks called Nubia "Ethiopia," the land of the Aethiopes, or burnt faces.

Lower Nubia was Wawat, administered from Aniba in the New Kingdom (1550-1069 B.C.E.). Upper Nubia became virtually everything south of the Second Cataract to the Blue and White Nile Rivers, dominated by an imposing Gebel Barkal, or Holy Mount, below the Fourth Cataract, where Napata developed. Lower Nubia had almost no arable land and Upper Nubia not much, but there were rich deposits of iron, good grazing land for cattle, sheep, and goats, and gold in the Nubian desert to the east. The western desert of Upper Nubia in the southern bend of the river is named Bayuda.

Early Nubia. The Lower Nubian Paleolithic period probably drew to a robust and culturally diverse close about 8000 B.C.E., followed by a hesitant and lingering terminal Paleolithic period until about 5000 B.C.E., some five hundred years later than in Upper Egypt. During this period, the Nile cut faster and deeper, and the valley took on something of its present size and climate and continued the gradual, inexorable desiccation of the previous era.

The Badarian culture of Upper Egypt, with its superlative thin red-and-black pottery, reed-matting-lined graves, and rectangular stone palettes, with all its prob-

able links to Mesopotamia and dynastic Egypt, still is not attested with certainty anywhere in Nubia, though some paleoarchaeologists assume a Badarian stage, or phase, in Lower Nubia and beyond. However, since just before World War I, when archaeologist George Andrew Reisner of Harvard University and the Boston Museum of Fine Arts first compared some fifty-eight Nubian cemeteries with those of Sir Flinders Petrie's predynastic Egypt, there has been no such hesitancy in matching up the subsequent Egyptian and Nubian Amratians (Petrie's Naqada I) with sites as far south as the Lower Nubian Khor-Bahan, nor with the Gerzeans (Naqada II), with all their advances, including gold and faience (earthenware with opaque colored glazes as decoration). Reisner called his parallels the Nubian Early and Middle Predynastics and their people the A-Group (Ta-Seti), while noting that Lower Nubia began to lag behind Egypt in the later prehistoric period. Archaeologist C. M. Firth, who built on Reisner's work, assumed that Lower Nubia's primitive, egalitarian society came to an end only under the impact of Egypt in the late Gerzean or early protodynastic period. In 1927, Firth dated his earliest "chiefly" grave to this period. Similarly, there is no evidence of advanced society in Upper Nubia before the Egyptians brought it there in the New Kingdom (1550-1069 B.C.E.).

Early dynasties. Nubia was a land of raiders and trade from the time of Aha, the first pharaoh of the First Dynasty (c. 3000-2686 B.C.E.). His successor Djer left his name on a battle scene at Wadi Halfa below the Second Cataract. By the end of the Second Dynasty (2890-2686 B.C.E.), Khasekhemwy, the last king of Abydos and the first builder of hard-stone monuments had led an army southward to found colonies and fortify trading posts, including Buhen near Djer's battle scene.

The Palermo stone describes 7,000 captives and 200,000 cattle that Pharaoh Snefru won from the Nubians at the beginning of the Fourth Dynasty (2613-2494 B.C.E.). He may also have begun copper smelting near Wadi Halfa, which may have continued through the Fifth Dynasty (2494-2345 B.C.E.). His son Khufu (Cheops) extracted diorite from a stone quarry northwest of Toshka. The Sixth Dynasty (2345-2181 B.C.E.) may have seen the first Nubian mercenaries in the Egyptian army. In the Nineteenth Dynasty, Rameses II was still using these mercenaries all over the empire. The Sixth Dynasty may also have seen the first Egyptian trading post above the Third Cataract, at Kerma, and the Weni narrative (third millennium B.C.E.; English translation in *Rank and Title in the Old Kingdom*, 1960) of the Sixth Dynasty alludes to at least five different tribes of Nubians.

In the time of Pepy II and throughout the First Intermediate period (2160-2055 B.C.E.), a new population, probably not black, known as the C-Group, seem to have taken possession of Wawat and perhaps even some of Upper Egypt. By the end of the period, there was probably a powerful chieftain, or king. The Egyptians began to call the south Kush and derived virtually all their gold from there.

Middle Kingdom and Intermediate period. The Middle Kingdom (2055-1650 B.C.E.) probably began with significant help from Nubian mercenaries. Toward the end of the Eleventh Dynasty (2055-1985 B.C.E.), Montuhotep I used them and so did the vizier of Montuhotep III. The first king of the Twelfth Dynasty (1986-1773 B.C.E.), Amenemhet I, who built on the southern connections of his Elephantine mother, subjugated Lower Nubia and founded the fortress of Semna beyond the Second Cataract, one of a series of great southern fortresses in which to station his Nubian troops. There were at least thirteen forts and depots between Syene and Semna alone, standing guard between the rich Upper Nubian trade and the dangerous Upper Nubian raiders. His son Sesostris I may have fortified the garrison of Buhen at Wadi Halfa. Conquest, fortification, commerce, and the Egyptianization of Nubia grew apace, reaching a zenith, perhaps, in the annexation of Lower Nubia by Sesostris III, who came to be worshiped as a god by the Nubians. He boasts of a southern frontier at the Second Cataract rather than the First and probably appointed a third vizier for the far south.

At the end of the Middle Kingdom or early in the Second Intermediate period (1650-1550 B.C.E.), while the Hyksos kings descended on the north, native kings captured, or recaptured, Kerma at the Third Cataract, where Amenemhet I had built and Amenemhet III had refurbished a great brick garrison and residence. There they indulged themselves with luxury Egyptian imports while creating native ceramics and other industrial endeavors and burying themselves in un-Egyptian barbaric splendor, sometimes with numerous human sacrifices of their own retainers, dominating not only their own country but also some of Upper Egypt, to judge from Kamose of Egypt's complaints at Thebes, until the consolidation of the New Kingdom (1550-1069 B.C.E.).

New Kingdom. In the Seventeenth Dynasty (c. 1580-1550 B.C.E.), Kamose used the Medjay Nubians, identical, perhaps, with the archaeologists' Pan-Grave people, against the Hyksos Asiatics. He may well have brought the south to book with a viceroy of Nubia before descending on the Hyksos, but he refers to a newly but firmly ensconced "chieftain of Kush," perhaps from Kerma, with ties to the Asiatics, who implored their Kushite correspondent to march northward against Kamose. Kamose's successor Ahmose I, founder of the Eighteenth Dynasty (1550-1295 B.C.E.) and the New Kingdom, crushed the last of the Nubians in Upper Egypt and marched against those in the south. His son and successor Amenhotep I reconquered Lower Nubia and colonized it. He may even have captured its king and appointed the first known "king's son of Kush," a title roughly analogous to the prince of Wales, though it did not necessarily signify royal birth or even the viceregency of Nubia.

Thutmose I tightened his grip on Nubia in the late sixteenth century B.C.E., especially on the Second, Third, and Fourth Cataracts, and draped a Nubian chieftain's body round the prow of his ship on the way home from one of his expeditions. Napata may well have begun as one of his outposts. The great warrior Thutmose III, who usually gets the credit for Napata about 1450 B.C.E., bettered the exploits of his predecessors in the south, where he not only commemorated some four hundred place names and built or improved at least six temples, but also redecorated that of Sesostris III at Semna in honour of the Nubian god Dedwen, perhaps for the Medjay Nubians he had campaigned with in Palestine.

Napata and Meroe. Napata's lowly beginnings are mysterious, but its future was assured, first as a crossroads of desert trade routes and an outpost of Egyptian control on the Nile to the Fifth Cataract during the New Kingdom, culminating, perhaps, in Rameses II's great Nineteenth Dynasty (1295-1186 B.C.E.) temples and statuary at Derr and Abu Simbel. Afterward, it became an increasingly native administrative capital of Egyptianized Kush and later a great religious center for the worship and priesthood of Amun-Re. Early in the fifteenth century B.C.E., blacks appear on the monuments of Thutmose III. By the end of that century, in the time of Amenhotep II, Napata was already important enough for the king to hang one of seven conquered princes on its walls as the southernmost frontier-city of Egypt. In the mid-fourteenth century B.C.E., Napata probably was not Akhenaton's Nubian City of the Sun,

Gem-Aten, which was somewhere near the Third Cataract, but at the end of that century, Tutankhamen still marked it as the boundary of Huy, his Lower Nubian viceroy at Aniba. In the middle of the thirteenth century B.C.E., the great pharaoh Rameses II built the southernmost of his five great Nubian mortuary temples there.

Napata's Egyptianized, Amun-Re-oriented, hybrid culture may well have developed more or less untrammeled after the collapse of the New Kingdom because of its religion and relative isolation. Ultimately Theban Amun-priest refugees seem to have shaped the virile religious and cultural conviction driving the kings of the Twenty-fifth or Ethiopian Dynasty (747-656 B.C.E.). By the middle of the eighth century B.C.E., King Kashta and his son the great warrior Piye were using Napata as their capital. They also seem to have made Meroe (a promising village of crops and cattle and iron deposits in the fork of the Nile and Atbara between the Fifth and Sixth Cataracts) into a second, southern city of Kush. Piye first conquered much of degenerate Egypt from Napata and then retired there, leaving his younger brother Shabaka to reconquer the whole and make himself pharaoh of Egypt in Thebes, perhaps in the year 711 B.C.E. By the time of the accession of Taharqa in 689 B.C.E., the Ethiopian dynasty's days were numbered, for all its anti-Assyrian intrigues with the Phoenicians and Israelites.

Esarhaddon drove Taharqa from Memphis, which he retook after the Assyrian died in 669 B.C.E., only to be driven out anew by Ashurbanipal in his first campaign. After Ashurbanipal went back to Nineveh, Tanutamun, the last king of the Twenty-fifth Dynasty, succeeded Taharqa and reoccupied Memphis, only to give way up the Nile before Ashurbanipal's second descent. Tanutamun abandoned Memphis, then Thebes, then Egypt. Like Piye before him, he retired to Napata, and the Ethiopians had to content themselves with Upper Nubia and develop the more defensible Meroe to the southeast as a refuge. They governed first from Napata until its destruction by the nationalist Egyptian king Psamtik II with his Greek and Carian mercenaries about 590 B.C.E., then from their new capital of Meroe, perhaps in the reign of their king Aspelta, even if Napata retained a great religious and economic significance.

ADDITIONAL RESOURCES

Adams, William L. *Nubia: Corridor to Africa.* London: Penguin, 1978.

Burstein, Stanley M., ed. *Ancient African Civilizations: Kush and Axum.* Princeton, N.J.: Markus Wiener, 1998.

Gardiner, Sir Alan. *Egypt of the Pharaohs.* London: Oxford University Press, 1961.

Harris, J. R., ed. *The Legacy of Egypt.* Oxford, England: Oxford University Press, 1971.

Taylor, John. *Egypt and Nubia.* London: The British Museum Press, 1991.

SEE ALSO: Akhenaton; Ashurbanipal; Assyria; Egypt, Prepharaonic; Esarhaddon; Ethiopia; Kerma; Napata and Meroe; Rameses II; Sesostris III; Shabaka; Snefru; Taharqa; Thutmose III; Tutankhamen; Wawat; Yam.

—*O. Kimball Armayor*

— O —

OCTAVIA

ALSO KNOWN AS: Octavia Minor
BORN: 69 B.C.E.; place unknown
DIED: 11 B.C.E.; Rome
RELATED CIVILIZATIONS: Republican and Imperial Rome
MAJOR ROLE/POSITION: Political figure

Life. Octavia was the daughter of the equestrian Gaius Octavius, praetor and governor of Macedonia, and Atia, the daughter of Julius Caesar's sister, Julia. Octavia's brother was Octavian (later Augustus), the first emperor of Rome. A woman of remarkable beauty and honored for her moral character, she was married first to Gaius Claudius Marcellus, consul in 50 B.C.E. Soon after Marcellus died in 40 B.C.E., Octavia was married to Marc Antony, to cement the Pact of Brundisium by which Antony surrendered Gaul to Octavian. The marriage at first was an amicable one. In 37 B.C.E., Octavia assisted in negotiating the Pact of Tarentum, by which Octavian and Antony reestablished their alliance. When Antony departed from Italy in 36 B.C.E. for the Parthian War, Octavia returned to Rome, where she stayed even when he returned to Rome's eastern provinces. Their relationship subsequently deteriorated. When Octavian sent her east with reinforcements for Antony's army, Antony forbade her to go beyond Athens. She rejected Octavian's advice to divorce Antony, but Antony divorced her in 32 B.C.E. After the divorce, she brought up with true affection all the children Antony had with his earlier wife Fulvia and with Cleopatra VII, queen of Egypt; their own two daughters; and her three children by Marcellus.

Influence. Augustus adopted her son, Marcus Claudius Marcellus, as his heir. Through her two daughters by Antony, Octavia became the grandmother of the emperors Caligula and Nero. Sometime after 27 B.C.E., to honor her, Octavian built the Porticus Octavia, which housed a famous collection of statues and paintings. Next to it, Octavian built a library in memory of her son, Marcellus, who died in 23 B.C.E.

ADDITIONAL RESOURCES
Dixon, Suzanne. *The Roman Mother.* Norman: University of Oklahoma Press, 1988.
Fantham, Elaine, et al. *Women in the Classical World.* Oxford, England: Oxford University Press, 1994.
Gardner, Jane F. *Women in Roman Law and Society.* Bloomington: Indiana University Press, 1991.
Kleiner, Diana E., and Susan B. Matheson, eds. *I, Claudia: Women in Ancient Rome.* New Haven, Conn.: Yale University Art Gallery, 1996.
Lefkowitz, Mary, and Maureen B. Fant. *Women's Life in Greece and Rome.* Baltimore: Johns Hopkins University Press, 1982.
Wood, Susan. *Imperial Women: A Study in Public Images 40 B.C.-A.D. 68.* Leiden: Brill, 1999.

SEE ALSO: Antony, Marc; Augustus; Caligula; Cleopatra VII; Nero; Parthia; Rome, Imperial; Rome, Republican.

—Judith Lynn Sebesta

ODOACER

ALSO KNOWN AS: Odovacar; Odovacer; Odovakar
BORN: c. 435 C.E.; place unknown
DIED: March 15, 493 C.E.; Ravenna, Italy
RELATED CIVILIZATION: Imperial Rome
MAJOR ROLE/POSITION: Adventurer, administrator

Life. The father of Odoacer (oh-doh-AY-sehr) seems to have been a Hun and his mother perhaps a Scirian, although Odoacer also is referred to as a Goth or a Rugian. He apparently is the Adovacrius who in the mid-460's C.E. led a band of Saxons in an attack on Angers in Gaul. By the early 470's C.E., he was in Roman service in Italy, where he became a member of the imperial bodyguard. In 476 C.E., he was proclaimed *rex*, or king, by the barbarian soldiers in Italy after their requests for land had been refused. Odoacer then deposed the young usurper Romulus Augustulus (r. 475-476 C.E.) and notified the Eastern emperor Zeno (r. 474-491 C.E.) that the West no longer needed an emperor of its own and that he, Odoacer, would be content to rule Italy in Zeno's name in the capacity of patrician. These terms were granted. In 489 C.E., Italy was invaded by Ostrogoth Theoderic the Great. After being besieged in Ravenna for three years, Odoacer finally surrendered in 493 C.E. on condition that the two would rule Italy jointly. Soon thereafter, however, he and his family were murdered by Theoderic.

Influence. Odovacar serves as an example par excellence of barbarian adventurers who successfully pursued their careers in the midst of the decay of the Western Roman Empire, which he was responsible for bringing to an end.

ADDITIONAL RESOURCES

Jones, Arnold H. M. "The Constitutional Position of Odoacer and Theoderic." *Journal of Roman Studies* 52 (1962); 126-130.

Moorhead, John. "Theoderic, Zeno, and Odovacer." *Byzantinische Zeitschrift* 77 (1984): 261-266.

SEE ALSO: Goths, Ostrogoths, Visigoths; Rome, Imperial; Romulus Augustulus; Theoderic the Great.

—*Ralph W. Mathisen*

ŌJIN TENNŌ

ALSO KNOWN AS: Honda Wake no Mikoto; Monuta; Homuda

BORN: late fourth century C.E.; place unknown

DIED: early fifth century C.E.; place unknown

RELATED CIVILIZATION: Japan

MAJOR ROLE/POSITION: Emperor

Life. Japanese tradition lists Ōjin as the fifteenth emperor of Japan and dates his reign to 270-310 C.E. Ōjin is said to have been born in 201 C.E. as the fourth son of the legendary emperor Chūai and empress Jingū. His personal name is Honda Wake no Mikoto, and he is also known as Monuta or Homuda.

Unlike some of his imperial predecessors, he is probably a historical rather than a mythic ruler. It is likely, however, that he reigned in the late fourth or early fifth century C.E. and is one of the five kings of Wa (Japan) who frequently sent ambassadors to China and are recorded in Chinese histories. He is associated with the establishment of the hereditary groups known as *amabe* (fishermen) and *yamabe* (hunters). He may have authorized a successful military campaign to expand imperial control into Kyūshū. His reign was probably

marked by significant immigration and importation from Korea. The most enduring Korean/Chinese introductions of this period were Buddhism and the Chinese writing system.

Ōjin's burial place may be in Habikino, Ōsaka Prefecture. This tomb, the second largest burial mound (*kofun*) of the Kofun period, is known as the Konda Gohyoyama Kofun or Emperor Ōjin's tomb. The largest is that of his traditional successor, Nintoku.

Influence. Ōjin is worshiped as Hachiman, the Shintō god of war.

ADDITIONAL RESOURCES

Aoki, Michiko Yamaguchi. *Ancient Myths and Early History of Japan.* New York: Exposition Press, 1974.

Brown, Delmer, ed. *Ancient Japan.* Vol. 1 in *The Cambridge History of Japan.* Cambridge, England: Cambridge University Press, 1988.

SEE ALSO: Japan; Kofun period; Nintoku; Shintō; Yamato court.

—*Thomas J. Sienkewicz*

OLD COPPER COMPLEX

DATE: 4000-1000 B.C.E.
LOCALE: Western Great Lakes, North America
RELATED CIVILIZATIONS: Archaic tradition, Lake Forest Archaic, Laurentian Archaic, Shield Archaic, Red Ocher complex, and Glacial Kame culture
SIGNIFICANCE: This series of Archaic hunter-gatherer cultures produced some of the oldest copper artifacts in North America.

The first human inhabitants arrived in the western Great Lakes during the end of the Pleistocene Epoch (last Ice Age) approximately 11,500 years ago. As glaciers receded north, new territories were opened up for habitation. Small groups of extended hunter-gatherer families began to settle into regional territories within this new landscape as early as 6500 B.C.E. Archaeologists refer to these post-Ice Age hunter-gatherer cultures collectively as the Archaic tradition. These cultures made a living by exploiting a wide variety of terrestrial game, migratory waterfowl, fish, and plants. The Archaic tradition lasted from 6500 to 1000 B.C.E. in the Great Lakes.

Great Lakes Archaic Indians were the first peoples in North America to experiment with metal fabrication technologies. Nearly pure native copper was discovered in the Lake Superior Basin in vein and nugget forms. Archaic peoples hot- and cold-hammered, ground, and polished the copper to produce a variety of projectile points, woodworking tools, harpoons, fishhooks, and pieces of jewelry. Many of these tools were used in addition to stone and bone tools for everyday subsistence activities; however, some copper goods were traded to cultures outside the region to obtain exotic materials such as marine shell and exotic chert.

The term Old Copper complex has been applied by archaeologists to the cultures that manufactured these ancient tools. From radiocarbon-dated materials recovered in close association with these copper artifacts, it is known that the Old Copper complex dates to between 3,000 and 6,000 years ago (4000-1000 B.C.E.). Most of the archaeological evidence has been recovered from mortuary sites and surface finds in Wisconsin, the Upper Peninsula of Michigan, and Ontario.

ADDITIONAL RESOURCES

Birmingham, Robert A., Carol I. Mason, and James B. Stoltman, eds. "Wisconsin Archaeology." *The Wisconsin Archaeologist* 78, nos. 1/2 (1999).

Halsey, John R., ed. *Retrieving Michigan's Buried Past: The Archaeology of the Great Lakes State.* Bulletin 64. Bloomfield Hills, Mich.: Cranbrook Institute of Science, 1999.

Martin, Susan R. *Wonderful Power: The Story of Ancient Copper Working in the Lake Superior Basin.* Detroit, Mich.: Wayne State University Press, 1999.

Martin, Susan R., and Thomas C. Pleger. "The Complex Formerly Known as a Culture: The Taxonomic Puzzle of 'Old Copper.'" In *Taming the Taxonomy: Toward a New Understanding of Great Lakes Archaeology,* edited by Ronald F. Williamson and Christopher M. Watts. Toronto: Eastend Books and the Ontario Archaeological Society, 1999.

Pleger, Thomas C. "Old Copper and Red Ocher Social Complexity." *Midcontinental Journal of Archaeology* 25, no. 2 (2000): 169-190.

SEE ALSO: Archaic North American culture; Archaic tradition, northern.

—Thomas C. Pleger

OLMECS

DATE: c. 1200-400 B.C.E.
LOCALE: Southern Gulf coast of Mexico
RELATED CIVILIZATIONS: Maya, Zapotec, Teotihuacán
SIGNIFICANCE: The Olmec culture, Mesoamerica's "mother culture," established the basic pattern for later high cultures in the region.

The Olmec heartland or core area extended along Mexico's southeastern Gulf coast lowlands, a humid and hot tropical environment abounding with lush vegetation and streams. The identity and origins of this early people are unknown. Olmec, a name applied by modern archaeologists, is a term from the Nahuatl language spoken by the Aztecs and other later peoples; it roughly

The Olmecs carved massive heads from volcanic basalt, the meaning and purpose of which are not known. (PhotoDisc)

translates "Rubber People" in reference to a product naturally found in this area.

History. During the time archaeologists denote as Early Formative (1500-900 B.C.E.), increased agricultural productivity in Mesoamerica gave rise to permanent villages whose inhabitants cultivated basic staples such as maize, beans, and squash. The Olmecs, however, were noticeably more advanced than the contemporary small village and farming cultures of this era. The fertile lowlands of southern Veracruz and Tabasco were rich enough to allow specialization in nonfarming activities such as the arts and commerce. It is believed that struggles for control of the area's limited but rich farmland gave rise to the dominant landowning class that shaped Mesoamerica's first high culture.

Olmec civilization initially flourished at the site of San Lorenzo Tenochtitlán in southern Veracruz province from 1200 to 900 B.C.E. Some radiocarbon dating indicates a presence as early as 1500 B.C.E., and early Olmec settlers may have inhabited the area even before this time. However, most of the site's monuments that distinguish this civilization date from the mid-1100's B.C.E. Another important Olmec center, La Venta, in

Tabasco province, functioned between 800-400 B.C.E. These Olmec sites were not true cities but impressive political and religious centers run by an elite of religious specialists and ruling families. Artisans and farmers also figured among their inhabitants. Monumental structures, such as huge platforms 3,000 feet (914 meters) long, 1,000 feet (305 meters) wide, and reaching heights of 150 feet (46 meters), as well as pyramids, altars, and tombs, indicate that these centers served as gathering places for religious rituals and burial sites for the leadership.

At San Lorenzo, elaborate drainage systems and hydraulic works were constructed from joined sections of U-shaped carved stones covered with capstones. These constructions served as aqueducts that channeled water into sacred and decorative pools and created fresh streams running throughout the complex for drinking and bathing. Some flow was also diverted for waste runoff. The scope of massive labor-intensive projects at these sites suggests the existence of Mesoamerica's first political state, which exercised strong governmental control and direction over the farming populace.

After 800 B.C.E., Olmec stylistic influence over the region waned, and the civilization ceased to be the cultural leader, although some centers continued to exist. By 300 B.C.E. the culture had disappeared. Nevertheless, other regional civilizations such as the Maya, Totonac, and Zapotec flourished during the Late Formative and Classic periods (300 B.C.E.-900 C.E.) and represented distinctive variations of a shared Olmec heritage.

Architecture and art. Most of what is known about this ancient culture derives from its monumental works and artistry. Skilled Olmec craftspeople and laborers, among the first to use stone in architecture and sculpture, produced impressive works from volcanic basalt, stone, and jade. Some monuments carved from basalt weigh as much as 44 tons (40 metric tons). The nearest source of this stone is located 50 to 60 miles (80 to 97 kilometers) to the northwest of San Lorenzo in the Tuxtla Mountains. Olmec specialists speculate that the massive boulders were dragged to one of the nearest navigable rivers and transported on large rafts to the vicinity of the ceremonial site.

The most striking and common stone carvings are colossal heads. The largest of these realistic portraits, believed to represent rulers, are about nine feet (three meters) in height and weigh close to twenty tons (eighteen metric tons). The lips are full, the noses are broad and flat, and the faces are flat and broad. Each is wearing headgear resembling a football helmet, which many believe to be part of the gear worn by ballplayers.

Calendars and chronology. Olmec intellectual and scientific achievements predate those of the Maya, who were once thought to have originated the most advanced features of Mesoamerican high cultures. In 1939, the archaeologist Matthew W. Stirling discovered an Olmec stela, or marker, at the Tres Zapotes site, containing numerals based on a bar-and-dot system. Stirling deciphered a date corresponding to the Maya calendar as 31 B.C.E.; this is more than a century before dated Maya inscriptions appear. The finding indicated to archaeologists that the famous Maya long-count system of dating, based on counting time from a specific starting date, may be an Olmec invention.

Religion and ritual. A very common theme in Olmec drawings and stone carvings is the figure of the were-jaguar, a half-animal and half-human figure with baby features and curved, snarling lips. The Olmecs believed themselves to be descended from the jaguar, an animal revered as sacred. This suggests that Olmec religion employed shamanistic practices whereby sha-

mans or curers were believed to have the power to transform their shapes into animal form and communicate with the spirit world.

Sports and entertainment. In part because of the colossal carved heads of rulers wearing ballplayers' gear, many experts believe that the popular and widespread Mesoamerican game that featured a solid rubber ball and opponents attired with protective gear originated with this culture located near the source of rubber. Rubber balls still giving off a strong smell of latex, as well as carved figurines representing ballplayers, have been excavated at Olmec sites. Archaeologists at La Venta have discovered what might be the remains of a ball court and speculated that these structures were also present at other Olmec centers.

Trade and commerce. Masters at carving in stone and jade, the Olmecs produced many fine and exquisite works of art, such as small figurines, ceremonial masks, jewelry, and burial items. Between 1100 and 800 B.C.E., the Olmecs developed an extensive trading network that spread their influence and led to cultural interaction with other parts of Mesoamerica. The aim was to secure access to valuable products and control the luxury trade in items such obsidian, green jade, and iron. Obsidian, imported from the Guatemala highlands, was used in making blades, flakes, and dart points. Iron ore was polished to make mirrors that could be pierced and worn around the neck. Serpentine and fine stones were needed for jewelry manufacture. Jade was highly prized, and the color green may have been considered sacred. Fine human and animal figures and axe heads were fashioned from jade.

To control trade routes and ensure the flow of goods to centers such as San Lorenzo, the Olmecs established trading stations garrisoned by troops. These sites, located in areas such as Puebla, the Valley of Mexico, and Morelos, were strategically located at the ends of valleys near or on major mountain passes. The largest of these sites is Chalcatzingo in Morelos, where an Olmec religious center was built. Huge boulders in the area display Olmec reliefs in the La Venta style. Olmec ceramics and figurines are found in burial sites at several places in the Valley of Mexico and Morelos. The Olmec presence also spread west into the provinces of Guerrero and Colima near the Pacific coast. Guerrero is the site of a spectacular cave painting depicting a characteristic Olmec figure and located almost a mile from the entrance. The southern highlands of Oaxaca and areas as far south as Guatemala and El Salvador also contain evidence of this early culture.

Writing systems. The Olmecs had an early form of hieroglyphic writing similar to that of the more complex and elaborate system the Maya later developed. Experts have identified 182 symbols with specific meanings. However, this script remains undeciphered and was probably in an early stage of development when the civilization declined.

Current views. Although Olmec artifacts were found as early as 1862, it was nearly a century before the scientific community discerned and recognized their distinct qualities and importance to Mesoamerican cultural development. Scholars now consider the Olmec culture to be perhaps the first great civilization of ancient North America.

It appears that the Olmecs contributed a number of features to the basic cultural pattern of later Mesoamerican cultures. In the area of religion, this culture revered a number of deities that are important in the later established Mesoamerican pantheon such as the fire god, rain god, corn god, and famous Feathered Serpent. Olmec religious practices also apparently included ritual warfare with mutilation of captives and some human sacrifice. Moreover, the ceremonial center of La Venta was built on an axial pattern of alignment that influenced urban development in Mesoamerica for many centuries to come.

ADDITIONAL RESOURCES

Coe, Michael. *America's First Civilization*. New York: American Heritage, 1968.

Luckert, Karl W. *Olmec Religion: A Key to Middle America and Beyond*. Norman: University of Oklahoma Press, 1976.

Piña Chan, Román. *The Olmec: Mother Culture of Mesoamerica*. New York: Rizzoli, 1989.

Soustelle, Jacques. *The Olmecs: The Oldest Civilization in Mexico*. Norman: University of Oklahoma Press, 1985.

Stuart, George S. "New Light on the Olmec." *National Geographic* 184, no. 5 (November, 1993): 88-115.

SEE ALSO: Ball game, Mesoamerican; Maya; Teotihuacán; Zapotecs.

—David A. Crain

OLYMPIAS

BORN: c. 375 B.C.E.; Epirus
DIED: 316 B.C.E.; Macedonia
RELATED CIVILIZATIONS: Classical and Hellenistic Greece
MAJOR ROLE/POSITION: Queen-mother

Life. Olympias, daughter of Neoptolemus of Epirus, married Philip II of Macedonia in 357 B.C.E. and in 356 B.C.E. gave birth to the future Alexander III (later the Great). Although only one of Philip's seven wives, Olympias enjoyed importance at the Macedonian court because she was the mother of the heir-apparent. When Philip married for the seventh time, in 337 B.C.E., Olympias seems to have resented the new bride and may have plotted with Alexander against Philip, who was assassinated in 336 B.C.E. Any thoughts she may have had of ruling Greece when Alexander left for Persia in 334 B.C.E. were dashed when he appointed Antipater as regent. In 331 B.C.E., Olympias returned to Epirus, where she exercised great power and continued to intervene in Greek affairs. On Alexander's death in 323 B.C.E., she opposed Antipater and then his son Cassander, siding with Polyperchon and returning to Macedonia in 318 B.C.E. At that time, she executed (among others) Philip III and his wife, Eurydice, and set up her grandson, Alexander IV, as king. Despite her great power as Alexander the Great's mother, Cassander defeated her, and she was put to death in 316 B.C.E.

Influence. Olympias was the mother of Alexander the Great, whose vast conquests as far east as India laid the foundations for the Hellenistic kingdoms.

ADDITIONAL RESOURCES

Errington, R. Malcolm. *A History of Macedonia*. Berkeley: University of California Press, 1990.

Green, Peter. *Alexander to Actium: The Historical Evolution of the Hellenistic Age*. Reprint. Berkeley: University of California Press, 1993.

Habicht, Christian. *Athens from Alexander to Antony*. Translated by Deborah Lucas Schneider. Cambridge, Mass.: Harvard University Press, 1999.

SEE ALSO: Alexander the Great; Antipater; Cassander; Greece, Classical; Greece, Hellenistic and Roman; Macedonia; Philip II.

—Ian Worthington

Olympic Games

Date: 776 B.C.E.-393 C.E.

Locale: Olympia, in the region of Ellis, Greece

Related civilizations: Archaic, Classical, Hellenistic, and Roman Greece

Significance: One of four Panhellenic (all-Greek) games, the quadrennial Olympic Games helped to provide unity in a country otherwise isolated into competing city-states.

Although it is unknown whether the Olympic Games actually began in 776 B.C.E., winners of each Olympic Festival were recorded from that year until 217 C.E. by the chronographer Eusebius of Caesarea. The festival provided an occasion for the disparate Greek city-states to celebrate their shared language, religion, and culture. Political disputes were suspended during all four Panhellenic athletic competitions, including the Olympic Games and Nemean Games honoring Zeus, the Pythian Games honoring Apollo, and the Isthmian Games dedicated to Poseidon at Corinth. The Olympic Games were the most prestigious and were held once every four years at the first full Moon after the summer solstice. The four-year period between Olympic Festivals was known as an Olympiad and could be used as a means of calculating dates.

Competition at these games was considered an act of worship as well as an athletic event. The poet Pindar often celebrated the physical achievement of these athletes in a religious or mythological context. City-states often supplemented the official prize (a wreath of olive leaves) with monetary awards so large that victors were rich for the rest of their lives.

Only free men (and, after 632 B.C.E., boys) whose native language was Greek were allowed to compete. In the Roman period, this restriction was waived for the Romans. Slaves and all women, except for the local priestess of Demeter, were forbidden from entering the sacred area while the Games were in progress. Those violating this prohibition were hurled to their deaths from the Typaeon Rock. The earliest events at Olympia appear to have been footraces, wrestling, and throwing events. As early as the seventh century B.C.E., races for chariots and individual horses occurred. It was always the owner of the horse, not its rider, who was awarded the victory.

From 472 B.C.E. onward, events at the Olympic Games were expanded to include horse races, the discus throw, the javelin throw, boxing, the pentathlon ("five contests": jumping, wrestling, the javelin, the discus, and running), and the *pankration* (a type of "no-holds-barred" wrestling). Contestants had to train for a minimum of ten months before their competition. For the last thirty days before the festival, athletes resided in a special gymnasium at Olympia itself, where they ran and threw the javelin or discus under the supervision of the Hellenodicae, a board of ten men who also served as referees during the Games themselves.

In 393 C.E., the Roman emperor Theodosius the Great, a Christian, ended all pagan athletic games in Greece.

Pentathlon

The pentathlon was held at the Olympic Games as well as at other ancient Greek games. According to Simonides, it consisted of five separate events: a running race about 180-200 yards (165-183 meters), a javelin throw, discus toss, long jump, and wrestling match. A pentathlete would claim overall victory if he won in three events. Training and competing were accompanied by music. The decathlon, a ten-event competition in the modern Olympics, includes some of the same events as the ancient pentathlon.

Additional resources

Drees, Ludwig. *Olympia: Gods, Artists, and Athletes.* New York: Praeger, 1968.

Golden, Mark. *Sport and Society in Ancient Greece.* New York: Cambridge University Press, 1998.

Schipper, Henry, producer. *Blood and Honor at the First Olympics.* Video. New York: Greystone Communications for A&E Network, 1996.

See also: Eusebius of Caesarea; Greece, Archaic; Greece, Classical; Greece, Hellenistic and Roman; Olympic shrine and Olympic Games; Pindar; Sports and entertainment; Theodosius the Great.

—*Thomas J. Sienkewicz*

OMOTIC PEOPLES

DATE: beginning c. 6000 B.C.E.
LOCALE: Northeastern Africa
SIGNIFICANCE: Contributed in prominent ways to the origins of agriculture and to the rise of early states in northeastern Africa.

The communities of the Omotic peoples of Ethiopia first took on historical importance in around the sixth millennium B.C.E. because of their independent invention of a distinctive agriculture. They based their agriculture on the cultivation of the *enset* and several other plants indigenous to the Ethiopian highlands. A plant outwardly resembling the banana, *enset* has an unappetizing fruit but an edible inner stem and bulb. From 5000 to 2000 B.C.E., the Omotic peoples expanded over a considerable portion of the highlands, carrying their agricultural practices along with them.

Between 2000 and 1 B.C.E., Omotic peoples living along the Ethiopian Rift Valley entered into a long period of close relations with Cushitic cattle raisers and grain cultivators. Out of these interactions, societies of mixed Omotic and Cushitic cultural heritage emerged. More important, these mixed communities brought into being major new developments in agricultural technology. They built stone-walled, terraced fields on the slopes of the Rift Valley, constructed irrigation works to water the fields, and used cattle manure to ensure their fields' fertility. They raised both grain crops and *enset* as staple foods.

Late in the period, in the highlands west of the Rift Valley, some Omotic peoples began to found small kingdoms, modifying an earlier position of clan ritual chief into that of a king with powerful ritual functions. Between about 100 and 700 C.E., these political ideas took hold in parts of the Rift Valley as well. By this period, trade with the Red Sea began to provide a material basis sufficient to support several larger, though still modest-sized kingdoms along and west of the Rift. Kingdoms of this Omotic type remained important into much later times, and some of their symbols and regalia were adopted by the medieval Christian Ethiopian kingdom in the thirteenth century C.E.

ADDITIONAL RESOURCES

Bander, M. Lionel. *Omotic*. Carbondale: University Museum, Southern Illinois University Press, 1975.
Hayward, R. J. *Omotic Language Studies*. London: School of Oriental and African Studies, 1990.

SEE ALSO: Afrasans; Africa, East and South; Africa, North; Cushites; Ethiopia; Rift Valley system.
—*Christopher Ehret*

ORIBASIUS

ALSO KNOWN AS: Oribase; Oreibasios; Oribasius of Pergamum
BORN: 325 C.E.; Pergamum, Turkey
DIED: c. 403 C.E.; place unknown
RELATED CIVILIZATIONS: Roman Greece, Imperial Rome
MAJOR ROLE/POSITION: Physician, medical encyclopedist

Life. Oribasius (ahr-eh-BAY-zhuhs) was born of an important family, probably studied medicine in Alexandria, Egypt, and had four children, including the physician Eustathius. He was personal physician to the Roman emperor Julian the Apostate and served during Julian's reign as quaestor in Constantinople. Banished after Julian's assassination, he was soon recalled because of his medical skill. He provided much information about Julian to the biographer Eunapius.

Oribasius was a prolific writer, but his works are compilations of the medical discoveries of other physicians, not reports of his own original work. Only twenty-two complete volumes and some fragments of his gigantic seventy-volume *Synagôgai iatrikai* (n.d., also known as *Collectiones medicae*; known in English as "Medical Collection") still exist. At Julian's suggestion, he prepared an abridged version, *Synopsis ad Eustathium* (n.d.; known in English as "The Synopsis"), which survives. Also extant is his pharmaceutical treatise, *Libri ad Eunapium* (n.d.).

Influence. If not for Oribasius, the contributions of many ancient medical authors, practitioners, and researchers would have been lost. He was frequently cited, republished, and anthologized during the Renaissance. In the sixteenth century, his surgical works were of particular importance. Guido Guidi translated them into Latin and commented on them (1544). Swiss physician Conrad Gesner excerpted them (1555).

ADDITIONAL RESOURCES

Allbutt, T. Clifford. *Greek Medicine in Rome*. London: Macmillan, 1921.
Grant, Mark. *Dieting for an Emperor: A Translation of Books 1 and 4 of Oribasius' Medical Compilations with an Introduction and Commentary*. Leiden, Netherlands: E. J. Brill, 1997.
Scarborough, John. *Roman Medicine*. London: Thames and Hudson, 1969.

SEE ALSO: Greece, Hellenistic and Roman; Julian the Apostate; Rome, Imperial; Science.

—Eric v.d. Luft

ORIGEN

BORN: c. 185 C.E.; Alexandria, Egypt
DIED: c. 254 C.E.; probably Tyre (modern Sur, Lebanon)
RELATED CIVILIZATIONS: Egypt, Imperial Rome
MAJOR ROLE/POSITION: Religious leader

Life. Born into a Christian family, Origen (AHR-eh-jehn) early engaged in the study of Scripture and theology. His father was martyred for his faith, and as Christians fled the persecution in Alexandria, Origen, at age eighteen, was left the head of a prestigious school. He quickly became an admired scholar and teacher. His ideas, however, caused controversy, and in 229 C.E., he was forced to leave Alexandria for Caesarea, in Palestine, where he remained until his death. He was arrested and tortured during the persecution of Christians under Emperor Decius. He was released in 251 C.E. but never recovered from the effects and died in 254.

Influence. Origen sought to show that Christian faith was compatible with human knowledge and understanding. To do so, he drew on Platonist philosophy and also developed the allegorical interpretation of Scriptures. He set forth his views in several works, including *Peri archōn* (220-230 C.E., also known as *De principiis*; *On First Principles*, 1936). He has had a profound influence on both Eastern and Western Christianity. He was one of the first people to propose a doctrine of universal salvation. He also believed in reincarnation.

ADDITIONAL RESOURCES

Butterworth, G. W., and Henry De Lubac. *Origen on First Principles*. Magnolia, Mass.: Smith, Peter, 1985.
Chadwick, Henry. *Early Christian Thought and Classical Tradition*. New York: Clarendon Press, 1984.
Crouzel, Henri. *Origen*. London: T and T Clark, 1999.
Greer, Rowan A. *Origen*. Mahwah, N.J.: Paulist Press, 1988.
Smith, John Clark. *The Ancient Wisdom of Origen*. Cranberry, N.J.: Bucknell University Press, 1992.

SEE ALSO: Christianity; Egypt; Gnosticism; Rome, Imperial.

—Charles L. Kammer III

ORPHISM

DATE: c. 500 B.C.E.-400 C.E.
LOCALE: The Greek-speaking world
RELATED CIVILIZATIONS: Classical and Hellenistic Greece
SIGNIFICANCE: An innovative movement within ancient polytheism, Orphism transformed the mystery religions.

Orphism (AWR-fih-zm) presented radical modifications of traditional Greek religion by granting authority to the mythical poet Orpheus and his reputed books; by professing the soul's immortality, its punishment for previous transgressions, and its reincarnation; and by requiring an ascetic vegetarian lifestyle that eschewed animal sacrifice. Starting from the earliest testimonia,

Orphism was inextricably conflated with Pythagoreanism and Bacchic mysteries.

In Orphic myth, Zeus mated with Demeter and then with their daughter Persephone to produce Dionysus or Zagreus. In a shocking development, the Titans dismembered, boiled, roasted, and ate the infant. However, Zeus blasted them with lightning, reconstituted his divine son, and created humanity from the soot. Thus mortals, sharing in both Dionysus's noble lineage and that of the troublesome Titanic brood, must pay penance to Persephone, queen of the dead.

Authors ranging from fifth century B.C.E. Athenians to Christian apologists resented the missionary zeal of Orphic initiators and presented biased descriptions. Scholars seriously doubt that the various rites and writings attributed to Orpheus from the sixth century B.C.E. to the fourth century C.E. and beyond represent a coherent movement. Archaeological finds from Olbia (1978) and Derveni (1982) have dramatically confirmed the relatively early presence of people called Orphics and cosmogonic Orphic texts.

ADDITIONAL RESOURCES

Alderink, L. J. *Creation and Salvation in Ancient Orphism*. Ann Arbor, Mich.: Scholars Press, 1981.

Guthrie, W. K. C. *Orpheus and Greek Religion*. Reprint. Princeton, N.J.: Princeton University Press, 1993.

Linforth, I. M. *The Arts of Orpheus*. Berkeley: University of California Press, 1941.

West, M. L. *The Orphic Poems*. Oxford, England: Clarendon Press, 1983.

SEE ALSO: Greece, Classical; Religion and ritual.

—*Jonathan Fenno*

OVID

ALSO KNOWN AS: Publius Ovidius Naso
BORN: March 20, 43 B.C.E.; Sulmo, Roman Empire (later Sulmona, Italy)
DIED: 17 C.E.; Tomis on the Black Sea, Moesia (later Constanţa, Romania)
RELATED CIVILIZATION: Imperial Rome
MAJOR ROLE/POSITION: Writer

Life. Ovid studied rhetoric in Rome, where his well established father wanted him to pursue politics. However, Ovid held only a few minor offices before abandoning public life for poetry. He impressed his cosmopolitan literary circle and the rest of Rome with his first publication, the witty *Amores* (c. 20 B.C.E.; English translation, 1597).

Next came the *Ars amatoria* (c. 2 B.C.E.; *Art of Love*, 1612), followed by the more original *Heroides* (before 8 C.E.; English translation, 1567) and *Remedia amoris* (before 8 C.E.; *Cure for Love*, 1600), both reprising the *Amores*'s erotic sophistication. In his forties, he started the *Fasti* (c. 8 C.E.; English translation, 1859), describing religious festivals, and masterfully wove 250 Greek and Roman myths together into the *Metamorphoses* (c. 8 C.E.; English translation, 1567).

Suddenly, in 8 C.E., Augustus exiled Ovid to Tomis, a Black Sea port (Constanţa, Romania), for what Ovid's

Ovid. (Kimberly Kurnizki)

poem *Tristia* (after 8 C.E.; *Sorrows*, 1859) calls a "mistake." Historians speculate that Ovid had unwittingly facilitated the adultery of Julia, the emperor's daughter. Additionally, Ovid's libertine persona defied Augustus's agenda for moral reform. In *Sorrow* and *Epistulae ex Ponto* (after 8 C.E.; *Letters from the Black Sea*, 1639), Ovid implored Augustus and then Tiberius, Augustus's successor, for a pardon—in vain.

Influence. Rome's second most popular poet after Vergil, Ovid was Christianized in the Middle Ages but made his deepest mark as a secular—even profane—poet. His immense influence on the troubadours, Jean de Meun, Petrarch, Geoffrey Chaucer, William Shakespeare, and others shaped medieval romance, courtly love, and Renaissance literature and drama.

ADDITIONAL RESOURCES

Mack, Sara. *Ovid*. New Haven, Conn.: Yale University Press, 1988.

Ovid. *Ovid in English*. Edited by Christopher Martin. New York: Penguin Books, 1998.

Wilkinson, L. P. *Ovid Surveyed*. Cambridge, England: Cambridge University Press, 1962.

SEE ALSO: Augustus; Rome, Imperial; Julia (daughter of Augustus); Tiberius; Vergil.

—Margaret Bozenna Goscilo

one years and then ascended to heaven. Legend has it that, seven days later, his remains fell from heaven to earth. People wanted to bury his remains together, but they were stopped by a huge snake. Consequently, the remains were buried at Five Tombs, also called the Snake Tombs, which are located at the Tamom Monastery.

Silla later conquered the other two kingdoms in the Three Kingdoms, Paekche in 660 C.E. and Koguryo in 668, thus unifying Korea.

ADDITIONAL RESOURCES

Banaschak, Peter. *Worthy Ancestors and Succession to the Throne: On the Office Ranks of the King's Ancestors in Early Silla Society.* New Brunswick, N.J.: Transaction, 1997.

Lee, Peter H. *From Early Times to the Sixteenth Century.* Vol. 1 in *Sourcebook of Korean Civilization.* New York: Columbia University Press, 1993.

SEE ALSO: Korea.

—*Chenyang Li*

PALENQUE

DATE: 400-800 C.E.
LOCALE: Chiapas, Mexico
RELATED CIVILIZATION: Maya
SIGNIFICANCE: In Palenque, one of the most important Classic Maya cities, King K'inich Janahb' Pakal was found buried in a vaulted tomb.

Palenque (pah-LEHN-kay) was small until King K'inich Janahb' Pakal assumed the throne in 615 C.E. and began an innovative building program that transformed the city into an imposing site. His most important building was the Temple of the Inscriptions, which contains pictorial and hieroglyphic carvings related to

his reign as well as his tomb and his sarcophagus, which has an elaborately carved lid showing him falling down into the Otherworld at the moment of his death.

Palenque was expanded by Pakal's son, K'inich Kan B'alam II, who is best known for building three distinctive temples called the Cross Group: the Temples of the Cross, Foliated Cross, and Sun. Inside each is a carved panel, showing Kan B'alam as a child and as an adult, which supported his legitimacy as ruler.

Later rulers continued to erect buildings and expanded the Great Palace, a multiroom residence with a unique four-story tower that may have been used as a watchtower and as a place for astronomical observance. The historical record ends at Palenque in the late eighth century C.E. Some of the longest hieroglyphic texts have been found at this site. Its buildings and carved monuments have provided significant information on Classic Maya history, religion, and dynastic rule.

ADDITIONAL RESOURCES

Coe, Michael D. *The Maya.* 6th ed. London: Thames and Hudson, 1999.

Schele, Linda, and Peter Mathews. *The Code of Kings: The Language of Seven Sacred Temples and Tombs.* New York: Scribner, 1998.

SEE ALSO: Maya.

—*Sandra L. Orellana*

The Temple of the Sun at Palenque, Chiapas, Mexico. (Corbis)

PALEO-INDIANS IN NORTH AMERICA

DATE: 11,500-8000 B.C.E.

LOCALE: North America

RELATED CIVILIZATIONS: Nenana, Clovis technological complex, Goshen, Folsom technological complex (Midland), Plainview (Milnesand), Agate Basin, Hell Gap, Cody (Scottsbluff and Firstview), Alberta, San Patrice, Dalton, Gainey, Cumberland, Barnes, Crowfield, Holcombe, Simpson, and Suwannee

SIGNIFICANCE: North American Paleo-Indians are the source of the first well-documented cultural traditions in North America.

Frank H. H. Roberts used "Paleo-Indian" in 1940 as a designation for artifact assemblages that appeared to be chronologically old on the basis of geology, fossils, or artifacts and for prehistoric cultures that were adapted to conditions unlike those prevailing in modern times. Today, "Paleo-Indian" is used to refer to the earliest well-documented cultures in the Americas, the characteristics of sites and artifact assemblages, and as a livelihood.

Paleo-Indian is the oldest unambiguous cultural tradition: It precedes all subsequent periods. Paleo-Indians adapted to a period of climatic oscillation, extremely fast environmental change, and global warming, and they explored virtually all types of topographic settings, from caves to mountainous terrain. Paleo-Indian sites have access to a high-quality stone source or an environmental magnet such as a spring, pond, or marsh, or they overlook a game crossing, stream, or confluence area. Base camps are located in areas that have access to multiple natural resources. Paleo-Indians procured high-quality chert, flint, rock crystal quartz, obsidian, quartzite, hematite, and other rock and mineral resources from a wide variety of geological situations.

Paleo-Indian settlement mobility was greater than that found among any modern hunter-gatherers. Paleo-Indian sites contain no evidence of formal houses and little refuse or features such as pits and fireplaces. Post molds and artifact distributions suggest that temporary shelters were built in a circular pattern. Paleo-Indian sites are small and scattered across the landscape. The low density of artifacts suggests that Paleo-Indian populations were sparse and scattered.

The discovery of Paleo-Indian sites on landscapes thought to have been environmentally stressful suggests a broad range of adaptive subsistence strategies. Basically, the diversity of sites and artifact assemblages from across North America demonstrates that Paleo-Indians were versatile hunter-gatherers capable of sustaining themselves in a number of ways, using whatever natural resources presented themselves.

Paleo-Indians narrowed their hunting preferences to large game animals, but their survival depended on a mixed foraging strategy that was extremely flexible and responsive to changes in ecological community structure. These changes included the extinction of large herbivores such as the mammoth, mastodon, ground sloth, horse, tapir, and camel. Paleo-Indian hunting most likely had a serious effect on species already in trouble. Ultimately, the impact of extinction on Paleo-Indian economies would have been highly variable and related to the diversity of the surviving plant and animal food resources and their response to climatic change.

Bifaces (stone tools with two faces, or edges) were the single most important Paleo-Indian utensil. They were used as weapons, knives, and a source of flakes that were recycled into myriad unifacial tools such as end scrapers, side scrapers, burins, gravers, and perforators. Use-wear studies show that plant fibers and animal skins were obtained and processed, possibly to make sacks, clothing, shelter, or traps. Bone, ivory, and stone beads were probably the most common ornament, but red ochre (hematite) was also extensively used. Red ochre was mined and commonly occurs in Paleo-Indian caches.

Paleo-Indians did not live in isolation. Contact between groups occupying neighboring areas would have been necessary to maintain an open exchange of information, raw material, and marriage partners. The only indication of Paleo-Indian trade is the presence of artifacts manufactured from exotic rocks and minerals. Although groups may have collected all their own local raw materials, the bulk of the exotic stone was probably obtained through exchange networks. Exotic stone artifacts are most common at base camps. Their presence suggests that intergroup contact and social interaction were confined to specific areas.

ADDITIONAL RESOURCES

Anderson, D. G., and K. E. Sassaman. *The Paleoindian and Early Archaic Southeast.* Tuscaloosa: University of Alabama Press, 1996.

Ellis, C., A. C. Goodyear, D. F. Morse, and K. B. Tankersley. "Archaeology of the Pleistocene-Holocene Transition in Eastern North America." *Quaternary International* 49/50 (1998): 151-166.

Frison, G. C. "Paleoindian Large Mammal Hunters on the Plains of North America." *Proceedings of the National Academy of Science* 95 (1998): 14576-14583.

_____. *Prehistoric Hunters of the High Plains*. 2d ed. San Diego, Calif.: Academic Press, 1991.

Tankersley, K. B. "Variation in the Early Paleoindian Economies of Late Pleistocene Eastern North America." *American Antiquity* 63 (1998): 7-20.

Tankersley, K. B., and B. L. Isaac. *Early Paleoindian Economies of Eastern North America*. Greenwich, Conn.: JAI Press, 1990.

SEE ALSO: Archaic North American culture; Clovis technological complex; Folsom technological complex.

—*Kenneth B. Tankersley*

PALEO-INDIANS IN SOUTH AMERICA

DATE: c. 14,000-7000 B.C.E.

LOCALE: South American continent

SIGNIFICANCE: The Paleo-Indians were the earliest inhabitants of the South American continent.

The term "Paleo-Indian" was originally coined by North American archaeologists working with early sites in the American Southwest in the 1920's. The archaeological culture said to represent this stage was called Clovis after an important site in New Mexico. Clovis, with its distinctive projectile points (subsequently radiocarbon-dated to c. 10,000-9000 B.C.E.), and "Paleo-Indian" remained synonymous for the next fifty years, and Clovis was believed to represent the earliest inhabitants of the Americas. However, new discoveries in both continents suggested that pre-Clovis archaeological cultures existed and that they were of substantial antiquity.

Although the controversy continues, it is generally accepted that the South American continent was occupied by pre-Clovis peoples no later than circa 14,000 B.C.E. The earliest widely accepted archaeological site dating to this period is Monte Verde, which is found in south-central Chile. Among the artifacts found here are narrow, lanceolate projectile points, fiber in the form of cords, carved wooden tent pegs, structures defined by logs, and grinding stones. The only other South American site with similar materials (projectile points) and acceptably early radiocarbon dates is Taima-Taima, in northern Venezuela, which is said to date circa 12,000-10,000 B.C.E. In addition to the points, the remains of a juvenile mastodon and stone artifacts were discovered. Although the data are sparse, the remains found from the sites indicate their inhabitants either killed or scavenged large animals and consumed plants such as the wild potato.

Sites with earlier dates, such as Pedra Furada in northeastern Brazil (c. 40,000-15,000 B.C.E.) and Pikimachay in the central Andean highlands (c. 18,000-13,000 B.C.E.), have been rejected by most archaeologists because of problems with excavation techniques and doubts about the likelihood that the artifacts found at them were in fact made or modified by humans. Similar doubts exist about an early component at Monte Verde (c. 30,000 B.C.E.), which is said to have crude pebble tools and purported hearths.

Although no classic Clovis sites have been found in South America, some archaeologists have speculated that certain projectile point forms, such as "fishtail" foliates found scattered across the continent from Venezuela to Tierra del Fuego, represent a derivative Clovis technological complex. Others have suggested these similarities are not caused by historical connections but instead by similarities in function.

Unfortunately, no human skeletal materials have been recovered from South American Paleo-Indian sites, and therefore, direct tests of the ancestry of these early peoples await new discoveries. However, data from North America strongly support an Asian origin for all New World peoples, although the number and source of early migrations are hotly debated.

ADDITIONAL RESOURCES

Dillehay, Tom D. *Monte Verde: A Late Pleistocene Settlement in Chile*. 2 vols. Washington, D.C.: Smithsonian Institution Press, 1989-1997.

Fiedel, S. "The Peopling of the New World: Present Evidence, New Theories, and Future Directions." *Journal of Archaeological Research* 8, no. 1 (2000): 39-103.

SEE ALSO: Archaic South American culture; Clovis technological complex; South America, southern; South American Intermediate Area.

—*Mark Aldenderfer*

PALERMO STONE

DATE: c. 2494-2345 B.C.E.
LOCALE: Egypt (exact origin unknown)
RELATED CIVILIZATIONS: Prepharaonic and Pharaonic Egypt
SIGNIFICANCE: The Palermo stone is an important source of chronology for the reigns of kings from prehistory to the Fifth Dynasty and of corresponding historic events.

The Palermo (pah-LEHR-moh) stone, housed in the Palermo Museum, Sicily, since 1877, is the principal fragment of a diorite slab containing hieroglyphic inscriptions that list the kings of Egypt from predynastic times to the Fifth Dynasty. The original slab was a freestanding oblong stele probably displayed in a temple and serving as official royal annals. This fragment provides valuable insight into the length of each king's reign, from Menes to Neferirkare, and the span of years covered by the first five dynasties.

Each side is divided horizontally into rows, or registers. The first row lists the predynastic kings by name only, with no additional information. The dynastic registers are further divided into compartments separated by vertical symbols meaning year. The name of the king presiding over each series of compartments is inscribed above each register. Hieroglyphics within each compartment record memorable events such as military victories, religious festivals, mining expeditions, erection of temples and palaces, building of ships, and the making of statues of kings and deities. The annual crest height of the Nile River is also noted. As the registers progress in time, the compartments become larger and list increasingly more accomplishments.

ADDITIONAL RESOURCES
Breasted, James Henry. *The First to the Seventeenth Dynasties.* Vol. 1 in *Ancient Records of Egypt: Historical Documents from the Earliest Times to the Persian Conquest.* Chicago: University of Chicago Press, 1906.
Gardiner, Sir Alan. *Egypt of the Pharoahs.* London: Oxford University Press, 1961.
Shaw, Ian, and Paul Nicholson. *Dictionary of Ancient Egypt.* New York: Harry Abrams, 1995.

SEE ALSO: Egypt, Pharaonic; Writing systems.

—*Barbara C. Beattie*

PALLADIUS, RUTILIUS TAURUS AEMILIANUS

BORN: c. 400? C.E.; place unknown
DIED: c. 460? C.E.; place unknown
RELATED CIVILIZATION: Imperial Rome
MAJOR ROLE/POSITION: Senator, author

Life. The "illustrious man" Rutilius Taurus Aemilianus Palladius (ruh-TIHL-ee-uhs TAWR-uhs ih-mihl-ee-AY-nuhs puh-LAY-dee-uhs), as he is named in his manuscripts, wrote a book on agriculture (c. mid-fifth century C.E.; *On Agriculture*, 1975). He probably is the Palladius, a young relative of the poet Rutilius Claudius Namatianus, who in 418 C.E. had come to Rome from Gaul to study law and was the son of Exsuperantius, praetorian prefect of Gaul in 424 C.E. Palladius's title of "illustrious" could suggest that he had held a high office, but no such Palladius can be found, so perhaps the title was honorary. He owned estates in Sardinia and Italy.

Palladius's handbook consists of fourteen chapters: an introduction, twelve chapters named after the months of the year, a poem, "On Grafting," and a final chapter, "On the Medicine of Herds." The introduction discusses basic agricultural practices, such as "on good water," "on the quality of land," "on the selection and location of fields," and "on winter and summer buildings." Although he drew material from previous agricultural writers such as Gargilius Martialis, Marcus Cetius Faventinus, Anatolius of Beirut, and, in particular, Columella, Palladius made much use of his own personal experience. His attempts to adhere to the dry and straightforward style of his models are complemented by a lively and varied manner of writing that reflect his rhetorical training.

Influence. Palladius was the last of a long line of ancient agricultural writers that ranged from Hesiod to Theophrastus, and from Cato the Censor and Marcus Terentius Varro to Columella and Gargilius Martialis. His work was popular in the Middle Ages, being greatly used, for example, by Albertus Magnus.

ADDITIONAL RESOURCES
Pommer, Hugh. *Vitruvius and Later Roman Building Manuals*. London: Cambridge University Press, 1996.
Rodgers, Robert Howard. *Introduction to Palladius*. London: London University Institute of Classical Studies, 1975.

SEE ALSO: Agriculture and animal husbandry; Cato the Censor; Columella; Hesiod; Rome, Imperial; Rutilius Claudius Namatianus; Theophrastus; Varro, Marcus Terentius.

—*Ralph W. Mathisen*

PALLAVA DYNASTY

DATE: c. 500-800 C.E.
LOCALE: India
RELATED CIVILIZATION: India
SIGNIFICANCE: This southeast Indian dynasty became prominent in southern India.

The Pallava (PAH-lah-vah) Dynasty flourished on south India's east coast between the Kisna and Penner Rivers, overlapping the modern Tamil Nādu in the south and southern Andhra Prakesh in the north and centering on the region surrounding the modern city Kanchipuram. Although of uncertain origin, the Pallavas did not speak a Dravidian language and all their records were kept in Prākrit, a simple form of Sanskrit. Classical Tamil literature of the Śaṅgam (or Caṅkam) age never refers to them, and local traditions speak of them as coming from the north.

The genealogy of the Pallavas is as disputed as their origins. They appear to have arisen out of indigenous Deccan tribes to the north, who moved into Andhra and then into Kanchi. Some sources identify a king Visnugopa who was defeated and then liberated the Gupta ruler Samudragupta (r. c. 330-c. 380 B.C.E.) in the middle of the fourth century C.E. A Pallava king Siṃhavarman is mentioned in the Sanskrit *Lokavibhāga* as reigning from 436 C.E. John Keay, in his history of India, charts a line from Pallavas from Siṃhavarman in the early fifth century C.E. to his son Visṇugopa to Siṃhavisṇu (r. c. 555-590), Mahendravarman I (r. c. 590-630), Narasiṃhavarman I (r. c. 630-688), Mahendravarman II (r. c. 660-670), Parameśvaravarman I (r. c. 670-700), Narasiṃhavarman II (r. c. 695-728), Parameśvaravarman II (r. c. 728-731), and finally Nandivarman (r. c. 731-796).

Socially and culturally, the Pallavas adapted Dravidian and Tamil ways. They were notable patrons of religion (Jainism, Buddhism, and Brahmanism), philosophy, Sanskrit literature, music, and arts. However, they were especially noted for their achievements in architecture, such as the Shore Temple, other temples carved from granite, and the Varaha cave at Mahabalipuram (Mamallapuram). They also encouraged overseas ventures and colonized areas of Hinterindia, Kamboja, Indonesia, Śrīvijaya, and Angkor.

In 740 C.E., the capture of Kanchi (Kanchipuram) by the contemporaneous kingdom of the Cālukyas to the northwest signaled the decline of the Pallava Dynasty. In 780 C.E., the Rāshtrakūtas broke their power and subjected the Pallavas to their rule. Around 900 C.E., the Pallava kingdom was annexed by the Cōḷas. Pallava princes continued as petty local chieftains until the thirteenth century.

ADDITIONAL RESOURCES
Keay, John. *India: A History*. New York: Atlantic Monthly Press, 2000.
Thaper, Romila. *A History of India*. Baltimore: Penguin Books, 1966.
Tinker, Hugh. *South Asia: A Short History*. New York: Praeger, 1966.

Walker, Benjamin. *Hindu World: An Encyclopedic Survey of Hinduism*. London: George Allen and Unwin, 1968.

SEE ALSO: Appar; Gupta emperors; India; Indian temple architecture; Mahendravarman I.

—Arthur W. Helweg

PANAETIUS OF RHODES

BORN: c. 185 B.C.E.; Lindus, Rhodes
DIED: 109 B.C.E.; Athens, Greece
RELATED CIVILIZATIONS: Hellenistic Greece, Republican Rome
MAJOR ROLE/POSITION: Stoic philosopher

Life. The son of Nicagoras, Panaetius (pah-NEE-shuhs) of Rhodes attended lectures in cosmopolitan Athens. There he became the student of Diogenes of Babylon, head of an important philosophical school, the Stoa. Eventually Panaetius journeyed to Rome and gained the friendship of Scipio Aemilianus, famed victor over Carthage in the Third Punic War (149-146 B.C.E.). Panaetius even accompanied Aemilianus on a celebrated embassy to the eastern Mediterranean, visiting Egypt, Rhodes, Pergamum, and Syria. Returning to the Stoa in 129 B.C.E., Panaetius spent the rest of his life serving as its head.

Influence. As teacher and philosopher, Panaetius was more concerned with practical morality than the ideal of the Stoic sage. Therefore, he helped to inaugurate the Middle Stoa, the second of three periods in the history of the school. He was influential beyond the school as well. Through friendship with Aemilianus, Panaetius inspired a contemporary generation of Roman nobles. Through his students, he affected numerous fields of study, and through his writings, which survive only in fragments, he swayed even the last generation of the Roman Republic, including the orator and statesman Cicero, who reveals his debt in *De officiis* (44 B.C.E.; *On Duties*, 1534).

ADDITIONAL RESOURCES

Dyck, Andrew A. *A Commentary on Cicero, "De Officiis."* Ann Arbor: University of Michigan Press, 1996.

Long, A. A. *Hellenistic Philosophy, Stoics, Epicureans, Sceptics*. 2d ed. Berkeley: University of California Press, 1986.

SEE ALSO: Cicero; Greece, Hellenistic and Roman; Philosophy; Punic Wars; Rome, Republican; Scipio Aemilianus.

—Denvy A. Bowman

PĀṆINI

ALSO KNOWN AS: Dākṣīputra Pāṇini
FLOURISHED: c. 500 B.C.E.; northwest India
RELATED CIVILIZATION: India
MAJOR ROLE/POSITION: Grammarian

Life. Little is known about the life of Pāṇini (PAW-nee-nee) except that he was born in a small town in the ancient province of Gandhāra (in modern Pakistan). Pāṇini's fame and importance derive from his authorship of the *Aṣṭādhyāyī* (c. 500 B.C.E.; *Astakam Paniniyam: Panini's Eight Books of Grammatical Sutras*, 1887), the earliest extant and most authoritative treatise in Sanskrit literature on grammar (*vyākaraṇa*). This work, composed in Sanskrit, consists of nearly four thousand concise rules or formulae that prescribe the correct forms of the spoken language known to Pāṇini. Evidence suggests that the text was composed orally; the brevity of its rules was thus an aid to memorization. Pāṇini and his presumed forerunners in India, stimulated by a religious sanction to preserve the correct interpretation of ritual texts, pioneered the systematic study of grammar.

Influence. Pāṇini's influence in India was immense. All later grammarians based their work on his system. When Sanskrit ceased to be a living language and became instead a literary and sacred language, his prescriptive rules, memorized by poets and scholars, established the standard for correct usage. Western knowledge of Pāṇini's system influenced the development of nineteenth century comparative linguistics. In the twentieth century, he interested theoretical linguists as a precursor of modern ideas.

ADDITIONAL RESOURCES
Cardona, George. *Recent Research in Paninian Studies*. Delhi, India: Motilal Banarsidass, 1999.

Mahulkar, D. D., ed. *Essays on Panini*. Simla, India: Indian Institute of Advanced Study, 1998.
Scharfe, Hartmut. *Grammatical Literature*. Wiesbaden, Germany: Harrassowitz, 1977.

SEE ALSO: India.

—*Burt Thorp*

PANTHEON

DATE: constructed 27 B.C.E.-c. 121 C.E.
LOCALE: Campus Martius in the city of Rome
RELATED CIVILIZATION: Imperial Rome
SIGNIFICANCE: This surviving ancient monument represents the Roman aim for perfection in structural integrity and philosophical harmony.

The Pantheon temple to "all the gods" (*pan theon*) was originally part of Augustus's plan to rebuild Rome in his image. Designed first by Marcus Vipsanius Agrippa, friend and general of Augustus whose inscription still fills the architrave above the portico, the monumental temple was finished a century later around 121 C.E. by the philhellene emperor Hadrian. That emperor envisioned it as a personal Pythagorean philosophical summation of what a Roman monument should entail and mean, with its Greek name and cosmopolitan Roman structure, as well as an imperial statement of power.

Consisting of three main architectural components—a *portico*, or porch, connected to a cylindrical drum in the *cella*, or main temple structure, and surmounted by a *rotunda,* or dome—the Pantheon was constructed of materials including brick, concrete, tufa, basalt, pumice, granite (columns), and leaded bronze (roof), with much of the structure veneered in marble. Hadrian intended mathematical polygons to be harmoniously seen—although the portico is not as carefully integrated with the drum—in the triangle of pedimental portico roof, rectangle of portico, and hemisphere of roof. The roof actually becomes a full sphere; the space between the roof and marble floor can be realized as a perfect 44-meter (48-yard) sphere, extending across the 44-meter width of the unusually cylindrical cella. The well-engineered foundations are of basalt, and the walls are of tufa, brick, and concrete. The coffered ceiling of light pumice is covered with leaded bronze sheets. There is also an *oculus*, or aperture, 9 meters (10

yards) long in the ceiling—open to sky—that was meant to mirror the round heaven. The marble inlaid *opus sectile* floor contains stone from all over the empire, including purple imperial porphyry and yellow Numidian marble in repeated squares and circles that echo the structural shapes.

After Rome became Christianized, the Pantheon became the Church of Santa Maria Rotunda, consecrated by command of the Byzantine emperor Phocas in 609 C.E., although the much-later seventeenth century dual towers were removed in the mid-twentieth century. The Pantheon contains the tombs of Raphael and Italian kings, which obscure the numerous original internal Roman apses containing shrines for major and minor gods. The entire internal area of the monument was 1,520 square meters (1,818 square yards) without any reinforcing support, and the internal diameter of its rotunda dome was not eclipsed until the twentieth century, although it was attempted unsuccessfully in the Duomo of Florence (42 meters, or 46 yards) in 1430 and by Saint Peter's (also 42 meters) in Rome in 1564. The massive Pantheon is undoubtedly the most impressive surviving Roman monumental building.

ADDITIONAL RESOURCES
Adam, Jean-Pierre. *Roman Construction: Material and Techniques*. 3d ed. London: Routledge, 1994.
Macdonald, William L. *The Pantheon: Design, Meaning and Progeny*. Reprint. Cambridge, Mass.: Harvard University Press, 1998.
Stierling, Henry. *The Pantheon*. Vol. 1 in *The Roman Empire*. Cologne, Germany: Taschen, 1996.

SEE ALSO: Agrippa, Marcus Vipsanius; Art and architecture; Augustus; Byzantine Empire; Christianity; Hadrian; Pythagoras; Rome, Imperial.

—*Patrick Norman Hunt*

PARIPĀṬAL

AUTHORSHIP: Kirantaiyar, Katuvan Ilaveyinanar, and others
DATE: fourth century C.E.
LOCALE: Tamil Nādu
RELATED CIVILIZATION: India (Tamil)
SIGNIFICANCE: The anthology of secular and religious poems is part of the larger anthology *Eṭṭūtokai*.

Paripāṭal (pah-ree-PAW-tahl) is a collection of seventy poems of the *akam* (internal), *puram* (external), and *bhakti* (devotional) genres of the Caṅkam era. Out of the seventy, only twenty-four complete poems and two long and eleven short fragments have survived the test of time. *Bhakti* poems in this anthology are the only collection of Tamil literature of this period that give detailed description about the birth of Lord Murukan and may be considered the first set of comprehensive Tamil devotional poems. This anthology includes eight hymns in praise of Lord Murukan, seven in praise of Lord Tirumal, and a few on the river Vaigai. The *Paripāṭal* meter is used and may be considered a development from the *akaval* and *vañci* meters of the early Caṅkam poems. *Paripāṭal* hymns were set to music and are a combination of *icai* (music) and *inniyal* (melodious poetry), also called *icai*-Tamil (musical Tamil). Narration and dialogues in this anthology seem to be more in the form of dramatic scenes and may be a development from the bardic poems of the early Caṅkam period to the *bhakti* poems of the later periods of Tamil literature.

ADDITIONAL RESOURCES

Hirosaka, Shu. *Paripatal*. Chennai, India: Institute of Asian Studies, 1996.

Kantaiya, A. *Cult and Worship of Murukan as Reflected in the Paripatal and the Tirumurukarruppatai*. Colombo, Sri Lanka: Government Press, 1984.

Sarangapani, R. *A Critical Study of Paripatal*. Madurai, India: Madurai Kamaraj University, 1984.

SEE ALSO: *Aiṅkururnūru*; Caṅkam; India; *Kalittokai*; *Kuruntokai*; *Patirruppattu*.

—*Salli Vargis*

PARMENIDES

ALSO KNOWN AS: Parmenides of Elea
BORN: c. 515 B.C.E.; Elea (also known as Velia)
DIED: after 436 B.C.E.; possibly Elea
RELATED CIVILIZATIONS: Classical Greece, southern Italy
MAJOR ROLE/POSITION: Philosopher

Life. Little is known of Parmenides' (pahr-MEHN-eh-deez) life except that he created some of the laws of his native Elea and perhaps visited Athens in 450 B.C.E. Diogenes Laertius states that he was a Pythagorean in his youth and a pupil of Xenophanes. Scholars note, however, that there are no significant Pythagorean elements in Parmenides' philosophy, and they question his relationship to Xenophanes. He wrote a poem under the traditional title, *Peri physeōs* (fifth century B.C.E.; *The Fragments of Parmenides*, 1869, commonly known as *On Nature*), one-third of which is extant. In the conventional form of epic hexameter, Parmenides promulgates his new philosophical ideas, which led to the foundation of the Eleatic School.

In *On Nature*, Parmenides introduces the theme of philosophical instruction: A young charioteer, the philosopher himself, embarks on a journey in the domain of the goddess of truth, justice, and retribution in order to learn the nature of true existence. Following Xenophanes' monotheistic understanding of the universe, Parmenides proclaims that true reality is solely "an object of thought and speech," and if "that which exists, cannot not-exist," then "there is not that which does not exist." This theoretical premise is announced by the just goddess, who teaches the young philosopher about the two ways of learning. One is the way toward true knowledge, that reality is "unoriginated, imperishable, whole, indivisible, steadfast and complete"; the other is the way toward false opinion, based on sense perceptions, that reality is originated, perishable, multiple, divisible, and in constant change over time and space.

Influence. Parmenides' denial of multiplicity was criticized by the pluralists, Empedocles, Anaxagoras, and the Atomists but was defended by his pupils of the Eleatic School. Zeno of Elea demonstrates logistically that multiplicity does not exist, for nothing can be both definite and indefinite. Melissus of Samos, the only member of the school outside Elea, elaborates on Parmenides' doctrine by explaining that the one, unoriginated and indivisible reality is not timeless but everlasting; that it is not limited but infinite because if it is unoriginated and imperishable, then it does not have beginning or an end; and that void and motion do not exist. Although Melissus is the last representative of the Eleatic School, Parmenides' philosophy lays the foundation for Plato's theory of forms and the epistemological dichotomy between true knowledge and false perceptual opinion by interrupting the Pre-Socratics' continuous interest in natural philosophy.

ADDITIONAL RESOURCES

Curd, P. K. *The Legacy of Parmenides: Eleatic Monism and Later Presocratic Thought.* Princeton, N.J.: Princeton University Press, 1998.

Gallop, D. *Parmenides of Elea.* Toronto: University of Toronto Press, 1984.

Guthrie, W. K. C. *A History of Greek Philosophy.* 6 vols. New York: Cambridge University Press, 1978-1990.

Kirk, G. S., J. E. Raven, and M. Schofield. *The Presocratic Philosophers.* 2d ed. Cambridge, England: Cambridge University Press, 1995.

Long, A. A. *The Cambridge Companion to Early Greek Philosophy.* Cambridge, England: Cambridge University Press, 1999.

SEE ALSO: Greece, Classical; Philosophy; Plato; Pre-Socratic philosophers; Zeno of Elea.

—*Svetla Slaveva-Griffin*

PARTHENON

DATE: construction, 447-432 B.C.E.
LOCALE: Athens, the Acropolis
RELATED CIVILIZATIONS: Classical Greece, Athens
SIGNIFICANCE: The Parthenon is a testament to Classical Greek humanism, which is the foundation of the Western tradition.

Situated atop the Acropolis (high city), the Parthenon is a temple dedicated to Athena Parthenos (the virgin), patron goddess of Athens. An earlier, unfinished Parthenon was destroyed in about 480 B.C.E. during the Persian invasion of Athens. In 447 B.C.E., under the direction of the statesman Pericles, the Athenians undertook a massive rebuilding project, which included razing the damaged building and constructing in its place the Parthenon that continues to grace the Athenian Acropolis. To pay for the project, Pericles used funds from the Delian League, an organization of Greek city-states formed for mutual defense in case of future invasions. In response, other Greek city-states, most notably Sparta, accused Athens of imperialism and thus began the Peloponnesian War (431-404 B.C.E.), which ended in the defeat of Athens.

The architects Ictinus and Callicrates oversaw the design and construction of the Parthenon, and the sculptor Phidias directed the building's sculptural pro-

grams. Constructed of Pentelic marble, which changes hue from white to gold depending on the light, the Parthenon was the most elaborate Greek temple of its day. In scale and detail, the Parthenon reflects Greek humanism. The Parthenon's simple Doric columns, typical of the Greek mainland, coupled with its elaborate Ionic elements, typical of Asia Minor, may have symbolized the dominance of Athens over all the Greek city-states, or perhaps these features represented the diverse origins of the Athenians themselves.

Following the classical canon of proportions, with modules based on the human form, the Parthenon has eight columns on each end and seventeen columns along each side ($x = 2y + 1$). Knowing that long, straight horizontal lines appear to sag in the middle, the designers compensated for this optical illusion by incorporating a slight upward curve toward the center of every horizontal element. The architects found that sunlight shining around a column makes it appear narrower, so they made the four corner columns widest. Every column has entasis (a slight bulge in the middle), which gives it the appearance of bearing weight.

The sculptural programs of the Parthenon related Greek myths such as the contest between Poseidon and Athena to be patron deity of Athens (west pediment) and the birth of Athena (east pediment), as well as ac-

The Parthenon in Athens, Greece, built by Pericles. (Corbis)

tual contemporary events such as the Panathenaic festival, a procession in celebration of Athena's birth (exterior cella wall frieze). Inside the Parthenon stood a magnificent chryselephantine (gold and ivory) statue of Athena, measuring 40 feet (12 meters) in height.

During the Middle Ages, the Parthenon was converted into a Christian church. Later, when the Ottoman Turks occupied Greece, the Parthenon served as an Islamic mosque. In 1687, the Venetians attacked Athens and blew up the Parthenon, which the Turks had been using as an ammunition dump. The worst damage to the Parthenon, however, has been caused by vehicle exhaust, industrial pollutants, and overvisitation by tourists.

ADDITIONAL RESOURCES

Boardman, John. *Oxford History of Classical Art.* Oxford, England: Oxford University Press, 1993.

Carpenter, Rhys. *The Architects of the Parthenon.* Harmondsworth, England: Penguin Books, 1970.

Dinsmoor, William Bell. *The Architecture of Ancient Greece.* New York: W. W. Norton, 1975.

Palagia, Olga. *The Pediments of the Parthenon.* Boston: Brill, 1998.

SEE ALSO: Art and architecture; Callicrates; Greece, Classical; Ictinus; Pericles; Phidias.

—*Sonia Sorrell*

PARTHIA

DATE: 400 B.C.E.-224 C.E.

LOCALE: Southwest Asia in modern-day northeastern Iran

SIGNIFICANCE: A revolt by the Parthians against the Seleucids established the Parthian kingdom. The Parthian victory at Carrhae in 53 B.C.E. blocked further Roman expansion to the east.

Following the death of Alexander the Great (323 B.C.E.), the Greek Empire was divided among his former generals. The eastern portion, corresponding to what had been the Achaemenian Empire established under Cyrus the Great, came under the control of Seleucus I. Within the Achaemenian Empire of the Persians, Parthia had at one time been ruled by Hystaspes (Vishtaspa), a member of Cyrus's extended family and father of Darius the Great, ruler of the Persian Empire.

Seleucus I was immediately faced with revolts in the satraps, the provinces that had been conquered by Alexander. These revolts resulted in part from rejection of Hellenism and its concept of a master race and also from the invasion of nomads from beyond the Jaxartes River, which marked the eastern boundary. A revolt led by Arsaces, chief of the Scythian Parni, in 245 B.C.E. resulted in the province of Parthia being established as a kingdom independent of the Seleucid Empire.

The establishment of the kingdom of Parthia (PAHR-thee-uh) was made possible by several developments. The precise boundaries of Parthia were largely undefined, and it was inhabited by a collection of peoples who were primarily nomads of ill-defined ethnicity. Their common goal in the initial struggle against the Seleucids was the removal of Greek/Macedonian domination. Their success was based on the combination of their own strengths and the concurrent rise of Rome in the western regions of the Seleucid Empire. The Parthians became known for their cataphracts, the mail-clad cavalry that developed the shoot-and-run tactics that proved effective against the Seleucids and later Rome.

Arsaces was instrumental in establishing the Parthian state, and even long after his death (c. 215 B.C.E.), he was considered the greatest of the Parthian rulers. The Arsacid era (c. 245 B.C.E.-224 C.E.) was named after him, and his image was found on Parthian coins for several hundred years.

The defeat (c. 225 B.C.E.) of Seleucus II by Arsaces was the start of decades of consolidation in the region, a process that continued under Arsaces' successor, Artabanus I. Hecatompylos, a city along the Silk Road, was established as Parthia's capital, and the fortress city of Dara (a later capital) and the city of Nisa (also an eventual capital) were founded. During the reign of Artabanus I, the region was marked by revolts of other satraps against Antiochus the Great (c. 242-187 B.C.E.), ruler of the Seleucids during the first decades of the second century B.C.E. A military campaign that captured Hecatompylos resulted in a peace treaty between Parthia and the Seleucids, who recognized the existence of Parthia in exchange for the inclusion of the Parthian cavalry in the Seleucid army.

The reign of Mithradates I (r. 171-138 B.C.E.) marked the beginning of the philhellenic period, an era that lasted some two hundred years and was characterized by the increasing influence of the Greek culture and language, even as the political influence of the Greeks began to wane. Mithradates took advantage of the weakening Seleucids by expanding the Parthian kingdom to the west, eventually occupying Media and Ecbatana (modern Hamadān). His opponent, Antiochus IV Epiphanes, was simultaneously dealing with revolts within other regions of his empire, including the Maccabean revolt in Judaea (c. 168-143 B.C.E.), a part of which became the basis of the Jewish holiday of Hanukkah.

The final attempt by the Greeks to maintain a foothold near Parthia occurred during the reign of Phraa-

tes II (r. c. 138-128 B.C.E.). Antiochus VII occupied Media, defeating Phraates in several small battles. However, a revolt of the Medes resulted in the death of Antiochus (c. 129 B.C.E.) and ended the last vestige of Greek political influence in the region.

The reign of Mithradates II (r. c. 124-87 B.C.E.) marked the apogee of the Parthian Empire. Mithradates' kingdom extended from modern-day India in the east to Asia Minor in the west. The Euphrates River was established as the boundary between Parthia and the growing Roman Empire. In the period following Mithradates' death, however, conflict began to grow with Rome. The Roman general Pompey the Great hoped to establish Parthia as a state friendly to Rome, if not an occupied buffer.

In 53 B.C.E., a Roman army under the triumvir Marcus Licinius Crassus passed through Armenia into Mesopotamia. His army of 44,000 men was attacked in the desert by a Parthian cavalry of 11,000 men at Carrhae. Crassus and some 30,000 of his men were either killed or captured, ending the attempt by Rome to incorporate Parthia into its empire. The Euphrates River remained a boundary between the two empires, and Rome would never have sufficient influence in the east to displace that of the Hellenists.

Subsequent decades of court intrigue weakened the political influence of Parthia. Though peace was again established with Rome, foreign influences from the east gradually replaced that of the Hellenists. The period between 12 and 160 C.E. was marked by increasing anti-Hellenism as Parthia broke into a succession of smaller states and kingdoms. An invasion by the emperor Trajan temporarily united the region in opposition (c. 120 C.E.) and allowed for a brief period of peace. However, the last years of the Parthian dynasties were marked by revolts and continuing hostilities with Rome. The death of Artabanus V (224 C.E.) in battle with the Persian Ardashīr I represented the end of the Arsacid era and the beginning of that of the Sāsānian shahs.

ADDITIONAL RESOURCES

Lepper, F. *Trajan's Parthian War*. Chicago: Ares, 1994.

Wilcox, Peter. *Rome's Enemies 3: Parthians and Sassanids*. Vol. 175. Oxford, England: Osprey, 1988.

Yarshater, Ehsan, ed. *The Seleucid, Parthian, and Sasanian Periods*. Vol. 3 in *The Cambridge History of Iran*. Cambridge, England: Cambridge University Press, 1983.

SEE ALSO: Achaemenian Dynasty; Alexander the Great; Ardashīr I; Artabanus I-V; Carrhae, Battle of; Crassus, Marcus Licinius; Cyrus the Great; Darius the Great; Greece, Hellenistic and Roman; Maccabees; Mithradates I; Mithradates II; Pompey the Great; Rome, Imperial; Sāsānian Empire; Seleucid Dynasty.

—*Richard Adler*

PĀRVATĪ DEVĪ TEMPLE

DATE: late fifth-early sixth centuries C.E.
LOCALE: Nachna Kuthara, Bundelkhand, India
RELATED CIVILIZATIONS: Gupta Dynasty, north India
SIGNIFICANCE: Early structural temple of the Gupta Dynasty.

The temple, although popularly named after the goddess Pārvatī Devī (PAWR-rah-tee DEH-vee), actually was dedicated to the Hindu god Śiva. A double-storied structure resting on a high plinth, the temple consists of a *garbha gṛha* (cella), a walled and roofed corridor for ritual circumambulation (*pradakhṣiṇāpatha*), and a *maṇḍapa* (porch). In addition, there was a second-story room above the cella, the purpose of which is not known. Both the inner corridor and the cella were lit by richly decorated stone grill windows. The temple is noted particularly for its splendidly embellished T-shaped doorway, a characteristic of Gupta architecture. It features lush floral ornamentation in which spiraling vines sprout leaves and tendrils that turn back on themselves, as well as graceful three-dimensional figural sculpture. Elegantly carved representations of guardians, flying celestial figures, the river goddesses Gaṅgā and Yamunā, *yakṣīs* (female nature spirits), loving couples (*mithunas*), and representations of the god Śiva and his wife, the Goddess Pārvatī, and adoring worshipers are clad in the courtly clothing, ornaments, and festoons of ringlets typical of Gupta fashion. The lively and sensuous sculptures are representative of the classic phase of Indian art, a period in which there is perfection and purity of form. Although the cella is empty now, it once held an icon of Śiva, probably in his lingam (phallic) form. The ornamentation on the plinth, consisting of rocky landscapes inhabited by wild animals, suggests that the overall temple was conceived of as Śiva's Himalayan abode, Mount Kailāsa.

ADDITIONAL RESOURCES

Mishra, Sudhakar Nath. *Gupta Art and Architecture.* Delhi, India: Agam Rala Prakashan, 1992.
Williams, Joanna Gottfried. *The Art of Gupta India: Empire and Province.* Princeton, N.J.: Princeton University Press, 1982.

SEE ALSO: Gupta emperors; Hinduism; India; Indian temple architecture.

—*Katherine Anne Harper*

PATIṈEṈKĪḺKKAṆAKKU

DATE: 300-700 C.E.
LOCALE: India
RELATED CIVILIZATIONS: Pre-Aryan Dravidian civilization, India
SIGNIFICANCE: This anthology of Tamil literature contains war poems in the *puram* style, poems in the *akam* style, and collections of maxims on private and public conduct, some of which have become quite popular.

Patiṉeṉkīḻkkaṇakku (pah-tee-NEHN-kihl-KAH-nah-kew), or the "eighteen shorter texts," can be classified into three main types of works: a war poem, six poems of the *akam* (internal) genre, and eleven collections of maxims on conduct. The war poem, which develops the *puram* (external) genre, is called *Kaḷavalinārpattu*, or "forty stanzas on the battleground," and is ascribed to Poykaiyar. Dedicated to the Battle of Kalumalam, fought by the Cōḷa king Cenkanan, this poem foreshadows later war poetry.

The work also contains six poems of the *akam* (internal) genre: *Karnarpattu*, or "forty stanzas on the rainy season," ascribed to Maturai Kaṇṇaṉ Kuttanar; *Aintiṇaiyeḻupatu*, or "seventy stanzas about the five settings," by Muvatiyar; *Aintiṇaiyaimpatu*, or "fifty stanzas about the five settings," by Maran Poraiyanar; *Tiṇaimoḻiyampathu*, by Kaṇṇaṉ Centanar; *Kainnilai*, which probably means "five attitudes of conduct," discovered as late as 1931, ascribed to Pullankatanar; and *Tiṉaimalainurraimpathu*, or "one hundred fifty stanzas on the garland of settings," by Kanimetaviyar. Composed in *venpa* meter, a four-line stanza that has gained almost absolute supremacy in the twentieth century, these poems are not valued highly for their poetic merit but are known for their didactic and instructive content.

The remaining eleven texts are collections of maxims on ethical and social conventions formulating rules of private and public conduct. Of these, *Tirukuraḷ* (third or fourth century C.E.; English translation, 1987), a comprehensive manual of ethics, polity, and love, consisting of 1,330 distichs divided into 133 sections of 10 couplets each, is undoubtedly the most exceptional in its literary merits. Next to *Tirukuraḷ*, the most popular book of moral maxims in Tamil is *Nālaṭiyār* (n.d.; *Naladiyar Four Hundred Quatrains in Tamil*, 1893), composed by Jain authors.

ADDITIONAL RESOURCES

Pope, G. U. *A Tamil Poetical Anthology: Naladiyar, Four Hundred Quatrains in Tamil*. Oxford, England: Clarendon Press, 1893.

Sundaram, P. S. *The Kural by Tiruvalluvar*. Harmondsworth, England: Penguin, 1991.

Thani Nayagam, Xavier S. *Landscape and Poetry: A Study of Nature in Classical Tamil Poetry*. 2d ed. New York: Asia Publishing House, 1966.

SEE ALSO: Caṅkam; India; Tiruvaḷḷuvar.

—Kokila Ravi

PATIRRUPPATTU

AUTHORSHIP: Kumatturk Kannanar, Palaik Kautamanar, Kappiyarruk Kappiyanar, Paranar, Kakkaipatiniyar Naccellaiyar, Kapilar, and others

DATE: second century B.C.E.-third century C.E.

LOCALE: Tamil Nāḍu

RELATED CIVILIZATION: India (Tamil)

SIGNIFICANCE: This anthology of poems on Cēra kings is part of the larger anthology *Eṭṭūtokai*.

Patirruppattu (pah-TEE-rew-PA-tew; English translation, 1984), or the "ten tens," is an anthology of poems of the *puram* (external) genre of Caṅkam literature and is part of the larger anthology called *Eṭṭūtokai*. Several verses have been lost, and in some cases, a few lines are missing. For the available verses, the line numbers are indicated at the end of every five lines. It is of tremendous historic significance because most of the verses are in praise of the Cēra kings of ancient Tamil Nāḍu. The anthology is divided into ten sections that narrate historic details during ten decades; the poems of the first and tenth decades are missing. The remaining poems vary in length from eight to fifty-seven lines and were probably composed by eight poets. The *patikams* (poetic prefaces or epilogues) that accompany each decade are of later origin but are useful because they established the historic and sociological framework of the verses that follow. The fifth decade of the *Patirruppattu* is extremely significant, as it helps establish the regnal years of Cenkuttuvan and the Caṅkam era.

ADDITIONAL RESOURCES

Hirosaka, Shu. *Tamil Poetry Through the Ages*. Chennai, India: Institute of Asian Studies, 1997.

Vacek, J., and S. V. Subramanian. *A Tamil Reader: Introducing Sangam Literature*. Chennai, India: Ulakat Tamilaraycci Niruvanam, 1989.

Zvelebil, Kamil Veith. *Companion Studies to the History of Tamil Literature*. Leiden: E. J. Brill, 1992.

SEE ALSO: *Aiṅkururnūru*; Caṅkam; India; *Kalittokai*; *Kuruntokai*; *Paripāṭal*.

—Salli Vargis

PATRICK, SAINT

BORN: c. 418-422 C.E.; England
DIED: March 17, 493 C.E.; Saul, Ireland
RELATED CIVILIZATION: Ireland
MAJOR ROLE/POSITION: Religious figure

Life. Patrick was born into a Celto-Roman family headed by Calpurnius, a Roman official. At age sixteen Patrick was captured by raiding sailors and sold into slavery at Antrim in Ireland. He was employed as a shepherd and began a lifelong habit of fervent prayer and deep meditation on his faith while tending his master's sheep. After six years of this life, Patrick was able to escape slavery.

He studied theology for some fourteen years at Auxerre in France. His principal teacher there, Saint Germain, ordained Patrick into the Roman Catholic priesthood. In 432 C.E., Patrick was made a bishop by Pope Celestine I, who sent him to Ireland to convert those people to the Roman Catholic faith.

Patrick landed in Ireland in the summer of 433 C.E. at the mouth of the Vantry River. He traveled inland, converting local chieftains and their followers, as he moved both north and west. In 444 C.E., he established his see at Armagh, where he built both a church and a monastery. Patrick's feast day is celebrated on March 17, the day of his death.

Influence. Although Saint Patrick is primarily celebrated for converting the Irish to the Roman Catholic faith, he is also known as the author of *Confessio* (fifth century C.E.; *The Confession* in *St. Patrick, the Writings*, 1887), in which he related the hardships he faced as a missionary.

Saint Patrick. (Library of Congress)

ADDITIONAL RESOURCES

Dumville, David N. *Saint Patrick,* A.D. *493-1993.* Rochester, N.Y.: Boydell Press, 1993.
Hopkin, Alannah. *The Living Legend of Saint Patrick.* New York: St. Martin's Press, 1989.

SEE ALSO: Christianity; Ireland.

—*Patricia E. Sweeney*

PAUL, SAINT

ALSO KNOWN AS: Paul the Apostle; Paul of Tarsus; Saul of Tarsus
BORN: early first century C.E.; Tarsus (later Turkey)
DIED: about 64 C.E.; Rome
RELATED CIVILIZATIONS: Israel, Anatolia, Hellenistic and Roman Greece, Imperial Rome
MAJOR ROLE/POSITION: Religious figure

Life. Any account of Saint Paul must rely mainly on the New Testament—not only on his occasional auto-

biographical comments in his letters (early 50's to early 60's C.E.) but also on the long but incomplete account in the Acts of the Apostles (about 80 C.E.).

Born a Jew and a Roman citizen in Cilicia (a province in Asia Minor), Paul probably came from a prosperous family and learned the craft of tent making. As a Pharisee, he eventually went to Jerusalem, where he studied Hebrew scripture under the eminent scholar Gamaliel. It was most likely in Jerusalem that Paul first encountered followers of Jesus

Saint Paul. (Library of Congress)

Jews but also to Gentiles. After a trip to Jerusalem to talk with the Jewish church leaders, before whom Paul defended his message that Gentile Christians should not bear the burden of Jewish law, he traveled again as a missionary through Asia Minor and then through Greece (both Macedonia and Achaia), accompanied by Silas and Timothy. Yet another trip took Paul once more to cities where he had previously preached and then to Jerusalem, where an attack on Paul by an anti-Christian mob led to his imprisonment by Roman authorities, first in Jerusalem and then, for two years, in Caesarea Maritima, Palestine, from which he sailed toward Rome, suffering storm and shipwreck on the way.

At Rome, waiting under house arrest until the emperor heard his appeal, Paul continued to serve Christ by proclaiming that everyone who had faith in him would share in his resurrection and enjoy eternal life. Although the account in Acts ends before the death of Paul, reliable tradition says that he died a martyr for his faith.

Influence. Through his evangelism and the theology in his letters to believers in several cities, Paul helped spread Christianity and to distinguish it from the Judaism from which it arose. Except for Jesus Christ, no one has influenced Christianity more than Paul.

of Nazareth and persecuted them as Jewish heretics.

According to Acts, Paul traveled from Jerusalem toward Damascus to arrest Jews who claimed that Jesus was the Christ, God's Anointed. Near Damascus, Acts says, Paul suddenly saw a brilliant light from above and heard the voice of Jesus asking why Paul was persecuting him. Soon, at Damascus, Paul received Christian baptism and began proclaiming the gospel he had so recently despised.

After a while, Paul returned to Jerusalem and met Peter and Jesus's brother James. Still later, following several years in his native province, Paul ministered in Syrian Antioch, where there was a thriving Christian congregation. It was from Antioch that Paul and Barnabas went on a missionary trip to Cyprus and south-central Asia Minor, where they preached not only to

ADDITIONAL RESOURCES

Hawthorne, Gerald F., Ralph P. Martin, and Daniel G. Reid, eds. *Dictionary of Paul and His Letters.* Downers Grove, Ill.: InterVarsity, 1993.

Meeks, Wayne A., et al. *The HarperCollins Study Bible: New Revised Standard Version.* New York: HarperCollins, 1993.

Roetzel, Calvin J. *Paul: The Man and the Myth.* Columbia: University of South Carolina Press, 1998.

SEE ALSO: Christianity; Jesus Christ; Judaism; Peter, Saint; Rome, Imperial.

—Victor Lindsey

Paulinus, Saint

Born: c. 584 C.E.; Rome, Italy
Died: 644 C.E.; Rochester, Kent, England
Related civilizations: Britain, Rome
Major role/position: Religious leader

Life. Saint Paulinus (paw-LI-nuhs) was an Italian priest sent by Gregory the Great in 601 C.E. to join Saint Augustine of Canterbury on his mission to convert the pagan Anglo-Saxons. After the mission succeeded in converting King Æthelbert I of Kent in 625 C.E., Paulinus was consecrated bishop and sent north to accompany Æthelbert's daughter, Princess Æthelbert, on her journey to marry the pagan king of Northumbria, Edwin. The first historian of the English church and people, the Venerable Bede, records that it was Paulinus's powerful preaching, as well as a dream that had prepared Edwin for meeting Paulinus, which resulted in the mass conversion of the Northumbrians in 627 C.E. near York. Paulinus established his seat at York, which henceforth became the second most important bishopric in the English church, after Canterbury. When Penda, the pagan king of neighboring Mercia, killed Edwin in 633 C.E., Paulinus retreated to Kent, where he died as the bishop of Rochester.

Influence. Although Paulinus's mission failed in his lifetime, the conversion experience was a deep one for the English, and his bishopric of York became ultimately one of the two archbishoprics in the English church. Paulinus was instrumental in following Pope Gregory the Great's admonition to "baptize the culture" of the Anglo-Saxons without destroying it, a policy that helped ensure the ultimate success of Christianity in England.

ADDITIONAL RESOURCES

Bede. *The Ecclesiastical History of the English People.* Edited by Judith McClure and Roger Collins. Oxford, England: Oxford University Press, 1999.
Campbell, James, ed. *The Anglo-Saxons.* London: Penguin, 1991.

SEE ALSO: Æthelbert; Augustine of Canterbury, Saint; Britain; Christianity; Edwin; Gregory the Great; Rome, Imperial.

—*James L. Persoon*

Paulinus of Nola, Saint

Born: c. 352 or 353 C.E.; Aquitania
Died: 431 C.E.; Nola, Italy
Related civilization: Imperial Rome
Major role/position: Bishop, poet

Life. Saint Paulinus of Nola (paw-LI-nuhs of NOH-lah) was born into a noble family in Aquitania, educated at Bordeaux, and by 380 C.E. was serving as consular governor of Campania. After marrying a Spanish woman named Therasia, Paulinus underwent a spiritual conversion. Following the death of their only son, he was ordained to the priesthood and the next year left Spain for Italy to pursue a monastic life at Nola at the tomb of Saint Felix. There Paulinus renounced sex, wealth, and other worldly concerns, including secular poetry, much to the dismay of his former teacher, Decimus Magnus Ausonius. He wrote a number of Christian poems, many of them in honor of Saint Felix, as well as fifty letters that have survived.

Influence. The conversion of such a conspicuous political figure as Paulinus to the monastic ideal scandalized some of his upper-class friends such as Ausonius, but Paulinus's spectacular repudiation of the world was celebrated by contemporaries, such as Saint Ambrose, who were interested in promoting asceticism in the West. Paulinus was a voluminous correspondent whose letters were compared by Saint Jerome to Cicero's. Among the Christian Latin poets of Late Antiquity, he is surpassed in his command of poetic form and diction only by Aurelius Clemens Prudentius.

ADDITIONAL RESOURCES

Lienhard, J. *Paulinus of Nola and Early Western Monasticism.* Cologne, Germany: Peter Hanstein Verlag, 1977.
Trout, D. *Paulinus of Nola: Life, Letters, and Poems.* Berkeley: University of California Press, 1999.

SEE ALSO: Ambrose; Ausonius, Decimus Magnus; Christianity; Cicero; Jerome, Saint; Prudentius, Aurelius Clemens.

—*Carl P. E. Springer*

PAUSANIAS OF SPARTA

BORN: late sixth century B.C.E.; Sparta
DIED: c. 470 B.C.E.; Sparta
RELATED CIVILIZATIONS: Classical Greece, Persia
MAJOR ROLE/POSITION: Regent, military leader

Life. Son of King Cleombrotus and regent for the minor son of Leonidas, Pausanias (paw-SAY-nee-uhs) of Sparta was given supreme command in 479 B.C.E., when Athens appealed to Sparta. At the Battle of Plataea, Pausanias rallied the Greek troops against daunting odds and led his Spartans to decisive victory over the Persian elite. Pausanias displayed honor by refusing to behead and crucify the Persian general Mardonius, as the Persians had done to Leonidas. He killed the traitors to the Greek cause at Thebes. Comparing a banquet that he ordered Mardonius's cooks to serve with a Spartan supper, Pausanias ridiculed the extravagant Persian for coming to rob poor Greeks.

Two years later, Pausanias commanded a Spartan/Athenian fleet, liberating Cypriot cities from Persian control, then Byzantium. There he became a ruthless tyrant, flaunting a Persian lifestyle. Proposing to marry Xerxes I's daughter and to subject all Greece to Xerxes, he was promised money and troops to attain the goal. The "liberated" peoples appealed to Athens, which Thucydides credits for the Athenian rise to supremacy. Recalled by Sparta, Pausanias was tried but acquitted. Venturing without authority to Byzantium and expelled by the Athenians, Pausanias submitted to Sparta's second recall, expecting to win by bribery or by fomenting a helot (serf-slave) insurrection. Only the testimony of a trusted servant gave the ephors (magistrates) sufficient cause to convict.

After fleeing to the temple of Athena, Pausanias was walled in and starved to death.

Influence. Though his success at Plataea saved Greece from Persian domination, Pausanias was remembered more for hubris and treachery.

ADDITIONAL RESOURCES
Green, Peter. *The Greco-Persian Wars*. Berkeley: University of California Press, 1996.
Hooker, J. T. *The Ancient Spartans*. London: J. M. Dent, 1980.

SEE ALSO: Greco-Persian Wars; Greece, Classical; Leonidas; Plataea, Battle of; Thucydides; Xerxes I.
—*Kenneth L. Burres*

Pausanias of Sparta, shown sacrificing to the gods before the battle, scored a decisive victory over the Persians at Plataea. (North Wind Picture Archives)

PAUSANIAS THE TRAVELER

BORN: early second century C.E.; Lydia
DIED: after 161 C.E.; possibly Rome
RELATED CIVILIZATIONS: Roman Greece, Imperial Rome
MAJOR ROLE/POSITION: Traveler, geographer

Life. All that is known of Pausanias (paw-SAY-nee-uhs) the Traveler is inferred from his *Periegesis Hellados* (between 143 and 161 C.E.; *Description of Greece*, 1794), the first known travel guide. After traveling in Asia Minor, Africa, Macedonia, and Greece,

Pausanias settled in Rome and composed his *Description of Greece* from three main sources: notes recording his personal observations, information obtained from innumerable conversations at every location, classical historians and poets such as Homer and Hesiod and contemporary writers such as Marcus Antonius Polemon. Pausanias's activity extends from the reign of Hadrian (before 138 C.E.) to that of Marcus Aurelius (after 161 C.E.). His itinerary proceeds from Attica throughout the Peloponnese and back north to Boeotia and Phocis.

Explicit directions guide the traveler from building to building and from city to city. More interested in human artifacts than the natural landscape, Pausanias concentrates on temples (some in ruins, he sadly notes), altars, sculptures of mortals and deities, monuments to victors, and all the pertinent local traditions. He is fond of the expression "worth seeing." Making no distinc-

tion between the myths of the heroic age and recent history, he is a literalist, though he notes conflicts among the traditions. He mentions offering his own sacrifices at various altars.

Influence. Through his writing, Pausanias provides copious information, much of it available nowhere else, about the art, religion, folklore, and politics of his and previous eras. Through him, it is revealed how much magnificent art has been lost.

ADDITIONAL RESOURCE

Pausanias. *Description of Greece.* 5 vols. Translated by W. H. S. Jones. Cambridge, Mass.: Harvard University Press, 1965-1966.

SEE ALSO: Greece, Hellenistic and Roman; Hadrian; Hesiod; Homer; Marcus Aurelius.

—Kenneth L. Burres

PELAGIANISM

DATE: coined c. 400-c. 525 C.E.
LOCALE: Western Europe, North Africa, Palestine
RELATED CIVILIZATION: Imperial Rome

Pelagianism (peh-LAY-jee-eh-nih-zm) is the name given to an early Christian theology that denies the doctrines of original sin, infant baptism, and the redemptive value of the death of Jesus Christ. The chief opponent to Pelagianism was Saint Augustine (354-430 C.E.), who taught that human beings were born sinful and have a propensity toward sin and that the only salvation from this state of sin is the grace of Christ, which comes through the sacraments. However, Pelagianism taught that far from being born with a predisposition toward sin, human beings are born, morally speaking, as a tabula rasa (blank slate), and it is their decisions in life that determine their fitness for heaven.

Pelagianism was condemned as heretical by early church councils from Carthage in North Africa (416 C.E.) to Orange in Gaul (529 C.E.), and the followers of

Pelagius's teachings were banned from the cities of Italy in 418 C.E. by the emperor Honorius (r. 393-423 C.E.) and from the Roman Empire in 430 C.E. by Theodosius II (r. 408-450 C.E.).

Pelagianism received its name from Pelagius (c. 355-c. 435 C.E.), a monk from the British Isles. He seems to have arrived in Rome circa 390 C.E. and taught there until 411 C.E. From Rome, he traveled through North Africa, where he met with Augustine several times, and settled in Palestine in 412 C.E. Although Pelagius disappears from history after 418 C.E., his chief disciple, Caelestius, carried on his teachings.

ADDITIONAL RESOURCE

Rees, B. R. *Pelagius: Life and Letters.* Rochester, N.Y.: Boydell Press, 1998.

SEE ALSO: Africa, North; Augustine, Saint; Christianity; Jesus Christ; Rome, Imperial; Theodosius II.

—Roger S. Evans

PELOPONNESIAN WAR

DATE: May, 431-September, 404 B.C.E.
LOCALE: Greece
RELATED CIVILIZATIONS: Athens, Sparta
SIGNIFICANCE: The Spartan victory over Athens destroyed its military and naval dominance and temporarily replaced a democracy with an oligarchy.

Background. The growth of an Athenian naval empire following the Greco-Persian Wars inevitably led to a military contest between Athens and its bitter rival Sparta.

Action. In 431 B.C.E., tensions between Athens and Sparta erupted into conflict on the Peloponnesian (PEH-leh-peh-nee-zhuhn) peninsula. Athens' military leader, Pericles, took to the sea, and Athenians withdrew behind the Long Walls, a defensive structure connecting the city to its port. After the first year, a plague erupted in the crowded Athens, killing perhaps one-quarter of the population, including Pericles. Without Pericles' guidance, the Athenians began to take increasingly brutal measures against their adversaries.

In 428 B.C.E., the city Mitylene attempted to free itself from the Athenian empire but was starved into submission. Although the Athenian assembly eventually rejected the severe punishments urged by the popular Athenian politician Cleon, within six years, such harsh penalties would be used against rebel cities as a matter of policy.

In 425 B.C.E., the Athenians were winning the war. The Athenian general Demosthenes, who had established a stronghold at Pylos on the southwest coast of the Peloponnese, could not be dislodged, and Sparta sued for a conditional peace. The Athenian general Nicias wanted the Athenian assembly to accept, but Cleon urged Athens to hold out for better terms. Placed in command of the Athenian force on the Peloponnese, Cleon arrived in Pylos to discover that the Athenians were about to attack the Spartans. Sparta lost nearly one-third of its troops and surrendered, providing the Athenians with hostages and, as a result, an unconditional peace in which Athens was allowed to keep its empire and possessions.

Cleon now suggested a campaign against the Spartans to compel them to yield territory. In 424 B.C.E., the Spartan general Brasidas captured an Athenian ally, Amphipolis, in northern Greece. In 422 B.C.E., in a second battle over Amphipolis, both Cleon and Brasidas were killed. With the death of Cleon, Sparta and Athens signed a treaty in March of 421 B.C.E. Known as the Peace of Nicias, the treaty held until the summer of 416 B.C.E. Then Athens attacked the island of Melos, killing all men of military age, enslaving all other citizens, and forcing Melos to join the empire.

The next year, the Athenians attempted to extend their empire into Sicily—but the Athenian general Alcibiades was recalled on suspicion of having profaned the religious rites of Demeter. Returning to Athens, Alcibiades slipped his guard and fled to Sparta. Partly because of Alcibiades' betrayal and partly because of the arrival of the Spartan commander Gylippus, a major portion of the Athenian fleet was destroyed in the campaign. Of a force of 40,000, only 7,000 soldiers survived; Nicias and Demosthenes were killed. The rest of the troops were imprisoned in a quarry, where many died.

Although its economy was nearly ruined, Athens built more ships and recruited soldiers. The Spartans' new commander, Lysander, captured the Athenian fleet at Aegospotomi along the Hellespont (Dardanelles) in 405 B.C.E. Some 170 ships were seized and 4,000 Athenian soldiers executed. Lysander then swept the coast of Asia Minor, forcing all Athenians and their supporters to return to Athens. With no means of importing food, Athens was starved out, finally offering unconditional surrender to Sparta in 404 B.C.E.

Consequences. Sparta's terms devastated the Athenians. Athens had to adopt Sparta's foreign policy, allow its exiles to return, breach the Long Walls, and reduce its fleet to twelve ships. The destruction of the once-mighty and expensive Athenian naval fleet spelled the end of the empire: Athens never again attained the political and military power it had wielded in the fifth century B.C.E.

ADDITIONAL RESOURCES

McGregor, Malcolm Francis. *The Athenians and Their Empire*. Vancouver: University of British Columbia Press, 1987.

Powell, Anton. *Athens and Sparta*. New York: Routledge, 1991.

Thucydides. "History of the Peloponnesian War." In *The Landmark Thucydides: A Comprehensive Guide to the Peloponnesian War*, edited by Robert B. Strassler. New York: Free Press, 1996.

_____."History of the Peloponnesian War." In *The Peloponnesian War: A New Translation, Backgrounds, Interpretations*, translated by Walter Blanco; edited by Walter Blanco and Jennifer Tolbert Roberts. New York: W. W. Norton, 1998.

SEE ALSO: Aegospotomi, Battle of; Alcibiades of Athens; Archidamian War; Brasidas of Sparta; Cleon of Athens; Greco-Persian Wars; Greece, Classical; Lysander of Sparta; Nicias of Athens; Pericles.

—Thomas J. Sienkewicz

PERIANDER OF CORINTH

BORN: c. 667 B.C.E.; place unknown
DIED: c. 587 B.C.E.; place unknown
RELATED CIVILIZATION: Archaic Greece
MAJOR ROLE/POSITION: Tyrant of Corinth

Life. Periander (pehr-ee-AN-dur) of Corinth inherited the tyranny from his father, Cypselus, who had seized control of the government from the Bacchiad oligarchy. A strong ruler, Periander (r. c. 627-c. 587 B.C.E.) promoted Corinth's economic development and political influence. Corinth's position on the isthmus, between the Corinthian and Saronic gulfs, made it naturally well suited for trade. Periander enhanced Corinth's natural advantages by constructing an artificial harbor and a passageway across the isthmus (the *diolkos*) that allowed ships to be dragged over land from one gulf to the other. He also levied taxes on the use of Corinthian harbors, markets, and the *diolkos*.

Periander built a fleet of triremes (warships), which he used to suppress piracy and to extend his political influence. By the end of his life, he controlled several colonies, including Corcyra (Corfu), Potidaea, Epidamnus (Durrës), and Epidaurus. At his death, the tyranny passed to his nephew, Psammetichus, who, after only three years in power, was killed by a popular uprising that ended the tyranny.

Influence. The brief span of Psammetichus's reign suggests that popular discontent had begun under Periander. Indeed, Periander had a reputation for ruthlessness and cruelty. He was supposed to have killed his wife, Melissa, in a fit of rage and caused the death of their son, Lycophron.

ADDITIONAL RESOURCES
Andrewes, A. *The Greek Tyrants*. London: Hutchinson, 1974.
Salmon, J. B. *Wealthy Corinth*. New York: Oxford University Press, 1984.

SEE ALSO: Cypselus of Corinth; Greece, Archaic; Thirty Tyrants.

—Susan O. Shapiro

PERICLES

BORN: c. 495 B.C.E.; Athens, Greece
DIED: 429 B.C.E.; Athens, Greece
RELATED CIVILIZATION: Classical Greece
MAJOR ROLE/POSITION: Statesman, admiral

Life. The most influential Athenian statesman of his time, Pericles (PEHR-eh-kleez) was of a distinguished family and conspicuous for his political acumen, self-control, oratorical powers, incorruptibility, and patriotism. By advocating popular causes, he gradually gained ascendancy over his conservative rivals as he brought to fruition the radical democracy that had long been developing and was characterized by the sovereignty of the assembly and the people's courts.

Under Pericles' leadership, Athens completed the transformation of the Delian League into a maritime empire and employed a portion of the tribute paid by member states for the beautification of the city with buildings and statuary. Convinced that the resources of Athens were adequate to winning a war with Sparta, Pericles guided his countrymen into the Peloponnesian War (431-404 B.C.E.). He died from the plague that

Pericles. (Library of Congress)

struck Athens in 430 B.C.E. while the population of Attica was packed within the city walls for protection from an invading Peloponnesian army.

Influence. Both the long and devastating Peloponnesian War and the democratic institutions of Athens, which were still flourishing a century after Pericles' death, were legacies of Periclean policy, as are the Parthenon and other public buildings that visitors to Athens have marveled at across the centuries.

ADDITIONAL RESOURCES

Scott-Kilvert, I., trans. *The Rise and Fall of Athens: Nine Greek Lives by Plutarch*. New York: Penguin, 1960.

Strassler, Robert B., ed. *The Landmark Thucydides*. Vols. 1-2. New York: Free Press, 1996.

SEE ALSO: Archidamian War; Aspasia of Miletus; Athens; Greece, Classical; Parthenon; Peloponnesian War.

—*Hubert M. Martin, Jr.*

PERSIA

DATE: 1000 B.C.E.-700 C.E.

LOCALE: Southwest region of modern Iran, bordering the Persian Gulf

SIGNIFICANCE: The Persians were a powerful eastern force against the Greeks and later the Romans. Under the Sāsānians, Persia enjoyed immense power and experienced an artistic renaissance.

The Parsa, an Indo-European nomadic group, moved into Persis (later Fārs) in what became southern Iran, in about 1000 B.C.E. The Parsa were first mentioned in the annals of an Assyrian king in 844 B.C.E.

History. By the sixth century B.C.E., the Parsa, or Persians, were able to assert themselves and defeat the Median king who had put an end to the Assyrian Empire through a coalition with other Near Eastern peoples, establishing the Achaemenian Dynasty (559-330 B.C.E.). Persian leader Cyrus the Great (r. 558-530 B.C.E.) subjugated the Medes and assumed the title of "king of kings" by capturing Lydia, Syria, Palestine,

and other regions in the Near East. He gave the Jews the freedom to return to Jerusalem to rebuild their temple, which had been destroyed during the Babylonian invasion of Palestine. Cyrus died in the east while fighting the Scythian tribes, and his son Cambyses II (r. 529-522 B.C.E.) ascended the throne.

Cambyses II was able to add Egypt to the Persian Empire, but with his sudden death (522 B.C.E.) in Egypt, Darius the Great (r. 522-486 B.C.E.), who was not directly related to Cyrus, was able to capture the throne. He left a long, trilingual testament to his feats in Old Persian, Elamite, and Akkadian called the Behistun inscription. He also finished building the famous Achaemenian Persian ceremonial capital, Persepolis. Darius the Great also established a postal system and the Royal Road, which connected Persia to the rest of the Near East.

During the time of Darius's successor, Xerxes I (r. 486-465 B.C.E.), the Greco-Persian Wars reached their height. The Persians had been annoyed that the

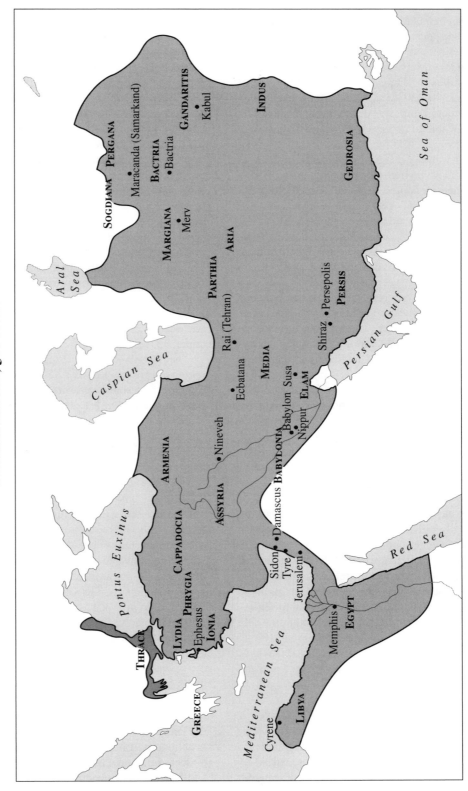

PERSIAN EMPIRE, 500 B.C.E.

Sea of Oman

GANDARITIS
Kabul
INDUS
BACTRIA
• Bactria
GEDROSIA
PERGANA
Maracanda (Samarkand)
SOGDIANA
MARGIANA
Merv
ARIA
PARTHIA
PERSIS
Aral Sea
Rai (Tehran) •
Persepolis
Shiraz •
Persian Gulf
Caspian Sea
Ecbatana •
MEDIA
Babylon Susa •
Nippur ELAM
Nineveh •
ARMENIA
BABYLONIA
ASSYRIA
Damascus •
Pontus Euxinus
CAPPADOCIA
Sidon •
PHRYGIA
Tyre •
LYDIA
Jerusalem •
Ephesus •
IONIA
EGYPT
Memphis •
THRACE
Red Sea
GREECE
Mediterranean Sea
Cyrene •
LIBYA

Greeks on the mainland had aided the Ionian Greeks in their rebellion against Persia. The Persians were able to sack and burn Athens, but generally the Greeks were able to defend themselves through a series of city-state alliances, such as the Delian League. By the reign of Darius III (r. 336-330 B.C.E.), the last Achaemenian king, the Persian Empire was in decline, and Alexander the Great was able to defeat the Persians in three successive battles.

Alexander wanted to legitimize himself in the eyes of the Persians, so he married the daughters of Darius III and reportedly adopted some Persian customs and dress. After Alexander's death, his empire was divided between his generals, and between 312 and 301 B.C.E., Seleucus I was able to control Babylonia and Persia. Alexander and the Seleucids are responsible for the spread of Hellenic culture and the Greek language in Persia.

By the third century B.C.E., the Seleucids had been pushed from Persia by the Parthians in the east. The Parthians gradually became the major power in Persia from 245 B.C.E. to 224 C.E. Although their language was Iranian, they were Hellenized and adopted the Greek language and culture during the early part of their rule. This is apparent from their coinage, which bears Greek legends, and the titles they adopted, such as Philhellenos, or "friend of the Greeks."

The Parthian kings ruled the various provinces of their empire through what has been called a feudal system. Although Arsaces is the first king in the dynasty, Mithradates I (r. 171-138 B.C.E.) is the real founder of the Parthian Empire and the king who reinstated the title "king of kings." From the time of his rule, the empire became more Iranian in character. The coins began to have Parthian legends, and Persian titles were adopted. The Parthians were often at war with Rome and in one instance were able to completely defeat a Roman army, resulting in the death of Marcus Licinius Crassus at the Battle of Carrhae in 53 B.C.E. by the general Surenas.

This Parthian power was apparent through the rule of the last king of kings, Artabanus V, who in 218 C.E. defeated the Romans at Nisibis. However, Artabanus V was defeated and killed by a Persian ruler from the province of Persis, Ardashīr I (r. 224-241 C.E.), in 224 C.E.

Ardashīr I, the founder of the Sāsānian Dynasty, was from Persis, the same province in which the Achaemenians originated. The Sāsānians were antihellenic and propagated Persian customs and the Zoroastrian religion, which had been the imperial religion during the Achaemenian period. The coins of Ardashīr and the succeeding Sāsānian kings have the bust of the ruler on the obverse and a fire temple on the reverse, demonstrating the close connection between the church and state.

Shāpūr I (r. 240-272 C.E.), the son of Ardashīr I, expanded the empire, defeated the Roman emperor Gordian in 244 C.E., and eventually captured the emperor Valerian in 260 C.E. Shāpūr I let religious leader Mani propagate his beliefs (Manichaeanism) throughout the empire, which caused dissatisfaction among the Zoroastrian priests. The Sāsānians exacted large sums of gold from the Romans from the third to the seventh centuries C.E.

In the fifth century C.E., the Hephthalites became a menace to the Sāsānians in the east, and the Persian Empire, much like the Roman Empire, had to defend its borders on several fronts. Armenia became a main point of contention between the Persians and the Romans, and by the fifth century, it was split in half, with the western portion under Rome and the eastern half under Persia.

The Sāsānian Empire reached its zenith during the reign of Khosrow I (r. 531-579 C.E.) who made fiscal, military, and social reforms. Some of these reforms were in reaction to Mazdak, a Zoroastrian priest who espoused an egalitarian society. Khosrow II (r. 590-628 C.E.) defeated a challenge by Bahrām VI, who was not a member of the Sāsānian family, with the aid of the Roman emperor Maurice. He then conquered Anatolia, Egypt, Palestine, Syria, and parts of Arabia. Even Constantinople came under attack, but the emperor Heraclius countered with a brilliant move and forced the Sāsānians to retreat.

In the seventh century, the Sāsānian Empire was in a state of anarchy and decline that coincided with the rise of Islam and the unification of the Arab tribes in the Arabian peninsula. The last Sāsānian king, Yazdegerd III (r. 633-651 C.E.), was not able to withstand the Arab Muslims and was forced to move from province to province to seek support. The Arab Muslims were able to defeat the Sāsānians at several important battles. These were the Battle of al-Qādisīyah, in which the famous general Rustam Farrokhzad was killed, and the Battle of Nahāvand in the heart of Persia. For the next fifty years, the Arab Muslims quelled local revolts by the Persian population while Yazdegerd's descendants sought help from the Chinese.

Religion and ritual. Zoroastrianism, the religion adopted by the Achaemenians and Parthians, spread throughout Persia, although other religions were tolerated. During the Sāsānian period (224-651 C.E.), Zoroastrianism and its doctrine were codified by priests and a Zoroastrian church was established with set rules and offices. One constant feature of Zoroastrianism was the worship of the deity Ahura Mazda (Ormazd). Such priests as Kerdir in the third century C.E. and Adur-

A Persian king with attendants. (North Wind Picture Archives)

Farranbag in the fourth century C.E. were responsible for the codification of the *Avesta*, the Zoroastrian holy text. Commentaries on the *Avesta*, designed to clarify various points, were written in Middle Persian.

During the rule of Shāpūr I in the third century C.E., Mani emerged as an important prophet who espoused a gnostic religion, Manichaeanism. His teaching focused on salvation and was eclectic, antimaterialistic, and apocalyptic. The Zoroastrian priest Kerdir caused the imprisonment and death of Mani, but the religion thrived outside the borders of Persia, especially in Central Asia and as far as China until the thirteenth century. A Zoroastrian priest in the sixth century C.E. by the name of Mazdak interpreted the *Avesta* quite differently and was able to gather a large following from the masses, and for a while, King Kavadh I (r. 488-531 C.E.) accepted his egalitarian ideas in order to reduce the power of the nobility.

Death and burial. According to the Zoroastrian doctrine, once a person had passed away, his body was deemed polluted and was not to come into contact with humans, the earth, or water. For this reason, the bodies of the dead were exposed to vultures and dogs in designated enclosures called *dakhma*. The bones were then collected and placed in a receptacle (*astodan*).

Language and literature. The most important writings regarding the Achaemenian period are the Old Persian royal inscriptions, including the longest of these, Darius the Great's Behistun inscription, and Xerxes I's Daiva inscription. All the inscriptions are formulaically constructed and repetitive and at times supply very little information. The Parthians left a few inscriptions in the Parthian and Greek languages, and some documents have been found in Central Asia. The Sāsānians left many more sources, including royal and priestly inscriptions in Middle Persian. There are hundreds of Middle Persian texts, many of which were redacted during the early Islamic period. They primarily concern themselves with religion, sacred history, geography, and law but are still important sources for Sāsānian history. Some Arabic and Persian historical texts also were translations of Sāsānian sources and chronicles.

Writing system. The Achaemenians adopted the cuneiform system of writing from their Mesopotamian neighbors and used it for the Old Persian languages. Aramaic was the language for imperial correspondence and the lingua franca of the ancient Near East. The Parthians and the Sāsānians used varied forms of the Aramaic script for inscriptions and texts. The Aramaic script used by the Sāsānians for the Middle Persian language evolved into a highly cursive script by the seventh century C.E.

Women's life. The Greek sources do not paint a favorable picture of the royal women in the Achaemenian period; however, this may be a reflection of Athenian prejudices. The Greeks depict royal women in the Achaemenian household as powerful and involved in matters of the state. In the Sāsānian period, several women ruled or had their portrait on coins. The most notable are queens Boran and Azarmidukht, who ruled in the seventh century C.E. Zoroastrian law was very much concerned with purity and pollution; therefore, women were restricted from daily activities during their menstrual periods. There are hundreds of seals belonging to women in the Sāsānian period that had either their name or portrait inscribed on them.

Daily life, customs, and traditions. The historian Herodotus tells us that the Achaemenian Persians' favorite celebration was birthdays. The Persians had specific customs for every occasion; for example, during meals, one was not to speak as that was viewed as a sin. Lying was the worst sin according to the Persians. Hair that had been cut off and nail clippings had to be collected and put in a particular spot or receptacle. Every Persian boy was taught the art of horsemanship and archery. Hunting was the royal sport in which the Persians engaged, and polo originated in a game played by the Sāsānian kings. Chess and backgammon were popularized and were part of a curriculum that the noblemen had to learn as part of the *frahang* "learning." The

Achaemenians practiced consanguineous marriages, and by the Sāsānian period, this had become common among the population. According to the Zoroastrian tradition, the ages of nine and fifteen, respectively, were the ideal age for a girl and a boy to be married.

ADDITIONAL RESOURCES

Briant, Pierre. *From Cyrus to Alexander: A History of the Persian Empire*. Winona Lake, Ind.: Eisenbrauns, 1998.

Gershvitch, Ilya, ed. *The Achaemenid Period*. Vol. 2 in *The Cambridge History of Iran*. Cambridge, England: Cambridge University Press, 1975.

Wiesehöfer, Josef. *Ancient Persia, from 550 B.C. to 650 A.D.* London: I. B. Tauris, 1996.

Yarshater, Ehsan, ed. *The Seleucid, Parthian, and Sasanian Periods*. Vol. 3 in *The Cambridge History of Iran*. Cambridge, England: Cambridge University Press, 1983.

SEE ALSO: Achaemenian Dynasty; Alexander the Great; Arabia; Ardashīr I; Arsacid Dynasty; Artabanus I-V; *Avesta*; Carrhae, Battle of; Crassus, Marcus Licinius; Cyrus the Great; Darius the Great; Darius III; Greco-Persian Wars; Greece, Hellenistic and Roman; Jerusalem, temple of; Manichaeanism; Mithradates I; Parthia; Sāsānian Empire; Seleucid Dynasty; Shāpūr I; Xerxes I; Zoroaster; Zoroastrianism.

—*Touraj Daryaee*

PERSIUS FLACCUS, AULUS

BORN: 34 C.E.; Volterrae (later Volterra, Italy)
DIED: 62 C.E.; Campania (later Champagne, France)
RELATED CIVILIZATION: Imperial Rome
MAJOR ROLE/POSITION: Poet

Life. One of the four major Roman satirists (the others are Gaius Lucilius, Horace, and Juvenal), Aulus Persius Flaccus (AW-luhs PEHR-shee-uhs FLAK-uhs) was born into an aristocratic Roman family but led a life withdrawn from the political and military affairs of his day. Like many of his contemporaries, he was attracted to the study of Stoic philosophy, learning from a leading Stoic of the day, Lucius Annaeus Cornutus.

He died young, leaving six satires that were coedited and published by his friend Cornutus. He was fortunate not to have lived through the failed conspiracy of Gaius Calpurnius Piso against the emperor Nero in 65 C.E., when many of Persius's Stoic friends were exiled (including Cornutus) or perished. Three more of the greatest writers of the day, Seneca the Younger, Lucan, and Petronius Arbiter, were forced to commit suicide. The absence of free political expression during much of Nero's reign severely constrained the political content of poetry. Therefore, it is not surprising that in his poetry Persius seeks to develop a personal morality. However, he still manages to express the disturbing "truth" of his society's literary bad taste and moral bankruptcy.

Influence. Even though the language and style of Persius's satires are difficult and compressed, the moral intensity of the *Satires* (n.d.; *The Satires*, 1693) made them popular throughout the ancient, late antique, and medieval worlds. Since the end of the seventeenth century, readers of satire have preferred Horace and Juvenal. However, there is no doubt that Persius's work is fundamental to the history of satire.

ADDITIONAL RESOURCES
Braund, S. H. *Roman Verse Satire.* Oxford, England: Oxford University Press, 1992.
Rudd, Niall, trans. *The Satires of Horace and Persius.* London: Penguin, 1974.

SEE ALSO: Horace; Juvenal; Lucan; Lucilius, Gaius (satirist); Nero; Petronius Arbiter; Rome, Imperial; Seneca the Younger.

—*Marc Mastrangelo*

PERUŇKATAI

AUTHORSHIP: Konguvelar from Vijayamankai in Kongumandalam
DATE: c. 900 C.E.
LOCALE: India
RELATED CIVILIZATION: India (Tamil)
SIGNIFICANCE: This epic poem explains the philosophical and moral teachings of Jainism.

Peruňkatai (peh-REWN-kah-tahi) in Tamil literally means "great story." This Jain epic is believed to be based on two Sanskrit works, the *Bṛhatkathā* (*The Brhatkatha: A Reconstruction from Brhatkathaslokasamgraha*, 1974) and *Utayana Kumara Kaviyam* (n.d.), which describe King Utayana of Kosambi city in Vattanatu. The *Bṛhatkathā*, ascribed to Guṇāḍhya, a poet of the Sātavāhana court, was originally written in Prākrit, and although that version was lost, fragments have been preserved in Sanskrit as *Bṛhatkathā manjari* (c. 1037 C.E.) and *Bṛhatkathā saṃgraha* (c. 1064-1081 C.E.; *The Brhatkatha*, 1974). The *Utayana Kumara Kaviyam* by Durvinta, a Gaṅga king in the first half of the seventh century C.E., extols the virtues of King Utayana. The Tamil epic loosely narrates the story of King Utayana and then his son, Naravanan. Utayana lives a perfect life, enjoying all the pleasures that his kingdom offers and achieving greatness in every walk of life only to become an ascetic in his later years, being satiated with life.

Celebrated only for a few beautiful passages, *Peruň katai* is not valued highly by scholars and critics because of its apparent lack of poetic or literary merit. However, although the poem extols the moral and philosophical tenets of Jainism, the poet resists the temptation to make the work a mere tool for propaganda but instead has attempted some characterization in the epic. The poem consists of 16,000 lines, is written in the *akaval* meter, with a four-foot line and a difference in rhyme, and in diction and meter displays some artistry.

ADDITIONAL RESOURCES
Ramanujam, A. K. *Poems of Love and War from the Eight Anthologies and the Ten Long Poems of Classical Tamil.* New York: Columbia University Press, 1985.
Zvelebil, Kamil Veith. *Tamil Literature.* Wiesbaden, Germany: Harrassowitz, 1974.

SEE ALSO: Guṇāḍhya; India; Jainism.

—*Kokila Ravi*

PETER, SAINT

ALSO KNOWN AS: Simeon; Simon
BORN: date unknown; Bethsaida, Galilee
DIED: 64 C.E.; Rome
RELATED CIVILIZATIONS: Israel, Imperial Rome
MAJOR ROLE/POSITION: Apostle, fisherman

Life. Peter was supporting his family as a fisherman when, according to the New Testament in the Bible, he was called by Jesus Christ to be one of the earliest disciples. He was renamed by Jesus as Cephas (translated from the Greek *Petros* as Peter), meaning "rock." Peter, along with John and James, was a leader among the twelve apostles and a close friend of Jesus. According to the Bible, Peter's ministry with Jesus vacillated from the heights—he confessed that Jesus was the Messiah and was consequently given great authority in the church by Jesus—to the depths—his denial of knowing Jesus led to Peter becoming a despondent, broken man.

Peter was the first apostle to enter the empty tomb of Jesus and was restored by Jesus to a position of prominence in the early church. It was Peter who delivered the first sermon during the birth of the Christian church at Pentecost, was one of the first to preach to non-Jews, and, according to Roman Catholic teaching, became the first Bishop of Rome. He is thought to have suffered

ROMAN CATHOLIC POPES (BISHOPS OF ROME), 1ST-8TH CENTURIES C.E.

First Century		*Fourth Century*		*Seventh Century*	
Peter	c. 33-67 C.E.	Marcellus I	308-309	Sabinianus	604-606
Linus	67-76	Eusebius	309?	Boniface III	607-607
Anacletus	76-88	Militiades	311-314	Boniface IV	608-615
Clement I	88-97	Sylvester I	314-335	Adeodatus	615-618
Evaristus	97-105	Marcus	336-336	Boniface V	619-625
		Julius I	337-352	Honorius I	625-638
Second Century		Liberius	352-366	Severinus	640-640
Alexander I	105-115	Damasus I	366-384	John IV	640-642
Sixtus I	115-125	Siricius	384-399	Theodore I	642-649
Telesphorus	125-136	Anastasius I	399-401	Mardn I	649-655
Hyginus	136-140			Eugene I	654-657
Pius I	140-155	*Fifth Century*		Vitalian	657-672
Anicetus	155-166	Innocent I	401-417	Adeodatus II	672-676
Soter	166-175	Zosimus	417-418	Donus	676-678
Eleutherius	175-189	Boniface I	418-422	Agatho	678-681
Victor I	189-199	Celestine I	422-432	Leo II	682-683
Zephyrinus	199-217	Sixtus III	432-440	Benedict II	684-685
		Leo I	461-483	John V	685-686
Third Century		Hilary	461-468	Conon	686-687
Calixtus	217-222	Simplicius	468-483	Sergius I	687-701
Urban I	222-230	Felix III	483-492		
Pontianus	230-235	Gelasius I	492-496	*Eighth Century*	
Anterus	235-236	Anastasius II	496-498	John VI	701-705
Fabian	236-250	Symmachus	498-514	John VII	705-707
Cornelius	251-253			Sisinnius	708-708
Lucius I	253-254	*Sixth Century*		Constantine	708-715
Stephen I	254-257	Hormisdas	514-523	Gregory II	715-731
Sixtus II	257-258	John I	523-526	Gregory III	731-741
Dionysius	259-268	Felix IV	526-530	Zachary	741-752
Felix I	269-274	Boniface II	530-532	Stephen II	752-752
Eutychian	275-283	John II	533-535	Stephen II (III)	752-757
Gaius	283-296	Agapitus I	535-536	Paul I	757-767
Marcellinus	296-304	Silarius	536-537	Stephen III	768-772
		Vigilius	537-555	Adrian I	772-795
		Pelagius I	556-561	Leo III	795-816
		John III	561-574		
		Benedict I	575-579		
		Pelauus II	579-590		
		Gregory I	590-604		

Saint Peter. (Library of Congress)

a martyr's death (crucified upside down) during Nero's persecution of Christians in 64 C.E.

Influence. Peter's legacy includes two New Testament letters, a primary role in founding the Christian faith, and, perhaps, the founding of the papacy.

ADDITIONAL RESOURCE

Perkins, P. *Peter: Apostle for the Whole Church.* Minneapolis, Minn.: Fortress Press, 2000.

SEE ALSO: Bible: New Testament; Christianity; Jesus Christ; John the Evangelist, Saint.

—*Paul John Chara, Jr.*

PETRONIUS ARBITER

ALSO KNOWN AS: Gaius Petronius Arbiter
BORN: date and place unknown
DIED: c. 66 C.E.; place unknown
RELATED CIVILIZATION: Imperial Rome
MAJOR ROLE/POSITION: Satirist

Life. Little is known about the life of Petronius Arbiter (peh-TROH-nee-uhs AHR-beht-ehr). Perhaps a senator with ties to the Neronian court, he is reputed to be the author of the *Satyricon* (c. 60 C.E.; *The Satyricon*, 1694). This lengthy but fragmentary Latin work combines both prose and poetry to recount the adventures of its hero and narrator Encolpius and assorted other characters as they travel about southern Italy.

Much of the *Satyricon* has been lost, but the extant portions of the work are episodic in nature and often depict contemporary Roman society with exaggerated realism. The most famous episode is the "Cena Trimalchionis" ("Trimalchio's Dinner Party"), in which the main characters are guests at an extravagant and vulgar dinner party. Other episodes are of a romantic or more graphically sexual nature, and the work features inserted tales and poetic interludes that derive from and reflect on the plot of the text.

Influence. The *Satyricon* satirized Roman social mores and parodied a variety of Greek literary works, including Homer's *Odyssey* (c. 800 B.C.E.; English

Petronius Arbiter. (Hulton Archive)

translation, 1616) and earlier prose fiction. Although the work was relatively unacknowledged in ancient times, its rediscovery in the Renaissance was met with great interest. Modern investigation of the text has revealed much information about colloquial Latin and about the development of the Roman novel as a genre.

ADDITIONAL RESOURCES

Hofmann, H. A., ed. *Latin Fiction: The Latin Novel in Context*. London: Routledge, 1999.

Slater, N. W. *Reading Petronius*. Baltimore: Johns Hopkins University Press, 1990.

Sullivan, J. P. *The Satyricon of Petronius*. Bloomington: Indiana University Press, 1968.

Walsh, P. G. *The Roman Novel*. Cambridge, England: Cambridge University Press, 1970.

SEE ALSO: Aristides of Miletus; Homer; Nero; Rome, Imperial.

—*John M. McMahon*

PEYAR

ALSO KNOWN AS: Pey; Kairavamuni; Mahādaḥvaya
FLOURISHED: sixth or seventh century C.E.
RELATED CIVILIZATION: South India
MAJOR ROLE/POSITION: Saint

Life. Peyar (PAY-yahr), whose name means "one who is mad or intoxicated with god," was one of the early Tamil *ālvārs* (literally, "one immersed in the experience of god"), or saints, devoted to the cult of the Hindu god Vishnu (Viṣṇu). Tradition asserts that Peyar was born from a red lotus in a temple tank or pond in Mylapore (modern Chennai). He and his contemporaries, Poykai and Pūtān, traveled from place to place, composing beautifully expressed poetic songs devoted to Vishnu. The three laid the foundation for the practice of religious mysticism or *bhakti* (devotion) in south India.

Peyar's ecstatic songs encouraged seeking a direct experience with god that is characterized by pure bliss and realization of a state of oneness with the divine. Peyar's songs record the ways of realizing the manifold personality of god, particularly the eternal bi-unity of the divine as both male and female. Thus, he exalted Nārāyaṇa, or Vishnu, and his consort Śrī, or Lakṣmī.

Peyar's realizations included a profound regard for the divine mother, the source of all. His poetic expressions became central to the entire theology of Śrī Vaishnavism, wherein Śrī is the principle of redemptive grace that operates on and through every function of the god Vishnu. Peyar also asserts that, at the heart of creation, there is a transcendent, transcending love that is supreme power.

Influence. Peyar was instrumental in establishing the Bhakti Movement and fostering the renaissance of Vishnu as an important deity in south India. In particular, he laid the theological foundations for the cult of Śrī Vaishnavism, which remains a powerful religious force in the twenty-first century.

ADDITIONAL RESOURCES

Prentiss, Karen Pechilis. *The Embodyment of Bhakti*. New York: Oxford University Press, 1999.

Varadachari, K. C. *Alwars of South India*. Bombay, India: Bharatiya Vidya Bhavan, 1976.

SEE ALSO: Hinduism; India; Nārāyaṇa; Poykai; Pūtān.

—*Katherine Anne Harper*

PHAEDRUS

ALSO KNOWN AS: Phaidros; Gaius Iulius Phaeder
BORN: c. 15 B.C.E.; Pieria, Thessaly, Macedonia
DIED: c. 55 C.E.; place unknown
RELATED CIVILIZATIONS: Roman Greece, Republican and Imperial Rome
MAJOR ROLE/POSITION: Fabulist

Life. Phaedrus (FEE-druhs) was brought to Rome as a child or a young man, perhaps as a slave or a freedman of the emperor Augustus. He was highly educated and was especially impressed by the comedy of Terence. Phaedrus translated Aesop's fables from Greek prose into Latin poetry, wrote many of his own, and added some stories and jokes. These were all collected in five books known as *Aesop's Fables*. He was generally conservative, but Lucius Aelius Seianus punished him for his topical allusions during the reign of Tiberius.

Influence. Renowned as a storyteller, Phaedrus wrote to teach morals and to entertain, not to create great literature. His iambic hexameter or senarius, a typical comic form of Latin poetry, was consistent and charming but not distinguished. Chiefly through the content of his works, not through their style, Phaedrus affected such authors as Seneca the Younger and Martial, as well as later fabulists such as Aulus Gellius and Avianus. His books, edited by Niccolò Perotti in the fifteenth century, were popular until the seventeenth, when his fables were eclipsed by those of Jean de La

Fontaine and when vernacular editions of Aesop became common.

ADDITIONAL RESOURCES

Rose, H. J. *A Handbook of Latin Literature from the Earliest Times to the Death of St. Augustine.* Wauconda, Ill.: Bolchazy-Carducci, 1996.

Widdows, P. F. *The Fables of Phaedrus.* Austin: University of Texas Press, 1992.

SEE ALSO: Aesop; Augustus; Gellius, Aulus; Greece, Hellenistic and Roman; Martial; Rome, Imperial; Rome, Republican; Seneca the Younger; Terence; Tiberius.

—*Eric v.d. Luft*

PHAROS OF ALEXANDRIA

DATE: constructed c. 300-285 B.C.E.
LOCALE: Alexandria, Egypt
RELATED CIVILIZATION: Hellenistic Greece

SIGNIFICANCE: Aided seagoing vessels in approaching Alexandria and served as a model for ancient harbor architecture.

This drawing (c. 1200 C.E.) is a representation of the lighthouse at Pharos, one of the Seven Wonders of the Ancient World. (Hulton Archive)

A prominent landmark of Hellenistic Alexandria was its famous lighthouse, or Pharos (FAR-uhs), erected at the beginning of the third century B.C.E. on the small island of the same name at the entrance to the double harbor of the city. The Pharos reflected the desire of Hellenistic rulers to create imposing monuments demonstrating their cities' wealth, power, and prestige. The architect, Sostratus of Cnidus, employed granite to construct the three-tiered lighthouse, crowned with a statue of Zeus the Savior (alternatively, the statue might have been Alexander the Great or Ptolemy I Soter). According to ancient records, the Pharos reached around 440 feet (134 meters) and was celebrated as one of the Seven Wonders of the World for its great height. The light of the signal fire maintained at the top was directed out to sea by an intricate curved metal mirror and was visible to mariners about twenty miles (thirty-two kilometers) from shore.

According to some sources, an earthquake toppled the third tier of the monumental edifice in 796 C.E., and later rebuilding enabled the structure to survive at a reduced height until its complete destruction following another earthquake in 1303. Although the dates of the lighthouse's destruction are not certain, parts of the Pharos are known to have been standing in the twelfth century.

ADDITIONAL RESOURCES

Clayton, Peter A., and Martin J. Price, eds. *The Seven Wonders of the Ancient World*. Reprint. New York: Routledge, 1998.

Empereur, Jean-Yves. *Alexandria Rediscovered*. Translated by Margaret Maehler. London: British Museum Press, 1998.

Fraser, P. M. *Ptolemaic Alexandria*. Oxford, England: Clarendon Press, 1972.

SEE ALSO: Alexander the Great; Alexandrian library; Art and architecture; Greece, Hellenistic and Roman.

—*William E. Dunstan*

PHARSALUS, BATTLE OF

DATE: August 9, 48 B.C.E.
LOCALE: Southern Thessaly
RELATED CIVILIZATION: Republican Rome
SIGNIFICANCE: The defeat of Pompey the Great at Pharsalus (fahr-SAY-luhs) essentially established Julius Caesar's supremacy over the Roman state.

Background. In January, 49 B.C.E., civil war erupted in the Roman Republic between Julius Caesar and senatorial forces led by Pompey the Great. The following year, the armies of the two great opponents clashed in a climactic battle near the community of Pharsalus in southern Thessaly.

Action. Pompey and a Republican army of 57,000 men engaged a force of 24,000 under the command of Caesar. Pompey placed his infantry in the center, with the right wing anchored on the Enipeus River and the left protected by a massive concentration of cavalry. Caesar deployed his nine legions in three lines, with a fourth line detached on the right in anticipation of a flank assault by Pompeian cavalry. As the opposing infantry engaged, the expected attack by Pompey's cavalry on the Caesarian right was decisively shattered by the detached infantry formation, which then attacked on the flank and rear of Pompey's main force of infantry. This action, combined with a fresh assault by Caesar's front line, collapsed all resistance. In the battle and ensuing rout, 15,000 Republican troops were killed, and some 23,000 taken captive.

Consequences. After his victory at Pharsalus and the subsequent assassination of Pompey by Ptolemy XIII of Egypt, Caesar had largely gained mastery of Rome, though fighting continued against Pompey's senatorial allies until 45 B.C.E.

ADDITIONAL RESOURCES

Dodge, Theodore A. *Caesar*. Mechanicsburg, Pa.: Stackpole Books, 1995.

Lucan. *The Civil War*. Translated by Nicholas Rowe. London: Everyman, 1998.

SEE ALSO: Caesar, Julius; Pompey the Great; Rome, Republican.

—*Donathan Taylor*